The Official Digital SAT

Study Guide™

COLLEGE BOARD, NEW YORK

ABOUT COLLEGE BOARD

College Board is a mission-driven not-for-profit organization that connects students to college success and opportunity. Founded in 1900, College Board was created to expand access to higher education. Today, the membership association is made up of over 6,000 of the world's leading educational institutions and is dedicated to promoting excellence and equity in education. Each year, College Board helps more than seven million students prepare for a successful transition to college through programs and services in college readiness and college success—including the SAT®, the Advanced Placement® Program, and BigFuture®. The organization also serves the education community through research and advocacy on behalf of students, educators, and schools. For further information, visit **collegeboard.org**.

Copies of this book are available from your bookseller or may be ordered from College Board Publications at **store.collegeboard.org** or by calling 800-323-7155.

Editorial inquiries concerning this book should be submitted to **sat.collegeboard.org/contact**.

This publication was written and edited by College Board. Primary authorship for this edition was by Jim Patterson and Dona Carling, with additional support from Sonia Wilson. Special thanks to Carolyn Lieberg, Sergio Frisoli, Jessica Marks, and Andrew Schwartz for contributions to prior editions. Cover and layout design: Joe Gagyi. Project manager: Linda Holbrook. Product owner: Nayoung Joe. Assistant editor: Samantha Herrera. Invaluable contributions and review from the College Board Assessment Design & Development team led by Sherral Miller, Laurie Moore, Jennifer Woodworth, and Nancy Burkholder.

ISBN-13: 978-1-4573-1670-8

Printed in the United States of America

1 2 3 4 5 6 7 8 9   23 22

Distributed by Macmillan

Dear Student,

Congratulations on taking an important step toward preparing for the SAT®. *The Official Digital SAT Study Guide*™ is a tool to help you practice for the latest version of the test. By investing in SAT practice, you're making a commitment to your college, career, and life success.

As you start to familiarize yourself with the test, we're excited to share with you some of the many benefits it has to offer. The questions that make up the assessment are modeled on the work you're already doing in school. You'll recognize topics and ideas from your math, English language arts, science, history, and social studies classes. These questions are also aligned with the capabilities that research says matter most for college and career readiness. This means that by practicing for the SAT, you're reinforcing the knowledge and skills that will help you excel both in your coursework and in your future pursuits.

The SAT is clearer than ever. The questions will not be tricky, nor will there be any obscure vocabulary or penalties for guessing. By being transparent about what is on the test and making preparation materials easily available, we're providing you the foundation for successful practice. The best source of information about the SAT is found right here in the pages of this book, and you've taken an important step by equipping yourself with these key facts.

The SAT is just one component of the College Board commitment to increasing students' access to and success in college and career. We have also partnered with colleges and universities to offer college application fee waivers to every income-eligible senior who takes the SAT (to learn more visit **sat.org/fee-waivers**). College Board wants you to succeed in your pursuits, and defraying the cost of admission for eligible students is just one way that we can make it easier for you to reach your goals.

Now that you have this great study guide as a tool, we encourage you to begin practicing today.

Keep up the good work.

Priscilla Rodriguez
Senior Vice President, College Readiness Assessments
College Board

Foreword

The Official Digital SAT Study Guide is the latest in a series of SAT preparation books put together by College Board, the makers of the test, to help you, the student, get ready to do your best work on the exam.

In putting this volume together, the various authors and contributors had a single goal in mind: giving students such as you all the information and advice you need to do well on test day. To that end, we've put together detailed overviews of the digital SAT and its components, provided walk-throughs of the various question formats and types you'll encounter on the test, and created opportunities for you to engage in authentic test practice.

The digital SAT itself has been crafted to give all students a fair, valid, and reliable way to demonstrate to colleges, career training programs, scholarship organizations, and others what they know and can do in reading and writing and in math. Designed and developed based on careful research and extensive input, including from students, the digital version of the SAT is easier to take, easier to give, more secure, and more relevant than ever before. The ultimate aim of the test is to give you the best possible opportunity to show what you know and can do, to stand out from your peers, and to be seen and recognized by the postsecondary institutions that interest you and that are a good match for your plans and capabilities.

Although the single best preparation for the digital SAT is engaging actively in a set of challenging high school courses, we've created this book to help you understand and get comfortable with the specific ways in which the digital SAT assesses your achievement. Equipped with this information and having taken advantage of one or more of the many opportunities this book offers to evaluate and hone your skills and knowledge, you'll be able to test with full confidence.

Jim Patterson, Ph.D.
Co-lead author, *The Official Digital SAT Study Guide*
College Board

Contents

PART 3   The Math Section

PART 4   Practice Tests

CHAPTER 1

Introduction

The Official Digital SAT Study Guide is designed to give you the information and tools you'll need to do your best on the SAT, a college and career readiness assessment. This book has been crafted by College Board, the makers of the SAT, and provides authoritative test-taking advice as well as official sample test questions and practice tests developed by the same College Board staff members who produce the actual tests. By using this book as part of your preparation for test day, you can be confident that you have access to all the resources you need to succeed.

A Word or Two about the Digital SAT

Before we dive into the specifics of preparing for the digital SAT, let's make sure that you know a little about the SAT and what testing digitally means for you.

The SAT is one, and the best known, of the tests in College Board's SAT Suite of Assessments. Along with the suite's other tests—the PSAT/NMSQT®, PSAT™ 10, and PSAT™ 8/9—the SAT is designed to measure what research indicates are essential academic requirements for college and career readiness in reading and writing and in math. This means that the SAT is intended to measure the extent to which you've obtained the skills and knowledge needed to be ready to succeed in college and in workforce training. Because the SAT shares the same goal as your high school courses—preparing you for the next stage of your educational career—you should expect that the questions on the SAT will ask you to demonstrate the same sorts of skills and knowledge you use every day in your classes. Moreover, because the SAT provides valuable information about your readiness to succeed in college and career, the results are highly relevant to you. In addition, the score report for the SAT serves as an important gateway to additional college-planning resources, which can help you make informed decisions supportive of your post–high school aspirations.

The SAT is designed to be an appropriately challenging test of your college and career readiness. The demands of college and workforce training programs are high, and the SAT must be similarly demanding.

At the same time, we've designed the SAT to be a fair test of what you know and can do. When test questions are challenging, it's because the content you're asked to work with, the questions you're posed, and the problems you're asked to solve require this level of understanding. The difficulty of SAT questions, in other words, comes from the sophistication of the skills and knowledge you're asked to demonstrate; by contrast, the wording of test passages and questions as well as the tasks you're presented with are meant to be as clear and comprehensible as possible. With appropriate familiarity with the test and its content, you'll be able to answer questions confidently and to the best of your ability.

The Structure of This Book

The Official Digital SAT Study Guide is divided into four parts.

- **Part 1: The Digital SAT** provides an overview of the digital SAT test itself, the scores it yields (and what to do with them), and the test day experience (e.g., what to bring and not bring to the test center). We also present some general test-taking strategies, which complement those specific to the test sections found in later chapters. Part 1 concludes with a discussion of how to use this book to prepare for either the PSAT/NMSQT or PSAT 10, two other, highly similar tests that are part of the SAT Suite of Assessments.

- **Part 2: The Reading and Writing Section** goes into depth on the features and elements of the literacy-focused section of the digital SAT. Part 2 begins with an overview of the test section. The next two chapters address Reading and Writing test passages and informational graphics in detail so you come away with a strong sense of the kinds of readings and graphics you'll be asked to engage with. After a brief introduction to the Reading and Writing section's four *content domains*—the categories into which we organize test questions by topic—we devote two chapters to each of these domains. The first chapter in each pair is a detailed look at the domain, including its purpose and focus and the kinds of questions you may encounter. The second chapter in each pair consists of drill questions in that domain. These questions are accompanied by answer explanations, so you can check your work. Our intent is for these drills to serve as immediate practice once you've read a given overview chapter. The number of drill questions varies somewhat by domain, and there's no real expectation that you answer these questions under timed conditions. Rather, our goal is just to get you familiar with the full range of questions you may encounter in each domain.

- **Part 3: The Math Section** includes a section overview as well as pairs of chapters devoted to the test section's four content domains. These pairs consist of domain overviews followed by drills with answer explanations. Two additional chapters round out Part 3. The first offers further discussion of the student-produced response (SPR) question format, which requires you to generate and enter your own answers (rather than select from multiple-choice options). The second describes your test-day calculator options, including the built-in Desmos Graphing Calculator.

- **Part 4: Practice Tests** consists of a series of official digital SAT practice tests accompanied by answer explanations and scoring guidelines. You may choose to use the paper versions of these tests included in this book, or, preferably, you can follow the provided directions to test digitally—just as you will on test day and using the same digital test application, Bluebook™. If you do choose to practice on paper, carefully read the introduction to this section of the book so that you're fully aware of the differences between practicing on paper and digitally.

How to Use This Book

First and foremost, this is your book, so you should use it in the way that makes you feel most confident in your preparation. We do, however, have some suggestions, depending on how much time you have before you test.

If you have **two months or more** to prepare, we recommend proceeding through this whole book. Read part 1 to get a clear sense of what the digital SAT is like, and then read parts 2 and 3 to become fully versed in how the Reading and Writing and Math sections of the test are put together. Answer the drill questions spread throughout parts 2 and 3 and use the provided answer explanations to assess your responses and identify areas of weakness to work on. Take a full-length practice test, either in Bluebook or in this book, under timed conditions to better understand how to pace yourself. Go through your answers and the provided explanations, figure out what you missed and got right, and identify skills and knowledge you need to brush up on and/or question formats and types you need more practice with. Visit Khan Academy® at **khanacademy.org/digital-sat**, the home for free Official Digital SAT Prep, to explore their resources, which include lessons and activities designed to assess and build your skills and knowledge. Take a second practice test to check for improvement and to identify any areas still needing work.

If you have roughly **one month** to prepare, we still recommend doing all the above, though you may need to push a little to get through everything. If you must prioritize, pay particular attention to the chapters providing overviews of the digital SAT (chapter 2), the Reading and Writing section (chapter 7), and the Math section (chapter 19) to ensure that you're familiar with the key features of the test and its two sections. Take a full-length practice test under timed conditions and analyze your results. Identify the areas where you need the most improvement and use the resources in this book and/or on Khan Academy to address your most critical shortcomings.

A NOTE ABOUT THE PRACTICE TESTS

Most students will take the digital SAT in **Bluebook**, a digital testing application downloaded onto an appropriate device. Because of this, we recommend that—unless you need to test on paper as an accommodation—you take the practice tests in Bluebook. This will get you familiar with the full testing experience, including the many ways Bluebook makes taking the test easy and efficient. If you choose to practice using the test forms included in this book, be sure to read "Introduction to the Practice Tests" in Part 4 for more information about how we've "adapted" the digital testing experience for paper.

If you have **a week or less** before test day, you'll need to be strategic in your preparation. Focus on the overview chapters (chapters 2, 7, and 19) mentioned above so that you have the key test features firmly in mind. Take a full-length practice test under timed conditions so that you have a better idea of how the test is put together and how to pace yourself effectively. Analyze your results and look for one to two areas in Reading and Writing and in Math that you feel you could improve on quickly. Use the drill questions and answer explanations found in various chapters in parts 2 and 3 to gain some quick practice with question formats and types you're not confident on but may be able to master with a bit of effort.

Some Additional Advice

There's a lot of information in this book as well as many options for getting ready for the digital SAT. We strongly suggest that you begin your preparation for taking the SAT at least a couple of months ahead of your test date so that you can practice at a relatively leisurely pace and have enough time and energy to evaluate and, where needed, improve on your reading and writing and math skills and knowledge.

Although we do recommend devoting effort to preparing for the digital SAT, we also want to reassure you that the questions you'll be asked are, in many respects, similar to those you'd encounter in challenging high school courses. Thus, **the single best preparation you can undertake for the digital SAT is what you're already doing: actively engaging in your classes.** The main purposes of specific preparation for the digital SAT are for you to (1) become comfortable with the kinds of questions we ask and how you're expected to respond and (2) learn to pace yourself during the test so that you have an opportunity to answer each question to the best of your ability.

Most of all, remember: You *can* do this.

PART 1

The Digital SAT

CHAPTER 2

Getting to Know the Digital SAT

In this chapter, we provide an overview of the digital SAT. We begin with a high-level discussion of the key components of the test, including its sections, timing, and number of questions. Following that, we describe some of these features in more detail, with a focus on how you can use this information to better prepare for test day.

The Digital SAT at a Glance

The digital SAT is composed of two sections:

- A **Reading and Writing section**, which measures your ability to apply reading and writing skills and knowledge you've gained in your classes in English language arts and other subjects.

- A **Math section**, which measures your ability to apply math skills and knowledge you've gained in your classes in math and in other subjects, such as science, where math is frequently used.

Questions in both sections test the skills and knowledge you've learned in your classes and that our research has found are necessary for you to have to be ready to succeed in college courses.

Table 1 summarizes key features of the digital SAT, while table 2 summarizes key features of each of the two test sections. These features are discussed in more detail below and throughout this book.

NOTE

Part 1 of this book focuses on the digital SAT in general terms. In parts 2 and 3, we cover the Reading and Writing section and the Math section, respectively, in depth, including offering you opportunities to immediately practice with questions in each of the test's *content domains*, the categories we use to conceptually organize test questions by topic.

Table 1. Key Features of the Digital SAT

Feature	Digital SAT
Administration	Two-stage adaptive testing
Number of questions	98 questions: 54 Reading and Writing 44 Math
Time allotted	134 minutes: 64 Reading and Writing 70 Math
Scores reported	Two **section scores**, each on a scale of 200–800: Reading and Writing Math A **total score**, which is the sum of the two section scores and is on a scale of 400–1600

Table 2. Key Features of the Digital SAT Sections

Feature	Reading and Writing Section	Math Section
Administration	Two-stage adaptive test design; each stage consists of a module of questions	Two-stage adaptive test design; each stage consists of a module of questions
Section composition	Questions divided into two modules, each timed separately	Questions divided into two modules, each timed separately
Number of questions	1st module: 27 questions (including 2 unscored questions) 2nd module: 27 questions (including 2 unscored questions)	1st module: 22 questions (including 2 unscored questions) 2nd module: 22 questions (including 2 unscored questions)
Time per module	1st module: 32 minutes 2nd module: 32 minutes	1st module: 35 minutes 2nd module: 35 minutes
Total number of questions	54 questions	44 questions
Total time allotted	64 minutes	70 minutes
Average time per question	1.19 minutes	1.59 minutes
Score reported	Reading and Writing section score, on a scale of 200–800	Math section score, on a scale of 200–800
Question type(s) used	Multiple-choice Each question is standalone (i.e., there are no question sets).	Multiple-choice (about 75% of the section) Student-produced response (about 25% of the section) Each question is standalone (i.e., there are no question sets).

Feature	Reading and Writing Section	Math Section
Subject areas for passages and contexts	Literature, history/social studies, the humanities, science	Science, social studies, real-world topics
Word count	25–150 words per passage (or pair of passages)	About 30% of questions are set in context; most of these contexts have 50 words or fewer.
Informational graphics	Yes; tables, bar graphs, line graphs	Yes; a wide range of data displays and geometric figures
Reading and Writing passage text complexity	Passages represent a range of text complexities from grades 6–8 through grades 12–14.	—

Key Features of the Digital SAT

In this section, we discuss the key features listed above in detail, with an emphasis on how this information can be used to enhance your preparation for test day.

Two-Stage Adaptive Testing

Traditionally, large-scale tests such as the SAT have been given in a paper and pencil format, and everyone who took a particular test form was presented with the exact same set of questions. Even when College Board started making the transition to digital testing for the SAT several years ago, these digital forms were essentially paper and pencil tests with some minor adjustments (e.g., answers being selected or entered onscreen rather than marked on a paper answer sheet). These sorts of test forms, whether printed on paper or displayed on a screen, are known as *linear* because there's only one "path" through the questions, and the test doesn't change in any way based on how the test taker is performing.

The main alternative to linear testing, and one that organizations such as College Board have increasingly turned to in recent years, is *adaptive* testing. You may have heard of such tests or taken one or more of them already. Adaptive tests (which are pretty much exclusively delivered on digital devices) are so called because, in one or more ways, they "adapt" during the test based on how the test taker is doing.

One critical way that adaptive tests such as the SAT improve the test-taking experience is by targeting questions to individual test takers' demonstrated achievement level. Put more simply, if a test taker is doing well on an adaptive test, they're given harder questions to determine the upper limits of their skills and knowledge; if a test taker is struggling, they're given easier questions to determine what they *do* know and can do, not just what they don't and can't.

By contrast, linear tests given to lots of test takers at a time must include a large number and broad range of questions of various challenge levels to assess everyone's achievement. In practice, this means that such tests are quite lengthy and that nearly all test takers end up being asked at least some questions that are either too easy or too hard for them, because the test doesn't change based on how any one test taker is doing during the exam.

The key benefit that the digital SAT's adaptive testing model offers you is a shorter exam that nonetheless measures your skills and knowledge as accurately as a longer test. While the last paper and pencil (linear) version of the SAT clocked in at three hours, the digital SAT is much closer to two.

There are various models for adaptive testing out there. The method we've chosen for the SAT is called *multistage adaptive testing* (MST). In MST, the digital test application adapts after test takers have completed a given *stage* of testing. The digital SAT uses a simple two-stage model, illustrated in figure 1, below.

Figure 1. The Digital SAT's Multistage Adaptive Testing Model

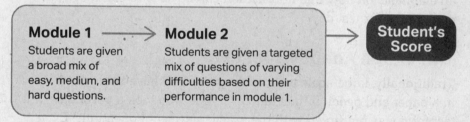

Each section of the digital SAT is divided into two stages, each of which consists of a *module* of questions. Each module contains half the section's test questions (27 Reading and Writing questions or 22 Math questions).

The first module in each test section consists of questions that are, on average, of medium difficulty. (We say "on average" because individual questions may be of high, medium, or low difficulty, but, overall, they average out to moderately challenging.) At the midpoint of each test section, the test application routes students to one of two possible second-stage modules of questions: one whose questions are, on average, of lower difficulty than those in the first module and the other whose questions are, on average, of higher difficulty than those in the first module. (Again, "on average" means that high-, medium- and low-difficulty questions may appear in either second-stage module.)

Each of the two modules in a test section is separately timed, so you'll be allotted half of the total time for each section for answering questions in the first module and the other half for answering questions in the second module. You'll have 32 minutes for each Reading and Writing module and 35 minutes for each Math module.

It's important to note here that the digital SAT only "adapts" once per test section and only after you've had a chance to answer half of the section's questions. This means that you'll have a good opportunity to show what you know and can do in each section before the digital testing app determines which of the two second-stage modules—higher or lower difficulty—you receive.

Besides reducing any stress you might feel about the adapting the test does, this feature allows you to move around freely among the questions in a given module. You can preview later questions in a module and flag and return to earlier questions if you wish, and even change your answers, as long as time permits.

The Fairness of Adaptive Testing

College Board is deeply committed to ensuring that all its tests, including the SAT, are fair to students from all backgrounds and achievement levels. Put simply, we believe that a test that's not fair is a bad test.

As part of this commitment, we've taken numerous steps to make sure that the adaptive testing model used for the digital SAT is fair to all students.

- All test takers begin each test section at the same place: with a medium-difficulty module.

- Because this medium-difficulty module contains a large number of questions as well as a mix of low-, medium-, and high-difficulty questions, every student has a fair chance to demonstrate their skills and knowledge.

- Test takers may navigate freely among the questions in a given module as time permits. They may preview later questions and flag, review, and change answers to earlier questions within a particular module.

- The test application only "adapts" once per test section, and only after each student has had a chance to answer many questions (27 in Reading and Writing, 22 in Math) and thereby give a strong indication of their achievement. This also means that you won't face a situation in which incorrectly answering the first few questions in a section sends you into a downward spiral of inappropriately easy questions, as could be the case if the test application adapted after each question.

- The specifications ("rules") that control how the digital SAT is put together ensure that every student, regardless of when or where they take the test, receives a highly comparable experience. In other words, no one receives a digital SAT test form that's significantly easier or harder than any other student's.

Timing and Pacing

For the Reading and Writing section, you'll have a total of 64 minutes to answer 54 questions. This averages out to 1.19 minutes per question. The questions and total time are evenly split between the two modules of questions in the test section, meaning that you'll have 32 minutes to answer the 27 questions in each module.

For the Math section, you'll have a total of 70 minutes to answer 44 questions. This averages out to 1.59 minutes per question. Like the Reading and Writing section, the Math section is divided evenly into two separately timed modules of questions. You'll have 35 minutes to answer the 22 questions in each module.

Remember that you won't be allowed to return to a given module of questions once time is up, and you won't be able to return to the Reading and Writing section once you've begun the Math section.

Question Types

All questions in the Reading and Writing section and about 75% of questions in the Math section are multiple-choice in format. Each of these multiple-choice questions has four answer choices (also known as options), of which one (and only one) is the best answer (*key*). The three other answer choices represent common errors that test takers make or common misconceptions that test takers hold, so they're intended to be plausible to varying degrees without any one of them being a second key.

The other approximately 25% of questions in the Math section are in a format we call *student-produced response* (SPR). These questions have no answer choices; you must solve each problem and enter your own answer into the test application. SPR questions may have more than one possible correct answer, but you'll only ever be asked to enter a single answer. We'll have more to say about SPR questions in chapter 29, and numerous examples of such questions appear throughout this book.

All digital SAT questions are standalone. (The technical term for this is *discrete*.) This means that each question can be answered independently, without reference to any other question. There are no sets of questions linked to a common passage or set of data. This means that you won't have to worry about answering several questions about a single Reading and Writing passage or Math context that perhaps you feel you don't fully understand. You'll instead be able to give your best effort on each question and then move on to the next. And as we'll discuss in chapter 5, there's no penalty for guessing on the digital SAT, so you should *always* answer every question, even if you must guess.

Context-Based Questions in the Math Section

Roughly a third of the questions in the Math section are set in context. By "in context," we're referring, loosely, to the sorts of questions commonly known as word problems. Although most questions in the section test "pure" math, in-context questions make an important contribution, as they help determine whether you can apply your math skills and knowledge to solving authentic problems in social studies and science as well as those based in real-world scenarios.

Subject Areas

All Reading and Writing questions and some Math questions are set in one of a range of academic subject areas, such as history/social studies and science. We do this for two main (and related) reasons. First, the digital SAT tests the skills and knowledge you've developed in your classes. It therefore makes sense—and is beneficial to you—to set questions in the subjects you've studied in school. Second, the digital SAT is a test of your college and career readiness. It therefore follows that your readiness should be tested in relation to the kinds of classes you'll have to take after high school.

It's important to note here that *no* digital SAT question tests your knowledge of specific topics within the various academic subjects sampled on the test. You won't, for instance, be asked to recall historical facts or scientific theories. All the information needed to answer a given question is provided in the question itself.

IMPORTANT!
We just said it, but it's a critical point worth emphasizing: All the information needed to answer a digital SAT question is in the question itself.

That said, we take great pains to ensure that digital SAT questions set in academic contexts are as authentic as possible. This means that Reading and Writing passages (and informational graphics—more on these below) as well as Math questions set in context present the kinds of topics and ask the kinds of questions that you'd encounter in challenging high school courses as well as in first-year courses at the college level. Your knowledge of and experience with these subjects, therefore, can be beneficial on the digital SAT, as courses in these subjects teach you how to read, write, and reason in the specific ways required in these fields. We'll have more to say about this later, particularly in chapter 8.

The Reading and Writing section includes passages and informational graphics in the subject areas of literature, history/social studies, the humanities, and science. Some Math section questions set in context address topics in the academic subjects of social studies and science, while others address real-world applications of mathematics. Examples of all of these appear in the chapters later in this book devoted to the Reading and Writing and the Math sections.

REMINDER

Each Reading and Writing passage and each Math context is connected to one and only one question. There are no question sets based on a common source, such as a long passage or a data set.

Passage/Context Word Count

On the digital SAT, we keep Reading and Writing passages and Math contexts short and focused so that you can concentrate on answering the associated questions. That doesn't mean that you won't encounter some challenging readings—more on that below—but it *does* mean that you'll be presented with only the most important information needed to answer a given question.

Reading and Writing passages are 25 to 150 words in length, while most Math contexts are 50 words or fewer.

Informational Graphics

The digital SAT includes informational graphics with select Reading and Writing and Math questions. That's because the ability to make skilled use of quantitative (numeric) data is a critical requirement of college and career readiness, not to mention effective participation in civic life.

In the Reading and Writing section, select questions will include a table, bar graph, or line graph. You'll be asked to do various things with the data displayed in these graphics, such as locate specific data points, recognize trends in data, and make connections between the information contained in a graphic with the information and ideas in an accompanying passage. What you *won't* have to do with these questions is perform calculations—and a calculator is neither permitted nor necessary to answer questions in this section. We've limited the types of graphics that appear in the Reading and Writing section to just the three listed above because these are the most common ways in which people in the subject areas sampled by the section organize and display data graphically.

The Math section, by contrast, includes a wider range of informational graphics (e.g., scatterplots, box plots). That's because mathematicians—as well as experts in other fields, such as science, in which math plays a large role—use numerous kinds of data displays, with the choice of which to use depending on what sorts of analyses are being performed. And, unlike in the Reading and Writing section, the Math section *will* require you to perform calculations involving these data. In doing so, you may make use of either the Desmos Graphing Calculator built into Bluebook or your own approved calculator. (In chapter 30, we'll discuss the features of the built-in graphing calculator as well as where you can find College Board's up-to-date calculator policy, that outlines which personal calculators are and aren't acceptable for use on the digital SAT.) In addition to data displays, select Math section questions may include geometric figures, such as triangles and circles.

Text Complexity (Reading and Writing Section)

The passages you encounter in the Reading and Writing section will vary in terms of how challenging they are to read. Some passages will be relatively straightforward, while others will exhibit a relatively high level of complexity. Technically speaking, passages in the section range in complexity from ones like those you might have encountered in grades 6–8 up to and including ones that are similar in difficulty to those you may be assigned in your first-year college classes. We include some highly challenging passages in the Reading and Writing section because research has shown that the ability to read complex texts is a key indicator of students' college and career readiness. (Text complexity in the Reading and Writing section is a topic we return to in chapter 8.)

Math contexts aren't formally rated for text complexity, in part because the presence of equations and other expressions limits the validity of the kinds of text complexity measures we use, and in part because that test section assesses math skills and knowledge, not reading achievement per se. Each Math context is, however, carefully examined by experts prior to its use to ensure that it's as clear and concise as possible, which helps keep the focus where it belongs: on the math itself.

CHAPTER 3

Understanding and Using Your Digital SAT Scores

In this chapter, we go over how the digital SAT is scored. We also examine the digital SAT score report, a critical tool enabling you both to understand your test performance better and to easily take advantage of the many SAT-related services College Board provides.

Your Scores

You'll need to understand your digital SAT scores to measure your progress toward college and career readiness and determine what your next steps should be. Table 1 shows the score details and score ranges.

Table 1. Digital SAT Scores.

SAT Score Reported	Details	Score Range
Section Scores (2)	• Reading and Writing	200–800
	• Math	200–800
Total Score	Sum of the two section scores	400–1600

Your score on each section is based on your performance on all questions in the section. Section scores for Reading and Writing and for Math are reported on a scale from 200 to 800. The two section scores are then added together to yield your total score. This total score ranges from 400 to 1600.

It's to your advantage to answer each question, even if you're not completely sure of your answer, as there's no guessing penalty.

IMPORTANT!

There's no scoring penalty for guessing on the digital SAT. It's therefore in your interest to answer each question to the best of your ability. As we'll discuss in more detail in chapter 5, educated guesses—ones based on having eliminated one or more incorrect answer choices (for multiple-choice questions)—are far better than random guesses; even so, you should never *not* provide an answer to a question.

Comparing Digital SAT and Paper and Pencil SAT Scores

Scores on the digital SAT are directly linked to scores on the paper and pencil version of the SAT that the digital test replaces. This means that scores on the paper and pencil SAT can be fairly compared to scores on the digital SAT. However, because the digital and paper and pencil SATs measure slightly different content and do so in somewhat different ways, a paper and pencil SAT score isn't a perfect predictor of how you'd perform on the digital test.

Your Score Report

Your score report gives the meaning behind the numbers by providing a summary of how you did on each section and on the test as a whole. It also serves as a portal connecting you with additional SAT-related services that College Board provides.

You can access your score report online through your College Board account. This account is the same one you use if you register to take the digital SAT on the weekend. (If you can't access your online score report, your school can print a copy for you.)

We briefly discuss some of the key features of the score report below.

Score Ranges

To better contextualize your actual test scores, we provide score ranges that account for the slight variations in your performance that could occur had you taken the digital SAT on a different day.

Score Comparisons

Score comparisons let you compare your total and section scores to the average scores of all students who took the same digital SAT administration, as applicable, at your school and in your district, state, and country as well as to all testers worldwide.

Percentiles

Percentiles represent the percentage of students whose score is equal to or lower than your own; the higher your percentile rank, the better. For example, if your score were at the 75th percentile for your state, this would mean that 75% of graduating seniors testing over the past three years in your state achieved scores at or below your score. Percentiles are provided, as applicable, at the state level, country level, and among testers worldwide, ranking your scores among the scores of graduating seniors over the last three years.

College and Career Readiness Benchmarks

Based on extensive, ongoing research, College Board has established college and career readiness benchmark scores for the Reading and Writing and Math sections of the digital SAT. These benchmarks—480 for the Reading and Writing section and 530 for the Math section—are the minimum scores our research indicates are required for students to have a high chance of succeeding in common entry-level credit-bearing college courses. Students are considered college and career ready when their digital SAT section scores meet both the Reading and Writing and the Math benchmarks. If your scores fall below one or both of these benchmarks, we recommend using the Knowledge and Skills section of your report (discussed below) to analyze your results further and to explore options for improving on your weaknesses.

Knowledge and Skills

By themselves, test scores are just numbers. As we illustrated above, test scores can be compared in various ways to give useful information about test performance. But the numbers remain abstractions unless looked at in the context of skills and knowledge they likely demonstrate.

That's why College Board has developed Skills Insight™ for the digital SAT (and the other tests of the digital SAT Suite of Assessments). Skills Insight is a set of statements, derived from careful analysis of student performance on hundreds of test questions, describing what test takers earning various scores on the digital SAT are likely to know and be able to do in reading and writing and in math. Accompanying these statements are sample test questions providing concrete examples of the kinds of skills and knowledge that students scoring in particular ranges on the digital SAT are typically able to demonstrate. The Skills Insight statements are generalizations, meaning that they don't precisely describe your performance or that of any single student, but they do provide a strong general sense of what students scoring in particular ranges probably know and can do.

The Knowledge and Skills portion of your score report, which is based on Skills Insight, allows you to better understand your performance across the digital SAT's eight content domains—four for Reading and Writing and four for Math. A link in your score report grants ready access to the Skills Insight Tool, which connects you to the statements and sample test questions associated with your scores.

Sharing Your Scores

Your digital SAT scores can help you better understand your readiness for college and workforce training and how you can further develop your skills and knowledge, but they become more useful still when shared with postsecondary institutions, such as colleges, universities, and scholarship organizations, that are a good match to your achievement and interests.

Sending Scores to Your High School

Your score report will automatically be delivered to your high school when you take the digital SAT.

Sending Scores to Colleges, Universities, and Scholarship Organizations

Sending your scores to colleges, universities, and scholarship organizations early in the college application process is a great way to show your interest in these institutions and their services. You'll have the opportunity when you take the digital SAT to choose up to four colleges/universities and/or scholarship organizations to receive your scores for free. You may also choose to send your scores to additional institutions for a fee.

For score sends requested when you take the digital SAT, only your scores from the requested test date will be sent, unless you specifically ask to send all your existing SAT scores.

If you want to change where your scores are sent, you have until nine days after your test date to alter the recipients of your four free score reports at no charge. After that, you'll be charged the additional score report request fee for any added or changed report requests.

Score Choice

If you take the SAT more than once, you have the option of Score Choice™. With Score Choice, you can choose which set(s) of scores you send to colleges.

Choose by test date for the digital SAT—but keep in mind that some colleges, universities, and scholarship organizations require you to send all your scores. If you don't use Score Choice, we'll send all your scores from your six most recent administrations. However, if you want only your highest set of scores to be seen, select Score Choice.

Each school or program has its own deadlines and policies for how scores are used. Information is listed on the score-sending site for each participating institution, but you should check with the individual school or scholarship organization to make sure you're following its guidelines.

IMPORTANT!
You can only choose which scores to send by test date. You can't send a Reading and Writing section score from one test date and a Math section score from another test date.

Sending Scores to College and University Systems

College Board doesn't use either your raw scores or your reported scaled scores by themselves or in combination with any other information to predict your individual future academic performance at specific postsecondary institutions. However, College Board does help individual colleges and universities use and interpret digital SAT scores.

In certain college and university systems, once you submit your scores to one school, other schools within that system will also have access to your scores. Please note, however, that if you are applying to more than one school within a college or university system, it's still important for you to send your digital SAT scores to each individual school. If you're not sure whether the specific school you're applying to is part of such a system, contact the school's admissions office.

Additionally, if you've decided to participate in Student Search Service (see the next section), colleges and universities may identify you to provide you with materials about college admission and financial aid at their institutions.

Connecting with Colleges, Universities, and Scholarship Organizations

College Board provides students with a range of ways to connect with colleges, universities, scholarship organizations, and other educational opportunities, including BigFuture® and Student Search Service. You will have the opportunity to opt into Student Search Service at any time (except during school day test administrations), including when you create a College Board account, when you register for SAT Weekend, and when you use BigFuture, our free career and college planning site.

BigFuture is a free online planning guide that helps all students take the right first step after high school. When students sign in, they can access a personalized dashboard with options to explore careers, plan for college, and pay for college. When students in tenth, eleventh, and twelfth grades sign in and complete specific steps on their dashboard, they automatically earn entries into monthly drawings for $500 and $40,000 BigFuture Scholarships. (Students must attend a high school in the United States or U.S. territories to be eligible for drawings.) Visit **bigfuture.org** to unlock your dashboard.

Thousands of colleges, universities, and scholarship organizations rely on Student Search Service to connect with millions of students who may be a good fit for their programs. By joining, you have the opportunity to hear directly from over 1,500 four-year colleges. Every year, $300 million in scholarships is available from colleges, universities, and scholarship organizations that use Student Search to find students.

When you join Student Search Service, you agree to share general information you provide when creating your College Board account, along with your score range on any College Board assessments that you've taken. You also agree to share institutions you've added to your college list on BigFuture to help colleges and universities see your demonstrated interest along with information about your high school performance and activities.

Colleges, universities, nonprofit scholarship programs, and nonprofit educational organizations pay for Student Search Service, but this service is available at no cost to you. Visit **cb.org/studentsearch** to join Student Search Service.

Key Facts about Student Search Service

- You can join for free and receive information from a diverse group of accredited colleges, universities, scholarship organizations, and other nonprofit education programs. No other organizations or companies are eligible to participate in Student Search Service.

- When you take a College Board test, you'll be asked to provide certain information about yourself during registration. Answers to some of the questions are optional; others are required.

- It's entirely up to you whether to opt in. The service is free to you, but education organizations pay us a licensing fee to use the service. We use those fees to support our nonprofit, mission-driven work, including providing fee waivers so that students from lower-income families can take the digital SAT for free.

- You can opt out of Student Search Service at any time.

- Being contacted by a college or university doesn't mean you've been admitted to that institution. You must submit an application to be considered for admission. Student Search Service is just a way for nonprofit education organizations to reach prospective students to let them know about the opportunities they offer.

How Student Search Service Works

- If you opt in, you may be identified by education organizations as a potential match for their programs and services.

- Education organizations generally look for groups of students based on expected graduation date, where they live, self-reported cumulative grade point average (GPA), test score ranges, intended college major, geography, and other limited parameters. This information comes from your registration and other information you provide to College Board. It may also include your college list, if you created one, on BigFuture, College Board's free career and college planning website.

- College Board never shares your actual test scores, grades, disability status, parent information, or telephone numbers. Please note that we *do* share test score ranges and GPA.

- If you've opted in and match an education organization's search criteria, we provide them your contact information so they can reach out to you by postal mail and/or email about their programs and services. These institutions are required to keep your data secure and may not share your data with any third parties (other than the education organization's own service providers).

- Colleges and universities may send you information about such things as

  - financial aid opportunities, scholarships, or other ways to make attending their institutions more affordable.

  - details on campus life and student services.

  - overviews of majors, courses, and degree options.

  - deadlines.

For more information, visit **bigfuture.collegeboard.org/student-search -service**.

If at any time you change your mind and want to stop participating in Student Search Service, please visit **my.collegeboard.org/profile /privacy** or contact us at **SearchCustomerService@collegeboard.org** or 866-825-8051. Please note that education organizations that have already received your name and other data may continue to send you information. You may contact such organizations directly to opt out of further communications from them.

CHAPTER 4

What to Expect on Test Day

In this chapter, we review important test day guidelines to help you understand the policies that cover your digital SAT testing experience. You should expect a similar experience to paper and pencil tests (e.g., prohibited behaviors such as attempting to cheat or communicate with other test takers are the same); however, the digital testing environment will include some unique elements that you should know about in advance.

Get Familiar with the Digital Testing App

To perform at your best on test day, you should be familiar with Bluebook, the digital application delivering the test to you.

Bluebook makes taking the digital SAT as easy as possible, allowing you to focus on demonstrating your skills and knowledge on test questions. And you don't need to wait till test day to try it out.

To begin your exploration, simply go to **bluebook.app.collegeboard.org** to download Bluebook and get started. This link will specify the hardware requirements your device must meet and then direct you on how to download and install the software. You'll need to sign in to or create a College Board account to use Bluebook for practice or official testing.

Test Day Items

Be prepared for test day by making sure you bring only what you need. Leave all prohibited items at home. You won't be able to use or access your phone during the test.

Here are some digital SAT regulations:

- For SAT Weekend, you can present your admission ticket on a mobile device instead of printing it. Your phone will be collected and stored away from your desk before testing begins.

- You should bring a pen or pencil for scratch work. (It doesn't have to be a No. 2 pencil.)

- You must have an eligible testing device (see below), with Bluebook already downloaded on it.

- A calculator isn't required but is allowed (see below).

IMPORTANT!

Most students taking the digital SAT will do so using Bluebook, the digital testing application. However, for those students who require paper and pencil testing as an accommodation, College Board makes linear versions of the digital SAT available. These linear tests use the exact same types of questions as found in the digital version of the SAT. The main difference is that linear tests, being in a different mode, are somewhat longer than their digital counterparts. The extra length is needed because linear tests aren't able to adapt to students' achievement levels during testing and therefore must include more questions to yield scores as valid and reliable as those from digital testing. The crucial point here is that if you expect to take the SAT digitally, you should, if you can, practice digitally.

Though not required, consider bringing

- snacks and drinks (which must be under your desk during testing).

- a power cord or portable charger for your eligible testing device.

- an acceptable calculator for use on the Math section of the test (if you prefer using a handheld calculator instead of using the Desmos Graphing Calculator embedded in Bluebook).*

- extra batteries and backup calculator.

*A battery-operated handheld calculator can be used for testing on the digital SAT Math section (only). No calculator power cords are allowed. If you have a calculator with characters that are 1 inch or higher, or if your calculator has a raised display that might be visible to other test takers, the testing staff will seat you in a location where other students can't see the display. All scientific calculators, which can perform complex mathematical functions but don't have a graphing feature, are acceptable if they don't have any prohibited features. For a list of acceptable graphing calculators and prohibited calculators, see **sat.org/calculator**. No other calculators are permitted. See also chapter 30 for more information on calculator options.

Eligible Testing Devices

You can take the digital SAT on a wide range of devices, including a personal or school-managed Windows laptop or tablet, a personal or school-managed Mac laptop, a personal or school-managed iPad, or a school-managed Chromebook. You'll need to download Bluebook onto your device before test day. If you're taking the test on a school-managed device, you'll need to ask your school's technology department to install the app for you. Your device must also be able to connect to Wi-Fi and hold a charge for roughly three hours. We recommend you bring a power cord or portable charger, but we can't guarantee you'll have access to an outlet. You're permitted to bring an external mouse for your device and an external keyboard if your device is a tablet. You can't use detachable device privacy screens. All other applications and programs must be closed during the test. You can't simultaneously test on multiple devices.

Testing Guidelines

This section summarizes important guidelines for digital SAT testing. Make sure you complete all the steps below to successfully prepare to take the test.

- Plan ahead and bring equipment that's in good working order and that has enough battery power to last for three hours. Your testing device must be able to connect to Wi-Fi, and you may need to update your operating system to support the digital test.

NOTE
A school-managed device is one owned and/or operated by your school, not a personal device you yourself own.

- If you're registering for SAT Weekend and think you'll need to borrow a testing device, you'll have a chance to request one. See "Borrowing a Device from College Board," below.

- If you're testing with extended time, bring a power cord; your testing site should provide an outlet for recharging if needed.

- You'll need to download Bluebook from **bluebook.app.collegeboard.org**.

- Between one and five days before the test, you'll need to sign in to the app, agree to the Application Terms and Conditions, and complete exam setup. You'll get access to your admission ticket once you've completed exam setup.

- On test day, you'll follow instructions to complete exam check-in on your testing device and connect to Wi-Fi. Then you'll type a brief statement saying that you agree to follow all test day rules.

- Store any snacks or drinks you bring out of sight in a paper bag under your desk. You may only eat snacks during breaks. The testing staff will tell you where you can go to have your snack.

- Keep your photo ID with you at all times. This is especially important if you leave the testing room. You may be asked to show your ID at any time while at the test site.

- If you're testing with a laptop, don't close your device during testing; leave it open during break time.

- Don't leave the testing room before you're dismissed; if you do, your scores will be canceled.

Borrowing a Device from College Board

For SAT Weekend, students who don't have access to an eligible testing device can request to borrow one from College Board. You may qualify to borrow a testing device if you submit a request at least thirty (30) days before the test date. Submitting a request, however, doesn't guarantee that College Board will grant such a request and provide you with a testing device. If a testing device is provided, additional rules relating to borrowing the device will apply to you. For more information, go to **satsuite.collegeboard.org/digital/device-lending**.

Technical Support on Test Day

The testing staff will provide additional support on test day. They will ensure the Wi-Fi network is working and will assist you if you encounter connectivity issues. Additionally, a help room will be available for you to fix device issues with the testing staff. We'll also have customer service resources ready to troubleshoot issues on test day. Before, during, and after testing, the Help icon in Bluebook enables users to review troubleshooting tips and FAQs.

Makeup Testing

During bad weather, natural disasters, power outages, or other unusual conditions, test sites may close. If a makeup date is confirmed, you'll be notified.

The following policies apply to makeup testing:

- The availability of makeup testing and the conditions that allow test takers to be eligible to take a makeup test are at the sole discretion of College Board.

- Access to scores from makeup administrations may be delayed by several weeks.

CHAPTER 5

Digital SAT Test-Taking Strategies

In this chapter, we offer suggestions for preparing for and taking the digital SAT. We begin with ways that you can get familiar with the digital SAT as you begin your preparation to take the test, and then we offer some tips for how you can demonstrate your best work on test day. We wrap up with a brief consideration of whether you should retest.

Getting Familiar with the Digital SAT

As you begin your digital SAT practice, you should become comfortable with several aspects of the test and how to take it.

Understand the Test's Purpose

The digital SAT is an assessment of your college and career readiness. It's designed to assess the extent to which you've obtained the necessary prerequisites in reading and writing and in math for success in college and workforce training programs. You should expect that the digital SAT will call on you to demonstrate academic skills and knowledge that the best available evidence indicates are necessary for you to have to be ready for postsecondary education.

The single best preparation for the digital SAT is actively participating in a challenging set of academic courses. Such classes and the digital SAT share the goal of helping ensure that you're ready to succeed in college and career training after you graduate from high school. This means that the skills and knowledge you'll be tested on in the digital SAT will closely resemble those you're called on to demonstrate in your current classes. While there are specific ways the digital SAT tests these skills and knowledge (which we'll go over throughout this book), the key point is that what you'll be tested on should be familiar to you from your classes. The test should also be clearly relevant to you since you'll need these same skills and knowledge to succeed in college and workforce training programs.

SECTION PREVIEW

In this section, we cover the following topics:

- Test purpose
- Test basics
- Bluebook
- Digital testing tools in Bluebook
- The adaptive test engine
- Test directions
- Question formats
- Question types

Know the Test Basics

Before taking the digital SAT (or any test), it's important to have a sense of the test's key features. Chapter 2 provides an overview and discussion of all those features. Here, we recap a few of the most relevant points as they pertain to your test preparation.

- **Test components:** A Reading and Writing section and a Math section

- **Number of questions:** 98 (54 Reading and Writing questions, 44 Math questions), with each test section divided into two equal-length, separately timed modules consisting of half the section's questions (27 questions for each Reading and Writing module, 22 questions for each Math module)

- **Time allotted:** 134 minutes (64 minutes for the Reading and Writing section, 70 minutes for the Math section), with each test section divided into two equal-length, separately timed modules of questions (32 minutes for each Reading and Writing module, 35 minutes for each Math module)

- **Scores**
  - Two section scores (Reading and Writing; Math), each on a 200–800 scale
  - A total score (sum of the Reading and Writing and Math section scores) on a 400–1600 scale

SAT Test Preview

One option offered by Bluebook—and one we strongly encourage you to make use of—is SAT Test Preview. SAT Test Preview gives you an untimed, stress-free option to explore Bluebook, try out the tools, and test out any assistive technology you might be using on test day. SAT Test Preview presents you with the directions for each test section and a small selection of sample questions. These questions aren't primarily to test your skills and knowledge but rather to get you up and running on how to appropriately respond to questions during your practice or on test day itself. You can also gain some experience with the app's tools for annotating text and for flagging questions to return to should time permit, and you can experiment with hiding and revealing the testing app's countdown timer, if you wish. When getting familiar with the Math section, you'll be able to learn how to use the built-in Demos Graphing Calculator as well as the reference sheet with common math formulas. (Neither of these tools is available—or needed—during the Reading and Writing section.) See chapter 30 for more on your calculator options and chapter 31 for a copy of the reference sheet.

When you finish each mini section in SAT Test Preview, you'll be reminded of questions you either flagged to return to and/or haven't yet answered. This feature helps ensure that you don't make careless mistakes when responding and will have the best chance to perform up to your achievement level.

STRATEGY

We **strongly recommend** that all students planning to take the SAT digitally spend some time exploring Bluebook using SAT Test Preview.

Official Full-Length Practice Tests

In addition to hosting SAT Test Preview, Bluebook is also your hub for official full-length SAT practice tests. Simply sign in to Bluebook to get started. The practice tests available via Bluebook have been written by the same developers College Board uses to produce the tests taken on test day, so you can be confident that you'll be measured on the same skills and knowledge, in the same ways, and at the same level of challenge as on test day. These Bluebook practice tests are also adaptive, like those on test day, meaning that you'll gain practical experience with how the adaptive test design used for the digital SAT works. Finally, because you'll be practicing in the same digital testing app as the one you'll be using on test day, you'll be gaining facility with the testing app while you practice. You can link to My Practice from Bluebook to access answer explanations and information about your estimated test scores to make the most of your practice in Bluebook.

Get Familiar with Digital Testing Tools

Bluebook offers several tools that you may choose to use to improve your testing experience. Among the key tools available to all students testing digitally are those that allow test takers to

- annotate text (Reading and Writing section only).

- cross out answer options in multiple-choice questions.

- display or (until the five-minutes-remaining mark) hide a countdown timer.

- access the test directions and the Math section's reference sheet during testing.

- flag questions within a given test module to return to.

- access a display informing you of how many questions in each test module you've either flagged or left unanswered and allowing you to jump to any question within a module.

- use the built-in Desmos Graphing Calculator (Math section only).

- adjust magnification (zoom with keyboard shortcuts on laptops or by pinching on tablets).

- modify color contrast using system settings before testing.

Remember that you're free to navigate among questions in a given test module as long as testing time remains. This means, for example, that you can preview upcoming questions or return to flagged or unanswered questions should time permit.

Understand the Nature of Adaptive SAT Testing

As discussed in chapter 2, the digital SAT uses a simple two-stage adaptive model to improve your testing experience, primarily by making it as short as possible while retaining the test's value as a fair, valid, and reliable measure of what you know and can do with respect to college and career readiness requirements.

LINEAR PRACTICE

For students preparing to take the SAT with pencil and paper, College Board has also made available a number of nonadaptive test forms. These forms are found in part 4 of this book and are also obtainable via free download **(satsuite.collegeboard.org/digital /digital-practice-preparation /practice-tests/linear)**. These linear versions of the tests are recommended only for those students who will be testing using paper and pencil. We recommend that all other students instead make use of the opportunity to take full-length practice via Bluebook. See "Introduction to the Practice Tests" in Part 4 for more information about these practice forms, including how they differ in terms of timing and number of questions from digital adaptive forms.

The key practical implication for you is that each of the two test sections on the digital SAT is divided into two separately timed, equal-length modules of questions. After you answer the questions in the first module of each test section, Bluebook will automatically route you to either a higher- or lower-difficulty second module of questions, depending on your performance on the first module's questions.

Each of the two possible second modules of questions contains a mix of easy, medium, and hard questions, although in different proportions. This means that when you move into the second module, you shouldn't expect to encounter only easy or only hard questions. In fact, the differences between the two possible modules, in terms of average question difficulty, are slight enough that you may not know which of the two possibilities you were routed to.

We suggest not thinking of the two modules in a test section as two separate tests, even though each has its own time limit. Rather, you should think about the two modules as two parts of a single test in either reading and writing or math. Your section scores are based on your performance on *all* test questions in the section. If you're routed to the higher-difficulty second module, you don't need to answer every question correctly to get a good score; conversely, if you're routed to the lower-difficulty second module, you'll have a full opportunity to answer questions in the module correctly and show what you know and can do.

A NOTE ON LINEAR SAT TEST FORMS

Linear (nonadaptive) versions of digital SAT test forms are available for students who require them as testing accommodations. These linear forms are longer in terms of number of questions and testing time due to their nonadaptive nature, but otherwise these linear forms are highly comparable to digital adaptive forms and also yield scores that can be reported to colleges and universities.

The essential point is that, in general terms, you'll get the same section and total scores on the digital SAT that you would've gotten had the test not been adaptive, except that the test would need to have been significantly longer to reach that conclusion. That's because in typical large-scale nonadaptive testing programs, such as the previous paper-based versions of the SAT, test makers must present each test taker with the same broad range of question difficulties, from very easy to very hard. While this works well enough for test takers in general, this approach isn't particularly efficient because any given individual is likely to encounter questions that are too easy or too hard for them. Such questions don't tell us much about the individual's capabilities. Correctly answering a too-easy question doesn't really help establish the upper limits of what the test taker knows and can do, and incorrectly answering a question that's too hard doesn't reveal much about what the test taker does know and can demonstrate.

The multistage adaptive model used in the digital SAT improves on this approach by targeting question difficulty more closely to the skills and knowledge of individual students than is possible in a nonadaptive test. This is beneficial to you because it means that the same information about your skills and knowledge can be obtained with fewer questions and less time. It also means you'll more likely be able to give your full effort and attention throughout the test than you would if the test were longer.

Learn the Test Directions Prior to Test Day

We strongly encourage you to become familiar with the directions for the digital SAT prior to test day. You won't have to memorize them because you'll have access to them throughout the test if you wish, but any time you spend reading directions on test day is time not spent answering questions.

The best way to become familiar with the test directions is through practice activities. SAT Test Preview, discussed above, allows you to read the test's directions in advance and to apply your understanding by answering a few sample test questions. Our official full-length practice tests, also discussed previously, contain the directions as well.

The directions for the digital SAT are straightforward. For most questions, you simply need to select the best (Reading and Writing) or correct (Math) option from among a set of provided answer choices. The exception to this is the SPR question format in Math. These questions lack answer options and require you to generate and enter your own answer. Directions for entering SPR answers in Bluebook can be found in chapter 29.

Know the Two Test Question Formats

Most digital SAT questions—all Reading and Writing questions and most Math questions—are in the multiple-choice format. Each of these questions has four answer choices, and your job is to determine which of these choices is the best (Reading and Writing) or correct (Math) answer.

About a quarter of Math questions are in the SPR format. As noted above, these questions lack answer options and instead require you to generate and enter your own answers. These questions are essentially tests of whether you can apply your math skills and knowledge in cases where the scaffolding and support of answer choices isn't provided. Examples of questions in the SPR format can be found throughout this book's discussion of the Math section, and chapter 29 is devoted to explaining how to properly enter your answers. Note that some SPR questions may have more than one possible answer, but you're only ever required to enter a single answer to each question in this format.

NOTE

Some Math multiple-choice questions also have more than one possible real-world answer, but only one correct answer will be provided among the options you're given.

Get Familiar with the Various Question Types

Chapter 7 (Reading and Writing) and chapter 19 (Math) provide overviews of the types of questions you'll be asked on test day, while subsequent chapters in parts 2 and 3 of this book go into detail about the skills and knowledge these question types require you to demonstrate and provide opportunities for immediate practice.

Becoming aware of and comfortable with the types of questions you'll be asked is a critical element of your preparation for several reasons. First, and most obviously, it's important for you to know what skills and knowledge you'll be required to demonstrate on the digital SAT. Second, it's important to know *how* these skills and knowledge are tested (i.e., in what types of questions) so that you're better prepared to answer correctly. Finally, an understanding of question types is helpful for practice, as you can hone your preparation on those topics that you may be struggling with.

The question drills in parts 2 (Reading and Writing) and 3 (Math) of this book are one way for you to gain this familiarity, as these practice sequences include a good representation of question types organized by content domain (e.g., Information and Ideas in Reading and Writing; Problem-Solving and Data Analysis in Math). Visiting Khan Academy for free Official Digital SAT Prep on Khan Academy at **khanacademy.org/digital-sat** is another excellent option.

Doing Your Best on Test Day

In this section, we focus on specific strategies that you can use on test day to maximize your performance.

Read Every Question Carefully

It's important that you read every question on the digital SAT carefully to know what you're being asked to demonstrate. Although this takes time and effort, there are compensations.

- You'll know exactly what you're being asked, so you're less likely to make a careless error when answering. This can be particularly important for multiple-choice questions, as the incorrect answers often play into common mistakes that test takers make or misconceptions that they hold.

- You may encounter some important contextual information that changes how you'd otherwise understand the question. This is true in both test sections. Some Reading and Writing questions, especially those associated with the literature subject area, supply important background information to make interpreting a given passage easier. In-context questions in Math, which constitute about 30% of questions in the section, require you to read and understand the scenarios presented in order to answer properly.

- You'll notice important qualifiers. A few Math questions, for example, may use "not" or "NOT" in the question to signal that you're looking for what's *not* the case. Missing out on that qualifier will leave you adrift in the question.

It's worth noting that College Board takes great pains to ensure the clarity and conciseness of each test question. In other words, we're not trying to trick or overload you with the wording of questions. We want the challenge posed by our test questions to come solely from the ease or difficulty of performing given tasks, not from students struggling to understand what they're being asked to do.

To this end, you may note that we make use of standardized question language whenever it makes sense to do so. For instance, in Rhetorical Synthesis questions in Reading and Writing (see chapter 15 for more details), you'll always be presented with a set of notes taken by a hypothetical student and asked to use relevant information from the notes to meet the student's goal as a writer, such as introducing an artist to an audience unfamiliar with that artist or their work. While the basic framing is the same from one Rhetorical Synthesis question to the next, the hypothetical student's goal varies from question to question, as will, of course, the student's notes and the topic they address. So you'll want to pay close attention to the specified goal in each question, as meeting this goal most effectively is the objective of answering the question.

Answer Every Question

There's no penalty for guessing on the digital SAT, so there's no reason not to answer every question in both sections. But what if you're not sure of the answer? There are a few things you can do to improve your odds of responding properly.

- First, you may find it beneficial to flag questions you're having trouble with to return to should time permit. You don't want to flag too many questions, but you don't want to get hung up on one or two questions about which you're uncertain when you could be answering other questions in a module with greater confidence.

- Second, for multiple-choice questions that you're not sure of the answer for, try to eliminate one or more incorrect answer choices. (The Bluebook testing application has an answer elimination option for this very reason.) You're much more likely to answer correctly if you can reduce your possible responses by two or even one than if you randomly guess.

- Third, as a last resort, randomly guess on multiple-choice questions that you're uncertain of the answer to and when time's running out. Admittedly, you're not likely to correctly answer many questions to which you randomly guessed the answer, but you'll definitely get none of the questions right that you don't answer at all.

After you've reached the end of a module but before time has expired, the questions you've flagged to return to and the questions you haven't answered at all will appear on your Check Your Work page. Use this information in the remaining moments of your testing to address as many of these questions as possible. Use your timed practice (see below) to get a better sense of when you should make this turn toward finalizing your answers to questions in each module.

Make Use of the Question Order

As also discussed in chapter 7 (Reading and Writing) and chapter 19 (Math), digital SAT questions are ordered in particular ways, and knowing these patterns can help you during testing.

In the Reading and Writing section, each module begins with Craft and Structure questions, followed by Information and Ideas, Standard English Conventions, and Expression of Ideas questions. Within all but the Standard English Conventions content domain, questions are further ordered by type, meaning that similar questions appear together. This is beneficial to you because it allows you to get into a rhythm by answering questions of the same type consecutively, with a minimum of context switching. This can also be an aid to pacing, as we discuss later. Note, however, that Reading and Writing questions aren't strictly ordered by question difficulty, so within each module you can expect to see easy, medium, and hard questions mingled.

In Math, questions are ordered by difficulty, from easiest to hardest, within each module. While you're free to navigate through the questions in each module and answer them in any order you choose, you may find more success working from the start of a given module to the end, given that the easier questions appear earlier than the harder ones. Of course, "easy" and "hard" are relative terms, and what's easy for one test taker may be hard for you and vice versa. Nonetheless, you may find that moving sequentially—question by question—through a Math module offers some benefit to you because of the ordering by difficulty.

Pace Yourself

Pacing is critical to success on the digital SAT. To get your best score, you need to spend the right amount of time on each question—no more, no less.

In Reading and Writing, you'll have about 1.2 minutes to read and answer each question, and you'll have about 1.6 minutes to read and answer each Math question. Since digital SAT questions are relatively brief, this should give you adequate time to give your best answer in each case as long as you're adequately prepared.

As we've argued, part of that preparation is understanding the purpose of the SAT; the test basics; Bluebook and its tools; the adaptive test engine; the test directions; and the question formats and types. Another crucial part is practice under timed conditions. The question drills throughout part 2 and part 3 of this book are geared toward untimed practice—in other words, the focus is intended to be on getting familiar with the way the digital SAT presents questions.

By contrast, the full-length practice test opportunities available through Bluebook and this book are ideal opportunities to practice under test-like conditions and to get a better handle on how long particular formats and types of questions are going to take you.

In general:

- Reading and Writing questions in the Information and Ideas content domain are usually the lengthiest and require the most time, on average, while questions in the Standard English Conventions domain are typically the briefest and take the least time, on average. Craft and Structure and Expression of Ideas questions usually fall somewhere in between.

- Math questions set in context are likely to take a bit longer to answer than Math questions not in context, as you'll have to spend some time and effort reading and understanding the scenarios being laid out.

Know When to Move On

Finally, it may sometimes be worth it to give up on particular test questions and move on to others for the sake of time. As mentioned above, we still suggest giving your best answer to every question, but there may be some that you really just don't know the answer to or perhaps even how to approach. When this happens, you should then take your best guess rather than not answer, particularly for multiple-choice questions. Grinding away on such questions is probably not worth it, even if you end up getting them right, as there's an opportunity cost in the form of other questions you might have answered more skillfully had you given them adequate time.

This may be obvious, but it's not necessary to get every question on the digital SAT correct to score well. In that spirit, don't let the perfect be the enemy of the good. Focus on your strengths and avoid getting bogged down in one or more questions that stump you.

Should I Retest?

Let's say you've done everything we suggested, practiced extensively, and taken the digital SAT. You've gotten your scores back, and while you're not unhappy with them, you feel as though you could've done better. Should you retest?

In general, College Board recommends that students take the SAT at least twice—in the spring of their junior year and the fall of their senior year. The most important reason for this is because research has shown that SAT test takers' scores tend to go up between tests, due to a combination of enhanced learning and greater familiarity with the test itself. What's more, colleges tend to use students' highest SAT scores as the basis for decision-making, and many use a practice known as superscoring in which a student's highest SAT Reading and Writing section score is paired with their highest SAT Math section score.

It's possible that your scores could increase between a first and second testing simply due to you becoming more familiar with the digital SAT itself. However, you're more likely to improve scores between testing if you spend the intervening time identifying and working on academic shortcomings associated with the digital SAT. This is where additional resources, such as your score report (discussed in more detail in chapter 3), full-length practice tests, and Official Digital SAT Prep on Khan Academy, can be hugely beneficial. These various resources can help you pinpoint weaknesses that you need to address and provide information and suggestions about how to improve on them.

CHAPTER 6

Using This Book to Prepare for the Digital PSAT/NMSQT or PSAT 10

Overview

The digital SAT is part of a system of tests—the SAT Suite of Assessments—created by College Board to assess students' progress toward college and career readiness. Two other important pieces of this suite are the digital Preliminary SAT/National Merit Scholarship Qualifying Test (PSAT/NMSQT) and PSAT 10. These two tests are the same in terms of content, differing mainly in when students take them and how they're used. The PSAT/NMSQT is administered in the fall of each year, typically to high school juniors, and serves as the qualifying test for entry to the National Merit® Scholarship Program conducted by National Merit Scholarship Corporation. The PSAT 10 is administered in the spring, typically to high school sophomores, and does *not* have any connection to this scholarship program.

Whether you take the digital PSAT/NMSQT or PSAT 10, the test and its results are useful to you in several ways. First, as we'll discuss in more detail below, the PSAT/NMSQT and PSAT 10 are highly similar in content to the SAT, meaning that preparation and practice for either of these earlier tests will carry over into getting ready for the SAT and that your PSAT/NMSQT or PSAT 10 scores are good indicators of how well you'd perform on the SAT if you'd taken it instead. Second, the PSAT/NMSQT and PSAT 10 provide important measures of your progress toward attaining college and career readiness. You can use the results to check in on your progress, engage in career exploration, identify areas of strength and weakness in your academic preparation, and plan steps to address any shortcomings. Third, as previously mentioned, taking the PSAT/NMSQT in the fall of your junior year is one requirement for entry to the National Merit Scholarship Corporation's annual scholarship program.

By design, the digital PSAT/NMSQT and PSAT 10 tests are very similar to the digital SAT. Among other things, this means that **you can use the content of this book, including the advice, sample questions, and practice tests, to help you prepare to take either the PSAT/NMSQT or PSAT 10**. There are just a few important differences worth noting.

Table 1 compares the digital SAT to the digital PSAT/NMSQT and PSAT 10. The few differences between the SAT and the two PSAT-related assessments are discussed afterward.

Table 1. Comparison of the Digital SAT and Digital PSAT/NMSQT and PSAT 10 Tests

Feature	SAT	PSAT/NMSQT and PSAT 10
Reading and Writing		
Number of questions	54	54
Total time allotted (minutes)	64	64
Average time per question (minutes)	1.19	1.19
Math		
Number of questions	44	44
Total time allotted (minutes)	70	70
Average time per question (minutes)	1.59	1.59
Score scales		
Section	200–800	160–760
Total	400–1600	320–1520
Question distribution—format		
READING AND WRITING:		
Multiple-choice	100%	100%
MATH:		
Multiple-choice	~75%	~75%
Student-produced response	~25%	~25%
Question distribution—content domain		
READING AND WRITING:		
Information and Ideas	~26%	~26%
Craft and Structure	~28%	~28%
Expression of Ideas	~24%	~24%
Standard English Conventions	~22%	~22%
MATH:		
Algebra	~35%	~35%
Advanced Math	~35%	~32.5%
Problem-Solving and Data Analysis	~15%	~20%
Geometry and Trigonometry	~15%	~12.5%
Administration	Two-stage adaptive test design; each stage consists of a module of questions	
Organization	Reading and Writing section, Math section	
	Each section consists of two separately timed modules of questions	
Scores reported	◆ Reading and Writing section score ◆ Math section score ◆ total score	
Skills and knowledge tested	Reading and Writing: ◆ No differences Math: Tested only on the digital SAT— ◆ margins of error ◆ evaluating statistical claims associated with observational studies and experiments ◆ circles	

Differences between the Digital SAT and the Digital PSAT/NMSQT and PSAT 10

There are only a few differences between the digital SAT and the digital PSAT/NMSQT and PSAT 10.

- **Score scales.** The tests of the digital SAT Suite of Assessments are on the same vertical scale. This means that your score on any one test in the suite is a good predictor of how well you'd score on a later test in the suite had you taken it instead. One consequence of the vertical scaling is that the tests' score scales are slightly different to allow for continued growth in subsequent tests. As a result, the digital PSAT/NMSQT and PSAT 10 have section scores that are on a 160–760 scale and total scores that are on a 320–1520 scale, whereas the digital SAT's section scores are on a 200–800 scale and its total score is on a 400–1600 scale.

- **Question distribution—content domains.** The approximate proportion of Reading and Writing questions in each of the section's four content domains is the same on the digital SAT and the digital PSAT/NMSQT and PSAT 10. The approximate proportion of Math questions in each of that section's four content domains varies slightly, with the digital SAT having slightly higher proportions of Advanced Math as well as Geometry and Trigonometry questions and a slightly lower proportion of Problem-Solving and Data Analysis questions.

- **Skills and knowledge tested.** The skills and knowledge tested in the Reading and Writing section are the same in the digital SAT and the digital PSAT/NMSQT and PSAT 10. The same is true for Math, with the following exceptions:

  - *Problem-Solving and Data Analysis.* The digital SAT (only) may have questions about margins of error and about evaluating statistical claims associated with observational studies and experiments.

  - *Geometry and Trigonometry.* The digital SAT (only) may have questions about circles.

NOTE

PSAT 8/9 is another test in the digital SAT Suite, one typically given to eighth and ninth graders. You don't need to study for the PSAT 8/9. The best way you can prepare is to pay attention in class and do your homework. The test is meant to assess the skills you are currently learning in school.

PART 2

Reading and Writing Section

CHAPTER 7

Reading and Writing: Overview

The Reading and Writing section of the digital SAT is, along with the Math section, one of the two main portions of the test. In the Reading and Writing section, you'll answer questions that test your ability to read, analyze, and use information and ideas in passages (texts); explain how and why authors make the choices that they do; revise passages to improve how information and ideas are expressed; and edit passages so that they meet expectations of Standard English sentence structure, usage, and punctuation.

In this chapter, we'll cover the whole Reading and Writing section at an overview level so that you'll have a general sense of what you'll be tested on and how. Subsequent chapters will go into more details about the passages, informational graphics, and questions found in the section.

The Section at a Glance

Table 1 provides an overview of the digital SAT Reading and Writing section. Each feature is discussed in the following subsections.

Number of Questions, Timing, and Pacing

Each Reading and Writing test section is divided into two equal-length *modules* of questions. Each of these modules is separately timed, so you'll have 32 minutes to answer the 27 questions in each module. That averages out to 1.19 minutes per question.

Score

You'll receive a Reading and Writing section score based on your performance. Section scores range from 200 to 800, in 10-point intervals. Your scores on the Reading and Writing and Math sections added together will give you your total score for the SAT, which is on a 400–1600 scale, also in 10-point intervals.

PREVIEW
Chapters 8 and 9 discuss in detail the kinds of passages and informational graphics found in the Reading and Writing section, respectively. Chapters 10–18 cover the kinds of questions you'll encounter and provide drills that you can use for immediate practice.

QUICK TAKE
You'll have **64 minutes** to answer **54 multiple-choice Reading and Writing questions**. This averages out to **1.19 minutes per question**. These questions will be divided into **two separately timed modules** of 32 minutes each.

FOR MORE INFORMATION
For an explanation of why the Reading and Writing (and Math) section is divided into two separately timed modules, see chapter 2.

Table 1. Reading and Writing Section Overview.

Feature	SAT Reading and Writing Section
Timing and Pacing	
Number of questions	1st module: 27 questions
	2nd module: 27 questions
	Total: 54 questions
Time per module	1st module: 32 minutes
	2nd module: 32 minutes
	Total: 64 minutes
Average time per question	1.19 minutes
Score	
Score	Reading and Writing section score (200–800 scale); one-half of the SAT total score
Passages	
Words per passage (or passage pair)	25–150
Passage subject areas	Literature
	History/social studies
	Humanities
	Science
Passage text type	Literary
	Informational/explanatory
	Argumentative
Text complexity bands	Grades 6–8
	Grades 9–11
	Grades 12–14
Informational graphics (included with select passages)	Tables
	Bar graphs
	Line graphs
Questions	
Question format	Four-option multiple-choice, each with a single best answer; all questions are independent of each other
Question content domains (categories)	Information and Ideas
	Craft and Structure
	Expression of Ideas
	Standard English Conventions

Passages

Each Reading and Writing question is accompanied by a brief *passage*, which questions in the Reading and Writing section refer to as a *text*. Each passage is short—as few as 25 words to a maximum of 150 words. Some questions will instead include a pair of passages on the same topic or similar topics; together, these passages will be 150 words or fewer in length.

Each passage has a number of important traits, which we'll describe here briefly and focus on in detail in chapter 8.

- Each passage has a **subject area**. This represents the nature of the topic being presented. Passages in the Reading and Writing section represent the subject areas of literature, history/social studies, the humanities, and science. It's helpful to pay attention to the subject area of a given passage because different subjects convey information and ideas in different ways, and knowing something about how each subject shares knowledge can give you an edge in responding to questions. You won't, however, be tested on what you already know about the topic of each passage, as all the information needed to answer each question is contained in the passage itself (and in any accompanying informational graphic).

- Each passage has a **text type**. The three text types represented in the Reading and Writing section are literary, informative/explanatory, and argumentative. It's useful to note the text type of a given passage because, as with subject area, the purpose for which a passage is written (e.g., to entertain, to explain, to convince) influences how its information and ideas are conveyed and organized as well as what kinds of details are included and what roles they serve.

- Each passage has a **text complexity** rating. *Text complexity* is a measure of how easy or difficult a given passage is. When we develop Reading and Writing passages, they get assigned to one of three text complexity bands: grades 6–8, grades 9–11, and grades 12–14. A given passage's text complexity is based on a number of factors, such as how long and sophisticated (or short and straightforward) its sentences are, how challenging (or familiar) its vocabulary is, and how much information it conveys and at what rate. You won't find text complexity ratings listed for passages on the test, and we don't advise paying too much attention to how easy or difficult any passage you encounter on test day is. Still, it's helpful to know that some passages will be relatively straightforward while others will be as challenging as those you'll be assigned in common first-year college courses.

The passages for certain questions will also include an **informational graphic**. Informational graphics in the Reading and Writing section consist of tables, bar graphs, and line graphs, which are among the most common tools authors use to display data visually.

A NOTE ON TERMINOLOGY

Reading and Writing questions refer to the brief readings they include as *texts*. In this guide, we use the term *passages* to refer to these texts in order to avoid possible confusion with other types of real-world texts you may encounter.

QUICK TAKE

Each passage has a **subject area**, **text type**, and **text complexity**, and some passages are accompanied by an **informational graphic**. Understanding these features can help you better prepare to read and understand the passages on test day.

Questions that include a graphic may ask you to locate data, interpret information (e.g., identify a trend), or combine data from the graphic with information in the passage in a meaningful way. You won't, however, have to "do math" with graphics in the Reading and Writing section. No question in the Reading and Writing section will ask you to perform calculations, and the use of a calculator isn't permitted in the section. Instead, you'll apply the numeracy skills you've acquired in various classes, including in history/social studies and science courses, to find and make strategic use of data from tables and graphs to come to a fuller understanding of the topics presented in passages.

Questions

All questions in the Reading and Writing section are multiple-choice. Each question has four answer choices and one (and only one) best answer, known as the *key*. The three incorrect answer choices represent common errors that students may make when answering a given question (which is why, in test maker lingo, incorrect multiple-choice options are sometimes called *distractors*, because they're meant to be at least somewhat tempting). Your task on test day will be figuring out the best answer for each question using your reading and writing skills and knowledge.

All Reading and Writing questions are independent of each other. (These sorts of questions are sometimes described as *discrete*.) This means that each question is self-contained and can be answered on its own, without reference to any other question. In practical terms, this means that instead of reading a few long passages and answering multiple questions about each one, you'll be reading many short passages and answering a single question about each. This has important implications for preparing for and taking the test: if you struggle with a particular passage, just give your best answer and move on (and possibly flag the question to return to if time permits).

Each Reading and Writing question tests a single skill. The skills tested by digital SAT Reading and Writing questions fall into four broad categories, or *content domains*. Each of these domains captures a "big idea" in reading and writing. We'll describe each of these briefly to orient you now and then unpack each content domain in later chapters.

Table 2 offers an overview of the four content domains in the Reading and Writing section, including the "big idea," or main focus, of each domain, the specific skills and knowledge on which you may be tested, and roughly how many questions of each domain appear in the test section.

QUICK TAKE

Each four-option multiple-choice Reading and Writing question has one (and only one) best answer. Your job is to determine which choice that is and to avoid being tempted by incorrect answers. All test questions are independent of each other; there are no question sets.

QUICK TAKE

Each Reading and Writing question falls into one of four categories, or *content domains*: Information and Ideas, Craft and Structure, Expression of Ideas, and Standard English Conventions. **Each question tests one (and only one) skill** (e.g., Central Ideas and Details).

The first two domains—Information and Ideas and Craft and Structure—mainly test reading skills, while the second two domains—Expression of Ideas and Standard English Conventions—mainly test writing skills.

Questions in each Reading and Writing test module will follow the sequence listed in table 3.

Within the content domains of Information and Ideas, Craft and Structure, and Expression of Ideas, questions testing the same skills (e.g., Central Ideas and Details in the Information and Ideas content domain) appear alongside each other. This is so you can concentrate on one type of question at a time, without having to switch back and forth among the various skills tested. Standard English Conventions questions, on the other hand, won't be organized by skill, so you might encounter Boundaries and Form, Structure, and Sense conventions questions in any order on your test form.

Being aware of this sequencing can help you manage your time since some question types can take longer to answer than others. However, it's important to be aware that the exact number of questions per skill within a module can vary.

Questions in each Reading and Writing module aren't strictly ordered by difficulty, so you may come across a hard question followed by an easier one and vice versa. Just do your best to answer each question, and remember that you can flag questions to return to if time permits.

IMPORTANT: UNSCORED QUESTIONS

Four Reading and Writing questions on each test form—two different questions per module—won't count toward your section score. These questions are ones that College Board is studying for potential use on future tests. Your answers to these questions won't impact your section score in any way. You won't be able to tell these questions apart from the ones in the section that do get scored, but there are few enough of them that their presence won't significantly affect your test taking.

Table 2. Reading and Writing Section Content Domains.

Reading and Writing Section Content Domain	The Big Idea	Skills and Knowledge Tested	Proportion of Test Section
Information and Ideas	Questions in this domain test your understanding of what you read.	Central Ideas and Details Command of Evidence ♦ Textual ♦ Quantitative Inferences	12–14 questions (about 26%)
Craft and Structure	Questions in this domain test your understanding of how and why authors write the way they do.	Words in Context Text Structure and Purpose Cross-Text Connections	13–15 questions (about 28%)
Expression of Ideas	Questions in this domain test your ability to revise passages to meet particular writing goals.	Rhetorical Synthesis Transitions	8–12 questions (about 20%)
Standard English Conventions	Questions in this domain test your ability to edit passages for conventional sentence structure, usage, and punctuation.	Boundaries Form, Structure, and Sense	11–15 questions (about 26%)

Table 3. Reading and Writing Section Question Order.

Reading and Writing Modules	Content Domain Sequence
1st module	Craft and Structure questions
	Information and Ideas questions
	Standard English Conventions questions
	Expression of Ideas questions
2nd module	Craft and Structure questions
	Information and Ideas questions
	Standard English Conventions questions
	Expression of Ideas questions

Summary: Reading and Writing Section

Timing and pacing

- 64 minutes to answer 54 questions across two separately timed modules of 32 minutes each

- An average of 1.19 minutes to answer each question

Score

- A Reading and Writing section score on a 200–800 scale, in 10-point intervals (one-half of the total score for the digital SAT, which is on an 800–1600 scale, also in 10-point intervals)

Passages

- 25–150 words per passage (or passage pair)

- Subject areas of literature, history/social studies, the humanities, and science

- An informational graphic (table, bar graph, or line graph) included with select passages

- Text complexities of grades 6–8, grades 9–11, and grades 12–14

Questions

- Four-option multiple-choice, each with a single best answer (*key*)

- All questions independent of each other (i.e., no question sets)

- Content domains of Information and Ideas, Craft and Structure, Expression of Ideas, and Standard English Conventions

  - On the test, Craft and Structure questions appear first in each module, followed by Information and Ideas, Standard English Conventions, and Expression of Ideas questions.

  - Except for Standard English Conventions questions, questions within each content domain are grouped together by skill (e.g., Central Ideas and Details) being tested.

- Each question tied to a single skill within one of the four content domains

- Easier and harder questions may appear alongside each other

- 4 unscored questions (2 different questions per module)

CHAPTER 8

Reading and Writing: Passages

This chapter examines the key features of the passages you'll be asked to work with in the Reading and Writing section. This information will help you unpack the passages you read during practice and on test day so that you're better prepared to answer associated test questions correctly. Over the course of this chapter, we'll demonstrate three strategies for unlocking the meaning of Reading and Writing passages: (1) determining a passage's main purpose, (2) identifying its central (main) idea, and (3) analyzing its structure. Using one or more of these strategies can help you obtain a high-level grasp of each passage, which can, in turn, help you answer whatever question you're ultimately presented with.

The Basics

Each Reading and Writing question includes a *passage* (which the test refers to as a *text*) or, in some cases, a pair of passages on the same topic. Each passage is tied to one (and only one) question, meaning that you can approach each question separately, without reference to any other question in the section.

As we noted in the previous chapter, all passages have three traits: a **subject area**, a **text type**, and a **text complexity**. Some passages also have a fourth trait: an **informational graphic**, which may be a table, bar graph, or line graph. We'll address the first three traits in this chapter and devote the next chapter to the informational graphics found in the Reading and Writing section.

All the information needed to answer each question is in the passage itself (and in any accompanying informational graphic). This benefits all test takers because it makes the Reading and Writing section a test of reading and writing skills and knowledge and not a test of what topics students such as you may or may not have had a chance to learn about in school.

This also means that you should **always answer questions based on what's stated or strongly implied in the passage (and any graphic)** rather than on what you know or believe about a topic.

Subject Area

Each passage belongs to one of four subject areas: literature, history/social studies, the humanities, and science. This is important because test passages (as well as real-world texts in these areas) convey information and ideas in differing ways by subject and have differing concerns, or things that authors writing in these subjects care about and are trying to communicate to readers.

Literature passages in the Reading and Writing section are excerpted from previously published works, such as novels, plays, and poems. Passages in all other subject areas are written specifically for the test in ways that simulate real-world texts in these areas.

As we analyze a sample passage from each of the four subject areas, we'll consider how we can determine the **main purpose** and the **central (main) idea** of each passage.

A statement of a passage's **main purpose** focuses on the author's aim in writing the text and is phrased in terms of what the author is trying to accomplish and why. Statements of purpose generally contain two elements:

- a verb signaling intent, such as "[to] persuade," "[to] convince," or "[to] explain," and

- a "that" or "in order to" clause signaling more specifically what the author is trying to do, such as "[to persuade readers] that the proposed policy should be adopted" or "[to explain why the experiment likely failed] in order to prevent similar failures by other scientists."

A statement of a passage's **central idea**, on the other hand, summarizes the informational content of the passage. In simpler terms, it conveys what the primary "message" of the passage is. Statements of central ideas are factual in content and are typically phrased as declarative sentences (e.g., "Researchers found that the new method of crop rotation increased yields by 30 percent on average").

The concepts of main purpose and central idea are closely related. Main purpose is about *why* the author is writing, whereas central idea is about *what* the author is trying to communicate.

With those two concepts in mind, let's examine sample passages from each of the four subject areas represented in the Reading and Writing section. As we look at each sample, we'll work to uncover the main purpose and central idea of each passage using only information and ideas in the passages themselves.

Literature

Authors write literary texts mainly to share ideas and experiences (real or fictional) in vivid, memorable ways that engage readers at many levels—intellectual, emotional, moral, and so on. Works of literature come in many forms, including novels, dramas, and poems. While these forms differ in many specifics, they all exhibit literary techniques such as evocative word choice, telling (revealing, characterizing) details, and figurative language (e.g., symbolism, metaphors). For literature questions in the Reading and Writing section, the reading skills you've developed in your English language arts classes are most applicable.

Literature passages in the Reading and Writing section include excerpts from previously published novels, short stories, plays, and poems as well as works of literary nonfiction (e.g., memoirs, personal essays). The original works from which literature passages are sampled represent a broad range of authors, styles, perspectives, and time periods and include works produced by writers from the United States and around the world; works originally in English as well as in translation; classic and contemporary works; and widely read and less familiar works. You don't need to have read any of the original works beforehand, however, as all the information needed to answer questions based on literature passages is, as always, included in the passages themselves.

Because they're excerpted from previously published works, literature passages in the Reading and Writing section will include some information about the author and the work, such as the author's name, the title of the work, and the year the work was first published. We suggest that you *not* skip over this information, as knowing who the author is and when the author was writing may help you properly set your expectations for what you'll read. For instance, if the work was originally published in the nineteenth century, you can reasonably expect that the vocabulary and style of writing will differ from what we typically find in more modern literature. In addition, this introductory material may include context that will help you understand the passage, such as a description of the setting or a quick summary of prior events to help set the scene.

Because Reading and Writing literature passages are so brief, don't expect to analyze them for complicated plot details or extended character development. Instead, these passages focus on specific moments, relationships, and characterizations that can be analyzed within a few sentences. You may be asked, for instance, to consider what a narrator's description tells us about a character's personality, how two characters feel about each other, or how a character reacts to an important event in their life.

Although the Reading and Writing section includes questions about selections from poems and dramas, you'll be asked to read and analyze these passages in ways similar to how you'd approach works of prose fiction, such as novels and short stories. In other words, you won't be asked to identify the meter or rhyme scheme of a poem, nor will you be asked to explain the conventions of drama, such as how plays are staged. Instead, you may be asked questions about ideas or experiences represented in the work, particular word choices that the author makes, or how one part of the passage relates to another.

QUICK TAKE

Literature passages in the Reading and Writing section convey ideas and experiences in expressive, memorable ways and are notable for their use of **evocative word choice, telling details, and figurative language.** These passages are excerpted from previously published works and include selections from novels, short stories, plays, poems, and works of literary nonfiction.

Don't worry: you don't need to have read these works beforehand. All the information needed to answer questions based on literature passages is in the passages themselves.

STRATEGY

Don't skip the introductory information about the authors and original texts from which literature passages in the Reading and Writing section are excerpted. This information may clue you in to the kind of reading experience you're about to have or provide useful context about the passage itself.

With that out of the way, let's examine a sample Reading and Writing literature passage.

Literature Sample Passage

> The following text is from F. Scott Fitzgerald's 1925 novel *The Great Gatsby*.
>
> [Jay Gatsby] was balancing himself on the dashboard of his car with that resourcefulness of movement that is so peculiarly American—that comes, I suppose, with the absence of lifting work in youth and, even more, with the formless grace of our nervous, sporadic games. This quality was continually breaking through his punctilious manner in the shape of restlessness.

This passage exhibits many of the qualities you'd expect to see in a challenging literary text, including uncommon vocabulary and sophisticated syntax (*syntax* being the arrangement of words, phrases, and clauses into sentences). Before digging into the details, though, let's consider the purpose of this passage in order to get a sense of the passage as a whole, which is useful regardless of the specific question you're being asked.

After reading the passage, we can conclude that its main purpose is to characterize Jay Gatsby. You can tell this (even if you find some of the vocabulary unfamiliar) by noting that all the details in the passage serve to describe Gatsby's manner, or the way in which he generally acts. The narrator indicates, for example, that Gatsby's manner is "peculiarly [i.e., uniquely] American," that he's lived a life of ease marked by participation in sports ("nervous, sporadic games") and freedom from hard labor ("absence of lifting work in youth"), and that he exhibits a kind of bored, infectious energy ("resourcefulness of movement," "formless grace") that fights against his tendency toward being reserved ("continually breaking through his punctilious manner in the shape of restlessness").

If we were asked to determine the central (main) idea of this passage, we could use the understanding we gained from identifying the passage's main purpose to assist us. We've already discovered that the author wants to describe Jay Gatsby's personality. We can now use that understanding to figure out what specifically the author is trying to tell us about that personality—that Gatsby's usual reserve ("his punctilious manner") is routinely disrupted by his restless energy. Going a bit deeper, we might also reasonably conclude that Gatsby is something of a contradictory figure, a person who's both restrained and energetic.

Note that even if you don't know what "punctilious" means, you should still be able to get the basic idea of the word (and the passage) from the more accessible information available to you. In this case, you can examine the language and structure of the passage's second sentence to figure out an approximate meaning for "punctilious."

Here's that last sentence again, with an example of how we might parse it.

> This quality was continually breaking through his punctilious manner in the shape of restlessness.

- "This quality" refers to "resourcefulness of movement," mentioned in the passage's first sentence.
- "Was continually breaking through" suggests a deviation from a pattern.
- "His punctilious manner" indicates Gatsby's usual behavior.
- "In the shape of restlessness" indicates how the pattern is broken.

At a minimum, then, we can discover that the second sentence of the passage describes Gatsby's self-presentation as somewhat contradictory. But we can do a little better than that, even if we don't know what "punctilious" means precisely. Because Gatsby's usual behavior ("his punctilious manner") is disrupted by restlessness, we can reasonably assume that "punctilious" carries a sense of being different from or perhaps the opposite of "restless." While this doesn't get us quite all the way to "reserved," we're much closer to understanding the gist of the passage even after encountering an unfamiliar word. The key point here—which applies generally to the Reading and Writing section—is, Don't give up if you come across a word or phrase whose meaning you don't know. There's probably a lot you *can* still figure out, and even getting a general sense of the main purpose or central idea of a passage can go a long way toward helping you eliminate incorrect answer choices.

STRATEGY
If you encounter something in a Reading and Writing passage that you don't know or understand, such as an unfamiliar vocabulary term, focus on what you *do* know and understand. That's often enough to answer the question correctly, or it will at least help you rule out one or more incorrect answer choices. Don't give up.

NOTE
While our focus here is on preparing for the digital SAT, this advice is true for any reading activity you undertake in or out of school. Use what you *do* know and *can* understand from a text to help you figure out what you don't (yet) know or understand.

AN ALTERNATE FORMAT FOR LITERATURE TEXTS IN THE READING AND WRITING SECTION

Above, we discussed what a typical passage in the literature subject area on the Reading and Writing section looks like. Some questions, however, may vary from that format, though these questions can still be approached in the same basic way we described.

Here's an example of an alternate presentation style you might encounter.

"Ghosts of the Old Year" is an early 1900s poem by James Weldon Johnson. In the poem, the speaker describes experiencing an ongoing cycle of anticipation followed by regretful reflection: _____

Which quotation from "Ghosts of the Old Year" most effectively illustrates the claim?

A) "The snow has ceased its fluttering flight, / The wind sunk to a whisper light, / An ominous stillness fills the night, / A pause—a hush."

B) "And so the years go swiftly by, / Each, coming, brings ambitions high, / And each, departing, leaves a sigh / Linked to the past."

C) "What does this brazen tongue declare, / That falling on the midnight air / Brings to my heart a sense of care / Akin to fright?"

D) "It tells of many a squandered day, / Of slighted gems and treasured clay, / Of precious stores not laid away, / Of fields unreaped."

Instead of being presented as a traditional passage, the literature content in this question is spread across the answer choices. In this case, you're looking for the evidence from the literary work (in the form of a quotation) that best supports the claim that the speaker in the poem experienced "an ongoing cycle of anticipation followed by regretful reflection." The best answer here is B, by the way, because that quotation describes both anticipation ("brings ambitions high") and regret ("and each, departing, leaves a sigh") occurring cyclically ("Each [year]").

History/Social Studies

Authors write history/social studies texts mainly to convey ideas and findings from research in the fields of history and social science, the latter including such areas of study as psychology, sociology, geography, and other subfields involving the study of people and societies.

Commonly found in many history/social studies passages are what we might describe collectively as elements of research reports: research questions, hypotheses, discussions of previous research, descriptions of methodology (i.e., how researchers went about conducting their study), data (e.g., statistics, observations), findings (i.e., what the researchers learned from the study), implications (i.e., the potential significance of the findings), and recommendations for further research. Because of their short length, individual Reading and Writing passages may not exhibit all these features, but you can expect to encounter many if not most of these elements across the history/social studies passages found on a test form.

In addition to these elements, you can expect to find a strong emphasis in history/social studies passages on establishing relationships. Passages may stress time or sequence relationships (e.g., what happened *before*, *after*, or *at the same time as* another event), causal relationships (e.g., one event happened *because* another event happened), and comparative relationships (e.g., one quantity was *greater* or *less than* another). Tracing these relationships is critical to success on many of the questions associated with history/social studies passages.

As always, all the information you'll need to answer questions about history/social studies passages is found in the passages themselves.

Reading and analyzing history/social studies passages will call most directly on your skill in and experience with reading texts in history and social studies classes. That's because history/social studies passages in the Reading and Writing section are designed to closely resemble the kinds of texts you'll read in high school and college history/social studies classes and because the associated questions require you to engage in the kinds of thinking typically expected in rich, challenging history/social studies courses.

QUICK TAKE

History/social studies passages in the Reading and Writing section aim to share ideas and findings from research in history and the social sciences. These passages tend to include several **elements of research reports**:

- **research questions** (what issue researchers are interested in studying).

- **hypotheses** (what researchers think will happen in their study).

- **discussion of previous research** (to put the study in context).

- **methodology** (how researchers performed the study).

- **data** (the information researchers collected in the study).

- **findings** (what researchers discovered in the study).

- **implications** (the impact the study may have on science and/or real life).

- **recommendations for future research** (to further address findings from a study).

History/social studies passages also establish important **sequential, causal, and comparative relationships**, an understanding of which is central to comprehending most of these passages.

All the information needed to answer questions based on history/social studies passages is in the passages themselves.

History/social studies passages in the Reading and Writing section are written specifically for the test. This means that the passages focus only on the most relevant information for answering the associated questions. It also means that we can tailor these passages for maximum clarity and precision while still presenting you with an appropriate challenge.

Let's examine a sample history/social studies passage in terms of structure, one of our three main strategies for analyzing Reading and Writing passages. After noting the research-based elements we find in this passage, we'll consider how the passage establishes and signals relationships between and among the pieces of information presented.

History/Social Studies Sample Passage

Some studies have suggested that posture can influence cognition, but we should not overstate this phenomenon. A case in point: In a 2014 study, Megan O'Brien and Alaa Ahmed had subjects stand or sit while making risky simulated economic decisions. Standing is more physically unstable and cognitively demanding than sitting; accordingly, O'Brien and Ahmed hypothesized that standing subjects would display more risk aversion during the decision-making tasks than sitting subjects did, since they would want to avoid further feelings of discomfort and complicated risk evaluations. But O'Brien and Ahmed actually found no difference in the groups' performance.

Let's unpack this passage, first, in terms of the elements of research reports that it exhibits.

- **Research question.** Does posture influence cognition (thinking)?

- **Methodology.** The researchers (O'Brien and Ahmed) had study participants stand or sit while making risky simulated economic decisions.

- **Discussion of previous research.** Some earlier studies have suggested that posture can influence cognition. Although not stated explicitly, we can also reasonably infer from the passage that prior studies have found standing to be more unstable and cognitively demanding than sitting.

- **Hypothesis.** The researchers expected that standing participants would be less likely to take risks than sitting participants. (To spell this out more fully: The researchers expected the hypothesized outcome *because* they knew, presumably from prior research, that standing is more difficult to endure than sitting, so standing participants, preoccupied at some level with the challenge of standing, would be less likely to take risks.)

- **Finding.** The researchers found no difference in the risk-taking behavior of the standing and sitting participants they studied.

NOTE

While many history/social studies passages describe the results of observational or experimental studies, some passages may instead take other approaches, such as discussing important historical events or sociological concepts.

NOTE

We're going deep into this passage for this exercise, and you may wish to do so yourself with other passages as part of your practice for the digital SAT, but we wouldn't expect that you'd analyze passages at this level of detail on test day.

The passage doesn't specifically tell us what data the researchers collected, and it doesn't explicitly describe implications of the study's finding.

Now let's take a look at another aspect of text structure: how the passage establishes and signals relationships between and among information and ideas. We'll number the sentences here for ease of reference and use boldface to call out important connectives in the passage, but neither of these features will appear in actual test passages.

> (1) Some studies have suggested that posture can influence cognition, **but** we should not overstate this phenomenon. (2) **A case in point:** In a 2014 study, Megan O'Brien and Alaa Ahmed had subjects stand or sit while making risky simulated economic decisions. (3) Standing is more physically unstable and cognitively demanding than sitting; **accordingly,** O'Brien and Ahmed hypothesized that standing subjects would display more risk aversion during the decision-making tasks than sitting subjects did, **since** they would want to avoid further feelings of discomfort and complicated risk evaluations. (4) **But** O'Brien and Ahmed actually found no difference in the groups' performance.

Sentence 1. Sentence 1 first makes a claim about previous investigations to provide context for the research study about to be described in the passage.

> Some studies have suggested that posture can influence cognition

The sentence then uses the coordinating conjunction *but* to introduce the second clause.

> **but** we should not overstate this phenomenon.

Let's consider the two ideas in sentence 1 separately for a moment, omitting the conjunction.

> Some studies have suggested that posture can influence cognition.

> We should not overstate this phenomenon.

If we paraphrase these ideas, or put them into simpler language that still accurately captures the meaning of the original ideas, we might come up with something such as the following.

> *Some research studies have found that a person's posture can affect cognition, or how the person thinks.*

> *It would be a mistake to think that posture always affects cognition.*

Just by examining the content and structure of this sentence, we can learn a lot about the passage.

- The use of a coordinating conjunction indicates that the two ideas presented in the sentence carry equal weight.

- The use of the conjunction *but* signals a contrast between the two ideas in the sentence.

The passage, in other words, is asking us to hold two ideas in our heads and to recognize (*but*) that the second idea should qualify our understanding of the first idea. We might rewrite (or mentally alter) sentence 1 for simplicity so that it reads something like the following.

> *Although some research studies have found that a person's posture can affect cognition, or how they think, it would be a mistake to think that posture always affects cognition.*

Sentence 2. Sentence 2 provides both some information about the specific study discussed in the passage and an important connective link to sentence 1.

> **A case in point:** In a 2014 study, Megan O'Brien and Alaa Ahmed had subjects stand or sit while making risky simulated economic decisions.

The information in the sentence itself is relatively straightforward: two researchers, Megan O'Brien and Alaa Ahmed, conducted a study in which participants either stood or sat while being asked to make economic decisions that carried (simulated) risk.

The phrase *a case in point* is the critical connector here. It acts as a bridge between sentences 1 and 2, letting us know that O'Brien and Ahmed's study is an example (*a case in point*) of the claim made in sentence 1. Recall that the claim, in our paraphrased version, was that although some research studies have found that a person's posture can affect cognition, that's not always true. *A case in point* signals to us, in other words, that sentence 2 (and beyond) provides an example of how it's not always the case that posture affects cognition.

Sentence 3. Due to its length and use of connectives, sentence 3 requires special attention.

> Standing is more physically unstable and cognitively demanding than sitting; **accordingly,** O'Brien and Ahmed hypothesized that standing subjects would display more risk aversion during the decision-making tasks than sitting subjects did, **since** they would want to avoid further feelings of discomfort and complicated risk evaluations.

We have several clauses linked by punctuation and conjunctions. Let's examine each idea separately, so as not to get overwhelmed, while momentarily leaving out the connectives.

> Standing is more physically unstable and cognitively demanding than sitting.

> O'Brien and Ahmed hypothesized that standing subjects would display more risk aversion during the decision-making tasks than sitting subjects did.

> They [standing study participants] would want to avoid further feelings of discomfort and complicated risk evaluations.

Although we need the connectives for a full understanding of the sentence, we can still get a lot of information out of the ideas considered separately. If we paraphrase them, we might come up with something like the following.

It's harder, both physically and mentally, to stand than to sit.

The researchers assumed that participants in the study who stood would be less likely to take risks during decision-making tasks than would participants who sat.

The researchers assumed that standing would make study participants feel even more uncomfortable when making complicated economic decisions and therefore encourage them to avoid risks during decision making.

Now let's consider how we might link these ideas with connectives. The original version of sentence 3 connects the first two ideas with *accordingly*, which here functions like the word "so."

*It's harder, both physically and mentally, to stand than to sit, **so** the researchers assumed that participants in the study who stood would be less likely to take risks during decision-making tasks than would participants who sat.*

This paraphrase now says, in essence, that *because* standing is harder than sitting, the researchers assumed (hypothesized) that standing would make participants less willing to take risks during the decision-making tasks.

Since is used in sentence 3 to link the last two ideas. *Since* is equivalent to "because" in this context, so let's just use that here as we work to tie the two ideas together.

*The researchers assumed that participants in the study who stood would be less likely to take risks during decision-making tasks than would participants who sat **because** standing would make study participants feel even more uncomfortable when making complicated economic decisions.*

Sentence 4. As we observed earlier, sentence 4 states the researchers' finding.

But O'Brien and Ahmed actually found no difference in the groups' performance.

But works here just as it did in sentence 1, signaling a contrast with what came before. Specifically, sentence 4 challenges the researchers' expectation expressed in sentence 3. Put another way, sentence 4 refutes the hypothesis the researchers laid out (sentence 3) by indicating that both sitting and standing participants showed similar degrees of risk tolerance.

As our analysis of this passage shows, paying close attention to text structure enables us to gain a rich understanding of the content of the passage. Even though you may have little or no prior familiarity with the topic of whether posture affects cognition, you can follow what the passage is saying by focusing on how the passage organizes and presents relationships among the ideas and information it discusses.

Humanities

Authors write humanities texts mainly to share ideas and insights about culture, literature, art, language, and philosophy. Texts in the humanities subject area aren't literary themselves, however. Instead, they inform readers about particular works of art or their creators, analyze the arguments of philosophers past and present, or make and support argumentative claims about cultural phenomena.

To make this distinction clearer, think about the differences between a movie and a movie review. Most movies are designed to entertain and to immerse viewers in a fictional (or fictionalized) narrative. Movie reviews, on the other hand, inform audiences by telling them what a given movie is about and make evaluative claims about the movie supported with evidence (e.g., discussion of plot details, standout performances, impactful scenes, and appealing filmmaking techniques). Humanities passages in the Reading and Writing section are more like movie reviews than movies themselves. They explain, illuminate, or make and defend claims about the products, expressions, and values of human cultures.

Like literature passages, humanities passages use vivid language and telling details, but because humanities passages seek to inform, explain, or convince, they also have a lot in common with history/social studies and science passages. For example, they present central ideas or claims, flesh out these points with support and evidence, and establish sequential, comparative, and cause-effect relationships.

All humanities passages in the Reading and Writing section are written specifically for the test.

Depending on the classes you've taken in high school, you may or may not have a lot of experience reading and analyzing humanities texts. If these types of texts are new to you, don't worry. As always, all the information you'll need to answer the questions is found in the passages themselves. You're not expected to have previous familiarity with any of the topics discussed in humanities passages.

Let's examine a sample humanities passage now to better understand how you can go about analyzing it productively. In our analysis, we'll focus first on determining the main purpose and the structure of the passage and then on distilling the central idea or claim. We'll again number the sentences in the passage for ease of reference during our discussion, but be aware that sentence numbers don't appear in actual test passages.

QUICK TAKE

Humanities passages in the Reading and Writing section aim to share ideas and insights about culture, literature, art, language, and philosophy.

Humanities passages are something of a hybrid between literature passages and history/social studies and science passages. Like literature passages, humanities passages tend to use **evocative language and telling details**. Like history/social studies and science passages, however, their **aim is to inform/explain or convince**.

All the information needed to answer questions based on humanities passages is in the passages themselves.

Humanities Sample Passage

> (1) To dye wool, Navajo (Diné) weaver Lillie Taylor uses plants and vegetables from Arizona, where she lives. (2) For example, she achieved the deep reds and browns featured in her 2003 rug *In the Path of the Four Seasons* by using Arizona dock roots, drying and grinding them before mixing the powder with water to create a dye bath. (3) To intensify the appearance of certain colors, Taylor also sometimes mixes in clay obtained from nearby soil.

As we noted in our introduction to humanities passages, these types of texts have as their main purpose either to inform or explain or to convince readers of something. Using that understanding, accompanied by an analysis of the passage's structure, you'll be better prepared to determine the passage's central idea or claim, which will help you regardless of the specific type of question that might be associated with the passage.

Sentence 1. Sentence 1 establishes a straightforward informative purpose for the passage.

> To dye wool, Navajo (Diné) weaver Lillie Taylor uses plants and vegetables from Arizona, where she lives.

While we haven't yet analyzed Reading and Writing passages by text type—that happens in the next section—it's clear here that the author's intent is to explain an artistic process. One clue is the language the author uses. Taylor's approach is described in a neutral and objective way. If the passage were argumentative in type, by contrast, we'd expect to find language that sets out a claim that can be both defended and challenged. There's nothing like that here. Instead, the author provides a statement of fact about how Taylor uses plants and vegetables from the state in which she lives to create dyes for the wool she uses in her art.

Having figured out the main purpose of the passage, we can make some educated guesses about what we're likely to find in the rest of the passage. Because the passage's purpose is to explain, we should expect the rest of the passage to supply additional facts, details, and examples related to Taylor's art and creative process. Furthermore, because sentence 1 signals that the passage will explain a process, we might also reasonably expect that the connectives the author uses will establish sequential or cause-effect relationships, since these are typically key to texts that seek to explain.

Sentences 2 and 3. As we anticipated, sentences 2 and 3 build on and support the point made in sentence 1 with examples. Specifically, we learn how Taylor got the deep reds and browns in her rug *In the Path of the Four Seasons* as well as how Taylor is able to intensify certain other colors.

> For example, she achieved the deep reds and browns featured in her 2003 rug *In the Path of the Four Seasons* by using Arizona dock roots, drying and grinding them before mixing the powder with water to create a dye bath.

To intensify the appearance of certain colors, Taylor also sometimes mixes in clay obtained from nearby soil.

The connective *for example* at the beginning of sentence 2 is important here for two reasons. First, it lets us know that what follows in the rest of the passage builds on and supports the point made in sentence 1. Second, in so doing, it lets us know (if we didn't already) that sentence 1 captures the central idea of the passage, because examples (sentences 2 and 3) can't fill that role.

Having now done this analysis, we recognize that the passage uses a simple structure of central idea (sentence 1) followed by supporting examples (sentences 2 and 3). The central idea itself is stated explicitly in sentence 1 and doesn't require much in the way of paraphrasing.

Science

Authors write science texts mainly to convey ideas and findings from research in the natural sciences, such as Earth science, biology, chemistry, and physics. Like history/social studies passages in the Reading and Writing section, science passages typically have elements of research reports: research questions, hypotheses, discussions of previous research, descriptions of methodology, data, findings, implications, and recommendations for future research. Because they're so brief, individual science passages may not have all these features, but you're likely to come across all of them at some point while reading the science passages in the Reading and Writing section.

One thing to note here is that although the general features of research reporting found in history/social studies and science passages are the same, the specific kinds of information and ideas presented often differ between the two subject areas. So instead of encountering data on consumer preferences or political movements, as in history/social studies passages, you may be presented with data on animal behavior or star formation.

You can expect to find relationships between and among information and ideas foregrounded in science passages, just as in history/social studies passages. Science passages, like their history/social studies counterparts, may stress time or sequence, cause-effect, or comparison-contrast relationships—or more than one type of relationship. Understanding these relationships is vital to understanding science passages and to answering many Reading and Writing test questions correctly.

Reading and analyzing science passages will call most directly on your skill in and experience with reading texts in science classes. That's because these classes help students such as you approach science writing with the tools, knowledge, and questions that professional researchers use in their own work. Science passages in the Reading and Writing section mimic the style and substance of real-world

QUICK TAKE

Science passages in the Reading and Writing section aim to share ideas and findings from research in Earth science, biology, chemistry, physics, and other natural science fields. Like history/social studies passages, science passages tend to include several **elements of research reports**:

- **research questions**.

- **hypotheses**.

- **discussion of previous research**.

- **methodology**.

- **data**.

- **findings**.

- **implications**.

- **recommendations for future research**.

Science passages (again like history/social studies passages) also establish important **sequential, causal, and comparative relationships**, an understanding of which is central to comprehending these texts. All the information needed to answer questions based on science passages is in the passages themselves.

scientific texts, meaning that "reading like a scientist" will help you successfully approach associated test questions. This doesn't mean, however, that you need specialized scientific knowledge or prior familiarity with the topics under discussion to answer the questions. As always, all the information you'll need to answer questions about science passages is found in the passages themselves.

Science passages in the Reading and Writing section are written specifically for the test.

Our analysis of a sample science passage will follow the same general approach as the one we used to examine a history/social studies passage. That's because, despite important differences in passage content, history/social studies and science passages in the Reading and Writing section tend to follow the same basic structure. We'll first look at the research reporting elements in the passage and then examine the relationships between and among information and ideas in the passage. We've again numbered the sentences for ease of reference, but these sentence numbers don't appear in actual test passages. Also note that we've modified this passage to include sentence 3, which is the correct answer (key) to the associated test question, in order to make the passage more complete.

Science Sample Passage

(1) Jan Gimsa, Robert Sleigh, and Ulrike Gimsa have hypothesized that the sail-like structure running down the back of the dinosaur *Spinosaurus aegyptiacus* improved the animal's success in underwater pursuits of prey species capable of making quick, evasive movements. (2) To evaluate their hypothesis, a second team of researchers constructed two battery-powered mechanical models of *S. aegyptiacus*, one with a sail and one without, and subjected the models to a series of identical tests in a water-filled tank. (3) The model with a sail took significantly less time to complete a sharp turn while submerged than the model without a sail did.

First, let's identify the research reporting elements found in this passage. When doing so, we'll note where the information can be found in the passage and paraphrase it if doing so seems helpful. This passage is fairly dense, so this will take a bit of time and effort.

Research question. The research question is the main thing the scientists are interested in finding out about. Such questions are usually broad, general statements, without a specific expected result in mind. Sentence 1 of this passage informs us that Gimsa, Sleigh, and Gimsa had previously made a claim (hypothesis) about the movement of a particular kind of dinosaur, *Spinosaurus aegyptiacus*, while sentences 2 and 3 tell us that another team of scientists carried out an experiment based on this hypothesis. Given that, we could reasonably formulate the research question as, How, if at all, was the movement of *S. aegyptiacus* affected by the presence of a sail-like structure running down its back?

Hypothesis. Hypotheses aren't the same as research questions, though they're related. A hypothesis puts the research question into terms that can be tested via observation or experimentation. The goal of the research, then, is to either support or refute (reject) the hypothesis using data collected in the study. This means that a hypothesis will indicate the result the researchers expect, with the rest of the study geared toward evaluating whether the results bolster or challenge that hypothesis.

Sentence 1 tells us that Gimsa, Sleigh, and Gimsa had a hypothesis about the role of *S. aegyptiacus*'s sail-like structure, and sentence 2 tells us that "a second team of researchers" set out to test this hypothesis. The hypothesis being tested is identified explicitly in sentence 1: "the sail-like structure running down the back of the dinosaur *Spinosaurus aegyptiacus* improved the animal's success in underwater pursuits of prey species capable of making quick, evasive movements." This statement passes our "test" for hypotheses because it's capable of being supported or refuted by research: a well-designed study will help determine whether the sail-like structure did or didn't help the dinosaur catch fast-moving prey underwater.

Discussion of previous research. This passage does mention earlier research, but it does so in a way that's a little subtle. The "earlier research" is actually that of Gimsa, Sleigh, and Gimsa, who came up with the hypothesis (sentence 1) that the "second team of researchers" (sentence 2) designed an experiment to test. This is how science often works, with one study building on another and the conclusion of one study serving to inspire the hypotheses of later studies. We don't know from the passage what the precise nature of Gimsa, Sleigh, and Gimsa's previous work was, only that it led them to the hypothesis stated in sentence 1. Because all the information needed to answer the associated test question is in the passage itself, this tells us that we don't have to worry about how those three scientists came up with their hypothesis, only that they did and that it led another team to test it.

Methodology. Sentence 2 tells us directly what approach the second team of researchers used. They "constructed two battery-powered mechanical models of *S. aegyptiacus*, one with a sail and one without, and subjected the models to a series of identical tests in a water-filled tank." In other words, the second team set up an experiment in which they compared the underwater movements of two dinosaur models, one that had a sail (which, remember, was hypothesized to aid the species' movement) and one that didn't (thereby serving as a control condition for the purpose of comparison).

Data. Sentence 3 says that "the model [dinosaur] with a sail took significantly less time to complete a sharp turn while submerged than the model without a sail did." Put more simply, the model with the sail (the experimental condition) outperformed the model without the sail (the control condition) in the experiment.

It's at this point that we run out of passage. We can, however, draw a reasonable, text-based inference as to what the **finding** was. A *finding* is a conclusion that scientists reach based on their data and hypothesis. We can safely conclude from what we've already read that the finding here was confirmation of the hypothesis. We can reach that conclusion in just a few steps. (You can probably make this leap more quickly than we illustrate below, but we think it's a useful exercise to sometimes slow down during practice to make our thinking and question-answering processes more explicit.)

- The hypothesis was that the sail-like structure on the dinosaur's back would help the dinosaur chase and catch quick-moving prey underwater.

- The second team of researchers designed an experiment to test this hypothesis.

- Data from the study showed that in tests of maneuverability, the dinosaur model with the sail outperformed the model without the sail.

- The finding, therefore, is that the hypothesis is supported.

We can't make any reasonable inferences from the passage about the **implication** of the study, nor are there any stated or implied **recommendations for future research**.

Now that we've studied the passage for elements of research reports, let's examine the relationships in the passage. We'll again highlight key connectives in boldface, though they won't be marked that way on actual test forms.

> Jan Gimsa, Robert Sleigh, and Ulrike Gimsa have hypothesized that the sail-like structure running down the back of the dinosaur *Spinosaurus aegyptiacus* **improved the animal's success** in underwater pursuits of prey species capable of making quick, evasive movements. **To evaluate their hypothesis**, a second team of researchers constructed two battery-powered mechanical models of *S. aegyptiacus*, one with a sail and one without, and subjected the models to a series of identical tests in a water-filled tank. The model with a sail took significantly **less time** to complete a sharp turn while submerged **than the model without a sail did**.

There are three relationship links we want to call attention to. Note that these links aren't in the form of common transitional words and phrases, such as *but* and *on the other hand*, like we identified in the history/social studies passage sample earlier, but these phrases establish similar kinds of relationships.

- **"improved the animal's success."** This phrase identifies an important comparative relationship: Gimsa, Sleigh, and Gimsa's hypothesis was that *S. aegyptiacus*'s sail-like structure would have made members of the species better able to catch fast-moving prey underwater than they otherwise would have been.

- **"To evaluate their hypothesis."** This phrase identifies an important causal relationship: the second team of researchers conducted their experiment because of Gimsa, Sleigh, and Gimsa's earlier hypothesis.

- **"less time . . . than the model without a sail did."** This phrase identifies another important comparative relationship: the experimental model with the sail made sharp turns faster than did the control-condition model lacking a sail.

Summary: Passage Subject Area

Literature passages

- Taken from previously published novels, short stories, dramas, poems, and works of literary nonfiction (e.g., memoirs, personal essays)

- Notable for evocative word choice, telling details, and figurative language

History/social studies and **science** passages

- Written for the test

- Differ from each other in that history/social studies passages focus on people and societies, while science passages focus on natural phenomena

- Tend to include elements of research reports: research questions, hypotheses, discussions of previous research, methodology, data, findings, implications, and recommendations for future research; may also discuss topics other than research (e.g., historical events, emerging theories)

- Signal important sequential, causal, and comparative relationships using common transitional words and phrases (e.g., *but*, *on the other hand*) as well as phrases unique to a given passage (e.g., *to evaluate the hypothesis*, *improved the animal's success*)

Humanities passages

- Written for the test

- Share information and insights about culture, literature, art, language, and philosophy

- Similar to literature passages in that they tend to feature evocative language and telling details

- Differ from literature passages in that their main aim is to inform/explain or convince

In reading and analyzing the sample passages, we used three main strategies, which we'll continue to employ throughout the rest of this chapter:

- Determining the main purpose of the passage
- Determining the central idea of the passage
- Analyzing the passage structurally

Text Type

In addition to having a subject area, each passage on the digital SAT has a **text type** closely tied to its main purpose.

Table 1 summarizes these text types and their associated main purposes.

Table 1. Passage Text Types and Main Purposes.

Text Type	Main Purpose
Literary	To share ideas and insights into the human condition in order to entertain or enlighten
Informative/explanatory	To convey factual information and ideas or to explain a process, procedure, or phenomenon
Argumentative	To convince readers to accept the "rightness" of a claim using logical reasoning and relevant evidence

As we observed when we examined passages by subject area, determining the main purpose of a passage allows us to get a high-level sense of the passage, or its gist. In this section, we'll apply that approach when examining sample passages by text type. We'll also consider the typical style and tone of each text type as well as features you'll commonly encounter in these passages.

Literary Passages

The literary category in the Reading and Writing section is the same as the literature subject area discussed earlier. The literary category includes excerpts from previously published novels, short stories, dramas, and poems as well as works of literary nonfiction, such as memoirs and personal essays.

In the classroom, there are important differences between how we approach, say, a novel and a poem, but in the Reading and Writing section, the focus of questions on literary passages, regardless of what kind of source the passage is taken from, will be similar: reading and understanding what the author says directly or strongly implies, and understanding and explaining how and why the author made the writing choices they did. In other words, you won't have to know what iambic pentameter is or consider how the set for a play might be constructed.

QUICK TAKE

Passages of the **literary text type** consist of passages in the literature subject area (i.e., excerpts from novels, short stories, dramas, poems, and works of literary nonfiction).

The **general main purpose** of literary texts **is to entertain or enlighten**. On the test, literary passages **have specific purposes as well**, such as to describe a character's personality.

The **style and tone** of literary passages **vary widely** from passage to passage.

Common features include **evocative word choice**, **telling details**, and **figurative language**.

Purpose. The **general main purpose** of literary texts— at least in the real world—**is to entertain or enlighten**. In the Reading and Writing section, we focus on the more specific purposes that particular literary passages have, such as describing

- the personality or actions of a character.

- how two characters interact.

- how one character views another character.

- what a particular setting (time, place) is like.

- how a series of events or actions unfolds.

Although this list is only a sampling of some of the more common purposes of literary passages, it should still give you a sense of the kinds of specific purposes found in literary passages in the Reading and Writing section.

Style and tone. Because literary passages in the Reading and Writing section are excerpted from previously published literature texts, their **styles and tones vary widely**. This makes sense because part of authors' goals in writing literary texts is to express ideas and describe experiences in unique ways.

Common features. You can expect that literary passages will use **evocative word choice**, **telling details**, and **figurative language**, among other features, to express ideas and points of view.

Let's consider how these elements play out in a sample literary passage.

Literary Sample Passage

The following text is from Herman Melville's 1854 short story "The Lightning-Rod Man."

The stranger still stood in the exact middle of the cottage, where he had first planted himself. His singularity impelled a closer scrutiny. A lean, gloomy figure. Hair dark and lank, mattedly streaked over his brow. His sunken pitfalls of eyes were ringed by indigo halos, and played with an innocuous sort of lightning: the gleam without the bolt. The whole man was dripping. He stood in a puddle on the bare oak floor: his strange walking-stick vertically resting at his side.

Before we examine the purpose and features of this passage, note the introductory information provided. Recall that this kind of information is offered only for literature passages because those are the only ones in the Reading and Writing section taken from previously published works. It's tempting to skip over that information and get right to the passage, but this information can provide some important clues about what the passage will contain.

STRATEGY

We recommend that you read the introductory information associated with literary passages, as this information can offer important clues to what you're about to read and/or useful context, such as details about the setting.

In this case, we're told that the passage was excerpted from a Herman Melville short story originally published in 1854. Melville was a famous nineteenth-century U.S. writer probably best known for the novel *Moby-Dick*, so you may know of him or have read some of his writing previously. If so, you might be better prepared for the writing style you encounter in the passage. Even if you don't know who Melville is, though, the fact that the passage is from a short story published in 1854 hints that you should expect to find language and literary techniques different from what you might find in a modern short story.

In addition to bibliographical information, the introductory material accompanying literature passages may include important contextual details, such as the setting of a short story or a brief recap of important events that occurred earlier in a novel. So don't skip this information.

Purpose. A close reading of this passage reveals a great many vivid details about "the stranger." We learn, for example, about his build ("lean"), demeanor ("gloomy"), hair ("dark and lank, mattedly streaked over his brow"), and face ("sunken pitfalls of eyes"). We're also told that "the whole man was dripping" and that he "stood in a puddle on the bare oak floor" and possessed an odd walking stick. Considering these details together, we can reasonably conclude that the (specific) main purpose of this passage is to describe the physical appearance of the character.

Common features. In this Melville passage, we find many examples of the three features commonly found in literary passages in the Reading and Writing section.

- **Evocative word choice.** The passage uses language in ways that we often associate with literature. In everyday conversations and in most nonfiction, it's uncommon, for example, to refer to hair being "mattedly streaked" over a brow or to characterize dark circles around the eyes as "indigo halos." The sentence "his singularity impelled a closer scrutiny" is a particularly strong turn of phrase, indicating that the stranger's oddness and uniqueness ("his singularity") inevitably drew ("impelled") careful looks ("a closer scrutiny"). (Even if the meaning of some of the words here is unfamiliar to you, you can still make a good guess about the intent of the sentence by observing that all the details that follow in the passage are related to the stranger's physical appearance.)

- **Telling details.** The passage uses numerous precise details to characterize the stranger. He's "lean" and "gloomy," with dark, lank, matted hair. The description of his eyes—"sunken pitfalls . . . ringed by indigo halos"—suggests that he's exhausted, perhaps due to lack of sleep. He's also described as "dripping," which indicates that he's been in the rain, on the water, or perhaps both.

- **Figurative language.** "Planted," in the passage's first sentence, is one example of figurative language in the passage. The stranger is obviously not "planted" in the literal sense. Instead, Melville uses the word to suggest that the stranger is unmoving, or fixed in place. "Pitfalls," in the passage's fifth sentence, is used in a similarly nonliteral way. According to the dictionary, a *pitfall* is either a trap, such as a pit, or a hidden danger. Based on how the rest of the passage characterizes the stranger, it's more likely that Melville means to indicate that the stranger is exhausted, as sunken eyes with dark rings are common signs of fatigue. The author also employs a metaphor: the stranger's eyes "played with an innocuous sort of lightning: the gleam without the bolt." In this metaphor, the stranger's eyes have a kind of light in them similar to that produced by lightning. However, we're also told that this "gleam" is "innocuous" and lacks the "bolt" associated with lightning. The general idea here is that while the stranger's eyes have a peculiar light to them, they lack the kind of energy, spark, and danger we think of when we think of lightning. Given that other details we've already examined suggest that the stranger is exhausted, it's reasonable to conclude that this detail is intended to add to that picture. (It's also possible that Melville was also or instead suggesting that the stranger is emotionally haunted by some experience that drained him of vitality, but we can't really tell that for sure without more context than the passage provides.)

Informative/Explanatory Passages

History/social studies, humanities, and science passages in the Reading and Writing section may be of the informative/explanatory text type.

Purpose. Informative/explanatory passages, as the name suggests, either **aim to share factual information and ideas or to explain a process, procedure, or phenomenon**. Passages of this type may, for example, describe the cause and consequence of a historical event, reveal how an artist created a particular work, or detail the steps in an experiment.

The chief difference between an informative/explanatory passage and an argumentative passage (which we'll discuss next) lies in their respective purposes. Informative/explanatory passages treat the information and ideas they share as factual, or as describing the real state of things in the world. Arguments, by contrast, deal with matters about which people can reasonably disagree. Whereas informative/explanatory passages assert and support central ideas (main points) that we as readers assume to be true, argumentative passages assert claims that readers must be convinced of the correctness of through logical reasoning and relevant evidence.

The difference is fairly easy to spot in practice. Consider again the following example from the humanities passage we analyzed earlier.

QUICK TAKE

Passages of the **informative/ explanatory text type** may come from the history/social studies, humanities, or science subject areas.

The **main purpose** of informative/ explanatory passages is to **share factual information and ideas or to explain a process, procedure, or phenomenon**.

Informative/explanatory passages tend to have a **formal style** and **objective tone**.

Common features include a **central idea** and **supporting details**.

> To dye wool, Navajo (Diné) weaver Lillie Taylor uses plants and vegetables from Arizona, where she lives.

As a statement of the central idea of an informative/explanatory text, the sentence simply relates a fact: Taylor uses plants and vegetables found in Arizona to make dyes for the wool she weaves. We'd expect—correctly, as we found out beforehand—that the rest of the passage offers factual details to support that central idea.

If, however, the passage had been written as an argument, we'd expect the author to assert a claim that reasonable people could challenge, such as the following hypothetical example.

> Navajo (Diné) weaver Lillie Taylor's use of local plant- and vegetable-based dyes makes her weavings among the most vibrant being made today.

This claim isn't factually true or false. It's an interpretation being made by the author. We can tell this, in part, by the author's use of subjective language. "Among the most vibrant" isn't something that can objectively be proved true (or false). It's an assertion based on the author's assessment. Given that, we'd expect the author to present logical reasoning and relevant evidence to back up that claim. The details found in the informative/explanatory version of the passage could, in fact, be recast into the argumentative mold.

> **Informative/explanatory:** For example, she achieved the deep reds and browns featured in her 2003 rug *In the Path of the Four Seasons* by using Arizona dock roots, drying and grinding them before mixing the powder with water to create a dye bath.
>
> **Argumentative:** For example, the deep browns and reds featured in Taylor's 2003 rug *In the Path of the Four Seasons* stand out far more than similar colors in other contemporary rugs, thanks to Taylor's use of dried and ground Arizona dock roots.
>
> ....
>
> **Informative/explanatory:** To intensify the appearance of certain colors, Taylor also sometimes mixes in clay obtained from nearby soil.
>
> **Argumentative:** Taylor's occasional use of locally sourced clay in her dyes further adds to the striking appearance of her weavings.

It should be clear by now that claims aren't limited to assertions about controversial topics, such as "pro" or "con" positions in a debate over a hotly contested issue. Claims can be found in any sort of text in which an author is offering their own interpretation or judgment, such as a critic's review of a movie or book, a historian's analysis of why something in the past happened, or a scientist's discussion about why the results of an experiment were different from what had been expected.

Style and tone. Informative/explanatory passages tend to have a **formal style** and **objective tone**. By "formal style," we mean that they tend to use language you'd find more often in academic settings than in everyday conversations, and by "objective tone," we mean that they attempt to describe things as they are in reality.

Common features. As suggested above, informative/explanatory passages contain a **central idea** and **supporting details.** The central idea is the main point the author is trying to make, while the supporting details flesh out that point. Continuing with the Lillie Taylor weaving sample, we can sketch out this structure. In doing so, we'll break down the supporting details into more distinct points than in the original passage to make their individual contributions to the passage clearer.

Central idea: To dye wool, Navajo (Diné) weaver Lillie Taylor uses plants and vegetables from Arizona, where she lives.

Supporting details:

- Taylor created the rug *In the Path of the Four Seasons* in 2003.

- This rug featured deep reds and browns.

- These reds and browns were achieved using Arizona dock roots.

- These dock roots were dried and ground by Taylor, who then mixed the resultant powder with water to create a dye bath.

- Taylor also sometimes mixes clay into her dyes.

- This clay is obtained from nearby soil.

- The use of this clay intensifies the appearance of certain colors.

Before we go on to the argumentative text type, two last points about informative/explanatory passages are worth making here:

- The central idea may be stated explicitly (as in the Lillie Taylor weaving sample), or you may need to infer it using evidence from the text.

- If stated explicitly, the central idea may appear anywhere in the passage, not just the first sentence. Although authors often begin paragraphs with topic sentences, sometimes the central idea appears at the end or even in the middle of a passage.

Argumentative Passages

History/social studies, humanities, and science passages in the Reading and Writing section may also be argumentative in nature instead of informative/explanatory. We've already discussed how arguments differ from informative/explanatory texts, but we'll recap here.

Purpose. Arguments seek to convince readers of the "rightness" of the author's point of view, interpretations, or recommendations.

QUICK TAKE

Passages of the **argumentative text type** may come from the history/social studies, humanities, or science subject areas.

The main purpose of argumentative passages is to **convince readers of the "rightness" of a claim** using logical reasoning and relevant evidence.

Argumentative passages tend to have a **formal style** and **objective tone**.

Common features include a **central claim**, **logical reasoning**, and **relevant evidence**.

We use "convince" here rather than "persuade" because arguments, unlike persuasive pieces, rely chiefly on logical reasoning and relevant evidence to support their claims. Persuasive pieces may use logical reasoning and evidence as well, but they may also draw on other writing techniques, such as appeals to emotion. While we find persuasive writing in many areas of our lives, such as in newspaper opinion columns, in politics, and in advertising, the argumentative mode is more typical of academic writing in the nonliterary subject areas sampled in the Reading and Writing section.

It's worth mentioning here explicitly that when we use the terms *argument* and *argumentative*, we're not using them in the sense of "fight" or "fighting," as in "I had an argument with my friend last night." Rather, we use them in a more technical way to refer to pieces of writing that make logical arguments or that use logical argumentation to assert and support claims. Arguments in this sense sometimes concern issues that people sharply disagree about, but that isn't always the case. As we observed earlier, authors of all sorts, writing texts serving many different purposes, use the argumentative form.

Style and tone. Like informative/explanatory passages, argumentative passages tend to have a formal style and objective tone. The latter is true even though arguments do tend to make greater use of subjective language, or the language of evaluation, than do informative/explanatory texts. Even when authors of arguments offer opinions or judgments, they do so in ways that suggest these assessments describe the way things really are; as part of the "bargain," readers who have weighed the claims and considered the reasoning and evidence supporting them are then free to accept or reject these assessments.

Common features. Argumentative passages contain a **central claim** that is backed up by **logical reasoning** and **relevant evidence**. The central claim is the main point the author is trying to convince readers of. As we noted earlier, this claim doesn't have to be about a controversial issue. It can, in fact, be any sort of assertion about which reasonable people can disagree.

The nature of evidence in arguments varies by subject area, as we've already observed. In other words, what counts as evidence in, for example, the humanities differs from what counts as evidence in science. In humanities passages, such as the Lillie Taylor sample, evidence may come in the form of analyses of specific works of art, such as Taylor's 2003 rug *In the Path of the Four Seasons*, whereas evidence in science passages may consist of data that support a hypothesis. To be meaningful, evidence must be relevant both to the topic and the subject area.

Logical reasoning is, metaphorically speaking, the connective tissue of an argument. It's the analysis—the "thinking"—that the author performs to connect the evidence being presented with the claim being asserted.

Let's consider the following sample argumentative passage in terms of its main purpose, style and tone, and key features.

Argumentative Sample Passage

> (1) Many animals, including humans, must sleep, and sleep is known to have a role in everything from healing injuries to encoding information in long-term memory. (2) But some scientists claim that, from an evolutionary standpoint, deep sleep for hours at a time leaves an animal so vulnerable that the known benefits of sleeping seem insufficient to explain why it became so widespread in the animal kingdom. (3) These scientists therefore imply that prolonged deep sleep is likely advantageous in ways that have yet to be discovered.

Note that we've added the answer to the question associated with this passage into the passage itself so that you can focus on how the text is put together. Also note that we've again numbered the passage's sentences here for ease of reference, but you won't find sentence numbers in the passages you read for practice or on test day.

Purpose. Given that this passage is an argument, we should expect that it would assert a debatable claim. This is, indeed, the case, but just what that central claim is requires some work to uncover.

Sentence 1 states that "many animals, including humans, must sleep" and "sleep is known to have a role in everything from healing injuries to encoding information in long-term memory." Although these statements might broadly be considered claims, neither qualifies as this passage's central claim. Reading through the rest of the passage, we learn that the information in sentence 1 is mostly background. It doesn't, in other words, capture the basic point of the passage.

How about sentence 2? This sentence even uses the word "claim," but it's not actually the passage's claim. It's the hypothesis that "some scientists" believe to be true. In the passage, sentence 2 mainly serves to qualify, or add considerations to, the commonly accepted ideas, cited in sentence 1, that many animals must sleep and that sleep has many known benefits. Sentence 2 doesn't directly challenge earlier findings that sleep is beneficial, but it does qualify these findings. To these scientists, the evolutionary danger to a species of long-lasting deep sleep is so profound that the benefits researchers have already found for sleep ("from healing injuries to encoding information in long-term memory") can't really explain why many species engage in such sleep.

That leaves us with sentence 3, which does, in fact, come closest to capturing the passage's central claim. It asserts that the scientists who found a problem with commonly accepted ideas about deep sleep believe ("imply") that there must be something else beneficial ("advantageous") to deep sleep that science has yet to discover.

If we string the various points made in the three sentences into a single statement of the passage's claim, we might come up with something like the following.

> Some scientists believe that long periods of deep sleep must have evolutionary benefits for animals beyond those already discovered.

This version of the claim leans heavily on sentence 3 but also incorporates ideas from the first two sentences—specifically, that deep sleep has benefits and that deep sleep also has evolutionary drawbacks (i.e., leaves animals vulnerable).

As a side note, it's worth calling out here that the passage doesn't actually explain how the scientists went about trying to prove their hypothesis, as in many passages in the Reading and Writing section. Instead, the focus here is on logical reasoning, and specifically on how these scientists came to believe that conventional explanations for why many animals engage in long periods of deep sleep are inadequate given that deep sleep is a profound evolutionary disadvantage.

Taking a structural approach to analyzing this passage, we might sketch out the following.

Sentence 1	Background: Sleep benefits animals.
Sentence 2	Problem: These benefits don't explain why some animals routinely engage in seemingly dangerous long periods of deep sleep.
Sentence 3	Qualification: While sleep does have known benefits for animals, science hasn't figured out yet why many animals engage in long periods of deep sleep, given how risky it is from an evolutionary standpoint.

Although this passage doesn't strictly follow the research report structure we discussed above, we can still find some research reporting elements.

Sentence 1	Discussion of previous research: Although we're not told directly that the benefits of sleep for animals were discovered by prior scientific research, it's a reasonable, text-supported conclusion.
Sentence 2	Implication: We can consider sentence 2 an implication since it points out a shortcoming of previous research.

REMINDER

Earlier in this chapter, we mentioned that not all science (or history/social studies) passages in the Reading and Writing section strictly follow the research reporting model. This argumentative passage is an example of one that doesn't.

Sentence 3   Recommendation for future research: Again, we're not told directly that "more research is needed," but the idea is strongly implicit, since scientists' understanding of the benefits of sleep for animals has been shown to be inadequate.

Style and tone. The passage clearly adopts a formal style and objective tone. The formality of the style is apparent in the sentence structures used and the vocabulary choices made by the author. Sentence 1 is a good example of an objective tone: the ideas that many animals must sleep and that sleep has many benefits for these animals are presented as facts, and while the passage goes on to point out a limitation of scientific understanding of sleep, it never questions the basic "rightness" of the ideas expressed in sentence 1. Overall, the passage takes on a tone of neutral reporting on a scientific phenomenon.

Common features. We've already discussed the passage's claim. Let's consider how logical reasoning and evidence are used.

The evidence here isn't in the form of data, such as results from an experiment or observational study. Instead, the evidence is in the form of a weakness found in current scientific explanations of the value of sleep to animals. Specifically, the evidence is that current explanations can't account for why some animals engage in long periods of deep sleep, which, from an evolutionary standpoint, is dangerous since it leaves animals defenseless for extended periods of time. We can reasonably infer from the passage that this evidence, as well as the current scientific explanations, are based on research even though the studies leading to those conclusions aren't discussed.

The logical reasoning used here is closely tied to the passage's structure, which we've already analyzed.

Sentence 1   Previous research has found that animals gain many benefits from sleep.

Sentence 2   **However,** some scientists believe that this previous research doesn't adequately explain why some animals engage in long periods of deep sleep.

Sentence 3   **Therefore,** more research is needed to find a better explanation for sleep in animals, one that accounts for why some animals engage in long periods of deep sleep.

We've highlighted the words *however* and *therefore* to call attention to the logical reasoning used in the passage. *However* highlights that sentence 2 challenges or undercuts sentence 1, while *therefore* highlights the conclusion that logically follows from sentence 2 being the case.

Summary: Passage Text Type

Literary passages (same features as for passages in the literature subject area)

- Purpose: In general, to entertain or enlighten; specific purposes vary by passage

- Style and tone: Vary widely from passage to passage

- Common features

  - Evocative word choice

  - Telling details

  - Figurative language

Informative/explanatory passages

- Purpose: To share factual information and ideas or to explain a process, procedure, or phenomenon

- Style and tone: Formal and objective

- Common features

  - A central idea

  - Supporting details

Argumentative passages

- Purpose: To convince readers of the "rightness" of a claim

- Style and tone: Formal and objective

- Common features

  - A central claim

  - Logical reasoning

  - Relevant evidence

Text Complexity

Our last topic specifically related to Reading and Writing passages is text complexity. You should be aware that passages in the Reading and Writing section may vary in terms of how challenging or easy the texts themselves are to read. Some passages may be relatively easy for most test takers, while others may pose a significant challenge. Since the SAT measures your readiness for college and careers, the challenge level of the texts you'll be asked to read on test day has to match the expectations that college instructors have for their incoming students and that employers have for people beginning workforce training programs.

This may sound daunting, especially if you don't feel you're a strong reader, but don't worry too much about this aspect of the test section. In this chapter, we've given you several ways to examine passages and break them down regardless of their difficulty, and most of the samples we presented were from the middle and the higher end of the text complexity range used in the Reading and Writing section. Remember, too, that all the information needed to answer test questions is found in their associated passages (and sometimes informational graphics, the topic of our next chapter), so even if you run into some unfamiliar words or difficult-to-understand concepts, you likely can use what you *do* know about passages in general and specific passages in particular to get a good handle on what the questions are asking and, at the very least, eliminate some incorrect answer choices, turning your response from a random guess into an educated one (and one with a vastly higher probability of success). Finally, because each Reading and Writing passage has only one question associated with it, you can give your best effort and move on from any one passage that you feel you don't understand well, as there's no penalty for guessing on the digital SAT.

Summary: Reading and Writing Passages

Each Reading and Writing passage has

- a **subject area** (literature, history/social studies, humanities, science)
  - ◆ **Literature** passages
    - – Purpose: To share ideas and experiences in vivid, memorable ways
    - – Style and tone: Vary widely from passage to passage
    - – Common features
      - • Evocative word choice
      - • Telling details
      - • Figurative language
  - ◆ **History/social studies** and **science** passages
    - – Purpose: To share ideas and findings from research
    - – Common features
      - • Elements of research reports
        - ○ Research questions
        - ○ Hypotheses
        - ○ Discussion of previous research
        - ○ Methodology
        - ○ Data
        - ○ Findings
        - ○ Implications
        - ○ Recommendations for future research
      - • Sequential, causal, and comparative relationships

- ◆ **Humanities** passages
  - – Purpose: To share ideas and insights about culture, literature, art, language, and philosophy
  - – Common features
    - • Evocative language
    - • Telling details
- ▪ a **text type** (literary, informative/explanatory, argumentative)
  - ◆ Literary passages
    - – Purpose
      - • In general, to entertain or enlighten
      - • Specific purpose varies by passage (e.g., to describe a character's personality)
    - – Style and tone: Vary widely from passage to passage
    - – Common features
      - • Evocative word choice
      - • Telling details
      - • Figurative language
  - ◆ Informative/explanatory passages
    - – Purpose: To share factual information and ideas or to explain a process, procedure, or phenomenon
    - – Style and tone: Formal and objective
    - – Common features
      - • A central idea
      - • Supporting details
  - ◆ Argumentative passages
    - – Purpose: To convince readers of the "rightness" of a claim
    - – Style and tone: Formal and objective
    - – Common features
      - • A central claim
      - • Logical reasoning
      - • Relevant evidence
- ▪ a **text complexity** (difficulty) ranging from relatively easy to significantly challenging

Some Reading and Writing passages include an informational graphic (**the** topic of our next chapter).

KEYS TO SUCCESS ON THE READING AND WRITING SECTION

- All the information needed to answer a given question is in the passage itself (or in an associated informational graphic).

- Base your answers to questions on what the passage says explicitly and what the passage strongly implies.

- If you struggle with a passage, give your best answer and move on. (You can always flag questions to return to if time permits.)

- Answer every question, even if you have to guess. Whenever possible, make educated rather than random guesses by focusing on what you *do* understand about a passage and eliminating incorrect answer choices. There's no penalty for guessing on the digital SAT.

- Remember that you *can* do this. You have the tools now (if you didn't before) to get the information you need from Reading and Writing passages to answer the associated questions.

CHAPTER 9

Reading and Writing: Informational Graphics

In this chapter, we'll discuss and walk through examples of the three kinds of informational graphics you may encounter in the Reading and Writing section: tables, bar graphs, and line graphs. We'll consider the important features common to all three graphics types so that you'll be better prepared to analyze such figures during practice and on test day. We'll then examine a sample of each type of graphic. We'll also talk about what you'll have to do with the graphics on test day—and what you won't, namely performing calculations (which is why a calculator isn't allowed for the Reading and Writing section).

Why Include Informational Graphics on a Test of Reading and Writing?

Before we get started, though, we should explain why informational graphics are included in the Reading and Writing section in the first place.

The SAT is a test of your college and career readiness. As we saw in the previous chapter, Reading and Writing passages simulate the kinds of reading and writing activities you not only engage in now in your high school classes but that you'll also participate in in college or workforce training. An important part of the way that many authors convey information and ideas in several of the subject areas represented in the Reading and Writing section is through the use of informational graphics. These graphics display data in ways that are typically easier to understand and work with than written descriptions are, and they often display more data than the author has an opportunity to discuss in writing (though extraneous data are minimized in graphics in the Reading and Writing section so that you can focus on the data relevant to answering a given question).

You'll also need to be able to read and analyze data from informational graphics in your everyday life. Tables, bar graphs, and line graphs— the three types of informational graphics in the Reading and Writing section—are among the most common ways authors in history/social studies, the humanities, and science as well as in workplace settings and popular media display data visually. You may not need to produce such data displays on your own, but you do need to be an informed consumer of such displays to navigate successfully in our increasingly data-driven world.

In short, the ability to make sense of and critically analyze data displays is important not only in your current and future classes but also in many other areas of your life after high school.

Common Features of Informational Graphics

Regardless of type, each informational graphic in the Reading and Writing section has a **title**, one or more **labels**, and **data**, while some graphics also have a **legend** and/or **additional information**. It's important to recognize and make use of these features, as they provide critical clues to how to read and interpret a given graphic.

To help make this discussion more concrete, we'll refer to the following sample table.

Informational Graphic Sample 1

Participants' Evaluation of the Likelihood That Robots
Can Work Effectively in Different Occupations

Occupation	Somewhat or very unlikely (%)	Neutral (%)	Somewhat or very likely (%)
Television news anchor	24	9	67
Teacher	37	16	47
Firefighter	62	9	30
Surgeon	74	9	16
Tour guide	10	8	82

Rows in table may not add up to 100 due to rounding.

Title. Each graphic has a title. This title lets you know what the general topic of the graphic is, but it often provides additional useful information.

Let's consider the title for the sample graphic above.

Participants' Evaluation of the Likelihood That Robots
Can Work Effectively in Different Occupations

Even without the graphic, we can draw some reasonable conclusions about the topic addressed and the kind of data displayed. The graphic focuses on people's perceptions of how likely robots are to successfully take on a range of jobs. Given that, it's likely that the data displayed will be quantitative and drawn from a survey or similar tool.

Labels. Although different kinds of informational graphics label key elements in different ways, all types of graphics use such labels to identify their constituent parts. These labels are vital to understanding what the displayed data represent.

Let's focus on a portion of the sample informational graphic above.

Occupation	Somewhat or very unlikely (%)	Neutral (%)	Somewhat or very likely (%)

This graphic uses the label "Occupation" for the leftmost column. Looking down the column, we see a list of five types of jobs: television news anchor, teacher, firefighter, surgeon, and tour guide. Examining the full graphic, we can reasonably conclude that participants in the study were asked their view of the likelihood that a robot could successfully perform each of those jobs.

The remaining columns are headed by three labels: "Somewhat or very unlikely (%)," "Neutral (%)," and "Somewhat or very likely (%)." Although this table lacks an overarching label for these three columns, we can reasonably infer that each of these columns corresponds to a possible response on the survey (or other tool) participants were given. The "(%)" symbol in each column tells us that the data are percentages, which isn't surprising given that we've already concluded that participants were given a survey (or the like) and asked to rate likelihood.

Data. Data are, of course, the heart of informational graphics. These data can take many forms and can be collected in many different ways. The data you encounter in informational graphics in the Reading and Writing section will typically be quantitative (numeric) in nature, although other types are possible. Quantitative data can consist of counts (e.g., how many times something occurred), percentages (e.g., what proportion of people behave in a given way), measurements (e.g., the body lengths of animals raised under different conditions), monetary values (e.g., the cost, in U.S. dollars, of various items), and so on. There's really no theoretical limit to the kinds of quantitative data that can be displayed.

As we've already determined, our sample table presents percentages— specifically, the percentages of participants who held certain views on the likelihood of robots successfully performing various types of jobs.

Occupation	Somewhat or very unlikely (%)	Neutral (%)	Somewhat or very likely (%)
Television news anchor	24	9	67

These rows from the full table represent the percentages of participants who rated the likelihood of a robot successfully performing the job of television news anchor as somewhat or very unlikely (24 percent) and somewhat or very likely (67 percent), as well as the percentage of participants who had no strong opinion on the matter ("neutral"; 9 percent).

Legend. Graphs used in the Reading and Writing section will also contain a legend. A *legend* is a guide to how to interpret the bars or lines in the figure, as in the sample below.

Informational Graphic Sample 2

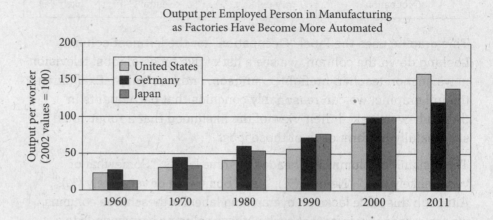

In this bar graph, which presents data about employee output in factories exhibiting greater levels of automation over time, the legend—the small box in the upper left-hand corner—tells us that the three bars for each year represent three different nations: the United States (light gray), Germany (black), and Japan (dark gray).

Additional information. Creators of informational graphics strive to make the data displayed as clear and understandable as possible. Sometimes, however, they supply additional information to guide how readers interpret the figures.

For example, in the sample table presented earlier in this chapter, we're given this additional information.

> Rows in table may not add up to 100 due to rounding.

This note is intended to allay concerns from attentive readers who discover (and may then be distracted by the fact) that the percentages in the table—specifically, the totals for the firefighter and surgeon rows—add up to something other than 100 percent (101 and 99, respectively). Pay attention to these notes, as they can significantly aid your understanding of a graphic and its data.

Informational Graphics in the Reading and Writing Section

Now let's examine each of the three types of informational graphics found in the Reading and Writing section: tables, bar graphs, and line graphs.

Tables

Authors use tables to organize and display a wide variety of data. These authors tend to favor using tables over graphs when the goal is to convey data precisely (e.g., exact percentages of survey participants answering in certain ways) or when they want to display data that don't share a common scale or unit of measurement, such as the length of selected passenger airline routes in miles alongside the average cost in U.S. dollars of tickets to fly those routes.

Let's examine another table, this time about changes to road capacity. Because we already studied a fairly simple table, we've selected a more complex one to discuss here. Bear with us on this because we're going to analyze this table in detail so that you get a better sense of just how much information you can obtain, even though no single question in the Reading and Writing section will require you to go into this much depth on test day.

Informational Graphic Sample 3

Effect of Route Capacity Reductions in Several Regions

Region	Vehicles per day on altered road		Vehicles per day on surrounding roads		Change in regional traffic
	Before alteration	After alteration	Before alteration	After alteration	
Rathausplatz, Nürnberg	24,584	0	67,284	55,824	−146.6%
Southampton city center	5,316	3,081	26,522	24,101	−87.5%
Tower Bridge, London	44,242	0	103,262	111,999	−80.3%
New York highway	110,000	50,000	540,000	560,000	−36.4%
Kinnaird Bridge, Edmonton	1,300	0	2,130	2,885	−41.9%

Title. The title tells us that the data in the table are intended to illustrate a cause-effect relationship ("effect of")—specifically, the impact that reductions in road capacity (i.e., restrictions on the amount of traffic that can use a given road) had on the numbers of vehicles per day on various roads in various regions. We can also reasonably expect, as turns out to be the case, that the data will be quantitative.

Labels. We need to pay attention to several labels here. The label for the leftmost column is "Region," and it heads a list of different locations around the world. Continuing from the left, the second and third columns have two labels. The topmost, "Vehicles per day on altered road," applies to both columns; each column also has its own label: "Before alteration" and "After alteration," respectively. This indicates that these columns display the average number of vehicles per day on an altered road, both before and after the alteration. (The numbers in the third column are all lower than the corresponding numbers in the second column because, as the table's title indicates, the "alteration" referred to involved reducing the traffic capacity of the road(s) in the locations listed in the leftmost column.) The fourth and fifth columns are labeled similarly to the second and third, but this time they describe the effect, in terms of vehicles per day, on roads surrounding those whose capacity was reduced. The rightmost column, "Change in regional traffic," lists negative percentages indicating reductions in traffic.

Data. The data displayed in this table are of two kinds. The first, found in the second through fifth columns (again counting from the left), are counts (or, more likely, estimated averages) of the number of vehicles using a road or roads in a given location (identified in the leftmost column) under various conditions. The second type of data, found in the rightmost column, consists of percentages indicating the extent of change in traffic. As we previously noted, these percentages are all negative because the data pertain to efforts to reduce traffic.

The big question here is, what can we make of these data?

First, let's reconsider the title. From it, we know that the table intends to show a cause-effect relationship between the amount of traffic on roads in several different regions and efforts to reduce the traffic capacity of those roads.

Second, let's consider some of the conclusions we're able to draw from the data. In doing so, we'll identify specific data points as well as patterns.

- Each of the listed regions experienced decreases in traffic on altered roads. For example, in Tower Bridge, London, traffic on an altered road decreased from 44,242 vehicles per day before the alteration to 0 after. (Presumably, the road was closed to vehicle traffic.)

- While some of the regions (e.g., Rathausplatz, Nürnberg) experienced a similar drop in traffic (in terms of number of vehicles per day) on surrounding roads after road alteration was complete, other regions (e.g., New York highway) saw increases in such traffic.

- The decrease in traffic across the regions varied from very high (e.g., −146.6% in Rathausplatz) to moderate (−36.4% for New York highway).

Now let's consider whether we can reach a "big picture" understanding of the data in the table, making use of the conclusions we've already drawn.

Let's first remind ourselves of what the table intends to illustrate. As we mentioned when we discussed the title, the table is meant to show a cause-effect relationship. Specifically, it's meant to show the effect of road capacity reduction efforts on the amount of traffic.

When we analyzed the labels and data in the table, we observed that the table not only indicates the effect of road capacity reduction efforts on specific roads but also on surrounding (neighboring) roads. This might lead us to wonder why both capacity-reduced roads and surrounding roads are included in the table. Given what we've already identified as the purpose of the table, the most likely reason is that if traffic is intentionally reduced on specific roads (columns 2 and 3 of the table) but actually goes up on surrounding roads (columns 4 and 5), the *total* amount of vehicle traffic may not be reduced as much as planners may have hoped, and thus road capacity reduction may not always lead to robust reductions in total traffic.

If we go back to our analysis of the data, we find that this was the case. While two regions in the table—Rathausplatz, Nürnberg, and Southampton city center—experienced reductions in both traffic on the altered road and surrounding roads, the other three regions in the table experienced an increase in the amount of traffic on surrounding roads once a given road was altered to reduce traffic. These latter three regions therefore also had smaller percentages in the "change in regional traffic" column.

From all of this, we can reasonably conclude that efforts to reduce vehicle capacity on roads are less likely to be successful in actually reducing vehicle traffic overall if changes to one road just lead drivers to move to surrounding roads. Thus, while all the road alterations presented in the table reduced overall traffic (as indicated by the negative percentages in the rightmost column), the more successful efforts in Rathausplatz and Southampton managed to reduce traffic on specific roads *and* keep displaced traffic from spilling over onto surrounding roads.

Bar Graphs

Authors use bar graphs to display data when they want to highlight comparisons in the data. In doing so, they sacrifice some of the precision of tables to make it easier for readers to grasp these comparisons visually.

Let's start with a straightforward example of a bar graph, which we'll analyze in terms of how the common features of graphics presented above are represented.

QUICK TAKE

Authors use **bar graphs** when they want readers to be able to easily make comparisons with data and when exact figures are less important than overall patterns.

Informational Graphic Sample 4

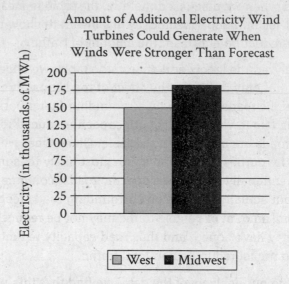

Amount of Additional Electricity Wind
Turbines Could Generate When
Winds Were Stronger Than Forecast

□ West   ■ Midwest

Title. The title for this graphic tells us that the data indicate how much extra electricity wind turbines can generate when the wind is stronger than forecasted. We note from this that the data do *not* represent the total amount of electricity generated by wind turbines but rather the "excess" amount produced when stronger-than-expected winds occur.

Labels. Bar graphs (and line graphs) include labels for one or more axes. In this simple graph, only one axis—the *y*-axis, or vertical axis— is so labeled: "Electricity (in thousands of MWh)." (*MWh* are megawatt hours.) This label is accompanied by a scale, which divides the graph into 25-unit increments from 0 to 200. Note, however, that the label indicates that these numerals represent *thousands* of MWh, so the scale actually ranges from 0 MWh to 200,000 MWh, not 0 to 200. Each increment on the graph represents 25,000 MWh.

Legend. The legend indicates that the first bar represents the "West," while the second bar represents the "Midwest." Paying attention to the legend not only allows us to make sense of the bars but also gives us an important hint about what's being compared in the graph—in this case, the additional electricity generated by wind turbines in two regions.

Data. Bringing the above analyses together, we can figure out that the graph is trying to tell us how two different regions (West, Midwest) compare in terms of the amount of "extra" electricity that wind turbines generate during stronger-than-forecasted winds. In this bar graph, we can simply compare the height of the two bars to see that the Midwest generates more such electricity than does the West. Because the bar for the West tops out exactly at the 150 mark, we can precisely determine that output; because the bar for the Midwest, by contrast, tops out at between 175 and 200, we can only really estimate the amount. (This is a key difference between a table and a graph, as we noted before. The graph was doubtlessly built from precise values, but these values have been somewhat obscured here because the exact values are less important than the comparison.)

Now let's take a quick look at another, slightly more complex bar graph.

Informational Graphic Sample 5

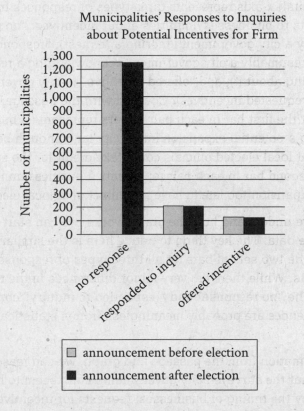

Municipalities' Responses to Inquiries about Potential Incentives for Firm

☐ announcement before election
■ announcement after election

To make sense of this graph, we'll need the context provided in the accompanying passage. This exercise is good practice for test day, as many graphics questions in the Reading and Writing section will not only require you to read and interpret graphics but also make connections between graphics and the passages that accompany them.

Here's the passage for that figure:

> In the United States, firms often seek incentives from municipal governments to expand to those municipalities. A team of political scientists hypothesized that municipalities are much more likely to respond to firms and offer incentives if expansions can be announced in time to benefit local elected officials than if they can't. The team contacted officials in thousands of municipalities, inquiring about incentives for a firm looking to expand and indicating that the firm would announce its expansion on a date either just before or just after the next election.

Pairing the information from the passage and the figure, we can make better sense of the graph's title, "Municipalities' Responses to Inquiries about Potential Incentives for Firm." We can figure out that the graph depicts how various city governments (municipalities) responded to business firms' requests for financial incentives to expand into their cities. By reading the labels, we see that the (vertical) *y*-axis represents number of city governments, in increments of one hundred, while the (horizontal) *x*-axis represents three types of responses from city governments to businesses' inquiries about incentives: "no response" (presumably a city government ignoring a request), "responded to inquiry" (presumably a city government acknowledging a request but doing nothing about it), and "offered incentive" (a city government giving out requested incentives). Coupled with the passage, the legend tells us that the first bar in each pair of bars represents a business announcing a potential expansion into a city long enough before an election that local elected officials could take credit for the expansion, while the second bar in each pair represents a business announcing a potential expansion too late to have an impact on a local election.

Now that we understand how the graph works, we can start to make sense of the data. The key thing to notice here is the similarity of the heights of the two sets of bars for all three types of responses from city governments. While there are very minor differences in the two bars' heights in the "no response" and "responded to inquiry" conditions, those differences are probably meaningless from a statistical standpoint.

Using information from the passage and graph, we can reasonably conclude that the surveyed city governments don't seem to have been motivated by the timing of businesses' requests for incentives. In the context of the passage, this would further lead us to conclude that the researchers' hypothesis—"municipalities are much more likely to respond to firms and offer incentives if expansions can be announced in time to benefit local elected officials than if they can't"—is incorrect. If the hypothesis *had* been correct, we would expect the first bars for at least the "responded to inquiry" and "offered incentive" conditions to be noticeably higher than the corresponding second bars. Instead, they're nearly or exactly equal.

Line Graphs

The third and final informational graphic type you may encounter in the Reading and Writing section is the line graph. Like bar graphs, line graphs prioritize illustrating comparisons, but line graphs also make it easy to spot trends in data.

Let's consider a relatively straightforward line graph.

QUICK TAKE
Authors use **line graphs** when they want to make it easy for readers to draw comparisons and/or identify trends in data, such as change over time.

Informational Graphic Sample 6

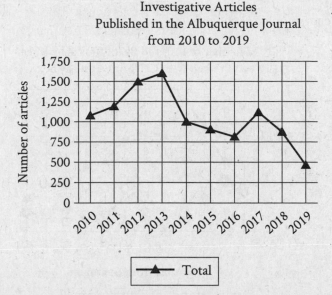

As we mentioned above, line graphs excel at illustrating trends. This graph's title informs us that the graph depicts the number of investigative articles published in the *Albuquerque Journal* in the time span from 2010 to 2019. The *y*-axis label tells us that the vertical axis represents the number of articles published, in increments of 250. Although unlabeled, the *x*-axis represents years from 2010 to 2019, inclusive. The legend indicates that each triangle in the graph represents the total number of investigative articles published in a given year. In terms of data, we can (roughly) identify the number of investigative articles published by the *Journal* each year, but the more interesting bit is analyzing how this number has changed over time. The overall trend isn't perfectly consistent, but the general pattern is a decrease in the number of investigative articles published, which reached a low (in the years represented) in 2019 after a peak in 2013.

A more complex line graph in the Reading and Writing section may look like the following.

Informational Graphic Sample 7

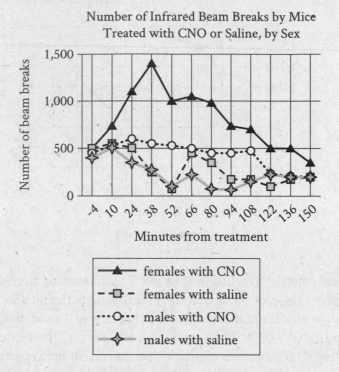

Rather than analyze this figure in detail, which would require working through the passage context, we really just want to illustrate here how line graphs can become more complex than the simple example we reviewed previously. But don't worry: more complex line graphs such as this will have the same basic features as simpler ones and can be evaluated in similar ways. The main difference is that in addition to being able to examine a single trend, such as the number of investigative articles a single newspaper published over time, you can compare multiple trends.

In this case, two variables are represented in the graph: (1) sex of the mice (male, female) and (2) treatment condition (treated with CNO, treated with saline). The combination of these two variables—females treated with CNO, females treated with saline, males treated with CNO, males treated with saline—results in the four lines graphed above. As the legend indicates, each of these lines has its own symbol (triangle, square, circle, diamond) and line style (solid black, dash, dot, solid gray), making it easier to tell them apart.

These lines are plotted against a grid in which the *y*-axis represents the number of infrared beam breaks by the mice, in increments of five hundred, and the *x*-axis represents time—specifically, minutes from the time at which the female and male mice were treated with either CNO or saline—in fourteen-minute increments.

Even without knowing more about the scientific study in question, we can both identify some specific data points and recognize some differences in how mice of different sexes responded to the two treatment conditions. For example, thirty-eight minutes after treatment (*x*-axis), female mice treated with CNO (solid black line with triangles) broke infrared beams approximately 1,450 times (*y*-axis). We can also recognize that during the period after the treatment, these mice broke infrared beams more often than did female mice treated with saline or male mice treated with either CNO or saline.

One interesting note about this graph is the inclusion of "−4 minutes" on the *x*-axis. Recall that the *x*-axis represents minutes from treatment. It's reasonable to conclude, then, that "−4 minutes from treatment" represents four minutes *before* the treatment with either CNO or saline was administered. Researchers likely included this information as a baseline—specifically, to indicate, for purposes of comparison, how the mice behaved just before receiving one of the two treatments.

What You Will and Won't Do with Reading and Writing Informational Graphics

Reading and Writing questions associated with informational graphics may ask you to do one or more of the following three things:

- **Locate data**, such as identifying a specific value from a table.

- **Interpret data**, such as recognizing trends in data and making comparisons.

- **Make connections** between data and the information and ideas in the associated passage.

To this point, we've focused primarily on the first two bullets, but you've probably already gotten some idea of how the information and ideas in the passages associated with graphics not only help you figure out what a given graphic means but also provide a context and a purpose for locating and interpreting data. We'll provide a few examples of this third type of task in chapters 11 and 12.

It's important to note here that **you *won't* be asked to perform calculations** with data from graphics in the Reading and Writing section. This means, for example, that you won't have to add, subtract, multiply, or divide using the data from graphics. For this reason, the use of a calculator isn't allowed (and wouldn't be beneficial) in the Reading and Writing section.

QUICK TAKE

When analyzing informational graphics in the Reading and Writing section, you may be asked to **locate data**, **interpret data**, and/or **make connections** between data and the associated passage.

You **won't**, however, have to perform calculations, and the use of a calculator isn't permitted in the Reading and Writing section (nor would it help to have access to one).

Summary: Reading and Writing Informational Graphics

Three types of informational graphics appear in the Reading and Writing section.

- **Tables**

- **Bar graphs**

- **Line graphs**

Regardless of type, informational graphics have certain features in common.

- A **title** indicating the purpose of the graphic

- **Labels** for a graphic's important elements (e.g., x- and y-axes)

- **Data**, typically in quantitative (numerical) form

- In addition, graphics may also have

  - a **legend** that explains the meaning of the bars or lines in a graph.

  - **additional information** that helps you interpret the graphic.

For graphics-related questions in the Reading and Writing section, you'll be asked to

- **locate data** (e.g., find a specific value in a table),

- **interpret data** (e.g., identify trends or make comparisons), and/or

- **make connections** between data and the information and ideas in the associated passage.

You *won't* be asked to perform calculations in the Reading and Writing section, and the use of a calculator isn't allowed in that section.

CHAPTER 10

Reading and Writing: Questions—Introduction

The following chapters discuss the kinds of questions you'll encounter in the Reading and Writing section and give you opportunities to immediately practice what you've learned.

Recall that the Reading and Writing section has questions in four broad categories, which we refer to as *content domains*. Each content domain has a "big idea," or common focus, tying all the questions in the domain together at a conceptual level. Table 1 summarizes the section's four content domains and the focus of their respective questions.

Table 1. Reading and Writing Section Content Domains.

Reading and Writing Content Domain	The Big Idea
Information and Ideas (chapters 11 and 12)	Testing your understanding of what you read
Craft and Structure (chapters 13 and 14)	Testing your understanding of how and why authors write the way they do
Expression of Ideas (chapters 15 and 16)	Testing your ability to revise passages to meet particular writing goals
Standard English Conventions (chapters 17 and 18)	Testing your ability to edit passages for conventional sentence structure, usage, and punctuation

Each of the following pairs of chapters will

- provide a broad overview of a particular content domain, including the "big idea" (focus) of the domain;

- indicate about how many questions you can expect to encounter from that domain on test day;

- identify the key types of questions included in the domain;

- offer a range of sample questions and answer explanations; and

- give you an opportunity to immediately practice by answering questions from that domain and reading the associated answer explanations.

CHAPTER 11

Reading and Writing: Questions— Information and Ideas

Overview

Reading and Writing questions in the **Information and Ideas** content domain are designed to test your ability to read and demonstrate understanding of passages that represent a range of subject areas, text types, and text complexities as well as of informational graphics. The main goal of these questions is to see whether you can **read carefully to determine what the passages say explicitly and what they strongly imply**.

REMINDER

For a full discussion of the kinds of passages you'll find in the Reading and Writing section as well as analysis of these passages' key features, see chapter 8.

Proportion of the Test Section

About 26 percent of the Reading and Writing section is made up of Information and Ideas questions. This translates to approximately **twelve to fourteen Information and Ideas questions** per test form.

Overview of Information and Ideas Question Types

The Information and Ideas content domain includes three main types of questions:

- **Central Ideas and Details** questions, which test your ability to locate or reasonably infer the main point of a passage and to identify and use supporting details.

- **Command of Evidence** questions, which test your ability to identify and use either textual evidence or quantitative data found in a passage and in any accompanying informational graphic to support or challenge points or claims.

- **Inferences** questions, which test your ability to draw reasonable, text-based conclusions from what you've read in passages.

All questions in this content domain (and in the Reading and Writing section in general) are multiple-choice in format. Each question has a single best answer (*key*) and three incorrect answer choices (*distractors*) that represent common errors students make when answering such questions. All the information needed to answer each question is in the passage (or in any accompanying informational graphic), so you should always base your answers on what a given passage (and/or graphic) says directly and what it strongly implies.

Information and Ideas Question Types in Detail

In this section, we'll discuss each of the three Information and Ideas question types in detail. We'll describe the general purpose of each type so that you understand better how to approach such questions on test day. As part of this discussion, we'll walk through some sample questions so that you get a strong sense of the kinds of skills and knowledge required to successfully answer questions of a given type.

Central Ideas and Details Questions

As the name suggests, **Central Ideas and Details** questions ask you to determine the main point of a given passage and to identify and make use of supporting details.

Questions about Central Ideas

When you're asked to determine the **main point (central idea)** of a passage, the answer you choose should capture all the important information and ideas in the passage. Answer choices that only reflect some of the information and ideas in the passage will be incorrect, as are, of course, choices that mischaracterize the passage or that make assertions about the passage that aren't supported in the text.

Let's begin with a fairly straightforward sample question.

Information and Ideas Sample Question 1

The following text is from Edith Nesbit's 1902 novel *Five Children and It*. Five young siblings have just moved with their parents from London to a house in the countryside that they call the White House.

It was not really a pretty house at all; it was quite ordinary, and mother thought it was rather inconvenient, and was quite annoyed at there being no shelves, to speak of, and hardly a cupboard in the place. Father used to say that the ironwork on the roof and coping was like an architect's nightmare. But the house was deep in the country, with no other house in sight, and the children had been in London for two years, without so much as once going to the seaside even for a day by an excursion train, and so the White House seemed to them a sort of Fairy Palace set down in an Earthly Paradise.

Which choice best states the main idea of the text?

A) The house is beautiful and well built, but the children miss their old home in London.

B) The children don't like the house nearly as much as their parents do.

C) Each member of the family admires a different characteristic of the house.

D) Although their parents believe the house has several drawbacks, the children are enchanted by it.

Now let's evaluate each of the answer choices. Recall that we're searching for the answer choice that best captures the main idea of the passage without introducing any misstatements or unsupported assertions.

In this case, choice D is the best answer, as it best reflects the passage's main idea. The passage makes two basic points. First, the parents are well aware of problems with the house. The mother calls the house "inconvenient," and the father describes the ironwork as "like an architect's nightmare." On the other hand, the children view the house as "a sort of Fairy Palace set down in an Earthly Paradise." Choice D clearly reflects both of those ideas.

The other three answer choices mischaracterize what the passage says, making them incorrect options for the main idea. Neither part of choice A is correct, per the passage. Even the narrator refers to the house as "quite ordinary," which undermines the idea that the house is beautiful, and, as we've already seen, both the father and mother recognize that the house has shortcomings. Additionally, nothing in the passage suggests that the children miss their former home in London. Choice B is similarly inaccurate, as the reverse is actually true: the children love the house more than do their parents. Choice C is also incorrect because while the children find things to admire about the house, all we know from the passage about the parents is that the mother finds the house "inconvenient" and that the father complains about the ironwork.

Part of the straightforwardness of this question comes from the fact that choices A, B, and C are simply wrong based on what we know from the passage. More challenging Central Ideas and Details questions focused on main ideas may also require you to distinguish the main idea from statements about the passage that are accurate but still not the best expression of the main idea. In other words, you'll also have to distinguish between a *main* idea and *subordinate* ideas or mere details.

Let's consider another example. This time, we'll have to consider both whether the choices are accurate, given what we know from the passage, and whether they appropriately capture the passage's main idea.

Information and Ideas Sample Question 2

In many of his sculptures, artist Richard Hunt uses broad forms rather than extreme accuracy to hint at specific people or ideas. In his first major work, *Arachne* (1956), Hunt constructed the mythical character Arachne, a weaver who was changed into a spider, by welding bits of steel together into something that, although vaguely human, is strange and machinelike. And his large bronze sculpture *The Light of Truth* (2021) commemorates activist and journalist Ida B. Wells using mainly flowing, curved pieces of metal that create stylized flames.

Which choice best states the text's main idea about Hunt?

A) He often depicts the subjects of his sculptures using an unrealistic style.

B) He uses different kinds of materials depending on what kind of sculpture he plans to create.

C) He tends to base his art on important historical figures rather than on fictional characters.

D) He has altered his approach to sculpture over time, and his works have become increasingly abstract.

When working on this question, it's helpful to remember our discussion in chapter 8 of the structure of passages and how we can use an understanding of structure to help us out. The passage's first sentence makes a general statement about Hunt and his creations, while the second and last sentences provide examples supporting this statement. Because the second and last sentences only offer supporting examples, it's unlikely that we'll find the main point of the passage there.

As it happens, choice A, which is the best answer, is a close paraphrase of the passage's first sentence. The first sentence makes a general statement about Hunt and his work—he often uses "broad forms rather than extreme accuracy" to depict his subjects—while the second and last sentences offer two examples illustrating that general statement. ("Unrealistic style" is a reasonable translation of "broad forms," with *broad* here suggesting a lack of precision or fidelity, in contrast to "extreme accuracy.")

Choice B is an example of a (mostly) accurate statement about the passage that still fails to capture the passage's main point. It's true, or at least highly probable, that Hunt uses different materials depending on the kind of sculpture he plans to create, and we observe from the two examples cited in the second and last sentences of the passage that *Arachne* and *The Light of Truth* do use different materials—steel and bronze, respectively. However, this choice focuses only on the examples and ignores the general statement in the passage's first sentence. Therefore, choice B can't be the best answer.

Choices C and D are more like the incorrect answer options we considered in the previous sample question. Choice C is incorrect because the passage doesn't say that Hunt tends to base his works on important historical figures rather than on fictional characters.

In fact, the passage's first example, *Arachne*, describes a work based on a figure from mythology. (Although you might know that Ida B. Wells is a famous historical figure, this knowledge isn't crucial to answering the question, as the answer choice is still inaccurate based only on what we find directly in the passage.) Choice D is incorrect because the passage gives no indication that Hunt has changed his approach over time.

Let's consider one final Central Ideas and Details example, this time on the more challenging side of things.

Information and Ideas Sample Question 3

In a study of new technology adoption, Davit Marikyan et al. examined negative disconfirmation (which occurs when experiences fall short of one's expectations) to determine whether it could lead to positive outcomes for users. The team focused on established users of "smart home" technology, which presents inherent utilization challenges but tends to attract users with high expectations, often leading to feelings of dissonance. The researchers found that many users employed cognitive mechanisms to mitigate those feelings, ultimately reversing their initial sense of disappointment.

Which choice best states the main idea of the text?

A) Research suggests that users with high expectations for a new technology can feel content with that technology even after experiencing negative disconfirmation.

B) Research suggests that most users of smart home technology will not achieve a feeling of satisfaction given the utilization challenges of such technology.

C) Although most smart home technology is aimed at meeting or exceeding users' high expectations, those expectations in general remain poorly understood.

D) Although negative disconfirmation has often been studied, little is known about the cognitive mechanisms shaping users' reactions to it in the context of new technology adoption.

NOTE

You may see the phrase "et al." in some passages about scientific (or social scientific) research (e.g., "Davit Marikyan et al." in this sample passage). This just means that the study being discussed was undertaken by several people, not all of whom are named. You may see slight variations on the same idea (e.g., "[researcher's name] and colleagues") in other questions.

Determining the main idea of this passage requires some persistence because of the complexity of the text itself. If you find some of the concepts, vocabulary, and sentence structures challenging, try to focus on the basic points and the connections between them.

In this case, we might say that the first sentence of the passage raises the question of whether "something bad" (negative disconfirmation) can be turned into "something good" (a positive outcome). The second sentence more or less just tells us that the subjects of the study were users of smart-home technology. For the purpose of understanding the passage and answering the associated question, it doesn't really matter what smart-home technology is, only that it's the case that Marikyan and colleagues studied users of this technology because those users are especially likely to experience the bad feeling described in the first sentence. At heart, the last sentence tells us that the researchers found that in many cases, the "something bad" (initial sense of disappointment) could be turned into "something good" (satisfaction).

STRATEGY

Don't get distracted by what a passage doesn't tell you. Focus on what it *does* tell you directly or what it strongly implies. That's all questions will ask you about.

We actually don't know from the passage the specific reason or reasons smart-home technology users' feelings changed, only that "many users employed cognitive mechanisms to mitigate those [negative] feelings." Because Reading and Writing passages are so short, expect that some details will be left out.

Now let's evaluate the answer choices for the question associated with this passage, keeping in mind that we're looking for the passage's main idea. Even from our simple breakdown of the passage above, we can recognize that choice A is the best answer, as it captures all the elements we traced. The first sentence of the passage tells us that the researchers were interested in negative feelings associated with the adoption of new technology. The second sentence informs us that smart-home technology users are prone to disappointment with the technology ("feelings of dissonance") when their high expectations aren't met. The third sentence lets us know that the researchers discovered that many smart-home technology users found a way to feel better about having adopted the technology.

You may have noticed that the key doesn't actually mention smart-home technology, and this might lead you away from choice A (and choice D) and toward choices B and C, which do refer directly to smart-home technology. The best way to avoid this misconception is to recognize that the researchers described in the passage were, first and foremost, interested in a phenomenon—negative disconfirmation—and that smart-home technology users are just one example of a category of people who, in the researchers' view, often experience this phenomenon.

All the other answer choices can be ruled out because they get the passage wrong. Choice B is incorrect because the passage says nearly the opposite: the passage's last sentence tells us that many smart-home technology users do, in fact, get over their initial disappointment. Both parts of choice C lack support in the passage. The passage doesn't tell us that smart-home technology is designed to meet or exceed users' high expectations, nor does it tell us that these expectations remain poorly understood.

Choice D is interesting—and tempting—because it plays into our assumptions, even though the passage doesn't directly support either idea it presents. We might guess that negative disconfirmation has been the subject of a lot of research just from the fact that it has a technical name and was something Marikyan and colleagues analyzed, but the passage never says that the phenomenon has "often" been studied. We might also assume that because the passage doesn't describe the "cognitive mechanisms" that allowed smart-home technology users to cope with their feelings of disappointment, little is known about these mechanisms. But, again, the passage doesn't say that. We therefore shouldn't jump to the conclusion that a lack of detail in the passage about the mechanisms means that scientists themselves don't understand the mechanisms.

Questions about Details

Questions about **details**, as opposed to ones about central ideas, will ask you to locate and use small bits of information from the passage. Sometimes the answer to a details-focused question will be explicitly stated in the passage; other times it will be strongly implicit.

In some cases, the best answer will be straightforward, as in the following example.

Information and Ideas Sample Question 4

Artist Justin Favela explained that he wanted to reclaim the importance of the piñata as a symbol in Latinx culture. To do so, he created numerous sculptures from strips of tissue paper, which is similar to the material used to create piñatas. In 2017, Favela created an impressive life-size, piñata-like sculpture of the Gypsy Rose lowrider car, which was displayed at the Petersen Automotive Museum in Los Angeles, California. The Gypsy Rose lowrider was famously driven by Jesse Valadez, an early president of the Los Angeles Imperials Car Club.

According to the text, which piece of Favela's art was on display in the Petersen Automotive Museum in 2017?

A) A painting of Los Angeles

B) A painting of a piñata

C) A sculpture of Jesse Valadez

D) A sculpture of a lowrider car

Here, we simply need to identify which answer choice is factually accurate per the passage. That option is choice D, as the passage's third sentence informs us that Favela "created an impressive life-size, piñata-like sculpture of the Gypsy Rose lowrider car" and that it was "displayed at the Petersen Automotive Museum." The other choices, by contrast, are inaccurate. The passage's only mentions of Los Angeles are as the location of the Petersen Automotive Museum and the Imperials Car Club, which rules out choice A. Choice B (as well as choice A) can be ruled out because the passage indicates that Favela is a sculptor, not a painter, and because no paintings are mentioned. Choice C is incorrect because the only reference in the passage to Valadez is as a driver of the Gypsy Rose lowrider car.

In other details-focused questions, you'll have to determine what the passage most strongly suggests. By "strongly suggests," we mean that the passage won't directly state the information or idea, but the information or idea will be heavily implied. Think of something "strongly suggested" as being a close paraphrase of what the passage directly says, a synthesis of multiple pieces of information found in the passage, or a statement that can be reasonably regarded as true given the information presented in the passage. The best answer will be put into different words than those found in the passage, but it will be closely connected to evidence in the passage, as in the following example.

Information and Ideas Sample Question 5

> In a paper about p-i-n planar perovskite solar cells (one of several perovskite cell architectures designed to collect and store solar power), Lyndsey McMillon-Brown et al. describe a method for fabricating the cell's electronic transport layer (ETL) using a spray coating. Conventional ETL fabrication is accomplished using a solution of nanoparticles. The process can result in a loss of up to 80% of the solution, increasing the cost of manufacturing at scale—an issue that may be obviated by spray coating fabrication, which the researchers describe as "highly reproducible, concise, and practical."
>
> What does the text most strongly suggest about conventional ETL fabrication?
>
> A) It typically entails a greater loss of nanoparticle solution than do other established approaches for ETL fabrication.
>
> B) It is less suitable for manufacturing large volumes of planar p-i-n perovskite solar cells than an alternative fabrication method may be.
>
> C) It is somewhat imprecise and therefore limits the potential effectiveness of p-i-n planar perovskite solar cells at capturing and storing solar power.
>
> D) It is more expensive when manufacturing at scale than are processes for fabricating ETLs used in other perovskite solar cell architectures.

The best answer to this question is choice B. Although this answer choice isn't stated word for word in the passage, it's strongly implied by the combination of the second and last sentences. The second sentence lets us know that "conventional ETL fabrication" involves using a solution of nanoparticles. The last sentence tells us that this process is inefficient because it results in "a loss of up to 80% of the solution," which raises the costs of manufacturing. We're also told in that sentence that the new process involving spray coating may represent an improvement. If we flip that around, it's basically the same as saying that the old process is worse ("less suitable") than the new one may be.

When you answer questions about Reading and Writing passages, don't fixate on what you don't know or understand. Focus on what you *do* know and understand. This can often be enough to answer a given question correctly, even if some details remain hazy.

Let's digress for a moment to talk about the word *obviated* in the passage's last sentence. You may or may not know that the verb *obviate* means to make something unnecessary. Even if you didn't know that going into the passage, however, you can get a good sense of the meaning of *obviated* from context clues in the passage. If the new spray coating process, as McMillon-Brown and colleagues claim, is "highly reproducible, concise, and practical," while the conventional solution-based process is inefficient, we can make a reasonable guess that *obviated* has something to do with making the problems associated with the solution-based process go away. We'll talk more about how to make use of context clues in chapter 13 when we discuss vocabulary-related questions.

Now let's consider the other answer choices for this question. Choice A is incorrect because the passage only talks about a single conventional (standard) process, not multiple established approaches. Choice C is incorrect because the passage describes the conventional process as inefficient and therefore wastefully expensive, not "imprecise" or ineffective per se. The old process seems to work; it's just costly.

Choice D is incorrect because the passage only discusses one type of perovskite solar cell architecture: p-i-n planar perovskite solar cells. Although the passage alludes to other types of architectures, it doesn't tell us anything about them.

Command of Evidence Questions

Command of Evidence questions assess your ability to make use of both textual evidence and quantitative data in passages and informational graphics to answer associated questions. This is an important set of skills because you'll frequently have to recognize and make use of evidence—facts, figures, quotations, data, and the like—as you read, write, participate in discussions, and make presentations in high school and college classes as well as in the workplace and everyday life.

Questions about Textual Evidence

As we noted in chapter 8, the nature of **textual evidence** varies by subject area. In the following example, we'll examine how this bears out in a literature passage.

Information and Ideas Sample Question 6

Sense and Sensibility is an 1811 novel by Jane Austen. In the novel, Austen describes Marianne Dashwood's ability to persuade others of the rightness of her artistic judgments, as is evident when Marianne visits with John Willoughby, a potential suitor: _____

Which quotation from *Sense and Sensibility* most effectively illustrates the claim?

A) "Above all, when she heard him declare, that of music and dancing he was passionately fond, she gave him such a look of approbation as secured the largest share of his discourse to herself for the rest of his stay."

B) "Their taste was strikingly alike. The same books, the same passages were idolized by each—or if any difference appeared, any objection arose, it lasted no longer than till the force of her arguments and the brightness of her eyes could be displayed."

C) "It was only necessary to mention any favourite amusement to engage her to talk. She could not be silent when such points were introduced, and she had neither shyness nor reserve in their discussion."

D) "They speedily discovered that their enjoyment of dancing and music was mutual, and that it arose from a general conformity of judgment in all that related to either. Encouraged by this to a further examination of his opinions, she proceeded to question him on the subject of books."

On first encountering this question, you may wonder where the passage you're supposed to read is and how you're supposed to answer this question if you haven't read *Sense and Sensibility*.

The format of this question is probably different from many you've encountered, but it shouldn't be intimidating. Remember that with all Reading and Writing questions, the information you need to answer correctly is always provided in the passages (and any graphics).

With a question such as this, your task is twofold:

- First, you'll be presented with a **claim** about the work of literature. In this case, the claim is that "Austen describes Marianne Dashwood's ability to persuade others of the rightness of her artistic judgments" and that this is made clear in a scene where Marianne talks with another character, John Willoughby. Recall from chapter 8 that a *claim* is an assertion—in this instance, an interpretation of a literary work—that people can reasonably disagree on.

- Second, you'll have to determine which of the answer choices best **supports** that claim in a way indicated by the question itself. In this case, you're asked to find which choice "most effectively illustrates the claim." The answer choices are carefully selected so that you can understand them on their own, whether or not you've read the literary work in question.

NOTE
It's always safe to assume with questions of this sort that the quotations in the answer choices are accurate excerpts from the literary work in question.

For this question, we're searching for the one quotation among the four offered in the answer choices that best illustrates that Marianne is able to convince others that her views on art are the correct ones.

Choice B does this most effectively. This quotation tells us, first, that Marianne and John have virtually identical opinions on art ("their taste was strikingly alike") and, second, that were John ever to disagree, Marianne's reasoning ("arguments") and physical appeal ("the brightness of her eyes") would quickly convince him to change his mind.

Choice A might seem like it's on the right track, but when we read it closely, we discover that this quotation merely indicates that Marianne approved of ("gave . . . a look of approbation" regarding) John being enthusiastic about ("passionately fond" of) music and dancing. In other words, there's nothing in this quotation about Marianne being persuasive. Choice C is incorrect because this quotation only tells us that Marianne herself was passionate about certain things ("favorite amusement[s]") and would talk boldly and at length about them with others. Again, this choice is in the right neighborhood, so to speak, but it doesn't illustrate Marianne persuading anyone, so it can't be the best answer. Choice D is tempting because, like choice B, it indicates that Marianne and John had a great deal in common, but, again, it doesn't support the point that Marianne was able to persuade John to accept her views on music and dancing.

Let's now shift to looking at a textual Command of Evidence question in a different subject area.

Information and Ideas Sample Question 7

In the 1980s, many musicians and journalists in the English-speaking world began to draw attention to music from around the globe—such as mbaqanga from South Africa and quan họ from Vietnam—that can't be easily categorized according to British or North American popular music genres, typically referring to such music as "world music." While some scholars have welcomed this development for bringing diverse musical forms to prominence in countries where they'd previously been overlooked, musicologist Su Zheng claims that the concept of world music homogenizes highly distinct traditions by reducing them all to a single category.

Which finding about mbaqanga and quan họ, if true, would most directly support Zheng's claim?

A) Mbaqanga is significantly more popular in the English-speaking world than quan họ is.

B) Mbaqanga and quan họ developed independently of each other and have little in common musically.

C) Mbaqanga and quan họ are now performed by a diverse array of musicians with no direct connections to South Africa or Vietnam.

D) Mbaqanga and quan họ are highly distinct from British and North American popular music genres but similar to each other.

NOTE

We use the phrase "if true" in questions such as this because we want to present a range of possibilities in the answer choices for you to consider without making you wonder about what actually happened in the study. At the same time, all the choices will be plausible—things that could reasonably have been discovered during research.

Let's begin by figuring out what the passage is trying to communicate. First, we're told that the category of "world music" was created by English-speaking musicians and journalists to describe types of music that didn't fit conventional British and North American popular music forms. Second, we learn that mbaqanga and quan họ are examples of two musical traditions that have both been categorized as "world music." Third, we're informed that Zheng objects to the concept of "world music" in general terms because, in Zheng's view, it ignores important differences between and among the musical traditions lumped into the category.

The question itself asks which finding about mbaqanga and quan họ, if true, would most directly support Zheng's claim, which is that it's inappropriate to homogenize (blend together) diverse musical traditions into the category of "world music." What we're looking for among the answer choices, in other words, is the best support for Zheng's claim.

Choice B is the best answer here. If mbaqanga and quan họ emerged separately and have little in common musically, this finding would support Zheng's criticism of conceiving of diverse musical traditions as belonging to the single category of "world music."

STRATEGY

When answering textual Command of Evidence questions such as this, read the passage carefully to determine what claim is being made. Then read the question closely to make sure you understand what you're looking for among the answer choices (e.g., support for the claim). And then carefully evaluate each answer choice to determine how it would affect the claim (support or weaken it)—or whether it's even relevant to the claim.

Choice A is incorrect because this finding wouldn't really affect Zheng's claim one way or the other, as the greater popularity of mbaqanga in the English-speaking world relative to quan họ would be irrelevant to what Zheng is arguing. Choice C is incorrect because it also wouldn't directly relate to Zheng's claim, which is about essential differences between and among diverse musical traditions and not about who performs the music. Choice D is incorrect because it would actually weaken Zheng's claim. Zheng asserts that highly distinct musical traditions shouldn't be lumped together, but the finding in choice D would indicate that mbaqanga and quan họ are actually similar to each other, which suggests it might not be such a bad thing to categorize them both as "world music."

Questions about Quantitative Evidence

While some Command of Evidence questions require you to work with textual evidence, others call on you to make use of **quantitative evidence** in the form of data obtained from informational graphics.

Let's examine a pair of examples.

Information and Ideas Sample Question 8

Comfort Range and Temperature-Adjustment Preferences from One Survey

Participant	Comfort rating	Preferred temperature adjustment
20	−2	Cooler
1	+1	Cooler
21	+1	Cooler

Nan Gao and her team conducted multiple surveys to determine participants' levels of comfort in a room where the temperature was regulated by a commercial climate control system. Participants filled out surveys several times a day to indicate their level of comfort on a scale from −3 (very cold) to +3 (very hot), with 0 indicating neutral (neither warm nor cool), and to indicate how they would prefer the temperature to be adjusted. The table shows three participants' responses in one of the surveys. According to the table, all three participants wanted the room to be cooler, _____.

Which choice most effectively uses data from the table to complete the statement?

A) and they each reported the same level of comfort.

B) even though each participant's ratings varied throughout the day.

C) but participant 20 reported feeling significantly colder than the other two participants did.

D) but participant 1 reported feeling warmer than the other two participants did.

REMINDER
Chapter 9 covers in detail how to work with informational graphics found in the Reading and Writing section.

NOTE
Some passages in the Reading and Writing section, such as this one, contain a blank. This blank is where the answer choice would go if it were added to the passage.

This question asks you to make some straightforward interpretations of data from the table in order to correctly complete the blank in the passage with the best answer choice.

Choice C is the best answer. According to the table, on the −3 (very cold) to +3 (very hot) scale used in the survey, participant 20 provided a response of −2 (near the "very cold" end of the scale), while the other two participants provided a response of +1 (on the "warm" side of the scale). Given that the scale only includes seven points (−3, −2, −1, 0, +1, +2, +3), a difference of three (−2, +1) can reasonably be considered significant, as choice C describes it.

The same rationale shows why choice A is incorrect. While participants 1 and 21 gave the same comfort rating response (+1), participant 20 gave a response of −2; this establishes clearly that one of the three participants experienced a different level of comfort than did the other two. Choice B is incorrect because the table provides only one rating per participant, so we can't tell whether perceptions changed throughout the day. Choice D is incorrect because participant 21 gave the same response (+1) as participant 1, meaning that participant 1 didn't feel warmer than both of the other participants (though participant 1 did feel warmer than participant 20 [−2]).

Other quantitative Command of Evidence questions, such as our next example, require more—and more complex—interpretation of data on your part.

Information and Ideas Sample Question 9

Distribution of Ecosystem Services Affected by Invasive Species by Service Type

Region (Overall)	Provisioning (75%)	Regulating (21%)	Cultural (4%)
West	73%	27%	0%
North	88%	12%	0%
South	79%	14%	7%
East	83%	6%	11%
Central	33%	67%	0%

To assess the impact of invasive species on ecosystems in Africa, Benis N. Egoh and colleagues reviewed government reports from those nations about how invasive species are undermining ecosystem services (aspects of the ecosystem on which residents depend). The services were sorted into three categories: provisioning (material resources from the ecosystem), regulating (natural processes such as cleaning the air or water), and cultural (nonmaterial benefits of ecosystems). Egoh and her team assert that countries in each region reported effects on provisioning services and that provisioning services represent the majority of the reported services.

Which choice best describes data from the table that support Egoh and colleagues' assertion?

A) Provisioning services represent 73% of the services reported for the West region and 33% of those for the Central region, but they represent 75% of the services reported overall.

B) None of the percentages shown for provisioning services are lower than 33%, and the overall percentage shown for provisioning services is 75%.

C) Provisioning services are shown for each region, while no cultural services are shown for some regions.

D) The greatest percentage shown for provisioning services is 88% for the North region, and the least shown for provisioning services is 33% for the Central region.

Let's consider first what main points the passage and table are trying to get across. The passage tells us that Egoh and colleagues were trying to determine the effects of invasive species on African ecosystems and that they used government reports to collect data about these effects. From these reports, the researchers calculated what percentage of reports of invasive species, by region, documented effects on three categories of ecosystem services: provisioning, regulating, and cultural. (The passage defines what each of these categories represents.) Let's use the West region as an example. Of the government reports from nations in the West region citing impacts of invasive species on ecosystem services, 73 percent of those reports were about impacts to provisioning services, while the other 27 percent were about impacts to regulating services (and no reports—0 percent—were about impacts to cultural services).

The top row of the table identifies the percentage of all the impact reports across regions that were about each of the three categories of services. According to those data, 75 percent of reports across regions were about impacts to provisioning services, 21 percent were about impacts to regulating services, and 4 percent were about impacts to cultural services. Continuing our previous example of the West region, we see that that the nations in that region reported impacts similar to those reported for Africa as a whole: 73 percent of reports described impacts to provisioning services, 27 percent to regulating services, and 0 percent to cultural services.

The claim the researchers make, as reported in the passage, is that (1) all regions experienced effects on provisioning services and that (2) impacts on provisioning services represent the majority of reports of affected ecosystem services. We're then directed to choose the answer that describes data from the table supporting the researchers' assertion (claim).

Now let's evaluate the answer choices. Choice B is the best answer, as it accurately uses data from the table to support both aspects of the researchers' assertion. We can tell, first, that provisioning services were affected in all regions listed on the table because all regions have a percentage greater than 0 for this category, with (as choice B alludes to) the Central region, at 33 percent, having the lowest percentage of reports of impacts on provisioning services. We can also tell, from the top row of the table, that 75 percent of reports across all regions related to provisioning services.

As we examine the other answer choices, keep in mind that the researchers' assertion (claim) was that each region reported effects on provisioning services and that reports of provisioning services impacts make up the majority of all impact reports.

Choice A is incorrect because it doesn't adequately support the researchers' assertion. Choice A only cites the percentage of impact reports relating to provisioning services for two regions and for the continent as a whole, not for each region. Choice C is incorrect because it also fails to support the assertion adequately. While choice C does mention that each region reported impacts on provisioning services, it doesn't support the part of the assertion that claims that reports of impacts on provisioning services represented the majority of all impact reports. Choice D is incorrect because although it does accurately list the range of percentages of impact reports by region related to provisioning services, it, like choice C, doesn't demonstrate that the majority of all impact reports were related to provisioning services.

Inferences Questions

Finally, let's look at **Inferences** questions. When a Reading and Writing question asks you to draw an inference, it's asking you to come to the most reasonable conclusion (represented by the question's key) based on information and ideas in the passage itself. You won't be asked to make giant leaps in logic or to provide your own subjective interpretation. Instead, you'll read carefully to determine what the passage says directly and what it strongly implies and then use that information to answer the question.

Let's first examine a relatively straightforward example to get a better sense of the kinds of inferences these questions will ask you to make.

Information and Ideas Sample Question 10

Researchers recently found that disruptions to an enjoyable experience, like a short series of advertisements during a television show, often increase viewers' reported enjoyment. Suspecting that disruptions to an unpleasant experience would have the opposite effect, the researchers had participants listen to construction noise for 30 minutes and anticipated that those whose listening experience was frequently interrupted with short breaks of silence would thus _____

Which choice most logically completes the text?

A) rate the listening experience as more negative than those whose listening experience was uninterrupted.

B) rate the experience of listening to construction noise as lasting for less time than it actually lasted.

C) perceive the volume of the construction noise as growing softer over time.

D) find the disruptions more irritating as time went on.

STRATEGY
Higher-complexity quantitative Command of Evidence questions, such as this one, will often present answer choices that accurately represent data from the informational graphic but that are still incorrect because they don't effectively answer the question. Remember that you're not just looking for an accurate statement but rather for one that is accurate *and* best meets the question's requirement (in this case, finding support in the table for a claim made by the researchers).

In questions with a blank, such as this, we need to select the answer choice that best completes that blank. In the case of Inferences questions, that answer will be the choice that represents the most reasonable inference based on the information and ideas we're supplied with in the passage.

The passage for this question presents a fairly simple scenario. Researchers have found that disruptions in enjoyable experiences often increase participants' perceptions of enjoying the experience. (The passage doesn't tell us why this is so, so we know we won't be asked about the reason.) The passage also tells us that researchers believe disruptions in unenjoyable experiences should have the opposite effect.

Before we consider the answer choices, let's think about what the passage is signaling about the right answer. If (1) interruptions to enjoyable experiences increase participants' positive perceptions of those experiences compared to the perceptions of those who had uninterrupted good experiences and if (2) researchers believe the opposite occurs when unenjoyable experiences are interrupted, we can reasonably conclude, or infer, that interruptions to unenjoyable experiences increase participants' *negative* perceptions of those experiences compared to the perceptions of those who had uninterrupted bad experiences. This is almost, in fact, what we find in choice A, which is the best answer to this question.

We can rule out choices B, C, and D on the same basic grounds. None of the inferences in these choices is supported by the passage, nor do any of the choices describe an effect opposite to the one described in the passage.

This question illustrates nicely two key takeaways about Inferences questions in general.

- The best answer to Inferences questions (as with all Reading and Writing questions) is based on what's explicitly stated and what's strongly implied in the associated passages.

- The best answer to Inferences questions is the choice that most logically completes the passage text (represented by the blank).

Choices B, C, and D might have some appeal because they sound like reasonable statements on their own, but they're neither supported by the passage nor the most logical way to fill in the passage's blank.

Let's now consider a more demanding Inferences question.

You may find it helpful to anticipate what the best answer to a question would look like before actually reading the answer choices. Doing so could help you find the right answer more quickly.

Information and Ideas Sample Question 11

As the name suggests, dramaturges originated in theater, where they continue to serve a variety of functions: conducting historical research for directors, compiling character biographies for actors, and perhaps most importantly, helping writers of plays and musicals to hone the works' stories and characters. Performance scholar Susan Manning observes that many choreographers, like playwrights and musical theater writers, are concerned with storytelling and characterization. In fact, some choreographers describe the dances they create as expressions of narrative through movement; it is therefore unsurprising that _____

Which choice most logically completes the text?

A) some directors and actors rely too heavily on dramaturges to complete certain research tasks.

B) choreographers developing dances with narrative elements frequently engage dramaturges to assist in refining those elements.

C) dramaturges can have a profound impact on the artistic direction of plays and musicals.

D) dances by choreographers who incorporate narrative elements are more accessible to audiences than dances by choreographers who do not.

Since this passage is more complex than the last one we analyzed, let's take the text apart to get a better idea of what it's saying.

We might sketch out the passage in these terms:

1. Dramaturges perform a variety of roles, including helping writers of plays and musicals develop stories and characters (first sentence).

2. Many choreographers, like writers of plays and musicals, care about storytelling and character development (second and last sentences).

3. It therefore shouldn't surprise us that _____. (last sentence).

The word *therefore* signals to us that what we place in the blank should be a logical consequence of the preceding information. Put another way, *therefore* tells us that if (1) and (2), above, are true, then (3) logically follows as a result or consequence.

The word *unsurprising* in the passage's last sentence is also useful to note here. The use of this word reinforces the point that what should fill the blank is predictable (unsurprising) based on the information we've been given.

We can figure out this logical consequence, even before considering the answer choices, just from what the passage tells us.

1. Dramaturges help writers of plays and musicals develop stories and characters.

2. Many choreographers also care about developing good stories and characters.

3. It therefore shouldn't surprise us that many choreographers work with dramaturges.

Choice B matches up pretty closely with our own passage-based inference making, and it turns out to be the best answer to the question. We'd expect (i.e., shouldn't be surprised by the fact that) many choreographers would turn to dramaturges for help since many choreographers, like writers of plays and musicals, care about good storytelling and strong characters.

Choice A is incorrect because it's not supported at all by the passage. Nothing in the passage suggests anyone is overly reliant on dramaturges, and the passage adopts a strongly positive tone toward them. Choice C is incorrect because although it's a reasonable assertion on its own, it doesn't make sense in the blank, which is leading us to draw a conclusion about the role of dramaturges in choreography. Choice D, like choice A, isn't supported by the passage, and, like choice C, it doesn't make sense in the blank.

Summary: Information and Ideas Questions

Main purpose: To assess whether you can read carefully to determine what passages (and sometimes informational graphics) say explicitly and what they strongly imply

Proportion of the test section: About 26 percent (approximately twelve to fourteen questions)

Question types

- Central Ideas and Details: Locate or reasonably infer the main point of a passage; identify and use supporting details

- Command of Evidence: Identify and use textual evidence and/or quantitative data to support or challenge points or claims

- Inferences: Draw reasonable, text-based conclusions from what you've read in passages

CHAPTER 12

Reading and Writing: Questions—Information and Ideas Drills

1

The ice melted on a Norwegian mountain during a particularly warm summer in 2019, revealing a 1,700-year-old sandal to a mountaineer looking for artifacts. The sandal would normally have degraded quickly, but it was instead well preserved for centuries by the surrounding ice. According to archaeologist Espen Finstad and his team, the sandal, like those worn by imperial Romans, wouldn't have offered any protection from the cold in the mountains, so some kind of insulation, like fabric or animal skin, would have needed to be worn on the feet with the sandal.

What does the text indicate about the discovery of the sandal?

A) The discovery revealed that the Roman Empire had more influence on Norway than archaeologists previously assumed.

B) The sandal would have degraded if it hadn't been removed from the ice.

C) Temperatures contributed to both protecting and revealing the sandal.

D) Archaeologists would have found the sandal eventually without help from the general public.

2

The following text is adapted from María Cristina Mena's 1914 short story "The Vine-Leaf."

It is a saying in the capital of Mexico that Dr. Malsufrido carries more family secrets under his hat than any archbishop.

The doctor's hat is, appropriately enough, uncommonly capacious, rising very high, and sinking so low that it seems to be supported by his ears and eyebrows, and it has a furry look, as if it had been brushed the wrong way, which is perhaps what happens to it if it is ever brushed at all. When the doctor takes it off, the family secrets do not fly out like a flock of parrots, but remain nicely bottled up beneath a dome of old and highly polished ivory.

Based on the text, how do people in the capital of Mexico most likely regard Dr. Malsufrido?

A) Few feel concerned that he will divulge their confidences.

B) Many have come to tolerate him despite his disheveled appearance.

C) Most would be unimpressed by him were it not for his professional expertise.

D) Some dislike how freely he discusses his own family.

3

NASA's *Cassini* probe has detected an unusual wobble in the rotation of Mimas, Saturn's smallest moon. Using a computer model to study Mimas's gravitational interactions with Saturn and tidal forces, geophysicist Alyssa Rhoden and colleagues have proposed that this wobble could be due to a liquid ocean moving beneath the moon's icy surface. The researchers believe other moons should be examined to see if they too might have oceans hidden beneath their surfaces.

Which choice best states the main idea of the text?

A) Rhoden and colleagues were the first to confirm that several of Saturn's moons contain hidden oceans.

B) Research has failed to identify signs that there is an ocean hidden beneath the surface of Mimas.

C) Rhoden and colleagues created a new computer model that identifies moons with hidden oceans without needing to analyze the moons' rotation.

D) Research has revealed that an oddity in the rotation of Mimas could be explained by an ocean hidden beneath its surface.

4

Hip-hop pedagogy is a form of teaching that's gaining popularity across school subjects. It involves incorporating hip-hop and rap music into lessons as well as using hip-hop elements when teaching other subject matters. For example, Quan Neloms's students look for college-level vocabulary and historical events in rap songs. Researchers claim that in addition to developing students' social justice awareness, <u>hip-hop pedagogy encourages student success by raising students' interest and engagement.</u>

Which finding, if true, would most strongly support the underlined claim?

A) Students tend to be more enthusiastic about rap music than they are about hip-hop music.

B) Educators report that they enjoy teaching courses that involve hip-hop and rap music more than teaching courses that don't.

C) Courses that incorporate hip-hop and rap music are among the courses with the highest enrollment and attendance rates.

D) Students who are highly interested in social justice issues typically don't sign up for courses that incorporate hip-hop and rap music.

5

Pulitzer Prize–winning writer Héctor Tobar has built a multifaceted career as both a journalist and an author of short stories and novels. In an essay about Tobar's work, a student claims that Tobar blends his areas of expertise by applying journalism techniques to his creation of works of fiction.

Which quotation from a literary critic best supports the student's claim?

A) "For one novel, an imagined account of a real person's global travels, Tobar approached his subject like a reporter, interviewing people the man had met along the way and researching the man's own writings."

B) "Tobar got his start as a volunteer for *El Tecolote*, a community newspaper in San Francisco, and wrote for newspapers for years before earning a degree in creative writing and starting to publish works of fiction."

C) "Many of Tobar's notable nonfiction articles are marked by the writer's use of techniques usually associated with fiction, such as complex narrative structures and the incorporation of symbolism."

D) "The protagonist of Tobar's third novel is a man who wants to be a novelist and keeps notes about interesting people he encounters so he can use them when developing characters for his stories."

6

Electra is a circa 420–410 BCE play by Sophocles, translated in 1870 by R.C. Jebb. Electra, who is in mourning for her dead father and her long-absent brother, is aware of the intensity of her grief but believes it to be justified: _____

Which quotation from *Electra* most effectively illustrates the claim?

A) "O thou pure sunlight, and thou air, earth's canopy, how often have ye heard the strains of my lament, the wild blows dealt against this bleeding breast, when dark night fails!"

B) "I know my own passion, it escapes me not; but, seeing that the causes are so dire, will never curb these frenzied plaints, while life is in me."

C) "Send to me my brother; for I have no more the strength to bear up alone against the load of grief that weighs me down."

D) "But never will I cease from dirge and sore lament, while I look on the trembling rays of the bright stars, or on this light of day."

7

Tadpole Body Mass and Toxin Production after Three Weeks in Ponds

Population density	Average tadpole body mass (milligrams)	Average number of distinct bufadienolide toxins per tadpole	Average amount of bufadienolide per tadpole (nanograms)	Average bufadienolide concentration (nanograms per milligram of tadpole body mass)
High	193.87	22.69	5,815.51	374.22
Medium	254.56	21.65	5,525.72	230.10
Low	258.97	22.08	4,664.99	171.43

Ecologist Veronika Bókony and colleagues investigated within-species competition among common toads (*Bufo bufo*), a species that secretes various unpleasant-tasting toxins called bufadienolides in response to threats. The researchers tested *B. bufo* tadpoles' responses to different levels of competition by creating ponds with different tadpole population densities but a fixed amount of food. Based on analysis of the tadpoles after three weeks, the researchers concluded that increased competition drove bufadienolide production at the expense of growth.

Which choice uses data from the table to most effectively support the researchers' conclusion?

A) The difference in average tadpole body mass was small between the low and medium population density conditions and substantially larger between the low and high population density conditions.

B) Tadpoles in the low and medium population density conditions had substantially lower average bufadienolide concentrations but had greater average body masses than those in the high population density condition.

C) Tadpoles in the high population density condition displayed a relatively modest increase in the average amount of bufadienolide but roughly double the average bufadienolide concentration compared to those in the low population density condition.

D) Tadpoles produced approximately the same number of different bufadienolide toxins per individual across the population density conditions, but average tadpole body mass decreased as population density increased.

8

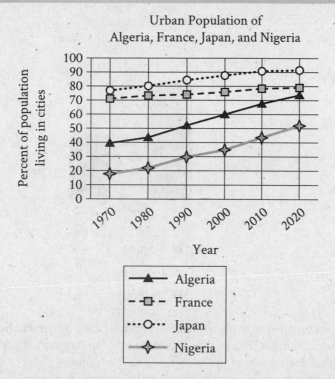

Urban Population of
Algeria, France, Japan, and Nigeria

Legend:
— ▲ — Algeria
– ☐ – France
··· ○ ··· Japan
— ✦ — Nigeria

The share of the world's population living in cities has increased dramatically since 1970, but this change has not been uniform. France and Japan, for example, were already heavily urbanized in 1970, with 70% or more of the population living in cities. The main contributors to the world's urbanization since 1970 have been countries like Algeria, whose population went from _____

Which choice most effectively uses data from the graph to complete the assertion?

A) less than 40% urban in 1970 to around 90% urban in 2020.

B) less than 20% urban in 1970 to more than 50% urban in 2020.

C) around 40% urban in 1970 to more than 70% urban in 2020.

D) around 50% urban in 1970 to around 90% urban in 2020.

9

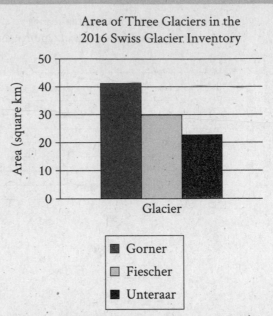

Area of Three Glaciers in the
2016 Swiss Glacier Inventory

To monitor changes to glaciers in Switzerland, the government periodically measures them for features like total area of ice and mean ice thickness, which are then reported in the Swiss Glacier Inventory. These measurements can be used to compare the glaciers. For example, the Gorner glacier had _____

Which choice most effectively uses data from the graph to complete the example?

A) a larger area than either the Fiescher glacier or the Unteraar glacier.

B) a smaller area than the Fiescher glacier but a larger area than the Unteraar glacier.

C) a smaller area than either the Fiescher glacier or the Unteraar glacier.

D) a larger area than the Fiescher glacier but a smaller area than the Unteraar glacier.

10

Henry Ossawa Tanner's 1893 painting *The Banjo Lesson*, which depicts an elderly man teaching a boy to play the banjo, is regarded as a landmark in the history of works by Black artists in the United States. Scholars should be cautious when ascribing political or ideological values to the painting, however: beliefs and assumptions that are commonly held now may have been unfamiliar to Tanner and his contemporaries, and vice versa. Scholars who forget this fact when discussing *The Banjo Lesson* therefore _____

Which choice most logically completes the text?

A) risk judging Tanner's painting by standards that may not be historically appropriate.

B) tend to conflate Tanner's political views with those of his contemporaries.

C) wrongly assume that Tanner's painting was intended as a critique of his fellow artists.

D) forgo analyzing Tanner's painting in favor of analyzing his political activity.

11

In many cultures, a handshake can create trust between people. Engineer João Avelino and his team are designing a robot to shake hands with a human in order to improve human-robot interactions. The robot hand adjusts its movements and pressure to better imitate the feel of a human hand. The researchers want the robot's handshake to feel realistic because _____.

Which choice most logically completes the text?

A) people are less likely to interact with robots that don't look like humans.

B) it's easier to program a robot to perform handshakes than it is to program a robot to perform some other types of greetings.

C) the robot in the researchers' study may have uses other than interacting with humans.

D) lifelike handshakes may make people more comfortable interacting with robots.

12

Tides can deposit large quantities of dead vegetation within a salt marsh, smothering healthy plants and leaving a salt panne—a depression devoid of plants that tends to trap standing water—in the marsh's interior. Ecologist Kathryn Beheshti and colleagues found that burrowing crabs living within these pannes improve drainage by loosening the soil, leading the pannes to shrink as marsh plants move back in. At salt marsh edges, however, crab-induced soil loosening can promote marsh loss by accelerating erosion, suggesting that the burrowing action of crabs _____.

Which choice most logically completes the text?

A) can be beneficial to marshes with small pannes but can be harmful to marshes with large pannes.

B) may promote increases in marsh plants or decreases in marsh plants, depending on the crabs' location.

C) tends to be more heavily concentrated in areas of marsh interiors with standing water than at marsh edges.

D) varies in intensity depending on the size of the panne relative to the size of the surrounding marsh.

Answer Explanations

QUESTION 1

Choice C is the best answer because it most clearly identifies what the passage indicates about the discovery of the sandal. A "particularly warm summer" revealed the sandal, and centuries of ice had kept the sandal "well preserved."

Choice A is incorrect because this choice doesn't reflect the information in the passage. The sandal is similar to Roman sandals in its lack of protection from cold, but there's no indication that the sandal itself or its design was a result of Roman influence. *Choice B* is incorrect because the passage says the opposite. The sandal had been preserved by the ice for centuries. *Choice D* is incorrect because there's no information in the passage suggesting that archaeologists would've found the sandal without the help of someone such as the treasure-hunting mountaineer.

QUESTION 2

Choice A is the best answer because it most accurately describes how, according to the passage, the people in the capital of Mexico regard Dr. Malsufrido. The passage cites a saying in the capital that Malsufrido keeps more secrets than any archbishop. It also says that when he takes off his hat, "the family secrets do not fly out . . . but remain nicely bottled up," suggesting that he won't reveal the secrets he's learned.

Choice B is incorrect because it doesn't reflect the passage. While the passage says Malsufrido's hat is large and appears to have been brushed in the wrong direction, it doesn't support a broader characterization of Malsufrido as being regarded as ill-dressed or disheveled. *Choice C* is incorrect because Malsufrido's professional expertise isn't discussed in the passage. *Choice D* is incorrect because the passage indicates that Malsufrido keeps (other) families' secrets "bottled up" in his head, not that he shares details about his own family.

QUESTION 3

Choice D is the best answer because it best states the main idea of the passage. The passage says researchers have proposed that Mimas's wobbly rotation "could be due to a liquid ocean moving beneath the moon's icy surface."

Choice A is incorrect because it doesn't reflect the passage. Rhoden and colleagues proposed, rather than confirmed, that one, and not several, of Saturn's moons may contain a hidden ocean. *Choice B* is incorrect because it conflicts with the passage. Researchers have identified at least one sign—the unusual wobble in Mimas's rotation—that may be due to a hidden ocean beneath the moon's surface. *Choice C* is incorrect because it doesn't reflect the passage. The model Rhoden and colleagues developed was limited to Mimas and was, in fact, the basis for them proposing a hypothesis regarding Mimas's wobbly rotation.

QUESTION 4

Choice C is the best answer because it presents the finding that would most strongly support the underlined claim. Courses incorporating hip-hop and rap music having among the highest enrollment and attendance rates would strongly suggest that these courses encourage student success by raising students' interest and engagement.

Choice A is incorrect because students being more enthusiastic about rap music than about hip-hop music wouldn't support the claim that hip-hop pedagogy, which includes both rap and hip-hop music, encourages student success by raising students' interest and engagement. *Choice B* is incorrect because educators' enthusiasm for hip-hop pedagogy isn't directly relevant to the claim that hip-hop pedagogy encourages student success by raising students' interest and engagement. *Choice D* is incorrect because some students opting out of taking courses influenced by hip-hop pedagogy wouldn't support the claim that hip-hop pedagogy encourages student success by raising the interest and engagement of those students who do take such courses.

QUESTION 5

Choice A is the best answer because it consists of the quotation from a literary critic that best supports the student's claim. The example of Tobar approaching the subject of one of his novels "like a reporter," including conducting interviews and research, shows Tobar applying journalism techniques to his fiction writing.

Choice B is incorrect because although it tells us about Tobar's initial career as a journalist and his transition to creative writing, it doesn't say anything directly about him applying journalism techniques to his fiction. *Choice C* is incorrect because it illustrates Tobar applying fiction techniques to his nonfiction writing, whereas the claim the student makes is that Tobar applied journalism techniques to his fiction writing. *Choice D* is incorrect because while it tells us that a character in one of Tobar's novels applied a journalism technique to his fiction writing, it doesn't tell us that Tobar himself did that.

QUESTION 6

Choice B is the best answer because it consists of the quotation from *Electra* that most effectively illustrates the claim. Electra states that she "know[s] her own passion," which shows that she's aware of the intensity of her grief. But she also claims that the "causes are so dire"—meaning the reasons for her grief are so awful—that she can't let it go, which shows that she believes her grief is justified.

Choice A is incorrect because although "strains of my lament" and "bleeding breast" show that Electra is aware of the intensity of her grief, this choice doesn't suggest that she believes she has a legitimate reason for feeling that way. *Choice C* is incorrect because although "load of grief that weighs me down" shows that Electra is aware of the intensity of her grief, this choice doesn't suggest that she believes she has a legitimate reason for feeling that way. *Choice D* is incorrect because although "dirge" and "sore lament" show that Electra is aware of the intensity of her grief, this choice doesn't suggest that she believes she has a legitimate reason for feeling that way.

QUESTION 7

Choice B is the best answer because it most effectively supports the researchers' conclusion with data from the table. According to the table, tadpoles in the high population density group—that is, the group with the most tadpoles and therefore the highest level of competition among them—had much higher average bufadienolide concentrations (374.22 nanograms per milligram of tadpole body mass) than did the tadpoles in the medium and low population density groups (230.10 and 171.43, respectively). Also according to the table, tadpoles in the high population density group had the lowest average body mass (193.87 mg) relative to the medium and low population density groups (254.56 and 258.97, respectively). These data support the claim that increased competition drove (i.e., increased) bufadienolide production at the expense of growth.

Choice A is incorrect because although this statement is supported by the table, it doesn't mention bufadienolide production, which it would need to do to support the claim. *Choice C* is incorrect because although this statement is supported by the table, it doesn't mention average body mass ("growth"), which it would need to do to support the claim. *Choice D* is incorrect because although this statement is supported by the table, the claim requires support regarding either the average amount of bufadienolide per tadpole or average bufadienolide concentration, not the average number of distinct bufadienolide toxins per tadpole, which is irrelevant to the claim.

QUESTION 8

Choice C is the best answer because it most effectively uses data from the graph to complete the assertion. In the graph, the line representing Algeria's urban population (third line from the top; dark solid line with triangles) indicates that the proportion of the population living in cities was 40 percent in 1970 and slightly above 70 percent in 2020.

Choices A, B, and *D* are incorrect because they each inaccurately represent data from the graph.

QUESTION 9

Choice A is the best answer because it most effectively uses data from the graph to complete the example. The graph displays area measurements (in square kilometers) for three glaciers. The leftmost (dark gray) bar in the graph, which represents the Gorner glacier, is taller than the two others, with a value of slightly above 40 square kilometers.

Choices B, C, and *D* are incorrect because the graph establishes that the Gorner glacier (more than 40 square kilometers) is larger than either the Fiescher glacier (middle, light gray bar; 30 square kilometers) or the Unteraar glacier (rightmost, black bar; somewhat more than 20 square kilometers).

QUESTION 10

Choice A is the best answer. The passage warns modern scholars against "ascribing [attributing] political or ideological values" to Tanner's 1893 painting *The Banjo Lesson* that may have been "unfamiliar to Tanner and his contemporaries." The passage's main concern, in other words, is that modern scholars may claim that the painting expresses ideas or values that Tanner may not have intended because he painted the work over a century ago, and thus those scholars may judge the painting by inappropriate standards.

Choice B is incorrect because Tanner's contemporaries are only briefly mentioned in the passage, and there's no suggestion that modern scholars are at risk of conflating (confusing) Tanner's views with those of his contemporaries. *Choice C* is incorrect because the passage offers no support for the idea that Tanner meant to critique his fellow artists with *The Banjo Lesson*, as the passage only briefly mentions Tanner's contemporaries. *Choice D* is incorrect because the passage is mainly concerned with how modern scholars interpret *The Banjo Lesson* and says nothing to suggest that modern scholars are at risk of focusing more on Tanner's political activity than on his painting.

QUESTION 11

Choice D is the best answer because it most logically completes the text. The passage says that handshakes can create trust and that the engineers' goal is to "improve human-robot interactions." This suggests that they want the robot's handshake to feel realistic because they want humans to trust the robot and therefore feel more comfortable interacting with it.

Choice A is incorrect because the passage never discusses the appearance of this robot or any other robots, so there's no basis to make this inference. *Choice B* is incorrect because the passage never discusses any other types of greetings, so there's no basis to make this inference. *Choice C* is incorrect because the passage never discusses any uses for the robot other than interacting with humans, so there's no basis to make this inference.

QUESTION 12

Choice B is the best answer because it most logically completes the text. The passage says that crab burrowing in the pannes enables marsh plants to grow there again. It also says that crab burrowing at the edges of salt marshes speeds up marsh loss. Taken together, these pieces of information suggest that burrowing crabs can either help or hurt marshes, depending on where the crabs are located.

Choice A is incorrect because the passage never discusses pannes of different sizes. *Choice C* is incorrect because the passage never suggests that crabs do more burrowing in the pannes (interior areas prone to standing water) than they do at salt marsh edges. *Choice D* is incorrect because the passage never discusses the intensity of crab burrowing, nor does it discuss the size of pannes relative to the size of surrounding salt marshes.

CHAPTER 13

Reading and Writing: Questions—Craft and Structure

Overview

Reading and Writing questions in the **Craft and Structure** content domain are designed to test your ability to demonstrate understanding of how and why authors write texts the way they do. The passages you'll consider for these questions represent a range of subject areas, text types, and text complexities. There are three main areas of focus in Craft and Structure questions: using and determining the meaning of vocabulary, analyzing the structure and purpose of passages, and making supportable connections between two topically related passages.

Proportion of the Test Section

About 28 percent of the Reading and Writing section is made up of Craft and Structure questions. This translates to approximately **thirteen to fifteen Craft and Structure questions** per test form.

Overview of Craft and Structure Question Types

The Craft and Structure content domain includes three main question types:

- **Words in Context** questions, which test your ability to use and determine the meaning of high-utility academic words and phrases in the contexts in which they appear.

- **Text Structure and Purpose** questions, which test your abilities to analyze and describe how and why passages are put together the way they are and to determine the main purpose of passages.

- **Cross-Text Connections** questions, which test your ability to draw supportable connections between two topically related passages.

All questions in this content domain (and in the Reading and Writing section in general) are multiple-choice in format. Each question has a single best answer (*key*) and three incorrect answer choices (*distractors*) that represent common errors students make when answering such questions. All the information needed to answer each question is in the passage (or passage pair), so you should always base your answers on what a given passage (or pair of passages) says directly and what it strongly implies.

Craft and Structure Question Types in Detail

In this section, we'll discuss each of the three Craft and Structure question types in detail. We'll describe the general purpose of each type so you'll better understand how to approach such questions on test day. As part of this discussion, we'll walk through some sample questions so you get a strong sense of the kinds of skills and knowledge required to answer questions of a given type.

Words in Context Questions

Words in Context questions ask you to either use or determine the meaning of high-utility academic words and phrases in the contexts in which they appear.

> ### WHAT ARE "HIGH-UTILITY ACADEMIC WORDS AND PHRASES"?
>
> We use the term *high-utility academic words and phrases* to describe the vocabulary tested in Words in Context questions in the Reading and Writing section. These words and phrases are ones that you'll encounter fairly often in your readings in class across a range of subject areas. Some examples of high-utility academic vocabulary are *analyze, dissent, simulate,* and *ambiguous.*
>
> The tested words and phrases are ones whose meaning has high value (utility) to you because they're often key to unlocking the meaning of texts you'll read, especially the more complex texts you'll encounter in your coursework in high school and college.
>
> By contrast, Words in Context questions *don't* test the meaning and use of words and phrases that are
>
> - common in casual, everyday speech.
> - specific to a given field of study (e.g., *isotope, magma, interest rate, lobbyist*).
> - so uncommon that learning their meaning isn't a high college and career readiness priority (e.g., *apricate, ultracrepidarian, lachrymose*).

To answer these questions, you'll need to pay close attention to the context, or the language surrounding the tested word or phrase, to get a clear sense of either what word or phrase (among the provided answer choices) should fill a given blank in a passage because it makes the most sense in context or what definition (among those provided in the answer choices) most nearly captures the meaning of the tested word or phrase as it's used in the passage.

It's crucial to note here that you can use clues from this context to help determine the best answer to each question. This is true even if you don't know the precise meaning of a tested word or phrase.

To be clear, strong vocabulary knowledge is beneficial with these sorts of questions, and students who know the meaning of and how to properly use more high-utility academic words and phrases than others will generally be more successful with these questions. However, context clues can help direct you to the answer, or at least help you eliminate incorrect answer choices, even when a tested word or phrase is unfamiliar to you.

STRATEGY
Passages for Words in Context questions will provide **context clues** that will help you understand the use or meaning of tested words and phrases.

PREPARING TO ANSWER WORDS IN CONTEXT QUESTIONS

The single best preparation you can undertake for answering Words in Context questions is reading, especially wide and/or deep reading of challenging texts. That's because the words and phrases tested in Words in Context questions are those you'll commonly find in texts in many different subject areas but not commonly hear or use in casual conversation. Vocabulary lessons in classes can also be beneficial, particularly if they focus on high-utility academic words and phrases (sometimes known as *tier two vocabulary*).

We won't say *not* to use word lists as a vocabulary-building tool, but there are a couple of things you should understand if you do decide to go that route.

First, College Board doesn't publish an official list of words and phrases tested on the digital SAT, so any list you find out there may or may not match up with the vocabulary you'll encounter in Reading and Writing questions. Many so-called SAT words, in fact, aren't actually ones we test because they're used so infrequently in the real world that knowing their meaning or how to use them yourself isn't particularly valuable in most circumstances.

Second, learning the isolated (out-of-context) meaning of words and phrases may not be particularly useful when encountering those words and phrases in particular contexts in the Reading and Writing section.

That said, any vocabulary learning is likely to be of at least some benefit to you, whether on the test, in classes, in the workplace, or in your everyday life.

Let's look at some examples of Words in Context questions, starting with those that ask you to fill in a passage's blank with the most logical and precise word or phrase from among the answer choices.

Craft and Structure Sample Question 1

Visual artist Gabriela Alemán states that the bold colors of comics, pop art, and Latinx culture have always fascinated her. This passion for the rich history and colors of her Latinx community translates into the _____ artworks she produces.

Which choice completes the text with the most logical and precise word or phrase?

A) unknown

B) reserved

C) definite

D) vivid

STRATEGY

"Most logical and precise" in this question reminds you that you're looking for the most contextually appropriate word or phrase from among the answer choices.

STRATEGY

Context clues are elements of a text that suggest the meaning of a particular word or phrase found in it. Context clues include, but aren't necessarily limited to, definitions, restatements, and synonyms and antonyms. In this case, the context clues come mainly in the form of the synonym "bold" and the related concept of "passion." Something that's bold and expresses passion is likely to be "vivid" and unlikely to be "unknown," "reserved," or "definite."

In questions such as this, you'll have to determine the answer choice that best fills in the blank in the most logical and precise way.

The gist of the passage is that Alemán produces art that reflects her "passion for the rich history and colors of her Latinx community." The position of the blank in the passage as well as the answer choices we're offered indicate that we're looking for an adjective—a descriptive word to modify the noun "artworks."

As we've previously noted, passages associated with Words in Context questions such as these will include context clues pointing to the word or phrase intended to fill the passage's blank. In this case, "bold colors" (first sentence of the passage) and "passion" and "rich history and colors" (last sentence) suggest that we want a word here that conveys the idea that Alemán's artworks are vibrant. This makes choice D the best option, as "vivid" effectively captures the ideas of boldness, vigor, and intensity.

The other choices aren't as logical or precise in this context. "Unknown" (choice A) and "definite" (choice C) make little sense in context, while "reserved" (choice B) suggests the opposite of what's intended by the context.

Here's a more challenging sample question that also asks you to determine the most logical and precise word or phrase in context.

Craft and Structure Sample Question 2

> Economist Marco Castillo and colleagues showed that nuisance costs—the time and effort people must spend to make donations—reduce charitable giving. Charities can mitigate this effect by compensating donors for nuisance costs, but those costs, though variable, are largely _____ donation size, so charities that compensate donors will likely favor attracting a few large donors over many small donors.
>
> Which choice completes the text with the most logical and precise word or phrase?
>
> A) predictive of
>
> B) subsumed in
>
> C) independent of
>
> D) supplemental to

Even though this question is more challenging than the first one we considered, you can approach it in the same way.

First, let's make sure we understand the passage. We're told that researchers found that charities can mitigate (reduce) the negative impact of nuisance costs on giving by compensating the donors for these costs. We're also told that because these costs have some kind of relationship to donation size, charities compensating for these costs would likely favor (prefer) working with a few large donors than a lot of small donors.

The blank in the passage before "donation size" indicates that we're going to need to choose the phrase from the answer options that makes the most sense in context. By doing so, we'll complete the passage logically by describing the relationship that's currently missing between nuisance costs and donation size.

At this point, we should be asking ourselves what kind of relationship between nuisance costs and donation size would lead charities to prefer taking money from a few large donors rather than many small donors. After considering all the choices, we find that choice C makes the most sense in context. "Independent of" indicates that the "amount" of nuisance cost doesn't depend on donation size. In other words, while nuisance costs vary, they're largely not tied to (i.e., are independent of) donation size. In practice, this would mean that charities would have to pay out roughly the same amount of compensation (in whatever form) to small donors as to large ones. Because the charities would be getting a lot of money from each of a few large donors, compensating these donors wouldn't have much impact on how much money the charities ultimately took in. On the other hand, these same charities would have to pay out roughly the same amount to each small donor, of whom there would be many more and each of whom would only be giving a little money. If the compensation were, say, a $5 gift card, the charity would be better off handing out a few $5 gift cards to a small number of big donors than a lot of $5 gift cards to many small donors.

None of the other answer choices makes sense in context. Nothing in the passage indicates that nuisance costs are predictive of (choice A), subsumed in (choice B), or supplemental to (choice D) donation size, and choosing any of those options for the key would leave the passage without a good explanation for why charities compensating donors for nuisance costs would likely prefer to work with fewer large donors than many smaller ones.

Now let's turn to a Words in Context example for which you must determine the context-based meaning of a word or phrase.

Craft and Structure Sample Question 3

The following text is from Booth Tarkington's 1921 novel *Alice Adams*.

Mrs. Adams had always been fond of vases, she said, and every year her husband's Christmas present to her was a vase of one sort or another—whatever the clerk showed him, underlined marked at about twelve or fourteen dollars.

As used in the text, what does the word "marked" most nearly mean?

A) Stained

B) Staged

C) Watched

D) Priced

STRATEGY

The context clues here aren't limited, as in the previous example, to synonyms and closely related concepts. For this question, it's important to use reading and reasoning skills to establish the intended relationship between nuisance costs and donation size. The passage as a whole suggests that nuisance costs have little relation to donation size, so "independent of" (choice C) is the best answer.

For questions such as this, we have to read carefully and consider the context in which the underlined word (in this case, "marked") appears in order to settle on the best definition for this word among the answer choices.

The passage informs us that Mrs. Adams really likes vases and that her husband gave her a vase each year as a present. The passage also informs us that Mrs. Adams's husband let a store clerk pick out each vase and that each vase was marked at around twelve or fourteen dollars.

The main context clue is right in the phrase in which the underlined word appears: "marked at about twelve to fourteen dollars." Choice D, "priced," makes obvious sense here, as what follows the underlined word is a range of costs that Mrs. Adams's husband paid. (Prices being "marked" on items for sale is also a common way in American English to indicate that these items have price tags of some sort on them, but even without that knowledge, you should easily recognize that "marked" in this context is closely related to price.)

By contrast, none of the other answer choices makes much sense in context, as it wouldn't be logical or customary to describe an item for sale as "stained" (choice A), "staged" (choice B), or "watched" (choice C) at about twelve or fourteen dollars. You can mark something by staining it, you can use marks in staging to indicate where actors should stand, and you can "mark" someone or something by observing them or it closely, but none of these options makes sense in relation to a listed price.

Text Structure and Purpose Questions

Text Structure and Purpose questions ask you to analyze the ways authors put texts together and for what reasons. You may be asked to describe the overall structure or purpose of a passage or to determine the impact on a passage of a particular element (e.g., a detail) in it.

Let's consider an example focusing on a passage-level main purpose.

Craft and Structure Sample Question 4

In 1973, poet Miguel Algarín started inviting other writers who, like him, were Nuyorican—a term for New Yorkers of Puerto Rican heritage—to gather in his apartment to present their work. The gatherings were so well attended that Algarín soon had to rent space in a cafe to accommodate them. Thus, the Nuyorican Poets Cafe was born. Moving to a permanent location in 1981, the Nuyorican Poets Cafe expanded its original scope beyond the written word, hosting art exhibitions and musical performances as well. Half a century since its inception, it continues to foster emerging Nuyorican talent.

Which choice best describes the overall purpose of the text?

A) To explain what motivated Algarín to found the Nuyorican Poets Cafe

B) To situate the Nuyorican Poets Cafe within the cultural life of New York as a whole

C) To discuss why the Nuyorican Poets Cafe expanded its scope to include art and music

D) To provide an overview of the founding and mission of the Nuyorican Poets Cafe

Main purpose questions are essentially central idea questions but with a focus on *why* rather than *what*. Like questions about passages' central ideas, main purpose questions require you to understand the passage as a whole and to provide a summary that incorporates the key ideas without leaving anything critical out or including anything extraneous. The difference is that main purpose questions address authors' intentions, or their aims for writing particular texts. Whereas central ideas questions will have answer choices that are (correct or incorrect) statements about the information and ideas contained in passages, each answer choice in main purpose questions will often begin with a verb (and the particle *to*)—"to explain," "to describe," "to argue," and so on.

REMINDER
Main purpose questions call on the same general skill as central ideas questions. You're looking for the answer choice that best captures the whole passage.

This passage narrates the development of the Nuyorican Poets Cafe from its informal founding in 1973 as a workshop for poets to its move in 1981 to a permanent location with an expanded focus on other art forms to its continued support for emerging artists over half a century. Choice D provides the best answer to the question, as the intent of the passage is to provide an overview of the birth and goal of the Nuyorican Poets Cafe.

Choice A is incorrect because Algarín's motivation for founding the cafe isn't specifically discussed in the passage and because the passage continues on from the cafe's founding to talk about its expansion and evolution. Choice B is incorrect because although the passage does mention that the cafe "continues to foster emerging Nuyorican talent," it doesn't do so in enough detail to qualify as situating (contextualizing) the cafe within New York City's cultural life, as the passage's focus is on the cafe itself. Choice C is incorrect because the passage doesn't tell us why the cafe expanded its scope to include art and music, only that it did so. In any case, the passage's overall focus is broader, addressing the cafe itself, its beginnings, and its development over time.

The important thing to note here is that, like central ideas questions, main purpose questions require you to not only determine what's factually correct per the passage but also differentiate the main purpose from subordinate, or minor, purposes. The incorrect answers in this example are primarily wrong on factual grounds (i.e., they aren't supported in the passage), but other main purpose questions— particularly more challenging ones—may ask you to distinguish between main and subordinate purposes. For example, an answer choice such as "To explain why Algarín had to rent space in a cafe for his gatherings of writers" would be true to the facts of the passage— which tells us that Algarín had to rent cafe space because the gatherings were so well attended—but would represent a subordinate purpose of the passage rather than the main purpose, since that explanation is merely one part of the larger account of the Nuyorican Poets Cafe that the passage provides.

STRATEGY
A key skill required to answer some main purpose questions, especially more challenging ones, is the ability to distinguish the *main* purpose from other, smaller purposes the passage might also be trying to accomplish (i.e., *subordinate* purposes).

While we're thinking about entire passages from a rhetorical standpoint, let's now consider an example about the overall structure of a passage.

Craft and Structure Sample Question 5

> Many films from the early 1900s have been lost. These losses include several films by the first wave of Black women filmmakers. We know about these lost movies only from small pieces of evidence. For example, an advertisement for Jennie Louise Touissant Welcome's documentary *Doing Their Bit* still exists. There's a reference in a magazine to Tressie Souders's film *A Woman's Error*. And Maria P. Williams's *The Flames of Wrath* is mentioned in a letter and a newspaper article, and one image from the movie was discovered in the 1990s.
>
> Which choice best describes the overall structure of the text?
>
> A) The text discusses several notable individuals, then explains commonly overlooked differences between those individuals.
>
> B) The text describes a general situation, then illustrates that situation with specific examples.
>
> C) The text identifies a complex problem, then presents examples of unsuccessful attempts to solve that problem.
>
> D) The text summarizes a debate among researchers, then gives reasons for supporting one side in that debate.

REMINDER

We spent a good deal of time discussing how to analyze the structure of passages in chapter 8.

This question asks us to pick the answer choice that best describes the overall structure of the passage. In chapter 8, we used text structure as one of a few key ways to analyze and make sense of passages. Here, our goal is to describe text structure itself.

The answer choices for this question all follow the same pattern. Each choice presents two ideas linked by the word *then*, which indicates sequence. First the passage does one thing, and then it does another thing.

Before turning to the answer choices, let's break down the passage's structure ourselves. The passage's first three sentences ("Many films . . . evidence") tell us that many early films, including films from "the first wave of Black women filmmakers," have been lost and that we only know those films existed because of "small pieces of evidence." The turning point in the passage is the fourth sentence, which begins with "for example" and introduces a series of cases of early films by Black women of which we have only scant evidence. Our preview of the answer choices led us to anticipate this circumstance, as we saw that each choice consisted of two ideas—two things the passage might do—linked by *then*.

Choice B closely tracks with our analysis of the passage's overall structure. The passage's first three sentences describe a general situation—the loss of many early films and, in particular, the near-total loss of those of many early Black women filmmakers—while the passage's last three sentences provide three examples of early films by Black women of which little trace remains.

Choice A is incorrect because the passage begins with a description of a general situation, not of several notable individuals, and because the passage concludes with examples of the general situation, not a discussion of differences among individuals. Moreover, the individuals mentioned in the passage's last three sentences are more alike than different, as each of their films has all but disappeared. Choice C is incorrect because the first three sentences of the passage present a regrettable set of facts more than a "problem" (complex or otherwise) to be solved and because the last three sentences offer examples illustrating the state of affairs rather than a series of failed solutions. Choice D is incorrect because no debate is presented in the passage.

Now let's examine the third type of Text Structure and Purpose question you may encounter in the Reading and Writing section: questions that ask you to determine the function (role) of part of a passage in relation to the passage as a whole. We'll number the sentences (and the underlined portion) for ease of reference in our discussion, but be aware that sentences in passages aren't numbered in actual test questions.

Craft and Structure Sample Question 6

(1) Horizontal gene transfer occurs when an organism of one species acquires genetic material from an organism of another species through nonreproductive means. (2) The genetic material can then be transferred "vertically" in the second species—that is, through reproductive inheritance. (3) Scientist Atma Ivancevic and her team have hypothesized infection by invertebrate parasites as a mechanism of horizontal gene transfer between vertebrate species: (4) while feeding, a parasite could acquire a gene from one host, then relocate to a host from a different vertebrate species and transfer the gene to it in turn.

Which choice best describes the function of the underlined portion in the text as a whole?

A) It explains why parasites are less susceptible to horizontal gene transfer than their hosts are.

B) It clarifies why some genes are more likely to be transferred horizontally than others are.

C) It contrasts how horizontal gene transfer occurs among vertebrates with how it occurs among invertebrates.

D) It describes a means by which horizontal gene transfer might occur among vertebrates.

Let's first break down the structure of this passage as a whole and then zero in on the role the underlined portion plays in the passage.

As with many opening sentences in Reading and Writing passages (and in real-world texts), sentence 1 here provides background—in this case, a brief explanation of the process of horizontal gene transfer. Sentence 2 continues the explanation by contrasting horizontal gene transfer with vertical transfer. From these sentences, we learn that while vertical gene transfer occurs through reproduction, horizontal gene transfer doesn't. Sentence 3 (before the colon) states the

STRATEGY

To answer questions about the function of parts of passages, you'll want to have a good sense of what the passage as a whole is trying to accomplish. The answer will be the main contribution the tested part of the passage makes to the whole passage.

hypothesis of Ivancevic and colleagues, which involves invertebrate parasites serving as a mechanism (means) for horizontal gene transfer between vertebrate species. In some sense, the parasites, the researchers speculate, act as a genetic "bridge" between other species.

The underlined portion, which we've numbered 4, is the part of the passage for which we need to determine a function in relation to the passage as a whole. In other words, we need to identify what the underlined portion mainly contributes to the passage.

Through careful reading, we can recognize that the underlined portion builds on sentence 3 by further explaining the mechanism posited by the researchers. There are several clues leading us to this interpretation. First, and most obviously, the content of the underlined portion describes a possible method by which parasites could be responsible for horizontal gene transfer: by gaining a gene from one host, moving to another host, and passing on the gene to the second host. Our second clue is the use of the colon in sentence 3. Colons can be used to introduce lists, for example, but their other main use in writing (especially in academic writing, which the Reading and Writing section's passages exemplify) is to introduce an elaboration. *Elaborations* are word(s), phrase(s), or even sentence(s) that build on or clarify the meaning of prior statements—in this case, the statement before the colon marked as sentence 3. This is exactly the role of the underlined portion in this passage. What follows the colon is an extension and clarification of what's said in sentence 3. While sentence 3 describes the way horizontal gene transfer involving parasites may occur, the underlined portion adds specific details about how that mechanism may work. A final clue to the role of sentence 4 is the use of the conditional mood verb "could acquire" in the underlined portion. "Could" here signals that what's being described in the underlined portion is a possible way in which horizontal gene transfer involving parasites may occur. This ties back nicely to sentence 3, which tells us that the researchers had a hypothesis about how parasites may facilitate horizontal gene transfer.

Choice D turns out to match very closely with the reasoning we just detailed and is the best answer to this question. Choice A is incorrect because it's not factually accurate. The passage does describe how parasites could be involved in horizontal gene transfer, but nothing in the passage suggests that parasites are "less susceptible" to such transfers, only that the parasites might facilitate such transfers. Choice B is incorrect because the passage doesn't tell us anything about which genes are capable of or prone to being transferred horizontally. Choice C is incorrect because the passage talks only about horizontal gene transfer among vertebrate species; the only reference to invertebrates is to the parasites themselves, and the only real comparison the passage makes is between horizontal and vertical gene transfer.

Cross-Text Connections Questions

Let's close out this chapter with the third and final main type of Craft and Structure question: questions that require you to make supportable text-based conclusions about how two passages on the same topic or similar topics relate to one another.

In **Cross-Text Connections** questions, you'll be presented with two brief passages that are related by topic. After reading both passages, you'll have to determine which of the question's answer choices is best supported by evidence in each of the passages. Individual questions of this type may focus on similarities or differences between the two passages, and these relationships may be fairly straightforward or quite subtle.

Let's consider some examples.

Craft and Structure Sample Question 7

Text 1
Today the starchy root cassava is found in many dishes across West Africa, but its rise to popularity was slow. Portuguese traders brought cassava from Brazil to the West African coast in the 1500s. But at this time, people living in the capitals further inland had little contact with coastal communities. Thus, cassava remained relatively unknown to most of the region's inhabitants until the 1800s.

Text 2
Cassava's slow adoption into the diet of West Africans is mainly due to the nature of the crop itself. If not cooked properly, cassava can be toxic. Knowledge of how to properly prepare cassava needed to spread before the food could grow in popularity. The arrival of formerly enslaved people from Brazil in the 1800s, who brought their knowledge of cassava and its preparation with them, thus directly fueled the spread of this crop.

Based on the texts, the author of Text 1 and the author of Text 2 would most likely agree with which statement?

A) The climate of the West African coast in the 1500s prevented cassava's spread in the region.

B) Several of the most commonly grown crops in West Africa are originally from Brazil.

C) The most commonly used methods to cook cassava today date to the 1500s.

D) Cassava did not become a significant crop in West Africa until long after it was first introduced.

Our general approach to this question will be similar to how we've tackled questions about single passages. We'll first consider what each passage says separately and then look for one or more supportable connections between the two texts.

The central idea of Text 1 is stated directly in the passage's last sentence: cassava remained relatively unknown in West Africa until the nineteenth century. In terms of purpose, Text 2 mainly serves to explain why cassava remained underutilized in West Africa until

STRATEGY

In many ways, Cross-Text Connections questions can be approached like other questions asking only about a single passage. You'll want to begin by getting a clear sense of the message of each passage separately as well as of the point of view or perspective expressed in each passage.

STRATEGY

Once you've grasped the message and point of view of each passage, think about how the two passages intersect. The second passage may, for example, offer details not included in the first passage, offer an example of what's described in the first passage, or support or challenge all or part of the first passage. In each case, the question itself will help guide you, as it will signal the kind of relationship you should be seeking.

the 1800s and why the situation changed with the arrival of formerly enslaved people from Brazil who knew how to prepare cassava safely. The two passages together give us a clearer view of the emergence of cassava in West Africa.

Now let's consider the question we're posed. Among the answer choices, we want to find the one that the author of Text 1 and the author of Text 2 would most likely agree on. Before we examine the answer choices closely, let's think about how the information in and the perspectives of the two passages relate. As we already noted, Text 1 focuses on the fact that cassava didn't become well known in West Africa until the 1800s, while Text 2 focuses on why cassava only emerged as an important West African food source in the 1800s. The two texts, in other words, are complementary, as they each present different parts of the story of cassava's introduction into the West African diet. Although the two passages contain different details, they agree on the main points.

Choice D is the best answer because it states a point that both authors would likely agree with. Both passages indicate that a lot of time passed between the introduction of cassava to West Africa and its widespread use as a source of food. Text 1 tells us directly that cassava was introduced to West Africa in the 1500s. Text 2 doesn't dispute that estimate and also characterizes the adoption of cassava as a food source in West Africa as "slow." In addition, Text 1 tells us directly that cassava "remained relatively unknown to most of the region's inhabitants until the 1800s," while Text 2 indicates that cassava didn't take off as a food source in West Africa until the arrival of formerly enslaved people from Brazil in the 1800s. Thus, both passages agree that it took a long time for cassava to become important to West Africans' diets.

Choice A, on the other hand, can be ruled out because neither passage suggests that climate prevented the spread of cassava: Text 1 suggests that the distance from the coasts to the inland capitals impeded the spread of cassava, while Text 2 suggests that cassava's toxicity kept it from being widely adopted as a food source. The passages also tell us only about a single crop, not several crops, coming to West Africa from Brazil, which rules out choice B. Text 2 establishes that successful methods for cooking cassava in West Africa emerged only in the 1800s with the arrival of formerly enslaved people from Brazil, which rules out choice C.

In the preceding example, only one answer choice, the key, was supported by textual evidence from the passages. In more challenging questions of this type, such as the following example, you'll have to consider more plausible choices that require more reasoning to dismiss.

Craft and Structure Sample Question 8

Text 1

Although food writing is one of the most widely read genres in the United States, literary scholars have long neglected it. And within this genre, cookbooks attract the least scholarly attention of all, regardless of how well written they may be. This is especially true of works dedicated to regional US cuisines, whose complexity and historical significance are often overlooked.

Text 2

With her 1976 cookbook *The Taste of Country Cooking*, Edna Lewis popularized the refined Southern cooking she had grown up with in Freetown, an all-Black community in Virginia. She also set a new standard for cookbook writing: the recipes and memoir passages interspersing them are written in prose more elegant than that of most novels. Yet despite its inarguable value as a piece of writing, Lewis's masterpiece has received almost no attention from literary scholars.

Based on the two texts, how would the author of Text 1 most likely regard the situation presented in the underlined sentence in Text 2?

A) As typical, because scholars are dismissive of literary works that achieve popularity with the general public

B) As unsurprising, because scholars tend to overlook the literary value of food writing in general and of regional cookbooks in particular

C) As justifiable, because Lewis incorporated memoir into *The Taste of Country Cooking*, thus undermining its status as a cookbook

D) As inevitable, because *The Taste of Country Cooking* was marketed to readers of food writing and not to readers of other genres

Recall that in our first Cross-Text Connections example, the two passages were quite similar in overall focus and perspective, differing only in details. In this example, the relationship between the two passages is more subtle and thus requires more reasoning to infer.

After reading both passages, we can say in broad terms that Text 1 describes a general state of affairs and that Text 2 provides a concrete example of that state. But there's a little bit more going on than that, and the text-based connection we're being asked to draw between the two passages requires a finer-level understanding of both passages.

Let's consider Text 1 first. The author describes a nested set of relationships concerning the esteem (or, rather, lack thereof) in which scholars hold certain forms of writing. Food writing, the broadest category of the three mentioned in Text 1, is "neglected." Within the category of food writing, cookbook writing is particularly devalued. And within the category of cookbook writing, regional cookbook writing is the most devalued. If we wanted to write this out using basic math symbology, we could come up with the following, which uses "greater than" signs to indicate the hierarchy described in Text 1.

(Other, esteemed forms of writing) > food writing > cookbook writing > regional cookbook writing

NOTE

In more challenging Cross-Text Connections questions, both the passages and the relationship between them tend to become more subtle and complex.

Once we've mapped out the relationships described in Text 1 (whether literally or in our heads), it's a fairly straightforward task to understand the intended connection to Text 2. Text 2 tells us that Edna Lewis published *The Art of Country Cooking*, a regional cookbook of "inarguable value," in 1976. Based only on our analysis of Text 1, we would anticipate that Lewis's cookbook wasn't highly valued by scholars, as regional cookbook writing was lowest in the hierarchy described in Text 1. This inference is borne out by evidence in Text 2, which tells us, in the underlined (last) sentence, that "Lewis's masterpiece has received almost no attention from literary scholars."

STRATEGY

While we strongly recommend that you read and consider the entirety of each answer choice to a given question, it's possible that some choices can be ruled out quickly based on (as here) a single key word or phrase that's clearly incorrect.

Let's consider now the answer choices. Each choice consists of two parts, which we might call a *characterization* and a *reason*. From the question itself, we learn that the characterizations—"typical," "unsurprising," "justifiable," and "inevitable"—are posed as possible reactions of the author of Text 1 to the situation described in the underlined sentence of Text 2 (Lewis's cookbook has been ignored by scholars despite its obvious quality). Even before we get to the reasons that follow each characterization, we can easily rule out choice C based on "justifiable." Nothing suggests that the author of Text 1 would regard scholarly neglect of a landmark regional cookbook as justified, as the author is critical of the scholarly neglect of cookbooks in general and regional cookbooks in particular.

To choose the best answer among the remaining choices, we need to consider the reasons—the "because" clauses—provided in each. In doing so, choice B turns out to be the best answer to the question. The underlined portion in Text 2 asserts that Lewis's work has been unfairly overlooked. Based on our analysis of the passages, it's reasonable to conclude that the author of Text 1 would find this neglect unsurprising, and the reason given in choice B—"because scholars tend to overlook the literary value of food writing in general and of regional cookbooks in particular"—tracks with our breakdown of the hierarchy of relationships depicted in Text 1.

STRATEGY

When answering Reading and Writing questions, especially more challenging ones, it's critical to distinguish between what *may* be possible or even plausible in the real world and what's actually supported in the passage(s). The key will be the answer choice with the firmest grounding in the passage(s).

Choice A is incorrect because while the characterization "typical" carries about the same meaning as "unsurprising" in choice B, the reason given in choice A is unsupported by Text 1. The author of Text 1 does mention that food writing is "one of the most widely read genres in the United States" but doesn't offer evidence that food writing is dismissed by scholars just because it's popular. It's *possible* that the author of Text 1 believes critics are biased against popular forms of writing, but the text doesn't directly say or strongly imply that, so we can safely rule out this answer option. As we've observed, the characterization "justifiable" in choice C immediately rules out this option, but we can also note that the reason provided— Lewis undermined the status of *The Taste of Country Cooking* by incorporating memoir into it—has no support in either text. Choice D is incorrect because the characterization "inevitable" is a little stronger than Text 1 supports and because there's no evidence in either text to support the assertion that *The Taste of Country Cooking* was marketed to readers of food writing and not to readers of other genres.

In our final example for this chapter, we'll examine a Cross-Text Connections question that, unlike the other two discussed, asks you to identify a difference in perspective between two passages.

Craft and Structure Sample Question 9

Text 1
Despite its beautiful prose, *The Guns of August*, Barbara Tuchman's 1962 analysis of the start of World War I, has certain weaknesses as a work of history. It fails to address events in Eastern Europe just before the outbreak of hostilities, thereby giving the impression that Germany was the war's principal instigator. Had Tuchman consulted secondary works available to her by scholars such as Luigi Albertini, she would not have neglected the influence of events in Eastern Europe on Germany's actions.

Text 2
Barbara Tuchman's *The Guns of August* is an engrossing if dated introduction to World War I. Tuchman's analysis of primary documents is laudable, but her main thesis that European powers committed themselves to a catastrophic outcome by refusing to deviate from military plans developed prior to the conflict is implausibly reductive.

Which choice best describes a difference in how the authors of Text 1 and Text 2 view Barbara Tuchman's *The Guns of August*?

A) The author of Text 1 believes that the scope of Tuchman's research led her to an incorrect interpretation, while the author of Text 2 believes that Tuchman's central argument is overly simplistic.

B) The author of Text 1 argues that Tuchman should have relied more on the work of other historians, while the author of Text 2 implies that Tuchman's most interesting claims result from her original research.

C) The author of Text 1 asserts that the writing style of *The Guns of August* makes it worthwhile to read despite any perceived deficiency in Tuchman's research, while the author of Text 2 focuses exclusively on the weakness of Tuchman's interpretation of events.

D) The author of Text 1 claims that Tuchman would agree that World War I was largely due to events in Eastern Europe, while the author of Text 2 maintains that Tuchman would say that Eastern European leaders were not committed to military plans in the same way that other leaders were.

Before we consider differences between the perspectives of the authors of the two passages in this question, let's identify some of the ways in which the two texts are similar in their views. Both authors describe *The Guns of August* as well written, with the author of Text 1 saying it has "beautiful prose" and the author of Text 2 calling it "engrossing." In addition, both authors agree that *The Guns of August* has serious limitations as a work of history. Text 1 argues that Tuchman paid too little attention to prewar events in Eastern Europe, while Text 2 contends that Tuchman gave too much credence to the idea that a refusal to deviate from military plans made before the outbreak of hostilities caused World War I.

STRATEGY

Authors of passages in Cross-Text Connections questions may agree or disagree in whole or in part. More challenging questions of this type will pair passages with subtle or complex relationships that you must use reading, reasoning, and text-based inferring to determine.

This discussion leads us to an important general point about Cross-Text Connections passages. Even when the authors of such passages disagree, this disagreement may only be partial. You may see pairs of passages in the Reading and Writing section in which two clearly opposing viewpoints are contrasted, but that's not always going to be the case, especially with more challenging questions of this type.

Choice A is the best answer to this question, as it captures an important difference between the two passages. The author of Text 1 objects to Tuchman's lack of attention to prewar events in Eastern Europe and attributes this to her failure to consult appropriate secondary sources. We can fairly conceptualize this, as choice A does, as a narrowness in the scope of Tuchman's work (i.e., not adequately considering secondary sources) led Tuchman to an incorrect interpretation (i.e., Germany was the war's primary instigator). We find support for the other half of choice A in Text 2, in which the author refers to Tuchman's central argument as "implausibly reductive." Even if the precise meaning of *reductive* (overly simplistic) eludes you, the adverb *implausibly* should clue you in to choice A being the best option.

Choice B is incorrect because although the first half of the answer choice is basically accurate—the author of Text 1 does argue that Tuchman should have consulted more secondary sources—the second half of the answer choice isn't really supported by Text 2. The author of Text 2 clearly respects *The Guns of August* at some level, but Text 2's emphasis is on the book's shortcomings as a work of history. Both halves of choice C are incorrect. The author of Text 1, as we've observed, does praise the prose of *The Guns of August*, but the author never says or implies anything as strongly worded as the proposition that the writing quality of the book transcends its weaknesses as history. Furthermore, although the author of Text 2 does focus primarily on the limitations of *The Guns of August* as a historical account, the author also praises the book, calling it "engrossing" and lauding Tuchman's analysis of primary sources. Choice D is incorrect because, like choice C, it's false on both counts. The author of Text 1 claims that Tuchman ignored prewar events in Eastern Europe, and the author of Text 2 never mentions Eastern Europe specifically, only Europe in general.

As we saw with this question, the most challenging Cross-Text Connections questions will require you to carefully evaluate two (potentially complex) passages while also sorting through answer choices that may be partially but not wholly right. But, as we've also shown, you can use the same basic approach to these questions regardless of the passages' content or the specific question you're asked: read each passage closely, and then establish the nature of the relationship between the two passages. Do they largely agree? Do they largely disagree? Do they simply cover different aspects of the same topic? Getting a strong sense of both passages' content and how the two texts relate will give you a solid basis for answering any question about the pairing.

Summary: Craft and Structure Questions

Main purpose: To test whether you can determine how and why authors write texts the way they do

Proportion of the test section: About 28 percent (approximately 13–15 questions)

Question types

- Words in Context: Use and determine the meaning of high-utility academic words and phrases in the contexts in which they appear

- Text Structure and Purpose: Analyze and describe how and why passages are put together the way they are; describe the main purpose of passages

- Cross-Text Connections: Draw supportable connections between two topically related passages

CHAPTER 14

Reading and Writing: Questions—Craft and Structure Drills

Biologist Jane Edgeloe and colleagues have located what is believed to be the largest individual plant in the world in the Shark Bay area of Australia. The plant is a type of seagrass called *Posidonia australis*, and it _____ approximately 200 square kilometers.

Which choice completes the text with the most logical and precise word or phrase?

A) acknowledges

B) produces

C) spans

D) advances

Osage Nation citizen Randy Tinker-Smith produced and directed the ballet *Wahzhazhe*, which vividly chronicles Osage history and culture. Telling Osage stories through ballet is _____ choice because two of the foremost ballet dancers of the twentieth century were Osage: sisters Maria and Marjorie Tallchief.

Which choice completes the text with the most logical and precise word or phrase?

A) an unpredictable

B) an arbitrary

C) a determined

D) a suitable

3

The following text is adapted from Zora Neale Hurston's 1921 short story "John Redding Goes to Sea." John wants to travel far beyond the village where he lives near his mother, Matty.

> [John] had on several occasions attempted to reconcile his mother to the notion, but found it a difficult task. Matty always took refuge in self-pity and tears. Her son's desires were incomprehensible to her, that was all.

As used in the text, what does the phrase "reconcile his mother to" most nearly mean?

A) Get his mother to accept

B) Get his mother to apologize for

C) Get his mother to match

D) Get his mother to reunite with

4

Michelene Pesantubbee, a historian and citizen of the Choctaw Nation, has identified a dilemma inherent to research on the status of women in her tribe during the 1600s and 1700s: the primary sources from that era, travel narratives and other accounts by male European colonizers, underestimate the degree of power conferred on Choctaw women by their traditional roles in political, civic, and ceremonial life. Pesantubbee argues that the Choctaw oral tradition and findings from archaeological sites in the tribe's homeland supplement the written record by providing crucial insights into those roles.

Which choice best describes the overall structure of the text?

A) It details the shortcomings of certain historical sources, then argues that research should avoid those sources altogether.

B) It describes a problem that arises in research on a particular topic, then sketches a historian's approach to addressing that problem.

C) It lists the advantages of a particular research method, then acknowledges a historian's criticism of that method.

D) It characterizes a particular topic as especially challenging to research, then suggests a related topic for historians to pursue instead.

5

The following text is from Srimati Svarna Kumari Devi's 1894 novel *The Fatal Garland* (translated by A. Christina Albers in 1910). Shakti is walking near a riverbank that she visited frequently during her childhood.

> She crossed the woods she knew so well. The trees seemed to extend their branches like welcoming arms. They greeted her as an old friend. Soon she reached the river-side.

Which choice best describes the function of the underlined portion in the text as a whole?

A) It suggests that Shakti feels uncomfortable near the river.

B) It indicates that Shakti has lost her sense of direction in the woods.

C) It emphasizes Shakti's sense of belonging in the landscape.

D) It conveys Shakti's appreciation for her long-term friendships.

6

The following text is adapted from Oscar Wilde's 1897 nonfiction work *De Profundis*.

> People whose desire is solely for self-realisation never know where they are going. They can't know. In one sense of the word it is of course necessary to know oneself: that is the first achievement of knowledge. But to recognise that the soul of a man is unknowable, is the ultimate achievement of wisdom. The final mystery is oneself. When one has weighed the sun in the balance, and measured the steps of the moon, and mapped out the seven heavens star by star, there still remains oneself. <u>Who can calculate the orbit of his own soul?</u>

Which choice best describes the function of the underlined question in the text as a whole?

A) It cautions readers that the text's directions for how to achieve self-knowledge are hard to follow.

B) It concedes that the definition of self-knowledge advanced in the text is unpopular.

C) It reinforces the text's skepticism about the possibility of truly achieving self-knowledge.

D) It speculates that some readers will share the doubts expressed in the text about the value of self-knowledge.

7

In many agricultural environments, the banks of streams are kept forested to protect water quality, but it's been unclear what effects these forests may have on stream biodiversity. To investigate the issue, biologist Xingli Giam and colleagues studied an Indonesian oil palm plantation, comparing the species richness of forested streams with that of nonforested streams. Giam and colleagues found that species richness was significantly higher in forested streams, a finding the researchers attribute to the role leaf litter plays in sheltering fish from predators and providing food resources.

Which choice best states the main purpose of the text?

A) It presents a study that addresses an unresolved question about the presence of forests along streams in agricultural environments.

B) It explains the differences between stream-protection strategies used in oil palm plantations and stream-protection strategies used in other kinds of agricultural environments.

C) It discusses research intended to settle a debate about how agricultural yields can be increased without negative effects on water quality.

D) It describes findings that challenge a previously held view about how fish that inhabit streams in agricultural environments attempt to avoid predators.

8

Text 1

Dance choreographer Alvin Ailey's deep admiration for jazz music can most clearly be felt in the rhythms and beats his works were set to. Ailey collaborated with some of the greatest jazz legends, like Charles Mingus, Charlie Parker, and perhaps his favorite, Duke Ellington. With his choice of music, Ailey helped bring jazz to life for his audiences.

Text 2

Jazz is present throughout Ailey's work, but it's most visible in Ailey's approach to choreography. Ailey often incorporated improvisation, a signature characteristic of jazz music, in his work. When managing his dance company, Ailey rarely forced his dancers to an exact set of specific moves. Instead, he encouraged his dancers to let their own skills and experiences shape their performances, as jazz musicians do.

Based on the texts, both authors would most likely agree with which statement?

A) Audiences were mostly unfamiliar with the jazz music in Ailey's works.

B) Ailey's work was strongly influenced by jazz.

C) Dancers who worked with Ailey greatly appreciated his supportive approach as a choreographer.

D) Ailey blended multiple genres of music together when choreographing dance pieces.

9

Text 1

The idea that time moves in only one direction is instinctively understood, yet it puzzles physicists. According to the second law of thermodynamics, at a macroscopic level some processes of heat transfer are irreversible due to the production of entropy—after a transfer we cannot rewind time and place molecules back exactly where they were before, just as we cannot unbreak dropped eggs. But laws of physics at a microscopic or quantum level hold that those processes *should* be reversible.

Text 2

In 2015, physicists Tiago Batalhão et al. performed an experiment in which they confirmed the irreversibility of thermodynamic processes at a quantum level, producing entropy by applying a rapidly oscillating magnetic field to a system of carbon-13 atoms in liquid chloroform. But the experiment "does not pinpoint . . . what causes [irreversibility] at the microscopic level," coauthor Mauro Paternostro said.

Based on the texts, what would the author of Text 1 most likely say about the experiment described in Text 2?

A) It is consistent with the current understanding of physics at a microscopic level but not at a macroscopic level.

B) It provides empirical evidence that the current understanding of an aspect of physics at a microscopic level must be incomplete.

C) It supports a claim about an isolated system of atoms in a laboratory, but that claim should not be extrapolated to a general claim about the universe.

D) It would suggest an interesting direction for future research were it not the case that two of the physicists who conducted the experiment disagree on the significance of its findings.

10

Text 1

Because literacy in Nahuatl script, the writing system of the Aztec Empire, was lost after Spain invaded central Mexico in the 1500s, it is unclear exactly how meaning was encoded in the script's symbols. Although many scholars had assumed that the symbols signified entire words, linguist Alfonso Lacadena theorized in 2008 that they signified units of language smaller than words: individual syllables.

Text 2

The growing consensus among scholars of Nahuatl script is that many of its symbols could signify either words or syllables, depending on syntax and content at any given site within a text. For example, the symbol signifying the word *huipil* (blouse) in some contexts could signify the syllable "pil" in others, as in the place name "Chipiltepec." Thus, for the Aztecs, reading required a determination of how such symbols functioned each time they appeared in a text.

Based on the texts, how would the author of Text 2 most likely characterize Lacadena's theory, as described in Text 1?

A) By praising the theory for recognizing that the script's symbols could represent entire words

B) By arguing that the theory is overly influenced by the work of earlier scholars

C) By approving of the theory's emphasis on how the script changed over time

D) By cautioning that the theory overlooks certain important aspects of how the script functioned

Answer Explanations

QUESTION 1

Choice C is the best answer because it completes the text with the most logical and precise word. "Spans" means "extends over a distance of" or "encompasses," which makes sense in describing the area covered by what's believed to be the world's largest individual plant.

Choice A is incorrect because "acknowledges" means "recognizes" or "admits the truth of." Either way, it doesn't make sense here, as a plant can't acknowledge an area. *Choice B* is incorrect because "produces" can mean "makes," "causes," or "presents," but none of those definitions makes sense here, as a plant can't make, cause, or present an area. *Choice D* is incorrect because "advances" means "moves forward" or "progresses," but the plant isn't necessarily moving forward or progressing. Rather, the passage indicates that it already covers an area of 200 square kilometers.

QUESTION 2

Choice D is the best answer because it completes the text with the most logical and precise phrase. "Suitable" means "appropriate for a particular purpose." Since the passage indicates that two of the best ballet dancers of the twentieth century were Osage, we can reasonably infer that the author believes that ballet is a suitable art form for telling Osage stories.

Choice A is incorrect because the passage never suggests that Tinker-Smith's choice was an "unpredictable" one. Rather, the fact that two of the best ballet dancers of the twentieth century were Osage makes ballet especially appropriate for telling Osage stories. *Choice B* is incorrect because the passage implies the opposite. An "arbitrary" choice is a choice based on whim rather than reason, but the passage gives a good reason behind the choice to tell Osage stories through ballet: two of the best ballet dancers of the twentieth century were Osage. *Choice C* is incorrect because the passage never suggests that Tinker-Smith's choice was a "determined" one, which would imply that Tinker-Smith initially faced some kind of obstacle or opposition, or that the choice was made for Tinker-Smith. Nothing like either of those ideas, however, is mentioned in or suggested by the passage.

QUESTION 3

Choice A is the best answer because it most nearly identifies what the underlined phrase means in context. The expression "reconcile . . . to" refers to causing someone to come to accept something difficult or disagreeable. The passage indicates that John wants his mother to accept his desire to travel even though she doesn't like the idea.

Choice B is incorrect because, per the passage, John doesn't want his mother to apologize for his own desire to travel; he just wants her to accept the idea. *Choice C* is incorrect because the passage doesn't suggest that John wants his mother to match, or share, his desire to travel. Rather, he wants her to accept his desire to travel even though she doesn't like the idea. *Choice D* is incorrect because a person can't really "reunite with" a notion, or idea; in any case, "reunite" illogically suggests that John's mother would be once again accepting the notion of John traveling, when the passage gives no indication that she'd previously accepted the idea.

QUESTION 4

Choice B is the best answer because it best describes the overall structure of the text. The passage begins by stating a problem with existing research on the status of Choctaw women during the 1600s and 1700s: because of the nature of their authorship, written primary sources underestimate the power Choctaw women had in their traditional roles. Then it presents one historian's solution: looking to oral tradition and archeological findings for additional insights into these roles.

Choice A is incorrect because the passage never says that research should avoid written primary sources altogether, just that research should also make use of oral tradition and archeological findings as sources. *Choice C* is incorrect because the passage never mentions the advantages of using written primary sources and because it goes beyond critiquing the use of such sources to suggest ways to supplement them. *Choice D* is incorrect because the passage never says that the status of Choctaw women during the 1600s and 1700s is unusually challenging to research compared to other historical topics and because it doesn't mention any other topics for historians to research instead.

QUESTION 5

Choice C is the best answer because it best describes the function of the underlined portion in the text as a whole. The phrase "welcoming arms" reinforces the passage's suggestion that Shakti feels a sense of belonging in the woods "she knew so well," as if the trees are embracing her.

Choice A is incorrect because the phrase "welcoming arms" suggests that Shakti is comfortable, not uncomfortable, in the woods. *Choice B* is incorrect because the phrase "welcoming arms" reinforces the passage's suggestion that the woods are familiar to Shakti, not that she's become lost. *Choice D* is incorrect because the underlined portion doesn't describe actual long-term friendships; it instead uses figurative language to emphasize Shakti's familiarity with the woods.

QUESTION 6

Choice C is the best answer because it best describes the function of the underlined question in the text as a whole. The passage repeatedly claims that true self-knowledge can't be achieved, and the rhetorical question in the underlined portion, which also expresses skepticism, emphasizes that point.

Choice A is incorrect because the passage doesn't provide directions for how to achieve self-knowledge; rather, it claims that true self-knowledge is impossible to achieve. *Choice B* is incorrect because the text doesn't really ever define self-knowledge, much less discuss the popularity of that nonexistent definition. *Choice D* is incorrect because the passage never expresses doubts about the value of self-knowledge; rather, the doubts expressed in the passage are about the possibility of achieving self-knowledge at all. Additionally, there's nothing in the passage to suggest that the author expects some readers to share his views.

QUESTION 7

Choice A is the best answer because it best states the main purpose of the text. The passage first describes an unresolved question: what effect do forests on stream banks have on stream biodiversity? Then the passage presents a study that answers the question: such forests increase stream biodiversity.

Choice B is incorrect because the passage never mentions any specific agricultural environments other than the one Giam and colleagues studied, which was an Indonesian oil palm plantation. *Choice C* is incorrect because the passage never mentions agricultural yields. *Choice D* is incorrect because the passage never mentions any previously held view about how fish in streams in agricultural environments try to avoid predators.

QUESTION 8

Choice B is the best answer because it identifies the statement with which the authors of the two texts would most likely agree. Text 1 states that Ailey had a "deep admiration for jazz music" and that he "helped bring jazz to life for his audiences" with the inclusion of jazz rhythms and beats in his works. Text 2 states that "jazz is present throughout Ailey's work."

Choice A is incorrect because neither passage mentions how familiar or unfamiliar audiences were with any aspect of Ailey's works. *Choice C* is incorrect because neither passage mentions how Ailey's dancers felt about his approach as a choreographer. *Choice D* is incorrect because neither passage mentions Ailey employing any genre of music other than jazz.

QUESTION 9

Choice B is the best answer because it identifies what the author of Text 1 would most likely say about the experiment described in Text 2. Text 1 describes a puzzle that physicists hadn't been able to solve: at a microscopic or quantum level, the laws of physics suggest that we should be able to reverse processes that aren't reversible at a macroscopic level. The researchers discussed in Text 2, however, provided empirical evidence that those processes aren't reversible even at the quantum level, for reasons the researchers themselves don't yet understand. It's reasonable to conclude, then, that the author of Text 1 would say that our understanding of the laws of physics is incomplete since this understanding led to an incorrect assumption.

Choice A is incorrect because the experiment described in Text 2 contradicts, rather than supports, what the physicists mentioned in Text 1 believed to be true at the microscopic or quantum level. Furthermore, per the passage, the experiment described in Text 2 didn't address the macroscopic level at all. *Choice C* is incorrect because neither passage distinguishes between laboratory findings and the way the universe works in general. *Choice D* is incorrect because although Text 2 mentions multiple physicists and that these physicists don't yet know what causes irreversibility at the microscopic level, there's no indication in Text 2 that two of the researchers disagree about the significance of their findings.

QUESTION 10

Choice D is the best answer because it identifies how the author of Text 2 would most likely characterize Lacadena's theory, as described in Text 1. Lacadena's theory is that Nahuatl script symbols signified syllables, but the consensus described in Text 2 is that they could signify either syllables or full words, depending on the context. The author of Text 2 would, therefore, likely consider Lacadena's theory too simplistic: it's missing the importance of context in determining the meaning of the symbols.

Choice A is incorrect because it conflicts with Text 1's description of Lacadena's theory, which is that Nahuatl script symbols signified only syllables. *Choice B* is incorrect because it conflicts with Text 1's description of Lacadena's theory. Text 1 states that Lacadena's theory differed from what earlier scholars had believed. *Choice C* is incorrect because neither passage mentions how or even whether the script changed over time.

CHAPTER 15

Reading and Writing: Questions— Expression of Ideas

Reading and Writing questions in the **Expression of Ideas** content domain are designed to test your ability to revise passages in order to improve how information and ideas are conveyed. There are two main areas of focus in Expression of Ideas questions: selectively using and combining provided information and ideas in order to best meet a specified rhetorical (writerly) goal and using the most logical transition word or phrase to connect information and ideas within a passage.

Proportion of the Test Section

About 20 percent of the Reading and Writing section is made up of Expression of Ideas questions. This translates to approximately **eight to twelve Expression of Ideas questions** per test form.

Overview of Expression of Ideas Question Types

The Expression of Ideas content domain includes two main question types:

- **Rhetorical Synthesis** questions, which test your ability to selectively use and combine provided information and ideas in order to meet specified writerly goals

- **Transitions** questions, which test your ability to provide the most logical transition word or phrase in order to link information and ideas in passages

All questions in this content domain (and in the Reading and Writing section in general) are multiple-choice in format. Each question has a single best answer (*key*) and three incorrect answer choices (*distractors*) that represent common errors students make when answering such questions. All the information needed to answer each question is in the passage, so you should always base your answers on what a given passage says directly and what it strongly implies.

Expression of Ideas Question Types in Detail

In this section, we'll discuss both Expression of Ideas question types in detail. We'll describe the general purpose of each type so that you understand better how to approach such questions on test day. As part of this discussion, we'll walk through some sample questions so that you get a strong sense of the kinds of skills and knowledge required to successfully answer questions of a given type.

Rhetorical Synthesis Questions

Rhetorical Synthesis questions ask you to selectively use and combine provided information and ideas into an effective single sentence that meets the writerly aim specified in the question itself.

A "passage" for a Rhetorical Synthesis question is made up of a bulleted list of statements about a topic. As the question reminds you, these statements are meant to simulate the kinds of notes a student like you might take during a reading assignment or research project. You'll draw on information and ideas in the statements to answer the question, but you'll need to do so selectively because—as is often the case when you take notes—not all the information and ideas may be needed to meet the writerly goal set forth in the question. You'll have to pay close attention to this goal because it will strongly influence how you answer the question. The answer choices in Rhetorical Synthesis questions will consist of single sentences that present differing ways to combine the information and ideas in the passage, but only one of these ways will best meet the specified writerly goal.

Let's begin with a relatively straightforward Rhetorical Synthesis example. Before going through how to answer the question itself, we'll point out the key features of questions of this type.

WHAT IS "RHETORIC"?

Rhetoric is simply the art of effective writing (and speaking). You may sometimes find people referring to empty arguments and insincere flowery language as "mere rhetoric," but the term has a broader and more positive meaning as well.

NOTE

Passages for Rhetorical Synthesis questions don't include the literature subject area.

Expression of Ideas Sample Question 1

While researching a topic, a student has taken the following notes:

- The painter Frida Kahlo is one of the most influential artists of the twentieth century.
- She was born in Coyoacán, Mexico, in 1907.
- She is best known for her vivid and richly symbolic self-portraits.
- *The Two Fridas* (1939) features two versions of Kahlo sitting together.
- One version wears a European-style dress and the other a traditional Tehuana dress.

The student wants to introduce Kahlo to an audience unfamiliar with the artist. Which choice most effectively uses relevant information from the notes to accomplish this goal?

A) The 1939 painting *The Two Fridas* is one example of a self-portrait by Frida Kahlo.

B) One painting by Frida Kahlo features two versions of herself, with one version wearing a European-style dress and the other a traditional Tehuana dress.

C) Known for being vivid and richly symbolic, Frida Kahlo's self-portraits include *The Two Fridas* (1939).

D) One of the most influential artists of the twentieth century, Mexican painter Frida Kahlo is best known for her self-portraits, which are vivid and richly symbolic.

Rhetorical Synthesis questions have several important features.

- *Framing.* The framing of the question, or how it's presented to you, asks you to approach this kind of question as if you were a student taking notes for an assignment. Although this framing isn't really necessary to answering the question, it helps to show you how answering the question is like something you've done many times already (and will continue to do) in your classes.

- *Bulleted list.* The statements in the bulleted list represent the kinds of notes you might take as you read about a topic. Just like real notes, this list includes information and ideas relevant to the specified writing goal and may include additional information and ideas that aren't particularly relevant to that goal. As the question itself reminds you, your job will be, in part, to distinguish between relevant and irrelevant information and ideas when answering. You can safely assume that all the information and ideas in these notes are accurate, and therefore you won't be asked to distinguish what's true from what's not.

- *Rhetorical goal.* The rhetorical (writerly) goal specified in the question is critically important to pay attention to. There are many potential ways that the information and ideas in the question's bulleted list *could* be combined into a single sentence, but only one of the four answer choices will do so in a way that most effectively meets the specified goal.

STRATEGY

Pay close attention to the writerly goal specified in Rhetorical Synthesis questions. There are many possible ways to combine the information and ideas in the bulleted list, but only one answer choice will do so in a way that best meets this goal.

NOTE

Rhetorical Synthesis questions don't test grammar, usage, and punctuation. All answer choices will be grammatical. Your job is to focus on meeting the specified writerly goal most effectively, not correcting sentence-level errors. (You'll do the latter in Standard English Conventions questions, the topic of subsequent chapters.)

STRATEGY

Before or while reading Rhetorical Synthesis answer choices, think about what meeting the writerly goal specified in the question might look like—in this case, how you might go about introducing an artist to an audience unfamiliar with her paintings.

- *Answer choices.* Each answer choice represents one possible way to use and combine information and ideas from the notes in the bulleted list. Each sentence is grammatical, and you won't be tested on conventions of sentence structure, usage, and punctuation in this type of question. Instead, you'll have to carefully consider the answer choices to determine which of them best meets the specified writerly goal.

Let's now turn to the particulars of this question.

The five statements in the bulleted list represent notes that a (hypothetical) student has taken about Frida Kahlo and some of her paintings. Before we set about trying to blend this information together, though, we need to consider the writerly goal specified in the question. In this case, the student wants to "introduce Kahlo to an audience unfamiliar with the artist."

This goal will shape how we evaluate the answer choices. We're not simply searching for the sentence among the answer choices that reads best to us but rather trying to meet the student's goal most effectively. Before (or at least while) reading the actual answer choices carefully, think about what it might mean to meet this goal. In this case, if you were to tell your classmates about an artist you'd researched, and you had good reason to think your fellow students wouldn't know who this artist was, you'd probably want to provide some general information about that artist to orient your listeners. You wouldn't just jump in by, say, describing some of this artist's works but instead would want to give your audience some sense of who the artist was, why they're important (to you or to others), and what they're known for.

Choice D, the best answer to this question, does all these things. It orients and informs readers in general terms about Kahlo and her artistry in a way suitable for an audience unfamiliar with her. This choice tells us that Kahlo was highly influential, worked in the twentieth century, was Mexican, and is best known for her self-portraits, and then characterizes her self-portraits as "vivid and richly symbolic."

Choice A is incorrect because it's simply a factual statement about one of Kahlo's paintings and doesn't provide any background about Kahlo, as the goal requires. Choice B is incorrect for a similar reason, as it jumps right to discussing one of Kahlo's paintings without any effort at an introduction. Choice C is incorrect as well. It gets closer than either choice A or choice B to offering an introductory statement, but it's a general statement about Kahlo's self-portraits, not, as the goal requires, about Kahlo herself, and the more successful choice D includes the same sort of information about Kahlo's self-portraits as choice C highlights.

Before we turn to another example, let's examine, statement by statement, how the information in the bulleted list was used (or not used) in the key to this question.

Bulleted-list statements	Use in the key
The painter Frida Kahlo is one of the most influential artists of the twentieth century.	This information is fully incorporated into the key.
She was born in Coyoacán, Mexico, in 1907.	The key uses the information that Kahlo was Mexican, but it leaves out her birthplace and the year she was born.
She is best known for her vivid and richly symbolic self-portraits.	This information is fully incorporated into the key.
The Two Fridas (1939) features two versions of Kahlo sitting together.	This information is left out of the key.
One version wears a European-style dress and the other a traditional Tehuana dress.	This information is left out of the key.

As you'll notice, although some information from the statements is used directly in the key, other pieces of information in the bulleted list are left out entirely, while one piece was only partly incorporated. This is normal: part of the task in Rhetorical Synthesis questions is to distinguish relevant from irrelevant information and ideas in terms of meeting the specified writerly goal.

We already implied this, but it's worth singling out and making more explicit: the best answer to a Rhetorical Synthesis question may, and likely will, selectively incorporate and/or paraphrase the information and ideas in its bulleted list. Although the first and the third bullets in the above example appear in the key nearly word for word, this won't always be the case—particularly for more challenging Rhetorical Synthesis questions, which may make greater use of paraphrasing. In addition, as with the second statement in the bulleted list, the best answer may use only part of the information found in some bulleted points. As we noted, Kahlo's Mexican heritage was relevant to meeting the writerly goal specified in the question, but her birthplace and the year she was born were extraneous details that wouldn't have contributed to the most effective introductory statement (choice D). And the best answer may, as we found in this example, leave out some bulleted statements entirely. In this case, the details about Kahlo's painting *The Two Fridas* were omitted because they were too specific and precise for an introductory statement about Kahlo herself.

Our second Rhetorical Synthesis example also highlights the need when answering this type of question to distinguish relevant from irrelevant information and ideas in order to meet the specified writerly goal.

STRATEGY
The best answer to a Rhetorical Synthesis question does *not* have to—and typically won't—use all the information and ideas found in its bulleted list. It may leave out some statements entirely, paraphrase elements of some statements (putting them into different words while still preserving the original meaning), and/or incorporate only the most relevant portions of some statements while leaving out less relevant portions.

Expression of Ideas Sample Question 2

While researching a topic, a student has taken the following notes:

- A wok is a cooking pan that originated in China during the Han dynasty (206 BCE–220 CE).
- The wok's round, wide base helps to cook food evenly.
- The wok's high, angled sides help to contain oil splatters.
- Grace Young is a cook and culinary historian.
- Her book *The Breath of a Wok* (2004) traces the history of the wok.

The student wants to describe the wok's shape. Which choice most effectively uses relevant information from the notes to accomplish this goal?

A) Grace Young's 2004 book, *The Breath of a Wok*, traces the history of the cooking pan.

B) A wok is a cooking pan with a round, wide base and high, angled sides.

C) The design of a wok, a type of cooking pan that originated in China during the Han dynasty, helps the pan cook food evenly and contain oil splatters.

D) Able to cook food evenly and contain oil splatters, the wok is the subject of Grace Young's 2004 book.

STRATEGY

Don't be afraid to leave out irrelevant information—even one or more whole statements—when answering Rhetorical Synthesis questions. Always keep the specified writerly goal in mind. You may even want to highlight or otherwise annotate the goal before answering to remind you of it.

Two of the five statements in the bulleted list pertain to Grace Young and her history of the wok. Given that forty percent of the information in the list is about Young and her writing, you might reasonably expect that the best answer would include that information somehow. But read the writerly goal closely. The student wants to describe the shape of a wok. Reading the last two sentences in the bulleted list again, we note that knowing that Young is a cook and culinary historian and that she wrote a history of the wok wouldn't add anything to a description of a wok's shape. It's interesting information, certainly, but it's not relevant to answering this particular question.

Choice B is the best answer because it sticks to describing the shape of a wok—it has a "round, wide base" and "high, angled sides." Choice A is incorrect because it focuses on Young's book and doesn't describe the shape of a wok. Choice C is incorrect because although it focuses on woks themselves, it doesn't describe the shape of a wok at all. Choice D is incorrect because it doesn't describe the shape of a wok and because it focuses as much on Young's book as it does on woks themselves.

Let's look at one final example.

Expression of Ideas Sample Question 3

While researching a topic, a student has taken the following notes:

- As engineered structures, many bird nests are uniquely flexible yet cohesive.
- A research team led by Yashraj Bhosale wanted to better understand the mechanics behind these structural properties.
- Bhosale's team used laboratory models that simulated the arrangement of flexible sticks into nest-like structures.
- The researchers analyzed the points where sticks touched one another.
- When pressure was applied to the model nests, the number of contact points between the sticks increased, making the structures stiffer.

The student wants to present the primary aim of the research study. Which choice most effectively uses relevant information from the notes to accomplish this goal?

A) The researchers used laboratory models that simulated the arrangement of flexible sticks and analyzed the points where sticks touched one another.

B) As analyzed by Bhosale's team, bird nests are uniquely flexible yet cohesive engineered structures.

C) Bhosale's team wanted to better understand the mechanics behind bird nests' uniquely flexible yet cohesive structural properties.

D) After analyzing the points where sticks touched, the researchers found that the structures became stiffer when pressure was applied.

This example again requires us to carefully differentiate relevant from irrelevant information in terms of the specified writerly goal. Given that this goal is to present the primary aim of the research study, we should be on the lookout for information about that in the bulleted list. The second statement in the list speaks directly to the researchers' motivation: they "wanted to better understand the mechanics behind" the structural properties of bird nests. We should, therefore, expect to find this statement strongly represented in the best answer.

The best answer to this question, choice C, does, in fact, include the second statement from the list, pairing it with the first statement's characterization of birds' nests as "uniquely flexible but cohesive."

Choice A is incorrect because it describes the researchers' approach during the study (i.e., their methodology), not their motivation for undertaking the study in the first place. Choice B is incorrect because it describes the nature of birds' nests, not the researchers' motivation for studying them. Choice D is incorrect because it describes a finding from the research, not the reason the researchers undertook the study.

STRATEGY

We've noted this before, but we think it's worth repeating: it's a good idea when answering Reading and Writing questions to have a sense of what the best answer ought to be (based on a close reading of the associated passage) before carefully examining the answer choices. Doing so may speed up your test taking and will likely make it easier for you to avoid being distracted by incorrect choices.

Transitions Questions

The other main type of Expression of Ideas question focuses on transitions, or the logical links between information and ideas in passages. In real-world texts, transitions serve to guide and smooth readers' movement between and among sentences, paragraphs, and larger sections of texts (such as chapters). In the Reading and Writing section, however, **Transitions** questions are focused on logical connections between and among sentences in brief passages. Let's study a Transitions example, returning to our strategy of analyzing the underlying structure of a passage to examine the relationship between the information and ideas presented and, more specifically, how the sentences themselves relate to one another.

COMMON TRANSITION WORDS AND PHRASES: AN INCOMPLETE LIST

Transitions questions in the Reading and Writing section make use of numerous common transition words and phrases. In linguistic terms, these take the form of conjunctions (e.g., *so, but, because*) and conjunctive adverbs (e.g., *however, as such, be that as it may*). Below is a list of some such transitions, though the list is only partial.

Accordingly	For example (for instance)	Moreover
Additionally	For that reason	Nevertheless (nonetheless)
After all	Furthermore	On the contrary
As a result	Hence	On the other hand
As such	In addition	So
Be that as it may	In conclusion (in the end)	Specifically
Because	In other words	That is
But	In summary (in sum) (to sum up)	Therefore
By contrast (in contrast)	In the meantime	Thus
Consequently	Indeed	To be sure
Conversely	Likewise	Yet
First (second, third, etc.)		

Expression of Ideas Sample Question 4

(1) Researchers believe that pieces of hull found off Oregon's coast are from a Spanish cargo ship that was lost in 1697. (2) Stories passed down among the area's Confederated Tribes of Siletz Indians support this belief. (3) _____ Siletz stories describe how blocks of beeswax, an item the ship had been carrying, began washing ashore after the ship was lost.

Which choice completes the text with the most logical transition?

A) For this reason,

B) For example,

C) However,

D) Likewise,

In our analysis, we'll omit some details to focus on the role each sentence serves. We've numbered the sentence for ease of reference, but they won't be so marked on test day.

Sentence 1:   Researchers make a claim about a discovered ship hull.

Sentence 2:   Researchers find evidence for the claim in stories.

Sentence 3:   ?

Sentence 2's main function is to provide evidence for the researchers' claim about the ship hull found off Oregon's coast. The passage makes this explicit by noting that stories of the Confederated Tribes of Siletz Indians "support" the researchers' claim.

What, then, is the role of sentence 3? Even with the blank, we can tell that that sentence offers additional detail about how the stories support the researchers' claim. It notes that stories about blocks of beeswax appearing on the shore align with the fact that the wrecked ship was carrying beeswax as cargo. In other words, sentence 3 provides a particular case in which the Siletz Indians' stories (sentence 2) support the researchers' claim (sentence 1).

Returning to our sketch of the passage's structure, we might update it as follows.

Sentence 1:   Researchers make a claim about a discovered ship hull.

Sentence 2:   Researchers find evidence for the claim in stories.

Sentence 3:   _____, these stories' description of beeswax blocks offers evidence for the claim.

We've left the blank where the transition word or phrase is needed. Since sentence 3 is a specific case of the general point made in sentence 2 about Siletz Indians' stories, we should expect to select the answer choice that most clearly signals that relationship.

After considering the answer choices, choice B emerges as the best answer. "For example" makes good sense as a transition phrase here because sentence 3 can be read as a particular instance of how the stories referred to in sentence 2 support the researchers' claim in sentence 1.

Choice A is incorrect. "For this reason" implies that the fact that Siletz Indians' stories support the researchers' claim led to the existence of particular stories describing beeswax blocks washing up on shore, which makes no sense in context. Choice C is incorrect because "however" implies that sentence 3 somehow contradicts or undermines sentence 2, which, as we've observed, isn't the case. Choice D is also incorrect. "Likewise" implies that Siletz Indians' stories in general (sentence 2) and their stories about beeswax blocks (sentence 3) are two separate if similar ("like") things supporting the researchers' claim. As we noted earlier, though, sentence 3 elaborates

STRATEGY
When answering Transitions questions, it can be helpful to consider the role of each sentence within the associated passage. In doing so, you can leave out or paraphrase some of the passage's details, as we've done here, in order to focus on the passage's underlying structure.

on sentence 2—we could say that sentence 3 is subordinate to sentence 2—and so it doesn't represent a second distinct example of support for the researchers' claim.

Now let's wrap up this chapter with one more Transitions example. We'll again number elements within the passage for ease of reference in our discussion.

Expression of Ideas Sample Question 5

(1) Seismologists Kaiqing Yuan and Barbara Romanowicz have proposed that the magma fueling Iceland's more than 30 active volcano systems emerges from deep within Earth. (2) The great depths involved—nearly 3,000 km—mark Iceland's volcanoes as extreme outliers; (3) _____ many of Earth's volcanoes are fed by shallow pockets of magma found less than 15 km below the surface.

Which choice completes the text with the most logical transition?

A) consequently,

B) in addition,

C) indeed,

D) nevertheless,

Let's once again sketch out the relationships among the passage's statements, leaving a blank where the transition word or phrase would appear.

Sentence 1:	Researchers make a claim about Iceland's active volcanoes.
Sentence 2:	The great depth of Iceland's active volcanoes makes them extreme outliers.
Sentence 3:	_____, many active volcanoes are much shallower than Iceland's.

The key task here is to ascertain the role of sentence 3 in relation to sentence 2 and the passage as a whole. Sentence 2 tells us that Iceland's active volcanoes are "extreme outliers" because of their great depth, while sentence 3 informs us that many active volcanoes are much shallower than Iceland's. From this, we realize that sentence 3 amplifies, or strengthens, the point made in sentence 2 by providing more details about shallower active volcanoes.

This might sound like another case in which sentence 3 provides a specific example in support of sentence 2, but that's not quite the case (and "for example" or something similar isn't an answer choice). Rather, sentence 3 essentially restates the point made in sentence 2, only this time with more specifics.

This makes choice C the best answer here. "Indeed" is often used to signal that the statement it introduces builds on what's been written or said previously by reaffirming the underlying truth or accuracy of these previous statements. In this sense, "indeed" is roughly synonymous with a phrase such as "in reality" or "in truth." This makes good sense in the context of this passage. Sentence 2 says that Iceland's active volcanoes are extreme outliers, while sentence 3 says that "in reality" or "in truth," many other active volcanoes are shallower than Iceland's.

Choice A is incorrect. "Consequently" signals a cause-effect relationship, but it's illogical to suggest that many active volcanoes outside of Iceland draw on shallow magma pools *because* Iceland's volcanoes are extreme outliers. Choice B is also incorrect. "In addition" illogically suggests that sentence 3 describes an additional factor related to the point made in sentence 2, but, as we've observed, sentence 3 serves to amplify sentence 2, meaning sentence 3 doesn't function as a separate, distinct point in the way that "in addition" would imply. Choice D is also incorrect. "Nevertheless" suggests that sentence 3 is true despite what's presented in sentence 2, but we've noted already that this isn't the case.

Summary: Expression of Ideas Questions

Main purpose: To test your ability to revise passages in order to improve how information and ideas are conveyed

Proportion of the test section: About 20 percent (eight to twelve questions)

Question types

- Rhetorical Synthesis: Selectively use and combine provided information and ideas in order to meet specified writerly goals

- Transitions: Provide the most logical transition word or phrase in order to link information and ideas in passages

CHAPTER 16

Reading and Writing: Questions—Expression of Ideas Drills

While researching a topic, a student has taken the following notes:

- Annie Wu is a prominent American flutist who graduated from the New England Conservatory.
- She has won multiple national flute competitions.
- She is best known for a 2011 YouTube video that has been viewed over two million times.
- The video shows her performing *Three Beats for Beatbox Flute,* an original work by composer Greg Pattillo.
- Wu combines flute playing and beatboxing in the video.

The student wants to emphasize Wu's most well-known achievement. Which choice most effectively uses relevant information from the notes to accomplish this goal?

A) Among her many achievements, prominent American flutist Annie Wu graduated from the New England Conservatory and has won multiple national flute competitions.

B) Annie Wu is best known for a 2011 YouTube video performance of *Three Beats for Beatbox Flute* that has been viewed over two million times.

C) Composer Greg Pattillo's original work *Three Beats for Beatbox Flute* combines flute playing and beatboxing.

D) Annie Wu, who has won multiple national flute competitions, has also combined flute playing and beatboxing.

2

While researching a topic, a student has taken the following notes:

- A thermal inversion is a phenomenon where a layer of atmosphere is warmer than the layer beneath it.
- In 2022, a team of researchers studied the presence of thermal inversions in twenty-five gas giants.
- Gas giants are planets largely composed of helium and hydrogen.
- The team found that gas giants featuring a thermal inversion were also likely to contain heat-absorbing metals.
- One explanation for this relationship is that these metals may reside in a planet's upper atmosphere, where their absorbed heat causes an increase in temperature.

The student wants to present the study's findings to an audience already familiar with thermal inversions. Which choice most effectively uses relevant information from the notes to accomplish this goal?

A) Gas giants were likely to contain heat-absorbing metals when they featured a layer of atmosphere warmer than the layer beneath it, researchers found; this phenomenon is known as a thermal inversion.

B) The team studied thermal inversions in twenty-five gas giants, which are largely composed of helium and hydrogen.

C) Researchers found that gas giants featuring a thermal inversion were likely to contain heat-absorbing metals, which may reside in the planets' upper atmospheres.

D) Heat-absorbing metals may reside in a planet's upper atmosphere.

3

While researching a topic, a student has taken the following notes:

- Muckrakers were journalists who sought to expose corruption in US institutions during the Progressive Era (1897–1920).

- Ida Tarbell was a muckraker who investigated the Standard Oil Company.

- She interviewed Standard Oil Company executives, oil industry workers, and public officials.

- She examined thousands of pages of the company's internal communications, including letters and financial records.

- Her book *The History of the Standard Oil Company* (1904) exposed the company's unfair business practices.

The student wants to emphasize the thoroughness of Ida Tarbell's investigation of the Standard Oil Company. Which choice most effectively uses relevant information from the notes to accomplish this goal?

A) Ida Tarbell not only interviewed Standard Oil executives, oil industry workers, and public officials but also examined thousands of pages of the company's internal communications.

B) As part of her investigation of the Standard Oil Company, muckraker Ida Tarbell conducted interviews.

C) Published in 1904, muckraker Ida Tarbell's book *The History of the Standard Oil Company* exposed the company's unfair business practices.

D) Ida Tarbell, who investigated the Standard Oil Company, was a muckraker (a journalist who sought to expose corruption in US institutions during the Progressive Era, 1897–1920).

4

While researching a topic, a student has taken the following notes:

- Platinum is a rare and expensive metal.
- It is used as a catalyst for chemical reactions.
- Platinum catalysts typically require a large amount of platinum to be effective.
- Researcher Jianbo Tang and his colleagues created a platinum catalyst that combines platinum with liquid gallium.
- Their catalyst was highly effective and required only trace amounts of platinum (0.0001% of the atoms in the mixture).

The student wants to explain an advantage of the new platinum catalyst developed by Jianbo Tang and his colleagues. Which choice most effectively uses relevant information from the notes to accomplish this goal?

A) Like other platinum catalysts, the new platinum catalyst requires a particular amount of the metal to be effective.

B) While still highly effective, the new platinum catalyst requires far less of the rare and expensive metal than do other platinum catalysts.

C) Platinum is a rare and expensive metal that is used as a catalyst for chemical reactions; however, platinum catalysts typically require a large amount of platinum to be effective.

D) Researcher Jianbo Tang and his colleagues created a platinum catalyst that combines platinum, a rare and expensive metal, with liquid gallium.

5

A 2017 study of sign language learners tested the role of iconicity—the similarity of a sign to the thing it represents—in language acquisition. The study found that the greater the iconicity of a sign, the more likely it was to have been learned. _____ the correlation between acquisition and iconicity was lower than that between acquisition and another factor studied: sign frequency.

Which choice completes the text with the most logical transition?

A) In fact,

B) In other words,

C) Granted,

D) As a result,

6

Before the 1847 introduction of the US postage stamp, the cost of postage was usually paid by the recipient of a letter rather than the sender, and recipients were not always able or willing to pay promptly. _____ collecting this fee could be slow and arduous, and heaps of unpaid-for, undeliverable mail piled up in post offices.

Which choice completes the text with the most logical transition?

A) Regardless,

B) On the contrary,

C) Consequently,

D) For example,

7

The number of dark spots that appear on the Sun, known as sunspots, can vary greatly. For example, there were about 180 sunspots in November 2001. _____ there were only about 2 sunspots in December 2008.

Which choice completes the text with the most logical transition?

A) In other words,

B) Similarly,

C) Therefore,

D) By comparison,

8

It has long been thought that humans first crossed a land bridge into the Americas approximately 13,000 years ago. _____ based on radiocarbon dating of samples uncovered in Mexico, a research team recently suggested that humans may have arrived more than 30,000 years ago—much earlier than previously thought.

Which choice completes the text with the most logical transition?

A) As a result,

B) Similarly,

C) However,

D) In conclusion,

Answer Explanations

QUESTION 1

Choice B is the best answer because it most effectively emphasizes Wu's most well-known achievement. This choice focuses directly on her 2011 YouTube video performance of *Three Beats for Beatbox Flute*, which the passage identifies as her best-known accomplishment.

Choices A and *D* are incorrect because although each choice mentions some of Wu's accomplishments, neither choice mentions her 2011 YouTube video performance of *Three Beats for Beatbox Flute*, which the passage identifies as what Wu is best known for. *Choice C* is incorrect because it doesn't mention Wu at all.

QUESTION 2

Choice C is the best answer because it most effectively presents the study's findings to an audience already familiar with thermal inversions. This choice presents the findings of the study without unnecessarily explaining what thermal inversions are.

Choice A is incorrect because it focuses on explaining what thermal inversions are, which is unnecessary for an audience already familiar with the concept. *Choice B* is incorrect because it describes the researchers' approach (methodology), not their findings. *Choice D* is incorrect because although it partially identifies the researchers' findings, it doesn't mention the study itself or link the information to the concept of thermal inversion.

QUESTION 3

Choice A is the best answer because it most effectively emphasizes the thoroughness of Ida Tarbell's investigation of the Standard Oil Company. This choice establishes that for *The History of the Standard Oil Company*, Tarbell interviewed many people from various occupations and reviewed a large amount of documentation.

Choice B is incorrect because it's less successful than choice A in establishing the thoroughness of Tarbell's investigation, as it mentions only that Tarbell conducted interviews (without indicating how many or what sorts of people she interviewed) and leaves out that she also analyzed a large number of documents. *Choice C* is incorrect because it merely describes *The History of the Standard Oil Company* without mentioning how much research went into writing it. *Choice D* is incorrect because it merely describes Tarbell and her work in general terms without mentioning how much research went into writing *The History of the Standard Oil Company*.

QUESTION 4

Choice B is the best answer because it most effectively explains an advantage of the new platinum catalyst developed by Jianbo Tang and his colleagues. This choice establishes such an advantage: the new catalyst is highly effective but requires much less of the rare and expensive metal platinum than do typical platinum catalysts.

Choices A and *D* are incorrect because each fails to establish an advantage of the new catalyst; choice A stresses a similarity between the new catalyst and other platinum catalysts, while choice D just describes how the new catalyst was created. *Choice C* is incorrect because it doesn't mention the new catalyst at all.

QUESTION 5

Choice C is the best answer because it completes the text with the most logical transition. The sentence with the blank concedes that sign frequency was found to be more important for sign language acquisition than was iconicity, the factor that the previous two sentences discuss. "Granted" means "admittedly" and would logically signal the kind of concession that the passage makes here.

Choice A is incorrect because "in fact" means "in truth" and would serve to emphasize the correctness of the previous sentences by adding new, amplifying details, which is roughly the opposite of the function the sentence with the blank actually performs in the passage. *Choice B* is incorrect because "in other words" would signal that the sentence with the blank restates in simpler language what's already been said in the passage, whereas the sentence with the blank offers a new piece of information. *Choice D* is incorrect because "as a result" would signal that the sentence with the blank describes the effect of a cause described in the previous sentences, whereas the sentence with a blank offers a concession.

QUESTION 6

Choice C is the best answer because it completes the text with the most logical transition. The sentence with the blank describes two effects—slow fee collection and "heaps" of undeliverable mail—that resulted from the past practice of having the recipient rather than the sender typically pay for postage. "Consequently" means "as a result" and would logically signal this cause-effect relationship.

Choice A is incorrect because "regardless" means "despite everything" and would signal that the sentence with the blank is true in spite of what's described in the previous sentence, whereas the sentence with the blank logically follows from what's already been presented in the passage. *Choice B* is incorrect because "on the contrary" means "just the opposite" and would signal that the sentence with the blank contradicts the previous sentence, whereas the sentence with the blank logically follows from what's already been presented in the passage. *Choice D* is incorrect because "for example" would signal that the sentence with the blank is an example of the situation described in the previous sentence, whereas the sentence with the blank describes a consequence of what's already been presented in the passage.

QUESTION 7

Choice D is the best answer because it completes the text with the most logical transition. The sentence with the blank completes a comparison between the number of sunspots in November 2001 and in December 2008. "By comparison" would logically signal this comparative relationship.

Choice A is incorrect because "in other words" would signal that the sentence with the blank restates in simpler language what's already been said in the passage, whereas the sentence with the blank provides a point of contrast. *Choice B* is incorrect because "similarly" would signal that what's described in the sentence with the blank is comparable to what's described in the previous sentences, whereas the sentence with the blank provides a point of contrast. *Choice C* is incorrect because "therefore" would signal a cause-effect relationship between the sentence with the blank and the previous sentences, whereas the sentence with the blank provides a point of contrast.

QUESTION 8

Choice C is the best answer because it completes the text with the most logical transition. The sentence with the blank offers evidence that contradicts the previous sentence's assertion that humans first crossed a land bridge into the Americas around 13,000 years ago. "However" means "in spite of that" and would logically signal this contrastive relationship.

Choice A is incorrect because "as a result" would signal a cause-effect relationship between the two sentences in the passage, whereas the sentence with the blank contradicts the previous sentence. *Choice B* is incorrect because "similarly" would signal that the sentence with the blank makes an assertion comparable to the one described in the previous sentence, whereas the sentence with the blank contradicts the previous sentence's assertion. *Choice D* is incorrect because "in conclusion" would signal that the sentence with the blank neatly wraps up the discussion begun in the previous sentence, but this makes no sense in context given that the sentence with the blank contradicts the previous sentence.

CHAPTER 17

Reading and Writing: Questions—Standard English Conventions

Reading and Writing questions in the **Standard English Conventions** content domain are designed to test your ability to edit passages so that they conform to core conventions of Standard English sentence structure, usage, and punctuation. There are two main areas of focus in Standard English Conventions questions: ensuring that sentences are conventionally complete and applying a range of usage and punctuation conventions.

Proportion of the Test Section

About 26 percent of the Reading and Writing section is made up of Standard English Conventions questions. This translates to approximately **eleven to fifteen Standard English Conventions questions** per test form.

Overview of Standard English Conventions Question Types

The Standard English Conventions content domain includes two main question types, each with several subtypes:

- **Boundaries** questions, which test your ability to form conventionally complete sentences

- **Form, Structure, and Sense** questions, which test your ability to edit text to conform to core usage and punctuation conventions

All questions in this content domain (and in the Reading and Writing section in general) are multiple-choice in format. Each question has a single best answer (*key*) and three incorrect answer choices (*distractors*) that represent common errors students make when answering such questions. All the information needed to answer each question is in the passage, so you won't need prior knowledge of the passages' topics to successfully answer associated questions.

"STANDARD ENGLISH" AND "CONVENTIONS"

Before we start examining test questions in this content domain, we need to be clear on a few key concepts.

Standard English is a specific form of formal English that's typically expected in academic and workplace settings. Because Standard English is widely understood and employed in these settings, it's useful as a tool of communication. Standard English isn't the only variety of English, and other forms of English are equally rich and sophisticated, but questions in the Reading and Writing section will only test your understanding of Standard English because of that variety's connection to college and career readiness.

Conventions in the sense we use the term describe the "rules" of Standard English. We put the word "rules" in quotation marks because these conventions aren't absolute and unchanging directives but rather agreed-on ways that most users of Standard English adopt to express things. For instance, one expectation of writers using Standard English is that their sentences will express complete thoughts and conform to certain requirements about how sentences are structured and marked with punctuation, such as the inclusion of ending punctuation (periods, question marks, and exclamation points) to denote the conclusion of a sentence. Knowing and applying these conventions makes writing (and, to some extent, speaking) more understandable to others who also know these conventions. In a real sense, the use of conventions is less about conforming to "rules" than it is about enhancing the communicative power of text. To underline that point, all Standard English Conventions questions in the Reading and Writing section appear within realistic contexts, and your task is to edit these contexts to improve their effectiveness.

Because conventions are simply (informal) agreements among writers and speakers about how to express ideas in standard ways, these conventions can—and do—change over time. A commonly cited example of this is the increasing acceptance of the use of the pronouns *they*, *them*, and *theirs* to refer to single individuals. A few language traditionalists still insist that such constructions as "a person . . . they" are incorrect, but the truth is that widely used languages, such as English, grow and evolve over time, and "singular *they*," as this usage is sometimes referred to, has come into much wider acceptance as part of Standard English. (From a linguistic standpoint, singular *they* actually fills a gap that otherwise exists in Standard English: the lack of a set of gender-neutral singular pronouns.)

The important thing to know here is that we won't ask you to try to apply conventions that are contested or rapidly changing. This means, to continue our previous example, that we won't test you on whether "they" is singular or plural in reference to a person whose gender hasn't been identified (and, to the fullest extent possible, we use the preferred pronouns of individuals mentioned in our passages).

Standard English Conventions Questions in Detail

In this section, we'll discuss both Standard English Conventions question types in detail. We'll describe the general purpose of each type so that you understand better how to approach such questions on test day. We'll also discuss the various subtypes of questions in each of these categories. As part of this discussion, we'll walk through some sample questions for each type so that you get a strong sense of the kinds of skills and knowledge required to answer questions of a given type.

Boundaries Questions

Boundaries questions test your ability to apply your understanding of Standard English conventions to ensure that sentences in test passages are conventionally complete. By *conventionally complete*, we mean that the sentences express complete thoughts, are structured in standard ways, and are set off from other sentences by appropriate punctuation.

Questions of this type may ask you to edit sentences in a variety of ways, some of which we'll illustrate below.

Standard English Conventions Sample Question 1

In the novel *Things Fall Apart* by Chinua Achebe, Okonkwo is a leader of Umuofia (a fictional Nigerian clan) and takes pride in his culture's traditions. However, when the arrival of European missionaries brings changes to Umuofia, the novel asks a central question; How _____

Which choice completes the text so that it conforms to the conventions of Standard English?

A) will Umuofia's traditions be affected?

B) Umuofia's traditions will be affected?

C) Umuofia's traditions will be affected.

D) will Umuofia's traditions be affected.

This question tests your ability to differentiate between two types of sentences: *declarative* sentences, which convey information and end with periods, and *interrogative* sentences, which pose questions and end with question marks.

The passage tells you, via "central question," that the statement in which the blank appears should be framed as a question (interrogative sentence).

To make this point clearer, consider the statement written in both declarative and interrogative forms.

> *Declarative:* Umuofia's traditions will be affected (in some unspecified way).

> *Interrogative:* How will Umuofia's traditions be affected?

You can observe that not only does the sentence's end punctuation differ between the two versions, but the word order (syntax) also changes.

Since we're told we're looking for a question here, let's consider choices A and B, which are framed as questions. Choice A results in "How will Umuofia's traditions be affected?" This choice matches our analysis and is the best answer because it's the conventionally appropriate choice. Although choice B is similarly presented as a question, it's not in standard interrogative form. "How Umuofia's traditions will be affected?" isn't a conventional way to phrase a question such as this, so choice B can be ruled out as incorrect. Choices C and D are presented as declarative, rather than interrogative, sentences, so we can quickly rule those options out as incorrect.

Standard English Conventions Sample Question 2

> Humans were long thought to have begun occupying the Peruvian settlement of Machu Picchu between 1440 and 1450 CE. However, a team led by anthropologist Dr. Richard Burger used accelerator mass spectrometry to uncover evidence that it was occupied _____ 1420 CE, according to Burger, humans were likely inhabiting the area.
>
> Which choice completes the text so that it conforms to the conventions of Standard English?
>
> A) earlier, which in
>
> B) earlier, in
>
> C) earlier. In
>
> D) earlier in

STRATEGY

Sometimes your "ear" for language may help you recognize obviously incorrect sentence structures. Even if that isn't always the case, it's still a good idea to (silently) read the various answer choices into the sentence by substituting them for the blank.

This question asks you to consider how best to join or separate two statements using words and sometimes punctuation. The passage makes two assertions, one before and one after the blank. To paraphrase:

> Researchers discovered that Machu Picchu was occupied earlier (than 1440–1450 CE).
>
> In 1420 CE, humans were inhabiting the area.

Choice C is the best answer because turning these two ideas into two separate, complete sentences is one conventional and effective way to structure the information.

The other answer choices violate convention in differing ways. Choice A would result in "it was occupied earlier, which in 1420 CE . . . humans were likely inhabiting the area," which is ungrammatical. *Which* is a relative pronoun, but in this case, it wouldn't precisely refer to anything (i.e., would lack a clear antecedent) in the preceding clause. The relative clause introduced by *which* would also be nonstandard. Choice B is incorrect because it results in a comma splice: two complete sentences joined only by a comma. Choice D is incorrect because it results in a run-on sentence: two complete sentences fused together without an appropriate conjunction and/or punctuation.

Standard English Conventions Sample Question 3

In a 2016 study, Eastern Washington University psychologist Amani El-Alayli found that, among the study participants who experienced frisson (a physiological response akin to goosebumps or getting the chills) while listening to music, there was one personality trait that they scored particularly _____ openness to experience.

Which choice completes the text so that it conforms to the conventions of Standard English?

A) high on;

B) high on

C) high. On

D) high on:

You may find this question more challenging than the previous two examples because it tests, in part, the appropriate use of colons and semicolons to link ideas. Colons and semicolons aren't common in informal writing and even in many published texts, but they make frequent appearance in academic (and, to a lesser extent, formal workplace) writing because they offer powerful ways to establish connections between and among ideas. The colon, for example, can be used to introduce a word, phrase, clause, or sentence (or more than one of these) that directly builds or elaborates on the statement made before the colon. This second word, phrase, clause, or sentence can be an example, a definition, a clarification, a restatement, or the like.

A semicolon, on the other hand, can be used to join two (or, less commonly, more) closely related sentences. Its effect is a little different from that of the colon because the semicolon suggests that the two (or more) sentences so connected carry equal weight, whereas the colon implies that what follows that punctuation mark is subordinate to (e.g., exemplifies, defines, clarifies, restates) the statement made before the colon.

Let's turn now to our answer choices for this question. It turns out that choice D, which employs the colon, is the best answer here. The phrase "openness to experience" clarifies what "personality trait" El-Alayli found to be closely associated with study participants who experienced frisson while listening to music.

Choice A is incorrect because a semicolon can't be used in this way to join an independent clause (beginning with "Eastern Washington University") to a phrase ("openness to experience"). As we previously mentioned, conventional use of the semicolon in this manner involves linking two (or more) closely related sentences, not two unequal sentence elements, such as (in this case) an independent clause and a phrase. Choice B is incorrect because some sort of punctuation is required between the independent clause beginning with "Eastern Washington University" and the phrase "openness to experience"; otherwise, the two ideas being expressed run together in a nonstandard and confusing way. Choice C is incorrect because the period after "high" results in two rhetorically unacceptable sentence fragments, one beginning with "in a 2016 study" and the other with "on openness."

Form, Structure, and Sense Questions

The second and final type of Standard English Conventions question consists of those in the **Form, Structure, and Sense** category. Questions of this type ask you to apply your knowledge of Standard English usage and punctuation conventions to a range of tasks. Specifically, these questions test

- subject-verb agreement.

- pronoun-antecedent agreement.

- verb finiteness (i.e., contextually appropriate uses of verbs and verbals [gerunds, participles, and infinitives]).

- verb tense and aspect (i.e., contextually proper choice of verb tense and aspect).

- subject-modifier placement (i.e., contextually appropriate placement of modifying elements in sentences).

- genitives and plurals (i.e., distinguishing between plural and possessive forms of nouns and pronouns, and using possessive determiners [e.g., *its*] conventionally).

NOTE

In published writing, especially literature, sentence fragments (incomplete sentences) are sometimes used for dramatic effect.

Like this, for example.

Standard English Conventions questions, however, won't offer a sentence fragment as the best answer.

We provide an example and discussion of each of these question subtypes below.

Standard English Conventions Sample Question 4

Wanda Diaz-Merced, an astrophysicist who is blind, has developed software that can translate astrophysical data into sound. Such tools _____ astrophysicists to detect subtle patterns in data—patterns that may not be evident in graphs and other visual formats.

Which choice completes the text so that it conforms to the conventions of Standard English?

A) has enabled

B) enable

C) is enabling

D) enables

This question primarily tests **subject-verb agreement**. When we talk about subjects and verbs agreeing, we mean that they have the same number: singular subjects take singular verbs, and plural subjects take plural verbs. Sometimes, as in this example, subject and verb are close together in the sentence, so it's fairly easy to find a match. In more challenging questions, however, the subject and verb may be separated by other words, phrases, and clauses, which makes maintaining the link harder. Sometimes this intervening text may seem to suggest a different number for the verb than is required by the subject itself. In a few cases, a verb may even come before its subject. These questions, though, are still answered the same way: by keeping track of the subject and ensuring that it agrees (matches) in number with the verb.

In this question, choice B is the best answer. The subject of the sentence with the blank is "tools," which is plural, and "enable" is a plural verb. Choices A, C, and D are incorrect because "has enabled," "is enabling," and "enables" are singular verbs that don't agree in number with the plural subject.

Standard English Conventions Sample Question 5

Official measurements of the Mississippi River's length vary: according to the US Geologic Survey, the river is 2,300 miles long, whereas the Environmental Protection Agency records its length as 2,320 miles. This disparity can be explained in part by the fact that rivers such as the Mississippi expand and contract as _____ sediment.

Which choice completes the text so that it conforms to the conventions of Standard English?

A) one accumulates

B) they accumulate

C) it accumulates

D) we accumulate

This question primarily tests **pronoun-antecedent agreement**. In Standard English, pronouns are expected to agree in number (singular, plural) and person (first person, second person, third person) with the antecedents they refer to. Note that antecedents typically come before the pronouns that rename them, but this isn't always the case.

Choice B is the best answer here. The antecedent for the pronoun that is to complete the text is "rivers," which is plural, and the plural pronoun "they" is the conventionally correct one to use to refer to a plural noun such as "rivers." Choice A is incorrect because "one" is singular, not plural. ("One" in this sense is typically used to refer to a generic person or thing, such as "One really ought to practice for the SAT.") Choice C is incorrect because "it," too, is singular. Choice D is incorrect because although "we" is plural, it doesn't make any sense in context to refer to "rivers" as "we." (Put slightly more technically, "we" is a first person pronoun, and all nouns referring to things take third person pronouns.)

Standard English Conventions Sample Question 6

In 1990, California native and researcher Ellen Ochoa left her position as chief of the Intelligent Systems Technology Branch at a NASA research center _____ the space agency's astronaut training program.

Which choice completes the text so that it conforms to the conventions of Standard English?

A) to join

B) is joining

C) joined

D) joins

This question primarily tests **verb finiteness**. *Finite verbs* are your average, garden-variety verbs. In a technical sense, verbs are finite when they agree with a subject and take a tense, such as past or present. Finite verbs contrast with a category of words known as *verbals*, which include gerunds (verbs functioning as nouns), participles (verbs functioning as adjectives or that are used as part of compound verbs [e.g., "is walking"]), and infinitives (base forms of verbs, such as "[to] be," that lack the characteristics of agreement or tense and that are used as nouns, adjectives, or adverbs). Conventional sentences require that there be at least one finite verb. Problems with verb finiteness arise when a sentence mistakenly uses a verbal in place of a finite verb, leaving the sentence either incomplete or poorly structured, and when finite verbs are used when verbals are instead called for.

In this case, choice A is the best answer because the context requires the use of the infinitive "to join." This infinitive signals Ochoa's intent in leaving one job for another and results in a conventional expression ("Ochoa left . . . to join"). Choices B, C, and D are incorrect because "is joining," "joined," and "joins" are finite verbs, whereas the context requires the infinitive "to join."

Standard English Conventions Sample Question 7

After winning the 1860 presidential election, Abraham Lincoln appointed Edward Bates, Salmon P. Chase, and William H. Seward to his cabinet. Lincoln's decision was surprising, since each of these men had run against him, but historians have praised it, noting that Lincoln _____ his rivals' diverse talents to strengthen his administration.

Which choice completes the text so that it conforms to the conventions of Standard English?

A) will leverage

B) is leveraging

C) has leveraged

D) leveraged

This question primarily tests **verb tense and aspect.** Verb *tense* identifies whether the verb describes something in the past, present, or future. Verb *aspect* can refine tense by adding a specific indication of whether the action took place once, more than once, or progressively over time. The basic guideline here is that verb tense and aspect have to make sense in context. You don't want a past tense verb to describe present action, for instance, nor do you want to use a verb in, say, the simple past tense (e.g., "ran") when the action took place over an extended time (e.g., "was running").

In this question, the best answer is choice D. The context describes how Lincoln made use of his rivals' talents by appointing several of his former opponents to his cabinet. This event occurred one time in the past (around 1860), so the simple past tense verb "leveraged" makes the most sense.

Choices A, B, and C are incorrect because the simple future tense verb "will leverage," the present progressive verb "is leveraging," and the present perfect verb "has leveraged" are inappropriate in this context, which describes a onetime historical event.

Standard English Conventions Sample Question 8

> In 2015, a team led by materials scientists Anirudha Sumant and Diana Berman succeeded in reducing the coefficient of friction (COF) between two surfaces to the lowest possible level—superlubricity. A nearly frictionless (and, as its name suggests, extremely slippery) state,
>
> _____
>
> Which choice completes the text so that it conforms to the conventions of Standard English?
>
> A) reaching superlubricity occurs when two surfaces' COF drops below 0.01.
>
> B) superlubricity is reached when two surfaces' COF drops below 0.01.
>
> C) when their COF drops below 0.01, two surfaces reach superlubricity.
>
> D) two surfaces, when their COF drops below 0.01, reach superlubricity.

This question primarily tests **subject-modifier placement**. Standard English conventions dictate that modifiers be placed as close as possible to the elements of the sentence they modify. Failure to meet this expectation often results in confusing—and sometimes unintentionally amusing—sentences in which the modifier appears to modify something other than what was intended.

In this question, "a nearly frictionless . . . state" is a phrase intended to modify, or describe, superlubricity. To construct this sentence in a conventional way, the modifying phrase should appear as close as possible to the word it modifies. This is accomplished by choice B, which is the best answer.

Choices A, C, and D are incorrect because they illogically result in "a nearly frictionless . . . state" modifying "reaching superlubricity" (choice A) and "two surfaces" (choices C and D). (In slightly more technical terms, "a nearly frictionless . . . state" becomes a dangling modifier under these circumstances.)

Sample Standard English Conventions Question 9

> When they were first discovered in Australia in 1798, duck-billed, beaver-tailed platypuses so defied categorization that one scientist assigned them the name *Ornithorhynchus paradoxus*: "paradoxical birdsnout." The animal, which lays eggs but also nurses _____ young with milk, has since been classified as belonging to the monotremes group.
>
> Which choice completes the text so that it conforms to the conventions of Standard English?
>
> A) it's
>
> B) their
>
> C) they're
>
> D) its

This question primarily tests appropriate uses of **genitives and plurals**. *Genitives* are a category of (usually) nouns with a range of uses, but for the purposes of answering questions in the Reading and Writing section, genitives are functionally equivalent to possessives—that is, they indicate that something "owns" something else, whether literally ("Alex's jacket") or more loosely, as in a trait ("Sofia's skill"). Essentially, this subtype of Form, Structure, and Sense questions asks you to knowledgeably distinguish among

- possessive nouns.

- plural nouns.

- the possessive determiners (sometimes called *possessive pronouns* and, occasionally, *possessive adjectives*) *my*, *your*, *his*, *her*, *its*, *our*, and *their*.

- the contractions *it's*, frequently confused with the possessive determiner *its*, and *they're*, frequently confused with the possessive determiner *their* or the adverb *there*.

The technical distinctions among these categories are fairly easy to grasp, but it's (its?) their (there? they're??) application that messes up many people, including some highly educated people and skilled writers. That's due in part to the fact that *its* and *it's* as well as *their*, *they're*, and *there* are indistinguishable to the ear and because *its* and *their* break the typical pattern of possessives in English, which generally take an apostrophe.

One common misapplication of genitives is sometimes described as the "grocer's apostrophe," so called because this category of error often appears in signs for the sale of such items as "banana's" and "apple's." The distinctions between *its* (determiner) and *it's* (contraction) as well as among *their* (determiner), *there* (adverb), and *they're* (contraction) are just things one has to learn to apply consistently, although asking yourself what function a given frequently confused word performs in a given sentence can help you spot or avoid errors.

Back to the sample question. We want to know which of the answer choices should precede the noun "young," as in offspring. This is a possessive (genitive) relationship—in a loose sense, the animal (platypus) "owns" its offspring—so the best answer here is the singular possessive determiner *its*, which is choice D.

Choices A and C are incorrect because "it's" and "they're" are contractions, not possessive determiners. Choice B is incorrect because although "their" is a possessive determiner, it's a plural one and therefore doesn't agree with the singular antecedent "animal."

STRATEGY

If you're one of the many people who struggle making these distinctions consistently in your writing, consider what role the word plays in the sentence. The possessive determiner *its*, for example, identifies "ownership" and typically precedes a noun (e.g., "its color is red"), whereas the contraction *it's* is a shortened form of either "it is" or "it has." One way to double-check whether *it's* rather than *its* is appropriate in context is to "read out" the contraction. "It is color is red" makes no sense, so *its* should be used instead. The same can be done with *they're* and *their*.

Summary: Standard English Conventions

Main purpose: To test your ability to edit passages so that they conform to core conventions of Standard English sentence structure, usage, and punctuation

Proportion of the test section: About 26 percent (11–15 questions)

Question types

- Boundaries: Form conventionally complete sentences

- Form, Structure, and Sense: Edit text to conform to core usage and punctuation conventions

CHAPTER 18

Reading and Writing: Questions—Standard English Conventions Drills

In 1959, marine biologist Dr. Albert Jones founded the Underwater Adventure Seekers, a scuba diving _____ that is the oldest club for Black divers in the United States and that has helped thousands of diving enthusiasts become certified in the field.

Which choice completes the text so that it conforms to the conventions of Standard English?

A) club

B) club, and

C) club—

D) club,

Photographer Ansel Adams's landscape portraits are iconic pieces of American art. However, many of the _____ of landscapes were intended not as art but as marketing; a concessions company at Yosemite National Park had hired Adams to take pictures of the park for restaurant menus and brochures.

Which choice completes the text so that it conforms to the conventions of Standard English?

A) photographers early photo's

B) photographers early photos

C) photographer's early photos

D) photographer's early photo's

3

The field of geological oceanography owes much to American _____ Marie Tharp, a pioneering oceanographic cartographer whose detailed topographical maps of the ocean floor and its multiple rift valleys helped garner acceptance for the theories of plate tectonics and continental drift.

Which choice completes the text so that it conforms to the conventions of Standard English?

A) geologist

B) geologist:

C) geologist;

D) geologist,

4

In her book *The Woman Warrior: Memoirs of a Girlhood Among Ghosts*, author Maxine Hong Kingston examines themes _____ childhood, womanhood, and Chinese American identity by intertwining autobiography and mythology.

Which choice completes the text so that it conforms to the conventions of Standard English?

A) of—

B) of

C) of:

D) of,

5

Classical composer Florence Price's 1927 move to Chicago marked a turning point in her career. It was there that Price premiered her First Symphony—a piece that was praised for blending traditional Romantic motifs with aspects of Black folk music—and _____ supportive relationships with other Black artists.

Which choice completes the text so that it conforms to the conventions of Standard English?

A) developing

B) developed

C) having developed

D) to develop

6

A subseasonal weather forecast attempts to predict weather conditions three to four weeks in _____ its predictions are therefore more short-term than those of the seasonal forecast, which attempts to predict the weather more than a month in advance.

Which choice completes the text so that it conforms to the conventions of Standard English?

A) advance and

B) advance

C) advance,

D) advance;

7

In 1881, French chemist Camille Faure redesigned the rechargeable lead-acid battery. Faure's design greatly increased the amount of electricity that the original battery, which the French physicist Gaston Planté _____ fifteen years earlier, could hold.

Which choice completes the text so that it conforms to the conventions of Standard English?

A) is inventing

B) will invent

C) had invented

D) invents

8

The African Games Co-production Market, one of over 180 annual international conferences supporting video game development, _____ the growth of the African gaming industry by helping start-up studios in Africa find partners.

Which choice completes the text so that it conforms to the conventions of Standard English?

A) promotes

B) promote

C) are promoting

D) have promoted

Answer Explanations

QUESTION 1

Choice A is the best answer because it completes the text so that it conforms to the conventions of Standard English. The two declarative content clauses ("that is the oldest club for Black divers in the United States," "that has helped thousands of diving enthusiasts become certified in the field") are essential sentence elements used to describe the Underwater Adventure Seekers and therefore shouldn't be separated from the noun "club" by either punctuation or a conjunction.

Choices B, C, and *D* are incorrect because each separates the noun "club" from the two declarative content clauses with punctuation, a conjunction, or both. *Choice D* is also incorrect because the comma after "club" turns "a scuba diving club" into a nonrestrictive appositive of "Underwater Adventure Seekers," which is inappropriate in this context. The relative clauses that follow ("that is the oldest club for Black divers in the United States," "that has helped thousands of diving enthusiasts become certified in the field") would need to be nonrestrictive themselves and each headed by "which" to make the resultant sentence grammatical.

QUESTION 2

Choice C is the best answer because it completes the text so that it conforms to the conventions of Standard English. The singular possessive noun "photographer's" and the plural noun "photos" are appropriate to indicate that a single photographer (Ansel Adams) took many photographs.

Choices A and *B* are incorrect because the singular possessive noun "photographer's," not the plural noun "photographers," is needed in this context. *Choices A* and *D* are incorrect because the plural noun "photos," not the singular possessive noun "photo's," is needed in this context.

QUESTION 3

Choice A is the best answer because it completes the text so that it conforms to the conventions of Standard English. The essential appositive "Marie Tharp" shouldn't be separated by punctuation from the noun phrase ("American geologist") it renames.

Choices B, C, and *D* are incorrect because each uses punctuation to separate the essential appositive from the noun phrase it renames.

QUESTION 4

Choice B is the best answer because it completes the text so that it conforms to the conventions of Standard English. No punctuation is needed between the preposition "of" and the words "childhood," "womanhood," and "Chinese American identity," each of which functions as an object of the preposition.

Choices A, C, and *D* are incorrect because each uses punctuation to separate the preposition "of" from its objects.

QUESTION 5

Choice B is the best answer because it completes the text so that it conforms to the conventions of Standard English. This choice establishes parallelism between the two verb phrases ("premiered her First Symphony," "developed supportive relationships with other Black artists") that describe what Price did in Chicago after her move there in 1927.

Choices A, C, and *D* are incorrect because the present participle "developing," the present perfect participle "having developed," and the infinitive "to develop" aren't parallel in form to the past tense verb "premiered."

QUESTION 6

Choice D is the best answer because it completes the text so that it conforms to the conventions of Standard English. The semicolon after "advance" is used in a conventional way to join the sentence's two closely related independent clauses, the first of which begins with "a subseasonal weather forecast" and the second of which begins with "its predictions."

Choice A is incorrect because it results in a rambling sentence. It's conventional to place a comma after the conjunction "and" when the conjunction is used to join two lengthy independent clauses. Even if that comma were present, however, the sentence would still be awkward, as the conjunction "and" and the conjunctive adverb "therefore" aren't both needed to establish the logical relationship between the two independent clauses. *Choice B* is incorrect because it results in a run-on sentence. *Choice C* is incorrect because it results in a comma splice.

QUESTION 7

Choice C is the best answer because it completes the text so that it conforms to the conventions of Standard English. The past perfect tense verb "had invented" is appropriate in this context to describe a past event that occurred before another event in the past. In this case, Planté invented the rechargeable lead-acid battery fifteen years before Faure improved on the design.

Choices A, B, and *D* are incorrect because the present progressive tense verb "is inventing," the simple future tense verb "will invent," and the simple present tense verb "invents" are inappropriate to describe a past event that took place before another event in the past.

QUESTION 8

Choice A is the best answer because it completes the text so that it conforms to the conventions of Standard English. The singular verb "promotes" agrees in number with the singular subject "African Games Co-production Market."

Choices B, C, and *D* are incorrect because "promote," "are promoting," and "have promoted" are plural verbs that don't agree in number with the singular subject "African Games Co-production Market."

PART 3

The Math Section

CHAPTER 19

Math: Overview

The Math section of the digital SAT is, alongside the Reading and Writing section, one of the two main portions of the test. In this test section, you'll answer questions that test your ability to solve problems involving algebra, advanced math, problem-solving and data analysis, and geometry and trigonometry.

In this chapter, we'll provide a high-level overview of the Math section. In the chapters that follow, we'll examine in detail each of the four broad content domains (areas) that compose the section, including the skills and knowledge covered by questions in each of the domains— Algebra, Advanced Math, Problem-Solving and Data Analysis, and Geometry and Trigonometry. Each content domain's overview chapter is followed by a chapter consisting of drill questions (and answer explanations) that you can use for immediate practice.

Three additional chapters round out our discussion of the Math section. The first provides additional details about responding to student-produced response, or SPR, questions in the Math section. As the name suggests, these questions require you to generate your own answers instead of selecting one of four multiple-choice answer options. You'll find samples of questions in this format throughout earlier chapters, but we want to make sure that you know how to properly enter your answers on test day. The second chapter provides an overview of the features of the graphing calculator built into the digital test platform, which you may choose to use on test day, as well as guidance about where to obtain up-to-date information on bringing your own approved calculator. The third chapter consists of a copy of the reference sheet with common math formulas that you have access to during testing.

At a Glance

Table 1 provides an overview of the digital SAT Math section. We then discuss each feature introduced in the table throughout the remainder of the chapter.

PREVIEW

Chapters 20–28 cover the various kinds of questions you'll encounter in the Math section and provide drills that you can use for immediate practice. Chapter 29 offers additional details about the student-produced response (SPR) question format and how to properly enter your answers. Chapter 30 provides an overview of the built-in graphing calculator available to you on the digital test platform as well as guidance about where to obtain up-to-date information on bringing our own approved calculator to test day should you choose to do so. Chapter 31 consists of a copy of the reference sheet available during testing that contains common math formulas.

QUICK TAKE

You'll have a total of **70 minutes** to answer **44 Math questions**, about 75 percent of which are in the multiple-choice format and the remaining roughly 25 percent in the student-produced response (SPR) format. This averages out to **1.59 minutes per question**. These questions will be divided into **two separately timed modules** of 35 minutes each.

Table 1. Math Section Overview.

Feature	SAT Math Section
Timing and Pacing	
Number of questions	1st module: 22 questions
	2nd module: 22 questions
	Total: 44 questions
Time per module	1st module: 35 minutes
	2nd module: 35 minutes
	Total: 70 minutes
Average time per question	1.59 minutes
Score	
Score	Math section score (200–800 scale); one-half of the SAT total score
Contexts	
Proportion of test section	About 30% of questions are in context ("word problems")
Words per context	A majority of in-context questions have 50 words or fewer
Context areas	Science
	Social studies
	Real-world topics
Graphics (included with select questions)	A wide range of types of informational graphics and geometric figures (e.g., *xy*-plane graphs, bar graphs, scatterplots)
Questions	
Question format	Four-option multiple-choice, each with a single correct answer (about 75% of section)
	Student-produced response (SPR) (about 25% of section)
Question content domains (categories)	Algebra
	Advanced Math
	Problem-Solving and Data Analysis
	Geometry and Trigonometry
Calculator Use	
A calculator is allowed throughout the Math section. You may use the graphing calculator built into the digital test platform, or you may bring your own approved calculator.	
Reference Sheet	
You'll have access to a set of common formulas used in math throughout the test section.	
Scratch (Scrap) Paper	
While you're taking the Math section, you'll have access to notepaper for performing calculations and the like.	

Discussion

In this section of the chapter, we'll go over each of the features in table 1.

Number of Questions, Timing, and Pacing

Each Math section is divided into two equal-length *modules* of questions. Each of these modules is separately timed, so you'll have 35 minutes to answer the 22 questions in each module. That averages out to 1.59 minutes per question.

Score

You'll receive a Math section score based on your performance on the section. This section score will range from 200 to 800, depending on how well you did. Your scores on the Math and Reading and Writing sections added together will give you your total score for the SAT, which is on a 400–1600 scale.

Contexts

About 30 percent of questions in the Math section are set in context. By *context*, we mean that the question presents a brief scenario that you have to read and analyze in order to solve the associated problem. These questions will ask you to consider topics in social studies, science, or real-world settings. Many of these contexts are quite short—a majority of in-context questions are 50 words or fewer—and all contexts are written to be clear and understandable without the need for prior knowledge of the topics being discussed. In other words, all topic-specific information needed to answer an in-context question correctly is in the question itself, and you won't need to have studied a given science, social studies, or real-world topic in school. These sorts of questions are included in the Math section because they help assess your ability to apply your math skills and knowledge in authentic situations. The remaining roughly 70 percent of questions are "pure" math problems without context.

> **QUICK TAKE**
>
> **About 30 percent** of Math questions are **set in context**. This context may consist of a **science, social studies, or real-world topic**. However, you won't need prior knowledge of these topics to be able to answer the associated questions correctly, as all relevant information about these topics is included in the contexts themselves.

Graphics

The Math section includes three main varieties of graphics with select questions. One category consists of informational graphics that display data. These include the same sorts of tables, line graphs, and bar graphs that you'll be presented with in the Reading and Writing section as well as other informational graphics types commonly encountered in math classes, such as scatterplots, dot plots, and histograms. The second category consists of graphs of functions in the *xy*-plane, while the third consists of geometric figures, such as triangles. You'll be expected to make skillful use of these graphics and the information they contain and represent to answer associated questions.

> **QUICK TAKE**
>
> Select Math questions are accompanied by one or more graphics. These may be **informational graphics** (data displays), **graphs of functions in the *xy*-plane**, or **geometric figures**, such as triangles.

Questions

Two question formats are used in the Math section. About 75 percent of the questions are in the multiple-choice format. Each of these questions has four answer choices (options), one (and only one) of which is the correct answer, or *key*. The three incorrect answer choices—which are sometimes called *distractors*—represent common errors that students often make in answering math questions, either in how they approach the question or how they calculate the answer. Your task in these questions is to use your math skills and knowledge to figure out which of the four choices is the correct answer.

The rest of the Math section's questions—about 25 percent of the total—use the student-produced response, or SPR, format. As the name suggests, these questions don't include answer choices to pick from. Instead, you'll have to find and enter your answers on your own. These questions are intended to find out whether you can successfully apply your math skills and knowledge without the structure of a set of options to choose from. We devote chapter 29 to discussing how to properly enter answers to questions in the SPR format, and examples of SPR questions are found throughout other chapters. For now, you just need to know that about one-quarter of the Math section's questions will require you to come up with and enter your own answer. Note that some SPR questions may have more than one possible correct answer, but you'll still enter only one answer per question.

All Math questions are independent of each other, or *discrete*. This means that there are no question sets built around a common source, such as a passage or graphic. This is good news for you because it means you can approach each question separately, give your best answer, and move on to the next question.

Each Math question, whether multiple-choice or student-produced response, primarily tests a single skill or element of knowledge (e.g., your ability to solve linear equations in one variable). The knowledge and skills tested by Math questions fall into four broad categories, which we call *content domains*. Each of these domains represents a major area of focus in math. Table 2 offers an overview of the four content domains in the Math section, including each domain's "big idea," or main focus; the skills and knowledge each domain covers; and the approximate proportion of the Math section devoted to questions in each domain. Subsequent chapters go into detail about each of the domains in turn and provide opportunities for immediate practice.

Table 2. Math Section Content Domains.

Math Section Content Domain	The Big Idea	Skills and Knowledge Tested	Proportion of Test Section
Algebra	Questions in this domain test your understanding of linear relationships.	• Linear equations in one variable • Linear equations in two variables • Linear functions • Systems of two linear equations in two variables • Linear inequalities in one or two variables	13–15 questions (about 35%)
Advanced Math	Questions in this domain test your understanding of nonlinear relationships.	• Equivalent expressions • Nonlinear equations in one variable and systems of equations in two variables • Nonlinear functions	13–15 questions (about 35%)
Problem-Solving and Data Analysis	Questions in this domain test your understanding of proportional relationships, percentages, and probability as well as your ability to use data to analyze and solve problems.	• Ratios, rates, proportional relationships, and units • Percentages • One-variable data: distributions and measures of center and spread • Two-variable data: models and scatterplots • Probability and conditional probability • Inference from sample statistics and margin of error • Evaluating statistical claims: observational studies and experiments	5–7 questions (about 15%)
Geometry and Trigonometry	Questions in this domain test your understanding of concepts central to geometry and trigonometry.	• Area and volume • Lines, angles, and triangles • Right triangles and trigonometry • Circles	5–7 questions (about 15%)

Questions from all four domains appear in each test module (i.e., in each of the two separately timed portions of the Math section). Questions in each module are ordered by difficulty from easiest to hardest, regardless of the content domain the question belongs to, so you may find it advantageous to answer questions in the order in which they appear.

IMPORTANT: UNSCORED QUESTIONS

Four Math questions on each test form—two different questions per module—won't count toward your section score. These questions are ones that College Board is studying for potential use on future tests. Your answers to these questions won't impact your section score in any way. You won't be able to tell these questions apart from the ones in the section that do get scored, but the small number of these unscored questions shouldn't affect your practice or test day performance. Just do your best on each question.

Calculator Use

You're allowed to use a calculator on all questions on the Math section. The digital test platform itself has a built-in graphing calculator that you can use if you wish, or you may instead use your own approved calculator. We recommend basing this choice on which tool you feel more comfortable with. We'll talk more about calculator options in chapter 30. The key thing for the moment is that you may use a calculator with all Math questions if you wish, although, as we'll talk about later, using a calculator won't always be the most efficient way to answer questions.

Reference Sheet

While you're taking the Math section, you'll have ready access to a reference sheet that includes a set of common math formulas that you can make use of anytime you want during the test. A copy of this reference sheet appears in chapter 31.

Scratch (Scrap) Paper

Even though you'll take the digital SAT on a laptop, desktop computer, or other device, you'll still have access on test day to notepaper for performing calculations, taking notes, and the like.

Summary: Math Section

Let's quickly recap the basics of the digital SAT's Math section:

Timing and pacing

- 70 minutes to answer 44 questions divided into two separately timed modules

- An average of 1.59 minutes to answer each question

Score

- A Math section score on a 200–800 scale (one-half of the total score for the digital SAT)

Contexts

- About 30 percent of Math questions set in context

- Majority of in-context questions have 50 words or fewer

- Contexts drawn from topics in science, social studies, and real-world settings

Graphics

- Informational graphics (data displays), graphs of functions in the *xy*-plane, or geometric figures included with select questions

Questions

- A mix of four-option multiple-choice questions (about 75 percent of the section total) and student-produced response (SPR) questions (about 25 percent of the section total)

  - Multiple-choice questions: A single correct answer (*key*)

  - SPR questions: May have more than one correct answer, although only a single answer is entered

- All questions independent of each other (i.e., no question sets)

- Content domains of Algebra, Advanced Math, Problem-Solving and Data Analysis, and Geometry and Trigonometry

- Ordered from easiest to hardest within each module

- 4 unscored questions (2 unique questions per module)

Calculators

- Allowed for all Math questions

- May choose between built-in graphing calculator and an approved personal calculator

Reference sheet

- A set of common formulas available anytime while taking the Math section

Scratch (scrap) paper

- Notepaper available during the Math section for making calculations, taking notes, and the like

CHAPTER 20

Math: Questions— Introduction

The following chapters discuss the kinds of questions you'll encounter in the Math section and give you opportunities to immediately practice what you've learned.

Recall that the Math section has questions in four broad categories, which we refer to as *content domains*. Each content domain has a "big idea," or common focus, tying all the questions in the domain together at a conceptual level. Table 1 summarizes the section's four content domains and the focus of their respective questions.

Table 1. Math Section Content Domains.

Math Content Domain	The Big Idea
Algebra (chapters 21 and 22)	Testing your understanding of linear relationships
Advanced Math (chapters 23 and 24)	Testing your understanding of nonlinear relationships
Problem-Solving and Data Analysis (chapters 25 and 26)	Testing your understanding of proportional relationships, percentages, and probability as well as your ability to use data to analyze and solve problems
Geometry and Trigonometry (chapters 27 and 28)	Testing your understanding of concepts central to geometry and trigonometry

Each of the following pairs of chapters will

- provide a broad overview of a particular content domain, including the "big idea" (focus) of the domain;

- indicate about how many questions you can expect to encounter from that domain on test day;

- identify the key types of questions included in the domain;

- offer a range of sample questions and answer explanations; and

- give you an opportunity to immediately practice by answering questions from that domain and reading the associated answer explanations.

CHAPTER 21

Math: Questions— Algebra

Algebra questions in the Math section focus on the mastery of linear equations and inequalities, linear functions, and systems of linear equations. The ability to interpret, create, use, and solve problems using linear representations and to make connections between different representations of linear relationships is essential for success in college and careers.

Across the Math section, Algebra questions vary significantly in form and appearance. They may be straightforward fluency exercises or pose challenges of strategy or understanding, such as interpreting the relationship between graphical and algebraic representations or solving as a process of reasoning. You'll be required to demonstrate both procedural skill and a deep understanding of concepts.

The questions in the Algebra content domain include both multiple-choice questions and student-produced response (SPR) questions.

Let's explore the content, skills, and knowledge assessed by Algebra questions.

Linear Equations, Linear Inequalities, and Linear Functions in Context

When you use algebra to analyze and solve a problem in real life, a key step is to represent the context of the problem algebraically. To do this, you may need to define one or more variables that represent quantities in the context. Then you may need to write one or more expressions, equations, inequalities, or functions that represent the relationships described in the context. For some algebra questions, you may need to rewrite an equation or interpret a given algebraic representation. For other questions, once you write an equation that represents the context, you then need to solve that equation. Then you may need to interpret the solution to the equation in terms of the context. Questions in the Math section may assess your ability to accomplish any or all of these steps.

QUICK TAKE

Questions in the Math section require you to demonstrate deep understanding of several core algebra topics, namely linear equations and inequalities, linear functions, and systems of linear equations. These topics are fundamental to the learning and work often required in college and careers.

REMINDER

Multiple-choice questions have four answer choices and one (and only one) correct answer, or *key*. Questions in the student-produced response (SPR) format require you to generate and enter your own answer.

STRATEGY

Many Algebra questions such as this one will require you to perform the following steps:

1. Define one or more variables that represent quantities in the question.

2. Write one or more equations, expressions, inequalities, or functions that represent the relationships described in the question.

3. Solve the equation.

4. Interpret the solution in terms of what the question is asking.

Ample practice with each of these steps will help you develop the math skills and knowledge needed to successfully answer questions in the Algebra content domain.

REMINDER

There are several different ways you may be tested on the same underlying algebra concepts. Practicing a variety of questions with different contexts is a good way to ensure you'll be ready for the questions you'll come across in the Math section.

Algebra Sample Question 1

In 2014, County X had 783 miles of paved roads. Starting in 2015, the county has been building 8 miles of new paved roads each year. At this rate, how many miles of paved road will County X have in 2030? (Assume that no paved roads go out of service.)

The first step in answering this question is to decide what variable or variables you need to define. Since the number of miles paved depends on the year, we can define a variable to represent the year. The number of years after 2014 can be represented using the variable n. Then, since the question says that County X had 783 miles of paved road in 2014 and has been building 8 miles of new paved roads each year, the expression $783 + 8n$ gives the number of miles of paved roads in County X in the year that is n years after 2014. The year 2030 is $2030 - 2014 = 16$ years after 2014; thus, the year 2030 corresponds to $n = 16$. Hence, to find the number of miles of paved roads in County X in 2030, substitute 16 for n in the expression $783 + 8n$, giving $783 + 8(16)$. This is equivalent to $783 + 128$, or 911. Therefore, at the given rate of building, County X will have 911 miles of paved roads in 2030.

Note that this example provides no answer choices. It's in the student-produced response format mentioned briefly above. To respond to this question, you would enter your answer in the digital test delivery platform. Directions for entering your answers to student-produced response questions are presented in chapter 29.

Note that the same context could have generated different sorts of questions, as in samples 2 and 3, below.

Algebra Sample Question 2

In 2014, County X had 783 miles of paved roads. Starting in 2015, the county has been building 8 miles of new paved roads each year. At this rate, which of the following functions f gives the number of miles of paved road there will be in County X n years after 2014? (Assume that no paved roads go out of service.)

A) $f(n) = 8 + 783n$

B) $f(n) = 2,014 + 783n$

C) $f(n) = 738 + 8n$

D) $f(n) = 2,014 + 8n$

This question already defines the variable and asks you to identify a function that describes the context. The discussion for sample 1 shows that the correct answer is choice C.

Algebra Sample Question 3

> In 2014, County X had 783 miles of paved roads. Starting in 2015, the county
> has been building 8 miles of new paved roads each year. At this rate, in which
> year will County X first have at least 1,000 miles of paved roads? (Assume that
> no paved roads go out of service.)

In this question, you must create and solve an inequality. As in sample 1,
let n be the number of years after 2014. Then the expression $783 + 8n$
gives the number of miles of paved roads in County X n years after
2014. The question is asking when there will first be at least 1,000 miles
of paved roads in County X. This condition can be represented by the
inequality $783 + 8n \geq 1{,}000$. To find the year in which there will first
be at least 1,000 miles of paved roads, you solve this inequality for n.
Subtracting 783 from each side of $783 + 8n \geq 1{,}000$ gives $8n \geq 217$.
Then dividing each side of $8n \geq 217$ by 8 gives $n \geq 27.125$. Note that an
important part of relating the inequality $783 + 8n \geq 1{,}000$ back to the
context is to notice that n is counting calendar years, and so the value of
n must be an integer. The least value of n that satisfies $783 + 8n \geq 1{,}000$
is 27.125, but the year $2014 + 27.125 = 2041.125$ does not make sense
as an answer, and in 2041, there would be only $783 + 8(27) = 999$ miles
of paved roads in the county. Therefore, the variable n needs to be
rounded up to the next integer, and so the least possible value of n is 28.
Therefore, the year that County X will first have at least 1,000 miles of
paved roads is 28 years after 2014, which is 2042.

In sample 1, once the variable n was defined, you needed to find an
expression that represents the number of miles of paved road in terms
of n. In other questions, creating the correct expression, equation, or
function may require a more insightful understanding of the context.

STRATEGY
Solving an equation or inequality
is often only part of the problem-
solving process. You'll also need to
interpret the solution in the context
of the question, so be sure to remind
yourself of the question's context
and the meaning of the variables
you solved for before selecting
your answer.

Algebra Sample Question 4

> To edit a manuscript, Miguel charges $50 for the first 2 hours and $20 per hour
> after the first 2 hours. Which of the following expresses the amount, C, in dollars,
> Miguel charges if it takes him x hours to edit a manuscript, where $x > 2$?
>
> A) $C = 20x$
> B) $C = 20x + 10$
> C) $C = 20x + 50$
> D) $C = 20x + 90$

The question defines the variables C and x and asks you to express
C in terms of x. To create the correct equation, you must note that
since the $50 that Miguel charges pays for his first 2 hours of editing,
he charges $20 per hour only *after* the first 2 hours. Thus, if it takes
x hours for Miguel to edit a manuscript, he charges $50 for the first
2 hours and $20 per hour for the remaining time, which is $x - 2$ hours.
Thus, his total charge, C, in dollars, can be written as $C = 50 + 20(x - 2)$,

STRATEGY
When the solution you arrive at
doesn't match any of the answer
choices provided in a given
multiple-choice question, consider
whether expanding, simplifying,
or rearranging your solution will
cause it to match an answer choice.
Sometimes this extra step is needed
to arrive at the correct answer.

where $x > 2$. This doesn't match any of the provided answer choices. But when you apply the distributive property to the right-hand side of $C = 50 + 20(x - 2)$, you get $C = 50 + 20x - 40$, or $C = 20x + 10$, which is choice B.

As with samples 1 to 3, different questions could have been asked about this context. For example, you could be asked to find how long it took Miguel to edit a manuscript if he charged $370.

In some questions in the Math section, you'll be given a function that represents a context and be asked to find the value of the output of the function given an input or, as in sample 5, below, the value of the input that corresponds to a given output.

Algebra Sample Question 5

A builder uses the function g defined by $g(x) = 110x + 10,000$ to estimate the cost $g(x)$, in dollars, to build a one-story home of planned floor area of x square feet in Stillwater. If the builder estimates that the cost to build a certain one-story home in Stillwater is $142,000, what is the planned floor area, in square feet, of the home?

This question asks you to find the value of the input of a function when you're given the value of the output and the equation of the function. The estimated cost of the home, in dollars, is the output of the function g for a one-story home of planned floor area of x square feet. That is, the output of the function, $g(x)$, is 142,000, and you need to find the value of the input x that gives an output of 142,000. To do this, substitute 142,000 for $g(x)$ in the equation that defines g: $142,000 = 110x + 10,000$. Now solve for x: First, subtract 10,000 from each side of the equation $142,000 = 110x + 10,000$, which gives $132,000 = 110x$. Then, divide each side of $132,000 = 110x$ by 110, which gives $1,200 = x$. Therefore, a one-story home with an estimated cost of $142,000 to build in Stillwater has a planned floor area of 1,200 square feet.

Systems of Linear Equations and Inequalities in Context

You may need to define more than one variable and create more than one equation or inequality to represent a context and answer a question. Questions on the Math section may require you to create and solve a system of equations or create a system of inequalities.

Algebra Sample Question 6

Maizah bought pants and a briefcase at a department store. The sum of the prices of the pants and the briefcase before sales tax was $130.00. There was no sales tax on the pants and a 9% sales tax on the briefcase. The total Maizah paid, including the sales tax, was $136.75. What was the price, in dollars, of the pants?

To answer the question, you first need to define the variables. The question discusses the prices of pants and a briefcase and asks you to find the price of the pants. So it's appropriate to let P be the price, in dollars, of the pants and to let B be the price, in dollars, of the briefcase. Since the sum of the prices before sales tax was $130.00, the equation $P + B = 130$ represents the sum of the prices. A sales tax of 9% was added to the price of the briefcase. Since 9% is equal to 0.09, the price of the briefcase with tax was $B + 0.09B = 1.09B$. There was no sales tax on the pants, and the total Maizah paid, including tax, was $136.75, so the equation $P + 1.09B = 136.75$ represents the total, in dollars, Maizah paid.

Now you need to solve the system

$$P + B = 130$$
$$P + 1.09B = 136.75$$

Subtracting the left- and right-hand sides of the first equation from the corresponding sides of the second equation gives you $(P + 1.09B) - (P + B) = 136.75 - 130$, which can be rewritten as $0.09B = 6.75$. Now you can divide each side of the equation $0.09B = 6.75$ by 0.09. This gives you $B = \dfrac{6.75}{0.09}$, or $B = 75$. Thus, the price, in dollars, of the briefcase is 75. The question asks for the price, in dollars, of the pants, which is P. You can substitute 75 for B in the equation $P + B = 130$, which gives you $P + 75 = 130$, or $P = 130 - 75$, or $P = 55$, so the price of the pants is $55.

Algebra Sample Question 7

Each morning, John jogs at 6 miles per hour and rides a bike at 12 miles per hour. His goal is to jog and ride his bike a total of at least 9 miles in no more than 1 hour. If John jogs j miles and rides his bike b miles, which of the following systems of inequalities represents John's goal?

A) $\dfrac{j}{6} + \dfrac{b}{12} \leq 1$
$j + b \geq 9$

B) $\dfrac{j}{6} + \dfrac{b}{12} \geq 1$
$j + b \leq 9$

C) $6j + 12b \geq 9$
$j + b \leq 1$

D) $6j + 12b \leq 1$
$j + b \geq 9$

It's given that John jogs j miles and rides his bike b miles. It's also given that his goal is to jog and ride his bike a total of at least 9 miles. This goal is represented by the inequality $j + b \geq 9$. This eliminates choices B and C.

You can use either of two approaches—combination or substitution—when solving a system of linear equations. One may get you to the answer more quickly than the other, depending on the equations you're working with and what you're solving for. Practice using both approaches to give you greater flexibility on test day.

STRATEGY

While this question may seem complex, as it involves numerous steps, solving it calls on the same underlying principles outlined earlier: defining variables, creating equations to represent relationships, solving equations, and interpreting the solution.

STRATEGY

In sample 7, the answer choices each contain two parts. Use this to your advantage by tackling one part at a time and eliminating answers that don't work.

Since rate × time = distance, it follows that time = $\dfrac{\text{distance}}{\text{rate}}$. John jogs j miles at 6 miles per hour, so the time he jogs is equal to $\dfrac{j \text{ miles}}{6 \text{ miles/hour}} = \dfrac{j}{6}$ hours. Similarly, since John rides his bike b miles at 12 miles per hour, the time he rides his bike is $\dfrac{b}{12}$ hours. Thus, John's goal to complete his jog and his bike ride in no more than 1 hour can be represented by the inequality $\dfrac{j}{6} + \dfrac{b}{12} \leq 1$. The system $j + b \geq 9$ and $\dfrac{j}{6} + \dfrac{b}{12} \leq 1$ is choice A.

Fluency in Solving Linear Equations, Linear Inequalities, and Systems of Linear Equations

Creating linear equations, linear inequalities, and systems of linear equations that represent a context are key skills for success in college and careers. It's also essential to be able to fluently solve these linear equations, linear inequalities, and systems of linear equations. Some of the Algebra questions in the Math section may also present equations, inequalities, or systems without a context and directly assess your fluency in solving them.

All such fluency questions in the Math section permit the use of a calculator, and some of them test your ability to solve equations, inequalities, and systems of equations. Even though a calculator is permitted for all Math section questions, you may be able to answer certain questions more quickly without using a calculator, such as in sample 9, below. Part of what the Math section assesses is your ability to decide whether using a calculator to answer a question offers efficiency or whether it's more efficient to solve by hand. Sample 8 is an example of a question that could be solved either by hand or by using a graphing calculator.

Algebra Sample Question 8

$$3\left(\frac{1}{2} - x\right) = \frac{3}{5} + 15x$$

What is the solution to the given equation?

Using the distributive property to rewrite the left-hand side of the equation gives $\dfrac{3}{2} - 3x = \dfrac{3}{5} + 15x$. Adding $3x$ to both sides of this equation and then subtracting $\dfrac{3}{5}$ from both sides of this equation gives $\dfrac{3}{2} - \dfrac{3}{5} = 18x$. The equation may be easier to solve if it's transformed into an equation without fractions; to do this, multiply each side of $\frac{3}{2} - \frac{3}{5} = 18x$ by 10, which is the least common multiple of the denominators 2 and 5. This gives $\frac{30}{2} - \frac{30}{5} = 180x$, which can be rewritten as $15 - 6 = 180x$, or $9 = 180x$. Dividing both sides of this equation by 180 gives $x = \frac{1}{20}$.

Alternatively, each side of the given equation can be set equal to y and entered in a graphing calculator. Then the problem can be solved by finding the intersection point of the two lines that each represent one side of the given equation. You would enter $y = 3\left(\frac{1}{2} - x\right)$ and $y = \frac{3}{5} + 15x$ in the graphing interface and draw the graphs. The intersection point is (0.05, 1.35), which means $x = 0.05$, which is equivalent to $x = \frac{1}{20}$. Note that .05 and 1/20 are examples of ways to enter a correct answer.

Algebra Sample Question 9

$$-2(3x + 2.4) = -3(3x + 2.4)$$

What is the solution to the given equation?

You could solve this in the same way as sample 8, by multiplying everything out and simplifying, or by graphing each side of the equation. But the structure of the equation reveals that −2 times a quantity, $3x \mp 2.4$, is equal to −3 times the same quantity. This is only possible if the quantity $3x + 2.4$ is equal to zero. Thus, $3x + 2.4 = 0$, or $3x = -2.4$. Therefore, the solution is $x = -0.8$.

Algebra Sample Question 10

$$-2x = 4y + 6$$
$$2(2y + 3) = 3x - 5$$

What is the solution (x, y) to the given system of equations?

A) (1, 2)

B) (1, −2)

C) (−1, −1)

D) (−1, 1)

This is an example of a system you can solve more efficiently by substitution than by using the elimination method demonstrated in sample 6. Since $-2x = 4y + 6$, it follows that $-x = 2y + 3$. Now you can substitute $-x$ for $2y + 3$ in the second equation. This gives you $2(-x) = 3x - 5$, which simplifies to $5x = 5$, or $x = 1$. Substituting 1 for x in the first equation gives you $-2 = 4y + 6$, which simplifies to $4y = -8$, or $y = -2$. Therefore, the solution to the system is (1, −2).

STRATEGY

While a calculator is permitted on all questions in the Math section, it's important to not rely too much on the tool. Some questions, such as sample 9, can be solved more efficiently without using a calculator. Your ability to choose when to use and when not to use a calculator is one of the things the Math section assesses, so be sure to practice this.

STRATEGY

In sample 6, the elimination method yields an efficient solution to the question. In sample 10, the substitution method turns out to be an efficient approach. These examples illustrate the benefits of knowing both approaches and thinking critically about which approach may be more efficient for a given question.

In the preceding examples, you found a unique solution to linear equations and to systems of two linear equations in two variables. But not all such equations and systems have solutions, and some have infinitely many solutions. Some questions in the Math section assess your ability to determine whether an equation or a system of linear equations has one solution, no solutions, or infinitely many solutions.

The Relationships among Linear Equations, Lines in the Coordinate Plane, and the Contexts They Describe

STRATEGY

Graphing systems of two linear equations is another effective approach to solving them. Practice arranging linear equations into $y = mx + b$ form and graphing them in the coordinate plane.

A system of two linear equations in two variables can be solved by graphing the lines in the coordinate plane. For example, you can graph the equations of the system in the xy-plane in sample 10, above.

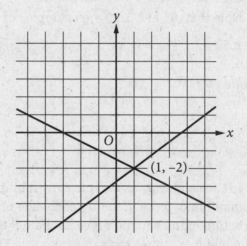

The point of intersection gives the solution to the system.

If the equations in a system of two linear equations in two variables are graphed, each graph will be a line. There are three possibilities:

1. The lines intersect at one point. In this case, the system has a unique solution.

2. The lines are parallel. In this case, the system has no solution.

3. The lines are identical. In this case, every point on the line is a solution, and so the system has infinitely many solutions.

One way that the second and third cases can be identified is by rewriting the equations of the system in slope-intercept form, $y = mx + b$, where m is the slope of the line and b is the y-coordinate of the y-intercept of the line when the system is graphed in the xy-plane. If the lines have the same slope and different y-coordinates of the y-intercepts, the lines are parallel; if both the slope and the y-coordinate of the y-intercept are the same, the lines are identical.

How are the second and third cases represented algebraically? Samples 11 and 12 answer this question.

Algebra Sample Question 11

$$2y + 6x = 3$$
$$y + 3x = 2$$

How many solutions (x, y) does the given system of equations have?

A) Zero

B) Exactly one

C) Exactly two

D) Infinitely many

To rewrite the second equation in slope-intercept form, subtract $3x$ from both sides of the equation, which gives $y = -3x + 2$. To rewrite the first equation in slope-intercept form, subtract $6x$ from both sides of the equation, which gives $2y = -6x + 3$. Next, divide both sides of this equation by 2, which gives $y = -3x + \frac{3}{2}$. Now that the two equations are written in slope-intercept form, you can identify that the slope of each line is -3 and that the y-coordinates of the y-intercepts are $\frac{3}{2}$ and 2.

Since the slopes are the same and the y-coordinates of the y-intercepts are different, the graphs of the lines will show distinct parallel lines. Because parallel lines never intersect, the system of equations has zero solutions.

Alternatively, if you multiply each side of $y + 3x = 2$ by 2, you get $2y + 6x = 4$. Then subtracting each side of $2y + 6x = 3$ from the corresponding side of $2y + 6x = 4$ gives $0 = 1$. This is a false statement. Therefore, the system has zero solutions (x, y).

You could also use graphing technology to graph the two equations. The graphs are parallel lines, so there are no points of intersection, and the system of equations has zero solutions.

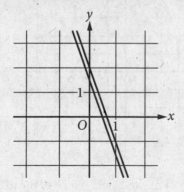

Algebra Sample Question 12

$$3s - 2t = a$$
$$-15s + bt = -7$$

In the given system of equations, a and b are constants. If the system has infinitely many solutions, what is the value of a?

STRATEGY

When the graphs of a system of two linear equations are distinct parallel lines, as in sample 11, the system has zero solutions. If the question states that a system of two linear equations has an infinite number of solutions, as in sample 12, the equations must be equivalent.

STRATEGY

The equations in the system in sample 11 are in a form that allows you to quickly find both the x-intercept and the y-intercept of the graph of the equation. For example, the graph of $y + 3x = 2$ has an x-intercept of $\left(\frac{2}{3}, 0\right)$ because if $y = 0$, then $3x = 2$ and $x = \frac{2}{3}$. Similarly, the graph has a y-intercept of $(0, 2)$ because if $x = 0$, then $y = 2$.

If a system of two linear equations in two variables has infinitely many solutions, the two equations in the system must be equivalent. Since the two equations are presented in the same form, the second equation must be equal to the first equation multiplied by a constant. Since the coefficient of s in the second equation is -5 times the coefficient of s in the first equation, multiply each side of the first equation by -5. This gives you the system

$$-15s + 10t = -5a$$
$$-15s + bt = -7$$

Since these two equations are equivalent and have the same coefficient of s, the coefficients of t and the constants on the right-hand side must also be the same. Thus, $b = 10$ and $-5a = -7$. Therefore, the value of a is $\frac{7}{5}$.

There may also be questions in the Math section that assess your knowledge of the relationship between the algebraic and the geometric representations of a line—that is, between an equation of a line and its graph. The key concepts are

- If the slopes of line ℓ and line k are each defined (that is, if neither line is a vertical line), then

    - Line ℓ and line k are parallel if and only if they have the same slope.

    - Line ℓ and line k are perpendicular if and only if the product of their slopes is -1.

Algebra Sample Question 13

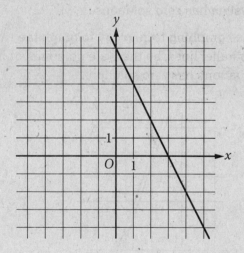

The graph of line k is shown in the xy-plane. Which of the following is an equation of a line that is perpendicular to line k?

A) $y = -2x + 1$

B) $y = -\frac{1}{2}x + 2$

C) $y = \frac{1}{2}x + 3$

D) $y = 2x + 4$

Note that the graph of line k passes through the points (0, 6) and (3, 0). Thus, the slope of line k is $\frac{0-6}{3-0} = -2$. Since the product of the slopes of perpendicular lines is −1, a line that is perpendicular to line k will have slope $\frac{1}{2}$. All the choices are in slope-intercept form, and so the coefficient of x is the slope of the line represented by the equation. Therefore, choice C, $y = \frac{1}{2}x + 3$, is an equation of a line with slope $\frac{1}{2}$, and thus this line is perpendicular to line k.

As we've noted, some contexts can be described with a linear equation. The graph of a linear equation is a line. A nonvertical line has geometric properties such as its slope and its y-intercept. These geometric properties can often be interpreted in terms of the context. The Math section may have questions that assess your ability to make these interpretations. For example, reconsider the contexts in samples 1 to 3. You created a linear function, $f(n) = 783 + 8n$, that describes the number of miles of paved road County X will have n years after 2014. This equation can be graphed in the coordinate plane, with n on the horizontal axis and $f(n)$ on the vertical axis. The points of this graph lie on a line with slope 8 and y-intercept of (0, 783). The slope, 8, gives the number of miles of new paved roads added each year, and the y-intercept gives the number of miles of paved roads in 2014, the year that corresponds to $n = 0$.

Algebra Sample Question 14

A voter registration drive was held in Town Y. The number of voters, V, registered T days after the drive began can be estimated by the equation $V = 3,450 + 65T$. What is the best interpretation of the number 65 in this context?

A) The estimated number of registered voters at the beginning of the registration drive

B) The estimated number of registered voters at the end of the registration drive

C) The total estimated number of voters registered during the drive

D) The estimated number of voters registered each day during the drive

The correct answer is choice D. For each day that passes, it's the next day of the registration drive, and so T increases by 1. In the given equation, when T, the number of days after the drive began, increases by 1, V, the estimated number of voters registered, becomes $V = 3,450 + 65(T + 1)$, or $V = 3,450 + 65T + 65$. That is, the estimated number of voters registered increases by 65 for each day of the drive. Therefore, 65 is the estimated number of voters registered each day during the drive.

You should note that choice A describes the number 3,450, and the numbers described by choices B and C can be found only if you know how many days the registration drive lasted; this information isn't given in the question.

The Math section will further assess your understanding of linear equations by, for instance, asking you to select a linear equation that describes a given graph, select a graph that describes a given linear equation, or determine how a graph may be affected by a change in its equation.

STRATEGY
Sample 13 requires a strong understanding of slope as well as the ability to calculate slope: slope is equal to rise over run, or the change in the y-value divided by the change in the x-value. Parallel lines have slopes that are equal. Perpendicular lines have slopes whose product is −1.

Summary: Algebra Questions

Main purpose: To assess your understanding of linear relationships

Proportion of the test section: About 35 percent (approximately thirteen to fifteen questions)

Question types

- Linear equations in one variable
- Linear equations in two variables
- Linear functions
- Systems of two linear equations in two variables
- Linear inequalities in one or two variables

CHAPTER 22

Math: Questions— Algebra Drills

1

$$3a + 4b = 25$$

A shipping company charged a customer \$25 to ship some small boxes and some large boxes. The given equation represents the relationship between a, the number of small boxes, and b, the number of large boxes, the customer had shipped. If the customer had 3 small boxes shipped, how many large boxes were shipped?

A) 3

B) 4

C) 5

D) 6

2

$$ax = 5$$

In the given equation, a is a constant. For which of the following values of a will the equation have no solution?

A) 0

B) 1

C) 5

D) 10

3

Tom scored 85, 78, and 98 on his first three exams in history class. Solving which inequality gives all the possible scores, G, that Tom could get on his fourth exam that will result in a mean score on all four exams of at least 90?

A) $90 - (85 + 78 + 98) \leq 4G$

B) $4G + 85 + 78 + 98 \geq 360$

C) $\dfrac{(G + 85 + 78 + 98)}{4} \geq 90$

D) $\dfrac{(85 + 78 + 98)}{4} \geq 90 - 4G$

4

If $3(3x + 5) = 2x - 8$, what is the value of x?

A) $-\frac{23}{7}$

B) $-\frac{15}{7}$

C) $-\frac{13}{7}$

D) $\frac{7}{11}$

5

On Monday, Jao walked a total of 11,400 steps. On Tuesday, Jao has a goal to walk at least 1,500 more steps than he did on Monday. What is the least number of steps Jao could walk on Tuesday to meet his goal?

6

$$x - 3y = 7$$
$$3y = 9$$

If (x, y) is the solution to the given system of equations, what is the value of x?

A) -2

B) 10

C) 16

D) 34

7

$$P = 1.20x + 5.00$$

The given equation gives the total monthly price P, in dollars, for using an online gaming service. The total monthly price for the online service consists of a flat monthly fee and a charge for each game played during a month. Of the following, which is the best interpretation of the value of x in this context?

A) The number of games played during a month

B) The charge, in dollars, for playing x games

C) The flat monthly fee, in dollars, for the gaming service

D) The number of months the gaming service was used

$$x + y = 4$$
$$x - y = 2$$

Which of the following is the graph in the *xy*-plane of the given system of equations?

A)

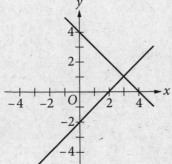

B)

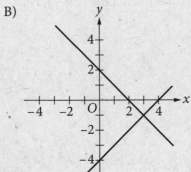

C)

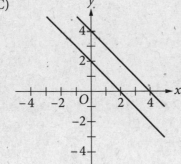

D)

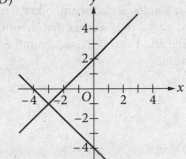

9

Nayya burns 5 kilocalories per minute running on a treadmill and 10 kilocalories per minute pedaling on a stationary bike. Which of the following equations represents the total number of kilocalories, T, Nayya has burned after running on the treadmill for 50 minutes and pedaling on the stationary bike for m minutes?

A) $T = 15m + 50$

B) $T = 50m + 50$

C) $T = 5m + 500$

D) $T = 10m + 250$

10

$$f(x) = \frac{(x+7)}{4}$$

For the function f defined as shown, what is the value of $f(9) - f(1)$?

A) 1

B) 2

C) $\frac{1}{4}$

D) $\frac{9}{4}$

11

In the xy-plane, line l contains the points (2, 6) and (8, 10). Which of the following is an equation of line l?

A) $y = \frac{2}{3}x + \frac{14}{3}$

B) $y = \frac{3}{2}x - 2$

C) $y = 2x + 6$

D) $y = 8x + 10$

12

During a month, Morgan ran r miles at 5 miles per hour and biked b miles at 10 miles per hour. She ran and biked a total of 200 miles that month, and she biked for twice as many hours as she ran. What is the total number of miles that Morgan biked during the month?

A) 80

B) 100

C) 120

D) 160

13

The equation $c = \frac{5}{4}x + 406$ gives the total cost c, in dollars, to produce a quantity of x units. If the quantity of units produced increases by 39 units, what is the corresponding increase in the total cost, in dollars?

14

$$kx - 3y = 4$$
$$4x - 5y = 7$$

In the given system of equations, k is a constant and x and y are variables. For what value of k will the system of equations have no solution?

A) $\frac{12}{5}$

B) $\frac{16}{7}$

C) $-\frac{16}{7}$

D) $-\frac{12}{5}$

15

x	y
-10	66
-5	45
5	3
10	-18

The table shows four values of x and their corresponding values of y. There is a linear relationship between x and y. If an equation representing this relationship is written in the form $Ax + 5y = C$, where A and C are constants, what is the value of C?

16

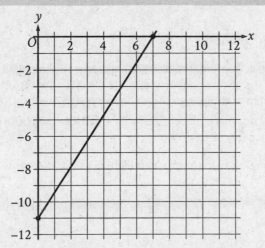

The point $(3, d)$ lies on the line shown. What is the value of d?

Answer Explanations

QUESTION 1

Choice B is correct. It's given that a represents the number of small boxes and b represents the number of large boxes the customer had shipped. If the customer had 3 small boxes shipped, then $a = 3$. Substituting 3 for a in the equation $3a + 4b = 25$ yields $3(3) + 4b = 25$, or $9 + 4b = 25$. Subtracting 9 from both sides of this equation yields $4b = 16$. Dividing both sides of this equation by 4 yields $b = 4$. Therefore, the customer had 4 large boxes shipped.

Choice A is incorrect. If the customer had 3 small boxes and 3 large boxes shipped, then the company would have charged the customer $21, not $25. *Choice C* is incorrect. If the customer had 3 small boxes and 5 large boxes shipped, then the company would have charged the customer $29, not $25. *Choice D* is incorrect. If the customer had 3 small boxes and 6 large boxes shipped, then the company would have charged the customer $33, not $25.

QUESTION 2

Choice A is correct. An equation has no solution when there is no value of x that produces a true statement. To solve the given equation for x, both sides of the equation can be divided by a, yielding $x = \frac{5}{a}$. Since 5 can be divided by any number except 0, it follows that the value of a can't be 0. Therefore, if the value of a is 0, the given equation will have no solution.

Alternate approach: Substituting 0 for a in the given equation yields $0x = 5$, or $0 = 5$, which isn't a true statement. Therefore, when $a = 0$, there is no solution to the given equation.

Choices B, C, and *D* are incorrect. These values of a yield exactly one solution rather than no solution.

QUESTION 3

Choice C is correct. The mean of the four scores (G, 85, 78, and 98) can be expressed as $\frac{G + 85 + 78 + 98}{4}$. Thus, an inequality that represents a mean score on all four exams of at least 90 can be written as $\frac{G + 85 + 78 + 98}{4} \geq 90$.

Choices A, B, and *D* are incorrect and may result from conceptual or calculation errors.

QUESTION 4

Choice A is correct. Applying the distributive property of multiplication on the left-hand side of the given equation yields $3(3x) + 3(5) = 2x - 8$, or $9x + 15 = 2x - 8$. Subtracting $2x$ from both sides of this equation yields $7x + 15 = -8$. Subtracting 15 from both sides of this equation yields $7x = -23$. Dividing both sides of this equation by 7 yields $x = -\frac{23}{7}$.

Choices B, C, and *D* are incorrect and may result from conceptual or calculation errors.

QUESTION 5

The correct answer is 12,900. It's given that Jao walked a total of 11,400 steps on Monday. It's also given that Jao has a goal to walk at least 1,500 more steps on Tuesday than he did on Monday. Let x represent the possible number of steps Jao could walk on Tuesday to meet his goal. This situation can be represented by the inequality $x \geq 11,400 + 1,500$, or $x \geq 12,900$. Thus, the least number of steps Jao could walk on Tuesday to meet his goal is 12,900.

QUESTION 6

Choice C is correct. From the given system of equations, adding the second equation, $3y = 9$, to the first equation, $x - 3y = 7$, yields $x - 3y + 3y = 7 + 9$, or $x = 16$.

Choices A, B, and *D* are incorrect and may result from conceptual or calculation errors.

QUESTION 7

Choice A is correct. It's given that the total monthly price P, in dollars, is the sum of a flat monthly fee and a charge for each game played during a month. A charge for each game played implies the multiplication of the rate, in dollars per game, and the number of games played. Therefore, $1.20 must be the charge per game, and x must be the number of games played during a month.

Choice B is incorrect. The charge, in dollars, for playing x games is $1.20x$. *Choice C* is incorrect. The flat monthly fee, in dollars, for the gaming service is $5.00. *Choice D* is incorrect. No information has been provided about the number of months the gaming service was used.

QUESTION 8

Choice A is correct. Each of the equations in the given system can be rewritten in the form $y = mx + b$, where m represents the slope and $(0, b)$ represents the y-intercept of the line. The first equation in the given system can be rewritten as $y = -x + 4$. It follows that this line has a slope of -1 and a y-intercept at $(0, 4)$. The second equation in the given system can be rewritten as $y = x - 2$. It follows that this line has a slope of 1 and a y-intercept at $(0, -2)$. Of the given choices, only the graph in choice A represents these lines.

Choices B and *D* are incorrect. These systems of equations represent lines with y-intercepts at $(0, 2)$ and $(0, -4)$ rather than $(0, 4)$ and $(0, -2)$. *Choice C* is incorrect. This system of equations represents lines with y-intercepts at $(0, 2)$ and $(0, 4)$ rather than $(0, 4)$ and $(0, -2)$.

QUESTION 9

Choice D is correct. It's given that Nayya burns 5 kilocalories per minute running on a treadmill. It follows that she will burn 5(50), or 250, kilocalories running on the treadmill for 50 minutes. It's also given that Nayya burns 10 kilocalories per minute pedaling on a stationary bike. It follows that she will burn $10m$ kilocalories pedaling on the stationary bike for m minutes. The sum of the kilocalories burned after running on the treadmill for 50 minutes, 250, and the kilocalories burned after pedaling on the stationary bike for m minutes, $10m$, gives the total number of kilocalories, T, Nayya burned. Therefore, $T = 250 + 10m$, or $T = 10m + 250$.

Choice A is incorrect. This equation represents the total number of kilocalories Nayya has burned if she burns 15, not 10, kilocalories per minute pedaling on a stationary bike and ran on the treadmill for 10, not 50, minutes. *Choice B* is incorrect. This equation represents the total number of kilocalories Nayya has burned if she burns 50, not 10, kilocalories per minute pedaling on a stationary bike and ran on the treadmill for 10, not 50, minutes. *Choice C* is incorrect. This equation represents the total number of kilocalories Nayya has burned if she burns 5, not 10, kilocalories per minute pedaling on a stationary bike and ran on the treadmill for 100, not 50, minutes.

QUESTION 10

Choice B is correct. The value of $f(9)$ represents the value of $f(x)$ when $x = 9$. Substituting 9 for x in the given function yields $f(9) = \frac{(9 + 7)}{4}$, which can be rewritten as $f(9) = \frac{16}{4}$, or $f(9) = 4$. Similarly, the value of $f(1)$ represents the value of $f(x)$ when $x = 1$. Substituting 1 for x in the given function yields $f(1) = \frac{(1 + 7)}{4}$, which can be rewritten as $f(1) = \frac{8}{4}$, or $f(1) = 2$. Therefore, $f(9) - f(1) = 4 - 2$, which is equivalent to 2.

Choices A, C, and *D* are incorrect and may result from conceptual or calculation errors.

QUESTION 11

Choice A is correct. The equation of a line in the *xy*-plane can be written as $y = mx + b$, where m represents the slope and b represents the y-coordinate of the y-intercept of the line. Given two points on a line, (x_1, y_1) and (x_2, y_2), the slope of the line can be calculated as $m = \frac{y_2 - y_1}{x_2 - x_1}$. Substituting (2, 6) for (x_1, y_1) and (8, 10) for (x_2, y_2) in the equation $m = \frac{y_2 - y_1}{x_2 - x_1}$ yields $m = \frac{10 - 6}{8 - 2}$, which is equivalent to $m = \frac{4}{6}$, or $m = \frac{2}{3}$. Substituting $\frac{2}{3}$ for m in the equation $y = mx + b$ yields $y = \frac{2}{3}x + b$. Since it's given that line *l* contains the point (2, 6), substituting 2 for x and 6 for y in $y = \frac{2}{3}x + b$ yields $6 = \frac{2}{3}(2) + b$, or $6 = \frac{4}{3} + b$. Subtracting $\frac{4}{3}$ from both sides of this equation yields $b = \frac{14}{3}$. Substituting $\frac{14}{3}$ for b in the equation $y = \frac{2}{3}x + b$ gives $y = \frac{2}{3}x + \frac{14}{3}$.

Choice B is incorrect and may result from reversing x and y when calculating the slope. *Choice C* is incorrect and may result from using the x- and y-coordinates of the first given point as the slope and constant, respectively, in the equation. *Choice D* is incorrect and may result from using the x- and y-coordinates of the second given point as the slope and constant, respectively, in the equation.

QUESTION 12

Choice D is correct. The number of hours Morgan spent running or biking can be calculated by dividing the distance, in miles, she traveled during that activity by her speed, in miles per hour, for that activity. It's given that Morgan ran r miles at 5 miles per hour and biked b miles at 10 miles per hour. It follows that the number of hours she ran can be represented by the expression $\frac{r}{5}$ and the number of hours she biked can be represented by the expression $\frac{b}{10}$. It's given that she biked for twice as many hours as she ran, so this can be represented by the equation $\frac{b}{10} = 2\left(\frac{r}{5}\right)$, which can be rewritten as $5b = 20r$, or $b = 4r$. It's also given that she ran and biked a total of 200 miles. This can be represented by the equation $r + b = 200$. Substituting $4r$ for b in this equation yields $r + 4r = 200$, or $5r = 200$. Dividing both sides of this equation by 5 yields $r = 40$. Determining the number of miles she biked, b, can be found by substituting 40 for r in the equation $r + b = 200$, which yields $40 + b = 200$. Subtracting 40 from both sides of this equation yields $b = 160$. Therefore, Morgan biked a total of 160 miles during the month.

Choices A, B, and C are incorrect because they don't satisfy the condition of Morgan biking for twice as many hours as she ran. If she had biked 80 miles (choice A), then she would have run 120 miles, which means she would have biked for 8 hours and run for 24 hours. If she had biked 100 miles (choice B), then she would have run 100 miles, which means she would have biked for 10 hours and run for 20 hours. If she had biked 120 miles (choice C), then she would have run 80 miles, which means she would have biked for 12 hours and run for 16 hours.

QUESTION 13

The correct answer is 48.75. It's given that the equation $c = \frac{5}{4}x + 406$ gives the total cost c, in dollars, to produce a quantity of x units. Since $c = \frac{5}{4}x + 406$ is a linear equation with a positive rate of change, $\frac{5}{4}$, it follows that the value of c increases by $\frac{5}{4}$ for every increase in x by 1. Therefore, if the value of x increases by 39, the value of c increases by $\frac{5}{4}(39)$, or $\frac{195}{4}$, which is equivalent to 48.75. Thus, if the quantity of units produced increases by 39, the corresponding increase in the total cost, in dollars, is 48.75. Note that 48.75 and 195/4 are examples of ways to enter a correct answer.

QUESTION 14

Choice A is correct. If a system of two linear equations has no solution, then the lines represented by the equations in the coordinate plane are parallel and distinct. The equation $kx - 3y = 4$ can be rewritten as $y = \frac{k}{3}x - \frac{4}{3}$, where $\frac{k}{3}$ is the slope and $\left(0, -\frac{4}{3}\right)$ is the y-intercept of the line. The equation $4x - 5y = 7$ can be rewritten as $y = \frac{4}{5}x - \frac{7}{5}$, where $\frac{4}{5}$ is the slope and $\left(0, -\frac{7}{5}\right)$ is the y-intercept of the line. If the two lines are parallel, then the lines have the same slope and different y-intercepts. Therefore, $\frac{k}{3} = \frac{4}{5}$, or $k = \frac{12}{5}$.

Choices B, C, and D are incorrect. These values of k each yield a system of equations that has exactly one solution rather than no solution.

QUESTION 15

The correct answer is 120. It's given that there is a linear relationship between x and y and that the table shows four values of x and their corresponding values of y. Based on the given table, when $x = -5$, the corresponding value of y is 45 and when $x = 5$, the corresponding value of y is 3. Substituting -5 for x and 45 for y in the equation $Ax + 5y = C$ yields $A(-5) + 5(45) = C$, or $-5A + 225 = C$. Substituting 5 for x and 3 for y in the equation $Ax + 5y = C$ yields $A(5) + 5(3) = C$, or $5A + 15 = C$. Since $-5A + 225 = C$ and $5A + 15 = C$, it follows that $-5A + 225 = 5A + 15$. Subtracting $5A$ and 225 from both sides of this equation yields $-10A = -210$. Dividing both sides of this equation by -10 yields $A = 21$. Substituting 21 for A in the equation $-5A + 225 = C$ yields $-5(21) + 225 = C$, which is equivalent to $-105 + 225 = C$, or $C = 120$. Therefore, if an equation representing this relationship is written in the form $Ax + 5y = C$, where A and C are constants, the value of C is 120.

QUESTION 16

The correct answer is $-\frac{44}{7}$. It's given from the graph that the points (7, 0) and (0, -11) lie on the line shown in the xy-plane. For two points on a line, (x_1, y_1) and (x_2, y_2), the slope, m, of the line can be calculated using the slope formula $m = \frac{y_2 - y_1}{x_2 - x_1}$. Substituting (7, 0) for (x_1, y_1) and (0, -11) for (x_2, y_2) in this formula, the slope of the line can be calculated as $m = \frac{-11 - 0}{0 - 7}$, or $m = \frac{11}{7}$. It's also given that the point (3, d) lies on the line. Substituting (7, 0) for (x_1, y_1), (3, d) for (x_2, y_2), and $\frac{11}{7}$ for m in the slope formula yields $\frac{11}{7} = \frac{d - 0}{3 - 7}$, or $\frac{11}{7} = \frac{d}{-4}$. Multiplying both sides of this equation by -4 yields $(-4)\left(\frac{11}{7}\right) = d$, or $d = -\frac{44}{7}$. Thus, the value of d is $-\frac{44}{7}$. Note that -44/7, -6.285, and -6.286 are examples of ways to enter a correct answer.

CHAPTER 23

Math: Questions— Advanced Math

Advanced Math questions in the Math section address topics that are especially important for students to master before studying higher-level math concepts. Chief among these topics is the understanding of the structure of expressions and the ability to analyze, manipulate, and rewrite these expressions. Questions in this content domain also include ones involving reasoning with more complex equations and interpreting and building functions.

Algebra questions focus on the mastery of linear equations and inequalities, systems of linear equations, and linear functions. By contrast, Advanced Math questions focus on the ability to work with and analyze more complex equations. Advanced Math questions may require you to demonstrate procedural skill in adding, subtracting, and multiplying polynomials and in factoring polynomials. You may also be required to work with expressions involving integer and rational exponents, radicals, or fractions with a variable in the denominator. Questions in this domain may ask you to solve quadratic, radical, rational, polynomial, or absolute value equations. They may also ask you to solve a system consisting of a linear equation and a nonlinear equation. You may also be required to manipulate an equation in several variables to isolate a quantity of interest.

Some questions in Advanced Math may ask you to build a quadratic or an exponential function or an equation that describes a context or to interpret the function, the graph of the function, or the solution to an equation in terms of the context.

Advanced Math questions may assess your ability to recognize structure. Expressions and equations that appear complex may use repeated terms or repeated expressions. By noticing these patterns, the complexity of a problem can be reduced. Structure may be used to factor or otherwise rewrite an expression, to solve a quadratic or other equation, or to draw conclusions about the context represented by an expression, equation, or function. You may be asked to identify or derive the form of an expression, equation, or function that reveals information about the expression, equation, or function or the context it represents.

Advanced Math questions may also assess your understanding of functions and their graphs. A question may require you to demonstrate your understanding of function notation, including interpreting an expression in which the argument of a function is an expression rather than a variable. The questions may assess your understanding of how the algebraic properties of a function relate to the geometric characteristics of its graph.

Advanced Math questions include both multiple-choice questions and student-produced response questions. Although you may always use a calculator in the Math section, you must decide whether using it is an effective strategy for a given question.

Let's consider the content, skills, and knowledge assessed by Advanced Math questions.

Operations with Polynomials and Rewriting Expressions

Questions in the Math section may assess your ability to add, subtract, and multiply polynomials.

Advanced Math Sample Question 1

$$x^3 + 6x^2 + 7x - 6 = (x^2 + bx - 2)(x + 3)$$

In the given equation, b is a constant. If the equation is true for all values of x, what is the value of b?

A) 2

B) 3

C) 7

D) 9

The given equation shows two polynomials that are equivalent. To find the value of b, use the distributive property to rewrite the polynomial on the right-hand side of the given equation and then combine like terms so that the polynomial on the right-hand side is in the same form as the polynomial on the left-hand side.

$$
\begin{aligned}
x^3 + 6x^2 + 7x - 6 &= (x^2 + bx - 2)(x + 3) \\
&= (x^3 + bx^2 - 2x) + (3x^2 + 3bx - 6) \\
&= x^3 + (3 + b)x^2 + (3b - 2)x - 6
\end{aligned}
$$

Since the two polynomials are equal for all values of x, the coefficient of matching powers of x should be the same. Therefore, comparing the coefficients of $x^3 + 6x^2 + 7x - 6$ and $x^3 + (3 + b)x^2 + (3b - 2)x - 6$ reveals that $3 + b = 6$ and $3b - 2 = 7$. Solving either of these equations gives $b = 3$, which is choice B.

STRATEGY

The skills and knowledge tested in Advanced Math questions build on the knowledge and skills tested by Algebra questions. Develop proficiency with the tested Algebra skills and knowledge before tackling Advanced Math questions.

Questions may also ask you to use structure to rewrite expressions. For example, the expression may be in the form of a common pattern, such as a difference of squares, where using the difference-of-squares structure allows for efficient rewriting of the expression as the product of two binomials, as shown in sample 2.

Advanced Math Sample Question 2

Which of the following is equivalent to $16s^4 - 4t^2$?

A) $4(s^2 - t)(4s^2 + t)$

B) $4(4s^2 - t)(s^2 + t)$

C) $4(2s^2 - t)(2s^2 + t)$

D) $(8s^2 - 2t)(8s^2 + 2t)$

A close examination reveals that the given expression follows the difference of two perfect squares pattern, $x^2 - y^2$, which factors as the product $(x - y)(x + y)$. The expression $16s^4 - 4t^2$ is also the difference of two squares: $16s^4 - 4t^2 = (4s^2)^2 - (2t)^2$. Therefore, it can be factored as $(4s^2)^2 - (2t)^2 = (4s^2 - 2t)(4s^2 + 2t)$. This expression can be rewritten as $(4s^2 - 2t)(4s^2 + 2t) = 2(2s^2 - t)(2)(2s^2 + t)$, or $4(2s^2 - t)(2s^2 + t)$, which is choice C.

Alternatively, a 4 could be factored out of the given expression: $4(4s^4 - t^2)$. The expression inside the parentheses is a difference of two squares. Therefore, it can be further factored as $4(2s^2 - t)(2s^2 + t)$.

Advanced Math Sample Question 3

Which expression is equivalent to $xy^2 + 2xy^2 + 3xy$?

A) $2xy^2 + 3xy$

B) $3xy^2 + 3xy$

C) $6xy^4$

D) $6xy^5$

There are three terms in the expression, the first two of which are like terms. The like terms can be added together by adding their coefficients: $xy^2 + 2xy^2 + 3xy = (xy^2 + 2xy^2) + 3xy$, which is equivalent to $3xy^2 + 3xy$. Therefore, choice B is correct.

Quadratic Functions and Equations

Advanced Math questions may require you to build a quadratic function or an equation to represent a context.

Advanced Math Sample Question 4

A car is traveling at x feet per second. The driver sees a red light ahead, and after 1.5 seconds reaction time, the driver applies the brake. After the brake is applied, the car takes $\frac{x}{24}$ seconds to stop, during which time the average speed of the car is $\frac{x}{2}$ feet per second. If the car travels 165 feet from the time the driver saw the red light to the time it comes to a complete stop, which of the following equations can be used to find the value of x?

A) $x^2 + 48x - 3,960 = 0$

B) $x^2 + 48x - 7,920 = 0$

C) $x^2 + 72x - 3,960 = 0$

D) $x^2 + 72x - 7,920 = 0$

STRATEGY

Sample 4 requires careful translation of an in-context problem into an algebraic equation. It pays to be deliberate and methodical when translating such problems in the Math section into equations.

During the 1.5-second reaction time, the car is still traveling at x feet per second, so it travels a total of $1.5x$ feet. The average speed of the car during the $\frac{x}{24}$-second braking interval is $\frac{x}{2}$ feet per second, so over this interval the car travels $\left(\frac{x}{2}\right)\left(\frac{x}{24}\right) = \frac{x^2}{48}$ feet. Since the total distance the car travels from the time the driver saw the red light to the time the car comes to a complete stop is 165 feet, you have the equation $\frac{x^2}{48} + 1.5x = 165$. This quadratic equation can be rewritten in standard form by subtracting 165 from each side and then multiplying each side by 48, giving $x^2 + 72x - 7,920 = 0$, which is choice D.

STRATEGY

Questions in the Advanced Math domain may ask you to solve a quadratic equation. Practice using the various methods (below) until you're comfortable with all of them.

1. Factoring
2. Completing the square
3. Using the quadratic formula
4. Graphing using technology
5. Using structure

Be prepared to identify which strategy may be the most effective for solving a given quadratic equation.

Some questions in the Advanced Math domain may ask you to solve a quadratic equation. You must determine an appropriate procedure: factoring, completing the square, using the quadratic formula, graphing using technology, or using structure. It may be more efficient to solve a quadratic equation if you can make use of one of the following facts:

- The sum of the distinct solutions of $x^2 + bx + c = 0$ is $-b$.

- The product of the distinct solutions of $x^2 + bx + c = 0$ is c.

Each of these facts can be observed from examining the factored form of a quadratic. If r and s are distinct solutions of $x^2 + bx + c = 0$, then $x^2 + bx + c = (x - r)(x - s)$. Thus, $b = -(r + s)$ and $c = (-r)(-s) = rs$. **Note:** To use either of these facts, the coefficient of x^2 must be equal to 1.

Advanced Math Sample Question 5

What are the solutions to the equation $x^2 - 3 = x$?

A) $\dfrac{-1 \pm \sqrt{11}}{2}$

B) $\dfrac{-1 \pm \sqrt{13}}{2}$

C) $\dfrac{1 \pm \sqrt{11}}{2}$

D) $\dfrac{1 \pm \sqrt{13}}{2}$

The equation can be solved by using the quadratic formula or by completing the square. Let's use the quadratic formula. First, subtract x from each side of $x^2 - 3 = x$ to put the equation into standard form: $x^2 - x - 3 = 0$. The quadratic formula states that the solutions, x, of the equation $ax^2 + bx + c = 0$ are $\frac{-b \pm \sqrt{b^2 - 4ac}}{2a}$. For the equation $x^2 - x - 3 = 0$, $a = 1$, $b = -1$, and $c = -3$. Substituting these values into the quadratic formula gives $x = \frac{-(-1) \pm \sqrt{(-1)^2 - 4(1)(-3)}}{2(1)}$. This equation can be rewritten as $x = \frac{1 \pm \sqrt{1-(-12)}}{2}$, or $x = \frac{1 \pm \sqrt{13}}{2}$, which is choice D.

REMINDER

The quadratic formula states that the solutions x of the equation $ax^2 + bx + c = 0$ are $x = \frac{-b \pm \sqrt{b^2 - 4ac}}{2a}$.

Advanced Math Sample Question 6

If $x > 0$ and $2x^2 + 3x - 2 = 0$, what is the value of x?

The left-hand side of the given equation can be factored: $2x^2 + 3x - 2 = (2x - 1)(x + 2)$. Therefore, the given equation can be rewritten as $(2x - 1)(x + 2) = 0$, which implies that either $2x - 1 = 0$, which gives $x = \frac{1}{2}$, or $x + 2 = 0$, which gives $x = -2$. Since $x > 0$, the value of x is $\frac{1}{2}$.

STRATEGY

Pay close attention to all the details in each question. In sample 6, x can equal $\frac{1}{2}$ or -2, but since the question states that $x > 0$, the value of x must be $\frac{1}{2}$.

Advanced Math Sample Question 7

What is the sum of the solutions to $(2x - 1)^2 = (x + 2)^2$?

If a and b are real numbers and $a^2 = b^2$, then either $a = b$ or $a = -b$. It follows then that since $(2x - 1)^2 = (x + 2)^2$, either $2x - 1 = x + 2$ or $2x - 1 = -(x + 2)$. In the first case, subtracting x and adding 1 to both sides of the equation yields $x = 3$. In the second case, applying the distributive property on the right side of the equation gives $2x - 1 = -x - 2$.

Adding x and 1 to both sides of this equation yields $3x = -1$, or $x = -\frac{1}{3}$.

Therefore, the sum of the solutions of $(2x - 1)^2 = (x + 2)^2$ is $3 + \left(-\frac{1}{3}\right) = \frac{8}{3}$.

Exponential Functions, Equations, and Expressions and Radicals

Some Advanced Math questions may ask you to build a function that models a given context. Exponential functions model situations in which a quantity is multiplied by a constant factor for each time period. An exponential function can be increasing with time, in which case it models exponential growth, or it can be decreasing with time, in which case it models exponential decay.

Advanced Math Sample Question 8

A researcher estimates that the population of a city is increasing at an annual rate of 0.6%. If the current population of the city is 80,000, which of the following expressions appropriately models the population of the city t years from now according to the researcher's estimate?

A) $80,000(1 + 0.006)^t$

B) $80,000(1 + 0.006^t)$

C) $80,000 + 1.006^t$

D) $80,000(0.006^t)$

REMINDER

A quantity that grows or decays by a fixed percent at regular intervals is said to exhibit exponential growth or decay, respectively.

Exponential growth is represented by the function $y = a(1 + r)^t$, while exponential decay is represented by the function $y = a(1 - r)^t$, where y is the new population, a is the initial population, r is the rate of growth or decay, and t is the number of time intervals that have elapsed.

According to the researcher's estimate, the population is increasing by 0.6% each year. Since 0.6% is equal to 0.006, after the first year the population is $80,000 + 0.006(80,000) = 80,000(1 + 0.006)$. After the second year, the population is $80,000(1 + 0.006) + 0.006(80,000)(1 + 0.006) = 80,000(1 + 0.006)^2$. Similarly, after t years, the population will be $80,000(1 + 0.006)^t$ according to the researcher's estimate. This is choice A.

A well-known example of exponential decay is the decay of a radioactive isotope. One example involves iodine-131, a radioactive isotope used in some medical treatments. The half-life of iodine-131 is 8.02 days; that is, after 8.02 days, half of the iodine-131 in a sample will have decayed. Suppose a sample with a mass of A milligrams of iodine-131 decays for d days. Every 8.02 days, the quantity of iodine-131 is multiplied by $\frac{1}{2}$, or 2^{-1}. In d days, a total of $\frac{d}{8.02}$ different 8.02-day periods will have passed, and so the original quantity will have been multiplied by 2^{-1} a total of $\frac{d}{8.02}$ times. Therefore, the mass, in milligrams, of iodine-131 remaining in the sample will be $A(2^{-1})^{\frac{d}{8.02}} = A\left(2^{-\frac{d}{8.02}}\right)$.

In the preceding discussion, we used the identity $\frac{1}{2} = 2^{-1}$. Advanced Math questions may require you to apply this and other laws of exponents as well as the relationship between powers and radicals.

Some Advanced Math questions may ask you to use properties of exponents to rewrite expressions.

Advanced Math Sample Question 9

Which of the following is equivalent to $\left(\frac{1}{\sqrt{x}}\right)^n$, where $x > 0$?

A) $x^{\frac{n}{2}}$

B) $x^{-\frac{n}{2}}$

C) $x^{n+\frac{1}{2}}$

D) $x^{n-\frac{1}{2}}$

The expression $\sqrt{x}$ is equal to $x^{\frac{1}{2}}$. Thus, $\frac{1}{\sqrt{x}} = x^{-\frac{1}{2}}$, and $\left(\frac{1}{\sqrt{x}}\right)^n = \left(x^{-\frac{1}{2}}\right)^n = x^{-\frac{n}{2}}$. Choice B is the correct answer.

An Advanced Math question may also ask you to solve a radical equation. In solving radical equations, you may square both sides of an equation. Since squaring both sides of an equation may result in an extraneous solution, you may end up with a root to the simplified equation that isn't a root to the original equation. Thus, when solving a radical equation, you must check any solution you get in the original equation.

Advanced Math Sample Question 10

$$x - 12 = \sqrt{x + 44}$$

What are all possible solutions to the given equation?

A) 5

B) 20

C) −5 and 20

D) 5 and 20

STRATEGY

Practice your exponent rules. Know, for instance, that $\sqrt{x} = x^{\frac{1}{2}}$ and that $\frac{1}{\sqrt{x}} = x^{-\frac{1}{2}}$.

Squaring each side of $x - 12 = \sqrt{x + 44}$ gives

$$(x - 12)^2 = (\sqrt{x + 44})^2$$

$$(x - 12)^2 = x + 44$$

$$x^2 - 24x + 144 = x + 44$$

$$x^2 - 25x + 100 = 0$$

$$(x - 5)(x - 20) = 0$$

The solutions to this quadratic equation are $x = 5$ and $x = 20$. However, since the first step was to square each side of the given equation, which may have introduced an extraneous solution, you need to check $x = 5$ and $x = 20$ in the original equation. Substituting 5 for x gives

$$5 - 12 = \sqrt{5 + 44}$$

$$-7 = \sqrt{49}$$

This isn't a true statement (since $\sqrt{49}$ represents the principal square root, or only the positive square root, 7), so $x = 5$ is *not* a solution to $x - 12 = \sqrt{x + 44}$. Substituting 20 for x gives

$$20 - 12 = \sqrt{20 + 44}$$

$$8 = \sqrt{64}$$

This is a true statement, so $x = 20$ is a solution to $x - 12 = \sqrt{x + 44}$. Therefore, the only solution to the given equation is 20, which is choice B.

STRATEGY

A good strategy to use when solving radical equations is to square both sides of the equation. When doing so, however, be sure to check the solutions in the original equation, as you may end up with a root that isn't a solution to the original equation.

Solving Rational Equations

Questions in the Advanced Math domain may assess your ability to work with rational expressions, including fractions with a variable in the denominator. This may include finding the solution to a rational equation.

Advanced Math Sample Question 11

$$\frac{3}{t+1} = \frac{2}{t+3} + \frac{1}{4}$$

If t is a solution to the given equation and $t > 0$, what is the value of t?

STRATEGY

When solving for a variable in an equation involving fractions, a good first step is to clear the variable out of the denominators of the fractions. Remember that you can only multiply both sides of an equation by an expression when you know the expression can't be equal to 0.

Since $t > 0$, both sides of the given equation can be multiplied by the lowest common denominator, which is $4(t + 1)(t + 3)$. The resulting equivalent equation won't have any fractions, and the variable will no longer be in the denominator. This gives $12(t + 3) = 8(t + 1) + (t + 1)(t + 3)$. This equation can be rewritten as $12t + 36 = (8t + 8) + (t^2 + 4t + 3)$, or $12t + 36 = t^2 + 12t + 11$. Subtracting $12t$ and 36 from both sides of this equation yields $0 = t^2 - 25$. This equation can be rewritten by factoring the right-hand side as $0 = (t - 5)(t + 5)$. By the zero product property, $t - 5 = 0$ or $t + 5 = 0$. Therefore, the solutions to the equation are $t = 5$ or $t = -5$. Since $t > 0$, the value of t is 5.

Systems of Equations

Questions in the Advanced Math domain may ask you to solve a system of equations in two variables in which one equation is linear and the other equation is quadratic or another nonlinear equation.

Advanced Math Sample Question 12

$$3x + y = -3$$
$$(x + 1)^2 - 4(x + 1) - 6 = y$$

If (x, y) is a solution to the given system of equations and $y > 0$, what is the value of y?

STRATEGY

The first step used to solve this example was substitution, an approach you may use on questions about finding the solution to a system of linear equations as well. The second step used to solve this example was taken after noticing that $(x + 1)$ can be treated as a variable.

One method for solving systems of equations is substitution. If the first equation is solved for y, it can be substituted in the second equation. Subtracting $3x$ from each side of the first equation gives you $y = -3 - 3x$, which can be rewritten as $y = -3(x + 1)$. Substituting $-3(x + 1)$ for y in the second equation gives you $(x + 1)^2 - 4(x + 1) - 6 = -3(x + 1)$. Since the factor $(x + 1)$ appears as a squared term and a linear term, the equation can be thought of as a quadratic equation in the variable $(x + 1)$, so collecting the terms and setting the expression equal to 0 gives you $(x + 1)^2 - (x + 1) - 6 = 0$. Rewriting this equation by factoring gives you $((x + 1) - 3)((x + 1) + 2) = 0$, or $(x - 2)(x + 3) = 0$. Thus, either $x = 2$, which gives $y = -3 - 3(2) = -9$; or $x = -3$, which gives $y = -3 - 3(-3) = 6$. Therefore, the solutions to the system are $(2, -9)$ and $(-3, 6)$. Since the question states that $y > 0$, the value of y is 6.

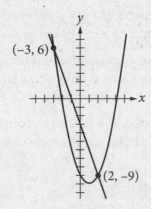

The solutions of the system are given by the intersection points of the two graphs. Questions in the digital SAT Math section may assess this or other relationships between algebraic and graphical representations of functions.

Relationships between Algebraic and Graphical Representations of Functions

A function f has a graph in the xy-plane, which is the graph of the equation $y = f(x)$, or, equivalently, consists of all ordered pairs $(x, f(x))$. Some Advanced Math questions may assess your ability to relate properties of the function f to properties of its graph and vice versa. You may be required to apply some of the following relationships:

- **Intercepts.** The x-intercepts of the graph of f correspond to values of x such that $f(x) = 0$, which corresponds to values of x where the graph intersects with the x-axis, also known as the function's zeros; if the function f has no zeros, its graph has no x-intercepts and vice versa. The y-intercept of the graph of f corresponds to the value of $f(0)$, or the value of y where the graph intersects with the y-axis. If $x = 0$ is not in the domain of f, the graph of f has no y-intercept and vice versa.

- **Domain and range.** The domain of f is the set of all x for which $f(x)$ is defined. The range of f is the set of all y such that $y = f(x)$ for some value of x in the domain. The domain and range can be found from the graph of f as the set of all x-coordinates and y-coordinates, respectively, of points on the graph.

- **Maximum and minimum values.** The maximum and minimum values of f can be found by locating the highest and the lowest points on the graph, respectively. For example, suppose P is the highest point on the graph of f. Then the y-coordinate of P is the maximum value of f, and the x-coordinate of P is where f takes on its maximum value.

- **Increasing and decreasing.** The graph of f shows the intervals over which the function f is increasing and decreasing.

REMINDER

The domain of a function is the set of all values for which the function is defined. The range of a function is the set of all values that correspond to the values in the domain, given the relationship defined by the function, or the set of all outputs that are associated with all the possible inputs.

- **End behavior.** The graph of f can indicate if $f(x)$ increases or decreases without limit as x increases or decreases without limit.

- **Transformations.** For a graph of a function f, a change of the form $f(x) + a$ will result in a vertical shift of a units, and a change of the form $f(x - a)$ will result in a horizontal shift of a units.

Note: The Math section uses the following conventions about graphs in the xy-plane unless a particular question clearly states or shows a different convention:

- The axes are perpendicular.

- Scales on the axes are linear scales.

- The size of the units on the two axes can't be assumed to be equal unless the question states they're equal or you're given enough information to conclude they're equal.

- The values on the horizontal axis increase as you move to the right.

- The values on the vertical axis increase as you move up.

Advanced Math Sample Question 13

The graph of which of the following functions in the xy-plane has x-intercepts at -4 and 5?

A) $f(x) = (x + 4)(x - 5)$

B) $g(x) = (x - 4)(x + 5)$

C) $h(x) = (x - 4)^2 + 5$

D) $k(x) = (x + 5)^2 - 4$

The x-intercepts of the graph of a function correspond to the zeros of the function. All the functions in the choices are defined by quadratic equations, so the answer must be a quadratic function. If a quadratic function has x-intercepts at -4 and 5, then the values of the function at -4 and 5 are each 0; that is, the zeros of the function occur at $x = -4$ and at $x = 5$. Since the function is defined by a quadratic equation and has zeros at $x = -4$ and $x = 5$, it must have $(x + 4)$ and $(x - 5)$ as factors. Therefore, choice A, $f(x) = (x + 4)(x - 5)$, is correct.

The graph in the xy-plane of each of the functions in the previous example is a parabola. Using the defining equations, you can tell that the graph of g has x-intercepts at 4 and -5; the graph of h has its vertex at $(4, 5)$; and the graph of k has its vertex at $(-5, -4)$.

STRATEGY

Don't assume the size of the units on the two axes are equal unless the question states they're equal or you can conclude they're equal from the information given.

STRATEGY

Another way to think of sample 13 is to ask yourself, "Which answer choice represents a function that has values of 0 when $x = -4$ and $x = 5$?"

Advanced Math Sample Question 14

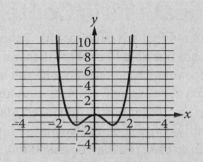

The function $f(x) = x^4 - 2.4x^2$ is graphed in the xy-plane where $y = f(x)$, as shown. If k is a constant such that the equation $f(x) = k$ has 4 solutions, which of the following could be the value of k?

A) 1

B) 0

C) −1

D) −2

Choice C is correct. Since $f(x) = x^4 - 2.4x^2$, the equation $f(x) = k$, or $x^4 - 2.4x^2 = k$, will have four solutions if and only if the graph of the horizontal line with equation $y = k$ intersects the graph of f at four points. The graph shows that of the given choices, only for choice C, −1, does the graph of $y = -1$ intersect the graph of f at four points.

Function Notation

The Math section may assess your understanding of function notation. In such cases, you must be able to evaluate a function given the rule that defines it, and if the function describes a context, you may need to interpret the value of the function in the context. A question may ask you to interpret a function when an expression, such as $2x$ or $x + 1$, is used as the argument instead of the variable x.

Advanced Math Sample Question 15

If $g(x) = 2x + 1$ and $f(x) = g(x) + 4$, what is $f(2)$?

You're given $f(x) = g(x) + 4$; therefore, $f(2) = g(2) + 4$. To determine the value of $g(2)$, use the function $g(x) = 2x + 1$. Thus, $g(2) = 2(2) + 1$, and therefore, $g(2) = 5$. Substituting $g(2)$ gives $f(2) = 5 + 4$, or $f(2) = 9$.

Alternatively, since $f(x) = g(x) + 4$ and $g(x) = 2x + 1$, it follows that $f(x)$ must equal $2x + 1 + 4$, or $2x + 5$. Therefore, $f(2) = 2(2) + 5 = 9$.

STRATEGY

What may seem at first to be a complex question could boil down to straightforward substitution.

Interpreting and Analyzing More Complex Equations in Context

Equations and functions that describe real-life contexts can be complex. Often, it's not possible to analyze them as completely as you can analyze a linear equation or function. You still can acquire key information about the context by interpreting and analyzing the equation or function that describes it. Advanced Math questions may ask you to identify connections between the function, its graph, and the context it describes. You may be asked to use an equation describing a context to determine how a change in one quantity affects another quantity. You may also be asked to manipulate an equation to isolate a quantity of interest on one side of the equation. You may be asked to produce or identify a form of an equation that reveals new information about the context it represents or about the graphical representation of the equation.

Advanced Math Sample Question 16

For a certain reservoir, the function f gives the water level $f(n)$, to the nearest whole percent of capacity, on the nth day of 2016. Which of the following is the best interpretation of $f(37) = 70$?

A) The water level of the reservoir was at 37% capacity for 70 days in 2016.

B) The water level of the reservoir was at 70% capacity for 37 days in 2016.

C) On the 37th day of 2016, the water level of the reservoir was at 70% capacity.

D) On the 70th day of 2016, the water level of the reservoir was at 37% capacity.

The function f gives the water level, to the nearest whole percent of capacity, on the nth day of 2016. It follows that $f(37) = 70$ means that on the 37th day of 2016, the water level of the reservoir was at 70% capacity. This statement is choice C.

Advanced Math Sample Question 17

If an object of mass m is moving at speed v, the object's kinetic energy (KE) is given by the equation $\text{KE} = \frac{1}{2}mv^2$. If the mass of the object is halved and its speed is doubled, how does the kinetic energy change?

A) The kinetic energy is halved.

B) The kinetic energy is unchanged.

C) The kinetic energy is doubled.

D) The kinetic energy is quadrupled (multiplied by a factor of 4).

STRATEGY

Another way to check your answer in sample 17 is to substitute simple numerical values for the variables m, v, and KE when those values are altered as indicated by the question. If the value 1 is substituted for both m and v, then KE is $\frac{1}{2}$. However, substituting $\frac{1}{2}$ for m and 2 for v yields a value for KE of 1. Since 1 is twice the value of $\frac{1}{2}$, you know that KE is doubled.

Choice C is correct. If the mass of the object is halved, the new mass is $\frac{m}{2}$. If the speed of the object is doubled, its new speed is $2v$. Therefore, the new kinetic energy is $\frac{1}{2}\left(\frac{m}{2}\right)(2v^2) = \frac{1}{2}\left(\frac{m}{2}\right)(4v^2) = mv^2$. This is double the original kinetic energy of the object, which was $\frac{1}{2}mv^2$.

Advanced Math Sample Question 18

A gas in a container will escape through holes of microscopic size, as long as the holes are larger than the gas molecules. This process is called effusion. If a gas of molar mass M_1 effuses at a rate of r_1 and a gas of molar mass M_2 effuses at a rate of r_2, then the following relationship holds.

$$\frac{r_1}{r_2} = \sqrt{\frac{M_2}{M_1}}$$

This is known as Graham's law. Which of the following correctly expresses M_2 in terms of M_1, r_1, and r_2?

A) $M_2 = M_1 \left(\dfrac{r_1^2}{r_2^2} \right)$

B) $M_2 = M_1 \left(\dfrac{r_2^2}{r_1^2} \right)$

C) $M_2 = \sqrt{M_1} \left(\dfrac{r_1}{r_2} \right)$

D) $M_2 = \sqrt{M_1} \left(\dfrac{r_2}{r_1} \right)$

Squaring each side of $\frac{r_1}{r_2} = \sqrt{\frac{M_2}{M_1}}$ gives $\left(\frac{r_1}{r_2} \right)^2 = \left(\sqrt{\frac{M_2}{M_1}} \right)^2$, which can be rewritten as $\frac{M_2}{M_1} = \frac{r_1^2}{r_2^2}$. Multiplying each side of $\frac{M_2}{M_1} = \frac{r_1^2}{r_2^2}$ by M_1 gives $M_2 = M_1 \left(\frac{r_1^2}{r_2^2} \right)$, which is choice A.

STRATEGY

Always start by identifying exactly what the question asks. In sample 18, you're being asked to isolate the variable M_2. Squaring both sides of the equation is a great first step, as it allows you to eliminate the radical sign.

Advanced Math Sample Question 19

A store manager estimates that if a video game is sold at a price of p dollars, the store will have weekly revenue, in dollars, of $r(p) = -4p^2 + 200p$ from the sale of the video game. Which of the following equivalent forms of $r(p)$ shows, as constants or coefficients, the maximum possible weekly revenue and the price that results in the maximum revenue?

A) $r(p) = 200p - 4p^2$
B) $r(p) = -2(2p^2 - 100p)$
C) $r(p) = -4(p^2 - 50p)$
D) $r(p) = -4(p - 25)^2 + 2{,}500$

Choice D is correct. The graph of r in the coordinate plane is a parabola that opens downward. The maximum value of revenue corresponds to the vertex of the parabola. Since the square of any real number is always nonnegative, the form $r(p) = -4(p - 25)^2 + 2{,}500$ shows that the vertex of the parabola is $(25, 2{,}500)$; that is, the maximum must occur where $-4(p - 25)^2$ is 0, which is $p = 25$, and this maximum is $r(25) = 2{,}500$. Thus, the maximum possible weekly revenue and the price that results in the maximum revenue occur as constants in the form $r(p) = -4(p - 25)^2 + 2{,}500$.

STRATEGY

The fact that the coefficient of the squared term is negative for this function indicates that the graph of r in the coordinate plane is a parabola that opens downward. Thus, the maximum value of revenue corresponds to the vertex of the parabola.

Summary: Advanced Math

Main purpose: To assess your understanding of nonlinear relationships

Proportion of the test section: About 35 percent (approximately thirteen to fifteen questions)

Question types

- Equivalent expressions
- Nonlinear equations in one variable and systems of equations in two variables
- Nonlinear functions

CHAPTER 24

Math: Questions—
Advanced Math Drills

1

Which of the following expressions is equivalent to $2(ab - 3) + 2$?

A) $2ab - 1$

B) $2ab - 4$

C) $2ab - 5$

D) $2ab - 8$

2

$$f(x) = (x + 0.25x)(50 - x)$$

The function f is defined as shown. What is the value of $f(20)$?

A) 250

B) 500

C) 750

D) 2,000

3

$$x^2 + 6x + 9 = 36$$

What is the positive solution to the given equation?

4

The function f is defined by $f(x) = \frac{22}{x+1}$. What is the value of $f(22)$?

5

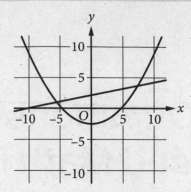

A system of equations consists of a quadratic equation and a linear equation. The equations in this system are graphed in the *xy*-plane shown. How many solutions does this system have?

A) 0

B) 1

C) 2

D) 3

6

$$S = 4\pi r^2$$

The formula shown gives the surface area, *S*, of a sphere in terms of the length of its radius, *r*. Which of the following gives the radius of the sphere in terms of its surface area?

A) $r = \sqrt{\dfrac{S}{4\pi}}$

B) $r = \sqrt{\dfrac{4\pi}{S}}$

C) $r = \dfrac{\sqrt{S}}{4\pi}$

D) $r = \dfrac{\sqrt{4\pi}}{S}$

7

$$\frac{4x}{2(x^2 - 1)} - \frac{3x}{3(x^2 - 1)}$$

Which of the following is equivalent to the given expression for $x \neq -1$ and $x \neq 1$?

A) $\dfrac{1}{6(x - 1)}$

B) $\dfrac{x}{6(x^2 - 1)}$

C) $\dfrac{1}{x - 1}$

D) $\dfrac{x}{x^2 - 1}$

8

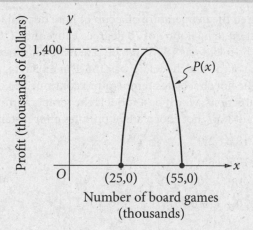

A company produces board games and sells them online and in stores. The quadratic function P models the company's monthly profits $P(x)$, in thousands of dollars, when x board games, in thousands, are produced and sold. The graph of $y = P(x)$, where $25 \le x \le 55$, is shown in the xy-plane. How many board games must the company produce and sell in order to earn the maximum profit estimated by the model?

A) 20,000

B) 40,000

C) 60,000

D) 1,400,000

9

$$y - x = 30$$
$$y = x^2 - 28x$$

The graphs of the equations in the given system intersect at the point (x, y) in the xy-plane. What is a possible value of y?

10

In the equation $9x^2 + 108x + \frac{c}{4} = 0$, c is a constant. If the equation has exactly one real solution, what is the value of c?

A) 0

B) 324

C) 1,296

D) 11,664

11

Kao measured the temperature of a cup of hot chocolate placed in a room with a constant temperature of 70 degrees Fahrenheit (°F). The temperature of the hot chocolate was 185°F at 6:00 p.m. when it started cooling. The temperature of the hot chocolate was 156°F at 6:05 p.m. and 135°F at 6:10 p.m. The hot chocolate's temperature continued to decrease. Of the following functions, which best models the temperature $T(m)$, in degrees Fahrenheit, of Kao's hot chocolate m minutes after it started cooling?

A) $T(m) = 185(1.25)^m$

B) $T(m) = 185(0.85)^m$

C) $T(m) = (185 - 70)(0.75)^{\frac{m}{5}}$

D) $T(m) = 70 + 115(0.75)^{\frac{m}{5}}$

12

$$\sqrt{5(x - k)} = x - k$$

In the given equation, k is a positive constant. The greatest solution to the equation is 12. What is the value of k?

13

$$g(x) = (5 - 2x)(14 + 2x)$$

The function g is defined by the given equation. For what value of x does $g(x)$ reach its maximum?

14

A rectangular volleyball court has an area of 162 square meters. If the length of the court is twice the width, what is the width of the court, in meters?

A) 9

B) 18

C) 27

D) 54

15

$$x^2 = 6x + y$$

$$y = -6x + 36$$

A solution to the given system of equations is (x, y). Which of the following is a possible value of xy?

A) 0

B) 6

C) 12

D) 36

16

The function f is defined by $f(x) = ax^2 + bx + c$, where a, b, and c are constants and $1 < a < 4$. The graph of $y = f(x)$ in the xy-plane passes through points $(11, 0)$ and $(-2, 0)$. If a is an integer, what could be the value of $a + b$?

Answer Explanations

QUESTION 1

Choice B is correct. Applying the distributive property to the given expression yields $2(ab) + 2(-3) + 2$, or $2ab - 6 + 2$. Adding the like terms -6 and 2 results in the expression $2ab - 4$.

Choice A is incorrect. This expression is equivalent to $2(ab - 3) + 5$. *Choice C* is incorrect. This expression is equivalent to $2(ab - 3) + 1$. *Choice D* is incorrect. This expression is equivalent to $2(ab - 3) - 2$.

QUESTION 2

Choice C is correct. Adding the like terms x and $0.25x$ yields the equation $f(x) = (1.25x)(50 - x)$. Substituting 20 for x yields $f(x) = (1.25(20))(50 - 20)$ or $f(20) = (25)(30)$, which is equivalent to $f(20) = 750$.

Choices A, B, and *D* are incorrect and may result from conceptual or calculation errors.

QUESTION 3

The correct answer is 3. Subtracting 36 from both sides of the given equation yields $x^2 + 6x - 27 = 0$. Two numbers whose product is -27 and whose sum is 6 are 9 and -3. Therefore, by factoring, the equation $x^2 + 6x - 27 = 0$ can be rewritten as $(x + 9)(x - 3) = 0$. By the zero product property, it follows that $x + 9 = 0$ or $x - 3 = 0$. Subtracting 9 from both sides of the equation $x + 9 = 0$ yields $x = -9$. Adding 3 to both sides of the equation $x - 3 = 0$ yields $x = 3$. Therefore, the two solutions to the given equation are -9 and 3. Thus, the positive solution to the given equation is 3.

Alternate approach: The left-hand side of the given equation is a perfect square trinomial. It follows that the given equation can be rewritten as $(x + 3)^2 = 36$. Taking the square root of both sides of this equation yields two equations: $x + 3 = 6$ and $x + 3 = -6$. Subtracting 3 from both sides of the equation $x + 3 = 6$ yields $x = 3$. Subtracting 3 from both sides of the equation $x + 3 = -6$ yields $x = -9$. Therefore, the two solutions to the given equation are 3 and -9. Thus, the positive solution to the given equation is 3.

QUESTION 4

The correct answer is $\frac{22}{23}$. For the given function f, the value of $f(22)$ is the value of $f(x)$ when $x = 22$. Substituting 22 for x in the equation $f(x) = \frac{22}{x+1}$ yields $f(22) = \frac{22}{(22)+1}$, or $f(22) = \frac{22}{23}$. Therefore, the value of $f(22)$ is $\frac{22}{23}$. Note that 22/23, .9565, 0.956, and 0.957 are examples of ways to enter a correct answer.

QUESTION 5

Choice C is correct. The solutions to a system of two equations correspond to points where the graphs of the equations intersect. The given graphs intersect at 2 points; therefore, the system has 2 solutions.

Choices A and *B* are incorrect because the given graphs intersect at more than one point. *Choice D* is incorrect. It's not possible for the graph of a quadratic equation and the graph of a linear equation to intersect at more than two points.

QUESTION 6

Choice A is correct. Solving the given formula for r yields the radius of the sphere in terms of its surface area. Dividing both sides of the given equation by 4π yields $\frac{S}{4\pi} = r^2$. Taking the square root of both sides of this equation yields $\sqrt{\frac{S}{4\pi}} = r$, which can be rewritten as $r = \sqrt{\frac{S}{4\pi}}$.

Choices B, C, and *D* are incorrect and may result from conceptual or calculation errors.

QUESTION 7

Choice D is correct. Multiplying the first fraction in the given expression by $\frac{3}{3}$ and multiplying the second fraction in the given expression by $\frac{2}{2}$ results in both fractions having a common denominator: $\frac{4x}{2(x^2-1)} - \frac{3x}{3(x^2-1)} = \frac{(3)(4x)}{(3)(2)(x^2-1)} - \frac{2(3x)}{(2)(3)(x^2-1)}$. Rewriting the right-hand side of this equation yields $\frac{12x}{6(x^2-1)} - \frac{6x}{6(x^2-1)}$, which is equivalent to $\frac{12x-6x}{6(x^2-1)}$, or $\frac{6x}{6(x^2-1)}$. Rewriting this fraction yields $\frac{x}{x^2-1}$.

Alternate approach: The given expression can be rewritten as $\frac{2x}{x^2-1} - \frac{x}{x^2-1}$. Since the fractions in this expression have a common denominator of x^2-1, it follows that this expression is equivalent to $\frac{2x-x}{x^2-1}$, or $\frac{x}{x^2-1}$.

Choices A, B, and *C* are incorrect and may result from conceptual or calculation errors.

QUESTION 8

Choice B is correct. For each point (x, y) on the graph shown, the x-coordinate gives the number of board games, in thousands, that the company produces and sells, and the y-coordinate gives the profit, in thousands of dollars, from the sale of these board games. The maximum profit is represented by the point on the graph with the greatest y-coordinate. Because P is a quadratic function, the graph of $y = P(x)$ is a parabola and the point with the greatest y-coordinate is the vertex. Because of the symmetry of the parabola, the x-coordinate of its vertex is the mean of the x-coordinates of any two symmetrical points on the graph. For example, the x-intercepts (25, 0) and (55, 0) are symmetrical points on the graph. Therefore, the x-coordinate of the vertex is $\frac{25+55}{2}$, or 40. It follows that the vertex of the graph is (40, 1,400). This means that the maximum profit of $1,400,000 is reached when the company produces and sells 40,000 board games.

Choices A and *C* are incorrect and may result from conceptual or calculation errors. *Choice D* is incorrect and may result from finding the maximum profit, in dollars, rather than the number of board games that need to be produced and sold to reach the maximum profit.

QUESTION 9

The correct answer is either 29 or 60. It's given that the graphs of the equations in the given system intersect at the point (x, y) in the xy-plane. Therefore, this intersection point represents a solution to the given system. The first equation, $y - x = 30$, can be rewritten as $y = x + 30$. Substituting $x + 30$ for y in the second equation, $y = x^2 - 28x$, yields $x + 30 = x^2 - 28x$. Subtracting x and 30 from both sides of this equation yields $0 = x^2 - 28x - x - 30$, or $0 = x^2 - 29x - 30$, which is equivalent to $0 = (x + 1)(x - 30)$. It follows that $x + 1 = 0$ or $x - 30 = 0$. Therefore, $x = -1$ or $x = 30$. Substituting -1 for x in the equation $y - x = 30$ yields

$y - (-1) = 30$, or $y + 1 = 30$, which is equivalent to $y = 29$. Therefore, the graphs of the equations in the given system intersect at the point $(-1, 29)$. Substituting 30 for x in the equation $y - x = 30$ yields $y - 30 = 30$, which is equivalent to $y = 60$. Therefore, the graphs of the equations in the given system intersect at the point $(30, 60)$. Thus, either 29 or 60 is a possible value of y. Note that 29 and 60 are examples of ways to enter a correct answer.

QUESTION 10

Choice C is correct. A quadratic equation of the form $Ax^2 + Bx + C = 0$, where A, B, and C are constants, has exactly one solution if and only if its discriminant, $B^2 - 4AC$, is equal to zero. The given equation is in this form, where $A = 9$, $B = 108$, and $C = \frac{c}{4}$. Substituting 9 for A, 108 for B, and $\frac{c}{4}$ for C into $B^2 - 4AC$ yields $(108)^2 - 4(9)\left(\frac{c}{4}\right)$, or $11{,}664 - 9c$. Therefore, if the given equation has exactly one solution, then $11{,}664 - 9c = 0$. Adding $9c$ to both sides of this equation yields $11{,}664 = 9c$. Dividing both sides of this equation by 9 yields $1{,}296 = c$. Therefore, if the equation has exactly one real solution, the value of c is 1,296.

Choice A is incorrect. This is the value of $9x^2 + 108x + \frac{c}{4}$, not c. *Choice B* is incorrect. This is the value of $\frac{c}{4}$, not c. *Choice D* is incorrect. This is the value of $(108)^2$, not c.

QUESTION 11

Choice D is correct. The temperature of the cup of hot chocolate, $T(m)$, will decrease as the number of minutes, m, after it starts cooling increases, since the temperature of the room is lower than the starting temperature of the cup of hot chocolate. Each of the answer choices involves the variable m in an exponent. Choices B, C, and D each have a function with the base of the exponent less than 1, so each of them is a decreasing function, where the value of $T(m)$ will decrease over time. It's given that the temperature of the hot chocolate was 185°F at 6:00 p.m. when it started cooling. It follows that $T(0) = 185$. It's also given that at 6:05 p.m., or 5 minutes after it started cooling, the temperature of the hot chocolate was 156°F and that at 6:10 p.m., or 10 minutes after it started cooling, the temperature was 135°F. Therefore, $T(5) = 156$ and $T(10) = 135$. For the function in choice D, substituting 0, 5, and 10 for m in the function yields $T(0) = 70 + 115(0.75)^{\frac{0}{5}}$, or 185; $T(5) = 70 + 115(0.75)^{\frac{5}{5}}$, which is approximately 156; and $T(10) = 70 + 115(0.75)^{\frac{10}{5}}$, which is approximately 135. Therefore, of the given choices, choice D best models the temperature of Kao's hot chocolate m minutes after it started cooling.

Choice A is incorrect because it's a function with the base of the exponent equal to 1.25, which results in the value of $T(m)$ increasing over time, rather than decreasing. *Choice B* is incorrect because substituting 0, 5, and 10 for m in this function yields approximately 185, 82, and 36, respectively, rather than 185, 156, and 135. *Choice C* is incorrect because substituting 0, 5, and 10 for m in this function yields approximately 115, 86, and 65, respectively, rather than 185, 156, and 135.

QUESTION 12

The correct answer is 7. Squaring both sides of the given equation yields $5(x - k) = (x - k)^2$, or $5(x - k) = (x - k)(x - k)$. Subtracting $5(x - k)$ from both sides of this equation yields $0 = (x - k)(x - k) - 5(x - k)$. Factoring out the common factor of $x - k$ from the terms on the right-hand side of this equation yields $0 = (x - k)(x - k - 5)$, or $0 = (x - k)(x - (k + 5))$. By the zero product property, it follows that $x - k = 0$ or $x - (k + 5) = 0$. Adding k to both sides of the equation $x - k = 0$ yields $x = k$. Adding $(k + 5)$ to both sides of the equation $x - (k + 5) = 0$ yields $x = k + 5$. Thus, the two solutions to the given equation are k and $k + 5$. It follows that the greatest solution to the given equation is $k + 5$. It's given that the greatest solution to the given equation is 12. Therefore, $k + 5 = 12$. Subtracting 5 from both sides of this equation yields $k = 7$. Thus, the value of k is 7.

QUESTION 13

The correct answer is $-\frac{9}{4}$. It's given that $g(x) = (5 - 2x)(14 + 2x)$, which can be rewritten as $g(x) = -4x^2 - 18x + 70$. Since the coefficient of the x^2-term is negative, the graph of $y = g(x)$ in the xy-plane opens downward and reaches a maximum value at its vertex. The x-coordinate of the vertex is the value of x such that $g(x)$ reaches its maximum. For the graph of an equation in the form $g(x) = ax^2 + bx + c$, where a, b, and c are constants, the x-coordinate of the vertex is $-\frac{b}{2a}$. For the equation $g(x) = -4x^2 - 18x + 70$, $a = -4$, $b = -18$, and $c = 70$. It follows that the x-coordinate of the vertex is $-\frac{-18}{2(-4)}$, or $-\frac{9}{4}$. Therefore, $g(x)$ reaches its maximum when the value of x is $-\frac{9}{4}$. Note that $-9/4$ and -2.25 are examples of ways to enter a correct answer.

QUESTION 14

Choice A is correct. It's given that the volleyball court is rectangular and has an area of 162 square meters. The formula for the area of a rectangle is $A = l \cdot w$, where A is the area, l is the length, and w is the width of the rectangle. It's also given that the length of the volleyball court is twice the width, thus $l = 2w$. Substituting 162 for A in the formula for the area of a rectangle and using the relationship between length and width for this rectangle yields $162 = (2w)(w)$. This equation can be rewritten as $162 = 2w^2$. Dividing both sides of this equation by 2 yields $81 = w^2$. Taking the square root of both sides of the equation yields $\pm 9 = w$. Since the width of the rectangle is a positive number, the width of the volleyball court is 9 meters.

Choice B is incorrect. This is the length, not the width, of the court. *Choice C* is incorrect and may result from using 162 as the perimeter, not the area, of the court. *Choice D* is incorrect and may result from solving for w in the equation $162 = 2w + w$ instead of $162 = (2w)(w)$.

QUESTION 15

Choice A is correct. Solutions to the given systems of equations are ordered pairs (x, y) that satisfy both equations in the system. Adding the left-hand and right-hand sides of the equations in the given system yields $x^2 + y = 6x + -6x + y + 36$, or $x^2 + y = y + 36$. Subtracting y from both sides of this equation yields $x^2 = 36$. Taking the square root of both sides of this equation yields $x = 6$ and $x = -6$. Therefore, there are two solutions to this system of equations, one with an x-coordinate of 6 and the other with an x-coordinate of -6. Substituting 6 for x in the second equation yields $y = -6(6) + 36$, or $y = 0$; therefore, one solution is $(6, 0)$. Similarly, substituting -6 for x in the second equation yields $y = -6(-6) + 36$, or $y = 72$; therefore, the other solution is $(-6, 72)$. Of these possible values of xy, only 0 is given as a choice.

Choice B is incorrect. This is the x-coordinate of one of the solutions, $(6, 0)$. *Choice C* is incorrect and may result from conceptual or calculation errors. *Choice D* is incorrect. This is the square of the x-coordinate of one of the solutions, $(6, 0)$.

QUESTION 16

The correct answer is either −16 or −24. It's given that the function f is defined by the equation $f(x) = ax^2 + bx + c$, where a, b, and c are constants, and $1 < a < 4$. It's also given that the graph of $y = f(x)$ in the xy-plane passes through the points $(11, 0)$ and $(−2, 0)$. Therefore, $f(11) = 0$ and $f(−2) = 0$. It follows that $x − 11$ and $x + 2$ are factors of $f(x)$, and the equation $f(x) = ax^2 + bx + c$ can be rewritten as $f(x) = a(x − 11)(x + 2)$. Applying the distributive property on the right-hand side of this equation yields $f(x) = a(x^2 − 9x − 22)$, or $f(x) = ax^2 − 9ax − 22a$. Since $1 < a < 4$, if a is an integer, it follows that the value of a is either 2 or 3. If $a = 2$, the equation defining f is $f(x) = (2)x^2 − 9(2)x − 22(2)$, or $f(x) = 2x^2 − 18x − 44$. Since it's given that $f(x) = ax^2 + bx + c$, it follows that $ax^2 + bx + c = 2x^2 − 18x − 44$. Therefore, if $a = 2$, then $b = −18$ and the value of $a + b$ is $2 + (−18)$, or −16. If $a = 3$, the equation defining f is $f(x) = (3)x^2 − 9(3)x − 22(3)$, or $f(x) = 3x^2 − 27x − 66$. Since it's given that $f(x) = ax^2 + bx + c$, it follows that $ax^2 + bx + c = 3x^2 − 27x − 66$. Therefore, if $a = 3$, then $b = −27$ and the value of $a + b$ is $3 + (−27)$, or −24. Thus, if a is an integer, then the value of $a + b$ is either −16 or −24. Note that −16 and −24 are examples of ways to enter a correct answer.

CHAPTER 25

Math: Questions— Problem-Solving and Data Analysis

Problem-Solving and Data Analysis questions in the Math section assess your ability to use your math skills and knowledge to solve problems, many of which are set in context. Some of the questions in this content domain may ask you to create a representation of a problem, consider the units involved, pay attention to the meaning of quantities, know and use different properties of mathematical operations and representations, and apply key principles of statistics and probability. Special focus in this domain is given to mathematical models. Models are representations of real-life contexts. They help us to explain or interpret the behavior of certain components of a system and to predict results that are as yet unobserved or unmeasured. You may be asked to create and use a model and to understand the distinction between the predictions of a model and the data that have been collected.

Some of the questions in this content domain may involve quantitative reasoning about ratios, rates, percentages, and proportional relationships and may require understanding and applying unit rates. Some problems may be set in contexts, which may address topics in science, social science, and real-world settings.

Some questions may present information about the relationship between two variables in a graph, scatterplot, table, or another form and ask you to analyze and draw conclusions about the given information. These questions assess your understanding of the key properties of, and the differences between, linear, quadratic, and exponential relationships and how these properties apply to the corresponding contexts.

The Problem-Solving and Data Analysis domain may also include questions that assess your understanding of essential concepts in statistics and probability. You may be asked to analyze univariate data (data involving one variable) presented in dot plots, histograms, box plots, bar graphs, and frequency tables, or bivariate data (data involving two variables) presented in scatterplots, line graphs, and two-way tables. This includes computing, comparing, and interpreting measures of center; interpreting measures of spread; describing overall patterns; and recognizing the effects of outliers on measures of center and spread. These questions may test your understanding of the conceptual meaning of standard deviation (although you won't be asked to calculate a standard deviation).

Other questions in this domain may ask you to estimate the probability of an event, employing different approaches, rules, or probability models. Special attention is given to the notion of conditional probability, which is tested using two-way tables and in other ways.

Some questions may present you with a description of a study and ask you to decide what conclusion is most appropriate based on the design of the study. Some questions may ask about using data from a sample to draw conclusions about an entire population. These questions may also assess conceptual understanding of the margin of error (although you won't be asked to calculate a margin of error) when a population mean or proportion is estimated from sample data. Other questions may ask about making conclusions about cause-and-effect relationships between two variables.

Problem-Solving and Data Analysis questions include both multiple-choice questions and student-produced response questions.

Let's explore the content, skills, and knowledge assessed by Problem-Solving and Data Analysis questions in the Math section.

Ratio, Proportion, Units, and Percentages

Ratio and proportion is one of the major ideas in math. Introduced well before high school, ratio and proportion is a theme throughout mathematics and has many applications in daily life, career work, and higher-level math courses.

Problem-Solving and Data Analysis Sample Question 1

On Thursday, 240 adults and children attended a show. The ratio of adults to children was 5 to 1. How many children attended the show?

A) 40

B) 48

C) 192

D) 200

REMINDER

A ratio represents a relationship between quantities, not the actual quantities themselves. Fractions are an especially effective way to represent and work with ratios.

Because the ratio of adults to children was 5 to 1, there were 5 adults for every 1 child. Thus, of every 6 people who attended the show, 5 were adults and 1 was a child. In fractions, $\frac{5}{6}$ of the 240 who attended were adults and $\frac{1}{6}$ were children. Therefore, $\frac{1}{6} \times 240$, or 40 children attended the show, which is choice A.

Ratios in the Math section may be expressed in the forms 3 to 1, 3:1, $\frac{3}{1}$, or simply 3.

Problem-Solving and Data Analysis Sample Question 2

On an architect's drawing of the floor plan for a house, 1 inch represents 3 feet. If a room is represented on the floor plan by a rectangle that has sides of lengths 3.5 inches and 5 inches, what is the actual floor area of the room, in square feet?

A) 17.5

B) 51.0

C) 52.5

D) 157.5

Because 1 inch represents 3 feet, the actual dimensions of the room are 3 × 3.5, or 10.5 feet, and 3 × 5, or 15 feet. Therefore, the floor area of the room is 10.5 × 15, or 157.5 square feet, which is choice D.

Another classic example of a ratio is the comparison of the length of an object to the length of its shadow. At a given location and time of day, it might be true that a fence post that has a height of 4 feet casts a shadow that is 6 feet long. This ratio of the height of the object to the length of its shadow, 4 to 6, or 2 to 3, remains the same for any object at the same location and time. This could be considered a unit rate: the ratio of the height of the object to the length of its shadow would be equivalent to 1 to $\frac{2}{3}$ or the unit rate $\frac{2}{3}$-foot change in height of the object for every 1-foot change in length of shadow. So, for example, a tree that casts a shadow that's 18 feet long has a height of 18 × $\frac{2}{3}$, or 12 feet. In this situation, in which one variable quantity is always a fixed constant times another variable quantity, the two quantities are said to be directly proportional.

Thus, if variables x and y are said to be directly proportional, then there exists some number k such that $y = kx$, where k is a nonzero constant. The constant k is called the constant of proportionality.

In the preceding example, you'd say that the height of an object is directly proportional to the length of the object's shadow, with constant of proportionality $\frac{2}{3}$. So if you let L be the length of the shadow and H be the height of the object, then $H = \frac{2}{3}L$.

Notice that both L and H are lengths, so the constant of proportionality, $\frac{H}{L} = \frac{2}{3}$, has no units. In contrast, let's consider sample 2 again. On the scale drawing, 1 inch represents 3 feet. The length of an actual measurement is directly proportional to its length on the scale drawing. But to find the constant of proportionality, you need to keep track of units: $\frac{3 \text{ feet}}{1 \text{ inch}} = \frac{36 \text{ inches}}{1 \text{ inch}} = 36$. Hence, if S is a length on the scale drawing that corresponds to an actual length of R, then $R = 36S$, where R and S have the same units.

Many questions in the Math section require you to pay attention to units. Some questions in the Problem-Solving and Data Analysis content domain require you to convert units either between the U.S. customary system and the metric system or within those systems.

Problem-Solving and Data Analysis Sample Question 3

> Scientists estimate that the Pacific Plate, one of Earth's tectonic plates, has moved about 1,060 kilometers in the past 10.3 million years. About how far, in <u>miles</u>, has the Pacific Plate moved during this same time period? (Use 1 mile = 1.6 kilometers.)
>
> A) 165
> B) 398
> C) 663
> D) 1,696

STRATEGY

Pay close attention to units, and convert units if required by the question. Writing out the unit conversion as a series of multiplication steps, as seen here, will help ensure accuracy. Intermediate units should cancel (as do the kilometers in sample 3), leaving you with the desired unit.

Because 1 mile = 1.6 kilometers, the distance is

$$1,060 \text{ kilometers} \times \frac{1 \text{ mile}}{1.6 \text{ kilometers}} = 662.5 \text{ miles, which is about}$$

663 miles. Therefore, the correct answer is choice C.

Problem-Solving and Data Analysis Sample Question 4

> County Y consists of two districts. One district has an area of 30 square miles and a population density of 370 people per square mile, and the other district has an area of 50 square miles and a population density of 290 people per square mile. What is the population density, in people per square mile, for all of County Y?

Note that this example is in the student-produced response (SPR) format and therefore has no answer choices. You have to generate and enter the response yourself.

The first district has an area of 30 square miles and a population density of 370 people per square mile, so its total population is

$30 \text{ square miles} \times \dfrac{370 \text{ people}}{\text{square mile}}$, or 11,100 people. The other district has an area of 50 square miles and a population density of 290 people per

square mile, so its total population is $50 \text{ square miles} \times \dfrac{290 \text{ people}}{\text{square mile}}$, or 14,500 people. Thus, County Y has a total population of 11,100 + 14,500 = 25,600 people and a total area of 30 + 50 = 80 square

miles. Therefore, the population density of County Y is $\dfrac{25,600}{80}$, or 320 people per square mile.

The Problem-Solving and Data Analysis domain also includes questions involving percentages, which are a type of proportion. These questions may involve the concepts of percentage increase and percentage decrease.

Problem-Solving and Data Analysis Sample Question 5

A furniture store buys its furniture from a wholesaler. For a particular style of table, the usual price of the table is 75% more than the cost of the table from the wholesaler. During a sale, the store sells the table for 15% more than the cost from the wholesaler. If the sale price of the table is $299, what is the usual price for the table?

A) $359

B) $455

C) $479

D) $524

The sale price of the table was $299. This is equal to the cost from the wholesaler plus 15%. Thus, $299 = 1.15 (cost from the wholesaler), and the cost from the wholesaler is $\frac{\$299}{1.15}$ = $260. The usual price is the cost from the wholesaler, $260, plus 75%. Therefore, the usual price the store charges for the table is 1.75 × $260 = $455, which is choice B.

Interpreting Relationships Presented in Scatterplots, Graphs, Tables, and Equations

The behavior of a variable and the relationship between two variables in a context may be explored by considering data presented in scatterplots, tables, and graphs.

The relationship between two quantitative variables may be modeled by a function or an equation. The model may allow very accurate predictions, as, for example, models used in physical sciences, or may only describe a general trend, with considerable variability between the actual and predicted values, as, for example, models used in behavioral and social sciences.

Questions in the Math section may assess your ability to understand and analyze relationships between two variables, the properties of the functions used to model these relationships, and the conditions under which a model is considered to be an appropriate representation of the data. Problem-Solving and Data Analysis questions of these sorts focus on linear, quadratic, and exponential relationships.

REMINDER

Percent is a type of proportion that means "per 100"; 20%, for instance, means 20 out of (or per) 100. Percent increase or decrease is calculated by finding the difference between two quantities, then dividing the difference by the original quantity and multiplying the result by 100.

REMINDER

The abilities of interpreting and synthesizing data from scatterplots, graphs, and tables are widely applicable in college and in many careers and thus are tested in the Math section.

Problem-Solving and Data Analysis Sample Question 6

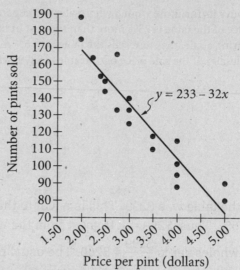

A grocery store sells pints of raspberries and sets the price per pint each week. The scatterplot above shows the price and the number of pints of raspberries sold for 19 weeks, along with a line of best fit for the data and an equation for the line of best fit.

Several different questions could be asked about this context.

A. According to the line of best fit, how many pints of raspberries would the grocery store be predicted to sell in a week when the price of raspberries is $4.50 per pint?

Because the line of best fit has equation $y = 233 - 32x$, where x is the price, in dollars, for a pint of raspberries and y is the predicted number of pints of raspberries sold, the number of pints the store would be predicted to sell in a week when the price of raspberries is $4.50 per pint is $233 - 32(4.50) = 89$ pints.

B. For how many of the 19 weeks shown was the number of pints of raspberries sold greater than the number predicted by the line of best fit?

For a given week, the number of pints of raspberries sold is greater than the number predicted by the line of best fit if and only if the point representing that week lies above the line of best fit. For example, at the price of $5 per pint, the number sold in two different weeks was approximately 80 and 90, which is more than the 73 predicted by the line of best fit. Of the 19 points, 8 lie above the line of best fit, so there were 8 weeks in which the number of pints sold was greater than what was predicted by the line of best fit.

C. What is the best interpretation of the slope of the line of best fit in this context?

In the Math section, this question would be followed by multiple-choice answer options. The slope of the line of best fit is −32. This means that the correct answer would state that for each dollar that the price of a pint of raspberries increases, the store is predicted to sell 32 fewer pints of raspberries.

D. What is the best interpretation of the y-intercept of the line of best fit in this context?

In the Math section, this question would be followed by multiple-choice answer options.

In this context, the y-intercept doesn't represent a likely scenario, so it can't be accurately interpreted in this context. According to the model, the y-intercept means that if the store sold raspberries for $0 per pint—that is, if the store gave raspberries away—233 people would be expected to accept the free raspberries. However, it's not realistic that the store would give away raspberries, and if it did, it's likely that far more people would accept the free raspberries. Also notice that in this case, the leftmost line on the graph is not the y-axis. The lower-left corner shows the x- and y-coordinates of (1.5, 70), not (0, 0).

The fact that the y-intercept indicates that 233 people would accept free raspberries is one limitation of the model. Another limitation is that for a price of $7.50 per pint or above, the model predicts that a negative number of people would buy raspberries, which is impossible. In general, you should be cautious about applying a model for values outside of the given data. In this example, you should only be confident in the prediction of sales for prices between $2 and $5 because those are the lowest and highest prices for which data are shown.

Giving a line of best fit, as in this example, assumes that the relationship between the variables is best modeled by a linear function, but that isn't always true. In the Math section, you may see data that are best modeled by a linear, quadratic, or exponential model.

Problem-Solving and Data Analysis Sample Question 7

Time (hours)	Number of bacteria
0	1,000
1	4,000
2	16,000
3	64,000

The table above gives the initial number (at time $t = 0$) of bacteria placed in a growth medium and the number of bacteria in the growth medium each hour for 3 hours. Which of the following functions best models the number of bacteria, $N(t)$, after t hours?

A) $N(t) = 4,000t$

B) $N(t) = 1,000 + 3,000t$

C) $N(t) = 1,000(4^{-t})$

D) $N(t) = 1,000(4^t)$

STRATEGY

To determine whether a relationship is linear or exponential, examine the change in the quantity between successive time periods. If the difference in the quantity is constant, the relationship is linear. If the ratio in the quantity is constant (for instance, 4 times greater than the preceding time period), the relationship is exponential.

The given choices are linear and exponential models. If a quantity is increasing linearly with time, then the *difference* in the quantity between successive time periods is constant. If a quantity is increasing exponentially with time, then the *ratio* in the quantity between successive time periods is constant. According to the table, after each hour, the number of bacteria in the culture is 4 times as great as it was the preceding hour: $\frac{4,000}{1,000} = \frac{16,000}{4,000} = \frac{64,000}{16,000} = 4$. That is, for each increase of 1 in t, the value of $N(t)$ is multiplied by 4. At $t = 0$, which corresponds to the time when the culture was placed in the medium, there were 1,000 bacteria. This is modeled by the exponential function $N(t) = 1,000(4^t)$, which has the value 1,000 at $t = 0$ and increases by a factor of 4 for each increase of 1 in the value of t. Choice D is the correct answer.

The Math section may include questions that require you to know the difference between linear and exponential growth.

Problem-Solving and Data Analysis Sample Question 8

Every month, Jamal adds two new books to his library. Which of the following types of functions best models the number of books in Jamal's library as a function of time?

A) Increasing linear

B) Decreasing linear

C) Increasing exponential

D) Decreasing exponential

Over equal intervals, linear functions increase or decrease by a constant amount, while exponential functions increase or decrease by a constant factor. Since the number of books is increasing by a constant amount (2 books) over equal intervals (each month), the function is linear. Also, since the number of books is increasing as time increases, the function is increasing, and therefore choice A is correct.

Problem-Solving and Data Analysis Sample Question 9

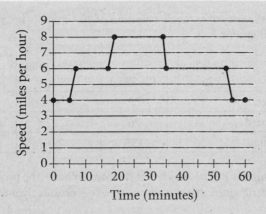

One evening, Maria walks, jogs, and runs for a total of 60 minutes. The graph above shows Maria's speed during the 60 minutes. Which segment of the graph represents the times when Maria's speed is the greatest?

A) The segment from (17, 6) to (19, 8)

B) The segment from (19, 8) to (34, 8)

C) The segment from (34, 8) to (35, 6)

D) The segment from (35, 6) to (54, 6)

The correct answer is choice B. Because the vertical coordinate represents Maria's speed, the part of the graph with the greatest vertical coordinate represents the times when Maria's speed is the greatest. This is the highest part of the graph, the segment from (19, 8) to (34, 8), when Maria runs at 8 miles per hour (mph). Choice A represents the time during which Maria's speed is increasing from 6 to 8 mph; choice C represents the time during which Maria's speed is decreasing from 8 to 6 mph; and choice D represents the longest period of Maria moving at the same speed (6 mph), not the times when Maria's speed is the greatest.

More Data and Statistics

Some questions in the Problem-Solving and Data Analysis domain may assess your ability to understand and analyze data presented in a table, bar graph, histogram, dot plot, box plot, line graph, or other display.

Problem-Solving and Data Analysis Sample Question 10

The given table summarizes the distribution of 200 animals by type of animal and mass, in kilograms.

	Less than 45 kg	45–55 kg	Greater than 55 kg	Total
Cheetah	12	59	4	75
Leopard	24	76	25	125
Total	36	135	29	200

One of these animals will be selected at random. What is the probability of selecting a leopard, given that the animal's mass is greater than 55 kilograms?

A) $\dfrac{25}{29}$

B) $\dfrac{1}{5}$

C) $\dfrac{29}{200}$

D) $\dfrac{1}{8}$

The probability of selecting a leopard given that the animal's mass is greater than 55 kg is the number of leopards with a mass greater than 55 kg divided by the total number of animals with a mass greater than 55 kg. According to the table, there are 29 animals with a mass greater than 55 kg. Of these 29 animals, 25 are leopards. Therefore, if the animal has a mass greater than 55 kg, the probability that the animal is a leopard is $\dfrac{25}{29}$. The correct answer is choice A.

Sample 10 is an example of a conditional probability, the probability of an event given that another event is known to have occurred. The question asks for the probability that an animal chosen at random is a leopard given that the animal has a mass greater than 55 kg.

REMINDER

Mean and median are measures of center for a data set, while range and standard deviation are measures of spread.

You may be asked to answer questions that involve a measure of center for a data set: the mean or the median. A question may ask you to draw conclusions about one or more of these measures of center even if the exact values cannot be calculated. To recall briefly:

- The *mean* of a set of numerical values is the sum of all the values divided by the number of values in the set.

- The *median* of a set of numerical values is the middle value when the values are listed in increasing (or decreasing) order. If the set has an even number of values, then the median is the average of the two middle values. While technically, the median could be any number between the two middle values, it is most often computed as the average of the two middle values and will always be computed this way for questions in the math section.

Problem-Solving and Data Analysis Sample Question 11

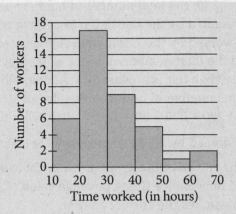

The histogram shown summarizes the distribution of time worked last week, in hours, by the 40 employees of a landscaping company. In the histogram, the first bar represents all workers who worked at least 10 hours but less than 20 hours; the second bar represents all workers who worked at least 20 hours but less than 30 hours; and so on. Which of the following could be the median and mean amount of time worked, in hours, for the 40 employees?

A) Median = 22, mean = 23

B) Median = 24, mean = 22

C) Median = 26, mean = 32

D) Median = 32, mean = 30

Note: In the Math section, all questions that include a histogram will include a description of the boundary condition if interpretation of the boundary is required. That is, the question will include a description of how to interpret the values represented by a bar and whether to include the left endpoint but not the right endpoint or the other way around.

If the number of hours the 40 employees worked is listed in increasing order, the median will be a value between the 20th and the 21st numbers in the list. The first 6 numbers in the list will be workers represented by the first bar; hence, each of the first 6 numbers will be at least 10 but less than 20. The next 17 numbers—that is, the 7th through the 23rd numbers in the list—will be workers represented by the second bar; hence, each of the next 17 numbers will be at least 20 but less than 30. Thus, the 20th and the 21st numbers in the list will be at least 20 but less than 30. Therefore, any of the median values in choices A, B, or C is possible, but the median value in choice D isn't.

Now let's find the possible values of the mean. Each of the 6 employees represented by the first bar worked at least 10 hours but less than 20 hours. Thus, the total number of hours worked by these 6 employees is at least 60. Similarly, the total number of hours worked by the 17 employees represented by the second bar is at least 340; the total

REMINDER

The distribution of a variable provides all possible values of the variable and how often they occur.

number of hours worked by the 9 employees represented by the third bar is at least 270; the total number of hours worked by the 5 employees represented by the fourth bar is at least 200; the total number of hours worked by the 1 employee represented by the fifth bar is at least 50; and the total number of hours worked by the 2 employees represented by the sixth bar is at least 120. Adding all these hours shows that the total number of hours worked by all 40 employees is at least $60 + 340 + 270 + 200 + 50 + 120 = 1{,}040$. Therefore, the mean number of hours worked by all 40 employees is at least $\frac{1{,}040}{40} = 26$. Therefore, only the values of the mean given in choices C and D are possible. Because only choice C has possible values for both the median and the mean, it's the correct answer.

A data set may have a few values that are much larger or smaller than the rest of the values in the set. These values are called *outliers*. An outlier may represent an important piece of data. For example, if a data set consists of rates of a certain illness in various cities, a data point with a very high value could indicate a serious health issue to be investigated.

In general, outliers affect the mean more than the median. Therefore, outliers that are larger than the rest of the points in the data set tend to make the mean greater than the median, and outliers that are smaller than the rest of the points in the data set tend to make the mean less than the median. In sample 11, the mean was larger than the median due to the unusually large amount of time worked by a few employees.

The mean and the median are different ways to describe the center of a data set. Another key characteristic of a data set is the amount of variability, or spread, in the data. One measure of spread is the range, which is equal to the maximum value minus the minimum value. Another measure of spread is the standard deviation, which is a measure of how dispersed, or far away, the points in the data set are from the mean value. A low standard deviation indicates the points in the data set are clustered around the mean value, and a high standard deviation indicates the points in the data set are more spread out from the mean value. In the Math section, you won't be asked to compute the standard deviation of a data set, but you do need to understand that a larger standard deviation corresponds to a data set whose values are more spread out from the mean value.

REMINDER

You won't be asked to calculate the standard deviation of a set of data in the Math section, but you will be expected to demonstrate an understanding of what standard deviation measures.

Problem-Solving and Data Analysis Sample Question 12

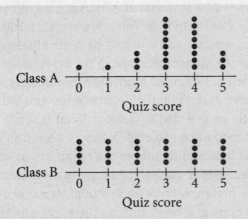

The dot plots show the distributions of scores on a current events quiz for two classes of 24 students each. Which of the following statements about the standard deviations of the two distributions is true?

A) The standard deviation of quiz scores in Class A is less than that of quiz scores in Class B.

B) The standard deviation of quiz scores in Class A is greater than that of quiz scores in Class B.

C) The standard deviation of quiz scores in Class A is equal to that of quiz scores in Class B.

D) There is not enough information to compare the standard deviations.

In Class A, the mean score is between 3 and 4. The large majority of scores are 3 and 4, with only a few scores of 0, 1, 2, and 5. In Class B, the mean score is 2.5, and scores are evenly distributed across all possible scores, with many scores not close to the mean score. Because the scores in Class A are more closely clustered around the mean, the standard deviation of the scores in Class A is smaller. The correct answer is choice A.

A *population parameter* is a numerical value that describes a characteristic of a population. For example, the percentage of registered voters who would vote for a certain candidate is a parameter describing the population of registered voters in an election. In another example, the average income of a household in a city is a parameter describing the population of households in that city. We often don't know the value of the population parameter; thus, an essential purpose of statistics is to estimate a population parameter based on a sample from the population. A common example is election polling, where researchers will interview a random sample of registered voters to estimate the proportion of all registered voters who plan to vote for a certain candidate. The precision of the estimate depends on the variability of the sample data and the sample size. For instance, if household incomes in a city vary widely or the sample is small, the estimate that comes from a sample may differ considerably from the actual value for the population parameter.

STRATEGY

When asked to compare the standard deviations of two data sets, first locate the mean approximately. Then ask yourself which data set has values that are more closely clustered around the mean. That data set will have the smaller standard deviation.

For example, a researcher wants to estimate the mean number of hours each week that the 1,200 students at a high school spend on campus engaged in after-school activities. Interviewing all 1,200 students would be time consuming, and it would be more efficient to survey a random sample of the students. Suppose the researcher has time to interview 80 students. Which 80 students? In order to have a sample that's representative of the population, students who will participate in the study should be selected at random. That is, each student must have the same chance to be selected. Random selection is essential in protecting against bias and increases the reliability of any estimates calculated. The researcher can select students at random in several different ways; for instance, write each student's name on a slip of paper, put all the slips in a bowl, mix up the slips, and then draw 80 names from the bowl. In practice, a computer is often used to select participants at random.

If you don't select a random sample, the sampling method used may introduce bias. For example, if you found 80 students from those attending a game of the school's football team, those people would be more likely to be interested in sports and, in turn, an interest in sports might be related to the average amount of time the students spend on the internet. The result would be that the average time those 80 students spend on the internet might not be an accurate estimate of the average amount of time all students at the school spend on the internet.

Suppose you select 80 students at random from the 1,200 students at the high school. You ask them how much time they spend on campus engaged in after-school activities each week, and you calculate that the mean time is 7.9 hours per week. You also find that 6 of the 80 students spend less than 1 hour each week on campus engaged in after-school activities. Based on these results, what conclusions should be made about the entire population of 1,200 students?

Because the sample was selected at random, the mean of 7.9 hours is a plausible estimate of the mean time spent each week on campus engaged in after-school activities by all 1,200 students. Also, we can use the sample data to estimate how many students spend less than 1 hour on campus engaged in after-school activities each week. In the sample, the percentage is $\frac{6}{80}$, or 7.5%. Applying this percentage to the entire population of 1,200 students, the best estimate is that 90 students at the school spend less than 1 hour per week on campus engaged in after-school activities.

However, the estimates of the population parameters need to be interpreted carefully. An essential part of statistics is accounting for the variability of the estimate. The estimates above are reasonable, but they're unlikely to be exactly correct. Statistical analysis can also describe how far from the estimates the actual values are expected at most to be. To describe the precision of an estimate, statisticians use the concept of *margin of error*. You won't be expected to compute a

REMINDER

You won't need to calculate margins of error in the Math section, but you should understand what the concept means and be able to interpret margins of error in context.

margin of error in the Math section, but you should understand how sample size affects margin of error and how to interpret a given margin of error in context.

If the example above had been part of a Math section question, you might have been given survey results indicating that for a random sample of 80 students, the estimated mean was 7.9 hours with an associated margin of error of 0.8 hours. An appropriate interpretation of these results is that it's plausible that the mean number of hours for all 1,200 students in the population is greater than 7.9 – 0.8, or 7.1 hours, but less than 7.9 + 0.8, or 8.7 hours. There are two key points to note.

1. The value of the margin of error is affected by two factors: the variability in the data and the sample size. The larger the standard deviation, the larger the margin of error; the smaller the standard deviation, the smaller the margin of error. Furthermore, increasing the size of the random sample provides more information and typically reduces the margin of error.

2. The margin of error applies to the estimated value of the population parameter only; it doesn't inform the estimated value for an individual. In the example, plausible values for the population mean are in the interval from 7.1 hours to 8.7 hours. The time, in hours, that an individual spends on the internet may or may not fall in this interval.

Problem-Solving and Data Analysis Sample Question 13

A quality control researcher at an electronics company is testing the life of the company's batteries in a certain camera. The researcher selects 100 batteries at random from the daily output of the batteries and finds that the life of the batteries has a mean of 342 pictures with an associated margin of error of 18 pictures. Which of the following is the most appropriate conclusion based on these data?

A) All the batteries produced by the company that day have a life between 324 and 360 pictures.

B) All the batteries ever produced by the company have a life between 324 and 360 pictures.

C) It is plausible that the mean life of batteries produced by the company that day is between 324 and 360 pictures.

D) It is plausible that the mean life of all the batteries ever produced by the company is between 324 and 360 pictures.

The correct answer is choice C. Choices A and B are incorrect because the margin of error gives information about the mean life of all batteries produced by the company that day, not about the life of any individual battery. Choice D is incorrect because the sample of batteries was taken from the population of all the batteries produced by the company on that day. The population of all batteries the company ever produced may have a different mean life because of changes in the formulation of the batteries, wear on machinery, improvements in production processes, and many other factors.

STRATEGY

When a margin of error is provided, determine the value to which the margin of error applies. If the margin of error is associated with a mean, then the margin of error describes the plausible values for individual values in the population.

The statistics examples discussed so far are largely based on investigations intended to estimate some characteristic of a group: the mean amount of time students spend on the internet, the mean life of a battery, and the percentage of registered voters who plan to vote for a candidate. Another primary focus of statistics is to investigate relationships between variables and to draw conclusions about cause and effect. For example, does a new type of physical therapy help people recover from knee surgery faster? For such a study, some people who have had knee surgery will be randomly assigned to the new therapy or to the usual therapy. The medical results of these patients can be compared. The key questions from a statistical viewpoint are

- Is it appropriate to generalize from the sample of patients in the study to the entire population of people who are recovering from knee surgery?
- Is it appropriate to conclude that the new therapy caused any difference in the results for the two groups of patients?

The answers depend on the use of random selection and random assignment.

- If the subjects in the sample of a study were selected at random from the entire population in question, the results can be generalized to the entire population because random sampling ensures that each individual has the same chance to be selected for the sample.
- If the subjects in the sample were randomly assigned to treatments, it may be appropriate to make conclusions about cause and effect because the treatment groups will be roughly equivalent at the beginning of the experiment other than the treatment they receive.

This can be summarized in the following table.

REMINDER

In order for the results of a study to be generalized to an entire population, random sampling is needed. In order for a cause-and-effect relationship to be established, random assignment of individuals to treatments is needed.

	Subjects selected at random	Subjects not selected at random
Subjects randomly assigned to treatments	• Results can be generalized to the entire population. • Conclusions about cause and effect can appropriately be drawn.	• Results *cannot* be generalized to the entire population. • Conclusions about cause and effect can appropriately be drawn.
Subjects not randomly assigned to treatments	• Results can be generalized to the entire population. • Conclusions about cause and effect should *not* be drawn.	• Results *cannot* be generalized to the entire population. • Conclusions about cause and effect should *not* be drawn.

The previous example discussed treatments in a medical experiment. The word *treatment* refers to any factor that is deliberately varied in an experiment.

Problem-Solving and Data Analysis Sample Question 14

A community center offers a Spanish course. This year, all students in the course were offered additional audio lessons they could take at home. The students who took these additional audio lessons did better in the course than students who didn't take the additional audio lessons. Based on these results, which of the following is the most appropriate conclusion?

A) Taking additional audio lessons will cause an improvement for any student who takes any foreign language course.

B) Taking additional audio lessons will cause an improvement for any student who takes a Spanish course.

C) Taking additional audio lessons was the cause of the improvement for the students at the community center who took the Spanish course.

D) No conclusion about cause and effect can be made regarding students at the community center who took the additional audio lessons at home and their performance in the Spanish course.

The correct answer is choice D. The better results of these students may have been a result of being more motivated, as shown in their willingness to do extra work, and not the additional audio lessons. Choice A is incorrect because no conclusion about cause and effect is possible without random assignment to treatments and because the sample was only students taking a Spanish course, so no conclusion can be appropriately made about students taking all foreign language courses. Choice B is incorrect because no conclusion about cause and effect is possible without random assignment to treatments and because the students taking a Spanish course at the community center is not a random sample of all students who take a Spanish course. Choice C is incorrect because the students taking the Spanish course at the community center weren't randomly assigned to use the additional audio lessons or to not use the additional audio lessons.

Summary: Problem-Solving and Data Analysis Questions

Main purpose: To assess your understanding of proportional relationships, percentages, and probability as well as your ability to use data to analyze and solve problems

Proportion of the test section: About 15 percent (approximately five to seven questions)

Question types

- Ratios, rates, proportional relationships, and units
- Percentages
- One-variable data: distributions and measures of center and spread
- Two-variable data: models and scatterplots
- Probability and conditional probability
- Inference from sample statistics and margin of error
- Evaluating statistical claims: observational studies and experiments

STRATEGY

Be wary of conclusions that claim a cause-and-effect relationship or that generalize a conclusion to a broader population. Before accepting a conclusion, assess whether the subjects were selected at random from the broader population and whether subjects were randomly assigned to treatments.

CHAPTER 26

Math: Questions— Problem-Solving and Data Analysis Drills

1

Makayla is planning an event in a 5,400-square-foot room. If there should be at least 8 square feet per person, what is the maximum number of people that could attend this event?

A) 588

B) 675

C) 15,274

D) 43,200

2

Water flows from a pipe at a rate of 6.0 gallons per minute. How many gallons of water will flow from the pipe in 8.4 minutes?

3

The bar graph shows the results from a survey in which a group of students was asked during which month they prefer to have the class picnic.

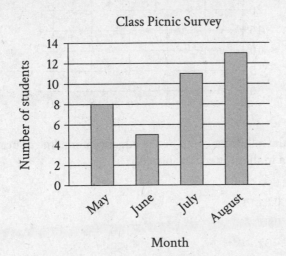

Class Picnic Survey

Based on the graph, how many students did <u>not</u> respond "May"?

4

A fish hatchery has three tanks for holding fish before they are introduced into the wild. Ten fish weighing less than 5 ounces are placed in tank A. Eleven fish weighing at least 5 ounces but no more than 13 ounces are placed in tank B. Twelve fish weighing more than 13 ounces are placed in tank C. Which of the following could be the median of the weights, in ounces, of these 33 fish?

A) 4.5

B) 8

C) 13.5

D) 15

5

A data set of 27 different numbers has a mean of 33 and a median of 33. A new data set is created by adding 7 to each number in the original data set that is greater than the median and subtracting 7 from each number in the original data set that is less than the median. Which of the following measures does NOT have the same value in both the original and new data sets?

A) Median

B) Mean

C) Sum of the numbers

D) Standard deviation

6

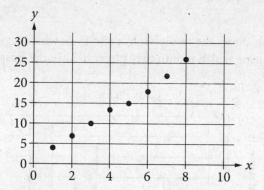

Which of the following could be the equation for a line of best fit for the data shown in the scatterplot above?

A) $y = 0.8 + 3x$

B) $y = 3 + 0.8x$

C) $y = 3 - 0.8x$

D) $y = 0.8 - 3x$

7

A sample of 40 fourth-grade students was selected at random from a certain school. The 40 students completed a survey about the morning announcements, and 32 thought the announcements were helpful. Which of the following is the largest population to which the results of the survey can be applied?

A) The 40 students who were surveyed

B) All fourth-grade students at the school

C) All students at the school

D) All fourth-grade students in the county in which the school is located

8

In which of the following tables is the relationship between the values of x and their corresponding y-values nonlinear?

A)

x	1	2	3	4
y	8	11	14	17

B)

x	1	2	3	4
y	4	8	12	16

C)

x	1	2	3	4
y	8	13	18	23

D)

x	1	2	3	4
y	6	12	24	48

9

A bag containing 10,000 beads of assorted colors is purchased from a craft store. To estimate the percent of red beads in the bag, a sample of beads is selected at random. The percent of red beads in the bag was estimated to be 15%, with an associated margin of error of 2%. If r is the actual number of red beads in the bag, which of the following is most plausible?

A) $r > 1,700$

B) $1,300 < r < 1,700$

C) $200 < r < 1,500$

D) $r < 1,300$

10

The table summarizes the distribution of people in a certain city by age group.

Age group	Percent
Less than 18 years old	27%
18–40 years old	22%
41–65 years old	26%
Greater than 65 years old	25%

If a person in this city is selected at random, what is the probability of selecting a person who is greater than 65 years old, given that the person is at least 18 years old? (Express your answer as a decimal or fraction, not as a percent.)

11

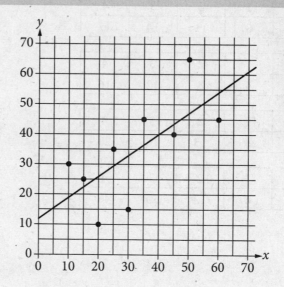

The scatterplot in the *xy*-plane above shows nine points (x, y) and a line of best fit. Of the following, which best estimates the amount by which the line underestimates the value of y when $x = 50$?

A) 8

B) 10

C) 13

D) 18

12

Sample	Percent in favor	Margin of error
A	52%	4.2%
B	48%	1.6%

The results of two random samples of votes for a proposition are shown. The samples were selected from the same population, and the margins of error were calculated using the same method. Which of the following is the most appropriate reason that the margin of error for sample A is greater than the margin of error for sample B?

A) Sample A had a smaller number of votes that could not be recorded.

B) Sample A had a higher percent of favorable responses.

C) Sample A had a larger sample size.

D) Sample A had a smaller sample size.

13

The number of crane flies in a wildlife sanctuary is 30% less than the number of ladybugs in the sanctuary. The number of honeybees in the sanctuary is 85% greater than the number of crane flies in the sanctuary. The number of honeybees in the sanctuary is how many times the number of ladybugs in the sanctuary?

14

The positive number a is 210% of the number b, and a is 30% of the number c. If c is $p\%$ of b, what is the value of p?

Answer Explanations

QUESTION 1

Choice B is correct. It's given that the event will be in a 5,400-square-foot room and that there should be at least 8 square feet per person. The maximum number of people that could attend the event can be found by dividing the total square feet in the room by the minimum number of square feet needed per person, which gives $\frac{5,400}{8}$, or 675.

Choices A and *C* are incorrect and may result from conceptual or calculation errors. *Choice D* is incorrect and may result from multiplying, rather than dividing, 5,400 by 8.

QUESTION 2

The correct answer is 50.4. It's given that water flows from a pipe at a rate of 6.0 gallons per minute. It follows that the number of gallons of water that will flow from the pipe in 8.4 minutes can be determined by multiplying the water flow rate by the number of minutes: $\left(\frac{6.0 \text{ gallons}}{1 \text{ minute}}\right)$(8.4 minutes), or 50.4 gallons.

Therefore, 50.4 gallons of water will flow from the pipe in 8.4 minutes. Note that 50.4 and 252/5 are examples of ways to enter a correct answer.

QUESTION 3

The correct answer is 29. It's given that the bar graph shows the results from a survey in which a group of students was asked during which month they prefer to have the class picnic. Based on the graph, 8 students responded "May," 5 students responded "June," 11 students responded "July," and 13 students responded "August." It follows that the number of students who did not respond "May" is the sum of the number of students who responded "June," "July," or "August," which yields 5 + 11 + 13, or 29. Therefore, 29 students did not respond "May."

QUESTION 4

Choice B is correct. The median of a set of numbers is the middle number when the values in the set are ordered from least to greatest. There are 33 fish, so in an ordered list of the weights, the 17th value would be the median weight. The 10 fish in tank A weigh the least, and these 10 weights would be the first 10 values on the ordered list. The 11 fish in tank B have the next set of greater weights and so would be the 11th through 21st weights in the ordered list, which includes the median weight as the 17th value. The fish in tank B weigh at least 5 ounces but no more than 13 ounces. Of the given choices, only 8 ounces falls within this range of values.

Choice A is incorrect. It's given that tank A has 10 fish weighing less than 5 ounces. Since there are more than 10 fish in tanks B and C combined, the median weight cannot be less than 5 ounces. *Choices C* and *D* are incorrect. It's given that tank C has 12 fish weighing more than 13 ounces. There are more than 12 fish in tanks A and B combined, so the median weight can't be more than 13 ounces.

QUESTION 5

Choice D is correct. When a data set has an odd number of elements, the median can be found by ordering the values from least to greatest and determining the middle value. Out of the 27 different numbers in this data set, 13 numbers are below the median, one number is exactly 33, and 13 numbers are above the median. When 7 is subtracted from each number below the median and added to each number above the median, the distance between these numbers and the median is larger in the new data set compared to the original data set. Since the median of this data set, 33, is equivalent to the mean of the data set, it follows that the distance between these numbers and the mean is larger in the new data set compared to the original data set. Since standard deviation is a measure of how spread out the data are from the mean, a greater spread from the mean indicates an increased standard deviation. Therefore, the standard deviation doesn't have the same value in both the original and new data sets.

Choice A is incorrect. All the numbers less than the median decrease and all the numbers greater than the median increase, but the median itself doesn't change. *Choices B and C* are incorrect. The mean of a data set is found by dividing the sum of the values by the number of values. The net change from subtracting 7 from 13 numbers and adding 7 to 13 numbers is zero. Therefore, neither the mean nor the sum of the numbers changes.

QUESTION 6

Choice A is correct. The data show a strong linear relationship between x and y. The line of best fit for a set of data is a linear equation that minimizes the distances from the data points to the line. An equation for the line of best fit can be written in slope-intercept form, $y = mx + b$, where m is the slope of the graph of the line and b is the y-coordinate of the y-intercept of the graph. Since, for the data shown, the y-values increase as the x-values increase, the slope of a line of best fit must be positive. The data shown lie almost in a line, so the slope can be roughly estimated using the formula for slope, $m = \frac{y_2 - y_1}{x_2 - x_1}$, where (x_1, y_1) and (x_2, y_2) represent two points on the line. The leftmost and rightmost data points have coordinates of about (1, 4) and (8, 26). Substituting (1, 4) for (x_1, y_1) and (8, 26) for (x_2, y_2) in the formula for slope yields $\frac{26 - 4}{8 - 1}$, or $\frac{22}{7}$. Thus, the slope is approximately $\frac{22}{7}$, which is a little greater than 3. Extension of the line to the left would intersect the y-axis at about (0, 1). Only choice A represents a line with a slope close to 3 and a y-intercept close to (0, 1).

Choice B is incorrect and may result from switching the slope and y-intercept. The line with a y-intercept of (0, 3) and a slope of 0.8 is farther from the data points than the line with a slope of 3 and a y-intercept of (0, 0.8). *Choices C and D* are incorrect. These equations represent lines with negative slopes, not positive slopes.

QUESTION 7

Choice B is correct. Selecting a sample of a reasonable size at random to use for a survey allows the results from that survey to be applied to the population from which the sample was selected, but not beyond this population. In this case, the population from which the sample was selected is all fourth-grade students at a certain school. Therefore, the results of the survey can be applied to all fourth-grade students at the school.

Choice A is incorrect. The results of the survey can be applied to the 40 students who were surveyed. However, this isn't the largest group to which the results of the survey can be applied. *Choices C* and *D* are incorrect. Since the sample was selected at random from among the fourth-grade students at a certain school, the results of the survey can't be applied to other students at the school or to other fourth-grade students who weren't represented in the survey results. Students in other grades in the school or other fourth-grade students in the county may feel differently about announcements than the fourth-grade students at the school do.

QUESTION 8

Choice D is correct. The relationship between the values of *x* and their corresponding *y*-values is nonlinear if the rate of change between these pairs of values isn't constant. The table for choice D gives four pairs of values: (1, 6), (2, 12), (3, 24), and (4, 48). Finding the rate of change, or slope, $\frac{y_2 - y_1}{x_2 - x_1}$, between $(x_1, y_1) = (1, 6)$ and $(x_2, y_2) = (2, 12)$ yields $\frac{12 - 6}{2 - 1}$, or 6. Finding the rate of change between $(x_1, y_1) = (2, 12)$ and $(x_2, y_2) = (3, 24)$ yields $\frac{24 - 12}{3 - 2}$, or 12. Finding the rate of change between $(x_1, y_1) = (3, 24)$ and $(x_2, y_2) = (4, 48)$ yields $\frac{48 - 24}{4 - 3}$, or 24. Since the rate of change isn't constant for these pairs of values, this table shows a nonlinear relationship.

Choices A, B, and *C* are incorrect. The rate of change between the values of *x* and their corresponding *y*-values in each of these tables is constant, with slopes of 3, 4, and 5, respectively. Therefore, each of these tables shows a linear relationship.

QUESTION 9

Choice B is correct. It was estimated that 15% of the beads in the bag are red. Since the bag contains 10,000 beads, it follows that there are an estimated 10,000 × 0.15 = 1,500 red beads. It's given that the associated margin of error is 2%, or 10,000 × 0.02 = 200 beads. If the estimate is too high, there could plausibly be 1,500 − 200 = 1,300 red beads. If the estimate is too low, there could plausibly be 1,500 + 200 = 1,700 red beads. Therefore, it is estimated that there are between 1,300 and 1,700 red beads in the bag. Since it's given that *r* represents the actual number of red beads in the bag, it follows that 1,300 < *r* < 1,700.

Choices A and *D* are incorrect and may result from conceptual or calculation errors. *Choice C* is incorrect because 200 is the associated margin of error for the number of red beads, not the lower bound of the range of red beads.

QUESTION 10

The correct answer is $\frac{25}{73}$. It's given that the table summarizes the distribution of people in a certain city by age group. If a person in this city is selected at random and the person is at least 18 years old, the person is either 18–40 years old, 41–65 years old, or greater than 65 years old. Therefore, the percent of the people in the city who are at least 18 years old is the sum of the percentages of the people who are 18–40 years old, 41–65 years old, and greater than 65 years old, which is 22% + 26% + 25%, or 73%. It follows that the proportion of people in the city who are at least 18 years old is $\frac{73}{100}$, or 0.73. Based on the table, 25% of the people in the city are greater than 65 years old. It follows that the proportion of people in the city who are greater than 65 years old is $\frac{25}{100}$, or 0.25. Therefore, the probability of selecting a person who is greater than 65 years old, given that the person is at least 18 years old, is the proportion of people in the city who are greater than 65 years old divided by the proportion of people in the city who are at least 18 years old, or $\frac{0.25}{0.73}$, which is equivalent to $\frac{25}{73}$. Note that 25/73, .3424, .3425, and 0.342 are examples of ways to enter a correct answer.

QUESTION 11

Choice D is correct. At $x = 50$, the point on the scatterplot is (50, 65) and the point on the line of best fit is approximately (50, 47). Therefore, the amount by which the line of best fit underestimates the value of y at $x = 50$ is approximately 65 − 47, or 18.

Choices A, B, and *C* are incorrect and may result from conceptual or calculation errors.

QUESTION 12

Choice D is correct. In general, a smaller sample size generally leads to a larger margin of error because the sample may be less representative of the whole population.

Choice A is incorrect. The margin of error will depend on the size of the sample of recorded votes, not the number of votes that could not be recorded. In any case, the smaller number of votes that could not be recorded for sample A would tend to decrease, not increase, the comparative size of the margin of error. *Choice B* is incorrect. Since the percent in favor for sample A is the same distance from 50% as the percent in favor for sample B, the percent of favorable responses doesn't affect the comparative size of the margin of error for the two samples. *Choice C* is incorrect and may result from a conceptual error.

QUESTION 13

The correct answer is 1.295. For this wildlife sanctuary, let x be the number of crane flies, y be the number of ladybugs, and z be the number of honeybees. It's given that the number of crane flies in the sanctuary is 30% less than the number of ladybugs. This means that the number of crane flies is (100 − 30)%, or 70%, of the number of ladybugs. The equation $x = \frac{70}{100}y$, or $x = 0.70y$, represents this situation. It's given that the number of honeybees in the sanctuary is 85% greater than the number of crane flies in the sanctuary. This means that the number of honeybees is (100 + 85)%, or 185%, of the number of crane flies. The equation $z = \frac{185}{100}x$, or $z = 1.85x$, represents this situation. Substituting 0.70y for x in the equation $z = 1.85x$ yields $z = 1.85(0.70y)$, or $z = 1.295y$. Therefore, the number of honeybees is 1.295 times the number of ladybugs in the sanctuary.

QUESTION 14

The correct answer is 700. It's given that the positive number a is 210% of the number b. Thus, $a = \frac{210}{100}b$. It's also given that a is 30% of the number c. Thus, $a = \frac{30}{100}c$. Since $a = \frac{210}{100}b$ and $a = \frac{30}{100}c$, it follows that $\frac{210}{100}b = \frac{30}{100}c$. Multiplying both sides of this equation by $\frac{100}{30}$ yields $\left(\frac{100}{30}\right)\left(\frac{210}{100}\right)b = c$, or $c = \frac{210}{30}b$. If c is p% of b, it follows that $\frac{p}{100} = \frac{210}{30}$. Multiplying both sides of this equation by 100 yields $p = \left(\frac{210}{30}\right)(100)$, or $p = 700$.

CHAPTER 27

Math: Questions—Geometry and Trigonometry

In addition to questions in Algebra, Advanced Math, and Problem-Solving and Data Analysis, the Math section includes several questions that are drawn from geometry and trigonometry. They include both multiple-choice and student-produced response questions.

Let's explore the content and skills assessed by these questions.

Geometry

The Math section includes questions that assess your understanding of the key concepts in the geometry of lines, angles, triangles, circles, and other geometric objects. Other questions may also ask you to find the area, surface area, or volume of an abstract figure or a real-life object. You don't need to memorize a large collection of formulas, but you should be comfortable understanding and using these formulas to solve various types of problems. Many of the geometry formulas are provided in the reference sheet available during testing, and less commonly used formulas required to answer particular questions are given in the questions themselves.

To answer geometry questions in the Math section, you should recall the geometry definitions learned before high school and know the essential concepts extended while learning geometry in high school. You should also be familiar with basic geometric notation.

Here are some of the areas that may be the focus of some geometry questions in the Math section.

- Lines and angles
    - Lengths and midpoints
    - Measures of angles
    - Vertical angles
    - Angle addition
    - Straight angles and the sum of the angles about a point
    - Properties of parallel lines and the angles formed when parallel lines are cut by a transversal
    - Properties of perpendicular lines

- Triangles and other polygons
  - Right triangles and the Pythagorean theorem
  - Properties of equilateral and isosceles triangles
  - Properties of 30°-60°-90° triangles and 45°-45°-90° triangles
  - Congruent triangles and other congruent figures
  - Similar triangles and other similar figures
  - The triangle inequality
  - Squares, rectangles, parallelograms, trapezoids, and other quadrilaterals
  - Regular polygons
- Circles
  - Radius, diameter, and circumference
  - Measure of central angles and inscribed angles
  - Arc length, arc measure, and area of sectors
  - Tangents and chords
- Area and volume
  - Area of plane figures
  - Volume of solids
  - Surface area of solids

You should be familiar with the geometric notation for points and lines, line segments, angles and their measures, and lengths.

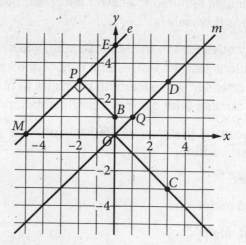

In the figure shown, the *xy*-plane has origin *O*. The values of *x* on the horizontal *x*-axis increase as you move to the right, and the values of *y* on the vertical *y*-axis increase as you move up. Line *e* contains point *P*, which has coordinates (−2, 3); point *E*, which has coordinates (0, 5); and point *M*, which has coordinates (−5, 0). Line *m* passes through the origin *O* (0, 0), the point *Q* (1, 1), and the point *D* (3, 3).

Lines *e* and *m* are parallel—they never meet. This is written *e* ‖ *m*.

You'll also need to know the following notation:

- $\overleftrightarrow{PE}$: The line containing the points *P* and *E* (this is the same as line *e*)

- $\overline{PE}$, or line segment *PE*: The line segment with endpoints *P* and *E*

- *PE*: The length of segment *PE* (you can write $PE = 2\sqrt{2}$)

- $\overrightarrow{PE}$: The ray starting at point *P* and extending indefinitely in the direction of point *E*

- $\overrightarrow{EP}$: The ray starting at point *E* and extending indefinitely in the direction of point *P*

- ∠*DOC*: The angle formed by $\overrightarrow{OD}$ and $\overrightarrow{OC}$

- △*PEB*: The triangle with vertices *P*, *E*, and *B*

- Quadrilateral *BPMO*: The quadrilateral with vertices *B*, *P*, *M*, and *O*

- $\overline{BP} \perp \overline{PM}$: Segment *BP* is perpendicular to segment *PM*. (You should also recognize that the right-angle box within ∠*BPM* means this angle is a right angle.)

STRATEGY
Familiarize yourself with these notations in order to avoid confusion on test day.

Geometry and Trigonometry Sample Question 1

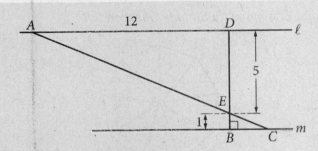

In the figure shown, line *ℓ* is parallel to line *m*, segment *BD* is perpendicular to line *m*, and segment *AC* and segment *BD* intersect at *E*. What is the length of segment *AC*?

Since segment *AC* and segment *BD* intersect at *E*, ∠*AED* and ∠*CEB* are vertical angles, and so the measure of ∠*AED* is equal to the measure of ∠*CEB*. Since line *ℓ* is parallel to line *m*, ∠*BCE* and ∠*DAE* are alternate interior angles of parallel lines cut by a transversal, and so the measure of ∠*BCE* is equal to the measure of ∠*DAE*. By the angle-angle similarity theorem, △*AED* is similar to △*CEB*, with vertices *A*, *E*, and *D* corresponding to vertices *C*, *E*, and *B*, respectively.

Also, △*AED* is a right triangle, so by the Pythagorean theorem, $AE = \sqrt{AD^2 + DE^2}$. Substituting values for the length of the line segments gives $\sqrt{12^2 + 5^2} = \sqrt{169}$, which means that *AE* = 13. Since △*AED* is similar to △*CEB*, the ratios of the lengths of corresponding sides of the two triangles are in the same proportion. Since $\frac{ED}{EB} = \frac{AE}{EC}$, then $\frac{5}{1} = \frac{13}{EC}$, and so $EC = \frac{13}{5}$. Therefore, *AC* = *AE* + *EC*, or $13 + \frac{13}{5} = \frac{78}{5}$.

STRATEGY
A shortcut here is remembering that 5, 12, 13 is a Pythagorean triple (5 and 12 are the lengths of the sides of the right triangle, and 13 is the length of the hypotenuse). Another common Pythagorean triple is 3, 4, 5.

Note how sample 1 requires the knowledge and application of numerous fundamental geometry concepts. Develop mastery of the fundamental concepts, and practice applying them on test-like questions.

Note some of the key concepts that were used in sample 1:

- Vertical angles have the same measure.

- When parallel lines are cut by a transversal, the alternate interior angles have the same measure.

- If two angles of a triangle are congruent to (have the same measure as) two angles of another triangle, the two triangles are similar.

- The Pythagorean theorem: $a^2 + b^2 = c^2$, where a and b are the lengths of the legs of a right triangle and c is the length of the hypotenuse.

- If two triangles are similar, then all ratios of lengths of corresponding sides are equal.

- If point E lies on line segment AC, then $AC = AE + EC$.

Note that if two triangles or other polygons are similar or congruent, the order in which the vertices are named does *not* necessarily indicate how the vertices correspond in the similarity or congruence. Thus, it was stated explicitly in sample 1 that "$\triangle AED$ is similar to $\triangle CEB$, with vertices A, E, and D corresponding to vertices C, E, and B, respectively."

Geometry and Trigonometry Sample Question 2

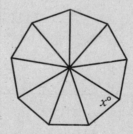

In the figure shown, a regular polygon with 9 sides has been divided into 9 congruent isosceles triangles by line segments drawn from the center of the polygon to its vertices. What is the value of x?

The sum of the measures of the angles around a point is 360°. Since the 9 triangles are congruent, the measures of each of the 9 angles around the center point are equal. Thus, the measure of each of the 9 angles around the center point is $\frac{360°}{9} = 40°$. In any triangle, the sum of the measures of the interior angles is 180°. So in each triangle, the sum of the measures of the remaining two angles is $180° - 40° = 140°$. Since each triangle is isosceles, the measure of each of these two angles is the same. Therefore, the measure of each of these angles is $\frac{140°}{2} = 70°$. Hence, the value of x is 70.

Note some of the key concepts that were used in sample 2:

- The sum of the measures of the angles about a point is 360°.

- Corresponding angles of congruent triangles have the same measure.

- The sum of the measure of the interior angles of any triangle is 180°.

- In an isosceles triangle, the angles opposite the sides of equal length are of equal measure.

Geometry and Trigonometry Sample Question 3

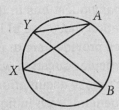

In the figure shown, $\angle AXB$ and $\angle AYB$ are inscribed in the circle. Which of the following statements is true?

A) The measure of $\angle AXB$ is greater than the measure of $\angle AYB$.

B) The measure of $\angle AXB$ is less than the measure of $\angle AYB$.

C) The measure of $\angle AXB$ is equal to the measure of $\angle AYB$.

D) There is not enough information to determine the relationship between the measure of $\angle AXB$ and the measure of $\angle AYB$.

Choice C is correct. Let the measure of arc AB be $d°$. Since $\angle AXB$ is inscribed in the circle and intercepts arc AB, the measure of $\angle AXB$ is equal to half the measure of arc AB. Thus, the measure of $\angle AXB$ is $\frac{d°}{2}$. Similarly, since $\angle AYB$ is also inscribed in the circle and intercepts arc AB, the measure of $\angle AYB$ is also $\frac{d°}{2}$. Therefore, the measure of $\angle AXB$ is equal to the measure of $\angle AYB$.

Note the key concept that was used in sample 3:

- The measure of an angle inscribed in a circle is equal to half the measure of its intercepted arc.

You also should know these related concepts:

- The measure of a central angle in a circle is equal to the measure of its intercepted arc.

- An arc is measured in degrees, while arc length is measured in linear units.

You should also be familiar with notation for arcs and circles for questions in the Math section.

- A circle may be identified by the point at its center—for instance, "the circle centered at point M" or "the circle with center at point M."

- An arc named with only its two endpoints, such as $\overset{\frown}{AB}$ or arc AB, will always refer to a minor arc. A minor arc has a measure that's less than 180°.

STRATEGY

At first glance, it may appear as though there's not enough information to determine the relationship between the two angle measures. One key to this question is identifying what's the same about the two angle measures. In this case, both angles intercept arc AB.

- An arc may also be named with three points: the two endpoints and a third point that the arc passes through. So $\overset{\frown}{ACB}$ or arc *ACB* has endpoints at *A* and *B* and passes through point *C*. Three points may be used to name a minor arc or an arc that has a measure of 180° or more.

In general, figures that accompany questions in the Math section are intended to provide information that's useful in answering the question. Sometimes figures provided are drawn to scale, and sometimes they're not. In a particular question when it's stated that the figure isn't drawn to scale, don't make assumptions about the relative size of angles or segments. In general, even in figures not drawn to scale, the relative positions of points and angles may be assumed to be in the order shown. Also, line segments that extend through points and appear to lie on the same line may be assumed to be on the same line. A point that appears to lie on a line or curve may be assumed to lie on the line or curve.

The text "Note: Figure not drawn to scale" is included with the figure when degree measures may not be accurately shown and specific lengths may not be drawn proportionally. The following example illustrates what information can and can't be assumed from a figure not drawn to scale.

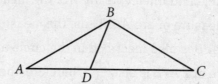

Note: Figure not drawn to scale.

A question may refer to a triangle such as *ABC* above. Although the note indicates that the figure isn't drawn to scale, you may assume the following from the figure:

- *ABD* and *DBC* are triangles.

- *A*, *D*, and *C* are points on a line.

- *D* is between *A* and *C*.

- The length of $\overline{AD}$ is less than the length of $\overline{AC}$.

- The measure of angle *ABD* is less than the measure of angle *ABC*.

You may *not* assume the following from the figure:

- The length of $\overline{AD}$ is less than the length of $\overline{DC}$.

- The measures of angles *BAD* and *DBA* are equal.

- The measure of angle *DBC* is greater than the measure of angle *ABD*.

- Angle *DBC* is a right angle.

Geometry and Trigonometry Sample Question 4

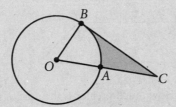

In the given figure, O is the center of the circle, segment BC is tangent to the circle at B, and A lies on segment OC. If the lengths of $\overline{OB}$ and $\overline{AC}$ are each 6, what is the area of the shaded region?

A) $18\sqrt{3} - 3\pi$

B) $18\sqrt{3} - 6\pi$

C) $36\sqrt{3} - 3\pi$

D) $36\sqrt{3} - 6\pi$

Since line segment BC is tangent to the circle at B, it follows that $\overline{BC} \perp \overline{OB}$, and so triangle OBC is a right triangle with its right angle at B. Since $OB = 6$ and $\overline{OB}$ and $\overline{OA}$ are both radii of the circle, $OA = 6$. Since $OC = OA + AC$, $OC = 6 + 6$, or 12. Thus, triangle OBC is a right triangle with the length of the hypotenuse ($OC = 12$) twice the length of one of its legs ($OB = 6$). It follows that triangle OBC is a 30°-60°-90° triangle with its 30° angle at C and its 60° angle at O. The area of the shaded region is the area of triangle OBC minus the area of the sector bounded by radii OA and OB.

In the 30°-60°-90° triangle OBC, the length of side OB, which is opposite the 30° angle, is 6. Thus, the length of side BC, which is opposite the 60° angle, is $6\sqrt{3}$. Hence, the area of triangle OBC is $\frac{1}{2}(6)(6\sqrt{3}) = 18\sqrt{3}$. Since the sector bounded by radii OA and OB has central angle 60°, the area of this sector is $\frac{60}{360} = \frac{1}{6}$ of the area of the circle. Since the circle has radius 6, its area is $\pi(6)^2 = 36\pi$, and so the area of the sector is $\frac{1}{6}(36\pi) = 6\pi$. Therefore, the area of the shaded region is $18\sqrt{3} - 6\pi$, which is choice B.

Note some of the key concepts that were used in sample 4:

- A tangent to a circle is perpendicular to the radius of the circle drawn to the point of tangency.
- Properties of 30°-60°-90° triangles.
- Area of a circle.
- The area of a sector with central angle $x°$ is equal to $\frac{x}{360}$ of the area of the entire circle.

STRATEGY

On complex multistep questions such as sample 4, start by identifying the task (finding the area of the shaded region) and considering the intermediate steps that you'll need to solve for (the area of triangle OBC and the area of sector OBA) in order to get to the final answer. Breaking up this question into a series of smaller questions will make it more manageable.

REMINDER

Arc length, area of a sector, and central angle are all proportional to each other in a circle. This proportionality is written as

$$\frac{\text{arc length}}{\text{circumference}} = \frac{\text{central angle}}{360 \text{ degrees}} = \frac{\text{area of a sector}}{\text{area of a circle}}.$$

Geometry and Trigonometry Sample Question 5

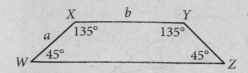

Trapezoid *WXYZ* is shown. How much greater is the area of this trapezoid than the area of a parallelogram with side lengths *a* and *b* and base angles of measures 45° and 135°?

A) $\frac{1}{2}a^2$

B) $\sqrt{2}a^2$

C) $\frac{1}{2}ab$

D) $\sqrt{2}ab$

STRATEGY

Note how drawing the parallelogram within trapezoid *WXYZ* makes it much easier to compare the areas of the two shapes, minimizing the amount of calculation needed to arrive at the solution. Be on the lookout for time-saving shortcuts such as this one.

In the figure, draw a line segment from *Y* to the point *P* on side *WZ* of the trapezoid such that ∠*YPW* has measure 135°, as shown in the figure below.

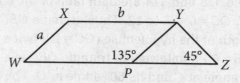

Since in trapezoid *WXYZ* side *XY* is parallel to side *WZ*, it follows that *WXYP* is a parallelogram with side lengths *a* and *b* and base angles of measure 45° and 135°. Thus, the area of the trapezoid is greater than the area of a parallelogram with side lengths *a* and *b* and base angles of measure 45° and 135° by the area of triangle *PYZ*. Since ∠*YPW* has measure 135°, it follows that ∠*YPZ* has measure 45°. Hence, triangle *PYZ* is a 45°-45°-90° triangle with legs of length *a*. Therefore, its area is $\frac{1}{2}a^2$, which is choice A.

Note some of the key concepts that were used in sample 5:

- Properties of trapezoids and parallelograms.

- Area of a 45°-45°-90° triangle.

Some questions in the Math section may ask you to find the area, surface area, or volume of an object, possibly in context.

Geometry and Trigonometry Sample Question 6

A laboratory supply company produces graduated cylinders, each with an internal radius of 2 inches and an internal height between 7.75 inches and 8 inches. What is one possible volume, rounded to the nearest cubic inch, of a graduated cylinder produced by this company?

The volume of a cylinder can be found by using the formula $V = \pi r^2 h$, where r is the radius of the circular base and h is the height of the cylinder. The smallest possible volume, in cubic inches, of a graduated cylinder produced by the laboratory supply company can be found by substituting 2 for r and 7.75 for h, giving $V = \pi(2^2)(7.75)$. This gives a volume of approximately 97.39 cubic inches, which rounds to 97 cubic inches. The largest possible volume, in cubic inches, can be found by substituting 2 for r and 8 for h, giving $V = \pi(2^2)(8)$. This gives a volume of approximately 100.53 cubic inches, which rounds to 101 cubic inches. Therefore, the possible volumes are all the integers greater than or equal to 97 and less than or equal to 101, which are 97, 98, 99, 100, and 101. Any of these numbers may be entered as the correct answer.

Coordinate Geometry

Questions in the Geometry and Trigonometry domain may ask you to use the coordinate plane and equations of lines and circles to describe figures. You may be asked to create the equation of a circle given the figure or use the structure of a given equation to determine a property of a figure in the coordinate plane. You should know that the graph of $(x - a)^2 + (y - b)^2 = r^2$ in the xy-plane is a circle with center (a, b) and radius r.

Geometry and Trigonometry Sample Question 7

$$x^2 + (y + 1)^2 = 4$$

The graph of the given equation in the xy-plane is a circle. A new circle is drawn whose center is 1 unit up from this circle and whose radius is 1 more than this circle. Which of the following is an equation of this new circle?

A) $x^2 + y^2 = 5$

B) $x^2 + y^2 = 9$

C) $x^2 + (y + 2)^2 = 5$

D) $x^2 + (y + 2)^2 = 9$

The graph of the given equation $x^2 + (y + 1)^2 = 4$ in the xy-plane is a circle with center $(0, -1)$ and radius $\sqrt{4} = 2$. If the center of the new circle is 1 unit up from the center of the given circle, the center of the new circle will be $(0, 0)$. If the radius of the new circle is 1 more than the given circle, the radius of the new circle will be 3. Therefore, an equation of the new circle in the xy-plane is $x^2 + y^2 = 3^2 = 9$, so choice B is correct.

Geometry and Trigonometry Sample Question 8

$$x^2 + 8x + y^2 - 6y = 24$$

The graph of the given equation in the xy-plane is a circle. What is the radius of the circle?

REMINDER

You should know that the graph of $(x - a)^2 + (y - b)^2 = r^2$ in the xy-plane is a circle with center (a, b) and radius r. You should also be comfortable finding the center or radius of a circle from an equation not written in "standard form" by using the method of completing the square to rewrite the equation in standard form.

The given equation isn't in the standard form $(x - a)^2 + (y - b)^2 = r^2$. You can put it in standard form by completing the square. Since the coefficient of x is 8 and the coefficient of y is -6, you can write the equation in terms of $(x + 4)^2$ and $(y - 3)^2$ as follows:

$$x^2 + 8x + y^2 - 6y = 24$$
$$(x^2 + 8x + 16) - 16 + (y^2 - 6y + 9) - 9 = 24$$
$$(x + 4)^2 - 16 + (y - 3)^2 - 9 = 24$$
$$(x + 4)^2 + (y - 3)^2 = 24 + 16 + 9$$
$$(x + 4)^2 + (y - 3)^2 = 49$$

Since $49 = 7^2$, the radius of the circle is 7. (Also, the center of the circle is $(-4, 3)$.)

Trigonometry and Radians

Questions in the Geometry and Trigonometry domain may ask you to apply the definitions from right triangle trigonometry. You should also know the definition of radian measure; you may also need to convert between angle measure in degrees and radians. You may need to evaluate trigonometric functions at benchmark angle measures such as 0, $\frac{\pi}{6}$, $\frac{\pi}{4}$, $\frac{\pi}{3}$, and $\frac{\pi}{2}$ radians (which are equal to the angle measures $0°$, $30°$, $45°$, $60°$, and $90°$, respectively). You will *not* be asked for values of trigonometric functions that require a calculator.

For an acute angle, the trigonometric functions sine, cosine, and tangent can be defined using right triangles. (Note the functions are often abbreviated as sin, cos, and tan, respectively.)

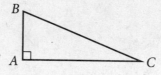

For $\angle C$ in the right triangle shown:

- $\sin \angle C = \dfrac{AB}{BC} = \dfrac{\text{length of leg opposite } \angle C}{\text{length of hypotenuse}}$

- $\cos \angle C = \dfrac{AC}{BC} = \dfrac{\text{length of leg adjacent to } \angle C}{\text{length of hypotenuse}}$

- $\tan \angle C = \dfrac{AB}{AC} = \dfrac{\text{length of leg opposite } \angle C}{\text{length of leg adjacent to } \angle C} = \dfrac{\sin \angle C}{\cos \angle C}$

The functions will often be written as sin C, cos C, and tan C, respectively.

Note that the trigonometric functions are actually functions of the *measures* of an angle, not the angle itself. Thus, if the measure of $\angle C$ is, say, $30°$, you can write sin $30°$, cos $30°$, and tan $30°$, respectively.

REMINDER

The acronym "SOHCAHTOA" may help you remember how to compute sine, cosine, and tangent. SOH stands for Sine equals Opposite over Hypotenuse, CAH stands for Cosine equals Adjacent over Hypotenuse, and TOA stands for Tangent equals Opposite over Adjacent.

Also note that sine and cosine are cofunctions and that

$\sin B = \dfrac{\text{length of leg opposite } \angle B}{\text{length of hypotenuse}} = \dfrac{AC}{BC} = \cos C.$ This is the

complementary angle relationship: $\sin x° = \cos (90° - x°).$

Geometry and Trigonometry Sample Question 9

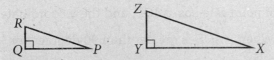

In the figure, right triangle *PQR* is similar to right triangle *XYZ*, with
vertices *P*, *Q*, and *R* corresponding to vertices *X*, *Y*, and *Z*, respectively.
If cos *R* = 0.263, what is the value of cos *Z*?

By the definition of cosine, $\cos R = \dfrac{RQ}{RP}$ and $\cos Z = \dfrac{ZY}{ZX}$. Since triangle

PQR is similar to triangle *XYZ*, with vertices *P*, *Q*, and *R* corresponding
to vertices *X*, *Y*, and *Z*, respectively, the ratios $\dfrac{RQ}{RP}$ and $\dfrac{ZY}{ZX}$ are

equal. Therefore, since $\cos R = \dfrac{RQ}{RP}$, or cos *R* = 0.263, it follows that

$\cos Z = \dfrac{ZY}{ZX}$, or cos *Z* = 0.263. Note that to find the values of the

trigonometric functions of *d*°, you can use *any* right triangle with an
acute angle of measure *d*° and then find the appropriate ratio of lengths
of sides.

Note that since an acute angle of a right triangle has a measure
between 0° and 90°, exclusive, right triangles can be used only to find
values of trigonometric functions for angles with measures between
0° and 90°, exclusive. The definitions of sine, cosine, and tangent can
be extended to all values. This is done using radian measure and the
unit circle.

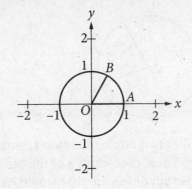

The circle above has radius 1 and is centered on the origin, *O*. An
angle in the coordinate plane is said to be in *standard position* if
it meets these two conditions: (1) its vertex lies at the origin and
(2) one of its sides lies along the positive *x*-axis. Since ∠*AOB*, above,
formed by segments *OA* and *OB*, meets both these conditions, it's in

standard position. As segment OB, also called the *terminal side* of $\angle AOB$, rotates counterclockwise about the circle, while OA is anchored along the x-axis, the *radian* measure of $\angle AOB$ is defined to be the length s of the arc that $\angle AOB$ intercepts on the unit circle. In other words, the measure of $\angle AOB$ is s radians.

When an acute $\angle AOB$ is in standard position within the unit circle, the x-coordinate of point B is cos $\angle AOB$, and the y-coordinate of point B is sin $\angle AOB$. When $\angle AOB$ is greater than 90 degrees (or $\frac{\pi}{2}$ radians), and point B extends beyond the boundaries of the positive x-axis and positive y-axis, the values of cos $\angle AOB$ and sin $\angle AOB$ may be negative depending on the coordinates of point B. For any $\angle AOB$, place $\angle AOB$ in standard position within the circle of radius 1 centered at the origin, with side OA along the positive x-axis and terminal side OB intersecting the circle at point B. Then the cosine of $\angle AOB$ is the x-coordinate of B, and the sine of $\angle AOB$ is the y-coordinate of B. The tangent of $\angle AOB$ is the sine of $\angle AOB$ divided by the cosine of $\angle AOB$.

An angle with a full rotation about point O has measure 360°. This angle intercepts the full circumference of the circle, which has length 2π. Thus, $\frac{\text{measure of an angle in radians}}{\text{measure of an angle in degrees}} = \frac{2\pi}{360°}$. It follows that the measure of an angle in radians is $\frac{2\pi}{360°} \times$ the measure of the angle in degrees and that the measure of an angle in degrees is $\frac{360°}{2\pi} \times$ the measure of the angle in radians.

Also note that since a rotation of 2π about point O brings you back to the same point on the unit circle, sin $(s + 2\pi) =$ sin s, cos $(s + 2\pi) =$ cos s, and tan $(s + 2\pi)$, for any radian measure s.

Let angle DEF be a central angle in a circle of radius r, as shown in the following figure.

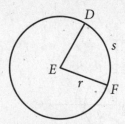

A circle of radius r is similar to a circle of radius 1, with constant of proportionality equal to r. Thus, the length s of the arc intercepted by angle DEF is r times the length of the arc that would be intercepted by an angle of the same measure in a circle of radius 1. Therefore, in the figure above, $s = r \times$ (radian measure of angle DEF), or radian measure of angle $DEF = \frac{s}{r}$.

Geometry and Trigonometry Sample Question 10

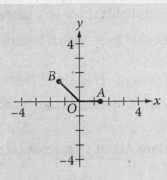

In the figure shown, the coordinates of point B are $(-\sqrt{2}, \sqrt{2})$. What is the measure, in radians, of angle AOB?

A) $\dfrac{\pi}{4}$

B) $\dfrac{\pi}{2}$

C) $\dfrac{3\pi}{4}$

D) $\dfrac{5\pi}{4}$

Let C be the point $(-\sqrt{2}, 0)$. Then triangle BOC, shown in the figure below, is a right triangle with both legs of length $\sqrt{2}$.

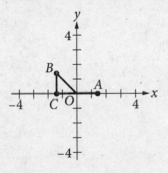

STRATEGY

Always be on the lookout for special right triangles. Here, noticing that segment OB is the hypotenuse of a 45°-45°-90° triangle makes this question easier to solve.

Hence, triangle BOC is a 45°-45°-90° triangle. Thus, angle COB has measure 45°, and angle AOB has measure 180° − 45° = 135°. Therefore, the measure of angle AOB in radians is $135° \times \dfrac{2\pi}{360°} = \dfrac{3\pi}{4}$, which is choice C.

Geometry and Trigonometry Sample Question 11

$$\sin x = \cos (K - x)$$

In the given equation, the angle measures are in radians and K is a constant. Which of the following could be the value of K?

A) 0

B) $\dfrac{\pi}{4}$

C) $\dfrac{\pi}{2}$

D) π

The complementary angle relationship for sine and cosine implies that the equation $\sin x = \cos (K - x)$ holds if $K = 90°$. Since $90° = \frac{2\pi}{360°} \times 90°$, or $\frac{\pi}{2}$ radians, the value of K could be $\frac{\pi}{2}$, which is choice C.

Summary: Geometry and Trigonometry Questions

Main purpose: To assess your understanding of concepts central to geometry and trigonometry

Proportion of the test section: About 15 percent (approximately five to seven questions)

Question types

- Area and volume

- Lines, angles, and triangles

- Right triangles and trigonometry

- Circles

CHAPTER 28

Math: Questions—Geometry and Trigonometry Drills

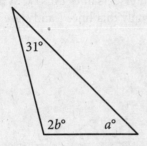

In the triangle shown, $a = 45$. What is the value of b?

A) 52

B) 59

C) 76

D) 104

A cube has a surface area of 54 square meters. What is the volume, in cubic meters, of the cube?

A) 18

B) 27

C) 36

D) 81

In the xy-plane, a circle with radius 5 has center $(-8, 6)$. Which of the following is an equation of the circle?

A) $(x - 8)^2 + (y + 6)^2 = 25$

B) $(x + 8)^2 + (y - 6)^2 = 25$

C) $(x - 8)^3 + (y + 6)^2 = 5$

D) $(x + 8)^2 + (y - 6)^2 = 5$

4

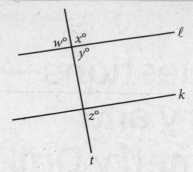

Note: Figure not drawn to scale.

In the figure shown, line t intersects lines ℓ and k. Which of the following statements, if true, would imply that lines ℓ and k are parallel?

A) $w = y$

B) $w = z$

C) $x = z$

D) $x + y = 180$

5

In a right triangle, the tangent of one of the two acute angles is $\frac{\sqrt{3}}{3}$. What is the tangent of the other acute angle?

A) $-\frac{\sqrt{3}}{3}$

B) $-\frac{3}{\sqrt{3}}$

C) $\frac{\sqrt{3}}{3}$

D) $\frac{3}{\sqrt{3}}$

6

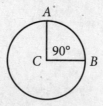

Point C is the center of the circle shown. What is the measure of angle ACB, in radians?

A) 2π

B) π

C) $\frac{\pi}{2}$

D) $\frac{\pi}{4}$

7

The length of one side of square M is 5 times the length of one side of square N. The area of square N is 361 square centimeters. What is the area, in square centimeters, of square M?

8

Triangle *KLM* is similar to triangle *QRS*, where angle *K* corresponds to angle *Q* and where angles *L* and *R* are right angles. If $\sin K = \frac{105}{233}$ and $\sin M = \frac{208}{233}$, what is the value of $\tan S$?

9

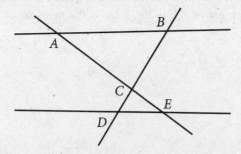

Note: Figure not drawn to scale.

In the figure shown, $\triangle ABC$ is similar to $\triangle EDC$, with $\angle BAC$ corresponding to $\angle CED$ and $\angle ABC$ corresponding to $\angle CDE$. Which of the following must be true?

A) $\overline{AE} \parallel \overline{BD}$

B) $\overline{AE} \perp \overline{BD}$

C) $\overline{AB} \parallel \overline{DE}$

D) $\overline{AB} \perp \overline{DE}$

10

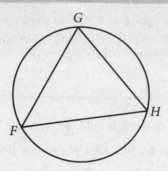

Note: Figure not drawn to scale.

Triangle *FGH* is inscribed in the circle shown. If arc *FG* is congruent to arc *GH* and the measure of ∠*G* is 30°, what is the measure of ∠*H*?

A) 30°

B) 60°

C) 75°

D) 120°

11

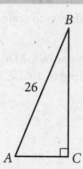

Triangle *ABC* shown is a right triangle, and $\sin B = \frac{5}{13}$. What is the length of side $\overline{BC}$?

12

An architect drew the sketch shown while designing a house roof. The dimensions shown are for the interior of the triangle.

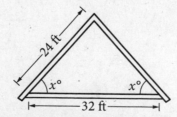

Note: Figure not drawn to scale.

What is the value of cos *x*?

13

Line ℓ is parallel to line m. Points A and B lie on line ℓ, and points P and Q lie on line m. If $\angle ABP$ and $\angle QAB$ each have measure 21° and $\angle AQB$ has measure 76°, what is the measure, in degrees, of $\angle PAQ$?

14

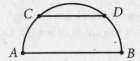

The semicircle shown has a radius of r inches, and chord $\overline{CD}$ is parallel to the diameter $\overline{AB}$. If the length of $\overline{CD}$ is $\frac{2}{3}$ of the length of $\overline{AB}$, what is the distance between the chord and the diameter in terms of r?

A) $\frac{1}{3}\pi r$

B) $\frac{2}{3}\pi r$

C) $\frac{\sqrt{2}}{2} r$

D) $\frac{\sqrt{5}}{3} r$

Answer Explanations

QUESTION 1

Choice A is correct. The sum of the measures of the three interior angles of a triangle is 180°. Therefore, $31 + 2b + a = 180$. Since it's given that $a = 45$, it follows that $31 + 2b + 45 = 180$, or $2b = 104$. Dividing both sides of this equation by 2 yields $b = 52$.

Choice B is incorrect and may result from conceptual or calculation errors. *Choice C* is incorrect. This is the value of $a + 31$. *Choice D* is incorrect. This is the value of $2b$.

QUESTION 2

Choice B is correct. The surface area of a cube with side length s is equal to $6s^2$. Since the surface area is given as 54 square meters, the equation $54 = 6s^2$ can be used to solve for s. Dividing both sides of this equation by 6 yields $9 = s^2$. Taking the square root of both sides of this equation yields $3 = s$ and $-3 = s$. Since the side length of a cube must be a positive value, it follows that $s = 3$. The volume of a cube with side length s is equal to s^3. Therefore, the volume of this cube, in cubic meters, is 3^3, or 27.

Choices A, C, and *D* are incorrect and may result from conceptual or calculation errors.

QUESTION 3

Choice B is correct. An equation of a circle in the xy-plane is $(x - h)^2 + (y - k)^2 = r^2$, where the center of the circle is (h, k) and the radius is r. It's given that the center of this circle is $(-8, 6)$ and the radius is 5. Substituting these values into the equation $(x - h)^2 + (y - k)^2 = r^2$ gives $(x - (-8))^2 + (y - 6)^2 = 5^2$, or $(x + 8)^2 + (y - 6)^2 = 25$.

Choice A is incorrect. This is an equation of a circle that has center $(8, -6)$. *Choice C* is incorrect. This is an equation of a circle that has center $(8, -6)$ and radius $\sqrt{5}$. *Choice D* is incorrect. This is an equation of a circle that has radius $\sqrt{5}$.

QUESTION 4

Choice B is correct. Two lines are parallel if the alternate exterior angles are congruent. The angles with measures of $w°$ and $z°$ are alternate exterior angles. If $w = z$, then these alternate exterior angles would be congruent, which would imply that the lines ℓ and k are parallel.

Choice A is incorrect. Although it's true that $w = y$, since vertical angles are congruent, this doesn't provide enough information to imply that lines ℓ and k are parallel. *Choice C* is incorrect. The angles with measures $x°$ and $z°$ must be supplementary, instead of congruent, to imply that lines ℓ and k are parallel. *Choice D* is incorrect. Although it's true that $x + y = 180$, since the sum of the measures of a linear pair of angles is 180°, this doesn't provide enough information to imply that lines ℓ and k are parallel.

QUESTION 5

Choice D is correct. The tangent of a non-right angle in a right triangle is defined as the ratio of the length of the leg opposite the angle to the length of the leg adjacent to the angle. Using this definition for tangent, in a right triangle with legs that have lengths a and b, the tangent of one acute angle is $\frac{a}{b}$ and the tangent for the other acute angle is $\frac{b}{a}$. It follows that the tangents of the acute angles in a right triangle are reciprocals of each other. Therefore, the tangent of the other acute angle in the given triangle is the reciprocal of $\frac{\sqrt{3}}{3}$, or $\frac{3}{\sqrt{3}}$.

Choices A, B, and C are incorrect and may result from conceptual or calculation errors.

QUESTION 6

Choice C is correct. It's given that the measure of angle *ACB* is 90°. Since 180° is equivalent to π radians and angle *ACB* is the equivalent of $\frac{180°}{2}$, it follows that the measure of angle *ACB*, in radians, is $\frac{\pi}{2}$.

Choices A, B, and D are incorrect and may result from conceptual or calculation errors.

QUESTION 7

The correct answer is 9,025. It's given that the length of one side of square M is 5 times the length of one side of square N. Let *m* and *n* represent the lengths, in centimeters, of each side of square M and square N, respectively. It follows that $m = 5n$ and the areas, in square centimeters, of squares M and N are m^2 and n^2, respectively. Squaring both sides of the equation $m = 5n$ yields $m^2 = (5n)^2$, which is equivalent to $m^2 = 25n^2$. It's given that the area of square N is 361 square centimeters. Substituting 361 for n^2 in the equation $m^2 = 25n^2$ yields $m^2 = 25(361)$, or $m^2 = 9,025$. Therefore, the area, in square centimeters, of square M is 9,025.

QUESTION 8

The correct answer is 1.981. It's given that triangle *KLM* is similar to triangle *QRS*, where angle *K* corresponds to angle *Q* and where angles *L* and *R* are right angles. Since corresponding angles in similar triangles have equal measures, the sines, cosines, and tangents, respectively, of corresponding angles are equivalent. Therefore, tan *S* = tan *M*. In a right triangle, the sine of an acute angle is the ratio of the length of the leg opposite the angle to the length of the hypotenuse. It follows that in triangle *KLM*, $\sin K = \frac{LM}{MK}$ and $\sin M = \frac{KL}{MK}$. If $\sin K = \frac{105}{233}$ and $\sin M = \frac{208}{233}$, then $\frac{LM}{MK} = \frac{105}{233}$ and $\frac{KL}{MK} = \frac{208}{233}$. It follows from these ratios that for some constant *d*, LM = 105*d*, MK = 233*d*, and KL = 208*d*.

The tangent of an acute angle in a right triangle is the ratio of the length of the leg opposite the angle to the length of the leg adjacent to the angle. It follows that in triangle *KLM*, $\tan M = \frac{KL}{LM}$. Thus, $\tan M = \frac{208d}{105d}$, or $\tan M = \frac{208}{105}$. Since tan *S* = tan *M*, the value of tan *S* is $\frac{208}{105}$, or approximately 1.981. Note that 1.981 and 1.98 are examples of ways to enter a correct answer.

QUESTION 9

Choice C is correct. It's given that ΔABC is similar to ΔEDC and that ∠BAC corresponds to ∠CED. Since the two triangles are similar, corresponding angles are congruent. Therefore, ∠BAC is congruent to ∠CED. The alternate interior angle theorem states that when two parallel lines are cut by a transversal, alternate interior angles are congruent. The converse of this theorem is also true, which implies that $\overline{AB}$ is parallel to $\overline{DE}$.

Choice A is incorrect. The figure shows that $\overline{AE}$ and $\overline{BD}$ intersect; therefore, they can't be parallel. *Choice B* is incorrect. While $\overline{AE}$ and $\overline{BD}$ appear to form a 90° angle, there isn't sufficient information to prove that $\overline{AE}$ is perpendicular to $\overline{BD}$. *Choice D* is incorrect. $\overline{AB}$ is parallel, not perpendicular, to $\overline{DE}$.

QUESTION 10

Choice C is correct. The measure of an inscribed angle is equal to half the measure of the arc the angle intercepts. Therefore, the measure of ∠H is equal to half the measure of arc *FG* and the measure of ∠F is equal to half the measure of arc *GH*. If arcs *FG* and *GH* are congruent, it follows that the measures of angles *H* and *F* must be equal. Let the measure of ∠H be $x°$. Therefore, the measure of ∠F is also $x°$. Since the sum of the three interior angles of a triangle is 180°, it follows that the sum of the measures of angles *F*, *G*, and *H* is 180°. Therefore, $x + x + 30 = 180$. Adding like terms on the left-hand side and subtracting 30 from both sides of this equation gives $2x = 150$. Dividing both sides of this equation by 2 yields $x = 75$. Therefore, the measure of ∠H is 75°.

Choice A is incorrect. This is the measure of ∠G, which isn't congruent to ∠H. *Choice B* is incorrect. This is twice the measure of ∠G, not the measure of ∠H. *Choice D* is incorrect and may result from a conceptual or calculation error.

QUESTION 11

The correct answer is 24. The sine of an acute angle in a right triangle is equal to the ratio of the length of the side opposite the angle to the length of the hypotenuse. In the triangle shown, the sine of angle *B*, or sin *B*, is equal to the ratio of the length of side *AC* to the length of side *AB*. It's given that the length of side *AB* is 26 and that $\sin(B) = \frac{5}{13}$. Therefore, $\frac{5}{13} = \frac{AC}{26}$. Multiplying both sides of this equation by 26 yields $AC = 10$. Using the Pythagorean theorem, it follows that $AB^2 = AC^2 + BC^2$. Substituting 26 for *AB* and 10 for *AC* in this equation gives $26^2 = 10^2 + BC^2$, or $676 = 100 + BC^2$. Subtracting 100 from both sides of $676 = 100 + BC^2$ yields $576 = BC^2$. Taking the square root of both sides of $576 = BC^2$ yields $-24 = BC$ or $24 = BC$. Since the side length of a triangle must be a positive value, the length of side *BC* is 24.

QUESTION 12

The correct answer is $\frac{2}{3}$. The given sketch of the house roof shows that the two base angles of the triangle are congruent, which means the triangle is isosceles. Constructing a perpendicular line from the vertex of the isosceles triangle to the opposite side will bisect the base of the triangle and create two smaller right triangles. In a right triangle, the cosine of an acute angle is equal to the ratio of the length of the side adjacent to the angle to the length of the hypotenuse. This gives $\cos x = \frac{16}{24}$, which can be rewritten as $\cos x = \frac{2}{3}$. Note that 2/3, 16/24, .6666, .6667, 0.666, and 0.667 are examples of ways to enter a correct answer.

QUESTION 13

The correct answer is 62. It's given that line ℓ is parallel to line m, where points A and B lie on line ℓ and points P and Q lie on line m. If a line segment is drawn from point B to point P and a line segment is drawn from point A to point Q, then angles ABP and QAB are formed. It's given that each of these angles has a measure of 21°. Let the intersection of $\overline{BP}$ and $\overline{AQ}$ be point T, which lies between lines ℓ and m. Since the sum of the interior angles of a triangle is 180°, it follows that in triangle ABT, the measure of angle ATB is equal to 180° − 2(21°), or 138°. Angles ATB and ATP are adjacent angles that form a straight line segment, $\overline{BP}$. Since a line segment is a straight angle that measures 180°, by the angle addition postulate, it follows that the measure of angle ATP is 180° − 138°, or 42°. Angles ATP and BTQ are vertical angles and are therefore congruent. Therefore, the measure of angle BTQ is also 42°. Angles ABP and BPQ are alternate interior angles. Since lines ℓ and m are parallel, angles ABP and BPQ are congruent. Therefore, the measure of angle BPQ is also 21°. Similarly, angles QAB and AQP are congruent alternate interior angles. Therefore, angle AQP also measures 21°. It follows that triangle ABT is an isosceles triangle, where $AT = BT$, and triangle PQT is an isosceles triangle, where $PT = QT$. If a line segment is drawn from point A to point P and a line segment is drawn from point B to point Q, then triangles ATP and BTQ are formed. Since $AT = BT$, $PT = QT$, and the measure of angle ATP is equal to the measure of angle BTQ, by the side-angle-side theorem, triangle ATP is congruent to triangle BTQ. In triangles ATP and BTQ, angle ATP corresponds to angle BTQ, angle TPA corresponds to angle TQB, and angle PAT corresponds to angle QBT. It's given that the measure of angle AQB is 76°. Since angle AQB and angle TQB are the same angle, the measure of angle TQB is 76°. Therefore, in triangle BTQ, by the triangle angle sum theorem, it follows that the measure of angle QBT is 180° − 42° − 76°, or 62°. In congruent triangles, corresponding angles have equal measure. Therefore, the measure of angle PAT is 62°. Since angle PAT and angle PAQ are the same angle, the measure, in degrees, of angle PAQ is 62.

QUESTION 14

Choice D is correct. Let the semicircle have center O. The diameter $\overline{AB}$ has length $2r$. If chord $\overline{CD}$ is $\frac{2}{3}$ of the length of the diameter, then $CD = \frac{2}{3}(2r)$, or $CD = \frac{4}{3}r$. It follows that $\frac{1}{2}CD = \frac{1}{2}\left(\frac{4}{3}\right)r$, or $\frac{1}{2}CD = \frac{2}{3}r$. The distance, x, between $\overline{AB}$ and $\overline{CD}$ can be found by drawing a right triangle connecting center O, the midpoint of chord $\overline{CD}$, and point C. Using the Pythagorean theorem, it follows that $r^2 = x^2 + \left(\frac{2}{3}r\right)^2$, or $r^2 = x^2 + \frac{4}{9}r^2$. Subtracting $\frac{4}{9}r^2$ from both sides of this equation yields $\frac{5}{9}r^2 = x^2$. Finally, taking the square root of both sides of this equation gives $x = \frac{\sqrt{5}}{3}r$ or $x = -\frac{\sqrt{5}}{3}r$. Since the distance between the chord and the diameter must be positive, this distance in terms of r is $\frac{\sqrt{5}}{3}r$.

Choices A, B, and C are incorrect and may result from conceptual or calculation errors.

CHAPTER 29

Math: Student-Produced Response (SPR) Questions

In earlier chapters, we presented numerous examples of Math section questions in the student-produced response, or SPR, format. In this brief chapter, we go over the directions for entering answers to these sorts of questions.

REMINDER

About 25 percent of questions in the Math section are in the student-produced response (SPR) format.

SPRs IN PRACTICE AND ACTUAL TESTS

The following describes how to enter SPR answers into Bluebook, the digital testing app. This guidance applies to taking a practice test digitally in Bluebook or an actual SAT digitally.

If you're using the paper-based practice test forms at the end of this book to prepare, write your answer to a given SPR question next to or under the question in this book. Once you've written your answer, circle it.

SPR Directions

You'll have ready access to the SPR directions while you take the digital SAT, so there's no need to memorize them in every detail prior to test day. However, as we discussed in chapter 5, being familiar with the directions in advance of testing is beneficial to you because it will both save you time—you can devote more time to answering questions—and make it less likely that you'll make a careless mistake when entering your answers.

Figure 1 displays the official directions for how to enter responses to SPR questions.

Figure 1. Math Section: Student-Produced Response (SPR) Entry Directions.

For student-produced response questions, solve each problem and enter your answer as described below.

- If you find **more than one correct answer,** enter only one answer.
- You can enter up to 5 characters for a **positive** answer and up to 6 characters (including the negative sign) for a **negative** answer.
- If your answer is a **fraction** that doesn't fit in the provided space, enter the decimal equivalent.
- If your answer is a **decimal** that doesn't fit in the provided space, enter it by truncating or rounding at the fourth digit.
- If your answer is a **mixed number** (such as $3\frac{1}{2}$), enter it as an improper fraction (7/2) or its decimal equivalent (3.5).
- Don't enter **symbols** such as a percent sign, comma, or dollar sign.

Examples

Answer	Acceptable ways to enter answer	Unacceptable: will NOT receive credit
3.5	3.5 3.50 7/2	31/2 3 1/2
$\frac{2}{3}$	2/3 .6666 .6667 0.666 0.667	0.66 .66 0.67 .67
$-\frac{1}{3}$	−1/3 −.3333 −0.333	−.33 −0.33

Unacceptable and Acceptable Answers

The directions themselves are clear on what can and can't be entered into an SPR answer field, but let's go over what disqualifies the "unacceptable" answers (as well as a few other examples) to clarify what makes them impermissible and to help you avoid making these (and similar) entry mistakes.

Table 1. Math Section: Examples of Unacceptable and Acceptable SPR Answers.

Intended answer	Unacceptable answer(s)	Reason	Acceptable answer(s)
3.5	31/2 3 1/2	Mixed numbers should be entered as improper fractions or as decimal equivalents.	7/2 (improper fraction that fits the space) 3.5 (decimal equivalent)
$\frac{2}{3}$	0.66 .66 0.67 .67	Decimals that don't fit the provided space should be truncated or rounded at the fourth digit.	2/3 (fraction that fits the space) .6666 (decimal truncated at the fourth digit) .6667 (decimal rounded at the fourth digit) 0.666 (decimal truncated at the fourth digit, includes leading zero) 0.667 (decimal rounded at the fourth digit, includes leading zero)
$-\frac{1}{3}$	−0.33	Decimals that don't fit the provided space should be truncated or rounded at the fourth digit.	−1/3 (fraction that fits the space) −.3333 (decimal rounded or truncated at the fourth digit) −0.333 (decimal rounded or truncated at the fourth digit, includes leading zero)
$2.53	$2.53	Answers may not include symbols such as a dollar sign.	2.53
68,132	68,132	Answers may not include symbols such as a comma.	68132
45%	45%	Answers may not include symbols such as a percent sign.	0.45

Confirming Your Answers

The Bluebook test application includes a feature called Answer Preview for each SPR question. Answer Preview shows you how the test interprets the response you entered to a given question so that you can confirm that your intended answer is properly reflected. If it's not, you'll have a chance to change it should time permit.

For example, to continue from the cases presented in the preceding table, let's assume that you had intended your answer to a given SPR question to be $3\frac{1}{2}$ and that, contrary to the guidelines above, you decided to enter this as 31/2, with the goal of representing your answer as a mixed number. Answer Preview would inform you that it interprets this response as the fraction $\frac{31}{2}$, which isn't what you intended.

Recognizing your error, you instead enter either 7/2, an improper fraction, or 3.5, the decimal equivalent of $3\frac{1}{2}$.

CHAPTER 30

Calculator Options

The use of a calculator is permitted throughout the Math section (but not the Reading and Writing section) of the digital SAT. You have two options in terms of tools on test day: (1) you may bring your own approved calculator or (2) you may use the Desmos Graphing Calculator built into Bluebook, the digital testing app. The choice you make should be based primarily on which tool you're more comfortable with. We recommend that you try out both options during your practice.

Bringing Your Own Calculator

College Board allows digital SAT test takers to use their own approved calculator on test day. To ensure that you have up-to-date information on which calculators are and aren't permitted, please visit **satsuite.collegeboard.org/digital/what-to-bring-do/calculator-policy**.

Using the Built-In Desmos Graphing Calculator

The embedded calculator available for test takers in Bluebook is the Desmos Graphing Calculator, a fully digital, accessible graphing calculator used for computational, graphing, statistical, and other mathematical purposes. You may already be familiar with the Desmos calculator from your classes, as it's an application commonly used in education as well as in other fields.

The Testing Calculator

The Desmos Graphing Calculator embedded in Bluebook mimics the experience users see at **desmos.com/calculator**, except that images, folders, and notes (usually available via the plus mark button—i.e., the "Add Icon" button atop the expression list) are removed in the testing calculator.

Figure 1. Desmos Graphing Calculator—Standard View in Bluebook with Keypad Open.

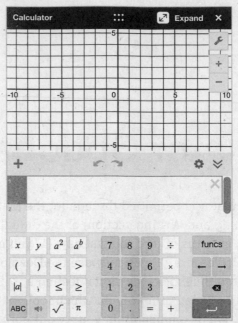

Figure 2. Desmos Graphing Calculator—Expanded View in Bluebook.

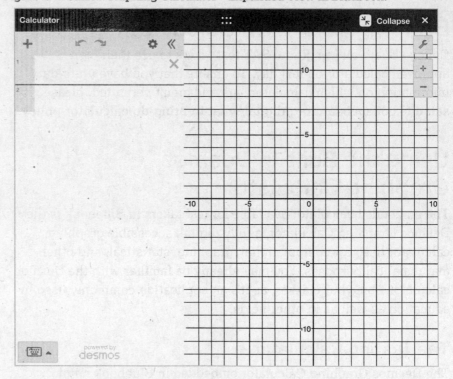

A PDF document explaining the slight differences between the online Demos Graphing Calculator and the one embedded in Bluebook, along with a practice calculator that mimics the exact version available in Bluebook, can be found at **desmos.com/testing**. The version of the Desmos Graphing Calculator for the digital SAT is also available at **desmos.com/practice** and on the Desmos Test Mode app available for Chromebooks (Chrome Web Store) and for iPads and iPhones (Apple's App Store).

Notable Features

For students and users new to the Desmos Graphing Calculator, please reference the frequently asked questions (FAQ) document (**help.desmos.com/hc/en-us/articles/4406360401677**) available at the Desmos Help Center to get started with basic functionality around plotting points, graphing lines and curves, adjusting display settings, and more.

Accessibility Settings

The Desmos Graphing Calculator was designed with all learners in mind. Accessibility features available to digital SAT test takers in the Desmos Graphing Calculator include

- Text-to-Speech and Audio Trace capabilities: **desmos.com/accessibility#setup**

- Enlarge Display, Reverse Contrast, and additional options: **help.desmos.com/hc/en-us/articles/5685797932813**

- Braille Mode: **desmos.com/braille-examples**

CHAPTER 31

Math: Reference Sheet

You'll have access to the following common formulas at any time as you take the digital SAT.

$A = \pi r^2$
$C = 2\pi r$

$A = \ell w$

$A = \frac{1}{2} bh$

$c^2 = a^2 + b^2$

Special Right Triangles

$V = \ell wh$

$V = \pi r^2 h$

$V = \frac{4}{3} \pi r^3$

$V = \frac{1}{3} \pi r^2 h$

$V = \frac{1}{3} \ell wh$

Practice Tests

Introduction to the Practice Tests

Part 4 of this book consists of four official full-length SAT practice tests accompanied by answer explanations and scoring guidelines. These practice tests were assembled using the same processes and standards College Board employs to construct actual SAT tests, so you can prepare for test day confident in the knowledge that your practice will be as authentic as possible.

We strongly recommend that you take at least one full-length practice test, under timed conditions, prior to test day to get a clear sense of how the test is put together and how to pace yourself.

About These Practice Tests

The four practice tests included in this book may be used as part of your preparation for test day. For the best and most realistic practice experience, however, **we strongly recommend that you take these tests digitally in the Bluebook test application** unless you know that you'll be taking the actual test on paper owing to a testing accommodation. Practicing in Bluebook gives you valuable exposure to the app's interface and tools in a low-stakes environment, allows you to experience how adaptive testing works, and yields section and total scores that you don't have to calculate yourself.

If you do use the practice tests printed in this book, please be aware that they aren't adaptive like the corresponding versions in Bluebook. While each test form begins with a medium-difficulty first-stage module, **Practice Tests 1 and 3 include (only) a lower-difficulty second-stage module, whereas Practice Tests 2 and 4 include (only) a higher-difficulty second-stage module.** To simulate (as best as possible on paper) the full test experience, we recommend taking *both* Practice Tests 1 and 2 or Practice Tests 3 and 4 in this guide so that you get a better sense of the full range of question difficulty found on the digital SAT administered in Bluebook. For more information on how adaptive testing in the digital SAT works, see chapter 2.

Important

College Board includes a small number of unscored questions in test forms—including these practice test forms—for research purposes. Your answers to these questions don't affect your score in any way.

In the scoring guides that follow each practice test in this book, the rows in the "SAT Practice Test Worksheet: Answer Key" corresponding to unscored questions are grayed out. You should **not** consider these questions when calculating your raw scores for the Reading and Writing and Math sections. (A reminder of this appears in each scoring guide.)

Note also that the placement of unscored questions within digital SAT test forms isn't fixed. This means that the locations of the unscored questions in the practice tests in this book are only examples and that such questions may appear in different locations in actual digital SAT test forms. You should give your best effort to answering each and every question on the test.

The SAT®

Practice Test #1

Make time to take the practice test.
It is one of the best ways to get ready for the SAT.

After you have taken the practice test, score it right away using materials provided in *The Official Digital SAT Study Guide*.

This version of the SAT Practice Test is for students using this guide. As a reminder, most students taking the digital SAT will do so using Bluebook™, the digital testing application. To best prepare for test day, download Bluebook at **bluebook.app.collegeboard.org** to take the practice test in the digital format.

Test begins on the next page.

Reading and Writing

27 QUESTIONS

DIRECTIONS

The questions in this section address a number of important reading and writing skills. Each question includes one or more passages, which may include a table or graph. Read each passage and question carefully, and then choose the best answer to the question based on the passage(s).

All questions in this section are multiple-choice with four answer choices. Each question has a single best answer.

1

Researchers and conservationists stress that biodiversity loss due to invasive species is _____. For example, people can take simple steps such as washing their footwear after travel to avoid introducing potentially invasive organisms into new environments.

Which choice completes the text with the most logical and precise word or phrase?

A) preventable

B) undeniable

C) common

D) concerning

2

It is by no means _____ to recognize the influence of Dutch painter Hieronymus Bosch on Ali Banisadr's paintings; indeed, Banisadr himself cites Bosch as an inspiration. However, some scholars have suggested that the ancient Mesopotamian poem *Epic of Gilgamesh* may have had a far greater impact on Banisadr's work.

Which choice completes the text with the most logical and precise word or phrase?

A) substantial

B) satisfying

C) unimportant

D) appropriate

3

Astronomers are confident that the star Betelgeuse will eventually consume all the helium in its core and explode in a supernova. <u>They are much less confident, however, about when this will happen, since that depends on internal characteristics of Betelgeuse that are largely unknown.</u> Astrophysicist Sarafina El-Badry Nance and colleagues recently investigated whether acoustic waves in the star could be used to determine internal stellar states but concluded that this method could not sufficiently reveal Betelgeuse's internal characteristics to allow its evolutionary state to be firmly fixed.

Which choice best describes the function of the second sentence in the overall structure of the text?

A) It explains how the work of Nance and colleagues was received by others in the field.

B) It presents the central finding reported by Nance and colleagues.

C) It identifies the problem that Nance and colleagues attempted to solve but did not.

D) It describes a serious limitation of the method used by Nance and colleagues.

CONTINUE ➔

The mimosa tree evolved in East Asia, where the beetle *Bruchidius terrenus* preys on its seeds. In 1785, mimosa tress were introduced to North America, far from any *B. terrenus*. But evolutionary links between predators and their prey can persist across centuries and continents. Around 2001, *B. terrenus* was introduced in southeastern North America near where botanist Shu-Mei Chang and colleagues had been monitoring mimosa trees. Within a year, 93 percent of the trees had been attacked by the beetles.

Which choice best describes the function of the third sentence in the overall structure of the text?

A) It states the hypothesis that Chang and colleagues had set out to investigate using mimosa trees and *B. terrenus*.

B) It presents a generalization that is exemplified by the discussion of the mimosa trees and *B. terrenus*.

C) It offers an alternative explanation for the findings of Chang and colleagues.

D) It provides context that clarifies why the species mentioned spread to new locations.

Text 1
When companies in the same industry propose merging with one another, they often claim that the merger will benefit consumers by increasing efficiency and therefore lowering prices. Economist Ying Fan investigated this notion in the context of the United States newspaper market. She modeled a hypothetical merger of Minneapolis-area newspapers and found that subscription prices would rise following a merger.

Text 2
Economist Dario Focarelli and Fabio Panetta have argued that research on the effect of mergers on prices has focused excessively on short-term effects, which tend to be adverse for consumers. Using the case of consumer banking in Italy, they show that over the long term (several years, in their study), the efficiency gains realized by merged companies do result in economic benefits for consumers.

Based on the texts, how would Focarelli and Panetta (Text 2) most likely respond to Fan's findings (Text 1)?

A) They would argue that over the long term the expenses incurred by the merged newspaper company will also increase.

B) They would recommend that Fan compare the near-term effect of a merger on subscription prices in the Minneapolis area with the effect of a merger in another newspaper market.

C) They would encourage Fan to investigate whether the projected effect on subscription prices persists over an extended period.

D) They would claim that mergers have a different effect on consumer prices in the newspaper industry than in most other industries.

CONTINUE

6

The following text is from Jane Austen's 1811 novel *Sense and Sensibility*. Elinor lives with her younger sisters and her mother, Mrs. Dashwood.

> Elinor, this eldest daughter, whose advice was so effectual, possessed a strength of understanding, and coolness of judgment, which qualified her, though only nineteen, to be the counsellor of her mother, and enabled her frequently to counteract, to the advantage of them all, that eagerness of mind in Mrs. Dashwood which must generally have led to imprudence. She had an excellent heart;—her disposition was affectionate, and her feelings were strong; but she knew how to govern them: it was a knowledge which her mother had yet to learn; and which one of her sisters had resolved never to be taught.

According to the text, what is true about Elinor?

A) Elinor often argues with her mother but fails to change her mind.

B) Elinor can be overly sensitive with regard to family matters.

C) Elinor thinks her mother is a bad role model.

D) Elinor is remarkably mature for her age.

7

The following text is adapted from Charles W. Chesnutt's 1901 novel *The Marrow of Tradition*.

> Mrs. Ochiltree was a woman of strong individuality, whose comments upon her acquaintance[s], present or absent, were marked by a frankness at times no less than startling. This characteristic caused her to be more or less avoided. Mrs. Ochiltree was aware of this sentiment on the part of her acquaintance[s], and rather exulted in it.

Based on the text, what is true about Mrs. Ochiltree's acquaintances?

A) They try to refrain from discussing topics that would upset Mrs. Ochiltree.

B) They are unable to spend as much time with Mrs. Ochiltree as she would like.

C) They are too preoccupied with their own concerns to speak with Mrs. Ochiltree.

D) They are likely offended by what Mrs. Ochiltree has said about them.

8

The following text is adapted from William Shakespeare's 1609 poem "Sonnet 27." The poem is addressed to a close friend as if he were physically present.

> Weary with toil, I [hurry] to my bed,
> The dear repose for limbs with travel tired;
> But then begins a journey in my head
> To work my mind, when body's work's expired:
> For then my thoughts—from far where I abide—
> [Begin] a zealous pilgrimage to thee,
> And keep my drooping eyelids open wide,

What is the main idea of the text?

A) The speaker is asleep and dreaming about traveling to see the friend.

B) The speaker is planning an upcoming trip to the friend's house.

C) The speaker is too fatigued to continue a discussion with the friend.

D) The speaker is thinking about the friend instead of immediately falling asleep.

Unauthorized copying or reuse of any part of this page is illegal.

CONTINUE ▶

324

9

Black beans (*Phaseolus vulgaris*) are a nutritionally dense food, but they are difficult to digest in part because of their high levels of soluble fiber and compounds like raffinose. They also contain antinutrients like tannins and trypsin inhibitors, which interfere with the body's ability to extract nutrients from foods. In a research article, Marisela Granito and Glenda Álvarez from Simón Bolívar University in Venezuela claim that inducing fermentation of black beans using lactic acid bacteria improves the digestibility of the beans and makes them more nutritious.

Which finding from Granito and Álvarez's research, if true, would most directly support their claim?

A) When cooked, fermented beans contained significantly more trypsin inhibitors and tannins but significantly less soluble fiber and raffinose than nonfermented beans.

B) Fermented beans contained significantly less soluble fiber and raffinose than nonfermented beans, and when cooked, the fermented beans also displayed a significant reduction in trypsin inhibitors and tannins.

C) When the fermented beans were analyzed, they were found to contain two microorganisms, *Lactobacillus casei* and *Lactobacillus plantarum*, that are theorized to increase the amount of nitrogen absorbed by the gut after eating beans.

D) Both fermented and nonfermented black beans contained significantly fewer trypsin inhibitors and tannins after being cooked at high pressure.

10

Ablation Rates for Three Elements in Cosmic Dust, by Dust Source

Element	SPC	AST	HTC	OCC
iron	20%	28%	90%	98%
potassium	44%	74%	97%	100%
sodium	45%	75%	99%	100%

Earth's atmosphere is bombarded by cosmic dust originating from several sources: short-period comets (SPCs), particles from the asteroid belt (ASTs), Halley-type comets (HTCs), and Oort cloud comets (OCCs). Some of the dust's material vaporizes in the atmosphere in a process called ablation, and the faster the particles move, the higher the rate of ablation. Astrophysicist Juan Diego Carrillo-Sánchez led a team that calculated average ablation rates for elements in the dust (such as iron and potassium) and showed that material in slower-moving SPC or AST dust has a lower rate than the same material in faster-moving HTC or OCC dust. For example, whereas the average ablation rate for iron from AST dust is 28%, the average rate for _____

Which choice most effectively uses data from the table to complete the example?

A) iron from SPC dust is 20%.

B) sodium from OCC dust is 100%.

C) iron from HTC dust is 90%.

D) sodium from AST dust is 75%.

CONTINUE

11

Economic Policy Uncertainty in the United Kingdom, 2005–2010

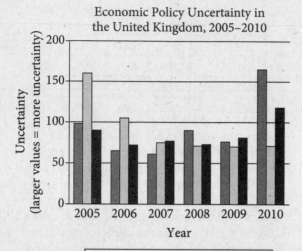

- ■ tax and public spending policy
- □ trade policy
- ■ general economic policy

High levels of public uncertainty about which economic policies a country will adopt can make planning difficult for businesses, but measures of such uncertainty have not tended to be very detailed. Recently, however, economist Sandile Hlatshwayo analyzed trends in news reports to derive measures not only for general economic policy uncertainty but also for uncertainty related to specific areas of economic policy, like tax or trade policy. One revelation of her work is that a general measure may not fully reflect uncertainty about specific areas of policy, as in the case of the United Kingdom, where general economic policy uncertainty _____

Which choice most effectively uses data from the graph to illustrate the claim?

A) aligned closely with uncertainty about tax and public spending policy in 2005 but differed from uncertainty about tax and public spending policy by a large amount in 2009.

B) was substantially lower than uncertainty about tax and public spending policy each year from 2005 to 2010.

C) reached its highest level between 2005 and 2010 in the same year that uncertainty about trade policy and tax and public spending policy reached their lowest levels.

D) was substantially lower than uncertainty about trade policy in 2005 and substantially higher than uncertainty about trade policy in 2010.

12

Average Number and Duration of Torpor Bouts and Arousal Episodes for Alaska Marmots and Arctic Ground Squirrels, 2008–2011

Feature	Alaska marmots	Arctic ground squirrels
torpor bouts	12	10.5
duration per bout	13.81 days	16.77 days
arousal episodes	11	9.5
duration per episode	21.2 hours	14.2 hours

When hibernating, Alaska marmots and Arctic ground squirrels enter a state called torpor, which minimizes the energy their bodies need to function. Often a hibernating animal will temporarily come out of torpor (called an arousal episode) and its metabolic rate will rise, burning more of the precious energy the animal needs to survive the winter. Alaska marmots hibernate in groups and therefore burn less energy keeping warm during these episodes than they would if they were alone. A researcher hypothesized that because Arctic ground squirrels hibernate alone, they would likely exhibit longer bouts of torpor and shorter arousal episodes than Alaska marmots.

Which choice best describes data from the table that support the researcher's hypothesis?

A) The Alaska marmots' arousal episodes lasted for days, while the Arctic ground squirrels' arousal episodes lasted less than a day.

B) The Alaska marmots and the Arctic ground squirrels both maintained torpor for several consecutive days per bout, on average.

C) The Alaska marmots had shorter torpor bouts and longer arousal episodes than the Arctic ground squirrels did.

D) The Alaska marmots had more torpor bouts than arousal episodes, but their arousal episodes were much shorter than their torpor bouts.

CONTINUE ▶

13

Employment by Sector in France and the United States, 1800–2012
(% of total employment)

Year	Agriculture in France	Manufacturing in France	Services in France	Agriculture in US	Manufacturing in US	Services in US
1800	64	22	14	68	18	13
1900	43	29	28	41	28	31
1950	32	33	35	14	33	53
2012	3	21	76	2	18	80

Rows in table may not add up to 100 due to rounding.

Over the past two hundred years, the percentage of the population employed in the agricultural sector has declined in both France and the United States, while employment in the service sector (which includes jobs in retail, consulting, real estate, etc.) has risen. However, this transition happened at very different rates in the two countries. This can be seen most clearly by comparing the employment by sector in both countries in _____

Which choice most effectively uses data from the table to complete the statement?

A) 1900 with the employment by sector in 1950.

B) 1800 with the employment by sector in 2012.

C) 1900 with the employment by sector in 2012.

D) 1800 with the employment by sector in 1900.

CONTINUE

14

Euphorbia esula (leafy spurge) is a Eurasian plant that has become invasive in North America, where it displaces native vegetation and sickens cattle. *E. esula* can be controlled with chemical herbicides, but that approach can also kill harmless plants nearby. Recent research on introducing engineered DNA into plant species to inhibit their reproduction may offer a path toward exclusively targeting *E. esula*, consequently _____

Which choice most logically completes the text?

A) making individual *E. esula* plants more susceptible to existing chemical herbicides.

B) enhancing the ecological benefits of *E. esula* in North America.

C) enabling cattle to consume *E. esula* without becoming sick.

D) reducing invasive *E. esula* numbers without harming other organisms.

15

Both Sona Charaipotra, an Indian American, and Dhonielle Clayton, an African American, grew up frustrated by the lack of diverse characters in books for young people. In 2011, these two writers joined forces to found CAKE Literary, a book packaging _____ specializes in the creation and promotion of stories told from diverse perspectives for children and young adults.

Which choice completes the text so that it conforms to the conventions of Standard English?

A) company,

B) company that

C) company

D) company, that

16

In 1930, Japanese American artist Chiura Obata depicted the natural beauty of Yosemite National Park in two memorable woodcuts: *Evening at Carl Inn* and *Lake Basin in the High Sierra*. In 2019, _____ exhibited alongside 150 of Obata's other works in a single-artist show at the Smithsonian American Art Museum.

Which choice completes the text so that it conforms to the conventions of Standard English?

A) it was

B) they were

C) this was

D) some were

17

American writer Edwidge Danticat, who emigrated from Haiti in 1981, has won acclaim for her powerful short stories, novels, and _____ her lyrical yet unflinching depictions of her native country's turbulent history, writer Robert Antoni has compared Danticat to Nobel Prize–winning novelist Toni Morrison.

Which choice completes the text so that it conforms to the conventions of Standard English?

A) essays, praising

B) essays and praising

C) essays praising

D) essays. Praising

CONTINUE →

18

In 1966, Emmett Ashford became the first African American to umpire a Major League Baseball game. His energetic gestures announcing when a player had struck out and his habit of barreling after a hit ball to see if it would land out of _____ transform the traditionally solemn umpire role into a dynamic one.

Which choice completes the text so that it conforms to the conventions of Standard English?

A) bounds helped

B) bounds, helping

C) bounds that helped

D) bounds to help

19

In crafting her fantasy fiction, Nigerian-born British author Helen Oyeyemi has drawn inspiration from the classic nineteenth-century fairy tales of the Brothers Grimm. Her 2014 novel *Boy, Snow, Bird*, for instance, is a complex retelling of the story of Snow White, while her 2019 novel _____ offers a delicious twist on the classic tale of Hansel and Gretel.

Which choice completes the text so that it conforms to the conventions of Standard English?

A) *Gingerbread—*

B) *Gingerbread,*

C) *Gingerbread*

D) *Gingerbread:*

20

The violins handmade in the seventeenth century by Italian craftsman Antonio Stradivari have been celebrated as some of the finest in the world. In close collaboration with musicians, Stradivari introduced changes to the shape of a traditional violin, flattening some of the instrument's curves and making _____ lighter overall.

Which choice completes the text so that it conforms to the conventions of Standard English?

A) those

B) one

C) them

D) it

21

During the English neoclassical period (1660–1789), many writers imitated the epic poetry and satires of ancient Greece and Rome. They were not the first in England to adopt the literary modes of classical _____ some of the most prominent figures of the earlier Renaissance period were also influenced by ancient Greek and Roman literature.

Which choice completes the text so that it conforms to the conventions of Standard English?

A) antiquity, however

B) antiquity, however,

C) antiquity, however;

D) antiquity; however,

CONTINUE

22

One poll taken after the first 1960 presidential debate suggested that John Kennedy lost badly: only 21 percent of those who listened on the radio rated him the winner. _____ the debate was ultimately considered a victory for the telegenic young senator, who rated higher than his opponent, Vice President Richard Nixon, among those watching on the new medium of television.

Which choice completes the text with the most logical transition?

A) In other words,

B) Therefore,

C) Likewise,

D) Nevertheless,

23

In November 1934, Amrita Sher-Gil was living in what must have seemed like the ideal city for a young artist: Paris. She was studying firsthand the color-saturated style of France's modernist masters and beginning to make a name for herself as a painter. _____ Sher-Gil longed to return to her childhood home of India; only there, she believed, could her art truly flourish.

Which choice completes the text with the most logical transition?

A) Still,

B) Therefore,

C) Indeed,

D) Furthermore,

24

In his 1925 book *The Morphology of Landscape*, US geographer Carl Sauer challenged prevailing views about how natural landscapes influence human cultures. _____ Sauer argued that instead of being shaped entirely by their natural surroundings, cultures play an active role in their own development by virtue of their interactions with the environment.

Which choice completes the text with the most logical transition?

A) Similarly,

B) Finally,

C) Therefore,

D) Specifically,

25

Although those who migrated to California in 1849 dreamed of finding gold nuggets in streambeds, the state's richest deposits were buried deeply in rock, beyond the reach of individual prospectors. _____ by 1852, many had given up their fortune-hunting dreams and gone to work for one of the large companies capable of managing California's complex mining operations.

Which choice completes the text with the most logical transition?

A) Furthermore,

B) Still,

C) Consequently,

D) Next,

CONTINUE

26

While researching a topic, a student has taken the following notes:

- In 2013, archaeologists studied cat bone fragments they had found in the ruins of Quanhucun, a Chinese farming village.
- The fragments were estimated to be 5,300 years old.
- A chemical analysis of the fragments revealed that the cats had consumed large amounts of grain.
- The grain consumption is evidence that the Quanhucun cats may have been domesticated.

The student wants to present the Quanhucun study and its conclusions. Which choice most effectively uses relevant information from the notes to accomplish this goal?

A) As part of a 2013 study of cat domestication, a chemical analysis was conducted on cat bone fragments found in Quanhucun, China.

B) A 2013 analysis of cat bone fragments found in Quanhucun, China, suggests that cats there may have been domesticated 5,300 years ago.

C) In 2013, archaeologists studied what cats in Quanhucun, China, had eaten more than 5,000 years ago.

D) Cat bone fragments estimated to be 5,300 years old were found in Quanhucun, China, in 2013.

27

While researching a topic, a student has taken the following notes:

- Started in 1925, the Scripps National Spelling Bee is a US-based spelling competition.
- The words used in the competition have diverse linguistic origins.
- In 2008, Sameer Mishra won by correctly spelling the word "guerdon."
- "Guerdon" derives from the Anglo-French word "guerdun."
- In 2009, Kavya Shivashankar won by correctly spelling the word "Laodicean."
- "Laodicean" derives from the ancient Greek word "Laodíkeia."

The student wants to emphasize a difference in the origins of the two words. Which choice most effectively uses relevant information from the notes to accomplish this goal?

A) "Guerdon," the final word of the 2008 Scripps National Spelling Bee, is of Anglo-French origin, while the following year's final word, "Laodicean," derives from ancient Greek.

B) In 2008, Sameer Mishra won the Scripps National Spelling Bee by correctly spelling the word "guerdon"; however, the following year, Kavya Shivashankar won based on spelling the word "Laodicean."

C) Kavya Shivashankar won the 2009 Scripps National Spelling Bee by correctly spelling "Laodicean," which derives from the ancient Greek word "Laodíkeia."

D) The Scripps National Spelling Bee uses words from diverse linguistic origins, such as "guerdon" and "Laodicean."

STOP

If you finish before time is called, you may check your work on this module only.
Do not turn to any other module in the test.

Reading and Writing

27 QUESTIONS

DIRECTIONS

The questions in this section address a number of important reading and writing skills. Each question includes one or more passages, which may include a table or graph. Read each passage and question carefully, and then choose the best answer to the question based on the passage(s).

All questions in this section are multiple-choice with four answer choices. Each question has a single best answer.

1

Due to their often strange images, highly experimental syntax, and opaque subject matter, many of John Ashbery's poems can be quite difficult to _____ and thus are the object of heated debate among scholars.

Which choice completes the text with the most logical and precise word or phrase?

A) delegate

B) compose

C) interpret

D) renounce

2

Mônica Lopes-Ferreira and others at Brazil's Butantan Institute are studying the freshwater stingray species *Potamotrygon rex* to determine whether biological characteristics such as the rays' age and sex have _____ effect on the toxicity of their venom—that is, to see if differences in these traits are associated with considerable variations in venom potency.

Which choice completes the text with the most logical and precise word or phrase?

A) a disconcerting

B) an acceptable

C) an imperceptible

D) a substantial

3

Former astronaut Ellen Ochoa says that although she doesn't have a definite idea of when it might happen, she _____ that humans will someday need to be able to live in other environments than those found on Earth. This conjecture informs her interest in future research missions to the moon.

Which choice completes the text with the most logical and precise word or phrase?

A) demands

B) speculates

C) doubts

D) establishes

4

Following the principles of community-based participatory research, tribal nations and research institutions are equal partners in health studies conducted on reservations. A collaboration between the Crow Tribe and Montana State University _____ this model: tribal citizens worked alongside scientists to design the methodology and continue to assist in data collection.

Which choice completes the text with the most logical and precise word or phrase?

A) circumvents

B) eclipses

C) fabricates

D) exemplifies

CONTINUE

5

Researchers have struggled to pinpoint specific causes for hiccups, which happen when a person's diaphragm contracts _____. However, neuroscientist Kimberley Whitehead has found that these uncontrollable contractions may play an important role in helping infants regulate their breathing.

Which choice completes the text with the most logical and precise word or phrase?

A) involuntarily

B) beneficially

C) strenuously

D) smoothly

6

The parasitic dodder plant increases its reproductive success by flowering at the same time as the host plant it has latched onto. In 2020, Jianqiang Wu and his colleagues determined that the tiny dodder achieves this _____ with its host by absorbing and utilizing a protein the host produces when it is about to flower.

Which choice completes the text with the most logical and precise word or phrase?

A) synchronization

B) hibernation

C) prediction

D) moderation

7

Ofelia Zepeda's contributions to the field of linguistics are _____: her many accomplishments include working as a linguistics professor and bilingual poet, authoring the first Tohono O'odham grammar book, and co-founding the American Indian Language Development Institute.

Which choice completes the text with the most logical and precise word or phrase?

A) pragmatic

B) controversial

C) extensive

D) universal

8

In the Indigenous intercropping system known as the Three Sisters, maize, squash, and beans form an _____ web of relations: maize provides the structure on which the bean vines grow; the squash vines cover the soil, discouraging competition from weeds; and the beans aid their two "sisters" by enriching the soil with essential nitrogen.

Which choice completes the text with the most logical and precise word or phrase?

A) indecipherable

B) ornamental

C) obscure

D) intricate

CONTINUE

9

The following text is adapted from Oscar Wilde's 1891 novel *The Picture of Dorian Gray*. Dorian Gray is taking his first look at a portrait that Hallward has painted of him.

Dorian passed listlessly in front of his picture and turned towards it. When he saw it he drew back, and his cheeks flushed for a moment with pleasure. A look of joy came into his eyes, as if he had recognized himself for the first time. He stood there motionless and in wonder, dimly conscious that Hallward was speaking to him, but not catching the meaning of his words. The sense of his own beauty came on him like a revelation. He had never felt it before.

According to the text, what is true about Dorian?

A) He wants to know Hallward's opinion of the portrait.

B) He is delighted by what he sees in the portrait.

C) He prefers portraits to other types of paintings.

D) He is uncertain of Hallward's talent as an artist.

10

"Often Rebuked, Yet Always Back Returning" is an 1846 poem by Emily Brontë. The poem conveys the speaker's determination to experience the countryside around her: _____

Which quotation from the poem most effectively illustrates the claim?

A) "Often rebuked, yet always back returning / To those first feelings that were born with me, / And leaving busy chase of wealth and learning / For idle dreams of things which cannot be."

B) "I'll walk, but not in old heroic traces, / And not in paths of high morality, / And not among the half-distinguished faces, / The clouded forms of long-past history."

C) "I'll walk where my own nature would be leading: / It vexes me to choose another guide: / Where the grey flocks in ferny glens are feeding; / Where the wild wind blows on the mountain side."

D) "To-day, I will seek not the shadowy region; / Its unsustaining vastness waxes drear; / And visions rising, legion after legion, / Bring the unreal world too strangely near."

11

"Mrs. Spring Fragrance" is a 1912 short story by Sui Sin Far. In the story, Mrs. Spring Fragrance, a Chinese immigrant living in Seattle, is traveling in California. In letters to her husband and friend, she demonstrates her concern for what's happening at her home in Seattle while she is away: _____

Which quotation from Mrs. Spring Fragrance's letters most effectively illustrates the claim?

A) "My honorable cousin is preparing for the Fifth Moon Festival, and wishes me to compound for the occasion some American 'fudge,' for which delectable sweet, made by my clumsy hands, you have sometimes shown a slight prejudice."

B) "Next week I accompany Ah Oi to the beauteous town of San José. There will we be met by the son of the Illustrious Teacher."

C) "Forget not to care for the cat, the birds, and the flowers. Do not eat too quickly nor fan too vigorously now that the weather is warming."

D) "I am enjoying a most agreeable visit, and American friends, as also our own, strive benevolently for the accomplishment of my pleasure."

12

Hedda Gabler is an 1890 play by Henrik Ibsen. As a woman in the Victorian era, Hedda, the play's central character, is unable to freely determine her own future. Instead, she seeks to influence another person's fate, as is evident when she says to another character, _____

Which quotation from a translation of *Hedda Gabler* most effectively illustrates the claim?

A) "Then what in heaven's name would you have me do with myself?"

B) "I want for once in my life to have power to mould a human destiny."

C) "Then I, poor creature, have no sort of power over you?"

D) "Faithful to your principles, now and for ever! Ah, that is how a man should be!"

CONTINUE →

13

If some artifacts recovered from excavations of the settlement of Kuulo Kataa, in modern Ghana, date from the thirteenth century CE, that may lend credence to claims that the settlement was founded before or around that time. There is other evidence, however, strongly supporting a fourteenth century CE founding date for Kuulo Kataa. If both the artifact dates and the fourteenth century CE founding date are correct, that would imply that _____

Which choice most logically completes the text?

A) artifacts from the fourteenth century CE are more commonly recovered than are artifacts from the thirteenth century CE.

B) the artifacts originated elsewhere and eventually reached Kuulo Kataa through trade or migration.

C) Kuulo Kataa was founded by people from a different region than had previously been assumed.

D) excavations at Kuulo Kataa may have inadvertently damaged some artifacts dating to the fourteenth century CE.

14

One theory behind human bipedalism speculates that it originated in a mostly ground-based ancestor that practiced four-legged "knuckle-walking," like chimpanzees and gorillas do today, and eventually evolved into moving upright on two legs. But recently, researchers observed orangutans, another relative of humans, standing on two legs on tree branches and using their arms for balance while they reached for fruits. These observations may suggest that _____

Which choice most logically completes the text?

A) bipedalism evolved because it was advantageous to a tree-dwelling ancestor of humans.

B) bipedalism must have evolved simultaneously with knuckle-walking and tree-climbing.

C) moving between the ground and the trees would have been difficult without bipedalism.

D) a knuckle-walking human ancestor could have easily moved bipedally in trees.

15

In a study of the cognitive abilities of white-faced capuchin monkeys (*Cebus imitator*), researchers neglected to control for the physical difficulty of the tasks they used to evaluate the monkeys. The cognitive abilities of monkeys given problems requiring little dexterity, such as sliding a panel to retrieve food, were judged by the same criteria as were those of monkeys given physically demanding problems, such as unscrewing a bottle and inserting a straw. The results of the study, therefore, _____

Which choice most logically completes the text?

A) could suggest that there are differences in cognitive ability among the monkeys even though such differences may not actually exist.

B) are useful for identifying tasks that the monkeys lack the cognitive capacity to perform but not for identifying tasks that the monkeys can perform.

C) should not be taken as indicative of the cognitive abilities of any monkey species other than *C. imitator*.

D) reveal more about the monkeys' cognitive abilities when solving artificial problems than when solving problems encountered in the wild.

16

The increased integration of digital technologies throughout the process of book creation in the late 20th and early 21st centuries lowered the costs of book production, but those decreased costs have been most significant in the manufacturing and distribution process, which occurs after the authoring, editing, and design of the book are complete. This suggests that in the late 20th and early 21st centuries, _____

Which choice most logically completes the text?

A) digital technologies made it easier than it had been previously for authors to write very long works and get them published.

B) customers generally expected the cost of books to decline relative to the cost of other consumer goods.

C) publishers increased the variety of their offerings by printing more unique titles but also printed fewer copies of each title.

D) the costs of writing, editing, and designing a book were less affected by the technologies used than were the costs of manufacturing and distributing a book.

CONTINUE

Unauthorized copying or reuse of any part of this page is illegal.

335

17

Public-awareness campaigns about the need to reduce single-use plastics can be successful, says researcher Kim Borg of Monash University in Australia, when these campaigns give consumers a choice: for example, Japan achieved a 40 percent reduction in plastic-bag use after cashiers were instructed to ask customers whether _____ wanted a bag.

Which choice completes the text so that it conforms to the conventions of Standard English?

A) they

B) one

C) you

D) it

18

A member of the Cherokee Nation, Mary Golda Ross is renowned for her contributions to NASA's Planetary Flight Handbook, which _____ detailed mathematical guidance for missions to Mars and Venus.

Which choice completes the text so that it conforms to the conventions of Standard English?

A) provided

B) having provided

C) to provide

D) providing

19

Typically, underlines, scribbles, and notes left in the margins by a former owner lower a book's _____ when the former owner is a famous poet like Walt Whitman, such markings, known as marginalia, can be a gold mine to literary scholars.

Which choice completes the text so that it conforms to the conventions of Standard English?

A) value, but

B) value

C) value,

D) value but

20

British scientists James Watson and Francis Crick won the Nobel Prize in part for their 1953 paper announcing the double helix structure of DNA, but it is misleading to say that Watson and Crick discovered the double helix. _____ findings were based on a famous X-ray image of DNA fibers, "Photo 51," developed by X-ray crystallographer Rosalind Franklin and her graduate student Raymond Gosling.

Which choice completes the text so that it conforms to the conventions of Standard English?

A) They're

B) It's

C) Their

D) Its

CONTINUE

21

In order to prevent nonnative fish species from moving freely between the Mediterranean and Red Seas, marine biologist Bella Galil has proposed that a saline lock system be installed along the Suez Canal in Egypt's Great Bitter Lakes. The lock would increase the salinity of the lakes and _____ a natural barrier of water most marine creatures would be unable to cross.

Which choice completes the text so that it conforms to the conventions of Standard English?

A) creates

B) create

C) creating

D) created

22

Lucía Michel of the University of Chile observed that alkaline soils contain an insoluble form of iron that blueberry plants cannot absorb, thus inhibiting blueberry growth. If these plants were grown in alkaline soil alongside grasses that aid in iron solubilization, _____ Michel was determined to find out.

Which choice completes the text so that it conforms to the conventions of Standard English?

A) could the blueberries thrive.

B) the blueberries could thrive.

C) the blueberries could thrive?

D) could the blueberries thrive?

23

The classic children's board game Chutes and Ladders is a version of an ancient Nepalese game, Paramapada Sopanapata. In both games, players encounter "good" or "bad" spaces while traveling along a path; landing on one of the good spaces _____ a player to skip ahead and arrive closer to the end goal.

Which choice completes the text so that it conforms to the conventions of Standard English?

A) allows

B) are allowing

C) have allowed

D) allow

24

In 1968, US Congressman John Conyers introduced a bill to establish a national holiday in honor of Dr. Martin Luther King Jr. The bill didn't make it to a vote, but Conyers was determined. He teamed up with Shirley Chisholm, the first Black woman to be elected to Congress, and they resubmitted the bill every session for the next fifteen years. _____ in 1983, the bill passed.

Which choice completes the text with the most logical transition?

A) Instead,

B) Likewise,

C) Finally,

D) Additionally,

CONTINUE

25

Most conifers (trees belonging to the phylum Coniferophyta) are evergreen. That is, they keep their green leaves or needles year-round. However, not all conifer species are evergreen. Larch trees, _____ lose their needles every fall.

Which choice completes the text with the most logical transition?

A) for instance,

B) nevertheless,

C) meanwhile,

D) in addition,

26

Samuel Coleridge-Taylor was a prominent classical music composer from England who toured the US three times in the early 1900s. The child of a West African father and an English mother, Coleridge-Taylor emphasized his mixed-race ancestry. For example, he referred to himself as Anglo-African. _____ he incorporated the sounds of traditional African music into his classical music compositions.

Which choice completes the text with the most logical transition?

A) In addition,

B) Actually,

C) However,

D) Regardless,

27

While researching a topic, a student has taken the following notes:

- British musicians John Lennon and Paul McCartney shared writing credit for numerous Beatles songs.

- Many Lennon-McCartney songs were actually written by either Lennon or McCartney, not by both.

- The exact authorship of specific parts of many Beatles songs, such as the verse for "In My Life," is disputed.

- Mark Glickman, Jason Brown, and Ryan Song used statistical methods to analyze the musical content of Beatles songs.

- They concluded that there is 18.9% probability that McCartney wrote the verse for "In My Life," stating that the verse is "consistent with Lennon's songwriting style."

The student wants to make a generalization about the kind of study conducted by Glickman, Brown, and Song. Which choice most effectively uses relevant information from the notes to accomplish this goal?

A) Based on statistical analysis, Glickman, Brown, and Song claim that John Lennon wrote the verse of "In My Life."

B) There is only an 18.9% probability that Paul McCartney wrote the verse for "In My Life"; John Lennon is the more likely author.

C) It is likely that John Lennon, not Paul McCartney, wrote the verse for "In My Life."

D) Researchers have used statistical methods to address questions of authorship within the field of music.

STOP

**If you finish before time is called, you may check your work on this module only.
Do not turn to any other module in the test.**

Test begins on the next page.

Math

22 QUESTIONS

DIRECTIONS

The questions in this section address a number of important math skills.
Use of a calculator is permitted for all questions.

NOTES

Unless otherwise indicated:

- All variables and expressions represent real numbers.

- Figures provided are drawn to scale.

- All figures lie in a plane.

- The domain of a given function f is the set of all real numbers x for which $f(x)$ is a real number.

REFERENCE

$A = \pi r^2$
$C = 2\pi r$

$A = \ell w$

$A = \frac{1}{2}bh$

b c a
$c^2 = a^2 + b^2$

Special Right Triangles

$V = \ell wh$

$V = \pi r^2 h$

$V = \frac{4}{3}\pi r^3$

$V = \frac{1}{3}\pi r^2 h$

$V = \frac{1}{3}\ell wh$

The number of degrees of arc in a circle is 360.

The number of radians of arc in a circle is 2π.

The sum of the measures in degrees of the angles of a triangle is 180.

CONTINUE ▶

For multiple-choice questions, solve each problem, choose the correct answer from the choices provided, and then circle your answer in this book. Circle only one answer for each question. If you change your mind, completely erase the circle. You will not get credit for questions with more than one answer circled, or for questions with no answers circled.

For student-produced response questions, solve each problem and write your answer next to or under the question in the test book as described below.

- Once you've written your answer, circle it clearly. You will not receive credit for anything written outside the circle, or for any questions with more than one circled answer.

- If you find **more than one correct answer**, write and circle only one answer.

- Your answer can be up to 5 characters for a **positive** answer and up to 6 characters (including the negative sign) for a **negative** answer, but no more.

- If your answer is a **fraction** that is too long (over 5 characters for positive, 6 characters for negative), write the decimal equivalent.

- If your answer is a **decimal** that is too long (over 5 characters for positive, 6 characters for negative), truncate it or round at the fourth digit.

- If your answer is a **mixed number** (such as $3\frac{1}{2}$), write it as an improper fraction (7/2) or its decimal equivalent (3.5).

- Don't include **symbols** such as a percent sign, comma, or dollar sign in your circled answer.

Unauthorized copying or reuse of any part of this page is illegal.

CONTINUE →

341

1

4, 4, 4, 4, 8, 8, 8, 13, 13

Which frequency table correctly represents the data listed?

A)

Number	Frequency
4	4
8	3
13	2

B)

Number	Frequency
4	4
3	8
2	13

C)

Number	Frequency
4	16
8	24
13	26

D)

Number	Frequency
16	4
24	8
26	13

2

Which expression is equivalent to $x^2 + 3x - 40$?

A) $(x - 4)(x + 10)$

B) $(x - 5)(x + 8)$

C) $(x - 8)(x + 5)$

D) $(x - 10)(x + 4)$

3

Jay walks at a speed of 3 miles per hour and runs at a speed of 5 miles per hour. He walks for w hours and runs for r hours for a combined total of 14 miles. Which equation represents this situation?

A) $3w + 5r = 14$

B) $\frac{1}{3}w + \frac{1}{5}r = 14$

C) $\frac{1}{3}w + \frac{1}{5}r = 112$

D) $3w + 5r = 112$

4

In triangle ABC, the measure of angle B is 52° and the measure of angle C is 17°. What is the measure of angle A?

A) 21°

B) 35°

C) 69°

D) 111°

Unauthorized copying or reuse of any part of this page is illegal.

CONTINUE

342

5

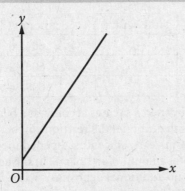

The graph represents the total charge, in dollars, by an electrician for x hours of work. The electrician charges a onetime fee plus an hourly rate. What is the best interpretation of the slope of the graph?

A) The electrician's hourly rate

B) The electrician's onetime fee

C) The maximum amount that the electrician charges

D) The total amount that the electrician charges

6

The table summarizes the distribution of color and shape for 100 tiles of equal area.

	Red	Blue	Yellow	Total
Square	10	20	25	55
Pentagon	20	10	15	45
Total	30	30	40	100

If one of these tiles is selected at random, what is the probability of selecting a red tile? (Express your answer as a decimal or fraction, not as a percent.)

7

From a population of 50,000 people, 1,000 were chosen at random and surveyed about a proposed piece of legislation. Based on the survey, it is estimated that 35% of people in the population support the legislation, with an associated margin of error of 3%. Based on these results, which of the following is a plausible value for the total number of people in the population who support the proposed legislation?

A) 350

B) 650

C) 16,750

D) 31,750

8

$$\frac{55}{x + 6} = x$$

What is the positive solution to the given equation?

9

An airplane descends from an altitude of 9,500 feet to 5,000 feet at a constant rate of 400 feet per minute. What type of function best models the relationship between the descending airplane's altitude and time?

A) Decreasing exponential

B) Decreasing linear

C) Increasing exponential

D) Increasing linear

10

$$g(x) = 11\left(\frac{1}{12}\right)^x$$

If the given function g is graphed in the xy-plane, where $y = g(x)$, what is the y-intercept of the graph?

A) $(0, 11)$

B) $(0, 132)$

C) $(0, 1)$

D) $(0, 12)$

CONTINUE

11

Note: Figure not drawn to scale.

The circle shown has center O, circumference 144π, and diameters PR and QS. The length of arc PS is twice the length of arc PQ. What is the length of arc QR?

A) 24π

B) 48π

C) 72π

D) 96π

12

A rectangle has a length of x units and a width of $(x - 15)$ units. If the rectangle has an area of 76 square units, what is the value of x?

A) 4

B) 19

C) 23

D) 76

13

Time (years)	Total amount (dollars)
0	604.00
1	606.42
2	608.84

Rosa opened a savings account at a bank. The table shows the exponential relationship between the time t, in years, since Rosa opened the account and the total amount n, in dollars, in the account. If Rosa made no additional deposits or withdrawals, which of the following equations best represents the relationship between t and n?

A) $n = (1 + 604)^t$

B) $n = (1 + 0.004)^t$

C) $n = 604(1 + 0.004)^t$

D) $n = 0.004(1 + 604)^t$

14

At how many points do the graphs of the equations $y = x + 20$ and $y = 8x$ intersect in the xy-plane?

A) 0

B) 1

C) 2

D) 8

15

$$5G + 45R = 380$$

At a school fair, students can win colored tokens that are worth a different number of points depending on the color. One student won G green tokens and R red tokens worth a total of 380 points. The given equation represents this situation. How many more points is a red token worth than a green token?

CONTINUE

16

The number of bacteria in a liquid medium doubles every day. There are 44,000 bacteria in the liquid medium at the start of an observation. Which represents the number of bacteria, y, in the liquid medium t days after the start of the observation?

A) $y = \frac{1}{2}(44{,}000)^t$

B) $y = 2(44{,}000)^t$

C) $y = 44{,}000\left(\frac{1}{2}\right)^t$

D) $y = 44{,}000(2)^t$

17

A cylinder has a diameter of 8 inches and a height of 12 inches. What is the volume, in cubic inches, of the cylinder?

A) 16π

B) 96π

C) 192π

D) 768π

18

$$6x + 7y = 28$$
$$2x + 2y = 10$$

The solution to the given system of equations is (x, y). What is the value of y?

A) -2

B) 7

C) 14

D) 18

19

In triangle JKL, $\cos(K) = \frac{24}{51}$ and angle J is a right angle. What is the value of $\cos(L)$?

20

$$f(x) = 4x^2 - 50x + 126$$

The given equation defines the function f. For what value of x does $f(x)$ reach its minimum?

21

In the xy-plane, line ℓ passes through the point $(0, 0)$ and is parallel to the line represented by the equation $y = 8x + 2$. If line ℓ also passes through the point $(3, d)$, what is the value of d?

22

In the xy-plane, a line with equation $2y = c$ for some constant c intersects a parabola at exactly one point. If the parabola has equation $y = -2x^2 + 9x$, what is the value of c?

STOP

**If you finish before time is called, you may check your work on this module only.
Do not turn to any other module in the test.**

Math

22 QUESTIONS

DIRECTIONS

The questions in this section address a number of important math skills.
Use of a calculator is permitted for all questions.

NOTES

Unless otherwise indicated:

- All variables and expressions represent real numbers.
- Figures provided are drawn to scale.
- All figures lie in a plane.
- The domain of a given function f is the set of all real numbers x for which $f(x)$ is a real number.

REFERENCE

    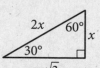

$A = \pi r^2$
$C = 2\pi r$

$A = \ell w$

$A = \frac{1}{2} bh$

$c^2 = a^2 + b^2$

Special Right Triangles

$V = \ell wh$

$V = \pi r^2 h$

$V = \frac{4}{3}\pi r^3$

$V = \frac{1}{3}\pi r^2 h$

$V = \frac{1}{3}\ell wh$

The number of degrees of arc in a circle is 360.

The number of radians of arc in a circle is 2π.

The sum of the measures in degrees of the angles of a triangle is 180.

CONTINUE →

For multiple-choice questions, solve each problem, choose the correct answer from the choices provided, and then circle your answer in this book. Circle only one answer for each question. If you change your mind, completely erase the circle. You will not get credit for questions with more than one answer circled, or for questions with no answers circled.

For student-produced response questions, solve each problem and write your answer next to or under the question in the test book as described below.

- Once you've written your answer, circle it clearly. You will not receive credit for anything written outside the circle, or for any questions with more than one circled answer.

- If you find **more than one correct answer**, write and circle only one answer.

- Your answer can be up to 5 characters for a **positive** answer and up to 6 characters (including the negative sign) for a **negative** answer, but no more.

- If your answer is a **fraction** that is too long (over 5 characters for positive, 6 characters for negative), write the decimal equivalent.

- If your answer is a **decimal** that is too long (over 5 characters for positive, 6 characters for negative), truncate it or round at the fourth digit.

- If your answer is a **mixed number** (such as $3\frac{1}{2}$), write it as an improper fraction (7/2) or its decimal equivalent (3.5).

- Don't include **symbols** such as a percent sign, comma, or dollar sign in your circled answer.

Unauthorized copying or reuse of any part of this page is illegal.

CONTINUE →

347

1

71, 72, 73, 76, 77, 79, 83, 87, 93

What is the median of the data shown?

A) 71

B) 77

C) 78

D) 79

2

$$x + 40 = 95$$

What value of x is the solution to the given equation?

3

What is the area of a rectangle with a length of 17 centimeters (cm) and a width of 7 cm?

A) 24 cm^2

B) 48 cm^2

C) 119 cm^2

D) 576 cm^2

4

Which expression is equivalent to $20w - (4w + 3w)$?

A) 10w

B) 13w

C) 19w

D) 21w

5

The number y is 84 less than the number x. Which equation represents the relationship between x and y?

A) $y = x + 84$

B) $y = \dfrac{1}{84}x$

C) $y = 84x$

D) $y = x - 84$

6

The expression $\dfrac{24}{6x + 42}$ is equivalent to $\dfrac{4}{x + b}$, where b is a constant and $x > 0$. What is the value of b?

A) 7

B) 10

C) 24

D) 252

7

Out of 300 seeds that were planted, 80% sprouted. How many of these seeds sprouted?

CONTINUE ➡

8

Ty set a goal to walk at least 24 kilometers every day to prepare for a multiday hike. On a certain day, Ty plans to walk at an average speed of 4 kilometers per hour. What is the minimum number of hours Ty must walk on that day to fulfill the daily goal?

A) 4

B) 6

C) 20

D) 24

9

If $6 + x = 9$, what is the value of $18 + 3x$?

10

The function f is defined by $f(x) = x^3 + 9$. What is the value of $f(2)$?

A) 14

B) 15

C) 17

D) 18

11

The total cost $f(x)$, in dollars, to lease a car for 36 months from a particular car dealership is given by $f(x) = 36x + 1,000$, where x is the monthly payment, in dollars. What is the total cost to lease a car when the monthly payment is $400?

A) $13,400

B) $13,000

C) $15,400

D) $37,400

12

The function g is defined by $g(x) = 10x + 8$. What is the value of $g(x)$ when $x = 8$?

A) 0

B) 8

C) 10

D) 88

13

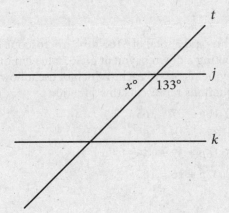

Note: Figure not drawn to scale.

In the figure, line j is parallel to line k. What is the value of x?

14

The graph of $7x + 2y = -31$ in the xy-plane has an x-intercept at $(a, 0)$ and a y-intercept at $(0, b)$, where a and b are constants. What is the value of $\dfrac{b}{a}$?

A) $-\dfrac{7}{2}$

B) $-\dfrac{2}{7}$

C) $\dfrac{2}{7}$

D) $\dfrac{7}{2}$

CONTINUE

15

An object travels at a constant speed of 12 centimeters per second. At this speed, what is the time, in seconds, that it would take for the object to travel 108 centimeters?

A) 9

B) 96

C) 120

D) 972

16

John paid a total of $165 for a microscope by making a down payment of $37 plus p monthly payments of $16 each. Which of the following equations represents this situation?

A) $16p - 37 = 165$

B) $37p - 16 = 165$

C) $16p + 37 = 165$

D) $37p + 16 = 165$

17

x	y
0	18
1	13
2	8

The table shows three values of x and their corresponding values of y. There is a linear relationship between x and y. Which of the following equations represents this relationship?

A) $y = 18x + 13$

B) $y = 18x + 18$

C) $y = -5x + 13$

D) $y = -5x + 18$

18

An object is kicked from a platform. The equation $h = -4.9t^2 + 7t + 9$ represents this situation, where h is the height of the object above the ground, in meters, t seconds after it is kicked. Which number represents the height, in meters, from which the object was kicked?

A) 0

B) 4.9

C) 7

D) 9

19

$$h(x) = x^2 - 3$$

Which table gives three values of x and their corresponding values of $h(x)$ for the given function h?

A)

x	1	2	3
$h(x)$	4	5	6

B)

x	1	2	3
$h(x)$	-2	1	6

C)

x	1	2	3
$h(x)$	-1	1	3

D)

x	1	2	3
$h(x)$	-2	1	3

CONTINUE

20

In the linear function f, $f(0) = 8$ and $f(1) = 12$. Which equation defines f?

A) $f(x) = 12x + 8$

B) $f(x) = 4x$

C) $f(x) = 4x + 12$

D) $f(x) = 4x + 8$

21

$$14j + 5k = m$$

The given equation relates the numbers j, k, and m. Which equation correctly expresses k in terms of j and m?

A) $k = \dfrac{m - 14j}{5}$

B) $k = \dfrac{1}{5}m - 14j$

C) $k = \dfrac{14j - m}{5}$

D) $k = 5m - 14j$

22

$$RS = 440$$
$$ST = 384$$
$$TR = 584$$

The side lengths of right triangle RST are given. Triangle RST is similar to triangle UVW, where S corresponds to V and T corresponds to W. What is the value of tan W?

A) $\dfrac{48}{73}$

B) $\dfrac{55}{73}$

C) $\dfrac{48}{55}$

D) $\dfrac{55}{48}$

STOP

If you finish before time is called, you may check your work on this module only. Do not turn to any other module in the test.

The SAT®

Practice Test #1

ANSWER EXPLANATIONS

These answer explanations are for students using
The Official Digital SAT Study Guide.

Reading and Writing

Module 1
(27 questions)

QUESTION 1

Choice A is the best answer because it most logically completes the text's discussion of how biodiversity loss due to invasive species can be avoided. As used in this context, "preventable" means able to be stopped or kept from happening. The text indicates that "people can take simple steps" to avoid bringing possible invasive species into new environments. It presents these steps as an example of how biodiversity loss due to invasive species is preventable.

Choice B is incorrect because it wouldn't make sense to say that a simple step like washing your shoes after traveling is an example of biodiversity loss due to invasive species being "undeniable," or something that can't be proved to be wrong. Although the text may suggest that biodiversity loss due to invasive species is something that really happens, the word that completes the text must make the first sentence into an assertion that is illustrated by the second sentence, and the second sentence illustrates the idea that biodiversity loss due to invasive species is preventable, not undeniable. *Choice C* is incorrect because it wouldn't make sense to say that a simple step like washing your shoes after traveling is an example of biodiversity loss due to invasive species being "common," or something that happens regularly. Additionally, the text doesn't provide any information about how frequently invasive species cause biodiversity loss. *Choice D* is incorrect because it wouldn't make sense to say that a simple step like washing your shoes after traveling is an example of biodiversity loss due to invasive species being "concerning," or something that is troubling or causes worry. Although the text implies that the phenomenon of biodiversity loss due to invasive species is itself a concerning phenomenon, the word that completes the text must make the first sentence into an assertion that is illustrated by the second sentence, and the second sentence illustrates the idea that biodiversity loss due to invasive species is preventable, not concerning.

QUESTION 2

Choice C is the best answer because it most logically completes the text's discussion of the influences on Banisadr's work. As used in this context, "unimportant" means trivial or lacking value. "It is by no means" establishes that the word that goes in the blank is contradicted by other information; the material that follows "indeed" later in that sentence provides the contradicting information—namely, that Banisadr himself cites Bosch as an inspiration. In other words, the sentence indicates that Bosch's influence on Banisadr is significant, and thus recognizing that influence is by no means unimportant.

Choice A is incorrect because it wouldn't make sense to say that recognizing Bosch's influence on Banisadr isn't "substantial," or meaningful. The text states that Banisadr himself cites Bosch as an influence. *Choice B* is incorrect because it wouldn't make sense to say that it isn't "satisfying," or pleasing, to recognize Bosch's influence on Banisadr. The text states that Banisadr himself cites Bosch as an influence. *Choice D* is incorrect because it wouldn't make sense to say that recognizing Bosch's influence on Banisadr isn't "appropriate," or suitable. The text indicates that Banisadr himself notes that Bosch's work has had an effect on him.

QUESTION 3

Choice C is the best answer because it best describes how the second sentence functions in the text as a whole. The first sentence establishes something astronomers believe with some certainty: that Betelgeuse will explode in a supernova. The second sentence then introduces a problem: astronomers aren't certain *when* Betelgeuse will explode because they don't have enough information about the star's internal characteristics. Finally, the third sentence indicates that researcher Sarafina El-Badry Nance and colleagues investigated a possible method of obtaining the necessary information about Betelgeuse's internal characteristics, though they found that the method wouldn't be sufficient. Thus, the function of the second sentence is to identify the problem that Nance and colleagues attempted to solve but didn't.

Choice A is incorrect because the second sentence doesn't indicate how other astronomers or astrophysicists responded to the work done by Nance and colleagues; the text doesn't address this information at all. *Choice B* is incorrect because the second sentence introduces the general problem Nance and colleagues hoped to solve, not the central finding they ultimately reported. It is the third sentence that presents Nance and colleagues' conclusion that a potential method for determining internal stellar states would be insufficient. *Choice D* is incorrect because the second sentence introduces the general problem Nance and colleagues hoped to solve, not a serious limitation of how Nance and colleagues tried to solve it. It is the third sentence that introduces Nance and colleagues, but no serious limitation of their approach to studying a method of determining internal stellar states is described.

QUESTION 4

Choice B is the best answer because it most accurately describes the function of the third sentence within the overall structure of the text. The third sentence makes a generalization, asserting that evolutionary links between predators and prey can persist across great expanses of time and distance. This generalization is exemplified by the text's discussion of the relationship between mimosa trees and *B. terrenus* beetles. When mimosa trees were introduced to North America in 1785, no *B. terrenus* beetles were present, so the relationship between the trees and the beetles that exists in their native East Asia was disrupted. When the beetles were introduced to North America more than 200 years later, however, they quickly attacked mimosa trees, illustrating the generalization that links between predators and prey "can persist across centuries and continents."

Choice A is incorrect because the third sentence doesn't indicate that Chang and colleagues were investigating any particular hypothesis. According to the text, Chang and colleagues were simply monitoring mimosa trees when the beetles happened to be introduced to the area. *Choice C* is incorrect because the third sentence offers a generalization about the relationship between predators and prey, not an explanation for the findings of Chang and colleagues that differs from an explanation presented elsewhere in the text. *Choice D* is incorrect because the third sentence doesn't discuss any particular species (either the species mentioned elsewhere in the text or any other) and doesn't help explain why species spread to new locations.

QUESTION 5

Choice C is the best answer because, based on the information presented in the texts, it represents how Focarelli and Panetta would most likely respond to Fan's findings. Text 1 indicates that Fan found that a newspaper merger would result in a rise in subscription prices. This rise wouldn't benefit customers, who would have to pay more for news after a merger. Text 2 presents Focarelli and Panetta's argument that merger research tends to focus too much on what happens immediately after the merger. Text 2 goes on to describe their finding that mergers can be economically beneficial for consumers over the long term. This suggests that Focarelli and Panetta would encourage Fan to investigate the long-term effect of the hypothetical newspaper merger on subscription prices.

Choice A is incorrect because Text 2 indicates that Focarelli and Panetta found that merged companies experience "efficiency gains" over the long term, meaning that their expenses go down relative to their output, not that their expenses increase. *Choice B* is incorrect because Text 2 doesn't indicate that Focarelli and Panetta connect the effects of mergers to specific locations. Instead, Focarelli and Panetta focus on the length of time over which the effects of mergers should be evaluated. *Choice D* is incorrect because there's no indication in Text 2 that Focarelli and Panetta believe that the newspaper industry is different from any other industry when it comes to the effects of mergers. Although their own research was about consumer banking, Text 2 suggests that they view their conclusions as applicable to mergers in general.

QUESTION 6

Choice D is the best answer because it provides a detail about Elinor that is established in the text. The text indicates that although Elinor is "only nineteen," she gives good advice and exhibits such a high level of understanding and judgment that she serves as "the counsellor of her mother." Thus, Elinor is mature beyond her years.

Choice A is incorrect because it isn't supported by the text: although the text says that Elinor advises her mother and often counteracts her mother's impulses, there's no mention of Elinor arguing with her mother or failing to change her mother's mind. *Choice B* is incorrect because it isn't supported by the text: although the text mentions that Elinor has strong feelings, it doesn't indicate that she's excessively sensitive when it comes to family issues. *Choice C* is incorrect because it isn't supported by the text: there's no mention of what Elinor thinks about her mother and no suggestion that she thinks her mother is a bad role model. Because she's described as having "an excellent heart," Elinor likely doesn't think ill of her mother.

QUESTION 7

Choice D is the best answer because it presents a statement about Mrs. Ochiltree's acquaintances that is supported by the text. The text indicates that Mrs. Ochiltree makes comments about her acquaintances that are frank, or direct and blunt, and sometimes startling. It also states that because of this behavior, the acquaintances tend to avoid Mrs. Ochiltree.

Together, these details suggest that the acquaintances choose not to be around Mrs. Ochiltree because they are offended by the things she has said about them.

Choice A is incorrect because the text doesn't suggest that Mrs. Ochiltree's acquaintances avoid discussing topics that would upset Mrs. Ochiltree; instead, it states that they avoid being around Mrs. Ochiltree. *Choice B* is incorrect because the text indicates that Mrs. Ochiltree knows her acquaintances often avoid her and is pleased about it (she "rather exulted in it"), not that she wants to spend more time with them. *Choice C* is incorrect because the text doesn't suggest that Mrs. Ochiltree's acquaintances avoid speaking with Mrs. Ochiltree because they are too focused on their own concerns, but rather because they don't like the frank comments she makes.

QUESTION 8

Choice D is the best answer because it most accurately states the main idea of the text. The speaker describes the experience of being "weary" and "tired" and going to bed to seek "dear repose" (that is, sleep), but instead of sleeping, the speaker is kept awake ("keep my drooping eyelids open wide") by thoughts of a friend ("my thoughts...[Begin] a zealous pilgrimage to thee").

Choice A is incorrect because the text makes it clear that the speaker isn't asleep; thoughts about the friend are keeping the speaker awake ("keep my drooping eyelids open wide"). *Choice B* is incorrect because the speaker isn't talking about taking a literal trip when referring to "a zealous pilgrimage." Rather, the speaker is referring to the experience of thinking about the friend, of taking "a journey in my head." *Choice C* is incorrect because the text indicates that the speaker and the friend aren't in the same place and having a conversation. Rather, the speaker is at home and thinking of the friend, who is somewhere else ("from far where I abide").

QUESTION 9

Choice B is the best answer because it presents a finding that would best support Granito and Álvarez's claim that fermenting black beans makes them easier to digest and more nutritious. The text indicates that high levels of soluble fiber and raffinose in black beans make the beans hard to digest and that tannins and trypsin inhibitors make it harder for the body to extract nutrients from the beans. If it were found that fermenting the beans significantly reduces their levels of soluble fiber, raffinose, trypsin inhibitors, and tannins when cooked, this would directly support the claim that fermentation improves the digestibility of the beans and makes them more nutritious.

Choice A is incorrect because the text indicates that trypsin inhibitors and tannins interfere with the body's ability to extract nutrients from black beans; if fermentation and cooking were found to increase these antinutrients, fermented beans would likely be less nutritious than unfermented ones, not more nutritious (as Granito and Álvarez claim). *Choice C* is incorrect because the text doesn't address the idea that greater nitrogen absorption in the gut has an effect on a food's digestibility or level of nutrition, so the discovery of the presence of microorganisms that may increase nitrogen absorption wouldn't provide relevant support for the claim that fermentation makes black beans easier to digest and more nutritious. *Choice D* is incorrect because Granito and Álvarez's claim focuses on the effect of fermenting black beans, but the finding that nonfermented black beans also have fewer trypsin inhibitors and tannins when cooked at high pressure would suggest that the role of the cooking method could be significant when it comes to nutrition; further, the finding wouldn't address the beans' digestibility.

QUESTION 10

Choice C is the best answer because it most effectively completes the example regarding the ablation rate of iron. The table shows the ablation rates for three elements—iron, potassium, and sodium—found in cosmic dust that comes from one of four sources. The text says that the ablation rate for a given element in slower-moving SPC or AST dust was lower than the ablation rate for that same element in faster-moving HTC or OCC dust. The text then presents the first part of an example of this pattern, describing an ablation rate of 28% for iron in AST dust. The information that iron from HTC dust had an ablation rate of 90% is therefore the most effective way to complete this example—the comparison of a relatively low ablation rate for iron in slower-moving AST dust with a relatively high ablation rate for iron in faster-moving HTC dust illustrates the tendency of ablation rates for a given element to be lower in slower-moving dust than in faster-moving dust.

Choice A is incorrect because the text indicates that SPC dust, like AST dust, moves relatively slowly; a comparison of the ablation rates of iron from two slower-moving dust sources could not be an example of the difference between ablation rates in slower-moving dust and faster-moving dust, which is the pattern that the example is supposed to illustrate. *Choice B* is incorrect because the example in the text is supposed to illustrate the difference in the ablation rates of the same element from slower-moving dust and faster-moving dust, and the first part of the example provides data about the ablation rate of iron, which means the second part of the example must also be about the ablation rate of iron, not the ablation rate of sodium. *Choice D* is incorrect because the example in the text is supposed to illustrate the difference in the ablation rates of the same element from slower-moving dust and faster-moving dust, and the first part of the example provides data about the ablation rate of iron, which means the second part of the example must also be about the ablation rate of iron, not the ablation rate of sodium. Additionally, any ablation rate from AST dust would be ineffective in this example since AST dust is referenced in the first part of the example and thus additional data focused on AST dust would not illustrate a variation across dust types.

QUESTION 11

Choice D is the best answer because it uses data from the graph to effectively illustrate the text's claim about general economic policy uncertainty in the United Kingdom. The graph presents values for economic policy uncertainty in tax and public spending policy, trade policy, and general economic policy in the UK from 2005 to 2010. The graph shows that in 2005, the value for general economic policy uncertainty (approximately 90) was substantially lower than the value for uncertainty about trade policy specifically (approximately 160). It also shows that in 2010, the value for general economic policy uncertainty (approximately 120) was substantially higher than the value for uncertainty about trade policy (approximately 70). The substantial differences between these values in 2005 and 2010 support the claim that a general measure may not fully reflect uncertainty about specific areas of policy.

Choice A is incorrect because the graph shows that the level of general economic policy uncertainty was similar to the level of uncertainty about tax and public spending policy in both 2005 (with values of approximately 90 and 100, respectively) and 2009 (with values of approximately 80 and 75, respectively). *Choice B* is incorrect because the graph shows that general economic policy uncertainty was higher than uncertainty about tax and public spending policy in 2006, 2007, and 2009, not that it was lower each year from 2005 to 2010. *Choice C* is incorrect because the graph shows that general economic policy uncertainty reached its highest level in 2010, which was when uncertainty about tax and public spending policy also reached its highest level, not its lowest level.

QUESTION 12

Choice C is the best answer because it describes data from the table that support the researcher's hypothesis. According to the text, the researcher hypothesized that Arctic ground squirrels would exhibit longer torpor bouts and shorter arousal episodes than Alaska marmots do—or, put the other way, that the marmots would show shorter torpor bouts and longer arousal episodes than the ground squirrels do. The table shows data about torpor bouts and arousal episodes for the two species from 2008 to 2011. According to the table, the average duration of torpor bouts was 13.81 days for Alaska marmots, shorter than the average of 16.77 days for Arctic ground squirrels, and the average duration of arousal episodes was 21.2 hours for Alaska marmots, longer than the average of 14.2 hours for Arctic ground squirrels. Thus, the table supports the researcher's hypothesis by showing that Alaska marmots had shorter bouts of torpor and longer arousal episodes than Arctic ground squirrels did.

Choice A is incorrect because it inaccurately describes data from the table and doesn't support the researcher's hypothesis. The table shows that the average duration of arousal episodes was less than a day for both Alaska marmots (21.2 hours) and Arctic ground squirrels (14.2 hours). Additionally, information about arousal episodes for Alaska marmots and Arctic ground squirrels isn't sufficient to support a hypothesis involving comparisons of both arousal episodes and torpor bouts for those animals. *Choice B* is incorrect because it doesn't support the researcher's hypothesis, which involves comparisons of arousal episodes as well as torpor bouts for Alaska marmots and Arctic ground squirrels. Noting that both animals had torpor bouts lasting several days, on average, doesn't address arousal episodes at all, nor does it reveal how the animals' torpor bouts compared. *Choice D* is incorrect because it doesn't support the researcher's hypothesis. Although the table does show that Alaska marmots had more torpor bouts (12) than arousal episodes (11) and that their arousal episodes were much shorter than their torpor bouts (21.2 hours and 13.81 days, respectively), comparing data across only Alaska marmot behaviors isn't sufficient to support a hypothesis about torpor and arousal behaviors of both Alaska marmots and Arctic ground squirrels.

QUESTION 13

Choice A is the best answer because it presents data from the table that most effectively complete the statement about the rates at which employment shifted in France and the United States. The text states that over the last two hundred years employment in the agricultural sector has declined while employment in the service sector has risen in both France and the US, and the data from the table reflect these trends. The text asserts, however, that the transition from agriculture to services "happened at very different rates in the two countries." This assertion is best supported by a comparison of data from 1900 and 1950: the table shows that in those years, employment in agriculture went from 43% to 32% in France (a decline of 11 percentage points) and from 41% to 14% in the US (a decline of 27 percentage points), and that employment in services went from 28% to 35% in France (an increase of 7 percentage points) and from 31% to 53% in the US (an increase of 22 percentage points). In other words, the rate of change was greater in the US than in France for both sectors.

Choice B is incorrect because comparing the data for 1800 and 2012 would suggest a similar rate of change in the two countries, not very different rates: employment in agriculture went from 64% in 1800 to 3% in 2012 in France, which is close to the change from 68% in 1800 to 2% in 2012 in the US, while employment in services went from 14% in 1800 to 76% in 2012 in France, which is close to the change from 13% in 1800 to 80% in 2012 in the US. *Choice C* is incorrect because comparing the data for 1900 and 2012 would suggest a similar rate of change in the two countries rather than very different rates: employment in agriculture went from 43% in 1900 to 3% in 2012 in France, which is close to the change from 41% in 1900 to 2% in 2012 in the US, while employment in services went from 28% in 1900 to 76% in 2012 in France, which is close to the change from 31% in 1900 to 80% in 2012 in the US. *Choice D* is incorrect because comparing the data for 1800 and 1900 would suggest a similar rate of change in the two countries, not very different rates: employment in agriculture went from 64% in 1800 to 43% in 1900 in France, which is fairly close to the change from 68% in 1800 to 41% in 1900 in the US, while employment in services went from 14% in 1800 to 28% in 1900 in France, which is close to the change from 13% in 1800 to 31% in 1900 in the US.

QUESTION 14

Choice D is the best answer because it presents the conclusion that most logically follows from the text's discussion of leafy spurge and engineered DNA. The text establishes that using chemical herbicides to control leafy spurge in North America can also harm other plants nearby. The text then indicates that it might be possible to use engineered DNA to prevent plants from reproducing, which would be useful for "exclusively targeting" leafy spurge. If it's possible to exclusively target leafy spurge with engineered DNA—meaning that only leafy spurge is affected by the engineered DNA—and prevent the plant from reproducing, then leafy spurge numbers could be reduced "without harming other organisms."

Choice A is incorrect because the text raises the possibility of using engineered DNA to prevent leafy spurge from reproducing, not to make individual leafy spurge plants more vulnerable to chemical herbicides that already exist. *Choice B* is incorrect because the text doesn't describe any ecological benefits of leafy spurge in North America; instead, the text is focused on using engineered DNA to prevent leafy spurge from reproducing and thereby reduce its numbers. The only ecological effects of leafy spurge in North America that are described in the text are harmful. *Choice C* is incorrect because the text describes the possibility of using engineered DNA to prevent leafy spurge from reproducing; it doesn't offer a way to enable cattle to eat leafy spurge without becoming sick.

QUESTION 15

Choice B is the best answer. The convention being tested is the use and punctuation of an integrated relative clause. This choice correctly uses the relative pronoun "that" and no punctuation to create an integrated relative clause that provides essential information about the noun phrase ("a book packaging company") that it modifies.

Choice A is incorrect because it doesn't use a relative pronoun to link the verb phrase beginning with "specializes" to the noun phrase that it modifies ("a book packaging company"). *Choice C* is incorrect because it doesn't use a relative pronoun to link the verb phrase beginning with "specializes" to the noun phrase that it modifies ("a book packaging company"). *Choice D* is incorrect because no punctuation is needed between the integrated relative clause beginning with "that specializes" and the noun phrase that it modifies ("a book packaging company").

QUESTION 16

Choice B is the best answer. The convention being tested is pronoun-antecedent agreement. The plural pronoun "they" agrees in number with the plural antecedent "woodcuts" and clearly identifies what was exhibited at the Smithsonian American Art Museum.

Choice A is incorrect because the singular pronoun "it" doesn't agree in number with the plural antecedent "woodcuts." *Choice C* is incorrect because the singular pronoun "this" doesn't agree in number with the plural antecedent "woodcuts." *Choice D* is incorrect because the plural pronoun "some" is illogical in this context (referring to "some" of only two woodcuts).

QUESTION 17

Choice D is the best answer. The convention being tested is punctuation use between sentences. In this choice, the period after "essays" is used correctly to mark the boundary between one sentence ("American…essays") and another ("Praising…Morrison"). The participial phrase beginning with "praising" modifies the subject of the second sentence, "writer Robert Antoni."

Choice A is incorrect because it results in a comma splice. A comma can't be used in this way to mark the boundary between sentences. *Choice B* is incorrect. Without a comma preceding it, the conjunction "and" can't be used in this way to join sentences. *Choice C* is incorrect because it results in a run-on sentence. The sentences ("American…essays" and "Praising…Morrison") are fused without punctuation and/or a conjunction.

QUESTION 18

Choice A is the best answer. The convention being tested is finite and nonfinite verb forms within a sentence. A main clause requires a finite verb to perform the action of the subject (in this case, Ashford's "gestures" and "habit"), and this choice supplies the finite past tense verb "helped" to indicate what Ashford's gestures and habit helped accomplish.

Choice B is incorrect because the nonfinite participle "helping" doesn't supply the main clause with a finite verb. *Choice C* is incorrect because the relative clause "that helped" doesn't supply the main clause with a finite verb. *Choice D* is incorrect because the nonfinite to-infinitive "to help" doesn't supply the main clause with a finite verb.

QUESTION 19

Choice C is the best answer. The convention being tested is punctuation between a subject and a verb. When, as in this case, a subject ("her 2019 novel *Gingerbread*") is immediately followed by a verb ("offers"), no punctuation is needed.

Choice A is incorrect because no punctuation is needed between the subject and the verb. *Choice B* is incorrect because no punctuation is needed between the subject and the verb. *Choice D* is incorrect because no punctuation is needed between the subject and the verb.

QUESTION 20

Choice D is the best answer. The convention being tested is pronoun-antecedent agreement. The singular pronoun "it" agrees in number with the singular antecedent "violin" and thus indicates that the traditional violin (and not its curves) was made lighter.

Choice A is incorrect because the plural pronoun "those" doesn't agree in number with the singular antecedent "violin." *Choice B* is incorrect because the singular pronoun "one" is ambiguous in this context; the resulting sentence leaves unclear what Stradivari made lighter. *Choice C* is incorrect because the plural pronoun "them" doesn't agree in number with the singular antecedent "violin."

QUESTION 21

Choice C is the best answer. The convention being tested is the punctuation of a supplementary word or phrase between two main clauses. This choice correctly uses a comma to separate the supplementary adverb "however" from the preceding main clause ("They...antiquity") and a semicolon to join the next main clause ("some...literature") to the rest of the sentence. Further, placing the semicolon after "however" indicates that the information in the preceding main clause (neoclassical writers were not the first to adopt classical literary modes) is contrary to what might be assumed from the information in the previous sentence (the neoclassical writers were unique in imitating classical epic poetry and satires).

Choice A is incorrect because it fails to mark the boundary between the two main clauses with appropriate punctuation. *Choice B* is incorrect because commas can't be used in this way to punctuate a supplementary word or phrase between two main clauses. *Choice D* is incorrect because placing the semicolon after "antiquity" illogically indicates that the information in the next main clause (prominent Renaissance figures were also influenced by classical literature) is contrary to the information in the previous clause (neoclassical writers were not the first to adopt classical literary modes).

QUESTION 22

Choice D is the best answer. "Nevertheless" logically signals that the claim in this sentence—that the telegenic Kennedy was ultimately considered the winner of the debate—is true despite the previous information about the poll of radio listeners.

Choice A is incorrect because "in other words" illogically signals that the claim in this sentence is a paraphrase of the previous information about the poll of radio listeners. Instead, Kennedy was ultimately considered the winner despite what that poll suggested about his performance. *Choice B* is incorrect because "therefore" illogically signals that the claim in this sentence is a result of the previous information about the poll of radio listeners. Instead, Kennedy was ultimately considered the winner despite what that poll suggested about his performance. *Choice C* is incorrect because "likewise" illogically signals that the claim in this sentence is similar to the previous information about the poll of radio listeners. Instead, Kennedy was ultimately considered the winner despite what that poll suggested about his performance.

QUESTION 23

Choice A is the best answer. "Still" logically signals that the information about Sher-Gil in this sentence—that she longed to leave Paris and return to India—contrasts with what one would expect after reading about Sher-Gil's experiences in Paris in the previous sentences.

Choice B is incorrect because "therefore" illogically signals that the information about Sher-Gil in this sentence is a result or consequence of the descriptions in the previous sentences. Instead, this information contrasts with what one would expect after reading about Sher-Gil's experiences in Paris. *Choice C* is incorrect because "indeed" illogically signals that the information about Sher-Gil in this sentence offers additional emphasis in support of the descriptions in the previous sentences. Instead, this information contrasts with what one would expect after reading about Sher-Gil's experiences in Paris. *Choice D* is incorrect because "furthermore" illogically signals that the information about Sher-Gil in this sentence offers additional support for or confirmation of the descriptions in the previous sentences. Instead, this information contrasts with what one would expect after reading about Sher-Gil's experiences in Paris.

QUESTION 24

Choice D is the best answer. "Specifically" logically signals that the information in this sentence about Sauer's argument—that, according to Sauer, cultures play a role in their own development, as opposed to being shaped solely by natural surroundings—provides specific, precise details elaborating on the more general information in the previous sentence about Sauer's challenge to prevailing views.

Choice A is incorrect because "similarly" illogically signals that the information in this sentence about Sauer's argument is similar to, but separate from, the more general information in the previous sentence. Instead, it provides specific, precise details elaborating on that information. *Choice B* is incorrect because "finally" illogically signals that the information in this sentence about Sauer's argument indicates a last step in a process or a concluding summary. Instead, it provides specific, precise details elaborating on the general information in the previous sentence. *Choice C* is incorrect because "therefore" illogically signals that the information in this sentence about Sauer's argument is a result of the more general information in the previous sentence. Instead, it provides specific, precise details elaborating on that information.

QUESTION 25

Choice C is the best answer. "Consequently" logically signals that the information in this sentence—that many individual gold prospectors gave up their fortune-hunting dreams and became employees of mining companies—is a result or consequence of the previous information about the inaccessibility of the state's gold deposits.

Choice A is incorrect because "furthermore" illogically signals that the information in this sentence merely adds to the previous information about the inaccessibility of the state's gold deposits. Instead, it's a result or consequence of that information. *Choice B* is incorrect because "still" illogically signals that the information in this sentence offers a contrast or exception to the previous information about the inaccessibility of the state's gold deposits. Instead, it's a result or consequence of that information. *Choice D* is incorrect because "next" illogically signals that the information in this sentence is the next step in a process. Instead, it's a result or consequence of the previous information about the inaccessibility of the state's gold deposits.

QUESTION 26

Choice B is the best answer. The sentence presents the study, describing it as a 2013 analysis of Quanhucun cat bone fragments, and its conclusions, indicating what the analysis suggests about cat domestication in Quanhucun.

Choice A is incorrect because the sentence focuses on the study's methodology; it doesn't present conclusions from the study. *Choice C* is incorrect. While the sentence provides a general overview of the study, it doesn't present conclusions from the study. *Choice D* is incorrect. The sentence describes a finding from the study; it doesn't present conclusions from the study.

QUESTION 27

Choice A is the best answer. Noting that "guerdon" is of Anglo-French origin and "Laodicean" is of ancient Greek origin, the sentence uses "while" to emphasize a difference in the origins of the two words.

Choice B is incorrect. While the sentence emphasizes two words used in the Scripps National Spelling Bee, it doesn't emphasize (or mention) the words' linguistic origins. *Choice C* is incorrect. While the sentence specifies the linguistic origin of one word used in the Scripps National Spelling Bee, it doesn't mention the other word or emphasize a difference in the two words' origins. *Choice D* is incorrect. While the sentence makes a generalization about words used in the Scripps National Spelling Bee, it doesn't emphasize a difference in the words' origins.

Reading and Writing

Module 2
(27 questions)

QUESTION 1

Choice C is the best answer because it most logically completes the text's discussion of John Ashbery's poems. As used in this context, "interpret" would mean decipher the meaning of. The text indicates that Ashbery's poems have many unusual features, that it's difficult to tell what exactly the poems' subject matter is, and that scholars strongly disagree about the poems. This context conveys the idea that it's difficult to interpret Ashbery's poems.

Choice A is incorrect because "delegate" means to assign someone as a representative of another person or to entrust something to someone else, neither of which would make sense in context. The text is focused only on the difficulty that readers have interpreting Ashbery's poems due to their many unusual features; it doesn't suggest anything about the poems being difficult to delegate. *Choice B* is incorrect because describing Ashbery's poems as difficult to "compose," or put together or produce, would make sense only if the text were about Ashbery's experience of writing the poems. It could be true that it was difficult for Ashbery to compose his poems, but the text doesn't address this; it instead discusses how readers interpret and engage with the poems. *Choice D* is incorrect because describing Ashbery's poems as being difficult to "renounce," or give up or refuse, wouldn't make sense in context. The text focuses on the idea that features of Ashbery's poems are odd or unclear and have caused heated scholarly debate. This context suggests that the poems are difficult to interpret, not that the poems are difficult to renounce.

QUESTION 2

Choice D is the best answer because it most logically completes the text's discussion of the research that Lopes-Ferreira and her colleagues are conducting on the stingray species *Potamotrygon rex*. As used in this context, "a substantial" effect means an effect that is sizable or noteworthy. The text indicates that the researchers are seeking to determine whether there are "considerable variations" in the potency of stingray venom that are associated with variation in the stingrays' age and sex. This context suggests that the researchers want to find out whether stingray age and sex have a substantial effect on venom toxicity.

Choice A is incorrect because there's nothing in the text that suggests that the researchers have been studying whether the stingrays' age and sex have "a disconcerting," or an unsettling and disturbing, effect on the stingrays' venom. The text indicates that the researchers wish to determine if stingray age and sex cause large variations in the toxicity of stingray venom, not if the effect of age and sex is disconcerting. *Choice B* is incorrect because the text indicates that researchers want to find out whether differences in stingray age and sex produce differences in stingray venom, not that the researchers want to find out whether age and sex have "an acceptable," or a satisfactory, effect on venom. The text makes no mention of what would make an effect on venom toxicity acceptable and gives no indication that the researchers are interested in that question. *Choice C* is incorrect because it wouldn't make sense in context for the researchers to be looking for "an imperceptible," or an unnoticeable, effect of age and sex on stingray venom. The text says that the researchers are trying to determine if there are "considerable variations" in venom toxicity linked to age and sex, not that the researchers are trying to find effects that they can't perceive.

QUESTION 3

Choice B is the best answer because it most logically completes the text's discussion of Ochoa's prediction that humans will one day need to live in places other than Earth. As used in this context, "speculates" would mean puts forward an idea without firm evidence. The text states that Ochoa "doesn't have a definite idea" about when humans might need to live in other environments and characterizes Ochoa's prediction as a "conjecture," or a conclusion presented without convincing evidence. This context indicates that Ochoa speculates when she makes this prediction.

Choice A is incorrect because saying that Ochoa "demands," or insists or requires, that humans will one day need to live in other environments than Earth's wouldn't make sense in context. The text indicates that she's unsure about the timing but hypothesizes that it will someday happen. *Choice C* is incorrect because saying that Ochoa "doubts," or questions or disbelieves, that humans will one day need to live in other environments than Earth's wouldn't make sense in context. The text indicates that although Ochoa is unsure about the timing, she hypothesizes that humans will need to live in places other than Earth and encourages research into future travel to the moon. *Choice D* is incorrect because saying that Ochoa "establishes," or proves, that humans will one day need to live in other environments than Earth's wouldn't make sense in context. Rather than stating that Ochoa discusses her idea with certainty and supports it with evidence, the text indicates that Ochoa is unsure about when humans might need to live in other environments.

QUESTION 4

Choice D is the best answer because it most logically completes the text's discussion of the collaboration between the Crow Tribe and Montana State University. As used in this context, "exemplifies" means demonstrates. The text conveys how the Crow Tribe–Montana State University collaboration serves to illustrate the model of community-based participatory research introduced earlier in the text and expanded on later in the text.

Choice A is incorrect because referring to "circumvents," or avoids, wouldn't make sense in context. The text suggests that the Crow Tribe–Montana State University collaboration serves as an example of the principles of community-based participatory research, not that the collaboration evades this model. *Choice B* is incorrect because referring to "eclipses," or overshadows, wouldn't make sense in context. The text describes the Crow Tribe–Montana

State University collaboration as an equal partnership, which indicates that it's an example of the community-based participatory research model, not that it overshadows the model. *Choice C* is incorrect because saying that the collaboration "fabricates," or creates, the model wouldn't make sense in context. The text indicates that the Crow Tribe–Montana State University collaboration serves as an example of the model, not that it created the model.

QUESTION 5

Choice A is the best answer because it most logically completes the text's discussion of diaphragm contractions and hiccups. In this context, "involuntarily" means done without any control, or by reflex. The text explains that when a person's diaphragm repeatedly contracts and results in hiccups (which may be beneficial for infants), those muscle contractions are "uncontrollable." This context indicates that the diaphragm contractions occur without the person's control.

Choice B is incorrect because it wouldn't support the logical relationship established in the text's discussion of diaphragm contractions and hiccups. The text indicates that although specific causes for hiccups haven't been identified, it may be the case that the muscle contractions that occur have an important purpose in infants. It wouldn't make sense to say that even though the contractions occur "beneficially," or with a good or helpful effect, they might play a positive role in infants' breathing regulation. *Choice C* is incorrect because the text indicates that the diaphragm contractions that result in hiccups are "uncontrollable." Because those muscle contractions are described as happening automatically and without the person's control, it wouldn't make sense to describe them as occurring "strenuously," or in a way that requires great effort or energy. *Choice D* is incorrect because the text doesn't describe the quality of the diaphragm contractions that result in hiccups beyond stating that they are "uncontrollable." Nothing in the text indicates that those muscle contractions occur "smoothly," or evenly and continuously.

QUESTION 6

Choice A is the best answer because it most logically completes the text's discussion of a relationship between the dodder plant and its host plant. As used in this context, "synchronization" means the act of things happening at the same time. The text indicates that the dodder and its host plant flower in unison and that this synchronization occurs because the dodder makes use of a protein produced by the host shortly before flowering.

Choice B is incorrect because referring to "hibernation," or the state of being dormant or inactive, wouldn't make sense in context. The text focuses on something the dodder plant actively engages in—making use of a protein and producing flowers. *Choice C* is incorrect because stating that the dodder plant and its host engage together in "prediction," or the act of declaring or indicating something in advance, wouldn't make sense in context. Rather than indicating that the dodder plant and its host plant make a prediction about flowering activity, the text suggests that the host produces a protein as part of its regular flowering process and that the dodder then absorbs and uses that protein to flower at the same time. *Choice D* is incorrect because referring to "moderation," or the act of causing something to become less intense or extreme, wouldn't make sense in context. Although the text states that the dodder plant absorbs and uses a protein made by its host plant, it doesn't suggest that the dodder lessens the host plant's flowering activity; the two plants simply flower in unison.

QUESTION 7

Choice C is the best answer because it most logically completes the text's discussion of how Ofelia Zepeda has contributed to the field of linguistics. As used in this context, "extensive" means having a wide or considerable extent. The text indicates that Zepeda's many accomplishments in linguistics are varied, including teaching linguistics, writing poetry in more than one language, creating a grammar book, and cofounding a language institute. This context supports the idea that Zepeda's contributions to the field are extensive.

Choice A is incorrect because the sentence presents Zepeda's accomplishments as examples to support the claim made in the first part of the sentence. It wouldn't make sense to say that achievements as a professor, poet and author, and co-founder of a language institute demonstrate that Zepeda's contributions in her field are "pragmatic," or related to practical matters and not involving intellectual or artistic matters. *Choice B* is incorrect because the sentence presents Zepeda's accomplishments as a professor, poet and author, and cofounder of a language institute as examples to support the claim made in the first part of the sentence. There's no reason to believe that the positive achievements listed demonstrate that Zepeda's contributions in her field are "controversial," or have caused disputes and opposing viewpoints. *Choice D* is incorrect because in this context, "universal" would mean including or covering everything in a group. The sentence presents Zepeda's accomplishments as examples to support the claim made in the first part of the sentence, and it wouldn't make sense to say that these specific achievements—particularly as the author of a grammar book specific to the Tohono O'odham language—demonstrate that Zepeda's contributions relate to everything in the field of linguistics.

QUESTION 8

Choice D is the best answer because it most logically completes the text's discussion of the Three Sisters intercropping system. As used in this context, "intricate" would mean made up of complexly related elements. The text indicates that in the Three Sisters system, maize, squash, and beans form a "web of relations" in which the crops interact in various ways. The text's description of these interactions—the bean vines growing on the maize stalks, the squash vines keeping weeds away, and the beans adding nutrients that the maize and squash use—provides context suggesting that this "web of relations" is intricate.

Choice A is incorrect because describing the relationship among the crops in the Three Sisters system as "indecipherable," or impossible to comprehend, would not make sense in context. Although the text presents the relationship as complex, the text's description of the role that each crop plays makes it clear that the relationship is well understood, not indecipherable. *Choice B* is incorrect because the text discusses the practical benefits that each plant in the Three Sisters system provides to other members of the system, showing that the relationship among the crops that make up the system is not "ornamental," or mainly serving a decorative purpose. *Choice C* is incorrect because describing the relationship among the crops in the Three Sisters system as "obscure," or unknown or poorly understood, would not make sense in context. Although the text presents the relationship as complex, the text's description of the role that each crop plays makes it clear that the relationship is well understood, not obscure.

QUESTION 9

Choice B is the best answer because it presents a statement about Dorian that is directly supported by the text. The narrator of the text says that when Dorian sees his portrait, "his cheeks flushed for a moment with pleasure" and "a look of joy came into his eyes." The narrator goes on to say that Dorian looked at the portrait "in wonder" and presents him as being so entranced by the portrait that he doesn't notice what Hallward is saying to him. These details support the description of Dorian as being delighted by what he sees in the portrait.

Choice A is incorrect because Dorian isn't depicted as interested in Hallward's opinion of the portrait; rather, he is so enraptured by the painting that he's hardly even aware of Hallward. *Choice C* is incorrect because the portrait of Dorian is the only painting mentioned in the text. Although Dorian is depicted as being delighted with this particular portrait, there's no evidence in the text that he likes portraits better than other kinds of paintings. *Choice D* is incorrect because nothing in the text suggests that Dorian is uncertain about Hallward's talent. Instead, the text is focused on Dorian's delight with the portrait.

QUESTION 10

Choice C is the best answer because it presents the quotation that best illustrates the claim that the speaker is determined to experience the countryside around her. In the quotation, the speaker makes it clear that she plans to walk somewhere based on her own wishes ("where my own nature would be leading") rather than follow anything else ("another guide"), and that she'll walk "in ferny glens" alongside the mountain.

Choice A is incorrect because this quotation suggests that the speaker wants to avoid pursuing money and education ("busy chase of wealth and learning") and instead return to some earlier interests (her "first feelings"); the quotation doesn't address her determination to experience the countryside. *Choice B* is incorrect because the speaker is describing the circumstances under which she won't walk, which doesn't address her determination to experience the countryside. *Choice D* is incorrect because rather than conveying her determination to experience the countryside, the speaker is explaining a particular thing she won't do ("seek not the shadowy region").

QUESTION 11

Choice C is the best answer because it presents a quotation that illustrates the claim that Mrs. Spring Fragrance demonstrates concern for what's happening at home while she's in California. By giving reminders to "care for the cat, the birds, and the flowers," "not eat too quickly," and avoid engaging in strenuous activity in the heat, Mrs. Spring Fragrance shows that she's thinking about what's happening at home and wants to ensure everything is taken care of.

Choice A is incorrect because the quotation, while it does suggest that Mrs. Spring Fragrance has made fudge at home before, is focused on preparations for an upcoming festival, not on concerns for anything happening at home while Mrs. Spring Fragrance is away. *Choice B* is incorrect because the quotation has to do with an upcoming event during Mrs. Spring Fragrance's trip—visiting San José and meeting someone new—rather than her concern for what's happening at home. *Choice D* is incorrect because the quotation is focused on how Mrs. Spring Fragrance feels about her trip and the friends she's seeing, not on her concern for what's happening at home.

QUESTION 12

Choice B is the best answer because it most effectively illustrates the claim in the text that Hedda seeks to influence another character's fate. In the quotation, Hedda says that she wants "to have power to mould a human destiny," or shape a person's fate, just as the text indicates. Additionally, the phrase "for once in my life" suggests that Hedda feels that she has never been able to shape anyone's life, including her own, supporting the text's assertion that she "is unable to freely determine her own future."

Choice A is incorrect because this quotation shows Hedda being uncertain about what to do with her own life, not wanting to influence another person's fate. *Choice C* is incorrect because while this quotation shows Hedda's interest in finding out whether she has any power over another character, it doesn't clearly show that she wants to influence that person's fate. In this quotation, Hedda seems to have inferred or concluded ("then") that she doesn't have any influence over the person to whom she's speaking, and she's asking that person to confirm her lack of influence. *Choice D* is incorrect because this quotation expresses Hedda's belief that a man should be true to his principles, not her desire to influence another person's fate.

QUESTION 13

Choice B is the best answer because it most logically completes the text's discussion of artifacts and Kuulo Kataa's founding date. If it were true both that Kuulo Kataa was founded in the fourteenth century CE and that artifacts found in excavations of the settlement are from the thirteenth century CE, it would be reasonable to conclude that the artifacts weren't created in the Kuulo Kataa settlement. That would suggest, then, that the artifacts originated somewhere else and eventually reached the settlement through trading or as people migrated.

Choice A is incorrect because the existence of thirteenth-century CE artifacts recovered during excavations of a settlement founded in the fourteenth century CE isn't logically connected to artifacts from one century being more commonly recovered than artifacts from another century. Rather than suggesting anything about how frequently artifacts from different times are found, the existence of artifacts confirmed as predating the settlement's founding suggests that those items arrived in Kuulo Kataa during or after its establishment. *Choice C* is incorrect because the text focuses on time periods and says nothing about which region the founders of Kuulo Kataa have been thought to come from; similarly, the text doesn't suggest anything about where the thirteenth-century CE artifacts originated other than not from Kuulo Kataa. Therefore, it isn't logical to conclude that the mere existence of artifacts confirmed as predating the Kuulo Kataa settlement suggests that the founders of the settlement came from a particular region other than one previously assumed. *Choice D* is incorrect because the existence of artifacts from the thirteenth century CE at a site dated to the fourteenth century CE doesn't imply that fourteenth-century objects were damaged during excavations. There's nothing in the text to suggest that any objects were damaged; rather, the existence of artifacts confirmed as predating the settlement's founding suggests that those items were brought to Kuulo Kataa during or after its establishment.

QUESTION 14

Choice A is the best answer because it most logically completes the text's discussion of the evolution of bipedalism in humans. According to the text, one potential explanation for humans walking upright on two legs is that the behavior evolved from an ancestor that mostly stayed on the ground and walked on four limbs, as modern chimpanzees and gorillas do. However, the finding that orangutans, also a relative of humans, sometimes stand on two legs in trees while using their arms to balance and reach for fruits suggests another possible explanation: perhaps a tree-dwelling ancestor of humans began moving on two legs because it offered an advantage, such as access to certain foods.

Choice B is incorrect because the finding that modern orangutans (a relative of humans) sometimes stand on two legs in trees doesn't offer any insight into when either bipedalism or tree-climbing behavior emerged in human ancestors.

Additionally, the text indicates that one theory is that bipedalism evolved from a mostly ground-based ancestor that was already practicing knuckle-walking, not that bipedalism and knuckle-walking developed at the same time. *Choice C* is incorrect because the finding that orangutans (a relative of humans) sometimes stand on two legs in trees doesn't offer any insight into how difficult it would've been to move between the ground and the trees without bipedalism; there's no suggestion that climbing or moving in trees depends on the ability to walk on two legs rather than four, even if that ability might be helpful in certain circumstances. *Choice D* is incorrect because the finding that orangutans (a relative of humans) sometimes stand on two legs in trees doesn't suggest that a knuckle-walking human ancestor could've easily moved on two legs in trees. Although the text indicates that bipedalism may have evolved from a human ancestor that mostly stayed on the ground and walked on four limbs, it gives no indication of how easy it would've been for such an ancestor to move bipedally in trees.

QUESTION 15

Choice A is the best answer because it presents the conclusion that most logically follows from the text's discussion of the study of capuchin monkeys' cognitive abilities. The text explains that the study failed to distinguish between outcomes for the tasks performed by the capuchin monkeys, such that simpler tasks requiring less dexterity, or skill, were judged by the same criteria as tasks that demanded more dexterity. Because the study didn't account for this discrepancy, the researchers might have assumed that observed differences in performance were due to the abilities of the monkeys rather than the complexity of the tasks. In other words, the results may suggest cognitive differences among the monkeys even though such differences may not really exist.

Choice B is incorrect because the text focuses on the fact that the tasks assigned to the capuchin monkeys in the study varied in difficulty and that the variety wasn't taken into consideration. The text doesn't suggest that the capuchin monkeys couldn't perform certain tasks, just that some tasks were more difficult to do. *Choice C* is incorrect because the text doesn't suggest that the study's results are indicative of the abilities of capuchin monkeys but not of other monkey species; in fact, the text suggests that the results may not even be an accurate reflection of capuchin monkeys' abilities. *Choice D* is incorrect because the text doesn't indicate that the researchers compared results for artificial tasks with those for tasks encountered in the wild, although the tasks described in the text—sliding a panel and putting a straw in a bottle—are presumably artificial.

QUESTION 16

Choice D is the best answer because it presents the conclusion that most logically follows from the text's discussion of how digital technologies affected the process of book creation. The text explains that in the late 20th and early 21st centuries digital technologies lowered book production costs most significantly in manufacturing and distribution. The text goes on to point out that authoring, editing, and book design are distinct steps in the process that occur before manufacturing and distribution. Because the savings connected to digital technologies have been most significant in manufacturing and distribution, it's reasonable to infer that those technologies had less of an effect on writing, editing, and designing books.

Choice A is incorrect because the text focuses on lowered book production costs that occur after authoring has taken place; there's no indication in the text whether digital technologies made writing and publishing lengthy books easier.

Choice B is incorrect. Although it's logical to conclude that customers would expect the cost of books to decline if production costs have declined, the text doesn't address customer expectations for the cost of books or any other consumer goods. *Choice C* is incorrect because the text focuses broadly on how digital technologies have affected the cost of the publishing process; it doesn't address the kinds of books being published or how many copies are printed.

QUESTION 17

Choice A is the best answer. The convention being tested is pronoun-antecedent agreement. The plural pronoun "they" agrees in number with the plural antecedent "customers."

Choice B is incorrect because the singular pronoun "one" doesn't agree in number with the plural antecedent "customers." *Choice C* is incorrect because the second person pronoun "you" isn't conventional as a substitute for "customers." It suggests that the audience ("you") is the customer. *Choice D* is incorrect because the singular pronoun "it" doesn't agree in number with the plural antecedent "customers."

QUESTION 18

Choice A is the best answer. The convention being tested is the use of finite and nonfinite verb forms within a sentence. Relative clauses, such as the one beginning with "which," require a finite verb, a verb that can function as the main verb of a clause. This choice correctly supplies the clause with the finite past tense verb "provided."

Choice B is incorrect because the nonfinite participle "having provided" doesn't supply the clause with a finite verb. *Choice C* is incorrect because the nonfinite to-infinitive "to provide" doesn't supply the clause with a finite verb. *Choice D* is incorrect because the nonfinite participle "providing" doesn't supply the clause with a finite verb.

QUESTION 19

Choice A is the best answer. The convention being tested is the coordination of clauses within a sentence. This choice correctly uses a comma and the coordinating conjunction "but" to join a main clause ("Typically...value") and a subordinate clause ("when...Whitman") that precedes a main clause ("such...scholars").

Choice B is incorrect because it results in a run-on sentence. A main clause is fused without punctuation and/or a conjunction to a subordinate clause that precedes a main clause. *Choice C* is incorrect because it results in a comma splice. A comma can't be used in this way to mark the boundary between a main clause and a subordinate clause that precedes a main clause. *Choice D* is incorrect. Without a comma preceding it, the conjunction "but" can't be used in this way to join a main clause and a subordinate clause that precedes a main clause.

QUESTION 20

Choice C is the best answer. The convention being tested is the use of possessive determiners. The plural possessive determiner "their" agrees in number with the plural conjoined noun phrase "Watson and Crick" and thus indicates that the findings were those of Watson and Crick.

Choice A is incorrect because "they're" is the contraction for "they are," not a possessive determiner. *Choice B* is incorrect because "it's" is the contraction for "it is" or "it has," not a possessive determiner. *Choice D* is incorrect because the singular possessive determiner "its" doesn't agree in number with the plural conjoined noun phrase "Watson and Crick."

QUESTION 21

Choice B is the best answer. The convention being tested is the use of finite and nonfinite verb forms within a sentence. The modal "would," which indicates the future from a perspective in the past, should be accompanied by a nonfinite base form verb. In this choice, the nonfinite base form verb "create" is used correctly in conjunction with the nonfinite base form verb "increase" to describe what the lock would do.

Choice A is incorrect because the finite present tense verb "creates" can't be used in this way with the modal "would" to describe what the lock would do. *Choice C* is incorrect because the present participle "creating" can't be used in this way with the modal "would" to describe what the lock would do. *Choice D* is incorrect because the finite past tense verb "created" can't be used in this way with the modal "would" to describe what the lock would do.

QUESTION 22

Choice D is the best answer. The convention being tested is end-of-sentence punctuation. This choice correctly uses a question mark to punctuate the interrogative clause "could the blueberries thrive," which asks a direct question at the end of the sentence.

Choice A is incorrect because a period can't be used in this way to punctuate an interrogative clause, such as "could the blueberries thrive," at the end of a sentence. *Choice B* is incorrect because the context requires an interrogative clause. The declarative clause "the blueberries could thrive" incorrectly indicates that it was known that the blueberries could thrive in alkaline soil, whereas Michel had yet to find this out. *Choice C* is incorrect because a question mark can't be used in this way to punctuate a declarative clause, such as "the blueberries could thrive," at the end of a sentence.

QUESTION 23

Choice A is the best answer. The convention being tested is subject–verb agreement. The singular verb "allows" agrees in number with the singular subject "landing."

Choice B is incorrect because the plural verb "are allowing" doesn't agree in number with the singular subject "landing." *Choice C* is incorrect because the plural verb "have allowed" doesn't agree in number with the singular subject "landing." *Choice D* is incorrect because the plural verb "allow" doesn't agree in number with the singular subject "landing."

QUESTION 24

Choice C is the best answer. "Finally" logically signals that the bill passing—following many attempts between 1968 and 1983—is the final, concluding event in the sequence described in the previous sentences.

Choice A is incorrect because "instead" illogically signals that the bill passing is an alternative to one of the events described in the previous sentences. It is the final event in the sequence. *Choice B* is incorrect because "likewise" illogically signals that the bill passing is similar to one of the events described in the previous sentences. Instead, it is the final event in the sequence. *Choice D* is incorrect because "additionally" illogically signals that the bill passing is merely another event described along with the events of the previous sentences. Instead, it is the final, concluding event in the sequence.

QUESTION 25

Choice A is the best answer. "For instance" logically signals that the information in this sentence—that larch trees lose their needles every fall—is an example supporting the claim in the previous sentence (that not all conifer species keep their leaves or needles year-round).

Choice B is incorrect because "nevertheless" illogically signals that the information in this sentence is true in spite of the claim about conifer species in the previous sentence. Instead, it's an example supporting that claim. *Choice C* is incorrect because "meanwhile" illogically signals that the information in this sentence is separate from (while occurring simultaneously with) the claim about conifer species in the previous sentence. Instead, it's an example supporting that claim. *Choice D* is incorrect because "in addition" illogically signals that the information in this sentence is merely an additional fact related to the claim about conifer species in the previous sentence. Instead, it's an example supporting that claim.

QUESTION 26

Choice A is the best answer. "In addition" logically signals that the detail in this sentence—that Coleridge-Taylor included traditional African music in his classical compositions—adds to the information in the previous sentence. Specifically, the previous sentence indicates one way in which Coleridge-Taylor emphasized his mixed-race ancestry, and the claim that follows indicates a second, additional way.

Choice B is incorrect because "actually" illogically signals that the detail in this sentence is surprising in light of the information in the previous sentence. Instead, the detail adds to the information, indicating a second, additional way in which Coleridge-Taylor emphasized his mixed-race ancestry. *Choice C* is incorrect because "however" illogically signals that the detail in this sentence contrasts with the information in the previous sentence. Instead, the detail adds to the information, indicating a second, additional way in which Coleridge-Taylor emphasized his mixed-race ancestry. *Choice D* is incorrect because "regardless" illogically signals that the detail in this sentence is true despite the information in the previous sentence. Instead, the detail adds to the information, indicating a second, additional way in which Coleridge-Taylor emphasized his mixed-race ancestry.

QUESTION 27

Choice D is the best answer. The sentence uses information from the notes to make a generalization about the kind of study Glickman, Brown, and Song conducted. Specifically, the sentence indicates that the study was of a kind that used statistical methods to address questions of authorship within the field of music.

Choice A is incorrect because the sentence summarizes the methodology and findings of a particular analysis of a single song; it doesn't make a generalization about the kind of study conducted. *Choice B* is incorrect because the sentence mentions the data and conclusion of a particular analysis of a single song; it doesn't make a generalization about the kind of study conducted. *Choice C* is incorrect because the sentence focuses on a specific conclusion from a particular analysis of a single song; it doesn't make a generalization about the kind of study conducted.

Math

Module 1
(22 questions)

QUESTION 1

Choice A is correct. A frequency table is a table that lists the data value and shows the number of times the data value occurs. In the data listed, the number 4 occurs four times, the number 8 occurs three times, and the number 13 occurs two times. This corresponds to the table in choice A.

Choice B is incorrect. This table has the values for number and frequency reversed. *Choice C* is incorrect because the frequency values don't represent the data listed. *Choice D* is incorrect. This table represents the listed number values as the frequency values.

QUESTION 2

Choice B is correct. The given expression may be rewritten as $x^2 + 8x - 5x - 40$. Since the first two terms of this expression have a common factor of x and the last two terms of this expression have a common factor of -5, this expression may be rewritten as $x(x) + x(8) - 5(x) - 5(8)$, or $x(x + 8) - 5(x + 8)$. Since each term of this expression has a common factor of $(x + 8)$, it may be rewritten as $(x - 5)(x + 8)$.

Alternate approach: An expression of the form $x^2 + bx + c$, where b and c are constants, can be factored if there are two values that add to give b and multiply to give c. In the given expression, $b = 3$ and $c = -40$. The values of -5 and 8 add to give 3 and multiply to give -40, so the expression can be factored as $(x - 5)(x + 8)$.

Choice A is incorrect. This expression is equivalent to $x^2 + 6x - 40$, not $x^2 + 3x - 40$. *Choice C* is incorrect. This expression is equivalent to $x^2 - 3x - 40$, not $x^2 + 3x - 40$. *Choice D* is incorrect. This expression is equivalent to $x^2 - 6x - 40$, not $x^2 + 3x - 40$.

QUESTION 3

Choice A is correct. Since Jay walks at a speed of 3 miles per hour for w hours, Jay walks a total of $3w$ miles. Since Jay runs at a speed of 5 miles per hour for r hours, Jay runs a total of $5r$ miles. Therefore, the total number of miles Jay travels can be represented by $3w + 5r$. Since the combined total number of miles is 14, the equation $3w + 5r = 14$ represents this situation.

Choice B is incorrect and may result from conceptual errors. *Choice C* is incorrect and may result from conceptual errors. *Choice D* is incorrect and may result from conceptual errors.

QUESTION 4

Choice D is correct. The sum of the angle measures of a triangle is 180°. Adding the measures of angles *B* and *C* gives 52 + 17 = 69°. Therefore, the measure of angle *A* is 180 − 69 = 111°.

Choice A is incorrect and may result from subtracting the sum of the measures of angles *B* and *C* from 90°, instead of from 180°. *Choice B* is incorrect and may result from subtracting the measure of angle *C* from the measure of angle *B*. *Choice C* is incorrect and may result from adding the measures of angles *B* and *C* but not subtracting the result from 180°.

QUESTION 5

Choice A is correct. It's given that the electrician charges a onetime fee plus an hourly rate. It's also given that the graph represents the total charge, in dollars, for *x* hours of work. This graph shows a linear relationship in the *xy*-plane. Thus, the total charge *y*, in dollars, for *x* hours of work can be represented as $y = mx + b$, where *m* is the slope and (0, *b*) is the *y*-intercept of the graph of the equation in the *xy*-plane. Since the given graph represents the total charge, in dollars, by an electrician for *x* hours of work, it follows that its slope is *m*, or the electrician's hourly rate.

Choice B is incorrect. The electrician's onetime fee is represented by the *y*-coordinate of the *y*-intercept, not the slope, of the graph. *Choice C* is incorrect and may result from conceptual errors. *Choice D* is incorrect and may result from conceptual errors.

QUESTION 6

The correct answer is $\frac{3}{10}$. It's given that there are a total of 100 tiles of equal area, which is the total number of possible outcomes. According to the table, there are a total of 30 red tiles. The probability of an event occurring is the ratio of the number of favorable outcomes to the total number of possible outcomes. By definition, the probability of selecting a red tile is given by $\frac{30}{100}$, or $\frac{3}{10}$. Note that 3/10 and .3 are examples of ways to enter a correct answer.

QUESTION 7

Choice C is correct. It's given that an estimated 35% of people in the population support the legislation, with an associated margin of error of 3%. Subtracting and adding the margin of error from the estimate gives an interval of plausible values for the true percentage of people in the population who support the legislation. Therefore, it's plausible that between 32% and 38% of people in this population support the legislation. The corresponding numbers of people represented by these percentages in the population can be calculated by multiplying the total population, 50,000, by 0.32 and by 0.38, which gives 50,000(0.32) = 16,000 and 50,000(0.38) = 19,000, respectively. It follows that any value in the interval 16,000 to 19,000 is a plausible value for the total number of people in the population who support the proposed legislation. Of the choices given, only 16,750 is in this interval.

Choice A is incorrect. This is the number of people in the sample, rather than in the population, who support the legislation. *Choice B* is incorrect. This is the number of people in the sample who do not support the legislation. *Choice D* is incorrect. This is a plausible value for the total number of people in the population who do not support the proposed legislation.

QUESTION 8

The correct answer is 5. Multiplying both sides of the given equation by $x + 6$ results in $55 = x(x + 6)$. Applying the distributive property of multiplication to the right-hand side of this equation results in $55 = x^2 + 6x$. Subtracting 55 from both sides of this equation results in $0 = x^2 + 6x - 55$. The right-hand side of this equation can be rewritten by factoring. The two values that multiply to -55 and add to 6 are 11 and -5. It follows that the equation $0 = x^2 + 6x - 55$ can be rewritten as $0 = (x + 11)(x - 5)$. Setting each factor equal to 0 yields two equations: $x + 11 = 0$ and $x - 5 = 0$. Subtracting 11 from both sides of the equation $x + 11 = 0$ results in $x = -11$. Adding 5 to both sides of the equation $x - 5 = 0$ results in $x = 5$. Therefore, the positive solution to the given equation is 5.

QUESTION 9

Choice B is correct. It's given that the airplane descends at a constant rate of 400 feet per minute. Since the altitude decreases by a constant amount during each fixed time period, the relationship between the airplane's altitude and time is linear. Since the airplane descends from an altitude of 9,500 feet to 5,000 feet, the airplane's altitude is decreasing with time. Thus, the relationship is best modeled by a decreasing linear function.

Choice A is incorrect and may result from conceptual or calculation errors.
Choice C is incorrect and may result from conceptual or calculation errors.
Choice D is incorrect and may result from conceptual or calculation errors.

QUESTION 10

Choice A is correct. The x-coordinate of any y-intercept of a graph is 0. Substituting 0 for x in the given equation yields $g(0) = 11\left(\frac{1}{12}\right)^0$. Since any nonzero number raised to the 0th power is 1, this gives $g(0) = 11 \cdot 1$, or $g(0) = 11$. The y-intercept of the graph is, therefore, the point $(0, 11)$.

Choice B is incorrect and may result from conceptual or calculation errors.
Choice C is incorrect and may result from conceptual or calculation errors.
Choice D is incorrect and may result from conceptual or calculation errors.

QUESTION 11

Choice B is correct. Since PR and QS are diameters of the circle shown, OS, OR, OP, and OQ are radii of the circle and are therefore congruent. Since $\angle SOP$ and $\angle ROQ$ are vertical angles, they are congruent. Therefore, arc PS and arc QR are formed by congruent radii and have the same angle measure, so they are congruent arcs. Similarly, $\angle SOR$ and $\angle POQ$ are vertical angles, so they are congruent. Therefore, arc SR and arc PQ are formed by congruent radii and have the same angle measure, so they are congruent arcs. Let x represent the length of arc SR. Since arc SR and arc PQ are congruent arcs, the length of arc PQ can also be represented by x. It's given that the length of arc PS is twice the length of arc PQ. Therefore, the length of arc PS can be represented by the expression $2x$. Since arc PS and arc QR are congruent arcs, the length of arc QR can also be represented by $2x$. This gives the expression $x + x + 2x + 2x$. Since it's given that the circumference is 144π, the expression $x + x + 2x + 2x$ is equal to 144π. Thus $x + x + 2x + 2x = 144\pi$, or $6x = 144\pi$. Dividing both sides of this equation by 6 yields $x = 24\pi$. Therefore, the length of arc QR is $2(24\pi)$, or 48π.

Choice A is incorrect. This is the length of arc PQ, not arc QR. *Choice C* is incorrect and may result from conceptual or calculation errors. *Choice D* is incorrect and may result from conceptual or calculation errors.

QUESTION 12

Choice B is correct. The area of a rectangle is equal to its length multiplied by its width. Multiplying the given length, x units, by the given width, $(x - 15)$ units, yields $x(x - 15)$ square units. If the rectangle has an area of 76 square units, it follows that $x(x - 15) = 76$, or $x^2 - 15x = 76$. Subtracting 76 from both sides of this equation yields $x^2 - 15x - 76 = 0$. Factoring the left-hand side of this equation yields $(x - 19)(x + 4) = 0$. Applying the zero product property to this equation yields two solutions: $x = 19$ and $x = -4$. Since x is the rectangle's length, in units, which must be positive, the value of x is 19.

Choice A is incorrect. This is the width, in units, of the rectangle, not the value of x. *Choice C* is incorrect and may result from conceptual or calculation errors. *Choice D* is incorrect. This is the area, in square units, of the rectangle, not the value of x.

QUESTION 13

Choice C is correct. It's given that the relationship between t and n is exponential. The table shows that the value of n increases as the value of t increases. Therefore, the relationship between t and n can be represented by an increasing exponential equation of the form $n = a(1 + b)^t$, where a and b are positive constants. The table shows that when $t = 0$, $n = 604$. Substituting 0 for t and 604 for n in the equation $n = a(1 + b)^t$ yields $604 = a(1 + b)^0$, which is equivalent to $604 = a(1)$, or $604 = a$. Substituting 604 for a in the equation $n = a(1 + b)^t$ yields $n = 604(1 + b)^t$. The table also shows that when $t = 1$, $n = 606.42$. Substituting 1 for t and 606.42 for n in the equation $n = 604(1 + b)^t$ yields $606.42 = 604(1 + b)^1$, or $606.42 = 604(1 + b)$. Dividing both sides of this equation by 604 yields approximately $1.004 = 1 + b$. Subtracting 1 from both sides of this equation yields that the value of b is approximately 0.004. Substituting 0.004 for b in the equation $n = 604(1 + b)^t$ yields $n = 604(1 + 0.004)^t$. Therefore, of the choices, choice C best represents the relationship between t and n.

Choice A is incorrect and may result from conceptual or calculation errors. *Choice B* is incorrect and may result from conceptual or calculation errors. *Choice D* is incorrect and may result from conceptual or calculation errors.

QUESTION 14

Choice B is correct. Each given equation is written in slope-intercept form, $y = mx + b$, where m is the slope and $(0, b)$ is the y-intercept of the graph of the equation in the xy-plane. The graphs of two lines that have different slopes will intersect at exactly one point. The graph of the first equation is a line with slope 1. The graph of the second equation is a line with slope 8. Since the graphs are lines with different slopes, they will intersect at exactly one point.

Choice A is incorrect because two graphs of linear equations have 0 intersection points only if they are parallel and therefore have the same slope. *Choice C* is incorrect because two graphs of linear equations in the xy-plane can have only 0, 1, or infinitely many points of intersection. *Choice D* is incorrect because two graphs of linear equations in the xy-plane can have only 0, 1, or infinitely many points of intersection.

QUESTION 15

The correct answer is 40. It's given that $5G + 45R = 380$, where G is the number of green tokens and R is the number of red tokens won by one student and these tokens are worth a total of 380 points. Since the equation represents the situation where the student won points with green tokens and red tokens for a total of 380 points, each term on the left-hand side of the equation represents the number of points won for one of the colors. Since the coefficient of *G* in the given equation is 5, a green token must be worth 5 points. Similarly, since the coefficient of *R* in the given equation is 45, a red token must be worth 45 points. Therefore, a red token is worth 45 − 5 points, or 40 points, more than a green token.

QUESTION 16

Choice D is correct. Since the number of bacteria doubles every day, the relationship between *t* and *y* can be represented by an exponential equation of the form $y = a(b)^t$, where *a* is the number of bacteria at the start of the observation and the number of bacteria increases by a factor of *b* every day. It's given that there are 44,000 bacteria at the start of the observation. Therefore, *a* = 44,000. It's also given that the number of bacteria doubles, or increases by a factor of 2, every day. Therefore, *b* = 2. Substituting 44,000 for *a* and 2 for *b* in the equation $y = a(b)^t$ yields $y = 44,000(2)^t$.

Choice A is incorrect and may result from conceptual or calculation errors. *Choice B* is incorrect and may result from conceptual or calculation errors. *Choice C* is incorrect. This equation represents a situation where the number of bacteria is decreasing by half, not doubling, every day.

QUESTION 17

Choice C is correct. The base of a cylinder is a circle with a diameter equal to the diameter of the cylinder. The volume, *V*, of a cylinder can be found by multiplying the area of the circular base, *A*, by the height of the cylinder, *h*, or $V = Ah$. The area of a circle can be found using the formula $A = \pi r^2$, where *r* is the radius of the circle. It's given that the diameter of the cylinder is 8 inches. Thus, the radius of this circle is 4 inches. Therefore, the area of the circular base of the cylinder is $A = \pi(4)^2$, or 16π square inches. It's given that the height *h* of the cylinder is 12 inches. Substituting 16π for *A* and 12 for *h* in the formula $V = Ah$ gives $V = 16\pi(12)$, or 192π cubic inches.

Choice A is incorrect. This is the area of the circular base of the cylinder. *Choice B* is incorrect and may result from using 8, instead of 16, as the value of r^2 in the formula for the area of a circle. *Choice D* is incorrect and may result from using 8, instead of 4, for the radius of the circular base.

QUESTION 18

Choice A is correct. The given system of linear equations can be solved by the elimination method. Multiplying each side of the second equation in the given system by 3 yields $(2x + 2y)(3) = (10)(3)$, or $6x + 6y = 30$. Subtracting this equation from the first equation in the given system yields $(6x + 7y) − (6x + 6y) = (28) − (30)$, which is equivalent to $(6x − 6x) + (7y − 6y) = 28 − 30$, or $y = −2$.

Choice B is incorrect. This is the value of *x*, not the value of *y*. *Choice C* is incorrect and may result from conceptual or calculation errors. *Choice D* is incorrect and may result from conceptual or calculation errors.

QUESTION 19

The correct answer is $\frac{15}{17}$. It's given that angle *J* is the right angle in triangle *JKL*.

Therefore, the acute angles of triangle *JKL* are angle *K* and angle *L*. The hypotenuse of a right triangle is the side opposite its right angle. Therefore, the hypotenuse of triangle *JKL* is side *KL*. The cosine of an acute angle in a right triangle is the ratio of the length of the side adjacent to the angle to the length of the hypotenuse. It's given that $\cos(K) = \frac{24}{51}$. This can be written as $\cos(K) = \frac{8}{17}$.

Since the cosine of angle K is a ratio, it follows that the length of the side adjacent to angle K is $8n$ and the length of the hypotenuse is $17n$, where n is a constant. Therefore, $JK = 8n$ and $KL = 17n$. The Pythagorean theorem states that in a right triangle, the square of the length of the hypotenuse is equal to the sum of the squares of the lengths of the other two sides. For triangle JKL, it follows that $(JK)^2 + (JL)^2 = (KL)^2$. Substituting $8n$ for JK and $17n$ for KL yields $(8n)^2 + (JL)^2 = (17n)^2$. This is equivalent to $64n^2 + (JL)^2 = 289n^2$. Subtracting $64n^2$ from each side of this equation yields $(JL)^2 = 225n^2$. Taking the square root of each side of this equation yields $JL = 15n$. Since $\cos(L) = \frac{JL}{KL}$, it follows that $\cos(L) = \frac{15n}{17n}$, which can be rewritten as $\cos(L) = \frac{15}{17}$. Note that 15/17, .8824, .8823, and 0.882 are examples of ways to enter a correct answer.

QUESTION 20

The correct answer is $\frac{25}{4}$. The given equation can be rewritten in the form $f(x) = a(x - h)^2 + k$, where a, h, and k are constants. When $a > 0$, h is the value of x for which $f(x)$ reaches its minimum. The given equation can be rewritten as $f(x) = 4\left(x^2 - \frac{50}{4}x\right) + 126$, which is equivalent to

$f(x) = 4\left(x^2 - \frac{50}{4}x + \left(\frac{50}{8}\right)^2 - \left(\frac{50}{8}\right)^2\right) + 126$. This equation can be rewritten as

$f(x) = 4\left(\left(x - \frac{50}{8}\right)^2 - \left(\frac{50}{8}\right)^2\right) + 126$, or $f(x) = 4\left(x - \frac{50}{8}\right)^2 - 4\left(\frac{50}{8}\right)^2 + 126$, which is

equivalent to $f(x) = 4\left(x - \frac{25}{4}\right)^2 - \frac{121}{4}$. Therefore, $h = \frac{25}{4}$, so the value of x for

which $f(x)$ reaches its minimum is $\frac{25}{4}$. Note that 25/4 and 6.25 are examples of ways to enter a correct answer.

QUESTION 21

The correct answer is 24. A line in the xy-plane can be defined by the equation $y = mx + b$, where m is the slope of the line and b is the y-coordinate of the y-intercept of the line. It's given that line ℓ passes through the point $(0, 0)$. Therefore, the y-coordinate of the y-intercept of line ℓ is 0. It's given that line ℓ is parallel to the line represented by the equation $y = 8x + 2$. Since parallel lines have the same slope, it follows that the slope of line ℓ is 8. Therefore, line ℓ can be defined by an equation in the form $y = mx + b$, where $m = 8$ and $b = 0$. Substituting 8 for m and 0 for b in $y = mx + b$ yields the equation $y = 8x + 0$, or $y = 8x$. If line ℓ passes through the point $(3, d)$, then when $x = 3$, $y = d$ for the equation $y = 8x$. Substituting 3 for x and d for y in the equation $y = 8x$ yields $d = 8(3)$, or $d = 24$.

QUESTION 22

The correct answer is $\frac{81}{4}$. The given linear equation is $2y = c$. Dividing both sides of this equation by 2 yields $y = \frac{c}{2}$. Substituting $\frac{c}{2}$ for y in the equation of the parabola yields $\frac{c}{2} = -2x^2 + 9x$. Adding $2x^2$ and $-9x$ to both sides of this equation yields $2x^2 - 9x + \dfrac{c}{2} = 0$. Since it's given that the line and the parabola intersect at exactly one point, the equation $2x^2 - 9x + \dfrac{c}{2} = 0$ must have exactly one solution. An equation of the form $Ax^2 + Bx + C = 0$, where A, B, and C are constants, has exactly one solution when the discriminant, $B^2 - 4AC$, is equal to 0. In the equation $2x^2 - 9x + \dfrac{c}{2} = 0$, where $A = 2$, $B = -9$, and $C = \dfrac{c}{2}$, the discriminant is $(-9)^2 - 4(2)\left(\dfrac{c}{2}\right)$. Setting the discriminant equal to 0 yields $(-9)^2 - 4(2)\left(\dfrac{c}{2}\right) = 0$, or $81 - 4c = 0$. Adding $4c$ to both sides of this equation yields $81 = 4c$. Dividing both sides of this equation by 4 yields $c = \dfrac{81}{4}$. Note that 81/4 and 20.25 are examples of ways to enter a correct answer.

Math

Module 2
(22 questions)

QUESTION 1

Choice B is correct. The median of a data set with an odd number of data values is defined as the middle value of the ordered list of values. The data set shown has nine values, so the median is the fifth value in the ordered list, which is 77.

Choice A is incorrect. This is the minimum value of the data set, not the median. *Choice C* is incorrect and may result from conceptual or calculation errors. *Choice D* is incorrect. This is the mean of the data set, not the median.

QUESTION 2

The correct answer is 55. Subtracting 40 from both sides of the given equation yields $x = 55$. Therefore, the value of x is 55.

QUESTION 3

Choice C is correct. The area of a rectangle with length ℓ and width w can be found using the formula $A = \ell w$. It's given that the rectangle has a length of 17 cm and a width of 7 cm. Therefore, the area of this rectangle is $A = 17(7)$, or 119 cm^2.

Choice A is incorrect. This is the sum of the length and width of the rectangle, not the area. *Choice B* is incorrect. This is the perimeter of the rectangle, not the area. *Choice D* is incorrect. This is the sum of the length and width of the rectangle squared, not the area.

QUESTION 4

Choice B is correct. Combining like terms inside the parentheses of the given expression, $20w - (4w + 3w)$, yields $20w - (7w)$. Combining like terms in this resulting expression yields $13w$.

Choice A is incorrect and may result from conceptual or calculation errors. *Choice C* is incorrect and may result from conceptual or calculation errors. *Choice D* is incorrect and may result from conceptual or calculation errors.

QUESTION 5

Choice D is correct. It's given that the number y is 84 less than the number x. A number that's 84 less than the number x is equivalent to 84 subtracted from the number x, or $x - 84$. Therefore, the equation $y = x - 84$ represents the relationship between x and y.

Choice A is incorrect and may result from conceptual errors.
Choice B is incorrect and may result from conceptual errors.
Choice C is incorrect and may result from conceptual errors.

QUESTION 6

Choice A is correct. Since the given expressions are equivalent and the numerator of the second expression is $\frac{1}{6}$ of the numerator of the first expression, the denominator of the second expression must also be $\frac{1}{6}$ of the denominator of the first expression. By the distributive property, $\frac{1}{6}(6x + 42)$ is equivalent to $\frac{1}{6}(6x) + \frac{1}{6}(42)$, or $x + 7$. Therefore, the value of b is 7.

Choice B is incorrect and may result from conceptual or calculation errors.
Choice C is incorrect and may result from conceptual or calculation errors.
Choice D is incorrect and may result from conceptual or calculation errors.

QUESTION 7

The correct answer is 240. It's given that 80% of the 300 seeds sprouted. Therefore, the number of seeds that sprouted can be calculated by multiplying the number of seeds that were planted by $\frac{80}{100}$, which gives $300\left(\frac{80}{100}\right)$, or 240.

QUESTION 8

Choice B is correct. It's given that Ty plans to walk at an average speed of 4 kilometers per hour. The number of kilometers Ty will walk is determined by the expression $4s$, where s is the number of hours Ty walks. The given goal of at least 24 kilometers means that the inequality $4s \geq 24$ represents the situation. Dividing both sides of this inequality by 4 gives $s \geq 6$, which corresponds to a minimum of 6 hours Ty must walk.

Choice A is incorrect and may result from conceptual or calculation errors.
Choice C is incorrect and may result from conceptual or calculation errors.
Choice D is incorrect and may result from conceptual or calculation errors.

QUESTION 9

The correct answer is 27. Multiplying both sides of the given equation by 3 yields $3(6 + x) = 3(9)$, or $18 + 3x = 27$. Therefore, the value of $18 + 3x$ is 27.

QUESTION 10

Choice C is correct. It's given that $f(x) = x^3 + 9$. Substituting 2 for x in this equation yields $f(2) = (2)^3 + 9$. This is equivalent to $f(2) = 8 + 9$, or $f(2) = 17$.

Choice A is incorrect. This is the value of $2 + 3 + 9$, not $2^3 + 9$.
Choice B is incorrect. This is the value of $2(3) + 9$, not $2^3 + 9$.
Choice D is incorrect. This is the value of $3^2 + 9$, not $2^3 + 9$.

QUESTION 11

Choice C is correct. It's given that $f(x)$ is the total cost, in dollars, to lease a car from this dealership with a monthly payment of x dollars. Therefore, the total cost, in dollars, to lease the car when the monthly payment is $400 is represented by the value of $f(x)$ when $x = 400$. Substituting 400 for x in the equation $f(x) = 36x + 1{,}000$ yields $f(400) = 36(400) + 1{,}000$, or $f(400) = 15{,}400$. Thus, when the monthly payment is $400, the total cost to lease a car is $15,400.

Choice A is incorrect and may result from conceptual or calculation errors. *Choice B* is incorrect and may result from conceptual or calculation errors. *Choice D* is incorrect and may result from conceptual or calculation errors.

QUESTION 12

Choice D is correct. The value of $g(x)$ when $x = 8$ can be found by substituting 8 for x in the given equation $g(x) = 10x + 8$. This yields $g(8) = 10(8) + 8$, or $g(8) = 88$. Therefore, when $x = 8$, the value of $g(x)$ is 88.

Choice A is incorrect. This is the value of x when $g(x) = 8$, rather than the value of $g(x)$ when $x = 8$. *Choice B* is incorrect and may result from conceptual or calculation errors. *Choice C* is incorrect and may result from conceptual or calculation errors.

QUESTION 13

The correct answer is 47. Based on the figure, the angle with measure $x°$ and the angle with measure $133°$ together form a straight line. Therefore, these two angles are supplementary, so the sum of their measures is $180°$. It follows that $x + 133 = 180$. Subtracting 133 from both sides of this equation yields $x = 47$.

QUESTION 14

Choice D is correct. The x-coordinate a of the x-intercept $(a, 0)$ can be found by substituting 0 for y in the given equation, which gives $7x + 2(0) = -31$, or $7x = -31$. Dividing both sides of this equation by 7 yields $x = -\dfrac{31}{7}$. Therefore, the value of a is $-\dfrac{31}{7}$. The y-coordinate b of the y-intercept $(0, b)$ can be found by substituting 0 for x in the given equation, which gives $7(0) + 2y = -31$, or $2y = -31$. Dividing both sides of this equation by 2 yields $y = -\dfrac{31}{2}$. Therefore, the value of b is $-\dfrac{31}{2}$. It follows that the value of $\dfrac{b}{a}$ is $\dfrac{-\dfrac{31}{2}}{-\dfrac{31}{7}}$, which is equivalent to $\left(\dfrac{31}{2}\right)\left(\dfrac{7}{31}\right)$, or $\dfrac{7}{2}$.

Choice A is incorrect and may result from conceptual or calculation errors. *Choice B* is incorrect and may result from conceptual or calculation errors. *Choice C* is incorrect and may result from conceptual or calculation errors.

QUESTION 15

Choice A is correct. If the object travels 108 centimeters at a speed of 12 centimeters per second, the time of travel can be determined by dividing the total distance by the speed. This results in $\dfrac{108 \text{ centimeters}}{12 \text{ centimeters/second}}$, which is 9 seconds.

Choice B is incorrect and may result from conceptual or calculation errors.
Choice C is incorrect and may result from conceptual or calculation errors.
Choice D is incorrect and may result from conceptual or calculation errors.

QUESTION 16

Choice C is correct. It's given that John made a $16 payment each month for p months. The total amount of these payments can be represented by the expression $16p$. The down payment can be added to that amount to find the total amount John paid, yielding the expression $16p + 37$. It's given that John paid a total of $165. Therefore, the expression for the total amount John paid can be set equal to that amount, yielding the equation $16p + 37 = 165$.

Choice A is incorrect and may result from conceptual or calculation errors.
Choice B is incorrect and may result from conceptual or calculation errors.
Choice D is incorrect and may result from conceptual or calculation errors.

QUESTION 17

Choice D is correct. A linear relationship can be represented by an equation of the form $y = mx + b$, where m and b are constants. It's given in the table that when $x = 0$, $y = 18$. Substituting 0 for x and 18 for y in $y = mx + b$ yields $18 = m(0) + b$, or $18 = b$. Substituting 18 for b in the equation $y = mx + b$ yields $y = mx + 18$. It's also given in the table that when $x = 1$, $y = 13$. Substituting 1 for x and 13 for y in the equation $y = mx + 18$ yields $13 = m(1) + 18$, or $13 = m + 18$. Subtracting 18 from both sides of this equation yields $-5 = m$. Therefore, the equation $y = -5x + 18$ represents the relationship between x and y.

Choice A is incorrect and may result from conceptual or calculation errors.
Choice B is incorrect and may result from conceptual or calculation errors.
Choice C is incorrect and may result from conceptual or calculation errors.

QUESTION 18

Choice D is correct. It's given that the equation $h = -4.9t^2 + 7t + 9$ represents this situation, where h is the height, in meters, of the object t seconds after it is kicked. It follows that the height, in meters, from which the object was kicked is the value of h when $t = 0$. Substituting 0 for t in the equation $h = -4.9t^2 + 7t + 9$ yields $h = -4.9(0)^2 + 7(0) + 9$, or $h = 9$. Therefore, the object was kicked from a height of 9 meters.

Choice A is incorrect and may result from conceptual or calculation errors.
Choice B is incorrect and may result from conceptual or calculation errors.
Choice C is incorrect and may result from conceptual or calculation errors.

QUESTION 19

Choice B is correct. It's given that $h(x) = x^2 - 3$. Each table gives 1, 2, and 3 as the three given values of x. Substituting 1 for x in the equation $h(x) = x^2 - 3$ yields $h(1) = (1)^2 - 3$, or $h(1) = -2$. Substituting 2 for x in the equation $h(x) = x^2 - 3$ yields $h(2) = (2)^2 - 3$, or $h(2) = 1$. Finally, substituting 3 for x in the equation $h(x) = x^2 - 3$ yields $h(3) = (3)^2 - 3$, or $h(3) = 6$. Therefore, $h(x)$ is -2 when x is 1, $h(x)$ is 1 when x is 2, and $h(x)$ is 6 when x is 3. Choice B is a table with these values of x and their corresponding values of $h(x)$.

Choice A is incorrect. This is a table of values for the function $h(x) = x + 3$, not $h(x) = x^2 - 3$. *Choice C* is incorrect. This is a table of values for the function $h(x) = 2x - 3$, not $h(x) = x^2 - 3$. *Choice D* is incorrect and may result from conceptual or calculation errors.

QUESTION 20

Choice D is correct. Since *f* is a linear function, it can be defined by an equation of the form $f(x) = ax + b$, where *a* and *b* are constants. It's given that $f(0) = 8$. Substituting 0 for *x* and 8 for $f(x)$ in the equation $f(x) = ax + b$ yields $8 = a(0) + b$, or $8 = b$. Substituting 8 for *b* in the equation $f(x) = ax + b$ yields $f(x) = ax + 8$. It's given that $f(1) = 12$. Substituting 1 for *x* and 12 for $f(x)$ in the equation $f(x) = ax + 8$ yields $12 = a(1) + 8$, or $12 = a + 8$. Subtracting 8 from both sides of this equation yields $a = 4$. Substituting 4 for *a* in the equation $f(x) = ax + 8$ yields $f(x) = 4x + 8$. Therefore, an equation that defines *f* is $f(x) = 4x + 8$.

Choice A is incorrect and may result from conceptual or calculation errors. Choice B is incorrect and may result from conceptual or calculation errors. Choice C is incorrect and may result from conceptual or calculation errors.

QUESTION 21

Choice A is correct. Subtracting $14j$ from each side of the given equation results in $5k = m - 14j$. Dividing each side of this equation by 5 results in

$$k = \frac{m - 14j}{5}.$$

Choice B is incorrect and may result from conceptual or calculation errors. Choice C is incorrect and may result from conceptual or calculation errors. Choice D is incorrect and may result from conceptual or calculation errors.

QUESTION 22

Choice D is correct. The hypotenuse of triangle *RST* is the longest side and is across from the right angle. The longest side length given is 584, which is the length of side *TR*. Therefore, the hypotenuse of triangle *RST* is side *TR*, so the right angle is angle *S*. The tangent of an acute angle in a right triangle is the ratio of the length of the opposite side, which is the side across from the angle, to the length of the adjacent side, which is the side closest to the angle that is not the hypotenuse. It follows that the opposite side of angle *T* is side *RS* and the adjacent side of angle *T* is side *ST*. Therefore, $\tan T = \frac{RS}{ST}$. Substituting 440 for *RS* and 384 for *ST* in this equation yields $\tan T = \frac{440}{384}$. This is equivalent to $\tan T = \frac{55}{48}$. It's given that triangle *RST* is similar to triangle *UVW*, where *S* corresponds to *V* and *T* corresponds to *W*. It follows that *R* corresponds to *U*. Therefore, the hypotenuse of triangle *UVW* is side *WU*, which means $\tan W = \frac{UV}{VW}$. Since the lengths of corresponding sides of similar triangles are proportional, $\frac{RS}{ST} = \frac{UV}{VW}$. Therefore, $\tan W = \frac{UV}{VW}$ is equivalent to $\tan W = \frac{RS}{ST}$, or $\tan W = \tan T$. Thus, $\tan W = \frac{55}{48}$.

Choice A is incorrect. This is the value of cos W, not tan W. Choice B is incorrect. This is the value of sin W, not tan W. Choice C is incorrect. This is the value of $\frac{1}{\tan W}$, not tan W.

Scoring Your Paper SAT Practice Test #1

Congratulations on completing an SAT® practice test.
To score your test, follow the instructions in this guide.

IMPORTANT: *This scoring guide is for students who completed the paper version of this digital SAT practice test.*

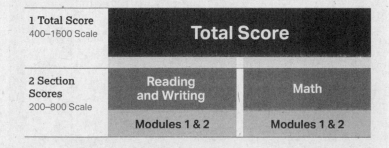

1 Total Score 400–1600 Scale	Total Score	
2 Section Scores 200–800 Scale	Reading and Writing	Math
	Modules 1 & 2	Modules 1 & 2

Scores Overview

Each assessment in the digital SAT Suite (SAT, PSAT/NMSQT®, PSAT™ 10, and PSAT™ 8/9) reports test scores on a common scale.

For more details about scores, visit **sat.org/scores**.

How to Calculate Your Practice Test Scores

The worksheets on pages 390 and 391 help you calculate your test scores.

GET SET UP

1 In addition to your practice test, you'll need the conversion tables and answer key at the end of this guide.

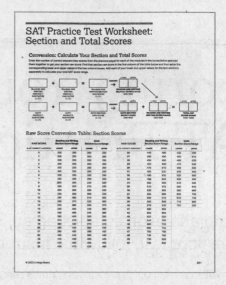

SCORE YOUR PRACTICE TEST

2 Compare your answers to the answer key on page 390, and count up the total number of correct answers for each section. Write the number of correct answers for each section in the answer key at the bottom of that section.

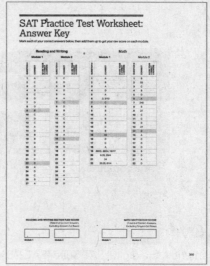

CALCULATE YOUR SCORES

3 Using your marked-up answer key and the conversion tables, follow the directions on page 391 to get your section and test scores.

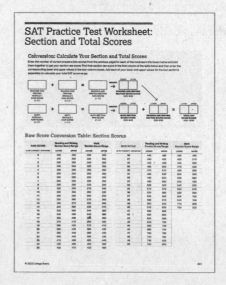

Get Section and Total Scores

Section and total scores for the paper version of this digital SAT practice test are expressed as ranges. That's because the scoring method described in this guide is a simplified (and therefore slightly less precise) version of the one used in Bluebook™, the digital test application.

To obtain your Reading and Writing and Math section scores, use the provided answer key to determine the number of questions you answered correctly in each section. These numbers constitute your *raw scores* for the two sections. Use the provided table to convert your raw score for each section into a *scaled score* range consisting of a "lower" and "upper" value. Add the two lower values together and the two upper values together to obtain your total score range.

GET YOUR READING AND WRITING SECTION SCORE

Calculate your SAT Reading and Writing section score (it's on a scale of 200–800).

1 Use the answer key on page 390 to find the number of questions in module 1 and module 2 that you answered correctly.

2 To determine your Reading and Writing raw score, add the number of correct answers you got on module 1 and module 2. **Exclude the questions in grayed-out rows from your calculation.**

3 Use the Raw Score Conversion Table: Section Scores on page 391 to turn your raw score into your Reading and Writing section score.

4 The "lower" and "upper" values associated with your raw score establish the range of scores you might expect to receive had this been an actual test.

GET YOUR MATH SECTION SCORE

Calculate your SAT Math section score (it's on a scale of 200–800).

1 Use the answer key on page 390 to find the number of questions in module 1 and module 2 that you answered correctly.

2 To determine your Math raw score, add the number of correct answers you got on module 1 and module 2. **Exclude the questions in grayed-out rows from your calculation.**

3 Use the Raw Score Conversion Table: Section Scores on page 391 to turn your raw score into your Math section score.

4 The "lower" and "upper" values associated with your raw score establish the range of scores you might expect to receive had this been an actual test.

GET YOUR TOTAL SCORE

Add together the "lower" values for the Reading and Writing and Math sections, and then add together the "upper" values for the two sections. The result is your total score, expressed as a range, for this SAT practice test. The total score is on a scale of 400–1600.

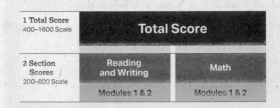

1 Total Score 400–1600 Scale	Total Score	
2 Section Scores 200–800 Scale	Reading and Writing	Math
	Modules 1 & 2	Modules 1 & 2

Your total score on this SAT practice test is the sum of your Reading and Writing section score and your Math section score. On this paper version of the digital SAT practice test, you'll receive a lower and upper score for each test section and the total score. This is the range of scores that you might expect to receive.

Use the worksheets on pages 390 and 391 to calculate your section and total scores.

SAT Practice Test Worksheet: Answer Key

Mark each of your correct answers below, then add them up to get your raw score on each module.

Reading and Writing

Module 1

QUESTION #	CORRECT	MARK YOUR CORRECT ANSWERS
1	A	
2	C	
3	C	
4	B	
5	C	
6	D	
7	D	
8	D	
9	B	
10	C	
11	D	
12	C	
13	A	
14	D	
15	B	
16	B	
17	D	
18	A	
19	C	
20	D	
21	C	
22	D	
23	A	
24	D	
25	C	
26	B	
27	A	

Module 2

QUESTION #	CORRECT	MARK YOUR CORRECT ANSWERS
1	C	
2	D	
3	B	
4	D	
5	A	
6	A	
7	C	
8	D	
9	B	
10	C	
11	C	
12	B	
13	B	
14	A	
15	A	
16	D	
17	A	
18	A	
19	A	
20	C	
21	B	
22	D	
23	A	
24	C	
25	A	
26	A	
27	D	

Math

Module 1

QUESTION #	CORRECT	MARK YOUR CORRECT ANSWERS
1	A	
2	B	
3	A	
4	D	
5	A	
6	.3, 3/10	
7	C	
8	5	
9	B	
10	A	
11	B	
12	B	
13	C	
14	B	
15	40	
16	D	
17	C	
18	A	
19	.8823, .8824, 15/17	
20	6.25, 25/4	
21	24	
22	20.25, 81/4	

Module 2

QUESTION #	CORRECT	MARK YOUR CORRECT ANSWERS
1	B	
2	55	
3	C	
4	B	
5	D	
6	A	
7	240	
8	B	
9	27	
10	C	
11	C	
12	D	
13	47	
14	D	
15	A	
16	C	
17	D	
18	D	
19	B	
20	D	
21	A	
22	D	

READING AND WRITING SECTION RAW SCORE
(Total # of Correct Answers,
Excluding Grayed-Out Rows)

Module 1

Module 2

MATH SECTION RAW SCORE
(Total # of Correct Answers,
Excluding Grayed-Out Rows)

Module 1

Module 2

SAT Practice Test Worksheet: Section and Total Scores

Conversion: Calculate Your Section and Total Scores

Enter the number of correct answers (raw scores from the previous page) for each of the modules in the boxes below and add them together to get your section raw score. Find that section raw score in the first column of the table below and then enter the corresponding lower and upper values in the two-column boxes. Add each of your lower and upper values for the test sections separately to calculate your total SAT score range.

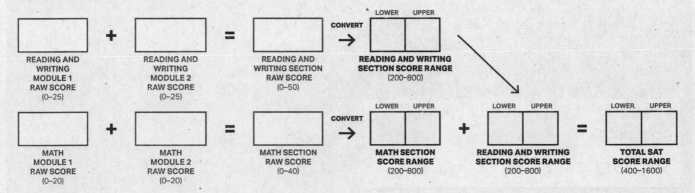

Raw Score Conversion Table: Section Scores

RAW SCORE (# OF CORRECT ANSWERS)	Reading and Writing Section Score Range		Math Section Score Range		RAW SCORE (# OF CORRECT ANSWERS)	Reading and Writing Section Score Range		Math Section Score Range	
	LOWER	UPPER	LOWER	UPPER		LOWER	UPPER	LOWER	UPPER
0	200	250	200	250	26	440	480	430	490
1	200	250	200	250	27	450	490	450	510
2	200	250	200	250	28	450	490	460	520
3	200	250	200	250	29	460	500	470	530
4	200	250	200	250	30	470	510	490	550
5	200	250	200	250	31	480	520	500	560
6	200	250	200	250	32	490	530	520	580
7	200	250	200	250	33	490	550	530	590
8	200	250	220	320	34	500	560	540	620
9	200	250	270	330	35	510	570	560	640
10	200	250	290	330	36	520	580	580	660
11	200	250	300	340	37	530	590	600	700
12	250	360	310	350	38	550	610	640	740
13	290	370	320	360	39	560	620	710	800
14	320	380	330	370	40	570	630	750	800
15	330	390	340	380	41	590	650		
16	340	400	340	380	42	600	660		
17	360	400	350	390	43	620	680		
18	370	410	360	400	44	640	700		
19	380	420	370	410	45	660	720		
20	380	420	380	420	46	680	740		
21	390	430	380	420	47	700	760		
22	400	440	390	430	48	720	780		
23	410	450	400	440	49	730	800		
24	420	460	400	460	50	750	800		
25	430	470	420	480					

The SAT®

Practice Test #2

Make time to take the practice test.
It is one of the best ways to get ready
for the SAT.

After you have taken the practice test, score it right away
using materials provided in *The Official Digital SAT Study Guide*.

This version of the SAT Practice Test is for students using
this guide. As a reminder, most students taking the
digital SAT will do so using Bluebook™, the digital testing
application. To best prepare for test day, download Bluebook
at **bluebook.app.collegeboard.org** to take the practice test in
the digital format.

Test begins on the next page.

Reading and Writing

27 QUESTIONS

1

In the early 1800s, the Cherokee scholar Sequoyah created the first script, or writing system, for an Indigenous language in the United States. Because it represented the sounds of spoken Cherokee so accurately, his script was easy to learn and thus quickly achieved _____ use: by 1830, over 90 percent of the Cherokee people could read and write it.

Which choice completes the text with the most logical and precise word or phrase?

A) widespread

B) careful

C) unintended

D) infrequent

2

Like the 1945 play it reimagines—Federico García Lorca's *The House of Bernarda Alba*—Marcus Gardley's 2014 play *The House That Will Not Stand* prominently features women. In both plays, the all-female cast _____ an array of female characters, including a strong mother and several daughters dealing with individual struggles.

Which choice completes the text with the most logical and precise word or phrase?

A) engulfs

B) encourages

C) comprises

D) provokes

Unauthorized copying or reuse of any part of this page is illegal.

396

CONTINUE

3

During a 2014 archaeological dig in Spain, Vicente Lull and his team uncovered the skeleton of a woman from El Algar, an Early Bronze Age society, buried with valuable objects signaling a high position of power. This finding may persuade researchers who have argued that Bronze Age societies were ruled by men to _____ that women may have also held leadership roles.

Which choice completes the text with the most logical and precise word or phrase?

A) waive

B) concede

C) refute

D) require

4

The following text is adapted from Oscar Wilde's 1895 play *The Importance of Being Earnest*.

CECILY: Have we got to part?

ALGERNON: I am afraid so. It's a very painful parting.

CECILY: It is always painful to part from people whom one has known for a very brief space of time. The absence of old friends one can endure with equanimity. But even a momentary separation from anyone to whom one has just been introduced is almost unbearable.

As used in the text, what does the word "endure" most nearly mean?

A) Regret

B) Persist

C) Tolerate

D) Encourage

5

The following text is from the 1924 poem "Cycle" by D'Arcy McNickle, who was a citizen of the Confederated Salish and Kootenai Tribes.

There shall be new roads wending,
A new beating of the drum—

Men's eyes shall have fresh seeing,
Grey lives reprise their span—
But under the new sun's being,
Completing what night began,

There'll be the same backs bending,
The same sad feet shall drum—
When this night finds its ending
And day shall have come.....

Which choice best states the main purpose of the text?

A) To consider how the repetitiveness inherent in human life can be both rewarding and challenging

B) To question whether activities completed at one time of day are more memorable than those completed at another time of day

C) To refute the idea that joy is a more commonly experienced emotion than sadness is

D) To demonstrate how the experiences of individuals relate to the experiences of their communities

CONTINUE

6

The following text is from Charlotte Forten Grimké's 1888 poem "At Newport."

Oh, deep delight to watch the gladsome waves
Exultant leap upon the rugged rocks;
Ever repulsed, yet ever rushing on—
Filled with a life that will not know defeat;
To see the glorious hues of sky and sea.
The distant snowy sails, glide spirit like,
Into an unknown world, to feel the sweet
Enchantment of the sea thrill all the soul,
Clearing the clouded brain, making the heart
Leap joyous as it own bright, singing waves!

Which choice best describes the function of the underlined portion in the text as a whole?

A) It portrays the surroundings as an imposing and intimidating scene.

B) It characterizes the sea's waves as a relentless and enduring force.

C) It conveys the speaker's ambivalence about the natural world.

D) It draws a contrast between the sea's waves and the speaker's thoughts.

7

The following text is adapted from Aphra Behn's 1689 novel *The Lucky Mistake*. Atlante and Rinaldo are neighbors who have been secretly exchanging letters through Charlot, Atlante's sister.

[Atlante] gave this letter to Charlot; who immediately ran into the balcony with it, where she still found Rinaldo in a melancholy posture, leaning his head on his hand: She showed him the letter, but was afraid to toss it to him, for fear it might fall to the ground; so he ran and fetched a long cane, which he cleft at one end, and held it while she put the letter into the cleft, and stayed not to hear what he said to it. But never was man so transported with joy, as he was at the reading of this letter; it gives him new wounds; for to the generous, nothing obliges love so much as love.

Which choice best describes the overall structure of the text?

A) It describes the delivery of a letter, and then portrays a character's happiness at reading that letter.

B) It establishes that a character is desperate to receive a letter, and then explains why another character has not yet written that letter.

C) It presents a character's concerns about delivering a letter, and then details the contents of that letter.

D) It reveals the inspiration behind a character's letter, and then emphasizes the excitement that another character feels upon receiving that letter.

Unauthorized copying or reuse of any part of this page is illegal.

CONTINUE

398

8

The following text is adapted from Frances Hodgson Burnett's 1911 novel *The Secret Garden*. Mary, a young girl, recently found an overgrown hidden garden.

Mary was an odd, determined little person, and now she had something interesting to be determined about, she was very much absorbed, indeed. She worked and dug and pulled up weeds steadily, only becoming more pleased with her work every hour instead of tiring of it. It seemed to her like a fascinating sort of play.

Which choice best states the main idea of the text?

A) Mary hides in the garden to avoid doing her chores.

B) Mary is getting bored with pulling up so many weeds in the garden.

C) Mary is clearing out the garden to create a space to play.

D) Mary feels very satisfied when she's taking care of the garden.

9

Believing that living in an impractical space can heighten awareness and even improve health, conceptual artists Madeline Gins and Shusaku Arakawa designed an apartment building in Japan to be more fanciful than functional. A kitchen counter is chest-high on one side and knee-high on the other; a ceiling has a door to nowhere. The effect is disorienting but invigorating: after four years there, filmmaker Nobu Yamaoka reported significant health benefits.

Which choice best states the main idea of the text?

A) Although inhabiting a home surrounded by fanciful features such as those designed by Gins and Arakawa can be rejuvenating, it is unsustainable.

B) Designing disorienting spaces like those in the Gins and Arakawa building is the most effective way to create a physically stimulating environment.

C) As a filmmaker, Yamaoka has long supported the designs of conceptual artists such as Gins and Arakawa.

D) Although impractical, the design of the apartment building by Gins and Arakawa may improve the well-being of the building's residents.

CONTINUE

10

The following text is from Maggie Pogue Johnson's 1910 poem "Poet of Our Race." In this poem, the speaker is addressing Paul Laurence Dunbar, a Black author.

> Thou, with stroke of mighty pen,
> Hast told of joy and mirth,
> And read the hearts and souls of men
> As cradled from their birth.
> The language of the flowers,
> Thou hast read them all,
> And e'en the little brook
> Responded to thy call.

Which choice best states the main purpose of the text?

A) To praise a certain writer for being especially perceptive regarding people and nature

B) To establish that a certain writer has read extensively about a variety of topics

C) To call attention to a certain writer's careful and elaborately detailed writing process

D) To recount fond memories of an afternoon spent in nature with a certain writer

11

"To You" is an 1856 poem by Walt Whitman. In the poem, Whitman suggests that he deeply understands the reader, whom he addresses directly, writing, _____

Which quotation from "To You" most effectively illustrates the claim?

A) "Your true soul and body appear before me."

B) "Whoever you are, now I place my hand upon you, that you be my poem."

C) "I should have made my way straight to you long ago."

D) "Whoever you are, I fear you are walking the walks of dreams."

12

Approximate Rates of Speech and Information Conveyed for Five Languages

Language	Rate of speech (syllables per second)	Rate of information conveyed (bits per second)
Serbian	7.2	39.1
Spanish	7.7	42.0
Vietnamese	5.3	42.5
Thai	4.7	33.8
Hungarian	5.9	34.6

A group of researchers working in Europe, Asia, and Oceania conducted a study to determine how quickly different Eurasian languages are typically spoken (in syllables per second) and how much information they can effectively convey (in bits per second). They found that, although languages vary widely in the speed at which they are spoken, the amount of information languages can effectively convey tends to vary much less. Thus, they claim that two languages with very different spoken rates can nonetheless convey the same amount of information in a given amount of time.

Which choice best describes data from the table that support the researchers' claim?

A) Among the five languages in the table, Thai and Hungarian have the lowest rates of speech and the lowest rates of information conveyed.

B) Vietnamese conveys information at approximately the same rate as Spanish despite being spoken at a slower rate.

C) Among the five languages in the table, the language that is spoken the fastest is also the language that conveys information the fastest.

D) Serbian and Spanish are spoken at approximately the same rate, but Serbian conveys information faster than Spanish does.

CONTINUE

13

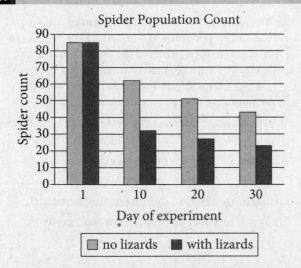

Spider Population Count

no lizards ■ with lizards

To investigate the effect of lizard predation on spider populations, a student in a biology class placed spiders in two enclosures, one with lizards and one without, and tracked the number of spiders in the enclosures for 30 days. The student concluded that the reduction in the spider population count in the enclosure with lizards by day 30 was entirely attributable to the presence of the lizards.

Which choice best describes data from the graph that weaken the student's conclusion?

A) The spider population count was the same in both enclosures on day 1.

B) The spider population count also substantially declined by day 30 in the enclosure without lizards.

C) The largest decline in spider population count in the enclosure with lizards occurred from day 1 to day 10.

D) The spider population count on day 30 was lower in the enclosure with lizards than in the enclosure without lizards.

14

Although military veterans make up a small proportion of the total population of the United States, they occupy a significantly higher proportion of the jobs in the civilian government. One possible explanation for this disproportionate representation is that military service familiarizes people with certain organizational structures that are also reflected in the civilian government bureaucracy, and this familiarity thus _____

Which choice most logically completes the text?

A) makes civilian government jobs especially appealing to military veterans.

B) alters the typical relationship between military service and subsequent career preferences.

C) encourages nonveterans applying for civilian government jobs to consider military service instead.

D) increases the number of civilian government jobs that require some amount of military experience to perform.

15

The city of Pompeii, which was buried in ash following the eruption of Mount Vesuvius in 79 CE, continues to be studied by archaeologists. Unfortunately, as _____ attest, archaeological excavations have disrupted ash deposits at the site, causing valuable information about the eruption to be lost.

Which choice completes the text so that it conforms to the conventions of Standard English?

A) researchers, Roberto Scandone and Christopher Kilburn,

B) researchers, Roberto Scandone and Christopher Kilburn

C) researchers Roberto Scandone and Christopher Kilburn

D) researchers Roberto Scandone, and Christopher Kilburn

CONTINUE

16

Seneca sculptor Marie Watt's blanket art comes in a range of shapes and sizes. In 2004, Watt sewed strips of blankets together to craft a 10-by-13-inch _____ in 2014, she arranged folded blankets into two large stacks and then cast them in bronze, creating two curving 18-foot-tall blue-bronze pillars.

Which choice completes the text so that it conforms to the conventions of Standard English?

A) sampler later,

B) sampler;

C) sampler,

D) sampler, later,

17

Gathering accurate data on water flow in the United States is challenging because of the country's millions of miles of _____ the volume and speed of water at any given location can vary drastically over time.

Which choice completes the text so that it conforms to the conventions of Standard English?

A) waterways and the fact that,

B) waterways, and the fact that,

C) waterways, and, the fact that

D) waterways and the fact that

18

In assessing the films of Japanese director Akira Kurosawa, _____ have missed his equally deep engagement with Japanese artistic traditions such as Noh theater.

Which choice completes the text so that it conforms to the conventions of Standard English?

A) many critics have focused on Kurosawa's use of Western literary sources but

B) Kurosawa's use of Western literary sources has been the focus of many critics, who

C) there are many critics who have focused on Kurosawa's use of Western literary sources, but they

D) the focus of many critics has been on Kurosawa's use of Western literary sources; they

19

Joshua Hinson, director of the language revitalization program of the Chickasaw Nation in Oklahoma, helped produce the world's first Indigenous-language instructional app, Chickasaw _____ Chickasaw TV, in 2010; and a Rosetta Stone language course in Chickasaw, in 2015.

Which choice completes the text so that it conforms to the conventions of Standard English?

A) Basic; in 2009, an online television network;

B) Basic; in 2009, an online television network,

C) Basic, in 2009; an online television network,

D) Basic, in 2009, an online television network,

20

A group of ecologists led by Axel Mithöfer at the Max Planck Institute for Chemical Ecology in Germany examined the defensive responses of two varieties of the sweet potato _____ TN57, which is known for its insect resistance, and TN66, which is much more susceptible to pests.

Which choice completes the text so that it conforms to the conventions of Standard English?

A) plant.

B) plant;

C) plant

D) plant:

21

When, in the 1800s, geologists first realized that much of Earth had once been covered by great sheets of ice, some theorized that the phenomenon was cyclical, occurring at regular intervals. Each Ice Age is so destructive, though, that it largely erases the geological evidence of its predecessor. _____ geologists were unable to confirm the theory of cyclical Ice Ages until the 1960s.

Which choice completes the text with the most logical transition?

A) Hence,

B) Moreover,

C) Nevertheless,

D) Next,

CONTINUE ▶

22

While researching a topic, a student has taken the following notes:

- The Seikan Tunnel is a rail tunnel in Japan.
- It connects the island of Honshu to the island of Hokkaido.
- It is roughly 33 miles long.
- The Channel Tunnel is a rail tunnel in Europe.
- It connects Folkestone, England, to Coquelles, France.
- It is about 31 miles long.

The student wants to compare the lengths of the two rail tunnels. Which choice most effectively uses relevant information from the notes to accomplish this goal?

A) Some of the world's rail tunnels, including one tunnel that extends from Folkestone, England, to Coquelles, France, are longer than 30 miles.

B) The Seikan Tunnel is roughly 33 miles long, while the slightly shorter Channel Tunnel is about 31 miles long.

C) The Seikan Tunnel, which is roughly 33 miles long, connects the Japanese islands of Honshu and Hokkaido.

D) Both the Seikan Tunnel, which is located in Japan, and the Channel Tunnel, which is located in Europe, are examples of rail tunnels.

23

While researching a topic, a student has taken the following notes:

- Ancient Native American and Australian Aboriginal cultures described the Pleiades star cluster as having seven stars.
- It was referred to as the Seven Sisters in the mythology of ancient Greece.
- Today, the cluster appears to have only six stars.
- Two of the stars have moved so close together that they now appear as one.

The student wants to specify the reason the Pleiades' appearance changed. Which choice most effectively uses relevant information from the notes to accomplish this goal?

A) Ancient Native American and Australian Aboriginal cultures described the Pleiades, which was referred to in Greek mythology as the Seven Sisters, as having seven stars.

B) Although once referred to as the Seven Sisters, the Pleiades appears to have only six stars today.

C) In the time since ancient cultures described the Pleiades as having seven stars, two of the cluster's stars have moved so close together that they now appear as one.

D) The Pleiades has seven stars, but two are so close together that they appear to be a single star.

CONTINUE →

While researching a topic, a student has taken the following notes:

- Pinnipeds, which include seals, sea lions, and walruses, live in and around water.

- Pinnipeds are descended not from sea animals but from four-legged, land-dwelling carnivores.

- Canadian paleobiologist Natalia Rybczynski recently found a fossil with four legs, webbed toes, and the skull and teeth of a seal.

- Rybczynski refers to her rare find as a "transitional fossil."

- The fossil illustrates an early stage in the evolution of pinnipeds from their land-dwelling ancestors.

The student wants to emphasize the fossil's significance. Which choice most effectively uses relevant information from the notes to accomplish this goal?

A) Canadian paleobiologist Natalia Rybczynski's fossil has the skull and teeth of a seal, which, like sea lions and walruses, is a pinniped.

B) Pinnipeds are descended from four-legged, land-dwelling carnivores; a fossil that resembles both was recently found.

C) Having four legs but the skull and teeth of a seal, the rare fossil illustrates an early stage in the evolution of pinnipeds from their land-dwelling ancestors.

D) A "transitional fossil" was recently found by paleobiologist Natalia Rybczynski.

While researching a topic, a student has taken the following notes:

- Gaspar Enriquez is an artist.

- He specializes in portraits of Mexican Americans.

- A portrait is an artistic representation of a person.

- Enriquez completed a painting of the sculptor Luis Jimenez in 2003.

- He completed a drawing of the writer Rudolfo Anaya in 2016.

The student wants to emphasize a difference between the two portraits. Which choice most effectively uses relevant information from the notes to accomplish this goal?

A) The portraits, or artistic representations, of Luis Jimenez and Rudolfo Anaya were both completed by Enriquez in the early 2000s.

B) Enriquez has completed portraits of numerous Mexican Americans, including sculptor Luis Jimenez and writer Rudolfo Anaya.

C) While both are by Enriquez, the 2003 portrait of Luis Jimenez is a painting, and the 2016 portrait of Rudolfo Anaya is a drawing.

D) Luis Jimenez was a Mexican American sculptor, and Rudolfo Anaya was a Mexican American writer.

CONTINUE

26

While researching a topic, a student has taken the following notes:

- *Las sergas de Esplandián* was a novel popular in sixteenth-century Spain.
- The novel featured a fictional island inhabited solely by Black women and known as California.
- That same century, Spanish explorers learned of an "island" off the west coast of Mexico.
- They called it California after the island in the novel.
- The "island" was actually the peninsula now known as Baja California ("Lower California"), which lies to the south of the US state of California.

The student wants to emphasize the role a misconception played in the naming of a place. Which choice most effectively uses relevant information from the notes to accomplish this goal?

A) The novel *Las sergas de Esplandián* featured a fictional island known as California.

B) To the south of the US state of California lies Baja California ("Lower California"), originally called California after a fictional place.

C) In the sixteenth century, Spanish explorers learned of a peninsula off the west coast of Mexico and called it California.

D) Thinking it was an island, Spanish explorers called a peninsula California after an island in a popular novel.

27

While researching a topic, a student has taken the following notes:

- In 1851, German American artist Emanuel Leutze painted *Washington Crossing the Delaware*.
- His huge painting (149 × 255 inches) depicts the first US president crossing a river with soldiers in the Revolutionary War.
- In 2019, Cree artist Kent Monkman painted *mistikôsiwak (Wooden Boat People): Resurgence of the People*.
- Monkman's huge painting (132 × 264 inches) was inspired by Leutze's.
- It portrays Indigenous people in a boat rescuing refugees.

The student wants to emphasize a similarity between the two paintings. Which choice most effectively uses relevant information from the notes to accomplish this goal?

A) Monkman, a Cree artist, finished his painting in 2019; Leutze, a German American artist, completed his in 1851.

B) Although Monkman's painting was inspired by Leutze's, the people and actions the two paintings portray are very different.

C) Leutze's and Monkman's paintings are both huge, measuring 149 × 255 inches and 132 × 264 inches, respectively.

D) Leutze's painting depicts Revolutionary War soldiers, while Monkman's depicts Indigenous people and refugees.

STOP

If you finish before time is called, you may check your work on this module only. Do not turn to any other module in the test.

Reading and Writing

27 QUESTIONS

The questions in this section address a number of important reading and writing skills. Each question includes one or more passages, which may include a table or graph. Read each passage and question carefully, and then choose the best answer to the question based on the passage(s).

All questions in this section are multiple-choice with four answer choices. Each question has a single best answer.

1

In addition to being an accomplished psychologist himself, Francis Cecil Sumner was a _____ increasing the opportunity for Black students to study psychology, helping to found the psychology department at Howard University, a historically Black university, in 1930.

Which choice completes the text with the most logical and precise word or phrase?

A) proponent of

B) supplement to

C) beneficiary of

D) distraction for

2

For her 2021 art installation *Anthem*, Wu Tsang joined forces with singer and composer Beverly Glenn-Copeland to produce a piece that critics found truly _____: they praised Tsang for creatively transforming a museum rotunda into a dynamic exhibit by projecting filmed images of Glenn-Copeland onto a massive 84-foot curtain and filling the space with the sounds of his and other voices singing.

Which choice completes the text with the most logical and precise word or phrase?

A) restrained

B) inventive

C) inexplicable

D) mystifying

3

Scholarly discussions of gender in Shakespeare's comedies often celebrate the rebellion of the playwright's characters against the rigid expectations _____ by Elizabethan society. Most of the comedies end in marriage, with characters returning to their socially dictated gender roles after previously defying them, but there are some notable exceptions.

Which choice completes the text with the most logical and precise word or phrase?

A) interjected

B) committed

C) illustrated

D) prescribed

4

The work of Kiowa painter T.C. Cannon derives its power in part from the tension among his _____ influences: classic European portraiture, with its realistic treatment of faces; the American pop art movement, with its vivid colors; and flatstyle, the intertribal painting style that rejects the effect of depth typically achieved through shading and perspective.

Which choice completes the text with the most logical and precise word or phrase?

A) complementary

B) unknown

C) disparate

D) interchangeable

CONTINUE ➡

5

Text 1

Conventional wisdom long held that human social systems evolved in stages, beginning with hunter-gatherers forming small bands of members with roughly equal status. The shift to agriculture about 12,000 years ago sparked population growth that led to the emergence of groups with hierarchical structures: associations of clans first, then chiefdoms, and finally, bureaucratic states.

Text 2

In a 2021 book, anthropologist David Graeber and archaeologist David Wengrow maintain that humans have always been socially flexible, alternately forming systems based on hierarchy and collective ones with decentralized leadership. The authors point to evidence that as far back as 50,000 years ago some hunter-gatherers adjusted their social structures seasonally, at times dispersing in small groups but also assembling into communities that included esteemed individuals.

Based on the texts, how would Graeber and Wengrow (Text 2) most likely respond to the "conventional wisdom" presented in Text 1?

A) By conceding the importance of hierarchical systems but asserting the greater significance of decentralized collective societies

B) By disputing the idea that developments in social structures have followed a linear progression through distinct stages

C) By acknowledging that hierarchical roles likely weren't a part of social systems before the rise of agriculture

D) By challenging the assumption that groupings of hunter-gatherers were among the earliest forms of social structure

6

In 1934 physicist Eugene Wigner posited the existence of a crystal consisting entirely of electrons in a honeycomb-like structure. The so-called Wigner crystal remained largely conjecture, however, until Feng Wang and colleagues announced in 2021 that they had captured an image of one. The researchers trapped electrons between two semiconductors and then cooled the apparatus, causing the electrons to settle into a crystalline structure. By inserting an ultrathin sheet of graphene above the crystal, the researchers obtained an impression—the first visual confirmation of the Wigner crystal.

Which choice best states the main idea of the text?

A) Researchers have obtained the most definitive evidence to date of the existence of the Wigner crystal.

B) Researchers have identified an innovative new method for working with unusual crystalline structures.

C) Graphene is the most important of the components required to capture an image of a Wigner crystal.

D) It's difficult to acquire an image of a Wigner crystal because of the crystal's honeycomb structure.

Unauthorized copying or reuse of any part of this page is illegal.

CONTINUE

407

7

For many years, the only existing fossil evidence of mixopterid eurypterids—an extinct family of large aquatic arthropods known as sea scorpions and related to modern arachnids and horseshoe crabs—came from four species living on the paleocontinent of Laurussia. In a discovery that expands our understanding of the geographical distribution of mixopterids, paleontologist Bo Wang and others have identified fossilized remains of a new mixopterid species, *Terropterus xiushanensis*, that lived over 400 million years ago on the paleocontinent of Gondwana.

According to the text, why was Wang and his team's discovery of the *Terropterus xiushanensis* fossil significant?

A) The fossil constitutes the first evidence found by scientists that mixopterids lived more than 400 million years ago.

B) The fossil helps establish that mixopterids are more closely related to modern arachnids and horseshoe crabs than previously thought.

C) The fossil helps establish a more accurate timeline of the evolution of mixopterids on the paleocontinents of Laurussia and Gondwana.

D) The fossil constitutes the first evidence found by scientists that mixopterids existed outside the paleocontinent of Laurussia.

8

The following text is adapted from Edith Nesbit's 1906 novel *The Railway Children*.

Mother did not spend all her time in paying dull [visits] to dull ladies, and sitting dully at home waiting for dull ladies to pay [visits] to her. She was almost always there, ready to play with the children, and read to them, and help them to do their home-lessons. Besides this she used to write stories for them while they were at school, and read them aloud after tea, and she always made up funny pieces of poetry for their birthdays and for other great occasions.

According to the text, what is true about Mother?

A) She wishes that more ladies would visit her.

B) Birthdays are her favorite special occasion.

C) She creates stories and poems for her children.

D) Reading to her children is her favorite activity.

9

"The Young Girl" is a 1920 short story by Katherine Mansfield. In the story, the narrator takes an unnamed seventeen-year-old girl and her younger brother out for a meal. In describing the teenager, Mansfield frequently contrasts the character's pleasant appearance with her unpleasant attitude, as when Mansfield writes of the teenager, _____

Which quotation from "The Young Girl" most effectively illustrates the claim?

A) "I heard her murmur, 'I can't bear flowers on a table.' They had evidently been giving her intense pain, for she positively closed her eyes as I moved them away."

B) "While we waited she took out a little, gold powder-box with a mirror in the lid, shook the poor little puff as though she loathed it, and dabbed her lovely nose."

C) "I saw, after that, she couldn't stand this place a moment longer, and, indeed, she jumped up and turned away while I went through the vulgar act of paying for the tea."

D) "She didn't even take her gloves off. She lowered her eyes and drummed on the table. When a faint violin sounded she winced and bit her lip again. Silence."

CONTINUE ➡

10

Estimates of Tyrannosaurid Bite Force

Study	Year	Estimation method	Approximate bite force (newtons)
Cost et al.	2019	muscular and skeletal modeling	35,000–63,000
Gignac and Erickson	2017	tooth-bone interaction analysis	8,000–34,000
Meers	2002	body-mass scaling	183,000–235,000
Bates and Falkingham	2012	muscular and skeletal modeling	35,000–57,000

The largest tyrannosaurids—the family of carnivorous dinosaurs that includes *Tarbosaurus*, *Albertosaurus*, and, most famously, *Tyrannosaurus rex*—are thought to have had the strongest bites of any land animals in Earth's history. Determining the bite force of extinct animals can be difficult, however, and paleontologists Paul Barrett and Emily Rayfield have suggested that an estimate of dinosaur bite force may be significantly influenced by the methodology used in generating that estimate.

Which choice best describes data from the table that support Barrett and Rayfield's suggestion?

A) The study by Meers used body-mass scaling and produced the lowest estimated maximum bite force, while the study by Cost et al. used muscular and skeletal modeling and produced the highest estimated maximum.

B) In their study, Gignac and Erickson used tooth-bone interaction analysis to produce an estimated bite force range with a minimum of 8,000 newtons and a maximum of 34,000 newtons.

C) The bite force estimates produced by Bates and Falkingham and by Cost et al. were similar to each other, while the estimates produced by Meers and by Gignac and Erickson each differed substantially from any other estimate.

D) The estimated maximum bite force produced by Cost et al. exceeded the estimated maximum produced by Bates and Falkingham, even though both groups of researchers used the same method to generate their estimates.

Unauthorized copying or reuse of any part of this page is illegal.

CONTINUE

409

11

When digging for clams, their primary food, sea otters damage the roots of eelgrass plants growing on the seafloor. Near Vancouver Island in Canada, the otter population is large and well established, yet the eelgrass meadows are healthier than those found elsewhere off Canada's coast. To explain this, conservation scientist Erin Foster and colleagues compared the Vancouver Island meadows to meadows where otters are absent or were reintroduced only recently. Finding that the Vancouver Island meadows have a more diverse gene pool than the others do, Foster hypothesized that damage to eelgrass roots increases the plant's rate of sexual reproduction; this, in turn, boosts genetic diversity, which benefits the meadow's health overall.

Which finding, if true, would most directly undermine Foster's hypothesis?

A) At some sites in the study, eelgrass meadows are found near otter populations that are small and have only recently been reintroduced.

B) At several sites not included in the study, there are large, well-established sea otter populations but no eelgrass meadows.

C) At several sites not included in the study, eelgrass meadows' health correlates negatively with the length of residence and size of otter populations.

D) At some sites in the study, the health of plants unrelated to eelgrass correlates negatively with the length of residence and size of otter populations.

12

In the mountains of Brazil, *Barbacenia tomentosa* and *Barbacenia macrantha*—two plants in the Velloziaceae family—establish themselves on soilless, nutrient-poor patches of quartzite rock. Plant ecologists Anna Abrahão and Patricia de Britto Costa used microscopic analysis to determine that the roots of *B. tomentosa* and *B. macrantha*, which grow directly into the quartzite, have clusters of fine hairs near the root tip; further analysis indicated that these hairs secrete both malic and citric acids. The researchers hypothesize that the plants depend on dissolving underlying rock with these acids, as the process not only creates channels for continued growth but also releases phosphates that provide the vital nutrient phosphorus.

Which finding, if true, would most directly support the researchers' hypothesis?

A) Other species in the Velloziaceae family are found in terrains with more soil but have root structures similar to those of *B. tomentosa* and *B. macrantha*.

B) Though *B. tomentosa* and *B. macrantha* both secrete citric and malic acids, each species produces the acids in different proportions.

C) The roots of *B. tomentosa* and *B. macrantha* carve new entry points into rocks even when cracks in the surface are readily available.

D) *B. tomentosa* and *B. macrantha* thrive even when transferred to the surfaces of rocks that do not contain phosphates.

CONTINUE

13

Ancestral Puebloans, the civilization from which present-day Pueblo tribes descended, emerged as early as 1500 B.C.E. in an area of what is now the southwestern United States and dispersed suddenly in the late 1200s C.E., abandoning established villages with systems for farming crops and turkeys. Recent analysis comparing turkey remains at Mesa Verde, one such village in southern Colorado, to samples from modern turkey populations in the Rio Grande Valley of north central New Mexico determined that the latter birds descended in part from turkeys cultivated at Mesa Verde, with shared genetic markers appearing only after 1280. Thus, researchers concluded that _____

Which choice most logically completes the text?

A) conditions of the terrains in the Rio Grande Valley and Mesa Verde had greater similarities in the past than they do today.

B) some Ancestral Puebloans migrated to the Rio Grande Valley in the late 1200s and carried farming practices with them.

C) Indigenous peoples living in the Rio Grande Valley primarily planted crops and did not cultivate turkeys before 1280.

D) the Ancestral Puebloans of Mesa Verde likely adopted the farming practices of Indigenous peoples living in other regions.

14

Ratified by more than 90 countries, the Nagoya Protocol is an international agreement ensuring that Indigenous communities are compensated when their agricultural resources and knowledge of wild plants and animals are utilized by agricultural corporations. However, the protocol has shortcomings. For example, it allows corporations to insist that their agreements with communities to conduct research on the commercial uses of the communities' resources and knowledge remain confidential. Therefore, some Indigenous advocates express concern that the protocol may have the unintended effect of _____

Which choice most logically completes the text?

A) diminishing the monetary reward that corporations might derive from their agreements with Indigenous communities.

B) limiting the research that corporations conduct on the resources of the Indigenous communities with which they have signed agreements.

C) preventing independent observers from determining whether the agreements guarantee equitable compensation for Indigenous communities.

D) discouraging Indigenous communities from learning new methods for harvesting plants and animals from their corporate partners.

CONTINUE

15

The domestic sweet potato (*Ipomoea batatas*) descends from a wild plant native to South America. It also populates the Polynesian Islands, where evidence confirms that Native Hawaiians and other Indigenous peoples were cultivating the plant centuries before seafaring first occurred over the thousands of miles of ocean separating them from South America. To explain how the sweet potato was first introduced in Polynesia, botanist Pablo Muñoz-Rodríguez and colleagues analyzed the DNA of numerous varieties of the plant, concluding that Polynesian varieties diverged from South American ones over 100,000 years ago. Given that Polynesia was peopled only in the last three thousand years, the team concluded that _____

Which choice most logically completes the text?

A) the cultivation of the sweet potato in Polynesia likely predates its cultivation in South America.

B) Polynesian peoples likely acquired the sweet potato from South American peoples only within the last three thousand years.

C) human activity likely played no role in the introduction of the sweet potato in Polynesia.

D) Polynesian sweet potato varieties likely descend from a single South American variety that was domesticated, not wild.

16

In Death Valley National Park's Racetrack Playa, a flat, dry lakebed, are 162 rocks—some weighing less than a pound but others almost 700 pounds—that move periodically from place to place, seemingly of their own volition. Racetrack-like trails in the _____ mysterious migration.

Which choice completes the text so that it conforms to the conventions of Standard English?

A) playas sediment mark the rock's

B) playa's sediment mark the rocks

C) playa's sediment mark the rocks'

D) playas' sediment mark the rocks'

17

Nigerian author Buchi Emecheta's celebrated literary oeuvre includes *The Joys of Motherhood*, a novel about the changing roles of women in 1950s _____ a television play about the private struggles of a newlywed couple in Nigeria; and *Head Above Water*, her autobiography.

Which choice completes the text so that it conforms to the conventions of Standard English?

A) Lagos, *A Kind of Marriage*,

B) Lagos; *A Kind of Marriage*,

C) Lagos, *A Kind of Marriage*:

D) Lagos; *A Kind of Marriage*

Unauthorized copying or reuse of any part of this page is illegal.

CONTINUE

412

18

In 2016, engineer Vanessa Galvez oversaw the installation of 164 bioswales, vegetated channels designed to absorb and divert stormwater, along the streets of Queens, New York. By reducing the runoff flowing into city sewers, _____

Which choice completes the text so that it conforms to the conventions of Standard English?

A) the mitigation of both street flooding and the resulting pollution of nearby waterways has been achieved by bioswales.

B) the bioswales have mitigated both street flooding and the resulting pollution of nearby waterways.

C) the bioswales' mitigation of both street flooding and the resulting pollution of nearby waterways has been achieved.

D) both street flooding and the resulting pollution of nearby waterways have been mitigated by bioswales.

19

From afar, African American fiber artist Bisa Butler's portraits look like paintings, their depictions of human faces, bodies, and clothing so intricate that it seems only a fine brush could have rendered them. When viewed up close, however, the portraits reveal themselves to be _____ stitching barely visible among the thousands of pieces of printed, microcut fabric.

Which choice completes the text so that it conforms to the conventions of Standard English?

A) quilts, and the

B) quilts, the

C) quilts; the

D) quilts. The

20

Compared to that of alumina glass, _____ silica glass atoms are so far apart that they are unable to re-form bonds after being separated.

Which choice completes the text so that it conforms to the conventions of Standard English?

A) silica glass is at a significant disadvantage due to its more dispersed atomic arrangement:

B) silica glass has a more dispersed atomic arrangement, resulting in a significant disadvantage:

C) a significant disadvantage of silica glass is that its atomic arrangement is more dispersed:

D) silica glass's atomic arrangement is more dispersed, resulting in a significant disadvantage:

21

In the historical novel *The Surrender Tree*, Cuban American author Margarita Engle uses poetry rather than prose _____ the true story of Cuban folk hero Rosa La Bayamesa.

Which choice completes the text so that it conforms to the conventions of Standard English?

A) tells

B) told

C) is telling

D) to tell

Unauthorized copying or reuse of any part of this page is illegal.

CONTINUE

413

22

Sociologist Alton Okinaka sits on the review board tasked with adding new sites to the Hawaiʻi Register of Historic Places, which includes Piʻilanihale Heiau and the ʻŌpaekaʻa Road Bridge. Okinaka doesn't make such decisions _____ all historical designations must be approved by a group of nine other experts from the fields of architecture, archaeology, history, and Hawaiian culture.

Which choice completes the text so that it conforms to the conventions of Standard English?

A) single-handedly, however;

B) single-handedly; however,

C) single-handedly, however,

D) single-handedly however

23

When Chinese director Chloé Zhao accepted the Oscar in 2021 for her film *Nomadland*, she made Academy Award history. _____ only one other woman, Kathryn Bigelow of the United States, had been named best director at the Oscars, making Zhao the second woman and the first Asian woman to win the award.

Which choice completes the text with the most logical transition?

A) As a result,

B) Previously,

C) However,

D) Likewise,

24

Researchers Helena Mihaljević-Brandt, Lucía Santamaría, and Marco Tullney report that while mathematicians may have traditionally worked alone, evidence points to a shift in the opposite direction. _____ mathematicians are choosing to collaborate with their peers—a trend illustrated by a rise in the number of mathematics publications credited to multiple authors.

Which choice completes the text with the most logical transition?

A) Similarly,

B) For this reason,

C) Furthermore,

D) Increasingly,

25

When soil becomes contaminated by toxic metals, it can be removed from the ground and disposed of in a landfill. _____ contaminated soil can be detoxified via phytoremediation: plants that can withstand high concentrations of metals absorb the pollutants and store them in their shoots, which are then cut off and safely disposed of, preserving the health of the plants.

Which choice completes the text with the most logical transition?

A) Alternatively,

B) Specifically,

C) For example,

D) As a result,

Unauthorized copying or reuse of any part of this page is illegal.

CONTINUE ▶

414

26

While researching a topic, a student has taken the following notes:

- In the late 1890s, over 14,000 unique varieties of apples were grown in the US.
- The rise of industrial agriculture in the mid-1900s narrowed the range of commercially grown crops.
- Thousands of apple varieties considered less suitable for commercial growth were lost.
- Today, only 15 apple varieties dominate the market, making up 90% of apples purchased in the US.
- The Lost Apple Project, based in Washington State, attempts to find and grow lost apple varieties.

The student wants to emphasize the decline in unique apple varieties in the US and specify why this decline occurred. Which choice most effectively uses relevant information from the notes to accomplish these goals?

A) The Lost Apple Project is dedicated to finding some of the apple varieties lost following a shift in agricultural practices in the mid-1900s.

B) While over 14,000 apple varieties were grown in the US in the late 1890s, only 15 unique varieties make up most of the apples sold today.

C) Since the rise of industrial agriculture, US farmers have mainly grown the same few unique apple varieties, resulting in the loss of thousands of varieties less suitable for commercial growth.

D) As industrial agriculture rose to prominence in the mid-1900s, the number of crops selected for cultivation decreased dramatically.

27

While researching a topic, a student has taken the following notes:

- The *Atlantic Monthly* magazine was first published in 1857.
- The magazine focused on politics, art, and literature.
- In 2019, historian Cathryn Halverson published the book *Faraway Women and the "Atlantic Monthly."*
- Its subject is female authors whose autobiographies appeared in the magazine in the early 1900s.
- One of the authors discussed is Juanita Harrison.

The student wants to introduce Cathryn Halverson's book to an audience already familiar with the *Atlantic Monthly*. Which choice most effectively uses relevant information from the notes to accomplish this goal?

A) Cathryn Halverson's *Faraway Women and the "Atlantic Monthly"* discusses female authors whose autobiographies appeared in the magazine in the early 1900s.

B) A magazine called the *Atlantic Monthly*, referred to in Cathryn Halverson's book title, was first published in 1857.

C) *Faraway Women and the "Atlantic Monthly"* features contributors to the *Atlantic Monthly*, first published in 1857 as a magazine focusing on politics, art, and literature.

D) An author discussed by Cathryn Halverson is Juanita Harrison, whose autobiography appeared in the *Atlantic Monthly* in the early 1900s.

STOP

**If you finish before time is called, you may check your work on this module only.
Do not turn to any other module in the test.**

Math

22 QUESTIONS

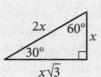

$A = \pi r^2$
$C = 2\pi r$

$A = \ell w$

$A = \frac{1}{2} bh$

$c^2 = a^2 + b^2$

Special Right Triangles

$V = \ell wh$

$V = \pi r^2 h$

$V = \frac{4}{3}\pi r^3$

$V = \frac{1}{3}\pi r^2 h$

$V = \frac{1}{3}\ell wh$

The number of degrees of arc in a circle is 360.

The number of radians of arc in a circle is 2π.

The sum of the measures in degrees of the angles of a triangle is 180.

Unauthorized copying or reuse of any part of this page is illegal.

416

CONTINUE

For multiple-choice questions, solve each problem, choose the correct answer from the choices provided, and then circle your answer in this book. Circle only one answer for each question. If you change your mind, completely erase the circle. You will not get credit for questions with more than one answer circled, or for questions with no answers circled.

For student-produced response questions, solve each problem and write your answer next to or under the question in the test book as described below.

- Once you've written your answer, circle it clearly. You will not receive credit for anything written outside the circle, or for any questions with more than one circled answer.

- If you find **more than one correct answer**, write and circle only one answer.

- Your answer can be up to 5 characters for a **positive** answer and up to 6 characters (including the negative sign) for a **negative** answer, but no more.

- If your answer is a **fraction** that is too long (over 5 characters for positive, 6 characters for negative), write the decimal equivalent.

- If your answer is a **decimal** that is too long (over 5 characters for positive, 6 characters for negative), truncate it or round at the fourth digit.

- If your answer is a **mixed number** (such as $3\frac{1}{2}$), write it as an improper fraction (7/2) or its decimal equivalent (3.5).

- Don't include **symbols** such as a percent sign, comma, or dollar sign in your circled answer.

Unauthorized copying or reuse of any part of this page is illegal.

CONTINUE

417

1

$$4x + 6 = 18$$

Which equation has the same solution as the given equation?

A) $4x = 108$

B) $4x = 24$

C) $4x = 12$

D) $4x = 3$

2

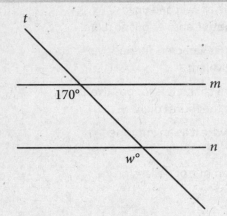

Note: Figure not drawn to scale.

In the figure, line m is parallel to line n. What is the value of w?

A) 17

B) 30

C) 70

D) 170

3

Each value in the data set shown represents the height, in centimeters, of a plant.

6, 10, 13, 2, 15, 22, 10, 4, 4, 4

What is the mean height, in centimeters, of these plants?

4

$$2.5b + 5r = 80$$

The given equation describes the relationship between the number of birds, b, and the number of reptiles, r, that can be cared for at a pet care business on a given day. If the business cares for 16 reptiles on a given day, how many birds can it care for on this day?

A) 0

B) 5

C) 40

D) 80

5

A cube has an edge length of 41 inches. What is the volume, in cubic inches, of the cube?

A) 164

B) 1,681

C) 10,086

D) 68,921

6

13 is p% of 25. What is the value of p?

7

A model predicts that the population of Springfield was 15,000 in 2005. The model also predicts that each year for the next 5 years, the population p increased by 4% of the previous year's population. Which equation best represents this model, where x is the number of years after 2005, for $x \le 5$?

A) $p = 0.96(15,000)^x$

B) $p = 1.04(15,000)^x$

C) $p = 15,000(0.96)^x$

D) $p = 15,000(1.04)^x$

CONTINUE

8

$$-4x^2 - 7x = -36$$

What is the positive solution to the given equation?

A) $\dfrac{7}{4}$

B) $\dfrac{9}{4}$

C) 4

D) 7

9

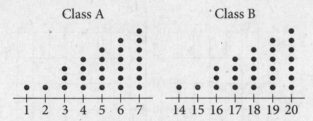

Class A   Class B

Each of the dot plots shown represents the number of glue sticks brought in by each student for two classes, class A and class B. Which statement best compares the standard deviations of the numbers of glue sticks brought in by each student for these two classes?

A) The standard deviation of the number of glue sticks brought in by each student for class A is less than the standard deviation of the number of glue sticks brought in by each student for class B.

B) The standard deviation of the number of glue sticks brought in by each student for class A is equal to the standard deviation of the number of glue sticks brought in by each student for class B.

C) The standard deviation of the number of glue sticks brought in by each student for class A is greater than the standard deviation of the number of glue sticks brought in by each student for class B.

D) There is not enough information to compare these standard deviations.

10

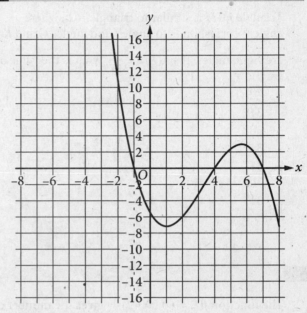

The graph of $y = f(x)$ is shown, where the function f is defined by $f(x) = ax^3 + bx^2 + cx + d$ and a, b, c, and d are constants. For how many values of x does $f(x) = 0$?

A) One

B) Two

C) Three

D) Four

11

The exponential function g is defined by $g(x) = 19 \cdot a^x$, where a is a positive constant. If $g(3) = 2{,}375$, what is the value of $g(4)$?

12

$$y = (x - 2)(x + 4)$$
$$y = 6x - 12$$

Which ordered pair (x, y) is the solution to the given system of equations?

A) $(0, 2)$

B) $(-4, 2)$

C) $(2, 0)$

D) $(2, -4)$

CONTINUE

13

Triangle *FGH* is similar to triangle *JKL*, where angle *F* corresponds to angle *J* and angles *G* and *K* are right angles. If $\sin(F) = \dfrac{308}{317}$, what is the value of $\sin(J)$?

A) $\dfrac{75}{317}$

B) $\dfrac{308}{317}$

C) $\dfrac{317}{308}$

D) $\dfrac{317}{75}$

14

The function $f(t) = 60{,}000(2)^{\frac{t}{410}}$ gives the number of bacteria in a population *t* minutes after an initial observation. How much time, in minutes, does it take for the number of bacteria in the population to double?

15

$$p = \dfrac{k}{4j + 9}$$

The given equation relates the distinct positive numbers *p*, *k*, and *j*. Which equation correctly expresses $4j + 9$ in terms of *p* and *k*?

A) $4j + 9 = \dfrac{k}{p}$

B) $4j + 9 = kp$

C) $4j + 9 = k - p$

D) $4j + 9 = \dfrac{p}{k}$

16

Line *p* is defined by $4y + 8x = 6$. Line *r* is perpendicular to line *p* in the *xy*-plane. What is the slope of line *r*?

17

Point *O* is the center of a circle. The measure of arc *RS* on this circle is 100°. What is the measure, in degrees, of its associated angle *ROS*?

18

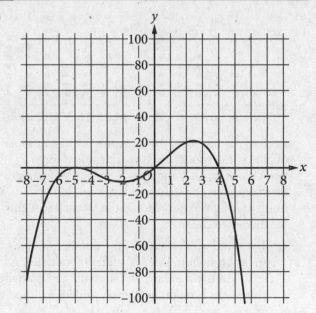

Which of the following could be the equation of the graph shown in the *xy*-plane?

A) $y = -\dfrac{1}{10}x(x - 4)(x + 5)$

B) $y = -\dfrac{1}{10}x(x - 4)(x + 5)^2$

C) $y = -\dfrac{1}{10}x(x - 5)(x + 4)$

D) $y = -\dfrac{1}{10}x(x - 5)^2(x + 4)$

CONTINUE ➤

19

For $x > 0$, the function f is defined as follows:

$f(x)$ equals 201% of x

Which of the following could describe this function?

A) Decreasing exponential

B) Decreasing linear

C) Increasing exponential

D) Increasing linear

20

$$f(x) = 4x^2 + 64x + 262$$

The function g is defined by $g(x) = f(x + 5)$. For what value of x does $g(x)$ reach its minimum?

A) -13

B) -8

C) -5

D) -3

21

Poll Results

Angel Cruz	483
Terry Smith	320

The table shows the results of a poll. A total of 803 voters selected at random were asked which candidate they would vote for in the upcoming election. According to the poll, if 6,424 people vote in the election, by how many votes would Angel Cruz be expected to win?

A) 163

B) 1,304

C) 3,864

D) 5,621

22

$$y = 2x^2 - 21x + 64$$
$$y = 3x + a$$

In the given system of equations, a is a constant. The graphs of the equations in the given system intersect at exactly one point, (x, y), in the xy-plane. What is the value of x?

A) -8

B) -6

C) 6

D) 8

STOP

If you finish before time is called, you may check your work on this module only.
Do not turn to any other module in the test.

Math

22 QUESTIONS

DIRECTIONS

The questions in this section address a number of important math skills.
Use of a calculator is permitted for all questions.

NOTES

Unless otherwise indicated:

- All variables and expressions represent real numbers.
- Figures provided are drawn to scale.
- All figures lie in a plane.
- The domain of a given function f is the set of all real numbers x for which $f(x)$ is a real number.

REFERENCE

    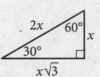

$A = \pi r^2$ $A = \ell w$ $A = \frac{1}{2}bh$ $c^2 = a^2 + b^2$ Special Right Triangles
$C = 2\pi r$

$V = \ell w h$ $V = \pi r^2 h$ $V = \frac{4}{3}\pi r^3$ $V = \frac{1}{3}\pi r^2 h$ $V = \frac{1}{3}\ell w h$

The number of degrees of arc in a circle is 360.

The number of radians of arc in a circle is 2π.

The sum of the measures in degrees of the angles of a triangle is 180.

CONTINUE ▶

For multiple-choice questions, solve each problem, choose the correct answer from the choices provided, and then circle your answer in this book. Circle only one answer for each question. If you change your mind, completely erase the circle. You will not get credit for questions with more than one answer circled, or for questions with no answers circled.

For student-produced response questions, solve each problem and write your answer next to or under the question in the test book as described below.

- Once you've written your answer, circle it clearly. You will not receive credit for anything written outside the circle, or for any questions with more than one circled answer.

- If you find **more than one correct answer**, write and circle only one answer.

- Your answer can be up to 5 characters for a **positive** answer and up to 6 characters (including the negative sign) for a **negative** answer, but no more.

- If your answer is a **fraction** that is too long (over 5 characters for positive, 6 characters for negative), write the decimal equivalent.

- If your answer is a **decimal** that is too long (over 5 characters for positive, 6 characters for negative), truncate it or round at the fourth digit.

- If your answer is a **mixed number** (such as $3\frac{1}{2}$), write it as an improper fraction (7/2) or its decimal equivalent (3.5).

- Don't include **symbols** such as a percent sign, comma, or dollar sign in your circled answer.

CONTINUE ➡

1

$$3x = 12$$
$$-3x + y = -6$$

The solution to the given system of equations is (x, y). What is the value of y?

A) -3

B) 6

C) 18

D) 30

2

Which expression is equivalent to $11x^3 - 5x^3$?

A) $16x^3$

B) $6x^3$

C) $6x^6$

D) $16x^6$

3

$$66x = 66x$$

How many solutions does the given equation have?

A) Exactly one

B) Exactly two

C) Infinitely many

D) Zero

4

A proposal for a new library was included on an election ballot. A radio show stated that 3 times as many people voted in favor of the proposal as people who voted against it. A social media post reported that 15,000 more people voted in favor of the proposal than voted against it. Based on these data, how many people voted against the proposal?

A) 7,500

B) 15,000

C) 22,500

D) 45,000

5

Caleb used juice to make popsicles. The function $f(x) = -5x + 30$ approximates the volume, in fluid ounces, of juice Caleb had remaining after making x popsicles. Which statement is the best interpretation of the y-intercept of the graph of $y = f(x)$ in the xy-plane in this context?

A) Caleb used approximately 5 fluid ounces of juice for each popsicle.

B) Caleb had approximately 5 fluid ounces of juice when he began to make the popsicles.

C) Caleb had approximately 30 fluid ounces of juice when he began to make the popsicles.

D) Caleb used approximately 30 fluid ounces of juice for each popsicle.

6

An angle has a measure of $\dfrac{16\pi}{15}$ radians. What is the measure of the angle, in <u>degrees</u>?

7

$$y \le x + 7$$
$$y \ge -2x - 1$$

Which point (x, y) is a solution to the given system of inequalities in the xy-plane?

A) $(-14, 0)$

B) $(0, -14)$

C) $(0, 14)$

D) $(14, 0)$

8

A right triangle has legs with lengths of 24 centimeters and 21 centimeters. If the length of this triangle's hypotenuse, in centimeters, can be written in the form $3\sqrt{d}$, where d is an integer, what is the value of d?

CONTINUE ▶

9

Value	Data set A frequency	Data set B frequency
30	2	9
34	4	7
38	5	5
42	7	4
46	9	2

Data set A and data set B each consist of 27 values. The table shows the frequencies of the values for each data set. Which of the following statements best compares the means of the two data sets?

A) The mean of data set A is greater than the mean of data set B.

B) The mean of data set A is less than the mean of data set B.

C) The mean of data set A is equal to the mean of data set B.

D) There is not enough information to compare the means of the data sets.

10

Triangle XYZ is similar to triangle RST such that X, Y, and Z correspond to R, S, and T, respectively. The measure of $\angle Z$ is 20° and $2XY = RS$. What is the measure of $\angle T$?

A) 2°

B) 10°

C) 20°

D) 40°

11

Keenan made 32 cups of vegetable broth. Keenan then filled x small jars and y large jars with all the vegetable broth he made. The equation $3x + 5y = 32$ represents this situation. Which is the best interpretation of $5y$ in this context?

A) The number of large jars Keenan filled

B) The number of small jars Keenan filled

C) The total number of cups of vegetable broth in the large jars

D) The total number of cups of vegetable broth in the small jars

12

$$x(x + 1) - 56 = 4x(x - 7)$$

What is the sum of the solutions to the given equation?

13

The function $f(x) = \frac{1}{9}(x - 7)^2 + 3$ gives a metal ball's height above the ground $f(x)$, in inches, x seconds after it started moving on a track, where $0 \le x \le 10$. Which of the following is the best interpretation of the vertex of the graph of $y = f(x)$ in the xy-plane?

A) The metal ball's minimum height was 3 inches above the ground.

B) The metal ball's minimum height was 7 inches above the ground.

C) The metal ball's height was 3 inches above the ground when it started moving.

D) The metal ball's height was 7 inches above the ground when it started moving.

CONTINUE

14

$$F(x) = \frac{9}{5}(x - 273.15) + 32$$

The function F gives the temperature, in degrees Fahrenheit, that corresponds to a temperature of x kelvins. If a temperature increased by 2.10 kelvins, by how much did the temperature increase, in degrees Fahrenheit?

A) 3.78

B) 35.78

C) 487.89

D) 519.89

15

x	y
k	13
$k + 7$	−15

The table gives the coordinates of two points on a line in the xy-plane. The y-intercept of the line is $(k - 5, b)$, where k and b are constants. What is the value of b?

16

One of the factors of $2x^3 + 42x^2 + 208x$ is $x + b$, where b is a positive constant. What is the smallest possible value of b?

17

The function f is defined by $f(x) = 7x - 84$. What is the x-intercept of the graph of $y = f(x)$ in the xy-plane?

A) $(-12, 0)$

B) $(-7, 0)$

C) $(7, 0)$

D) $(12, 0)$

18

A certain park has an area of 11,863,808 square yards. What is the area, in <u>square miles</u>, of this park? (1 mile = 1,760 yards)

A) 1.96

B) 3.83

C) 3,444.39

D) 6,740.8

19

One gallon of paint will cover 220 square feet of a surface. A room has a total wall area of w square feet. Which equation represents the total amount of paint P, in gallons, needed to paint the walls of the room twice?

A) $P = \dfrac{w}{110}$

B) $P = 440w$

C) $P = \dfrac{w}{220}$

D) $P = 220w$

CONTINUE

20

$$48x - 72y = 30y + 24$$

$$ry = \frac{1}{6} - 16x$$

In the given system of equations, r is a constant. If the system has no solution, what is the value of r?

21

$$\frac{x^2}{\sqrt{x^2 - c^2}} = \frac{c^2}{\sqrt{x^2 - c^2}} + 39$$

In the given equation, c is a positive constant. Which of the following is one of the solutions to the given equation?

A) $-c$

B) $-c^2 - 39^2$

C) $-\sqrt{39^2 - c^2}$

D) $-\sqrt{c^2 + 39^2}$

22

$$f(x) = ax^2 + 4x + c$$

In the given quadratic function, a and c are constants. The graph of $y = f(x)$ in the xy-plane is a parabola that opens upward and has a vertex at the point (h, k), where h and k are constants. If $k < 0$ and $f(-9) = f(3)$, which of the following must be true?

  I. $c < 0$

  II. $a \geq 1$

A) I only

B) II only

C) I and II

D) Neither I nor 11

STOP

If you finish before time is called, you may check your work on this module only.
Do not turn to any other module in the test.

The SAT®

Practice Test #2

ANSWER EXPLANATIONS

These answer explanations are for students using
The Official Digital SAT Study Guide.

Reading and Writing

Module 1
(27 questions)

QUESTION 1

Choice A is the best answer because it most logically completes the text's discussion of the writing system created by Sequoyah. In this context, "widespread" means widely accepted or practiced. The text indicates that because Sequoyah's script accurately represented the spoken sounds of the Cherokee language and was easy to learn, nearly all Cherokee people were able to read and write it soon after it was created. This context demonstrates that the script was widely used by the Cherokee people.

Choice B is incorrect. In this context, "careful" would mean exercised with care and attentive concern. Although the work of creating a writing system likely involved great care, the text indicates that the system was "easy to learn," which conflicts with the idea that using this system requires a noteworthy amount of care. *Choice C* is incorrect because in this context "unintended" means not deliberate. The idea that using Sequoyah's script was unintentional conflicts directly with the claim that it was easy to learn and used by "over 90% of the Cherokee people" by 1830. In fact, because one had to learn this system, it's not clear how one could use it unintentionally. *Choice D* is incorrect because in this context "infrequent" means rare or not occurring often, which conflicts directly with the claim that "over 90% of the Cherokee people" were using Sequoyah's script by 1830.

QUESTION 2

Choice C is the best answer because it most logically completes the text's discussion of Gardley's play. In this context, "comprises" means constitutes or makes up the totality of, and the text indicates that *The House That Will Not Stand* had an "all-female cast" that stands in some relationship to "an array of female characters" in the play. Because all cast members are female, the characters must be played by these female cast members; therefore the cast constitutes, or comprises, the collection of characters.

Choice A is incorrect. In this context, "engulfs" would mean encloses or overwhelms, and although it is fairly common to describe an actor as embodying (or personifying realistically) a character, there is nothing in the text to suggest that the cast members enclosed or overwhelmed the characters they played. *Choice B* is incorrect because in this context, "encourages" would mean inspires with courage or hope. Although the text does mention "a strong mother and several daughters dealing with individual struggles," which might suggest that there are moments of encouragement among the characters during the play, there is nothing to suggest that the cast members encouraged the characters they portrayed. *Choice D* is incorrect because, in this context, "provokes" would mean instigates or incites to anger. Nothing in the text addresses provocation or what it might mean for actors to provoke the characters they are playing.

QUESTION 3

Choice B is the best answer because it most logically completes the text's discussion of the significance of the 2014 archaeological finding at El Algar. In this context, "concede" means to admit something is true after first resisting that admission. The text indicates that some researchers believe "Bronze Age societies were ruled by men." But the Bronze Age burial of a woman at El Algar included "valuable objects signaling a high position of power," which would raise the possibility that "women may have also held leadership roles." Thus, the text is calling into question the notion that only men were leaders in these societies and speculating that people holding this view may reconsider their opinion.

Choice A is incorrect because "waive" means to refrain from insisting that something, such as a right or a requirement, be observed; the word isn't used, however, in contexts where someone acknowledges that an opinion they hold may be invalid, as is the case in the text. *Choice C* is incorrect. According to the text, the finding from the El Algar burial site undermines the view that Bronze Age societies were exclusively ruled by men. However, "refute" means to demonstrate that something is false and would not make sense in context. Lull and team's finding supports the view that women may have also held leadership roles, not that they did not participate in such roles. *Choice D* is incorrect because in this context, "require" means to demand or specify as mandatory. However, it would not make sense for contemporary researchers to demand that Bronze Age "women may have also held leadership roles."

QUESTION 4

Choice C is the best answer because as used in the text, "endure" most nearly means tolerate. In the text, Cecily and Algernon discuss parting, or saying goodbye. Cecily remarks on the deep pain of saying goodbye to people whom one has only known briefly and then comments on the equanimity, or calm steadiness, one experiences when separated from old friends. The text sets up an ironic contrast: one can easily tolerate, or put up with, the absence of close friends, but even a very short separation from a new acquaintance is unbearable.

Choice A is incorrect. Nothing in the text suggests that Cecily associates regret, or a feeling of sorrow, with the absence of old friends. Rather, the text sets up an ironic contrast between the feeling of calm steadiness one feels when separated from old friends and the unbearable pain of being separated from new acquaintances. *Choice B* is incorrect. Although in some contexts "endure" can mean persist, or proceed stubbornly, it doesn't have that meaning in this context because what is being endured is the absence of old friends. Whereas one can persist *despite* the absence of someone else, one can't persist the absence itself. *Choice D* is incorrect because the text doesn't convey that Cecily encourages, or urges, old friends to be absent. Although it may be that Cecily prefers new acquaintances to friends she has known for a long time, the text focuses on her feelings as a result of others' absences, not on her treatment of others.

QUESTION 5

Choice A is the best answer because it accurately states the main purpose of the text. The text begins by discussing the promise of the future, with positive references to renewal such as "new roads," "new beating of the drum," and "fresh seeing." But with the "new sun," the text continues, there will still be "the same backs bending" and "the same sad feet" drumming, indicating that these difficulties will follow people into this new day. The poem thus considers both the rewards and challenges associated with the repetitiveness of human life.

Choice B is incorrect because the text doesn't say anything about how memorable activities are, let alone compare the memorability of activities completed at different times of the day. *Choice C* is incorrect. Although the text contrasts hope with difficulty, it does not compare the relative frequency of joyful feelings with that of sad feelings. *Choice D* is incorrect because the text makes no distinction between the experiences of individuals and the experiences of their communities.

QUESTION 6

Choice B is the best answer because it most accurately describes how the underlined portion functions in the text as a whole. The text presents the speaker's experience of viewing the sea. In the underlined portion, the speaker focuses on the idea that the waves hitting rocks on the shore are a relentless and enduring force: they are constantly pushed back ("ever repulsed") but always return ("ever rushing on"), as though they have an energy that can't be overcome ("a life that will not know defeat").

Choice A is incorrect. Although the underlined portion characterizes the waves as a relentless force (always "repulsed" but still "rushing on" and never being defeated), the speaker doesn't suggest that the surroundings are intimidating. Instead, the speaker presents the scene in a positive way, describing the "deep delight" of the "gladsome," or cheerful, waves and feeling "the heart / Leap joyous" while viewing the sea. *Choice C* is incorrect because the underlined portion doesn't suggest that the speaker is ambivalent, or has mixed feelings about, the natural world. Instead, it presents a single view of one part of the immediate surroundings: the speaker characterizes the sea's waves as an unstoppable force, since they are constantly pushed back but always return ("ever repulsed, yet ever rushing on"). *Choice D* is incorrect. Although the text later suggests the speaker's view of her own thoughts by referring to a "clouded brain" and a heart that leaps joyously, this reference neither occurs within the underlined portion nor establishes a clear contrast with the relentless determination of the waves. The underlined portion addresses only the speaker's view of the waves and doesn't suggest what her own thoughts might be.

QUESTION 7

Choice A is the best answer because it most accurately describes the overall structure of the text. The narrator begins by explaining how Charlot carefully delivers Atlante's letter to Rinaldo, and then relates that Rinaldo feels "transported with joy" after reading the letter. Therefore, the overall structure of the text is best described as a description of the delivery of a letter followed by the portrayal of a character's happiness after reading the letter.

Choice B is incorrect because the text indicates that the letter has been written; there's no explanation why another character hasn't written one. In addition, the text's description of Rinaldo "in a melancholy posture" suggests that he's sad and thoughtful, not that he's desperate to receive the letter. *Choice C* is incorrect.

Although the text states that Charlot won't toss the letter to Rinaldo because she doesn't want it to fall, the text doesn't refer to the contents of the letter. Instead, the text describes how happy Rinaldo feels after reading it. *Choice D* is incorrect. Although the text does describe Rinaldo's reaction to the letter, the text doesn't begin by discussing Atlante's inspiration for writing the letter. Instead, the text begins by discussing the delivery of the letter.

QUESTION 8

Choice D is the best answer because it most accurately states the main idea of the text. The text describes Mary's activities in an overgrown hidden garden, saying that she was "very much absorbed" and was "only becoming more pleased with her work every hour" rather than getting tired of it. She also thinks of garden activities as a "fascinating sort of play." Thus, the main idea of the text is that Mary feels very satisfied when taking care of the garden.

Choice A is incorrect because the text never makes any mention of Mary's chores. *Choice B* is incorrect because the text indicates that Mary finds pulling up weeds to be fascinating, not boring. *Choice C* is incorrect because Mary thinks of garden activities in and of themselves as play, not as something necessary to do to create a space to play.

QUESTION 9

Choice D is the best answer because it most accurately states the main idea of the text. According to the text, conceptual artists Gins and Arakawa have designed an apartment building that is disorienting because of several unconventional elements, such as uneven kitchen counters and "a door to nowhere." The text goes on to suggest that there may be benefits to this kind of design because filmmaker Yamaoka lived in the apartment building for four years and reported health benefits. Thus, although the design is impractical, it may improve the well-being of the apartment building's residents.

Choice A is incorrect. Although the text mentions that Yamaoka lived in the apartment for four years, it doesn't address how long someone can beneficially live in a home surrounded by fanciful features or whether doing so can be sustained. *Choice B* is incorrect. Although the text mentions the potential benefits of living in a home with disorienting design features, it doesn't suggest that this is the most effective method to create a physically stimulating environment. *Choice C* is incorrect because the text refers to Yamaoka to support the claim that Gins and Arakawa's apartment building design may be beneficial, but the text doesn't indicate that Yamaoka supports the designs of other conceptual artists.

QUESTION 10

Choice A is the best answer because it most accurately states the main purpose of the text. In the first part of the text, the speaker addresses Paul Laurence Dunbar's ability to understand people (he has "read the hearts and souls of men" and written of their "joy and mirth"). In the second part of the text, the speaker describes Dunbar's thorough understanding of the natural world (he has read "the language of the flowers" and engaged with "the little brook"). Thus, the text mainly praises Dunbar for being especially perceptive about people and nature.

Choice B is incorrect because the speaker describes Dunbar has having read the "hearts and souls of men" and the "language of flowers" to convey Dunbar's ability to comprehend people and nature, not to suggest that Dunbar has literally read any of these things or has read a great deal about them.

Choice C is incorrect because the text notes how well Dunbar has made sense of the topics he's written about but doesn't address any specific parts of Dunbar's writing process beyond the suggestion that he used a pen. *Choice D* is incorrect because the text focuses on Dunbar's understanding of people and nature as expressed in his writing. Nothing in the text suggests that the speaker is recalling a particular afternoon actually spent in nature with Dunbar; even if there had been a shared experience, the text isn't focused on reminiscing.

QUESTION 11

Choice A is the best answer because it most directly illustrates the text's claim about Whitman's poem, "To You." The text says that in this poem, Whitman suggests that he deeply understands the poem's reader. This quotation says that the reader's "true soul and body appear before" Whitman, thereby asserting that he can see the reader as the reader truly is, suggesting that he deeply understands the reader.

Choice B is incorrect because this quotation describes Whitman making the reader the subject of the poem ("you be my poem"), not Whitman deeply understanding the reader. *Choice C* is incorrect because instead of suggesting that Whitman deeply understands the reader, it emphasizes Whitman's regret at not having addressed the reader sooner. *Choice D* is incorrect. Although this quotation shows Whitman directly addressing the reader and expressing concern about the reader, it doesn't illustrate the idea that Whitman suggests that he deeply understands the reader. The quotation is simply expressing concern about the reader, which doesn't necessarily imply deep understanding of the reader.

QUESTION 12

Choice B is the best answer because it provides the most direct support from the table for the claim that two languages can convey similar amounts of information even if they're spoken at different rates. The table shows the approximate rates at which five languages are spoken and the rates at which those five languages convey information. Vietnamese is spoken at around 5.3 syllables per second, whereas Spanish is spoken at around 7.7 syllables per second, but the two languages convey information at very similar rates: Vietnamese at a rate of around 42.5 bits per second and Spanish at a rate of around 42.0 bits per second. Thus, the description of Vietnamese conveying information at around the same rate that Spanish does despite being spoken more slowly supports the claim in the text that languages can convey the same amount of information even if spoken at different rates.

Choice A is incorrect because it isn't true that Thai and Hungarian have the lowest rates of speech of the five languages shown. According to the table, Hungarian is spoken at around 5.9 syllables per second, which is faster than Vietnamese (5.3 syllables per second). Additionally, even if this statement were true, the assertion that two languages are spoken the slowest and convey information the slowest wouldn't support the claim that languages can convey the same amount of information even if they're spoken at different rates. *Choice C* is incorrect because it isn't true that the fastest-spoken language (Spanish, at 7.7 syllables per second) also conveys information the fastest: Spanish conveys information at 42.0 bits per second, which is slower than the 42.5 bits-per-second rate at which Vietnamese conveys information. Additionally, even if this statement were true, the assertion that the language spoken the fastest also conveys information the fastest has no bearing on the claim that languages can convey the same amount of information even if they're spoken at different rates. *Choice D* is incorrect because it isn't true that Serbian conveys information faster than Spanish does. According to the table, Serbian conveys information at a rate of around 39.1 bits per second, which is slower than the 42.0 bits-per-second rate at which Spanish conveys information.

QUESTION 13

Choice B is the best answer because it describes data from the graph that weaken the student's conclusion about the reduction in the spider population in the enclosure with lizards. The graph shows that the enclosure with lizards and the enclosure without lizards each began with about 85 spiders, and that the number of spiders in each enclosure fell over the 30 days of the study. The student's claim is that the reduction in spiders in the enclosure with lizards is "entirely attributable to the presence of the lizards," meaning that the spider population wouldn't have declined except for the presence of the lizards. This claim is weakened, however, by the fact that the enclosure without lizards also saw a substantial reduction in the number of spiders. Since the number of spiders fell in the enclosure without lizards as well as in the enclosure with lizards, there must be some other factor than just the presence of the lizards that contributed to the reduction in the spider population.

Choice A is incorrect because the fact that the two enclosures started with the same number of spiders is irrelevant to the claim that the reduction in spider population by day 30 in the enclosure with lizards can be entirely attributed to the lizards. *Choice C* is incorrect because the fact that the spider population in the enclosure with lizards fell more between days 1 and 10 than in other periods has nothing to do with the student's claim that the reduction in spiders in that enclosure by day 30 can be entirely attributed to the lizards. *Choice D* is incorrect. Although it's true that on day 30 the spider population was lower in the enclosure with lizards than in the enclosure without lizards, this fact doesn't weaken the student's claim that the reduction in the spider population in the enclosure with lizards can be entirely attributed to the lizards. Indeed, the lower spider population in the enclosure with lizards suggests that the lizards are contributing to the reduction in the spider population, though the fact that the spider population also fell substantially in the other enclosure means that the lizards aren't the only cause of the reduction.

QUESTION 14

Choice A is the best answer because it presents the conclusion that most logically follows from the text's discussion of military veterans working in civilian government jobs in the United States. The text indicates that the proportion of military veterans working in civilian government jobs is considerably higher than the proportion of military veterans in the population as a whole. The text also notes that the unusually high representation of military veterans in these jobs may be a result of the organizational structures shared by civilian government entities and the military. Hence, it's reasonable to infer that it's the familiarity of the structures of civilian government that makes jobs there particularly attractive to military veterans.

Choice B is incorrect because the text doesn't address what a typical relationship between military service and later career preferences would be, and there's no indication that it's atypical for veterans to work in civilian government jobs after they've left the military. On the contrary, the text suggests that many military veterans are drawn to such jobs. *Choice C* is incorrect because the text is focused on the high representation of military veterans in civilian government jobs and doesn't address nonveterans or their possible interest in military service. *Choice D* is incorrect because the text conveys that military veterans may be particularly interested in civilian government jobs due to the familiarity of organizational structures that are already in place, but there's no reason to think that this interest would mean that more civilian government jobs will start to require military experience.

QUESTION 15

Choice C is the best answer. The convention being tested is the punctuation of a restrictive coordinated noun phrase. No punctuation is needed within or around the coordinated noun phrase "researchers Roberto Scandone and Christopher Kilburn" because it would create an illogical separation between the noun "researchers" and the coordinated noun phrase "Roberto Scandone and Christopher Kilburn."

Choice A is incorrect because no punctuation is needed. Placing a pair of commas around the coordinated noun phrase "Roberto Scandone and Christopher Kilburn" creates an illogical separation between the noun "researchers" and the aforementioned coordinated noun phrase. In this case, it illogically suggests that researchers in general bear the specific names Roberto Scandone and Christopher Kilburn. *Choice B* is incorrect because no punctuation is needed between the noun "researchers" and the coordinated noun phrase "Roberto Scandone and Christopher Kilburn." *Choice D* is incorrect because no punctuation is needed within the coordinated noun phrase "Roberto Scandone and Christopher Kilburn."

QUESTION 16

Choice B is the best answer. The convention being tested is the coordination of main clauses within a sentence. This choice uses a semicolon in a conventional way to join the first main clause ("In 2004…sampler") and the second main clause ("in 2014…pillars").

Choice A is incorrect because it results in a comma splice. Without a conjunction following it, a comma can't be used in this way to join two main clauses. The word "later" is an adverb and cannot be used to join two main clauses unless it is preceded by a conjunction. *Choice C* is incorrect because it results in a comma splice. Without a conjunction following it, a comma can't be used in this way to join two main clauses. *Choice D* is incorrect because it results in a comma splice. Without a conjunction following it, a comma can't be used in this way to join two main clauses. The word "later" is an adverb and cannot be used to join two main clauses unless it is preceded by a conjunction.

QUESTION 17

Choice D is the best answer. The convention being tested is punctuation within two coordinated noun phrases. When, as in this case, a noun phrase ("the country's millions of miles of waterways") is coordinated with another noun phrase ("the fact") followed by an integrated relative clause ("that the volume… time"), no punctuation is needed.

Choice A is incorrect because no punctuation is needed. *Choice B* is incorrect because no punctuation is needed. *Choice C* is incorrect because no punctuation is needed.

QUESTION 18

Choice A is the best answer. The convention being tested is subject-modifier placement. This choice makes the noun phrase "many critics" the subject of the sentence and places it immediately after the modifying phrase "in assessing… Kurosawa." In doing so, this choice clearly establishes that it is the critics—and not another noun in the sentence—who assess Kurosawa's films.

Choice B is incorrect because it results in a dangling modifier. The placement of the noun phrase "Kurosawa's...sources" immediately after the modifying phrase illogically suggests that his use of Western literary sources is what assesses Kurosawa's films. *Choice C* is incorrect because it results in a dangling modifier. The placement of the function word "there" immediately after the modifying phrase illogically suggests that "there" is what assesses Kurosawa's films. *Choice D* is incorrect because it results in a dangling modifier. The placement of the noun phrase "the focus...critics" immediately after the modifying phrase illogically suggests that the critics' focus is what assesses Kurosawa's films.

QUESTION 19

Choice C is the best answer. The convention being tested is the punctuation of items in a complex series. It's conventional to use a semicolon to separate items in a complex series with internal punctuation, and in this choice, the semicolon after "2009" is conventionally used to separate the first item ("the world's...2009") and the second item ("an online...2010") in the series of things that Hinson helped create. Further, the comma after "Basic" correctly pairs with the comma after "app," and the comma after "network" correctly pairs with the comma after "TV" to set off the supplemental elements ("Chickasaw Basic" and "Chickasaw TV") that provide the names of the app and the TV network, respectively. Altogether, the punctuation in this choice results in a sentence that clearly indicates that Hinson helped make a language app in 2009, an online TV network in 2010, and a language course in 2015.

Choice A is incorrect because it fails to punctuate the complex series in a way that makes clear that Hinson helped make a language app in 2009, an online TV network in 2010, and a language course in 2015. *Choice B* is incorrect because it fails to punctuate the complex series in a way that makes clear that Hinson helped make a language app in 2009, an online TV network in 2010, and a language course in 2015. *Choice D* is incorrect because the comma after "2009" doesn't match the semicolon used to separate the second and third items in the complex series.

QUESTION 20

Choice D is the best answer. The convention being tested is punctuation use between a main clause and a supplementary phrase. In this choice, a colon is correctly used to mark the boundary between the main clause ("A group... plant") and the supplementary element ("TN57...pests") and to introduce the following elaboration on the specific varieties of sweet potato plants that were examined.

Choice A is incorrect because it results in a rhetorically unacceptable sentence fragment beginning with "TN57." *Choice B* is incorrect because a semicolon can't be used in this way to join the main clause ("A group...plant") and the supplementary element ("TN57...pests"). A semicolon is conventionally used to join two main clauses, whereas a colon is conventionally used to introduce an element that explains or amplifies the information in the preceding clause. *Choice C* is incorrect because it fails to mark the boundary between the main clause ("A group...plant") and the supplementary element ("TN57...pests") with appropriate punctuation.

QUESTION 21

Choice A is the best answer. "Hence" logically signals that the information in this sentence—that geologists couldn't confirm the theory of cyclical Ice Ages until the 1960s—is a consequence of the previous information about the destructiveness of each Ice Age and the erasure of necessary geological evidence.

Choice B is incorrect because "moreover" illogically signals that the information in this sentence is merely additional to the previous information about the destructiveness of each Ice Age. Instead, the sentence identifies a specific consequence of that information. *Choice C* is incorrect because "nevertheless" illogically signals that the information in this sentence is true despite the previous information about the destructiveness of each Ice Age. Instead, the sentence identifies a specific consequence of that information. *Choice D* is incorrect because "next" illogically signals that the information in this sentence is the next step in a process. Instead, the sentence identifies a specific consequence of the previous information.

QUESTION 22

Choice B is the best answer. The sentence compares the lengths of the two rail tunnels, noting that the Channel Tunnel (about 31 miles long) is slightly shorter than the Seikan Tunnel (roughly 33 miles long).

Choice A is incorrect. The sentence makes a generalization about the length of some rail tunnels; it doesn't compare the lengths of the two rail tunnels. *Choice C* is incorrect. The sentence describes a single rail tunnel; it doesn't compare the lengths of the two rail tunnels. *Choice D* is incorrect. While the sentence mentions the two rail tunnels, it doesn't compare their lengths.

QUESTION 23

Choice C is the best answer. The sentence specifies the reason the Pleiades' appearance changed, noting that two of the cluster's stars have moved so close together that they now appear as one star.

Choice A is incorrect. The sentence specifies how ancient Native American and Australian Aboriginal cultures described the Pleiades; it doesn't specify the reason the Pleiades' appearance changed. *Choice B* is incorrect. The sentence describes the appearance of the Pleiades today; it doesn't specify the reason the Pleiades' appearance changed. *Choice D* is incorrect. The sentence explains why two of the Pleiades' stars appear to be a single star; it doesn't specify the reason the Pleiades' appearance changed.

QUESTION 24

Choice C is the best answer. The sentence effectively emphasizes the fossil's significance, explaining that the fossil is rare and illustrates an early stage in the evolution of pinnipeds from their land-dwelling ancestors.

Choice A is incorrect. The sentence describes the fossil Rybczynski found; it doesn't emphasize the fossil's significance. *Choice B* is incorrect. The sentence mentions that a fossil resembling both pinnipeds and their ancestors was found; it doesn't emphasize the fossil's significance. *Choice D* is incorrect. The sentence notes a term used to describe the fossil Rybczynski found; it doesn't emphasize the fossil's significance.

QUESTION 25

Choice C is the best answer. The sentence emphasizes a difference between the portraits, noting that one is a painting and the other is a drawing.

Choice A is incorrect. The sentence emphasizes a similarity between the two portraits rather than a difference. *Choice B* is incorrect. The sentence makes a generalization about Enriquez's portraits; it doesn't emphasize a difference between the portraits of Jimenez and Anaya. *Choice D* is incorrect. While the sentence notes a difference between Jimenez and Anaya, it doesn't emphasize a difference between, or even mention, their portraits.

QUESTION 26

Choice D is the best answer. The sentence emphasizes the role a misconception played in the naming of a place, explaining that Spanish explorers mistook a peninsula for an island and, as a result, named the peninsula after a fictional island, California.

Choice A is incorrect. The sentence mentions a novel that featured a fictional island, California; it doesn't emphasize the role a misconception played in the naming of a place. *Choice B* is incorrect. The sentence notes that Baja California was originally named after a fictional place; it doesn't emphasize the role a misconception—specifically, the Spanish explorers' mistaken belief that the peninsula was an island—played in the naming of a place. *Choice C* is incorrect. The sentence indicates when Spanish explorers learned of the peninsula they called California; it doesn't emphasize the role a misconception played in the naming of a place.

QUESTION 27

Choice C is the best answer. The sentence emphasizes a similarity between the two paintings, noting that Leutze's painting (which measures 149 × 255 inches) and Monkman's painting (which measures 132 × 264 inches) are both very large.

Choice A is incorrect. The sentence mentions that Monkman's painting was completed in 2019 and Leutze's was completed in 1851; it doesn't emphasize a similarity between the two paintings. *Choice B* is incorrect. While the sentence acknowledges that one painting was inspired by the other, it emphasizes differences between the two paintings; it doesn't emphasize a similarity between them. *Choice D* is incorrect. The sentence mentions a difference between the two paintings; it doesn't emphasize a similarity between them.

Reading and Writing

Module 2

(27 questions)

QUESTION 1

Choice A is the best answer because it most logically completes the text's discussion of Francis Cecil Sumner. As used in this context, "proponent of" means supporter of. The text says that Sumner helped to found the psychology department at historically Black Howard University in 1930. This is evidence that Sumner supported increasing the opportunity for Black students to study psychology.

Choice B is incorrect because the phrase "supplement to," or addition to, wouldn't make sense in context. The text discusses Sumner's efforts to increase the number of Black psychology students, but it doesn't make sense to describe him as an addition to his efforts. *Choice C* is incorrect because Sumner was already an accomplished psychologist himself when he helped to found the Howard University psychology department. While Black students were the beneficiaries of his efforts—that is, they received help because of his efforts—it wouldn't make sense in this context to describe Sumner as a "beneficiary of" opportunities, because he was the one doing the helping. *Choice D* is incorrect because founding a psychology department at Howard University wouldn't be a "distraction for" Sumner's aim to increase the opportunity for Black students to study psychology—that is, it wouldn't be something that draws Sumner's attention away from that goal, but rather the opposite.

QUESTION 2

Choice B is the best answer because it most logically completes the text's discussion of the art installation *Anthem*. In this context, "inventive" means characterized by invention and creativity. The text explains that critics' responses to the installation involved praise for Tsang's creative transformation of a space into a dynamic exhibit with huge images and lots of sound. This context conveys that the critics found the piece particularly creative.

Choice A is incorrect because the text indicates that critics praised the installation for being dynamic and including huge images and lots of sound, and it wouldn't make sense to describe such an exhibit as "restrained," or limited and not extravagant or showy. *Choice C* is incorrect because it wouldn't make sense to say that critics found the installation "inexplicable," or incapable of being explained or interpreted, since the critics were able to explain their praise for the installation's transformation of a space with huge images and lots of sound. *Choice D* is incorrect because the text focuses on the idea that critics praised Tsang for creatively transforming a space into a dynamic exhibit, not that they found the installation "mystifying," or bewildering and hard to understand. Nothing in the text suggests that the critics couldn't understand the piece.

QUESTION 3

Choice D is the best answer because it most logically completes the text's discussion of gender roles in Shakespeare's comedies. As used in this context, "prescribed" would mean laid down as rules. The text indicates that the characters in the comedies often defy gender roles that are "socially dictated" (even if most characters do return to those roles eventually) and that scholars have been very interested in these acts of defiance. This context indicates that what the characters are rebelling against are standards of behavior prescribed by the society of the time.

Choice A is incorrect because saying that expectations about gender were "interjected," or suddenly inserted between other things, wouldn't make sense in context. There's no suggestion in the text that the issue of gender roles was inserted between other things or was an interruption in a larger discussion. *Choice B* is incorrect because the text indicates that Shakespeare depicts characters rebelling against expectations about gender that have been "socially dictated," not expectations that society has "committed," or carried out, entrusted, or promised. *Choice C* is incorrect because the text indicates that Shakespeare depicts characters rebelling against expectations about gender that have been "socially dictated," not expectations that have been "illustrated," or clarified with examples. Although it's possible for expectations about gender roles to be illustrated, there's nothing in the text to indicate that characters in Shakespeare's comedies rebel against illustrations of gender expectations.

QUESTION 4

Choice C is the best answer because it most logically completes the text's discussion of the artistic styles that have influenced Cannon's work. As used in this context, "disparate" means distinct or dissimilar. The text indicates that a tension exists among the styles that have influenced Cannon's work and goes on to describe how those styles differ: classic European portraiture favors realism, American pop art uses vivid colors, and intertribal flatstyle rejects the use of shading and perspective to achieve depth. This context suggests that the styles that have influenced Cannon's work are disparate.

Choice A is incorrect because the text indicates that there is a tension among the influences on Cannon's artwork, so it wouldn't make sense to say that the influences are "complementary," or that they complete one another or make up for one another's deficiencies. *Choice B* is incorrect because it wouldn't make sense to characterize Cannon's influences as "unknown," or not familiar; it's clear that the influences are known because the text goes on to list them. *Choice D* is incorrect because the text indicates that there is a tension among the influences on Cannon's work, not that they are "interchangeable," or capable of being used in one another's place.

QUESTION 5

Choice B is the best answer because it describes the most likely way that Graeber and Wengrow (Text 2) would respond to the "conventional wisdom" presented in Text 1. According to Text 1, the conventional wisdom about human social systems is that they developed through stages, beginning with hunter-gatherer bands, then moving to clan associations, then chiefdoms, and finally arriving at states with bureaucratic structures. Text 2 indicates that Graeber and Wengrow believe that human social systems have been flexible, shifting between different types of structures, including both hierarchical and collective systems, and that these shifts may have even occurred seasonally. This suggests that Graeber and Wengrow would dispute the idea that developments in social structures have followed a linear progression through distinct stages.

Choice A is incorrect because nothing in Text 2 suggests that Graeber and Wengrow believe that decentralized collective societies are more significant than hierarchical systems. Text 2 is focused on Graeber and Wengrow's view that humans have flexibly shifted among various social structures, not on the importance of particular structures relative to others. *Choice C* is incorrect because Text 2 doesn't include any information suggesting that Graeber and Wengrow believe that hierarchies didn't emerge until after the rise of agriculture. In fact, Text 2 indicates that Graeber and Wengrow cite evidence suggesting that some hunter-gatherer groups formed social structures with hierarchical elements ("communities that included esteemed individuals") 50,000 years ago, long before the rise of agriculture, which Text 1 says occurred around 12,000 years ago. *Choice D* is incorrect because there's no information in Text 2 suggesting that Graeber and Wengrow would challenge the assumption that groupings of hunter-gatherers were among the earliest forms of social structure. Although Text 1 does indicate that hunter-gatherer groups are assumed to be the earliest human social system, Text 2 says only that Graeber and Wengrow believe that some hunter-gatherer groups made use of different social structures at different times. Text 2 doesn't imply that Graeber and Wengrow doubt that hunter-gatherer groups preceded most other social structures.

QUESTION 6

Choice A is the best answer because it most accurately states the main idea of the text. According to the text, Eugene Wigner hypothesized that a crystal could exist that would be composed of electrons and have a honeycomb-like shape. The text goes on to say that the existence of the Wigner crystal remained unconfirmed until Feng Wang and colleagues were able to make an impression of one using two semiconductors and an ultrathin sheet of graphene. Thus, the main idea is that researchers have obtained the most definitive evidence to date of the existence of the Wigner crystal.

Choice B is incorrect because the text focuses on one kind of crystal—the Wigner crystal—and doesn't discuss crystalline structures in general. And although the text conveys that Wang and colleagues figured out a way to capture an image of a Wigner crystal, it doesn't address the idea of applying this approach to other types of crystals. *Choice C* is incorrect because the text describes in general the process Wang and colleagues followed to obtain an impression of the Wigner crystal; it doesn't address the relative importance of each component in that process. *Choice D* is incorrect because the text doesn't state that researchers had a hard time getting an impression of the Wigner crystal because of its honeycomb structure. Nothing in the text indicates why it took so long to prove the existence of this crystal or take an impression of it.

QUESTION 7

Choice D is the best answer because it states why Wang and his team's discovery of the *Terropterus xiushanensis* fossil was significant. The text explains that up until Wang and his team's discovery, the only fossil evidence of mixopterids came from the paleocontinent of Laurussia. Wang and his team, however, identified fossil remains of a mixopterid species from the paleocontinent Gondwana. Therefore, the team's discovery was significant because the fossil remains of a mixopterid species were outside of the paleocontinent Laurussia.

Choice A is incorrect. Although the text states that Wang and his team identified fossilized remains of a mixopterid species that lived more than 400 million years ago, it doesn't indicate that mixopterid fossils previously found by scientists dated to a more recent period than that. *Choice B* is incorrect. Although the text states that mixopterids are related to modern arachnids and horseshoe crabs, it doesn't suggest that the fossil discovered by Wang and his team confirmed that this relationship is closer than scientists had previously thought. *Choice C* is incorrect because the team's fossil established the presence of mixopterids on Gondwana, not on Laurussia. Moreover, the text only discusses the fossil in relation to the geographical distribution of mixopterids, not in relation to their evolution.

QUESTION 8

Choice C is the best answer because it describes something that is true of Mother, as presented in the text. The text indicates that in addition to other activities, Mother writes stories for her children while they are at school and makes up "funny pieces of poetry" for certain occasions.

Choice A is incorrect because the text suggests that Mother prefers to spend her time with her children and doesn't sit at home hoping that ladies will visit her. *Choice B* is incorrect because the text says only that Mother makes up poetry for the children's birthdays, not that she likes birthdays more than other special occasions. *Choice D* is incorrect because the text doesn't suggest that Mother prefers reading to her children over the other activities she does with them, such as playing with them and writing stories and poems for them.

QUESTION 9

Choice B is the best answer because it most effectively illustrates the claim in the text that in describing the teenaged girl, Mansfield contrasts the character's pleasant appearance with her unpleasant attitude. In the quotation, Mansfield describes the teenager as having a "lovely nose" (a compliment about her appearance) but also as treating her makeup puff "as though she loathed it" (a judgment suggesting her unpleasant attitude).

Choice A is incorrect because the teenager's reaction to the flowers doesn't make it clear that she has an unpleasant attitude, and nothing in the quotation indicates that any part of her appearance is pleasant. *Choice C* is incorrect because the quotation suggests that the teenager has an unpleasant attitude (being upset with the location and leaving the table before the narrator has paid for the meal) but doesn't give any indication that she has a pleasant appearance. *Choice D* is incorrect because the quotation suggests that the teenager may have an unpleasant attitude (lowering her eyes, wincing, and sitting in silence) but doesn't give any indication that any part of her appearance is pleasant.

QUESTION 10

Choice C is the best answer because it accurately describes data from the table that support Barrett and Rayfield's suggestion about bite force estimates. According to the text, Barrett and Rayfield believe that estimates of dinosaur bite force may be strongly influenced by the methods used to produce them— that is, that different methods may produce significantly different results. The table shows that the studies by Bates and Falkingham and by Cost et al.

used the same estimation method (muscular and skeletal modeling) and produced similar bite force estimates (approximately 35,000–57,000 newtons and 35,000–63,000 newtons, respectively). The study by Meers, however, used body-mass scaling and produced a much higher bite force estimate (183,000–235,000 newtons), while the study by Gignac and Erickson used tooth-bone interaction analysis and produced a much lower bite force estimate (8,000–34,000 newtons). The fact that one method produced similar estimates in two different studies and that two different methods used in other studies produced substantially different estimates supports the idea that dinosaur bite force estimates are significantly influenced by the methodology used to produce them.

Choice A is incorrect because it inaccurately describes data from the table. The table does show that the studies by Meers and by Cost et al. used different estimation methods and produced very different ranges of estimated dinosaur bite force, which would support Barrett and Rayfield's suggestion that different methodologies may produce significantly different estimates. However, the table doesn't show that the study by Meers produced the lowest estimated maximum bite force while the study by Cost et al. produced the highest. In fact, the study by Meers estimated a maximum bite force of approximately 235,000 newtons, which is the highest of all the estimated maximums. *Choice B* is incorrect. Although the data from Gignac and Ericson's study are accurately described, a single set of findings from one study using only one methodology can't show that different methodologies may produce significantly different dinosaur bite force estimates, as Barrett and Rayfield suggest. *Choice D* is incorrect. Although the table shows that the maximum bite force estimated by Cost et al. was higher than that estimated by Bates and Falkingham, the difference is relatively small; in fact, both teams estimated a minimum bite force of approximately 35,000 newtons and a maximum bite force close to approximately 60,000 newtons. Because these findings demonstrate that a single methodology (muscular and skeletal modeling) produced similar overall results in two studies, the findings don't support Barrett and Rayfield's suggestion that different methodologies may produce significantly different dinosaur bite force estimates.

QUESTION 11

Choice C is the best answer because it presents a finding that, if true, would weaken Foster's hypothesis that damage to eelgrass roots improves the health of eelgrass meadows by boosting genetic diversity. The text indicates that sea otters damage eelgrass roots but that eelgrass meadows near Vancouver Island, where there's a large otter population, are comparatively healthy. When Foster and her colleagues compared the Vancouver Island eelgrass meadows to those that don't have established otter populations, the researchers found that the Vancouver Island meadows are more genetically diverse than the other meadows are. This finding led Foster to hypothesize that damage to the eelgrass roots encourages eelgrass reproduction, thereby improving genetic diversity and the health of the meadows. If, however, other meadows not included in the study are less healthy the larger the local otter population is and the longer the otters have been in residence, that would suggest that damage to the eelgrass roots, which would be expected to increase with the size and residential duration of the otter population, isn't leading meadows to be healthier. Such a finding would therefore weaken Foster's hypothesis.

Choice A is incorrect because finding that small, recently introduced otter populations are near other eelgrass meadows in the study wouldn't weaken Foster's hypothesis. If otter populations were small and only recently established, they wouldn't be expected to have caused much damage to eelgrass roots, so even if those eelgrass meadows were less healthy than the Vancouver Island meadows, that wouldn't undermine Foster's hypothesis. In fact, it would be consistent with Foster's hypothesis since it would suggest that the greater damage caused by larger, more established otter populations is associated with healthier meadows. *Choice B* is incorrect because the existence of areas with otters but without eelgrass meadows wouldn't reveal anything about whether the damage that otters cause to eelgrass roots ultimately benefits eelgrass meadows. *Choice D* is incorrect because the health of plants other than eelgrass would have no bearing on Foster's hypothesis that damage to eelgrass roots leads to greater genetic diversity and meadow health. It would be possible for otters to have a negative effect on other plants while nevertheless improving the health of eelgrass meadows by damaging eelgrass roots.

QUESTION 12

Choice C is the best answer because it presents a finding that, if true, would support the researchers' hypothesis about the plants' dependence on dissolving rock. The text indicates that the roots of the two plant species grow directly into quartzite rock, where hairs on the roots secrete acids that dissolve the rock. The researchers hypothesize that the plants depend on this process because dissolving rock opens spaces for the roots to grow and releases phosphates that provide the plants with phosphorous, a vital nutrient. If the plants carry out this process of dissolving rock even when the rock already has spaces into which the roots could grow, that would support the researchers' hypothesis because it suggests that the plants are getting some advantage—such as access to phosphorous—from the action of dissolving rock. If the plants don't benefit from dissolving rock, they would be expected to grow in the cracks that already exist, as doing so would mean that the plants don't have to spend energy creating and secreting acids; if, however, the plants create new entry points by dissolving rock even when cracks already exist, that would support the hypothesis that they depend on dissolving rock for some benefit.

Choice A is incorrect because the existence of soil-inhabiting members of the Velloziaceae family with similar root structures to those of the two species discussed in the text wouldn't support the researchers' hypothesis that the species discussed in the text depend on dissolving rock. If other such members exist, that might suggest that the root structures can serve more functions than secreting acids to dissolve rock (since dissolving rock may not be necessary for plants living in soil), but that wouldn't suggest anything about whether the species discussed in the text benefit from dissolving rock. *Choice B* is incorrect because differences in the proportions of citric and malic acid secreted by the two species would be irrelevant to the hypothesis that the plants depend on dissolving rock. There's no information in the text to suggest that the proportion of each acid has any bearing on the process of dissolving rock or on any benefits the plants might receive from that process. *Choice D* is incorrect because if the two species thrive on rocks without phosphates, that would weaken the researchers' hypothesis that the plants depend on dissolving rock partly because dissolving rock gives them access to phosphates. If the plants can survive on rocks without getting a vital nutrient by dissolving those rocks, then either the nutrient isn't actually vital for those plants or they can get the nutrient in some way other than by dissolving rocks.

QUESTION 13

Choice B is the best answer because it presents the conclusion that most logically follows from the text's discussion of Ancestral Puebloans' migration to the Rio Grande Valley. The text states that in the late 1200s C.E., the Ancestral

Puebloan civilization abandoned villages in its original homeland, which included the Mesa Verde site. The text goes on to say that recent genetic analysis has demonstrated that the modern turkey population in the Rio Grande Valley descends partly from the ancient turkeys raised at Mesa Verde, and that the genetic markers shared by the two turkey populations first appeared at Mesa Verde only after 1280 C.E. Therefore, it can reasonably be concluded that some Ancestral Puebloans migrated to the Rio Grande Valley in the late 1200s and carried their agricultural practices—including the farming of turkeys— to their new home.

Choice A is incorrect because the text never compares the condition of the Rio Grande Valley's terrain to that of Mesa Verde's terrain, either in the present or in the past. *Choice C* is incorrect. Although genetic analysis has demonstrated that the modern turkey population in the Rio Grande valley descended in part from the turkey population raised by the Ancestral Puebloans of Mesa Verde before their migration to the valley in 1280, this finding doesn't eliminate the possibility that Indigenous peoples living in the valley before 1280 might also have farmed turkeys. *Choice D* is incorrect. The text doesn't consider the possibility that before their migration to the Rio Grande Valley after 1280, the Ancestral Puebloans of Mesa Verde might have adopted turkey farming from an outside Indigenous civilization in another region; instead, the text provides evidence suggesting that the Ancestral Puebloans brought turkey farming to another region— the Rio Grande Valley—after 1280.

QUESTION 14

Choice C is the best answer because it most logically completes the argument about an unintended effect of the Nagoya Protocol. The text explains that the Nagoya Protocol is an agreement ensuring that Indigenous communities are compensated when their agricultural resources and knowledge are used by corporations. The text then states that the protocol allows corporations to keep their agreements with Indigenous communities confidential, about which some Indigenous advocates express concern. Choice C, when inserted into the blank, gives a good justification for the advocates' concern: such secrecy could mean that the public is unable to determine whether participating Indigenous communities were properly compensated under these agreements.

Choice A is incorrect. The text suggests that because corporations can keep their agreements with Indigenous communities confidential, Indigenous communities, not corporations, might not be compensated fairly. *Choice B* is incorrect because the text doesn't suggest that the ability of corporations to keep their agreements with Indigenous communities confidential would place limits on how much research corporations can undertake. *Choice D* is incorrect because the text doesn't indicate that Indigenous communities aim to learn new harvesting methods from their corporate partners. Rather, the text suggests that corporations use the knowledge of Indigenous communities for their research.

QUESTION 15

Choice C is the best answer because it most logically completes the text's discussion of the sweet potato in Polynesia. The text indicates that the sweet potato is found in Polynesia but originated in South America, and that the sweet potato was being cultivated by Native Hawaiians and other Indigenous peoples in Polynesia long before sea voyages between South America and Polynesia began. The text goes on to note that research by Muñoz-Rodríguez and colleagues has established that the Polynesian varieties of sweet potato split from South American varieties more than 100,000 years ago, which is thousands of years before humans settled in Polynesia. If Polynesian peoples were cultivating the sweet potato before sea voyages between Polynesia and South America began, and if Polynesian varieties of sweet potato diverged from South American varieties well before people were in Polynesia, it can reasonably be concluded that humans didn't play a role in bringing the sweet potato to Polynesia.

Choice A is incorrect. The text doesn't provide any information about when the sweet potato began to be cultivated in South America, so there's no support for the conclusion that cultivation began in Polynesia before it began in South America. *Choice B* is incorrect because the text indicates that the sweet potato was being cultivated in Polynesia long before sea journeys between Polynesia and South America began. Therefore, it wouldn't be reasonable to conclude that Polynesian peoples acquired the sweet potato from South American peoples. Additionally, the text indicates that the Polynesian varieties of sweet potato diverged from the South American varieties thousands of years before people settled in Polynesia, which suggests that the sweet potato was already present in Polynesia when people arrived. *Choice D* is incorrect because the text states that the domestic sweet potato, which is found in Polynesia, descends from a wild South American plant, not from a domesticated South American plant. The only people that the text describes as cultivating the sweet potato are Native Hawaiians and other Indigenous peoples of Polynesia.

QUESTION 16

Choice C is the best answer. The convention being tested is the use of plural and possessive nouns. The singular possessive noun "playa's" and the plural possessive noun "rocks'" correctly indicate that the sediment is that of one playa (the Racetrack Playa) and that there are multiple rocks that have mysteriously migrated across the sediment.

Choice A is incorrect because the context requires the singular possessive noun "playa's" and the plural possessive noun "rocks'," not the plural noun "playas" and the singular possessive noun "rock's." *Choice B* is incorrect because the context requires the plural possessive noun "rocks'," not the plural noun "rocks." *Choice D* is incorrect because the context requires the singular possessive noun "playa's," not the plural possessive noun "playas'."

QUESTION 17

Choice B is the best answer. The convention being tested is the punctuation of items in a complex series (a series including internal punctuation). In this choice, the semicolon after "Lagos" is conventionally used to separate the first item ("*The Joys*...Lagos") and the second item ("*A Kind*...Nigeria") in the series. Further, the comma after "*Marriage*" correctly separates the title "*A Kind of Marriage*" from the supplementary phrase ("a television...Nigeria") that describes it.

Choice A is incorrect because the comma after "Lagos" doesn't match the semicolon used later in the series to separate the second item ("*A Kind*... Nigeria") from the third item ("and...autobiography"). *Choice C* is incorrect because the comma after "Lagos" doesn't match the semicolon used later in the series to separate the second item ("*A Kind*...Nigeria") from the third item ("and...autobiography"). Additionally, a colon can't be used in this way to separate the title "*A Kind of Marriage*" from the supplementary phrase ("a television...Nigeria") that describes it. *Choice D* is incorrect because it fails to use appropriate punctuation to separate the title "*A Kind of Marriage*" from the supplementary phrase ("a television...Nigeria") that describes it.

QUESTION 18

Choice B is the best answer. The convention being tested is subject-modifier placement. This choice makes the noun phrase "the bioswales" the subject of the sentence and places it immediately after the modifying phrase "By reducing...sewers." In doing so, this choice clearly establishes that the bioswales—and not another noun in the sentence—are reducing runoff flowing into city sewers.

Choice A is incorrect because it results in a dangling modifier. The placement of the noun phrase "the mitigation...waterways" immediately after the modifying phrase results in unclear modification. The resulting sentence makes it hard to determine what is responsible for "reducing the runoff": the bioswales or some other noun in the sentence. *Choice C* is incorrect because it results in a dangling modifier. The placement of the noun phrase "the bioswales' mitigation...waterways" immediately after the modifying phrase results in unclear modification. The resulting sentence makes it hard to determine what is responsible for "reducing the runoff": the bioswales or some other noun in the sentence. *Choice D* is incorrect because it results in a dangling modifier. The placement of the noun phrase "street flooding and the resulting pollution" immediately after the modifying phrase illogically suggests that the "flooding and pollution" are reducing runoff flowing into city sewers.

QUESTION 19

Choice B is the best answer. The convention being tested is punctuation use between a main clause and a supplementary phrase. This choice correctly uses a comma to mark the boundary between the main clause ("the portraits...quilts") and the supplementary noun phrase ("the stitching...fabric") that provides a further description of how the portraits can be identified as quilts.

Choice A is incorrect. A comma and the conjunction "and" can't be used in this way to join a main clause and a supplementary noun phrase. *Choice C* is incorrect because a semicolon can't be used in this way to join a main clause and a supplementary noun phrase. *Choice D* is incorrect because it results in a rhetorically unacceptable sentence fragment beginning with "the stitching."

QUESTION 20

Choice D is the best answer. The convention being tested is subject-modifier placement. This choice makes "silica glass's atomic arrangement" the subject of the sentence and places it immediately after the modifying phrase "compared to that of alumina glass." In doing so, this choice clearly establishes that silica glass's atomic arrangement—and not another noun in the sentence—is being compared to the atomic arrangement ("that") of alumina glass.

Choice A is incorrect because it results in a dangling modifier. The placement of the noun phrase "silica glass" immediately after the modifying phrase illogically suggests that silica glass itself (rather than its atomic arrangement) is being compared to alumina glass's atomic arrangement. *Choice B* is incorrect because it results in a dangling modifier. The placement of the noun phrase "silica glass" immediately after the modifying phrase illogically suggests that silica glass itself (rather than its atomic arrangement) is being compared to alumina glass's atomic arrangement. *Choice C* is incorrect because it results in a dangling modifier. The placement of the noun phrase "a significant disadvantage" immediately after the modifying phrase illogically suggests that "a significant disadvantage" is being compared to alumina glass's atomic arrangement.

QUESTION 21

Choice D is the best answer. The convention being tested is the use of finite and nonfinite verb forms within a sentence. The nonfinite to-infinitive "to tell" is correctly used to form a nonfinite (infinitive) clause that explains the reason Engle uses poetry in her novel.

Choice A is incorrect because the finite present tense verb "tells" can't be used in this way to explain the reason that Engle uses poetry in her novel. *Choice B* is incorrect because the finite past tense verb "told" can't be used in this way to explain the reason that Engle uses poetry in her novel. *Choice C* is incorrect because the finite present progressive tense verb "is telling" can't be used in this way to explain the reason that Engle uses poetry in her novel.

QUESTION 22

Choice A is the best answer. The convention being tested is the punctuation of a supplementary word or phrase between two main clauses. This choice correctly uses a comma to separate the supplementary adverb "however" from the preceding main clause ("Okinaka doesn't...single-handedly") and a semicolon to join the next main clause ("all...culture") to the rest of the sentence. Further, placing the semicolon after "however" correctly indicates that the information in the preceding main clause (Okinaka doesn't make such decisions single-handedly) is contrary to what might be assumed from the information in the previous sentence (Okinaka sits on the review board that adds new sites to the Hawaii Register of Historic Places).

Choice B is incorrect because placing the semicolon after "single-handedly" and the comma after "however" illogically indicates that the information in the next main clause (all historical designations must be approved by a group of experts) is contrary to the information in the previous clause (Okinaka doesn't make such decisions single-handedly). *Choice C* is incorrect because it results in a comma splice. Commas can't be used in this way to punctuate a supplementary word or phrase between two main clauses. *Choice D* is incorrect because it results in a run-on sentence. The two main clauses are fused without punctuation and/or a conjunction.

QUESTION 23

Choice B is the best answer. "Previously" logically signals that the event described in this sentence—Bigelow being named best director—occurred before Zhao's win. The fact that only one other woman had won the award before puts Zhao's win in perspective.

Choice A is incorrect because "as a result" illogically signals that the event described in this sentence occurred as a result or consequence of Zhao's win. Instead, it occurred before Zhao was named best director and puts Zhao's win in perspective. *Choice C* is incorrect because "however" illogically signals that the event described in this sentence occurred in spite of or in contrast to Zhao's win. Instead, it occurred before Zhao was named best director and puts Zhao's win in perspective. *Choice D* is incorrect because "likewise" illogically signals that this sentence merely adds a second, similar piece of information to the information about Zhao's win. Instead, the fact that only one other woman had won the award before puts Zhao's win in perspective.

QUESTION 24

Choice D is the best answer. "Increasingly" logically signals that the claim in this sentence—that mathematicians are collaborating with their peers—marks a change relative to what was traditionally done. As the previous sentence explains, while mathematicians may have traditionally worked alone, evidence points to a shift in the opposite direction. The claim describes the shift: a rise in collaboration.

Choice A is incorrect because "similarly" illogically signals that the claim in this sentence is similar to, but separate from, the previous claim about the shift away from mathematicians working alone. Instead, the claim about the rise in collaboration elaborates on the previous claim, describing the shift. *Choice B* is incorrect because "for this reason" illogically signals that the claim in this sentence is caused by the previous claim about the shift away from mathematicians working alone. Instead, the claim about the rise in collaboration elaborates on the previous claim, describing the shift. *Choice C* is incorrect because "furthermore" illogically signals that the claim in this sentence is in addition to the previous claim about the shift away from mathematicians working alone. Instead, the claim about the rise in collaboration elaborates on the previous claim, describing the shift.

QUESTION 25

Choice A is the best answer. "Alternatively" logically signals that the soil decontamination method described in this sentence—removing toxic metals from the soil via phytoremediation—offers an alternative to the previously described method (removing the contaminated soil from the ground).

Choice B is incorrect because "specifically" illogically signals that the soil decontamination method described in this sentence specifies or elaborates on an aspect of the previously described method (removing the contaminated soil from the ground). Instead, phytoremediation is an alternative to that method. *Choice C* is incorrect because "for example" illogically signals that the soil decontamination method described in this sentence is an example of the previously described method (removing the contaminated soil from the ground). Instead, phytoremediation is an alternative to that method. *Choice D* is incorrect because "as a result" illogically signals that the soil decontamination method described in this sentence is a result or consequence of the previously described method (removing the contaminated soil from the ground). Instead, phytoremediation is an alternative to that method.

QUESTION 26

Choice C is the best answer. The sentence emphasizes the decline in unique apple varieties in the US and specifies why this decline occurred, noting that thousands of apple varieties were lost because US farmers started mainly growing the same few unique varieties.

Choice A is incorrect. The sentence introduces the Lost Apple Project; it doesn't emphasize the decline in unique apple varieties in the US and specify why this decline occurred. *Choice B* is incorrect. While the sentence emphasizes the decline in unique apple varieties in the US, it doesn't explain why this decline occurred. *Choice D* is incorrect. The sentence emphasizes the general decline of crop varieties in the mid-1900s; it doesn't emphasize the specific decline in unique apple varieties in the US.

QUESTION 27

Choice A is the best answer. The sentence effectively introduces Cathryn Halverson's book to an audience already familiar with the *Atlantic Monthly*, noting the title of Halverson's book and describing its content without providing background information about the *Atlantic Monthly*.

Choice B is incorrect. The sentence introduces the *Atlantic Monthly* and mentions that it's referred to in Cathryn Halverson's book title; it doesn't effectively introduce Halverson's book. *Choice C* is incorrect. The sentence assumes that the audience is unfamiliar with the *Atlantic Monthly*, providing background information about the magazine; it doesn't effectively introduce Halverson's book to an audience already familiar with the *Atlantic Monthly*. *Choice D* is incorrect. While the sentence assumes that the audience is familiar with the *Atlantic Monthly*, it doesn't effectively introduce Cathryn Halverson's book.

Math

Module 1
(22 questions)

QUESTION 1

Choice C is correct. Subtracting 6 from both sides of the given equation yields $4x = 12$, which is the equation given in choice C. Since this equation is equivalent to the given equation, it has the same solution as the given equation.

Choice A is incorrect and may result from conceptual or calculation errors.
Choice B is incorrect and may result from conceptual or calculation errors.
Choice D is incorrect and may result from conceptual or calculation errors.

QUESTION 2

Choice D is correct. It's given that lines m and n are parallel. Since line t intersects both lines m and n, it's a transversal. The angles in the figure marked as 170° and w° are on the same side of the transversal, where one is an interior angle with line m as a side, and the other is an exterior angle with line n as a side. Thus, the marked angles are corresponding angles. When two parallel lines are intersected by a transversal, corresponding angles are congruent and, therefore, have equal measure. It follows that w° = 170°. Therefore, the value of w is 170.

Choice A is incorrect and may result from conceptual or calculation errors.
Choice B is incorrect and may result from conceptual or calculation errors.
Choice C is incorrect and may result from conceptual or calculation errors.

QUESTION 3

The correct answer is 9. The mean of a data set is the sum of the values in the data set divided by the number of values in the data set. It follows that the mean height, in centimeters, of these plants is the sum of the heights, in centimeters, of each plant, $6 + 10 + 13 + 2 + 15 + 22 + 10 + 4 + 4 + 4$, or 90, divided by the number of plants in the data set, 10. Therefore, the mean height, in centimeters, of these plants is $\frac{90}{10}$, or 9.

QUESTION 4

Choice A is correct. The number of birds can be found by calculating the value of b when $r = 16$ in the given equation. Substituting 16 for r in the given equation yields $2.5b + 5(16) = 80$, or $2.5b + 80 = 80$. Subtracting 80 from both sides of this equation yields 2.5b = 0. Dividing both sides of this equation by 2.5 yields b = 0. Therefore, if the business cares for 16 reptiles on a given day, it can care for 0 birds on this day.

Choice B is incorrect and may result from conceptual or calculation errors.
Choice C is incorrect and may result from conceptual or calculation errors.
Choice D is incorrect and may result from conceptual or calculation errors.

QUESTION 5

Choice D is correct. The volume, V, of a cube can be found using the formula $V = s^3$, where s is the edge length of the cube. It's given that a cube has an edge length of 41 inches. Substituting 41 inches for s in this equation yields $V = 41^3$ cubic inches, or $V = 68{,}921$ cubic inches. Therefore, the volume of the cube is 68,921 cubic inches.

Choice A is incorrect. This is the perimeter, in inches, of the cube.
Choice B is incorrect. This is the area, in square inches, of a face of the cube.
Choice C is incorrect. This is the surface area, in square inches, of the cube.

QUESTION 6

The correct answer is 52. It's given that 13 is p% of 25. It follows that $\frac{13}{25} = \frac{p}{100}$. Multiplying both sides of this equation by 100 gives 52 = p. Therefore, the value of p is 52.

QUESTION 7

Choice D is correct. It's given that a model predicts the population of Springfield in 2005 was 15,000. The model also predicts that each year for the next 5 years, the population increased by 4% of the previous year's population. The predicted population in one of these years can be found by multiplying the predicted population from the previous year by 1.04. Since the predicted population in 2005 was 15,000, the predicted population 1 year later is 15,000(1.04). The predicted population 2 years later is this value times 1.04, which is 15,000(1.04)(1.04), or 15,000(1.04)^2. The predicted population 3 years later is this value times 1.04, or 15,000(1.04)^3. More generally, the predicted population, p, x years after 2005 is represented by the equation $p = 15{,}000(1.04)^x$.

Choice A is incorrect. Substituting 0 for x in this equation indicates the predicted population in 2005 was 0.96 rather than 15,000. *Choice B* is incorrect. Substituting 0 for x in this equation indicates the predicted population in 2005 was 1.04 rather than 15,000. *Choice C* is incorrect. This equation indicates the predicted population is decreasing, rather than increasing, by 4% each year.

QUESTION 8

Choice B is correct. Multiplying each side of the given equation by −16 yields $64x^2 + 112x = 576$. To complete the square, adding 49 to each side of this equation yields $64x^2 + 112x + 49 = 576 + 49$, or $(8x + 7)^2 = 625$. Taking the square root of each side of this equation yields two equations: $8x + 7 = 25$ and $8x + 7 = -25$. Subtracting 7 from each side of the equation $8x + 7 = 25$ yields $8x = 18$. Dividing each side of this equation by 8 yields $x = \frac{18}{8}$, or $x = \frac{9}{4}$.

Therefore, $\frac{9}{4}$ is a solution to the given equation. Subtracting 7 from each side of the equation $8x + 7 = -25$ yields $8x = -32$. Dividing each side of this equation by 8 yields $x = -4$. Therefore, the given equation has two solutions, $\frac{9}{4}$ and -4. Since $\frac{9}{4}$ is positive, it follows that $\frac{9}{4}$ is the positive solution to the given equation.

Alternate approach: Adding $4x^2$ and $7x$ to each side of the given equation yields $0 = 4x^2 + 7x - 36$. The right-hand side of this equation can be rewritten as $4x^2 + 16x - 9x - 36$. Factoring out the common factor of $4x$ from the first two terms of this expression and the common factor of -9 from the second two terms yields $4x(x + 4) - 9(x + 4)$. Factoring out the common factor of $(x + 4)$ from these two terms yields the expression $(4x - 9)(x + 4)$. Since this expression is equal to 0, it follows that either $4x - 9 = 0$ or $x + 4 = 0$. Adding 9 to each side of the equation $4x - 9 = 0$ yields $4x = 9$. Dividing each side of this equation by 4 yields $x = \frac{9}{4}$. Therefore, $\frac{9}{4}$ is a positive solution to the given equation. Subtracting 4 from each side of the equation $x + 4 = 0$ yields $x = -4$. Therefore, the given equation has two solutions, $\frac{9}{4}$ and -4. Since $\frac{9}{4}$ is positive, it follows that $\frac{9}{4}$ is the positive solution to the given equation.

Choice A is incorrect. Substituting $\frac{7}{4}$ for x in the given equation yields $-\frac{49}{2} = -36$, which is false. *Choice C* is incorrect. Substituting 4 for x in the given equation yields $-92 = -36$, which is false. *Choice D* is incorrect: Substituting 7 for x in the given equation yields $-245 = -36$, which is false.

QUESTION 9

Choice B is correct. Standard deviation is a measure of the spread of a data set from its mean. The dot plot for class A and the dot plot for class B have the same shape. Thus, the frequency distributions for both class A and class B are the same. Since both class A and class B have the same frequency distribution of glue sticks brought in by each student, it follows that both class A and class B have the same spread of the number of glue sticks brought in by each student from their respective means. Therefore, the standard deviation of the number of glue sticks brought in by each student for class A is equal to the standard deviation of the number of glue sticks brought in by each student for class B.

Choice A is incorrect and may result from conceptual or calculation errors. *Choice C* is incorrect and may result from conceptual or calculation errors. *Choice D* is incorrect and may result from conceptual or calculation errors.

QUESTION 10

Choice C is correct. If a value of x satisfies $f(x) = 0$, the graph of $y = f(x)$ will contain a point $(x, 0)$ and thus touch the x-axis. Since there are 3 points at which this graph touches the x-axis, there are 3 values of x for which $f(x) = 0$.

Choice A is incorrect and may result from conceptual or calculation errors. *Choice B* is incorrect and may result from conceptual or calculation errors. *Choice D* is incorrect and may result from conceptual or calculation errors.

QUESTION 11

The correct answer is 11,875. It's given that the exponential function g is defined by $g(x) = 19 \cdot a^x$, where a is a positive constant, and $g(3) = 2,375$. It follows that when $x = 3$, $g(x) = 2,375$. Substituting 3 for x and 2,375 for $g(x)$ in the given equation yields 2,375 = 19 · a^3. Dividing each side of this equation by 19 yields 125 = a^3. Taking the cube root of both sides of this equation gives a = 5. Substituting 4 for x and 5 for a in the equation $g(x)$ = 19 · a^x yields $g(4)$ = 19 · 5^4, or $g(4)$ = 11,875. Therefore, the value of $g(4)$ is 11,875.

QUESTION 12

Choice C is correct. The second equation in the given system of equations is y = 6x – 12. Substituting 6x – 12 for y in the first equation of the given system yields 6x – 12 = (x – 2)(x + 4). Factoring 6 out of the left-hand side of this equation yields 6(x – 2) = (x – 2)(x + 4). An expression with a factor of the form (x – a) is equal to zero when x = a. Each side of this equation has a factor of (x – 2), so each side of the equation is equal to zero when x = 2. Substituting 2 for x into the equation 6(x – 2) = (x – 2)(x + 4) yields 6(2 – 2) = (2 – 2)(2 + 4), or 0 = 0, which is true. Substituting 2 for x into the second equation in the given system of equations yields y = 6(2) – 12, or y = 0. Therefore, the solution to the system of equations is the ordered pair (2, 0).

Choice A is incorrect and may result from switching the order of the solutions for x and y. *Choice B* is incorrect and may result from conceptual or calculation errors. *Choice D* is incorrect and may result from conceptual or calculation errors.

QUESTION 13

Choice B is correct. If two triangles are similar, then their corresponding angles are congruent. It's given that right triangle *FGH* is similar to right triangle *JKL* and angle *F* corresponds to angle *J*. It follows that angle *F* is congruent to angle *J* and, therefore, the measure of angle *F* is equal to the measure of angle *J*. The sine ratios of angles of equal measure are equal. Since the measure of angle *F* is equal to the measure of angle *J*, sin(F) = sin(J). It's given that sin(F) = $\frac{308}{317}$. Therefore, sin(J) is $\frac{308}{317}$.

Choice A is incorrect. This is the value of cos(J), not the value of sin(J). *Choice C* is incorrect. This is the reciprocal of the value of sin(J), not the value of sin(J). *Choice D* is incorrect. This is the reciprocal of the value of cos(J), not the value of sin(J).

QUESTION 14

The correct answer is 410. It's given that t minutes after an initial observation, the number of bacteria in a population is $60{,}000(2)^{\frac{t}{410}}$. This expression consists of the initial number of bacteria, 60,000, multiplied by the expression $2^{\frac{t}{410}}$. The time it takes for the number of bacteria to double is the increase in the value of t that causes the expression $2^{\frac{t}{410}}$ to double. Since the base of the expression $2^{\frac{t}{410}}$ is 2, the expression $2^{\frac{t}{410}}$ will double when the exponent increases by 1. Since the exponent of the expression $2^{\frac{t}{410}}$ is $\frac{t}{410}$, the exponent will increase by 1 when t increases by 410. Therefore the time, in minutes, it takes for the number of bacteria in the population to double is 410.

QUESTION 15

Choice A is correct. To express 4j + 9 in terms of p and k, the given equation must be solved for 4j + 9. Since it's given that j is a positive number, 4j + 9 is not equal to zero. Therefore, multiplying both sides of the given equation by 4j + 9 yields the equivalent equation $p(4j + 9) = k$. Since it's given that p is a positive number, p is not equal to zero. Therefore, dividing each side of the equation

$p(4j + 9) = k$ by p yields the equivalent equation $4j + 9 = \dfrac{k}{p}$.

Choice B is incorrect. This equation is equivalent to $p = \dfrac{4j + 9}{k}$.

Choice C is incorrect. This equation is equivalent to $p = k - 4j - 9$.
Choice D is incorrect. This equation is equivalent to $p = k(4j + 9)$.

QUESTION 16

The correct answer is $\dfrac{1}{2}$. For an equation in slope-intercept form $y = mx + b$,

m represents the slope of the line in the xy-plane defined by this equation. It's given that line p is defined by $4y + 8x = 6$. Subtracting $8x$ from both sides of this equation yields $4y = -8x + 6$. Dividing both sides of this equation by 4 yields

$y = -\dfrac{8}{4}x + \dfrac{6}{4}$, or $y = -2x + \dfrac{3}{2}$. Thus, the slope of line p is -2. If line r is perpendicular

to line p, then the slope of line r is the negative reciprocal of the slope of line p.

The negative reciprocal of -2 is $-\dfrac{1}{(-2)} = \dfrac{1}{2}$. Note that 1/2 and .5 are examples of

ways to enter a correct answer.

QUESTION 17

The correct answer is 100. It's given that point O is the center of a circle and the measure of arc RS on the circle is 100°. It follows that points R and S lie on the circle. Therefore, OR and OS are radii of the circle. A central angle is an angle formed by two radii of a circle, with its vertex at the center of the circle. Therefore, $\angle ROS$ is a central angle. Because the degree measure of an arc is equal to the measure of its associated central angle, it follows that the measure, in degrees, of $\angle ROS$ is 100.

QUESTION 18

Choice B is correct. Each of the given choices is an equation of the form

$y = -\dfrac{1}{10}x(x - a)^m(x + b)^n$, where a, b, m, and n are positive constants. In the

xy-plane, the graph of an equation of this form has x-intercepts at $x = 0$, $x = a$, and $x = -b$. The graph shown has x-intercepts at $x = 0$, $x = 4$, and $x = -5$. Therefore, $a = 4$ and $b = 5$. Of the given choices, only choices A and B have

$a = 4$ and $b = 5$. For an equation in the form $y = -\dfrac{1}{10}x(x - a)^m(x + b)^n$, if all values

of x that are less than $-b$ or greater than a correspond to negative y-values, then the sum of all the exponents of the factors on the right-hand side of the equation is even. In the graph shown, all values of x less than -5 or greater than 4 correspond to negative y-values. Therefore, the sum of all the exponents of

the factors on the right-hand side of the equation $y = -\dfrac{1}{10}x(x - 4)^m(x + 5)^n$ must

be even. For choice A, the sum of these exponents is $1 + 1 + 1$, or 3, which is odd. For choice B, the sum of these exponents is $1 + 1 + 2$, or 4, which is even.

Therefore, $y = -\dfrac{1}{10}x(x - 4)(x + 5)^2$ could be the equation of the graph shown.

Choice A is incorrect. For the graph of this equation, all values of x less than -5 correspond to positive, not negative, y-values. *Choice C* is incorrect. The graph of this equation has x-intercepts at $x = -4$, $x = 0$, and $x = 5$, rather than x-intercepts at $x = -5$, $x = 0$, and $x = 4$. *Choice D* is incorrect. The graph of this equation has x-intercepts at $x = -4$, $x = 0$, and $x = 5$, rather than x-intercepts at $x = -5$, $x = 0$, and $x = 4$.

QUESTION 19

Choice D is correct. It's given that for $x > 0$, $f(x)$ is equal to 201% of x. This is equivalent to $f(x) = \frac{201}{100}x$, or $f(x) = 2.01x$, for $x > 0$. This function indicates that as x increases, $f(x)$ also increases, which means f is an increasing function. Furthermore, $f(x)$ increases at a constant rate of 2.01 for each increase of x by 1. A function with a constant rate of change is linear. Thus, the function f can be described as an increasing linear function.

Choice A is incorrect and may result from conceptual errors. *Choice B* is incorrect and may result from conceptual errors. *Choice C* is incorrect. This could describe the function $f(x) = (2.1)^x$, where $f(x)$ is equal to 201% of $f(x - 1)$, not x, for $x > 0$.

QUESTION 20

Choice A is correct. It's given that $g(x) = f(x + 5)$. Since $f(x) = 4x^2 + 64x + 262$, it follows that $f(x + 5) = 4(x + 5)^2 + 64(x + 5) + 262$. Expanding the quantity $(x + 5)^2$ in this equation yields $f(x + 5) = 4(x^2 + 10x + 25) + 64(x + 5) + 262$. Distributing the 4 and the 64 yields $f(x + 5) = 4x^2 + 40x + 100 + 64x + 320 + 262$. Combining like terms yields $f(x + 5) = 4x^2 + 104x + 682$. Therefore, $g(x) = 4x^2 + 104x + 682$. For a quadratic function defined by an equation of the form $g(x) = a(x - h)^2 + k$, where a, h, and k are constants and a is positive, $g(x)$ reaches its minimum, k, when the value of x is h. The equation $g(x) = 4x^2 + 104x + 682$ can be rewritten in this form by completing the square. This equation is equivalent to $g(x) = 4(x^2 + 26) + 682$, or $g(x) = 4(x^2 + 26x + 169 - 169) + 682$. This equation can be rewritten as $g(x) = 4\big((x + 13)^2 - 169\big) + 682$, or $g(x) = 4(x + 13)^2 - 4(169) + 682$, which is equivalent to $g(x) = 4(x + 13)^2 + 6$. This equation is in the form $g(x) = a(x - h)^2 + k$, where $a = 4$, $h = -13$, and $k = 6$. Therefore, $g(x)$ reaches its minimum when the value of x is -13.

Choice B is incorrect. This is the value of x for which $f(x)$, rather than $g(x)$, reaches its minimum. *Choice C* is incorrect and may result from conceptual or calculation errors. *Choice D* is incorrect. This is the value of x for which $f(x - 5)$, rather than $f(x + 5)$, reaches its minimum.

QUESTION 21

Choice B is correct. It's given that 483 out of 803 voters responded that they would vote for Angel Cruz. Therefore, the proportion of voters from the poll who responded they would vote for Angel Cruz is $\frac{483}{803}$. It's also given that there are a total of 6,424 voters in the election. Therefore, the total number of people who would be expected to vote for Angel Cruz is $6{,}424\left(\frac{483}{803}\right)$, or 3,864. Since 3,864 of the 6,424 total voters would be expected to vote for Angel Cruz, it follows that $6{,}424 - 3{,}864$, or 2,560 voters would be expected not to vote for Angel Cruz. The difference in the number of votes for and against Angel Cruz is $3{,}864 - 2{,}560$, or 1,304 votes. Therefore, if 6,424 people vote in the election, Angel Cruz would be expected to win by 1,304 votes.

Choice A is incorrect. This is the difference in the number of voters from the poll who responded that they would vote for and against Angel Cruz. *Choice C* is incorrect. This is the total number of people who would be expected to vote for Angel Cruz. *Choice D* is incorrect. This is the difference between the total number of people who.vote in the election and the number of voters from the poll.

QUESTION 22

Choice C is correct. It's given that the graphs of the equations in the given system intersect at exactly one point, (x, y), in the xy-plane. Therefore, (x, y) is the only solution to the given system of equations. The given system of equations can be solved by subtracting the second equation, $y = 3x + a$, from the first equation, $y = 2x^2 - 21x + 64$. This yields $y - y = (2x^2 - 21x + 64) - (3x + a)$, or $0 = 2x^2 - 24x + 64 - a$. Since the given system has only one solution, this equation has only one solution. A quadratic equation in the form $rx^2 + sx + t = 0$, where r, s, and t are constants, has one solution if and only if the discriminant, $s^2 - 4rt$, is equal to zero. Substituting 2 for r, -24 for s, and $-a + 64$ for t in the expression $s^2 - 4rt$ yields $(-24)^2 - (4)(2)(64 - a)$. Setting this expression equal to zero yields $(-24)^2 - (4)(2)(64 - a) = 0$, or $8a + 64 = 0$. Subtracting 64 from both sides of this equation yields $8a = -64$. Dividing both sides of this equation by 8 yields $a = -8$. Substituting -8 for a in the equation $0 = 2x^2 - 24x + 64 - a$ yields $0 = 2x^2 - 24x + 64 + 8$, or $0 = 2x^2 - 24x + 72$. Factoring 2 from the right-hand side of this equation yields $0 = 2(x^2 - 12x + 36)$. Dividing both sides of this equation by 2 yields $0 = x^2 - 12x + 36$, which is equivalent to $0 = (x - 6)(x - 6)$, or $0 = (x - 6)^2$. Taking the square root of both sides of this equation yields $0 = x - 6$. Adding 6 to both sides of this equation yields $x = 6$.

Choice A is incorrect. This is the value of a, not x. *Choice B* is incorrect and may result from conceptual or calculation errors. *Choice D* is incorrect and may result from conceptual or calculation errors.

Math

Module 2
(22 questions)

QUESTION 1

Choice B is correct. Adding the second equation in the given system to the first equation in the given system yields $3x + (-3x + y) = 12 + (-6)$, which is equivalent to $y = 6$.

Choice A is incorrect and may result from conceptual or calculation errors.
Choice C is incorrect and may result from conceptual or calculation errors.
Choice D is incorrect and may result from conceptual or calculation errors.

QUESTION 2

Choice B is correct. The given expression can be rewritten as $11x^3 + (-5)x^3$. Since the two terms of this expression are both constant multiples of x^3, they are like terms and can, therefore, be combined through addition. Adding like terms in the expression $11x^3 + (-5)x^3$ yields $6x^3$.

Choice A is incorrect. This is equivalent to $11x^3 + 5x^3$, not $11x^3 - 5x^3$.
Choice C is incorrect. This is equivalent to $11x^6 - 5x^6$, not $11x^3 - 5x^3$.
Choice D is incorrect. This is equivalent to $11x^6 + 5x^6$, not $11x^3 - 5x^3$.

QUESTION 3

Choice C is correct. If the two sides of a linear equation are equivalent, then the equation is true for any value. If an equation is true for any value, it has infinitely many solutions. Since the two sides of the given linear equation $66x = 66x$ are equivalent, the given equation has infinitely many solutions.

Choice A is incorrect and may result from conceptual or calculation errors.
Choice B is incorrect and may result from conceptual or calculation errors.
Choice D is incorrect and may result from conceptual or calculation errors.

QUESTION 4

Choice A is correct. It's given that a radio show stated that 3 times as many people voted in favor of the proposal as people who voted against it. Let x represent the number of people who voted against the proposal. It follows that $3x$ is the number of people who voted in favor of the proposal and $3x - x$, or $2x$, is how many more people voted in favor of the proposal than voted against it. It's also given that a social media post reported that 15,000 more people voted in favor of the proposal than voted against it. Thus, $2x = 15,000$. Since $2x = 15,000$, the value of x must be half of 15,000, or 7,500. Therefore, 7,500 people voted against the proposal.

Choice B is incorrect. This is how many more people voted in favor of the proposal than voted against it, not the number of people who voted against the proposal. *Choice C* is incorrect. This is the number of people who voted in favor of the proposal, not the number of people who voted against the proposal. *Choice D* is incorrect and may result from conceptual or calculation errors.

QUESTION 5

Choice C is correct. An equation that defines a linear function f can be written in the form $f(x) = mx + b$, where m represents the slope and b represents the y-intercept, $(0, b)$, of the line of $y = f(x)$ in the xy-plane. The function $f(x) = -5x + 30$ is linear. Therefore, the graph of the given function $y = f(x)$ in the xy-plane has a y-intercept of $(0, 30)$. It's given that $f(x)$ gives the approximate volume, in fluid ounces, of juice Caleb had remaining after making x popsicles. It follows that the y-intercept of $(0, 30)$ means that Caleb had approximately 30 fluid ounces of juice remaining after making 0 popsicles. In other words, Caleb had approximately 30 fluid ounces of juice when he began to make the popsicles.

Choice A is incorrect. This is an interpretation of the slope, rather than the y-intercept, of the graph of $y = f(x)$ in the xy-plane. *Choice B* is incorrect and may result from conceptual errors. *Choice D* is incorrect and may result from conceptual errors.

QUESTION 6

The correct answer is 192. The measure of an angle, in degrees, can be found by multiplying its measure, in radians, by $\dfrac{180 \text{ degrees}}{\pi \text{ radians}}$. Multiplying the given angle measure, $\dfrac{16\pi}{15}$ radians, by $\dfrac{180 \text{ degrees}}{\pi \text{ radians}}$ yields $\left(\dfrac{16\pi}{15} \text{ radians}\right)\left(\dfrac{180 \text{ degrees}}{\pi \text{ radians}}\right)$, which simplifies to 192 degrees.

QUESTION 7

Choice D is correct. A point (x, y) is a solution to a system of inequalities in the xy-plane if substituting the x-coordinate and the y-coordinate of the point for x and y, respectively, in each inequality makes both of the inequalities true. Substituting the x-coordinate and the y-coordinate of choice D, 14 and 0, for x and y, respectively, in the first inequality in the given system, $y \le x + 7$, yields $0 \le 14 + 7$, or $0 \le 21$, which is true. Substituting 14 for x and 0 for y in the second inequality in the given system, $y \ge -2x - 1$, yields $0 \ge -2(14) - 1$, or $0 \ge -29$, which is true. Therefore, the point $(14, 0)$ is a solution to the given system of inequalities in the xy-plane.

Choice A is incorrect. Substituting -14 for x and 0 for y in the inequality $y \le x + 7$ yields $0 \le -14 + 7$, or $0 \le -7$, which is not true. *Choice B* is incorrect. Substituting 0 for x and -14 for y in the inequality $y \ge -2x - 1$ yields $-14 \ge -2(0) - 1$, or $-14 \ge -1$, which is not true. *Choice C* is incorrect. Substituting 0 for x and 14 for y in the inequality $y \le x + 7$ yields $14 \le 0 + 7$, or $14 \le 7$, which is not true.

QUESTION 8

The correct answer is 113. It's given that the legs of a right triangle have lengths 24 centimeters and 21 centimeters. In a right triangle, the square of the length of the hypotenuse is equal to the sum of the squares of the lengths of the two legs. It follows that if h represents the length, in centimeters, of the hypotenuse of the right triangle, $h^2 = 24^2 + 21^2$. This equation is equivalent to $h^2 = 1{,}017$. Taking the square root of each side of this equation yields $h = \sqrt{1{,}017}$. This equation can be rewritten as $h = \sqrt{9 \cdot 113}$, or $h = \sqrt{9} \cdot \sqrt{113}$. This equation is equivalent to $h = 3\sqrt{113}$. It's given that the length of the triangle's hypotenuse, in centimeters, can be written in the form $3\sqrt{d}$. It follows that the value of d is 113.

QUESTION 9

Choice A is correct. The mean value of a data set is the sum of the values of the data set divided by the number of values in the data set. When a data set is represented in a frequency table, the sum of the values in the data set is the sum of the products of each value and its frequency. For data set A, the sum of products of each value and its frequency is $30(2) + 34(4) + 38(5) + 42(7) + 46(9)$, or 1,094. It's given that there are 27 values in data set A. Therefore, the mean of data set A is $\frac{1{,}094}{27}$, or approximately 40.52. Similarly, the mean of data B is $\frac{958}{27}$, or approximately 35.48. Therefore, the mean of data set A is greater than the mean of data set B.

Choice B is incorrect and may result from conceptual or calculation errors.
Choice C is incorrect and may result from conceptual or calculation errors.
Choice D is incorrect and may result from conceptual or calculation errors.

QUESTION 10

Choice C is correct. It's given that triangle XYZ is similar to triangle RST, such that X, Y, and Z correspond to R, S, and T, respectively. Since corresponding angles of similar triangles are congruent, it follows that the measure of $\angle Z$ is congruent to the measure of $\angle T$. It's given that the measure of $\angle Z$ is 20°. Therefore, the measure of $\angle T$ is 20°.

Choice A is incorrect and may result from a conceptual error.
Choice B is incorrect. This is half the measure of $\angle Z$.
Choice D is incorrect. This is twice the measure of $\angle Z$.

QUESTION 11

Choice C is correct. It's given that the equation $3x + 5y = 32$ represents the situation where Keenan filled x small jars and y large jars with all the vegetable broth he made, which was 32 cups. Therefore, $3x$ represents the total number of cups of vegetable broth in the small jars and $5y$ represents the total number of cups of vegetable broth in the large jars.

Choice A is incorrect. The number of large jars Keenan filled is represented by y, not $5y$. *Choice B* is incorrect. The number of small jars Keenan filled is represented by x, not $5y$. *Choice D* is incorrect. The total number of cups of vegetable broth in the small jars is represented by $3x$, not $5y$.

QUESTION 12

The correct answer is $\frac{29}{3}$. Applying the distributive property to the left-hand

side of the given equation, $x(x + 1) - 56$, yields $x^2 + x - 56$. Applying the distributive property to the right-hand side of the given equation, $4x(x - 7)$, yields $4x^2 - 28x$. Thus, the equation becomes $x^2 + x - 56 = 4x^2 - 28x$. Combining like terms on the left- and right-hand sides of this equation yields $0 = (4x^2 - x^2) + (-28x - x) + 56$, or $3x^2 - 29x + 56 = 0$. For a quadratic equation in the form $ax^2 + bx + c = 0$, where a, b, and c are constants, the quadratic

formula gives the solutions to the equation in the form $x = \frac{\left(-b \pm \sqrt{b^2 - 4ac}\right)}{2a}$.

Substituting 3 for a, -29 for b, and 56 for c from the equation $3x^2 - 29x + 56 = 0$

into the quadratic formula yields $x = \frac{\left(29 \pm \sqrt{(-29)^2 - 4(3)(56)}\right)}{2(3)}$, or $x = \frac{29}{6} \pm \frac{13}{6}$. It

follows that the solutions to the given equation are $\frac{29}{6} + \frac{13}{6}$ and $\frac{29}{6} - \frac{13}{6}$. Adding

these two solutions gives the sum of the solutions: $\frac{29}{6} + \frac{13}{6} + \frac{29}{6} - \frac{13}{6}$, which is

equivalent to $\frac{29}{6} + \frac{29}{6}$, or $\frac{29}{3}$. Note that 29/3, 9.666, and 9.667 are examples of ways to enter a correct answer.

QUESTION 13

Choice A is correct. The graph of a quadratic equation in the form $y = a(x - h)^2 + k$, where a, h, and k are positive constants, is a parabola that

opens upward with vertex (h, k). The given function $f(x) = \frac{1}{9}(x - 7)^2 + 3$ is in the

form $y = a(x - h)^2 + k$, where $y = f(x)$, $a = \frac{1}{9}$, $h = 7$, and $k = 3$. Therefore, the graph

of $y = f(x)$ is a parabola that opens upward with vertex $(7, 3)$. Since the parabola opens upward, the vertex is the lowest point on the graph. It follows that the y-coordinate of the vertex of the graph of $y = f(x)$ is the minimum value of $f(x)$.

Therefore, the minimum value of $f(x)$ is 3. It's given that $f(x) = \frac{1}{9}(x - 7)^2 + 3$

represents the metal ball's height above the ground, in inches, x seconds after it started moving on a track. Therefore, the best interpretation of the vertex of the graph of $y = f(x)$ is that the metal ball's minimum height was 3 inches above the ground.

Choice B is incorrect and may result from conceptual or calculation errors. *Choice C* is incorrect and may result from conceptual or calculation errors. *Choice D* is incorrect and may result from conceptual or calculation errors

QUESTION 14

Choice A is correct. It's given that the function $F(x) = \frac{9}{5}(x - 273.15) + 32$ gives

the temperature, in degrees Fahrenheit, that corresponds to a temperature of x kelvins. A temperature that increased by 2.10 kelvins means that the value of x increased by 2.10 kelvins. It follows that an increase in x by 2.10 increases

$F(x)$ by $\frac{9}{5}(2.10)$, or 3.78. Therefore, if a temperature increased by 2.10 kelvins,

the temperature increased by 3.78 degrees Fahrenheit.

Choice B is incorrect and may result from conceptual or calculation errors.
Choice C is incorrect and may result from conceptual or calculation errors.
Choice D is incorrect and may result from conceptual or calculation errors.

QUESTION 15

The correct answer is 33. It's given in the table that the coordinates of two points on a line in the xy-plane are $(k, 13)$ and $(k + 7, -15)$. The y-intercept is another point on the line. The slope computed using any pair of points from the line will be the same. The slope of a line, m, between any two points, (x_1, y_1) and (x_2, y_2), on the line can be calculated using the slope formula, $m = \frac{(y_2 - y_1)}{(x_2 - x_1)}$. It follows that the slope of the line with the given points from the table, $(k, 13)$ and $(k + 7, -15)$, is $m = \frac{-15 - 13}{k + 7 - k}$, which is equivalent to $m = \frac{-28}{7}$, or $m = -4$. It's given that the y-intercept of the line is $(k - 5, b)$. Substituting -4 for m and the coordinates of the points $(k - 5, b)$ and $(k, 13)$ into the slope formula yields $-4 = \frac{13 - b}{k - (k - 5)}$, which is equivalent to $-4 = \frac{13 - b}{k - k + 5}$, or $-4 = \frac{13 - b}{5}$. Multiplying both sides of this equation by 5 yields $-20 = 13 - b$. Subtracting 13 from both sides of this equation yields $-33 = -b$. Dividing both sides of this equation by -1 yields $b = 33$. Therefore, the value of b is 33.

QUESTION 16

The correct answer is 8. Since each term of the given expression, $2x^3 + 42x^2 + 208x$, has a factor of $2x$, the expression can be rewritten as $2x(x^2) + 2x(21x) + 2x(104)$, or $2x(x^2 + 21x + 104)$. Since the values 8 and 13 have a sum of 21 and a product of 104, the expression $x^2 + 21x + 104$ can be factored as $(x + 8)(x + 13)$. Therefore, the given expression can be factored as $2x(x + 8)(x + 13)$. It follows that the factors of the given expression are $2, x, x + 8$, and $x + 13$. Of these factors, only $x + 8$ and $x + 13$ are of the form $x + b$, where b is a positive constant. Therefore, the possible values of b are 8 and 13. Thus, the smallest possible value of b is 8.

QUESTION 17

Choice D is correct. The given function f is a linear function. Therefore, the graph of $y = f(x)$ in the xy-plane has one x-intercept at the point $(k, 0)$, where k is a constant. Substituting 0 for $f(x)$ and k for x in the given function yields $0 = 7k - 84$. Adding 84 to both sides of this equation yields $84 = 7k$. Dividing both sides of this equation by 7 yields $12 = k$. Therefore, the x-intercept of the graph of $y = f(x)$ in the xy-plane is $(12, 0)$.

Choice A is incorrect and may result from conceptual or calculation errors.
Choice B is incorrect and may result from conceptual or calculation errors.
Choice C is incorrect and may result from conceptual or calculation errors.

QUESTION 18

Choice B is correct. Since 1 mile is equal to 1,760 yards, 1 square mile is equal to $1,760^2$, or 3,097,600, square yards. It's given that the park has an area of 11,863,808 square yards. Therefore, the park has an area of (11,863,808 square yards) $\left(\frac{1 \text{ square mile}}{3,097,600 \text{ square yards}}\right)$, or $\frac{11,863,808}{3,097,600}$ square miles. Thus, the area, in square miles, of the park is 3.83.

Choice A is incorrect and may result from conceptual or calculation errors. *Choice C* is incorrect. This is the square root of the area of the park in square yards, not the area of the park in square miles. *Choice D* is incorrect and may result from converting 11,863,808 yards to miles, rather than converting 11,863,808 square yards to square miles.

QUESTION 19

Choice A is correct. It's given that w represents the total wall area, in square feet. Since the walls of the room will be painted twice, the amount of paint, in gallons, needs to cover $2w$ square feet. It's also given that one gallon of paint will cover 220 square feet. Dividing the total area, in square feet, of the surface to be painted by the number of square feet covered by one gallon of paint gives the number of gallons of paint that will be needed. Dividing $2w$ by 220 yields $\frac{2w}{220}$, or $\frac{w}{110}$. Therefore, the equation that represents the total amount of paint P, in gallons, needed to paint the walls of the room twice is $P = \frac{w}{110}$.

Choice B is incorrect and may result from conceptual or calculation errors. *Choice C* is incorrect and may result from finding the amount of paint needed to paint the walls once rather than twice. *Choice D* is incorrect and may result from conceptual or calculation errors.

QUESTION 20

The correct answer is −34. A system of two linear equations in two variables, x and y, has no solution if the lines represented by the equations in the xy-plane are distinct and parallel. Two lines represented by equations in standard form $Ax + By = C$, where A, B, and C are constants, are parallel if the coefficients for x and y in one equation are proportional to the corresponding coefficients in the other equation. The first equation in the given system can be written in standard form by subtracting $30y$ from both sides of the equation to yield $48x - 102y = 24$. The second equation in the given system can be written in standard form by adding $16x$ to both sides of the equation to yield $16x + ry = \frac{1}{6}$. The coefficient of x in this second equation, 16, is $\frac{1}{3}$ times the coefficient of x in the first equation, 48. For the lines to be parallel the coefficient of y in the second equation, r, must also be $\frac{1}{3}$ times the coefficient of y in the first equation, −102. Thus, $r = \frac{1}{3}(-102)$, or $r = -34$. Therefore, if the given system has no solution, the value of r is −34.

QUESTION 21

Choice D is correct. If $x^2 - c^2 \leq 0$, then neither side of the given equation is defined and there can be no solution. Therefore, $x^2 - c^2 > 0$. Subtracting $\frac{c^2}{\sqrt{x^2 - c^2}}$ from both sides of the given equation yields $\frac{x^2}{\sqrt{x^2 - c^2}} - \frac{c^2}{\sqrt{x^2 - c^2}} = 39$, or $\frac{x^2 - c^2}{\sqrt{x^2 - c^2}} = 39$. Squaring both sides of this equation yields $\left(\frac{x^2 - c^2}{\sqrt{x^2 - c^2}}\right) = 39^2$, or $\frac{(x^2 - c^2)(x^2 - c^2)}{x^2 - c^2} = 39^2$. Since $x^2 - c^2$ is positive and, therefore, nonzero, the expression $\frac{x^2 - c^2}{x^2 - c^2}$ is defined and equivalent to 1. It follows that the equation

$\frac{(x^2 - c^2)(x^2 - c^2)}{x^2 - c^2} = 39^2$ can be rewritten as $\left(\frac{x^2 - c^2}{x^2 - c^2}\right)(x^2 - c^2) = 39^2$,

or $(1)(x^2 - c^2) = 39^2$, which is equivalent to $x^2 - c^2 = 39^2$. Adding c^2 to both sides of this equation yields $x^2 = c^2 + 39^2$. Taking the square root of both sides of this equation yields two solutions: $x = \sqrt{c^2 + 39^2}$ and $x = -\sqrt{c^2 + 39^2}$. Therefore, of the given choices, $-\sqrt{c^2 + 39^2}$ is one of the solutions to the given equation.

Choice A is incorrect and may result from conceptual or calculation errors.
Choice B is incorrect and may result from conceptual or calculation errors.
Choice C is incorrect and may result from conceptual or calculation errors.

QUESTION 22

Choice D is correct. It's given that the graph of $y = f(x)$ in the xy-plane is a parabola with vertex (h, k). If $f(-9) = f(3)$, then for the graph of $y = f(x)$, the point with an x-coordinate of -9 and the point with an x-coordinate of 3 have the same y-coordinate. In the xy-plane, a parabola is a symmetric graph such that when two points have the same y-coordinate, these points are equidistant from the vertex, and the x-coordinate of the vertex is halfway between the x-coordinates of these two points. Therefore, for the graph of $y = f(x)$, the points with x-coordinates -9 and 3 are equidistant from the vertex, (h, k), and h is halfway between -9 and 3. The value that is halfway between -9

and 3 is $\frac{-9 + 3}{2}$, or -3. Therefore, $h = -3$. The equation defining f can also be written in vertex form, $f(x) = a(x - h)^2 + k$. Substituting -3 for h in this equation yields $f(x) = a(x - (-3))^2 + k$, or $f(x) = a(x + 3)^2 + k$. This equation is equivalent to $f(x) = a(x^2 + 6x + 9) + k$, or $f(x) = ax^2 + 6ax + 9a + k$. Since $f(x) = ax^2 + 4x + c$, it follows that $6a = 4$ and $9a + k = c$. Dividing both sides of the equation $6a = 4$ by

6 yields $a = \frac{4}{6}$, or $a = \frac{2}{3}$. Since $\frac{2}{3} < 1$, it's not true that $a \geq 1$. Therefore, statement II isn't true. Substituting $\frac{2}{3}$ for a in the equation $9a + k = c$ yields $9\left(\frac{2}{3}\right) + k = c$, or

$6 + k = c$. Subtracting 6 from both sides of this equation yields $k = c - 6$. If $k < 0$, then $c - 6 < 0$, or $c < 6$. Since c could be any value less than 6, it's not necessarily true that $c < 0$. Therefore, statement I isn't necessarily true. Thus, neither I nor II must be true.

Choice A is incorrect and may result from conceptual or calculation errors.
Choice B is incorrect and may result from conceptual or calculation errors.
Choice C is incorrect and may result from conceptual or calculation errors.

Scoring Your Paper SAT Practice Test #2

Congratulations on completing an SAT® practice test.
To score your test, follow the instructions in this guide.

IMPORTANT: *This scoring guide is for students who completed the paper version of this digital SAT practice test.*

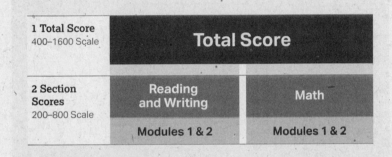

Scores Overview

Each assessment in the digital SAT Suite (SAT, PSAT/NMSQT®, PSAT™ 10, and PSAT™ 8/9) reports test scores on a common scale.

For more details about scores, visit **sat.org/scores**.

How to Calculate Your Practice Test Scores

The worksheets on pages 470 and 471 help you calculate your test scores.

GET SET UP

1 In addition to your practice test, you'll need the conversion tables and answer key at the end of this guide.

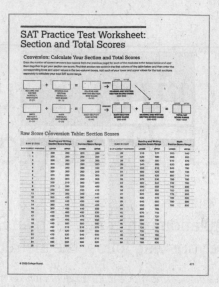

SCORE YOUR PRACTICE TEST

2 Compare your answers to the answer key on page 470, and count up the total number of correct answers for each section. Write the number of correct answers for each section in the answer key at the bottom of that section.

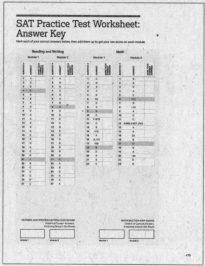

CALCULATE YOUR SCORES

3 Using your marked-up answer key and the conversion tables, follow the directions on page 471 to get your section and test scores.

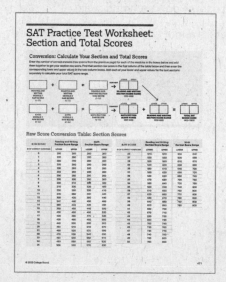

Get Section and Total Scores

Section and total scores for the paper version of this digital SAT practice test are expressed as ranges. That's because the scoring method described in this guide is a simplified (and therefore slightly less precise) version of the one used in Bluebook™, the digital test application.

To obtain your Reading and Writing and Math section scores, use the provided answer key to determine the number of questions you answered correctly in each section. These numbers constitute your *raw scores* for the two sections. Use the provided table to convert your raw score for each section into a *scaled score* range consisting of a "lower" and "upper" value. Add the two lower values together and the two upper values together to obtain your total score range.

GET YOUR READING AND WRITING SECTION SCORE

Calculate your SAT Reading and Writing section score (it's on a scale of 200–800).

1. Use the answer key on page 470 to find the number of questions in module 1 and module 2 that you answered correctly.

2. To determine your Reading and Writing raw score, add the number of correct answers you got on module 1 and module 2. **Exclude the questions in grayed-out rows from your calculation.**

3. Use the Raw Score Conversion Table: Section Scores on page 471 to turn your raw score into your Reading and Writing section score.

4. The "lower" and "upper" values associated with your raw score establish the range of scores you might expect to receive had this been an actual test.

GET YOUR MATH SECTION SCORE

Calculate your SAT Math section score (it's on a scale of 200–800).

1. Use the answer key on page 470 to find the number of questions in module 1 and module 2 that you answered correctly.

2. To determine your Math raw score, add the number of correct answers you got on module 1 and module 2. **Exclude the questions in grayed-out rows from your calculation.**

3. Use the Raw Score Conversion Table: Section Scores on page 471 to turn your raw score into your Math section score.

4. The "lower" and "upper" values associated with your raw score establish the range of scores you might expect to receive had this been an actual test.

GET YOUR TOTAL SCORE

Add together the "lower" values for the Reading and Writing and Math sections, and then add together the "upper" values for the two sections. The result is your total score, expressed as a range, for this SAT practice test. The total score is on a scale of 400–1600.

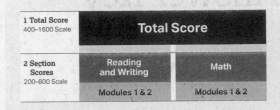

1 Total Score 400–1600 Scale	Total Score	
2 Section Scores 200–800 Scale	Reading and Writing	Math
	Modules 1 & 2	Modules 1 & 2

Your total score on this SAT practice test is the sum of your Reading and Writing section score and your Math section score. On this paper version of the digital SAT practice test, you'll receive a lower and upper score for each test section and the total score. This is the range of scores that you might expect to receive.

Use the worksheets on pages 470 and 471 to calculate your section and total scores.

SAT Practice Test Worksheet: Answer Key

Mark each of your correct answers below, then add them up to get your raw score on each module.

Reading and Writing

Module 1

QUESTION #	CORRECT	MARK YOUR CORRECT ANSWERS
1	A	
2	C	
3	B	
4	C	
5	A	
6	B	
7	A	
8	D	
9	D	
10	A	
11	A	
12	B	
13	B	
14	A	
15	C	
16	B	
17	D	
18	A	
19	C	
20	D	
21	A	
22	B	
23	C	
24	C	
25	C	
26	D	
27	C	

Module 2

QUESTION #	CORRECT	MARK YOUR CORRECT ANSWERS
1	A	
2	B	
3	D	
4	C	
5	B	
6	A	
7	D	
8	C	
9	B	
10	C	
11	C	
12	C	
13	B	
14	C	
15	C	
16	C	
17	B	
18	B	
19	B	
20	D	
21	D	
22	A	
23	B	
24	D	
25	A	
26	C	
27	A	

Math

Module 1

QUESTION #	CORRECT	MARK YOUR CORRECT ANSWERS
1	C	
2	D	
3	9	
4	A	
5	D	
6	52	
7	D	
8	B	
9	B	
10	C	
11	11875	
12	C	
13	B	
14	410	
15	A	
16	.5, 1/2	
17	100	
18	B	
19	D	
20	A	
21	B	
22	C	

Module 2

QUESTION #	CORRECT	MARK YOUR CORRECT ANSWERS
1	B	
2	B	
3	C	
4	A	
5	C	
6	192	
7	D	
8	113	
9	A	
10	C	
11	C	
12	9.666, 9.667, 29/3	
13	A	
14	A	
15	33	
16	8	
17	D	
18	B	
19	A	
20	−34	
21	D	
22	D	

READING AND WRITING SECTION RAW SCORE
(Total # of Correct Answers, Excluding Grayed-Out Rows)

Module 1

Module 2

MATH SECTION RAW SCORE
(Total # of Correct Answers, Excluding Grayed-Out Rows)

Module 1

Module 2

SAT Practice Test Worksheet: Section and Total Scores

Conversion: Calculate Your Section and Total Scores

Enter the number of correct answers (raw scores from the previous page) for each of the modules in the boxes below and add them together to get your section raw score. Find that section raw score in the first column of the table below and then enter the corresponding lower and upper values in the two-column boxes. Add each of your lower and upper values for the test sections separately to calculate your total SAT score range.

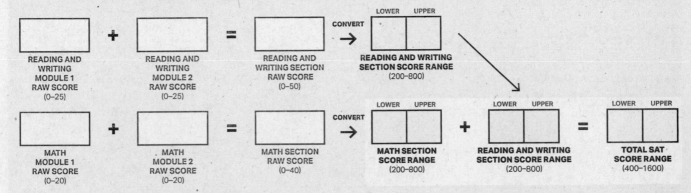

Raw Score Conversion Table: Section Scores

RAW SCORE	Reading and Writing Section Score Range		Math Section Score Range	
(# OF CORRECT ANSWERS)	LOWER	UPPER	LOWER	UPPER
0	200	260	200	260
1	200	260	200	260
2	200	260	200	260
3	200	260	200	260
4	200	260	200	260
5	200	260	200	260
6	200	280	200	260
7	200	300	260	360
8	200	310	300	380
9	210	330	320	400
10	230	350	330	410
11	240	360	360	440
12	300	420	380	440
13	340	440	400	460
14	360	440	420	480
15	380	460	440	500
16	400	460	460	520
17	420	480	470	530
18	430	490	490	550
19	440	500	500	560
20	450	510	510	570
21	460	520	530	590
22	470	530	540	600
23	480	540	550	610
24	490	550	560	620
25	500	560	570	630

RAW SCORE	Reading and Writing Section Score Range		Math Section Score Range	
(# OF CORRECT ANSWERS)	LOWER	UPPER	LOWER	UPPER
26	510	570	580	640
27	520	580	600	660
28	530	590	610	670
29	540	600	630	690
30	550	610	640	700
31	560	620	660	720
32	560	620	680	740
33	570	630	700	760
34	580	640	720	780
35	590	650	740	800
36	610	650	760	800
37	620	660	770	800
38	630	670	780	800
39	640	680	780	800
40	650	690	780	800
41	660	700		
42	670	710		
43	680	720		
44	690	730		
45	700	740		
46	720	760		
47	730	770		
48	740	780		
49	760	800		
50	780	800		

The SAT®

Practice Test #3

Make time to take the practice test.
It is one of the best ways to get ready for the SAT.

After you have taken the practice test, score it right away using materials provided in *The Official Digital SAT Study Guide*.

This version of the SAT Practice Test is for students using this guide. As a reminder, most students taking the digital SAT will do so using Bluebook™, the digital testing application. To best prepare for test day, download Bluebook at **bluebook.app.collegeboard.org** to take the practice test in the digital format.

Test begins on the next page.

Reading and Writing

27 QUESTIONS

The questions in this section address a number of important reading and writing skills. Each question includes one or more passages, which may include a table or graph. Read each passage and question carefully, and then choose the best answer to the question based on the passage(s).

All questions in this section are multiple-choice with four answer choices. Each question has a single best answer.

1

Artist Marilyn Dingle's intricate, coiled baskets are _____ sweetgrass and palmetto palm. Following a Gullah technique that originated in West Africa, Dingle skillfully winds a thin palm frond around a bunch of sweetgrass with the help of a "sewing bone" to create the basket's signature look that no factory can reproduce.

Which choice completes the text with the most logical and precise word or phrase?

A) indicated by

B) handmade from

C) represented by

D) collected with

2

Some researchers believe that the genes that enable groundhogs and certain other mammals to hibernate through the winter by slowing their breathing and heart rates and lowering their body temperature may be _____ in humans: present yet having essentially no effect on our bodily processes.

Which choice completes the text with the most logical and precise word or phrase?

A) decisive

B) lacking

C) variable

D) dormant

3

Diego Velázquez was the leading artist in the court of King Philip IV of Spain during the seventeenth century, but his influence was hardly _____ Spain: realist and impressionist painters around the world employed his techniques and echoed elements of his style.

Which choice completes the text with the most logical and precise word or phrase?

A) derived from

B) recognized in

C) confined to

D) repressed by

4

Although science fiction was dominated mostly by white male authors when Octavia Butler, a Black woman, began writing, she did not view the genre as _____: Butler broke into the field with the publication of several short stories and her 1976 novel *Patternmaster*, and she later became the first science fiction writer to win a prestigious MacArthur Fellowship.

Which choice completes the text with the most logical and precise word or phrase?

A) legitimate

B) impenetrable

C) compelling

D) indecipherable

CONTINUE ▶

5

The following text is adapted from Nathaniel Hawthorne's 1844 short story "Drowne's Wooden Image." Drowne, a young man, is carving a wooden figure to decorate the front of a ship.

> Day by day, the work <u>assumed</u> greater precision, and settled its irregular and misty outline into distincter grace and beauty. The general design was now obvious to the common eye.

As used in the text, what does the word "assumed" most nearly mean?

A) Acquired

B) Acknowledged

C) Imitated

D) Speculated

6

The following text is from Walt Whitman's 1860 poem "Calamus 24."

> I HEAR it is charged against me that I seek to destroy institutions;
>
> But really I am neither for nor against institutions
>
> (What indeed have I in common with them?— Or what with the destruction of them?),
>
> Only I will establish in the Mannahatta [Manhattan] and in every city of These States, inland and seaboard,
>
> And in the fields and woods, and above every keel [ship] little or large, that dents the water,
>
> Without edifices, or rules, or trustees, or any argument,
>
> The institution of the dear love of comrades.

Which choice best describes the overall structure of the text?

A) The speaker questions an increasingly prevalent attitude, then summarizes his worldview.

B) The speaker regrets his isolation from others, then predicts a profound change in society.

C) The speaker concedes his personal shortcomings, then boasts of his many achievements.

D) The speaker addresses a criticism leveled against him, then announces a grand ambition of his.

7

Utah is home to Pando, a colony of about 47,000 quaking aspen trees that all share a single root system. Pando is one of the largest single organisms by mass on Earth, but ecologists are worried that its growth is declining in part because of grazing by animals. The ecologists say that strong fences could prevent deer from eating young trees and help Pando start thriving again.

According to the text, why are ecologists worried about Pando?

A) It isn't growing at the same rate it used to.

B) It isn't producing young trees anymore.

C) It can't grow into new areas because it is blocked by fences.

D) Its root system can't support many more new trees.

8

Cats can judge unseen people's positions in space by the sound of their voices and thus react with surprise when the same person calls to them from two different locations in a short span of time. Saho Takagi and colleagues reached this conclusion by measuring cats' levels of surprise based on their ear and head movements while the cats heard recordings of their owners' voices from two speakers spaced far apart. Cats exhibited a low level of surprise when owners' voices were played twice from the same speaker, but they showed a high level of surprise when the voice was played once each from the two different speakers.

According to the text, how did the researchers determine the level of surprise displayed by the cats in the study?

A) They watched how each cat moved its ears and head.

B) They examined how each cat reacted to the voice of a stranger.

C) They studied how each cat physically interacted with its owner.

D) They tracked how each cat moved around the room.

CONTINUE

Culinary anthropologist Vertamae Smart-Grosvenor may be known for her decades of work in national public television and radio, but her book *Vibration Cooking: or, the Travel Notes of a Geechee Girl* is likely her most influential project. The 1970 book, whose title refers to Smart-Grosvenor's roots in the Low Country of South Carolina, was unusual for its time. It combined memoir, recipes, travel writing, and social commentary and challenged notions about conventions of food and cooking. Long admired by many, the book and its author have shaped contemporary approaches to writing about cuisine.

Which choice best describes the main idea of the text?

A) Smart-Grosvenor's unconventional book *Vibration Cooking: or, the Travel Notes of a Geechee Girl* is an important contribution to food writing.

B) Smart-Grosvenor held many different positions over her life, including reporter and food writer.

C) Smart-Grosvenor's groundbreaking book *Vibration Cooking: or, the Travel Notes of a Geechee Girl* didn't receive the praise it deserved when it was first published in 1970.

D) Smart-Grosvenor was a talented chef whose work inspired many people to start cooking for themselves.

O Pioneers! is a 1913 novel by Willa Cather. In the novel, Cather depicts Alexandra Bergson as a person who takes comfort in understanding the world around her: _____

Which quotation from *O Pioneers!* most effectively illustrates the claim?

A) "She looked fixedly up the bleak street as if she were gathering her strength to face something, as if she were trying with all her might to grasp a situation which, no matter how painful, must be met and dealt with somehow."

B) "She had never known before how much the country meant to her. The chirping of the insects down in the long grass had been like the sweetest music. She had felt as if her heart were hiding down there, somewhere, with the quail and the plover and all the little wild things that crooned or buzzed in the sun. Under the long shaggy ridges, she felt the future stirring."

C) "Alexandra drove off alone. The rattle of her wagon was lost in the howling of the wind, but her lantern, held firmly between her feet, made a moving point of light along the highway, going deeper and deeper into the dark country."

D) "Alexandra drew her shawl closer about her and stood leaning against the frame of the mill, looking at the stars which glittered so keenly through the frosty autumn air. She always loved to watch them, to think of their vastness and distance, and of their ordered march. It fortified her to reflect upon the great operations of nature, and when she thought of the law that lay behind them, she felt a sense of personal security."

Unauthorized copying or reuse of any part of this page is illegal.

478

CONTINUE ▶

11

Several artworks found among the ruins of the ancient Roman city of Pompeii depict a female figure fishing with a cupid nearby. Some scholars have asserted that the figure is the goddess Venus, since she is known to have been linked with cupids in Roman culture, but University of Leicester archaeologist Carla Brain suggests that cupids may have also been associated with fishing generally. The fact that a cupid is shown near the female figure, therefore, _____

Which choice most logically completes the text?

A) is not conclusive evidence that the figure is Venus.

B) suggests that Venus was often depicted fishing.

C) eliminates the possibility that the figure is Venus.

D) would be difficult to account for if the figure is not Venus.

12

In documents called judicial opinions, judges explain the reasoning behind their legal rulings, and in those explanations they sometimes cite and discuss historical and contemporary philosophers. Legal scholar and philosopher Anita L. Allen argues that while judges are naturally inclined to mention philosophers whose views align with their own positions, the strongest judicial opinions consider and rebut potential objections; discussing philosophers whose views conflict with judges' views could therefore _____

Which choice most logically completes the text?

A) allow judges to craft judicial opinions without needing to consult philosophical works.

B) help judges improve the arguments they put forward in their judicial opinions.

C) make judicial opinions more comprehensible to readers without legal or philosophical training.

D) bring judicial opinions in line with views that are broadly held among philosophers.

13

Many of William Shakespeare's tragedies address broad themes that still appeal to today's audiences. For instance, *Romeo and Juliet,* which is set in the Italy of Shakespeare's time, tackles the themes of parents versus children and love versus hate, and the play continues to be read and produced widely around the world. But understanding Shakespeare's so-called history plays can require a knowledge of several centuries of English history. Consequently, _____

Which choice most logically completes the text?

A) many theatergoers and readers today are likely to find Shakespeare's history plays less engaging than the tragedies.

B) some of Shakespeare's tragedies are more relevant to today's audiences than twentieth-century plays.

C) *Romeo and Juliet* is the most thematically accessible of all Shakespeare's tragedies.

D) experts in English history tend to prefer Shakespeare's history plays to his other works.

14

In her analysis of Edith Wharton's *The House of Mirth* (1905), scholar Candace Waid observes that the novel depicts the upper classes of New York society as "consumed by the appetite of a soulless _____ an apt assessment given that *The House of Mirth* is set during the Gilded Age, a period marked by rapid industrialization, economic greed, and widening wealth disparities.

Which choice completes the text so that it conforms to the conventions of Standard English?

A) materialism"; and

B) materialism" and

C) materialism,"

D) materialism"

Unauthorized copying or reuse of any part of this page is illegal.

CONTINUE

479

15

Based on genetic evidence, archaeologists have generally agreed that reindeer domestication began in the eleventh century CE. However, since uncovering fragments of a 2,000-year-old reindeer training harness in northern Siberia, _____ may have begun much earlier.

Which choice completes the text so that it conforms to the conventions of Standard English?

A) researcher Robert Losey has argued that domestication

B) researcher Robert Losey's argument is that domestication

C) domestication, researcher Robert Losey has argued,

D) the argument researcher Robert Losey has made is that domestication

16

A conceptual artist and designer embraced by both the art world and the fashion _____ Mary Ping was chosen to curate the exhibition *Front Row: Chinese American Designers* for the Museum of Chinese in America.

Which choice completes the text so that it conforms to the conventions of Standard English?

A) world

B) world:

C) world;

D) world,

17

Professional American football player Fred Cox invented one of the world's most popular toys. In the 1970s, he came up with the idea for the Nerf football, which _____ of the harder and heavier regulation football.

Which choice completes the text so that it conforms to the conventions of Standard English?

A) were a smaller, foam version

B) are smaller, foam versions

C) were smaller, foam versions

D) is a smaller, foam version

18

Beatrix Potter is perhaps best known for writing and illustrating children's books such as *The Tale of Peter Rabbit* (1902), but she also dedicated herself to mycology, the study of _____ more than 350 paintings of the fungal species she observed in nature and submitting her research on spore germination to the Linnean Society of London.

Which choice completes the text so that it conforms to the conventions of Standard English?

A) fungi; producing

B) fungi. Producing

C) fungi producing

D) fungi, producing

19

African American Percy Julian was a scientist and entrepreneur whose work helped people around the world to see. Named in 1999 as one of the greatest achievements by a US chemist in the past hundred years, _____ led to the first mass-produced treatment for glaucoma.

Which choice completes the text so that it conforms to the conventions of Standard English?

A) Julian synthesized the alkaloid physostigmine in 1935; it

B) in 1935 Julian synthesized the alkaloid physostigmine, which

C) Julian's 1935 synthesis of the alkaloid physostigmine

D) the alkaloid physostigmine was synthesized by Julian in 1935 and

CONTINUE

20

The first computerized spreadsheet, Dan Bricklin's *VisiCalc*, improved financial recordkeeping not only by providing users with an easy means of adjusting data in spreadsheets but also by automatically updating all calculations that were dependent on these _____ to VisiCalc's release, changing a paper spreadsheet often required redoing the entire sheet by hand, a process that could take days.

Which choice completes the text so that it conforms to the conventions of Standard English?

A) adjustments prior

B) adjustments, prior

C) adjustments. Prior

D) adjustments and prior

21

Neuroscientist Karen Konkoly wanted to determine whether individuals can understand and respond to questions during REM sleep. She first taught volunteers eye movements they would use to respond to basic math problems while asleep (a single left-right eye movement indicated the number one). _____ she attached electrodes to the volunteers' faces to record their eye movements during sleep.

Which choice completes the text with the most logical transition?

A) Specifically,

B) Next,

C) For instance,

D) In sum,

22

Archaeologist Sue Brunning explains why the seventh-century ship burial site at Sutton Hoo in England was likely the tomb of a king. First, the gold artifacts inside the ship suggest that the person buried with them was a wealthy and respected leader. _____ the massive effort required to bury the ship would likely only have been undertaken for a king.

Which choice completes the text with the most logical transition?

A) Instead,

B) Still,

C) Specifically,

D) Second,

23

Every chemical compound has a spectroscopic fingerprint, a pattern of reflected light unique to that compound. _____ upon analyzing the light reflected by the bright regions on the surface of the dwarf planet Ceres, Maria Cristina De Sanctis of Rome's National Institute of Astrophysics was able to determine that the regions contain large amounts of the compound sodium carbonate.

Which choice completes the text with the most logical transition?

A) Regardless,

B) Meanwhile,

C) Thus,

D) In comparison,

CONTINUE

24

While researching a topic, a student has taken the following notes:

- Severo Ochoa discovered the enzyme PNPase in 1955.
- PNPase is involved in both the creation and degradation of mRNA.
- Ochoa incorrectly hypothesized that PNPase provides the genetic blueprints for mRNA.
- The discovery of PNPase proved critical to deciphering the human genetic code.
- Deciphering the genetic code has led to a better understanding of how genetic variations affect human health.

The student wants to emphasize the significance of Ochoa's discovery. Which choice most effectively uses relevant information from the notes to accomplish this goal?

A) Ochoa's 1955 discovery of PNPase proved critical to deciphering the human genetic code, leading to a better understanding of how genetic variations affect human health.

B) Ochoa first discovered PNPase, an enzyme that he hypothesized contained the genetic blueprints for mRNA, in 1955.

C) In 1955, Ochoa discovered the PNPase enzyme, which is involved in both the creation and degradation of mRNA.

D) Though his discovery of PNPase was critical to deciphering the human genetic code, Ochoa incorrectly hypothesized that the enzyme was the source of mRNA's genetic blueprints.

25

While researching a topic, a student has taken the following notes:

- Physicist Muluneh Abebe was working on a garment suited for both warm and cold conditions.
- He analyzed the emissivity, or ability to emit heat, of the materials he planned to use.
- Abebe found that reflective metal fibers emitted almost no heat and had an emissivity of 0.02.
- He found that silicon carbide fibers absorbed large amounts of heat and had an emissivity of 0.74.
- The amount of heat a material absorbs is equal to the amount of heat it emits.

The student wants to contrast the emissivity of reflective metal fibers with that of silicon carbide fibers. Which choice most effectively uses relevant information from the notes to accomplish this goal?

A) The ability of reflective metal fibers and silicon carbide fibers to emit heat was determined by an analysis of each material's emissivity.

B) The amount of heat a material absorbs is equal to the amount it emits, as evidenced in Abebe's analyses.

C) Though the reflective metal fibers and silicon carbide fibers had different rates of emissivity, Abebe planned to use both in a garment.

D) Whereas the reflective metal fibers had an emissivity of just 0.02, the silicon carbide fibers absorbed large amounts of heat, resulting in an emissivity of 0.74.

CONTINUE

26

While researching a topic, a student has taken the following notes:

- In the early 1960s, the US had a strict national-origins quota system for immigrants.
- The number of new immigrants allowed from a country each year was based on how many people from that country lived in the US in 1890.
- This system favored immigrants from northern Europe.
- Almost 70% of slots were reserved for immigrants from Great Britain, Ireland, and Germany.
- The 1965 Hart-Celler Act abolished the national-origins quota system.

The student wants to present the significance of the Hart-Celler Act to an audience unfamiliar with the history of US immigration. Which choice most effectively uses relevant information from the notes to accomplish this goal?

A) Almost 70% of slots were reserved for immigrants from Great Britain, Ireland, and Germany at the time the Hart-Celler Act was proposed.

B) Prior to the Hart-Celler Act, new immigration quotas were based on how many people from each country lived in the US in 1890.

C) The quota system in place in the early 1960s was abolished by the 1965 Hart-Celler Act.

D) The 1965 Hart-Celler Act abolished the national-origins quota system, which favored immigrants from northern Europe.

27

While researching a topic, a student has taken the following notes:

- In 2020, theater students at Radford and Virginia Tech chose an interactive, online format to present a play about woman suffrage activists.
- Their "Women and the Vote" website featured an interactive digital drawing of a Victorian-style house.
- Audiences were asked to focus on a room of their choice and select from that room an artifact related to the suffrage movement.
- One click took them to video clips, songs, artwork, and texts associated with the artifact.
- The play was popular with audiences because the format allowed them to control the experience.

The student wants to explain an advantage of the "Women and the Vote" format. Which choice most effectively uses relevant information from the notes to accomplish this goal?

A) "Women and the Vote" featured a drawing of a Victorian-style house with several rooms, each containing suffrage artifacts.

B) To access video clips, songs, artwork, and texts, audiences had to first click on an artifact.

C) The "Women and the Vote" format appealed to audiences because it allowed them to control the experience.

D) Using an interactive format, theater students at Radford and Virginia Tech created "Women and the Vote," a play about woman suffrage activists.

STOP

If you finish before time is called, you may check your work on this module only. Do not turn to any other module in the test.

Reading and Writing
27 QUESTIONS

The questions in this section address a number of important reading and writing skills. Each question includes one or more passages, which may include a table or graph. Read each passage and question carefully, and then choose the best answer to the question based on the passage(s).

All questions in this section are multiple-choice with four answer choices. Each question has a single best answer.

1

For painter Jacob Lawrence, being _____ was an important part of the artistic process. Because he paid close attention to all the details of his Harlem neighborhood, Lawrence's artwork captured nuances in the beauty and vitality of the Black experience during the Harlem Renaissance and the Great Migration.

Which choice completes the text with the most logical and precise word or phrase?

A) skeptical

B) observant

C) critical

D) confident

2

Particle physicists like Ayana Holloway Arce and Aida El-Khadra spend much of their time _____ what is invisible to the naked eye: using sophisticated technology, they closely examine the behavior of subatomic particles, the smallest detectable parts of matter.

Which choice completes the text with the most logical and precise word or phrase?

A) selecting

B) inspecting

C) creating

D) deciding

3

Beginning in the 1950s, Navajo Nation legislator Annie Dodge Wauneka continuously worked to promote public health; this _____ effort involved traveling throughout the vast Navajo homeland and writing a medical dictionary for speakers of *Diné bizaad*, the Navajo language.

Which choice completes the text with the most logical and precise word or phrase?

A) impartial

B) offhand

C) persistent

D) mandatory

4

The process of mechanically recycling plastics is often considered _____ because of the environmental impact and the loss of material quality that often occurs. But chemist Takunda Chazovachii has helped develop a cleaner process of chemical recycling that converts superabsorbent polymers from diapers into a desirable reusable adhesive.

Which choice completes the text with the most logical and precise word or phrase?

A) resilient

B) inadequate

C) dynamic

D) satisfactory

Unauthorized copying or reuse of any part of this page is illegal.

484

CONTINUE ➔

5

Novelist N. K. Jemisin declines to _____ the conventions of the science fiction genre in which she writes, and she has suggested that her readers appreciate her work precisely because of this willingness to thwart expectations and avoid formulaic plots and themes.

Which choice completes the text with the most logical and precise word or phrase?

A) question

B) react to

C) perceive

D) conform to

6

In 1929 the *Atlantic Monthly* published several articles based on newly discovered letters allegedly exchanged between President Abraham Lincoln and a woman named Ann Rutledge. Historians were unable to _____ the authenticity of the letters, however, and quickly dismissed them as a hoax.

Which choice completes the text with the most logical and precise word or phrase?

A) validate

B) interpret

C) relate

D) accommodate

7

The following text is from Georgia Douglas Johnson's 1922 poem "Benediction."

> Go forth, my son,
> Winged by my heart's desire!
> Great reaches, yet unknown,
> Await
> For your possession.
> I may not, if I would,
> Retrace the way with you,
> My pilgrimage is through,
> But life is calling you!

Which choice best states the main purpose of the text?

A) To express hope that a child will have the same accomplishments as his parent did

B) To suggest that raising a child involves many struggles

C) To warn a child that he will face many challenges throughout his life

D) To encourage a child to embrace the experiences life will offer

8

In 2007, computer scientist Luis von Ahn was working on converting printed books into a digital format. He found that some words were distorted enough that digital scanners couldn't recognize them, but most humans could easily read them. Based on that finding, von Ahn invented a simple security test to keep automated "bots" out of websites. The first version of the reCAPTCHA test asked users to type one known word and one of the many words scanners couldn't recognize. Correct answers proved the users were humans and added data to the book-digitizing project.

Which choice best states the main purpose of the text?

A) To discuss von Ahn's invention of reCAPTCHA

B) To explain how digital scanners work

C) To call attention to von Ahn's book-digitizing project

D) To indicate how popular reCAPTCHA is

CONTINUE

9

Text 1

A tiny, unusual fossil in a piece of 99-million-year-old amber is of the extinct species *Oculudentavis khaungraae*. The *O. khaungraae* fossil consists of a rounded skull with a thin snout and a large eye socket. Because these features look like they are avian, or related to birds, researchers initially thought that the fossil might be the smallest avian dinosaur ever found.

Text 2

Paleontologists were excited to discover a second small fossil that is similar to the strange *O. khaungraae* fossil but has part of the lower body along with a birdlike skull. Detailed studies of both fossils revealed several traits that are found in lizards but not in dinosaurs or birds. Therefore, paleontologists think the two creatures were probably unusual lizards, even though the skulls looked avian at first.

Based on the texts, what would the paleontologists in Text 2 most likely say about the researchers' initial thought in Text 1?

A) It is understandable because the fossil does look like it could be related to birds, even though *O. khaungraae* is probably a lizard.

B) It is confusing because it isn't clear what caused the researchers to think that *O. khaungraae* might be related to birds.

C) It is flawed because the researchers mistakenly assumed that *O. khaungraae* must be a lizard.

D) It is reasonable because the *O. khaungraae* skull is about the same size as the skull of the second fossil but is shaped differently.

10

The following text is from Ezra Pound's 1909 poem "Hymn III," based on the work of Marcantonio Flaminio.

> As a fragile and lovely flower unfolds its gleaming foliage on the breast of the fostering earth, if the dew and the rain draw it forth;
> So doth my tender mind flourish, if it be fed with the sweet dew of the fostering spirit,
> Lacking this, it beginneth straightway to languish, even as a floweret born upon dry earth, if the dew and the rain tend it not.

Based on the text, in what way is the human mind like a flower?

A) It becomes increasingly vigorous with the passage of time.

B) It draws strength from changes in the weather.

C) It requires proper nourishment in order to thrive.

D) It perseveres despite challenging circumstances.

11

Maximum Height of Maple Trees
When Fully Grown

Tree type	Maximum height (feet)	Native to North America
Sugar maple	75	yes
Silver maple	70	yes
Red maple	60	yes
Japanese maple	25	no
Norway maple	50	no

For a school project, a forestry student needs to recommend a maple tree that is native to North America and won't grow more than 60 feet in height. Based on the characteristics of five common maple trees, she has decided to select a _____

Which choice most effectively uses data from the table to complete the text?

A) silver maple.

B) sugar maple.

C) red maple.

D) Norway maple.

Unauthorized copying or reuse of any part of this page is illegal.

CONTINUE

486

12

A student is examining a long, challenging poem that was initially published in a quarterly journal without explanatory notes, then later republished in a stand-alone volume containing only that poem and accompanying explanatory notes written by the poet. The student asserts that the explanatory notes were included in the republication primarily as a marketing device to help sell the stand-alone volume.

Which statement, if true, would most directly support the student's claim?

A) The text of the poem as published in the quarterly journal is not identical to the text of the poem published in the stand-alone volume.

B) Many critics believe that the poet's explanatory notes remove certain ambiguities of the poem and make it less interesting as a result.

C) The publishers of the stand-alone volume requested the explanatory notes from the poet in order to make the book attractive to readers who already had a copy of the poem in a journal issue.

D) Correspondence between the poet and the publisher reveals that the poet's explanatory notes went through several drafts.

13

The Post Office is a 1912 play by Rabindranath Tagore, originally written in Bengali. The character Amal is a young boy who imagines that the people he sees passing the window of his home are carefree even when engaged in work or chores, as is evident when he says to the daughter of a flower seller, _____

Which quotation from *The Post Office* most effectively illustrates the claim?

A) "I see, you don't wish to stop; I don't care to stay on here either."

B) "Oh, flower gathering? That is why your feet seem so glad and your anklets jingle so merrily as you walk."

C) "I'll pay when I grow up—before I leave to look for work out on the other side of that stream there."

D) "Wish I could be out too. Then I would pick some flowers for you from the very topmost branches right out of sight."

Unauthorized copying or reuse of any part of this page is illegal.

CONTINUE

487

14

Characteristics of Five Recently Discovered Gas Exoplanets

Exoplanet designation	Mass (Jupiters)	Radius (Jupiters)	Orbital period (days)	Distance from the Sun (parsecs)
TOI-640 b	0.88	1.771	5.003	340
TOI-1601 b	0.99	1.239	5.331	336
TOI-628 b	6.33	1.060	3.409	178
TOI-1478 b	0.85	1.060	10.180	153
TOI-1333 b	2.37	1.396	4.720	200

"Hot Jupiters" are gas planets that have a mass of at least 0.25 Jupiters (meaning that their mass is at least 25% of that of Jupiter) and an orbital period of less than 10 days (meaning that they complete one orbit around their star in less than 10 days), while "warm Jupiters" are gas planets that meet the same mass criterion but have orbital periods of more than 10 days. In 2021, Michigan State University astronomer Joseph Rodriguez and colleagues announced the discovery of five new gas exoplanets and asserted that four are hot Jupiters and one is a warm Jupiter.

Which choice best describes data from the table that support Rodriguez and colleagues' assertion?

A) None of the planets have an orbital period of more than 10 days, and TOI-628 b has a mass of 6.33 Jupiters.

B) TOI-1478 b has an orbital period of 153 days, and the masses of all the planets range from 0.85 to 6.33 Jupiters.

C) All the planets have a radius between 1.060 and 1.771 Jupiters, and only TOI-1333 b has an orbital period of more than 10 days.

D) Each of the planets has a mass greater than 0.25 Jupiters, and all except for TOI-1478 b have an orbital period of less than 10 days.

Unauthorized copying or reuse of any part of this page is illegal.

CONTINUE

488

15

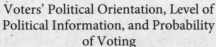

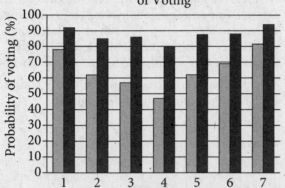

Voters' Political Orientation, Level of
Political Information, and Probability
of Voting

Voters' political orientation
(1 = strong Democrat/liberal;
4 = independent;
7 = strong Republican/conservative)

Economists Kerwin Kofi Charles and Melvin
Stephens Jr. investigated a variety of factors that
influence voter turnout in the United States. Using
survey data that revealed whether respondents voted
in national elections and how knowledgeable
respondents are about politics, Charles and Stephens
claim that the likelihood of voting is driven in part
by potential voters' confidence in their assessments
of candidates—essentially, the more informed voters
are about politics, the more confident they are at
evaluating whether candidates share their views, and
thus the more likely they are to vote.

Which choice best describes data in the graph that
support Charles and Stephens's claim?

A) At each point on the political orientation scale,
high-information voters were more likely than
low-information voters to vote.

B) Only low-information voters who identify as
independents had a voting probability below 50%.

C) The closer that low-information voters are to the
ends of the political orientation scale, the more
likely they were to vote.

D) High-information voters were more likely to
identify as strong Democrats or strong
Republicans than low-information voters were.

16

In the "language nest" model of education,
Indigenous children learn the language of their
people by using it as the medium of instruction and
socialization at pre-K or elementary levels. In their
2016 study of a school in an Anishinaabe
community in Ontario, Canada, scholars Lindsay
Morcom and Stephanie Roy (who are Anishinaabe
themselves) found that the model not only imparted
fluency in the Anishinaabe language but also
enhanced students' pride in Anishinaabe culture
overall. Given these positive effects, Morcom and
Roy predict that the model increases the probability
that as adults, former students of the school will
transmit the language to younger generations in
their community.

Which finding, if true, would most strongly support
the researchers' prediction?

A) Anishinaabe adults who didn't attend the school
feel roughly the same degree of cultural pride as
the former students of the school feel.

B) After transferring to the school, new students
experience an increase in both fluency and
academic performance overall.

C) As adults, former students of the school are just
as likely to continue living in their community as
individuals who didn't attend the school.

D) As they complete secondary and higher
education, former students of the school
experience no loss of fluency or cultural pride.

CONTINUE

17

Choctaw/Cherokee artist Jeffrey Gibson turns punching bags used by boxers into art by decorating them with beadwork and elements of Native dressmaking. These elements include leather fringe and jingles, the metal cones that cover the dresses worn in the jingle dance, a women's dance of the Ojibwe people. Thus, Gibson combines an object commonly associated with masculinity (a punching bag) with art forms traditionally practiced by women in most Native communities (beadwork and dressmaking). In this way, he rejects the division of male and female gender roles.

Which choice best describes Gibson's approach to art, as presented in the text?

A) He draws from traditional Native art forms to create his original works.

B) He finds inspiration from boxing in designing the dresses he makes.

C) He rejects expectations about color and pattern when incorporating beadwork.

D) He has been influenced by Native and non-Native artists equally.

18

For thousands of years, people in the Americas _____ the bottle gourd, a large bitter fruit with a thick rind, to make bottles, other types of containers, and even musical instruments. Oddly, there is no evidence that any type of bottle gourd is native to the Western Hemisphere; either the fruit or its seeds must have somehow been carried from Asia or Africa.

Which choice completes the text so that it conforms to the conventions of Standard English?

A) to use

B) have used

C) having used

D) using

19

The Alvarez theory, developed in 1980 by physicist Luis Walter Alvarez and his geologist son Walter Alvarez, maintained that the secondary effects of an asteroid impact caused many dinosaurs and other animals to die _____ it left unexplored the question of whether unrelated volcanic activity might have also contributed to the mass extinctions.

Which choice completes the text so that it conforms to the conventions of Standard English?

A) out but

B) out, but

C) out

D) out,

20

To survive when water is scarce, embryos inside African turquoise killifish eggs _____ a dormant state known as diapause. In this state, embryonic development is paused for as long as two years— longer than the life span of an adult killifish.

Which choice completes the text so that it conforms to the conventions of Standard English?

A) enter

B) to enter

C) having entered

D) entering

21

In his 1963 exhibition *Exposition of Music— Electronic Television*, Korean American artist Nam June Paik showed how television images could be manipulated to express an artist's perspective. Today, Paik _____ considered the first video artist.

Which choice completes the text so that it conforms to the conventions of Standard English?

A) will be

B) had been

C) was

D) is

CONTINUE ▶

22

As British scientist Peter Whibberley has observed, "the Earth is not a very good timekeeper." Earth's slightly irregular rotation rate means that measurements of time must be periodically adjusted. Specifically, an extra "leap second" (the 86,401st second of the day) is _____ time based on the planet's rotation lags a full nine-tenths of a second behind time kept by precise atomic clocks.

Which choice completes the text so that it conforms to the conventions of Standard English?

A) added, whenever

B) added; whenever

C) added. Whenever

D) added whenever

23

Like other amphibians, the wood frog (*Rana sylvatica*) is unable to generate its own heat, so during periods of subfreezing temperatures, it _____ by producing large amounts of glucose, a sugar that helps prevent damaging ice from forming inside its cells.

Which choice completes the text so that it conforms to the conventions of Standard English?

A) had survived

B) survived

C) would survive

D) survives

24

Chimamanda Ngozi Adichie's 2013 novel *Americanah* chronicles the divergent experiences of Ifemelu and Obinze, a young Nigerian couple, after high school. Ifemelu moves to the United States to attend a prestigious university. _____ Obinze travels to London, hoping to start a career there. However, frustrated with the lack of opportunities, he soon returns to Nigeria.

Which choice completes the text with the most logical transition?

A) Meanwhile,

B) Nevertheless,

C) Secondly,

D) In fact,

25

Before California's 1911 election to approve a proposition granting women the right to vote, activists across the state sold tea to promote the cause of suffrage. In San Francisco, the Woman's Suffrage Party sold Equality Tea at local fairs. _____ in Los Angeles, activist Nancy Tuttle Craig, who ran one of California's largest grocery store firms, distributed Votes for Women Tea.

Which choice completes the text with the most logical transition?

A) For example,

B) To conclude,

C) Similarly,

D) In other words,

CONTINUE

26

While researching a topic, a student has taken the following notes:

- Some sandstone arches in Utah's Arches National Park have been defaced by tourists' carvings.
- Park rangers can smooth away some carvings using power grinders.
- For deep carvings, power grinding is not always feasible because it can greatly alter or damage the rock.
- Park rangers can use an infilling technique, which involves filling in carvings with ground sandstone and a bonding agent.
- This technique is minimally invasive.

The student wants to explain an advantage of the infilling technique. Which choice most effectively uses relevant information from the notes to accomplish this goal?

A) To remove carvings from sandstone arches in Utah's Arches National Park, power grinding is not always feasible.

B) Filling in carvings with ground sandstone and a bonding agent is less invasive than smoothing them away with a power grinder, which can greatly alter or damage the sandstone arches.

C) Park rangers can use a power grinding technique to smooth away carvings or fill them in with ground sandstone and a bonding agent.

D) As methods for removing carvings from sandstone, power grinding and infilling differ in their level of invasiveness.

27

While researching a topic, a student has taken the following notes:

- Soo Sunny Park is a Korean American artist who uses light as her primary medium of expression.
- She created her work *Unwoven Light* in 2013.
- *Unwoven Light* featured a chain-link fence fitted with iridescent plexiglass tiles.
- When light passed through the fence, colorful prisms formed.

The student wants to describe *Unwoven Light* to an audience unfamiliar with Soo Sunny Park. Which choice most effectively uses relevant information from the notes to accomplish this goal?

A) Park's 2013 installation *Unwoven Light*, which included a chain-link fence and iridescent tiles made from plexiglass, featured light as its primary medium of expression.

B) Korean American light artist Soo Sunny Park created *Unwoven Light* in 2013.

C) The chain-link fence in Soo Sunny Park's *Unwoven Light* was fitted with tiles made from iridescent plexiglass.

D) In *Unwoven Light*, a 2013 work by Korean American artist Soo Sunny Park, light formed colorful prisms as it passed through a fence Park had fitted with iridescent tiles.

STOP

**If you finish before time is called, you may check your work on this module only.
Do not turn to any other module in the test.**

Test begins on the next page.

Math

22 QUESTIONS

DIRECTIONS

The questions in this section address a number of important math skills.
Use of a calculator is permitted for all questions.

NOTES

Unless otherwise indicated:

- All variables and expressions represent real numbers.

- Figures provided are drawn to scale.

- All figures lie in a plane.

- The domain of a given function f is the set of all real numbers x for which $f(x)$ is a real number.

REFERENCE

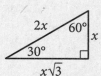

$A = \pi r^2$
$C = 2\pi r$

$A = \ell w$

$A = \dfrac{1}{2}bh$

$c^2 = a^2 + b^2$

Special Right Triangles

$V = \ell wh$

$V = \pi r^2 h$

$V = \dfrac{4}{3}\pi r^3$

$V = \dfrac{1}{3}\pi r^2 h$

$V = \dfrac{1}{3}\ell wh$

The number of degrees of arc in a circle is 360.

The number of radians of arc in a circle is 2π.

The sum of the measures in degrees of the angles of a triangle is 180.

CONTINUE →

For multiple-choice questions, solve each problem, choose the correct answer from the choices provided, and then circle your answer in this book. Circle only one answer for each question. If you change your mind, completely erase the circle. You will not get credit for questions with more than one answer circled, or for questions with no answers circled.

For student-produced response questions, solve each problem and write your answer next to or under the question in the test book as described below.

- Once you've written your answer, circle it clearly. You will not receive credit for anything written outside the circle, or for any questions with more than one circled answer.

- If you find **more than one correct answer**, write and circle only one answer.

- Your answer can be up to 5 characters for a **positive** answer and up to 6 characters (including the negative sign) for a **negative** answer, but no more.

- If your answer is a **fraction** that is too long (over 5 characters for positive, 6 characters for negative), write the decimal equivalent.

- If your answer is a **decimal** that is too long (over 5 characters for positive, 6 characters for negative), truncate it or round at the fourth digit.

- If your answer is a **mixed number** (such as $3\frac{1}{2}$), write it as an improper fraction (7/2) or its decimal equivalent (3.5).

- Don't include **symbols** such as a percent sign, comma, or dollar sign in your circled answer.

1

A bus is traveling at a constant speed along a straight portion of road. The equation $d = 30t$ gives the distance d, in feet from a road marker, that the bus will be t seconds after passing the marker. How many feet from the marker will the bus be 2 seconds after passing the marker?

A) 30

B) 32

C) 60

D) 90

2

A line in the xy-plane has a slope of $\frac{1}{9}$ and passes through the point $(0, 14)$. Which equation represents this line?

A) $y = -\frac{1}{9}x - 14$

B) $y = -\frac{1}{9}x + 14$

C) $y = \frac{1}{9}x - 14$

D) $y = \frac{1}{9}x + 14$

3

If $\frac{x}{8} = 5$, what is the value of $\frac{8}{x}$?

4

Triangles ABC and DEF are congruent, where A corresponds to D, and B and E are right angles. The measure of angle A is 18°. What is the measure of angle F?

A) 18°

B) 72°

C) 90°

D) 162°

5

Which expression is equivalent to $(m^4 q^4 z^{-1})(mq^5 z^3)$, where m, q, and z are positive?

A) $m^4 q^{20} z^{-3}$

B) $m^5 q^9 z^2$

C) $m^6 q^8 z^{-1}$

D) $m^{20} q^{12} z^{-2}$

6

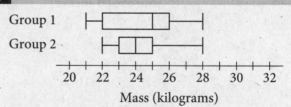

The box plots summarize the masses, in kilograms, of two groups of gazelles. Based on the box plots, which of the following statements must be true?

A) The mean mass of group 1 is greater than the mean mass of group 2.

B) The mean mass of group 1 is less than the mean mass of group 2.

C) The median mass of group 1 is greater than the median mass of group 2.

D) The median mass of group 1 is less than the median mass of group 2.

CONTINUE

7

$$y = 76$$
$$y = x^2 - 5$$

The graphs of the given equations in the xy-plane intersect at the point (x, y). What is a possible value of x?

A) $-\dfrac{76}{5}$

B) -9

C) 5

D) 76

8

To estimate the proportion of a population that has a certain characteristic, a random sample was selected from the population. Based on the sample, it is estimated that the proportion of the population that has the characteristic is 0.49, with an associated margin of error of 0.04. Based on this estimate and margin of error, which of the following is the most appropriate conclusion about the proportion of the population that has the characteristic?

A) It is plausible that the proportion is between 0.45 and 0.53.

B) It is plausible that the proportion is less than 0.45.

C) The proportion is exactly 0.49.

D) It is plausible that the proportion is greater than 0.53.

9

$$y = 2x + 10$$
$$y = 2x - 1$$

At how many points do the graphs of the given equations intersect in the xy-plane?

A) Zero

B) Exactly one

C) Exactly two

D) Infinitely many

10

In the xy-plane, the graph of the linear function f contains the points $(0, 2)$ and $(8, 34)$. Which equation defines f, where $y = f(x)$?

A) $f(x) = 2x + 42$

B) $f(x) = 32x + 36$

C) $f(x) = 4x + 2$

D) $f(x) = 8x + 2$

11

If $\dfrac{x}{y} = 4$ and $\dfrac{24x}{ny} = 4$, what is the value of n?

12

$$w(t) = 300 - 4t$$

The function w models the volume of liquid, in milliliters, in a container t seconds after it begins draining from a hole at the bottom. According to the model, what is the predicted volume, in milliliters, draining from the container each second?

A) 300

B) 296

C) 75

D) 4

Unauthorized copying or reuse of any part of this page is illegal.

CONTINUE

497

13

Each year, the value of an investment increases by 0.49% of its value the previous year. Which of the following functions best models how the value of the investment changes over time?

A) Decreasing exponential

B) Decreasing linear

C) Increasing exponential

D) Increasing linear

14

$$24x + y = 48$$
$$6x + y = 72$$

The solution to the given system of equations is (x, y). What is the value of y?

15

$$y = x^2 - 14x + 22$$

The given equation relates the variables x and y. For what value of x does the value of y reach its minimum?

16

The function h is defined by $h(x) = 4x + 28$. The graph of $y = h(x)$ in the xy-plane has an x-intercept at $(a, 0)$ and a y-intercept at $(0, b)$, where a and b are constants. What is the value of $a + b$?

A) 21

B) 28

C) 32

D) 35

17

Square A has side lengths that are 166 times the side lengths of square B. The area of square A is k times the area of square B. What is the value of k?

18

The scatterplot shows the relationship between two variables, x and y. A line of best fit for the data is also shown.

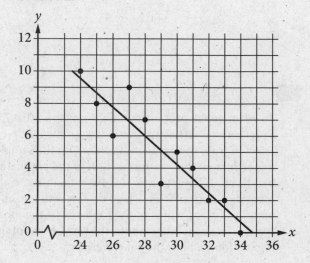

At $x = 25.5$, which of the following is closest to the y-value predicted by the line of best fit?

A) 6.2

B) 7.3

C) 8.2

D) 9.1

CONTINUE

19

The measure of angle R is $\frac{2\pi}{3}$ radians. The measure of angle T is $\frac{5\pi}{12}$ radians greater than the measure of angle R. What is the measure of angle T, in <u>degrees</u>?

A) 75

B) 120

C) 195

D) 390

20

A scientist initially measures 12,000 bacteria in a growth medium. 4 hours later, the scientist measures 24,000 bacteria. Assuming exponential growth, the formula $P = C(2)^{rt}$ gives the number of bacteria in the growth medium, where r and C are constants and P is the number of bacteria t hours after the initial measurement. What is the value of r?

A) $\dfrac{1}{12,000}$

B) $\dfrac{1}{4}$

C) 4

D) 12,000

21

$$\sqrt{(x-2)^2} = \sqrt{3x + 34}$$

What is the smallest solution to the given equation?

22

$$x - 29 = (x - a)(x - 29)$$

Which of the following are solutions to the given equation, where a is a constant and $a > 30$?

   I. a

   II. $a + 1$

   III. 29

A) I and II only

B) I and III only

C) II and III only

D) I, II, and III

STOP

If you finish before time is called, you may check your work on this module only.
Do not turn to any other module in the test.

Math

22 QUESTIONS

DIRECTIONS

The questions in this section address a number of important math skills.
Use of a calculator is permitted for all questions.

NOTES

Unless otherwise indicated:

- All variables and expressions represent real numbers.
- Figures provided are drawn to scale.
- All figures lie in a plane.
- The domain of a given function f is the set of all real numbers x for which $f(x)$ is a real number.

REFERENCE

$A = \pi r^2$
$C = 2\pi r$

$A = \ell w$

$A = \frac{1}{2}bh$

$c^2 = a^2 + b^2$

Special Right Triangles

$V = \ell wh$

$V = \pi r^2 h$

$V = \frac{4}{3}\pi r^3$

$V = \frac{1}{3}\pi r^2 h$

$V = \frac{1}{3}\ell wh$

The number of degrees of arc in a circle is 360.

The number of radians of arc in a circle is 2π.

The sum of the measures in degrees of the angles of a triangle is 180.

CONTINUE

For multiple-choice questions, solve each problem, choose the correct answer from the choices provided, and then circle your answer in this book. Circle only one answer for each question. If you change your mind, completely erase the circle. You will not get credit for questions with more than one answer circled, or for questions with no answers circled.

For student-produced response questions, solve each problem and write your answer next to or under the question in the test book as described below.

- Once you've written your answer, circle it clearly. You will not receive credit for anything written outside the circle, or for any questions with more than one circled answer.

- If you find **more than one correct answer**, write and circle only one answer.

- Your answer can be up to 5 characters for a **positive** answer and up to 6 characters (including the negative sign) for a **negative** answer, but no more.

- If your answer is a **fraction** that is too long (over 5 characters for positive, 6 characters for negative), write the decimal equivalent.

- If your answer is a **decimal** that is too long (over 5 characters for positive, 6 characters for negative), truncate it or round at the fourth digit.

- If your answer is a **mixed number** (such as $3\frac{1}{2}$), write it as an improper fraction (7/2) or its decimal equivalent (3.5).

- Don't include **symbols** such as a percent sign, comma, or dollar sign in your circled answer.

Unauthorized copying or reuse of any part of this page is illegal.

CONTINUE

501

1

What is 10% of 470?

A) 37

B) 47

C) 423

D) 460

2

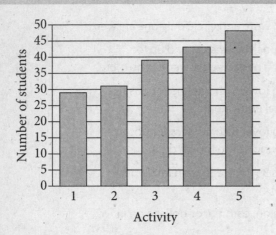

A group of students voted on five after-school activities. The bar graph shows the number of students who voted for each of the five activities. How many students chose activity 3?

A) 25

B) 39

C) 48

D) 50

3

$$4x + 5 = 165$$

What is the solution to the given equation?

4

A customer spent $27 to purchase oranges at $3 per pound. How many pounds of oranges did the customer purchase?

5

The function f is defined by $f(x) = 4x$. For what value of x does $f(x) = 8$?

6

The function g is defined by $g(x) = x^2 + 9$. For which value of x is $g(x) = 25$?

A) 4

B) 5

C) 9

D) 13

CONTINUE

7

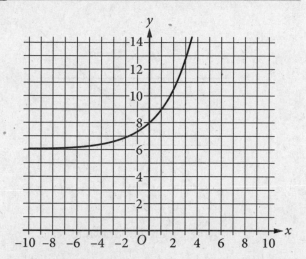

What is the *y*-intercept of the graph shown?

A) $(-8, 0)$

B) $(-6, 0)$

C) $(0, 6)$

D) $(0, 8)$

8

Sean rents a tent at a cost of $11 per day plus a onetime insurance fee of $10. Which equation represents the total cost *c*, in dollars, to rent the tent with insurance for *d* days?

A) $c = 11(d + 10)$

B) $c = 10(d + 11)$

C) $c = 11d + 10$

D) $c = 10d + 11$

9

Which expression is equivalent to $\dfrac{4}{4x - 5} - \dfrac{1}{x + 1}$?

A) $\dfrac{1}{(x + 1)(4x - 5)}$

B) $\dfrac{3}{3x - 6}$

C) $-\dfrac{1}{(x + 1)(4x - 5)}$

D) $\dfrac{9}{(x + 1)(4x - 5)}$

CONTINUE

10

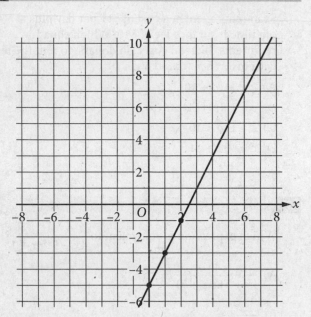

The graph shows the linear relationship between x and y. Which table gives three values of x and their corresponding values of y for this relationship?

A)

x	y
0	0
1	−7
2	−9

B)

x	y
0	0
1	−3
2	−1

C)

x	y
0	−5
1	−7
2	−9

D)

x	y
0	−5
1	−3
2	−1

11

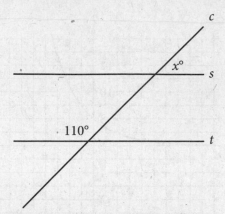

Note: Figure not drawn to scale.

In the figure shown, line c intersects parallel lines s and t. What is the value of x?

12

What is the perimeter, in inches, of a rectangle with a length of 4 inches and a width of 9 inches?

A) 13

B) 17

C) 22

D) 26

13

$$8j = k + 15m$$

The given equation relates the distinct positive numbers j, k, and m. Which equation correctly expresses j in terms of k and m?

A) $j = \dfrac{k}{8} + 15m$

B) $j = k + \dfrac{15m}{8}$

C) $j = 8(k + 15m)$

D) $j = \dfrac{k + 15m}{8}$

Unauthorized copying or reuse of any part of this page is illegal.

504

CONTINUE

14

The point (8, 2) in the *xy*-plane is a solution to which of the following systems of inequalities?

A) $x > 0$
$y > 0$

B) $x > 0$
$y < 0$

C) $x < 0$
$y > 0$

D) $x < 0$
$y < 0$

15

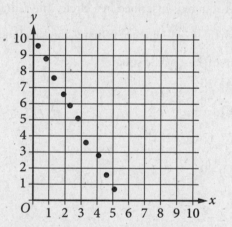

Which of the following equations is the most appropriate linear model for the data shown in the scatterplot?

A) $y = -1.9x - 10.1$

B) $y = -1.9x + 10.1$

C) $y = 1.9x - 10.1$

D) $y = 1.9x + 10.1$

16

A company opens an account with an initial balance of $36,100.00. The account earns interest, and no additional deposits or withdrawals are made. The account balance is given by an exponential function *A*, where $A(t)$ is the account balance, in dollars, *t* years after the account is opened. The account balance after 13 years is $68,071.93. Which equation could define *A*?

A) $A(t) = 36{,}100.00(1.05)^t$

B) $A(t) = 31{,}971.93(1.05)^t$

C) $A(t) = 31{,}971.93(0.05)^t$

D) $A(t) = 36{,}100.00(0.05)^t$

17

$$2|4 - x| + 3|4 - x| = 25$$

What is the positive solution to the given equation?

18

The expression $90y^5 - 54y^4$ is equivalent to $ry^4(15y - 9)$, where *r* is a constant. What is the value of *r*?

19

The area *A*, in square centimeters, of a rectangular cutting board can be represented by the expression $w(w + 9)$, where *w* is the width, in centimeters, of the cutting board. Which expression represents the length, in centimeters, of the cutting board?

A) $w(w + 9)$

B) w

C) 9

D) $(w + 9)$

CONTINUE

20

$$y > 13x - 18$$

For which of the following tables are all the values of x and their corresponding values of y solutions to the given inequality?

A)

x	y
3	21
5	47
8	86

B)

x	y
3	26
5	42
8	86

C)

x	y
3	16
5	42
8	81

D)

x	y
3	26
5	52
8	91

21

Function f is defined by $f(x) = (x + 6)(x + 5)(x + 1)$. Function g is defined by $g(x) = f(x - 1)$. The graph of $y = g(x)$ in the xy-plane has x-intercepts at $(a, 0)$, $(b, 0)$, and $(c, 0)$, where a, b, and c are distinct constants. What is the value of $a + b + c$?

A) -15

B) -9

C) 11

D) 15

22

A square is inscribed in a circle. The radius of the circle is $\frac{20\sqrt{2}}{2}$ inches. What is the side length, in inches, of the square?

A) 20

B) $\frac{20\sqrt{2}}{2}$

C) $20\sqrt{2}$

D) 40

STOP

If you finish before time is called, you may check your work on this module only.
Do not turn to any other module in the test.

The SAT

Practice Test #3

ANSWER EXPLANATIONS

These answer explanations are for students using
The Official Digital SAT Study Guide.

Reading and Writing

Module 1
(27 questions)

QUESTION 1

Choice B is the best answer because it most logically completes the text's discussion of Marilyn Dingle's baskets. In this context, to say that Dingle's baskets are "handmade from" particular plants means that Dingle creates baskets herself using those plants but without using machines. The text says that Dingle "skillfully winds" parts of palmetto palm plants around sweetgrass plants to make baskets with an appearance that "no factory can reproduce." This context suggests that Dingle's baskets are handmade from sweetgrass and palmetto palm.

Choice A is incorrect because the text describes how Dingle uses sweetgrass and palmetto palm to create her baskets, not how her baskets are "indicated by," or signified by, sweetgrass and palmetto palm. *Choice C* is incorrect. Although Dingle's baskets are described as being made using sweetgrass and palm, there's nothing in the text to suggest that the baskets are "represented by," or exemplified or portrayed by, sweetgrass and palmetto palm. Instead, the focus of the text is on Dingle's use of sweetgrass and palmetto palm and the impossibility of replicating the appearance of her baskets using machines. *Choice D* is incorrect because there's nothing in the text to suggest that Dingle's baskets are "collected with," or brought together in a group with, sweetgrass and palmetto palm. Instead, the text describes how Dingle uses those plants to make her baskets.

QUESTION 2

Choice D is the best answer because it logically completes the text's discussion about genes related to hibernation. In this context, "dormant" means inactive. The text explains that the same genes that enable certain nonhuman mammal species to hibernate during the winter by altering their bodily processes are also found in our species but have "essentially no effect" on humans' bodily processes. In other words, these genes don't function in humans.

Choice A is incorrect because in this context, "decisive" means has the power to affect the outcome of something, but the text states that genes related to hibernation are instead inactive in humans—that is, the genes don't affect humans' bodily processes, although they are present in their bodies. *Choice B* is incorrect because in this context, "lacking" means missing, but the text states that the genes are present in humans, though inactive. *Choice C* is incorrect because "variable" means characterized by the potential to change, but the text indicates that these genes don't change in their effect on humans' bodily processes; instead, the genes are consistently inactive in humans.

QUESTION 3

Choice C is the best answer because it most logically completes the discussion of the artist Diego Velázquez's influence outside Spain. As used in this context, "confined to" means restricted to. The text says that Velázquez was the leading artist in the Spanish court during the seventeenth century, but it also notes that other painters around the world were influenced by his techniques and style. Thus, Velázquez's influence was hardly (or almost not) confined to, or restricted to, Spain.

Choice A is incorrect because if Velázquez was a leading artist in Spain, it doesn't make logical sense to claim that his influence was hardly (or almost not) derived from, or obtained from, Spain. Moreover, the other painters around the world who employed Velázquez's techniques would by definition be influenced by Spanish style. *Choice B* is incorrect because if Velázquez was a leading artist in the court of King Philip IV of Spain, then his influence must have been widely recognized, or acknowledged, rather than being hardly (or almost not) recognized. *Choice D* is incorrect because the text gives no indication that deliberately limiting Velázquez's influence outside Spain was ever considered by anyone. Thus, even if it is true that his influence was not repressed, or restrained, it doesn't make logical sense to say so in this context.

QUESTION 4

Choice B is the best answer because it most logically completes the discussion of Octavia Butler's career. In this context, "impenetrable" means impossible to enter. The text indicates that the field of science fiction was dominated by white males when Butler, a Black woman, started writing, but she published several science fiction short stories and a novel and later won a prestigious award; that is, Butler pursued science fiction writing and had success. This context suggests that Butler didn't view the genre as impossible to enter.

Choice A is incorrect. In this context, "legitimate" would mean genuinely good or valid. Nothing in the text suggests that Butler didn't think the science fiction genre was good or valid; in fact, it indicates that she pursued and made a successful career of publishing work in that field. *Choice C* is incorrect. In this context, "compelling" would mean attracting or demanding attention. The text indicates that Butler chose to write science fiction, so it wouldn't make sense to say that she didn't see the field as drawing her attention. *Choice D* is incorrect. To say that Butler didn't consider science fiction "indecipherable," or impossible to understand, would suggest that Butler did understand it. However, the text doesn't address Butler's ability to interpret works in the genre; rather, it focuses on Butler's successful pursuit of writing science fiction.

QUESTION 5

Choice A is the best answer because as used in the text, "assumed" most nearly means acquired, or came to possess. The text portrays a character named Drowne carving a figure out of wood. At first "irregular and misty," or haphazard and indistinct, the figure's outline gradually showed "distincter grace and beauty" until the general design of the carved object "was now obvious to the common eye," or plainly recognizable to anyone. In other words, as Drowne continued to carve, the wooden object came to possess, or acquired, greater precision, changing from an indistinct outline or shape into a graceful, beautiful, and clearly recognizable form.

Choice B is incorrect. Although in some contexts "assumed" can mean acknowledged, or recognized, it doesn't have that meaning in this context because an inanimate object like the wooden figure can't acknowledge its own precision. *Choice C* is incorrect because there's nothing in the text to suggest that the wooden figure merely imitated, or mimicked, precision. Rather, the text suggests that as Drowne carved his wooden figure, it gradually became more precise. *Choice D* is incorrect. Although in some contexts "assumed" can mean speculated, or supposed based on incomplete information, it doesn't have that meaning in this context because an inanimate object like the wooden figure can't speculate about its own precision.

QUESTION 6

Choice D is the best answer because it best describes the overall structure of the text. The speaker begins by stating that he has heard that others are accusing him of seeking to destroy institutions. The speaker then addresses this criticism by stating that he is "neither for nor against institutions." Instead, the speaker states that his ultimate goal is to instill "the institution of the dear love of comrades" everywhere in the country. Therefore, the overall structure of the text is best described as an address of criticism followed by an announcement of a grand ambition.

Choice A is incorrect. While the speaker does address an opinion of him that he believes to be untrue, he doesn't indicate that this attitude has become increasingly prevalent. The speaker also concludes by explaining his goal for the future rather than his current worldview. *Choice B* is incorrect because the text doesn't portray the speaker as isolated or regretful, and the speaker gestures toward a hope for societal change but doesn't offer an explicit prediction that it will happen. *Choice C* is incorrect because the speaker addresses a criticism of him that he believes to be false; he doesn't admit any personal shortcomings. Moreover, the speaker concludes by stating a goal he has rather than showcasing his achievements.

QUESTION 7

Choice A is the best answer because it presents an explanation that is directly stated in the text for why ecologists are worried about Pando. The text states that Pando is a colony of about 47,000 quaking aspen trees that represents one of the largest organisms on Earth. According to the text, ecologists are worried that Pando's growth is declining, partly because animals are feeding on the trees. In other words, the ecologists are worried that Pando isn't growing at the same rate it used to.

Choice B is incorrect. Rather than indicating that Pando isn't producing young trees anymore, the text reveals that Pando is indeed producing young trees, stating that those trees can be protected from grazing deer by strong fences. *Choice C* is incorrect because the text states that fences can be used to prevent deer from eating Pando's young trees, not that Pando itself can't grow in new areas because it's blocked by fences. *Choice D* is incorrect because the text offers no evidence that Pando's root system is incapable of supporting new trees or is otherwise a cause of worry for ecologists.

QUESTION 8

Choice A is the best answer because It explains how the researchers determined the level of surprise displayed by the cats in the study. The text states that Saho Takagi and colleagues played recordings of the voice of each cat's owner and measured how surprised the cat was by the recording based on how it moved its ears and head.

Choice B is incorrect because, as the text explains, the recordings played for each cat in the study were of the voice of the cat's owner, not a stranger's voice. *Choice C* is incorrect because the text explains that during the study, the cats didn't interact directly with their owners; instead, the cats listened to recordings of their owners' voices. *Choice D* is incorrect because the text doesn't indicate that the researchers monitored the cats' movement around the room in which the study was conducted.

QUESTION 9

Choice A is the best answer because it most accurately states the main idea of the text. The text describes the book *Vibration Cooking: or, the Travel Notes of a Geechee Girl* as Smart-Grosvenor's "most influential project" and as "unusual for its time." The text also notes that the book and author have influenced contemporary approaches to writing about food and cooking. Therefore, the text mainly conveys that *Vibration Cooking: or, the Travel Notes of a Geechee Girl* is an unconventional and important contribution to food writing.

Choice B is incorrect. Although the text mentions that Smart-Grosvenor worked in national public television and radio and was a food writer, these details aren't the main focus. Rather than focusing on Smart-Grosvenor's various jobs, the text focuses specifically on one specific book she wrote. *Choice C* is incorrect. Although the text suggests that *Vibration Cooking: or, the Travel Notes of a Geechee Girl* was groundbreaking, it doesn't suggest that the book didn't receive praise when it was published. In fact, the text states that the book is "long admired." *Choice D* is incorrect because the text states that Smart-Grosvenor was a culinary anthropologist and that her book influenced later approaches to food writing but doesn't indicate that Smart-Grosvenor or her book influenced people to begin cooking for themselves.

QUESTION 10

Choice D is the best answer because it most effectively uses a quotation from *O Pioneers!* to illustrate the claim that Alexandra Bergson takes comfort in understanding the world around her. In the quotation, Alexandra is described as enjoying looking at the stars and feeling a "sense of personal security" when she contemplates nature's order and its governing laws. This suggests that Alexandra takes comfort in understanding the world around her.

Choice A is incorrect because the quotation expresses how Alexandra Bergson attempts to meet difficult situations with determination, not how she takes comfort in understanding the world around her. *Choice B* is incorrect because the quotation expresses "how much the country meant to" Alexandra Bergson, not how she takes comfort in understanding the world around her. In detailing some of the wildlife surrounding Alexandra, the quotation conveys that nature is important to her but not necessarily that it gives her comfort. *Choice C* is incorrect because the quotation describes Alexandra driving her wagon down a highway at night; it doesn't describe how she takes comfort in understanding the world around her or address how she's feeling as she drives off.

QUESTION 11

Choice A is the best answer because it presents the conclusion that most logically completes the text's discussion about the significance of the cupid found at Pompeii. The text indicates that the cupid is near a statue of a female figure who is fishing, and it goes on to indicate that because Venus is associated with cupids, some scholars believe the female figure to be the goddess Venus. But the text then says that, according to archaeologist Carla Brain, cupids may have also been associated with the activity of fishing, which, if true, would suggest that the mere appearance of a cupid near a female figure engaged in fishing does not indicate with certainty that the figure is Venus (that is, the cupid might be associated with fishing, and the figure might be anyone at all).

Choice B is incorrect because the text says nothing about how often Venus was depicted fishing in Roman art: it only implies that in certain instances a female figure may or may not be Venus. *Choice C* is incorrect because Carla Brain's proposed explanation for the presence of the cupids makes no reference to the female figure, and so the possibility that the figure in the artworks is in fact Venus cannot be definitively eliminated. *Choice D* is incorrect because there is nothing in the text to suggest that the only reasonable way to interpret the figure is as Venus.

QUESTION 12

Choice B is the best answer because it most logically completes the text's discussion of Anita Allen's argument about judges citing philosophers in their judicial opinions. The text indicates that judges sometimes cite philosophers when writing their judicial opinions and that, according to Allen, judges tend to cite philosophers whose views are in agreement with those of the judges themselves. Allen claims, however, that the best judicial opinions consider potential objections and rebut them, which suggests that judges may be able to strengthen their opinions by including discussions of philosophers with views contrary to their own.

Choice A is incorrect because Allen's claim is that judges could improve their judicial opinions by citing philosophers who disagree with the views expressed in the opinions, which would necessarily require judges to consult philosophical works. *Choice C* is incorrect because there's no discussion in the text about making judicial opinions more easily understood by any particular group of readers. The focus of the text is on Allen's claim that judicial opinions could be strengthened by the inclusion of discussions of philosophers whose views disagree with those of the judges authoring the opinions. *Choice D* is incorrect because the text presents Allen's argument that discussing philosophers whose views judges disagree with could strengthen judicial opinions, not that doing so could bring those opinions into line with views that are popular among philosophers.

QUESTION 13

Choice A is the best answer because it most logically completes the text's discussion of the relative appeal of different kinds of plays by Shakespeare to today's audiences. According to the text, Shakespeare's tragedies address broad themes that continue to appeal to today's audiences. Indeed, the text suggests that these themes are timeless, as illustrated by the example of *Romeo and Juliet*, which the text states is still read and widely performed despite being set in the Italy of Shakespeare's time. In contrast, the text indicates that audiences and readers may need to be familiar with several centuries of English history in order to understand Shakespeare's history plays. Because many theatergoers and readers are unlikely to possess such extensive historical knowledge, it follows that they are likely to find Shakespeare's history plays less engaging than his more accessible tragedies.

Choice B is incorrect because the text never introduces a comparison between Shakespeare's tragedies and twentieth-century plays, only between Shakespeare's tragedies and his history plays. Since twentieth-century plays aren't mentioned, there's no basis in the text for the idea that some of Shakespeare's tragedies are more relevant than twentieth-century plays to today's audiences. *Choice C* is incorrect. Although the text indicates that *Romeo and Juliet* is thematically accessible to today's audiences, it doesn't suggest that *Romeo and Juliet* is more accessible than Shakespeare's other tragedies. Rather, the text presents *Romeo and Juliet* as an example to support the idea that Shakespeare's tragedies hold continued appeal for today's readers and theatergoers. *Choice D* is incorrect. Although experts in English history would likely possess the knowledge needed to understand Shakespeare's history plays, the text never mentions such experts or suggests that they would enjoy the history plays more than Shakespeare's other works.

QUESTION 14

Choice C is the best answer. The convention being tested is punctuation between a main clause and a supplementary noun phrase. This choice correctly uses a comma to mark the boundary between the main clause ("scholar...materialism") and the supplementary noun phrase ("an apt assessment") that describes Waid's observation about how *The House of Mirth* depicts the upper classes of New York society.

Choice A is incorrect because a semicolon and the conjunction "and" can't be used in this way to mark the boundary between a main clause and a supplementary noun phrase. *Choice B* is incorrect. Joining the main clause ("scholar...materialism") and the following noun phrase with the conjunction "and" results in a confusing and illogical sentence that suggests that the novel depicts the upper classes of New York society as "an apt assessment," which doesn't make sense in this context. *Choice D* is incorrect because it fails to mark the boundary between the main clause and the supplementary noun phrase with appropriate punctuation.

QUESTION 15

Choice A is the best answer. The convention being tested is subject-modifier placement. This choice makes the noun phrase "researcher Robert Losey" the subject of the sentence and places it immediately after the modifying phrase "since...Siberia." In doing so, this choice clearly establishes that researcher Robert Losey—and not another noun in the sentence—is who uncovered fragments of a 2,000-year-old reindeer training harness in northern Siberia.

Choice B is incorrect because it results in a dangling modifier. The placement of the noun phrase "researcher Robert Losey's argument" immediately after the modifying phrase illogically suggests that the "argument" is what uncovered fragments of a 2,000-year-old reindeer training harness in northern Siberia. *Choice C* is incorrect because it results in a dangling modifier. The placement of the noun "domestication" immediately after the modifying phrase illogically suggests that "domestication" is what uncovered fragments of a 2,000-year-old reindeer training harness in northern Siberia. *Choice D* is incorrect because it results in a dangling modifier. The placement of the noun phrase "the argument" immediately after the modifying phrase illogically suggests that the "argument" is what uncovered fragments of a 2,000-year-old reindeer training harness in northern Siberia.

QUESTION 16

Choice D is the best answer. The convention being tested is punctuation between a supplementary phrase and a main clause. This choice correctly uses a comma to mark the boundary between the supplementary phrase ("A conceptual artist...world"), which describes Mary Ping, and the main clause ("Mary...America").

Choice A is incorrect because it fails to mark the boundary between the supplementary phrase ("A conceptual artist...world") and the main clause ("Mary...America") with appropriate punctuation. *Choice B* is incorrect because a colon can't be used in this way to join the supplementary phrase

("A conceptual artist...world") and the main clause ("Mary...America"). In this context, the colon incorrectly suggests that the information in the supplementary phrase is an explanation or amplification of the information in the main clause (Mary Ping being chosen to curate the exhibition), which isn't the case. *Choice C* is incorrect because a semicolon can't be used in this way to join the supplementary phrase ("A conceptual artist...world") and the main clause ("Mary...America"). Semicolons are conventionally used to separate two main clauses or to separate items in a complex series.

QUESTION 17

Choice D is the best answer. The convention being tested is subject-verb agreement and agreement between nouns. The singular verb "is" and the singular noun "version" both agree in number with the relative pronoun "which." In this context, "which" functions as a singular subject because it refers to the singular noun "the Nerf football."

Choice A is incorrect because the plural verb "were" doesn't agree in number with the singular noun phrase "the Nerf football" that it's modifying. *Choice B* is incorrect because the plural verb "are" and the plural noun "versions" don't agree in number with the singular noun phrase "the Nerf football" that they're modifying. *Choice C* is incorrect because the plural verb "were" and the plural noun "versions" don't agree in number with the singular noun phrase "the Nerf football" that they're modifying.

QUESTION 18

Choice D is the best answer. The convention being tested is punctuation use between two supplementary phrases following the coordinate clause ("but she...mycology"). This choice correctly uses a comma to mark the boundary between the supplementary noun phrase ("the study of fungi") that defines the term "mycology" and the supplementary participial phrase ("producing...London") that provides additional information about the extent to which Potter dedicated herself to mycology.

Choice A is incorrect because a semicolon can't be used in this way to join two supplementary phrases following a coordinate clause. *Choice B* is incorrect because it results in a rhetorically unacceptable sentence fragment beginning with "producing." *Choice C* is incorrect. The lack of punctuation results in a sentence that illogically suggests that the study of fungi is producing more than 350 paintings.

QUESTION 19

Choice C is the best answer. The convention being tested is subject-modifier placement. This choice makes the noun phrase "Julian's 1935 synthesis" the subject of the sentence and places it immediately after the modifying phrase "named...years." In doing so, this choice clearly establishes that Julian's 1935 synthesis of the alkaloid physostigmine—and not another noun in the sentence—was named in 1999 as one of the greatest achievements by a US chemist in the past hundred years.

Choice A is incorrect because it results in a dangling modifier. The placement of the noun "Julian" immediately after the modifying phrase illogically suggests that Julian himself was named as one of the greatest achievements by a US chemist in the past hundred years. *Choice B* is incorrect because it results in a dangling modifier. The placement of the prepositional phrase "in 1935" immediately after the modifying phrase illogically and confusingly suggests that "in 1935" was named as one of the greatest achievements by a US chemist in the past hundred years. *Choice D* is incorrect because it results in a dangling modifier. The placement of the noun phrase "the alkaloid physostigmine" immediately after the modifying phrase illogically and confusingly suggests that the alkaloid physostigmine itself (not the synthesis of it) was named as one of the greatest achievements by a US chemist in the past hundred years.

QUESTION 20

Choice C is the best answer. The convention being tested is punctuation use between sentences. In this choice, the period is used correctly to mark the boundary between the first sentence ("The...adjustments") and the second sentence ("Prior...days"). Because the adverbial phrase beginning with "prior" indicates when changing a spreadsheet required redoing the sheet by hand, that phrase belongs with the second sentence.

Choice A is incorrect because it results in a run-on sentence. Two sentences are fused without punctuation and/or a conjunction. *Choice B* is incorrect because it results in a comma splice. A comma can't be used in this way to mark the boundary between sentences. *Choice D* is incorrect. Without a comma preceding it, the conjunction "and" can't be used in this way to join the sentences.

QUESTION 21

Choice B is the best answer. "Next" logically signals that the action described in this sentence—Konkoly recording participants' eye movements—is the next step in Konkoly's experiment.

Choice A is incorrect because "specifically" illogically signals that this sentence specifies or elaborates on an aspect of the action described in the previous sentence. Instead, it describes the next step in Konkoly's experiment. *Choice C* is incorrect because "for instance" illogically signals that the action described in this sentence is an example of the action described in the previous sentence. Instead, it is the next step in Konkoly's experiment. *Choice D* is incorrect because "in sum" illogically signals that this sentence summarizes or concludes the action described in the previous sentence. Instead, it describes the next step in Konkoly's experiment.

QUESTION 22

Choice D is the best answer. "Second" logically signals that the information in this sentence—that the effort to bury the ship would likely only have been made for a king—joins the information in the previous sentence ("first...") in supporting Brunning's claim that the burial site was likely the tomb of a king.

Choice A is incorrect because "instead" illogically signals that the information in this sentence presents an alternative or substitute to the previous information about the gold artifacts inside the ship. Rather, this sentence presents a second piece of information that supports Brunning's claim. *Choice B* is incorrect because "still" illogically signals that the information in this sentence exists in contrast to or despite the previous information about the gold artifacts inside the ship. Instead, this sentence presents a second piece of information that supports Brunning's claim. *Choice C* is incorrect because "specifically" illogically signals that the information in this sentence specifies or elaborates on the previous information about the gold artifacts inside the ship. Instead, this sentence presents a second piece of information that supports Brunning's claim.

QUESTION 23

Choice C is the best answer. "Thus" logically signals that the action described in this sentence—the researcher being able to determine the chemical makeup of the planet's bright regions based on how they reflect light—is a result or consequence of the previous information about spectroscopic fingerprints.

Choice A is incorrect because "regardless" illogically signals that the action described in this sentence occurs despite the previous information about spectroscopic fingerprints. Instead, the finding in this sentence is a result or consequence of that information. *Choice B* is incorrect because "meanwhile" illogically signals that the action described in this sentence either occurs at the same time as or offers an alternative to the previous information about spectroscopic fingerprints. Instead, the finding in this sentence is a result or consequence of that information. *Choice D* is incorrect because "in comparison" illogically signals that the action described in this sentence is being compared with the previous information about spectroscopic fingerprints. Instead, the finding in this sentence is a result or consequence of that information.

QUESTION 24

Choice A is the best answer. The sentence emphasizes the significance of Ochoa's discovery, noting that it proved critical to deciphering the human genetic code, which resulted in a better understanding of how genetic variations affect human health.

Choice B is incorrect. While the sentence explains what Ochoa discovered, it doesn't emphasize the significance of the discovery. *Choice C* is incorrect. While the sentence explains what Ochoa discovered, it doesn't emphasize the significance of the discovery. *Choice D* is incorrect. While the sentence mentions that Ochoa's discovery was crucial, it emphasizes Ochoa's incorrect hypothesis, not the significance of the discovery.

QUESTION 25

Choice D is the best answer. The sentence uses "whereas" to contrast the emissivities of the two fibers, noting that the emissivity of the reflective metal fibers was just 0.02, far lower than that of the silicon carbide fibers (0.74).

Choice A is incorrect. The sentence emphasizes the ability of reflective metal fibers and silicon carbide fibers to emit heat; it doesn't contrast the emissivities of the two fibers. *Choice B* is incorrect. The sentence states a law of thermodynamics: the amount of heat a material absorbs is equal to the amount it emits. The sentence doesn't contrast the emissivity of reflective metal fibers with that of silicon carbide fibers. *Choice C* is incorrect. While the sentence includes a generalization about the emissivities of reflective metal fibers and silicon carbide fibers, it emphasizes Abebe's plans for their use in a garment; it doesn't contrast the emissivities of the two fibers.

QUESTION 26

Choice D is the best answer. The sentence presents the significance of the Hart-Celler Act to an audience unfamiliar with the history of US immigration, noting that the 1965 act abolished the national-origins quota system and explaining why that mattered, historically: because the old quota system had favored immigrants from northern Europe.

Choice A is incorrect. The sentence describes an aspect of immigration policy at the time the Hart-Celler Act was proposed; it doesn't present the significance of the Hart-Celler Act to an audience unfamiliar with the history of US immigration. *Choice B* is incorrect. The sentence describes an aspect of immigration policy before the Hart-Celler Act; it doesn't describe or present the significance of the act to an audience unfamiliar with the history of US immigration. *Choice C* is incorrect. While the sentence indicates that the Hart-Celler Act abolished the old quota system, it doesn't explain the act or the quota system to an audience unfamiliar with the history of US immigration.

QUESTION 27

Choice C is the best answer. The sentence explains an advantage of the "Women and the Vote" format, noting that the format appealed to audiences because it allowed them to control the experience.

Choice A is incorrect. The sentence describes a digital drawing on the "Women and the Vote" website; it doesn't explain an advantage of the play's format. *Choice B* is incorrect. The sentence explains how audiences interacted with the "Women and the Vote" website; it doesn't explain an advantage of the play's format. *Choice D* is incorrect. While the sentence mentions that "Women and the Vote" had an interactive format, it doesn't explain what advantage this format might have.

Reading and Writing

Module 2
(27 questions)

QUESTION 1

Choice B is the best answer because it most logically completes the text's discussion of Jacob Lawrence's artistic process. In this context, "observant" means watchful and perceptive. The text emphasizes that the "close attention" Lawrence paid to "all the details" of his neighborhood allowed him to reflect subtle elements of "the beauty and vitality of the Black experience" in his artwork. This context indicates that being observant of his surroundings was an important part of Lawrence's work as an artist.

Choice A is incorrect because the text gives no indication that Lawrence was "skeptical," or had an attitude of doubt in general or about particular things, let alone that skepticism was important to him as an artist. Rather than indicating that he was skeptical, the text focuses on how Lawrence paid careful attention to everything around him and reflected his observations in his artwork. *Choice C* is incorrect because the text gives no indication that Lawrence was "critical," which in this context would mean inclined to criticize harshly or unfairly. Rather than indicating that Lawrence found fault in things, the text suggests that he paid careful attention to everything around him and that his artwork reflects this careful attention. *Choice D* is incorrect because the text doesn't suggest that Lawrence was "confident," or self-assured. Rather than addressing how Lawrence felt about himself and how that feeling affected his artistic process, the text emphasizes the careful attention Lawrence paid to everything around him—attention that allowed him to capture subtle elements of a particular place and time in his artwork.

QUESTION 2

Choice B is the best answer because it most logically completes the text's discussion of the work of particle physicists. In this context, "inspecting" means viewing closely in order to examine. The text indicates that as particle physicists, Arce and El-Khadra's work involves using advanced technology to "closely examine" subatomic particles. In other words, they use technology to inspect small parts of matter that can't be seen by the naked eye.

Choice A is incorrect because nothing in the text suggests that Arce and El-Khadra spend time "selecting," or choosing, subatomic particles for some purpose; the text simply states that the particle physicists use advanced technology to see and study the behavior of those tiny parts of matter. *Choice C* is incorrect because nothing in the text suggests that Arce and El-Khadra spend time "creating" subatomic particles, or bringing them into existence; the text simply states that the particle physicists use advanced technology to see and study the behavior of those tiny parts of matter. *Choice D is incorrect.* In this context, "deciding" would mean making a final choice or judgment about something. It wouldn't make sense to say that particle physicists get to choose what is and isn't visible to the naked eye, especially when the text presents it as fact that subatomic particles are "the smallest detectable parts of matter" and would therefore be invisible. The text focuses on Arce and El-Khadra's close observation of those particles, not on any decisions they might make.

QUESTION 3

Choice C is the best answer because it most logically completes the text's discussion of Annie Dodge Wauneka's work as a Navajo Nation legislator. As used in this context, "persistent" means existing continuously. The text states that Wauneka "continuously worked to promote public health," traveling extensively and authoring a medical dictionary; this indicates that Wauneka's effort was persistent.

Choice A is incorrect because describing Wauneka's effort related to public health as "impartial," or not partial or biased and treating all things equally, wouldn't make sense in context. The text suggests that Wauneka's continuous work was partial in one way, as she focused specifically on promoting public health throughout the Navajo homeland and to speakers of the Navajo language. *Choice B is incorrect* because the text emphasizes that Wauneka's effort to promote public health as a Navajo Nation legislator was continuous and extensive, involving wide travels and the authoring of a medical dictionary. Because this work clearly involved care and dedication, it wouldn't make sense to describe it as "offhand," or casual and informal. *Choice D is incorrect* because nothing in the text suggests that Wauneka's effort to promote public health was "mandatory," or required by law or rule, even though Wauneka was a Navajo Nation legislator. Rather than suggesting that Wauneka's effort was required for any reason, the text emphasizes the continuous and extensive nature of her work.

QUESTION 4

Choice B is the best answer because it most logically completes the text's discussion about recycling plastics. In this context, "inadequate" means not satisfactory. The text indicates that the mechanical plastic-recycling process affects the environment and causes "the loss of material quality." The text contrasts that with Chazovachii's chemical plastic-recycling process, which is cleaner and produces a desirable product. The text's emphasis on the negative aspects of mechanical recycling suggests that it is inadequate in terms of environmental impact and the quality of the material the process yields.

Choice A is incorrect because in this context "resilient" would mean able to withstand difficulty and the text does not characterize the plastic-recycling process as having this quality or describe any difficulties that these processes might need to overcome. *Choice C is incorrect* because in this context "dynamic" would mean constantly changing. Although the text suggests that there have been changes in the field of recycling, as is the case with the advent of Chazovachii's chemical recycling process, there is nothing to suggest that the mechanical process itself has changed or is prone to change. *Choice D is incorrect* because in this context "satisfactory" would mean acceptable but not perfect. The text mentions only shortcomings of the mechanical process (environmental effects and lower material quality), so the text more strongly supports a negative view of this process and provides no evidence that it would be considered satisfactory.

QUESTION 5

Choice D is the best answer because it most logically completes the text's discussion of Jemisin's writing. In this context, "conform to" means to act in accordance with something. The text suggests that in her science fiction writing, Jemisin's willingness to go against expectations and not use plots and themes that seem to follow a formula reflects how she treats the standard practices of the genre. This context conveys that Jemisin chooses not to act in accordance with those conventions.

Choice A is incorrect. In this context, "question" would mean doubt or object to. The text indicates that Jemisin is willing to go against expectations and not use formulaic plots and themes in her science fiction writing, suggesting that she may actually object to those conventions of the genre, not that she chooses not to question them. *Choice B* is incorrect because the text indicates that in her science fiction writing, Jemisin is willing to go against expectations and not use formulaic plots and themes. Rather than suggesting that Jemisin chooses not to "react to," or act in response to, the standard practices of the genre, this context suggests that she is acting in response to such conventions by deliberately avoiding them. *Choice C* is incorrect. In this context, "perceive" would mean become aware of or understand. The text indicates that in her science fiction writing, Jemisin is willing to go against expectations and not use formulaic plots and themes. This context conveys that Jemisin is aware of and deliberately avoids those conventions of the genre, not that she chooses not to be aware of them.

QUESTION 6

Choice A is the best answer because it most logically completes the text's discussion of letters allegedly exchanged between President Lincoln and Rutledge. In this context, "validate" means to confirm that something is real or correct. According to the text, it was alleged, or claimed, that the newly discovered letters had been written by Lincoln and Rutledge. The text also indicates that historians ultimately decided the letters were a hoax, or fraudulent. This context suggests that the historians couldn't confirm that the letters were authentic.

Choice B is incorrect. The text focuses on the authenticity of the letters, which were claimed to have been written by Lincoln and Rutledge and were then quickly dismissed as fraudulent by historians. Rather than conveying that the historians simply weren't able to "interpret," or explain in an understandable way, the letters' authenticity, the text suggests that the historians decided the letters lacked authenticity altogether. *Choice C* is incorrect. The text states that the historians quickly dismissed the letters claimed to have been written by Lincoln and Rutledge as fraudulent; this suggests that rather than being unable to "relate," or tell others about, the letters' authenticity, the historians were able to share what they'd decided about the letters. *Choice D* is incorrect because it wouldn't make sense to suggest that the historians couldn't "accommodate," or give consideration to, the authenticity of the letters claimed to have been written by Lincoln and Rutledge; the text states that the historians decided that the letters were fraudulent, which indicates that they *did* consider whether the letters were authentic.

QUESTION 7

Choice D is the best answer because it accurately states the text's main purpose. The poem begins with the speaker urging a child to "go forth" with her encouragement ("my heart's desire"). The speaker goes on to suggest that new experiences ("Great reaches, yet unknown") lie ahead for the son that "life is calling" him to seek out. Thus, the main purpose is to encourage a child to embrace the experiences available to him in his life.

Choice A is incorrect because the speaker encourages the child to pursue new experiences ("Great reaches") without knowing exactly what those experiences will be ("yet unknown") or suggesting that they should match the speaker's own accomplishments. *Choice B* is incorrect because the speaker focuses on positive possibilities for her son ("Great reaches, yet unknown") and her enthusiastic encouragement to embrace those possibilities ("life is calling you!"), while there is no mention of raising a child or associated struggles. *Choice C* is incorrect because the speaker frames the possibilities for her son in a positive light when she says that "great reaches, yet unknown" are waiting for him, and this positive outlook for the son is consistent throughout the text.

QUESTION 8

Choice A is the best answer because it most accurately states the main purpose of the text. After providing a brief introduction to computer scientist Luis von Ahn, the text focuses on discussing how von Ahn's digitization work led to the invention of a digital security test known as reCAPTCHA.

Choice B is incorrect because the text doesn't address how digital scanners work. *Choice C* is incorrect. Although the text mentions von Ahn's book-digitizing project, that information is provided as a detail, not as the main purpose of the text. *Choice D* is incorrect because the text doesn't provide any indication of reCAPTCHA's popularity; instead, it describes reCAPTCHA's origin.

QUESTION 9

Choice A is the best answer because it reflects what the paleontologists in Text 2 would most likely say about what the researchers in Text 1 initially thought. Text 1 focuses on the discovery of a strange fossil consisting of the skull of the extinct species *Oculudentavis khaungraae*. According to Text 1, the fossil has features that appear to be avian, or related to birds, which led researchers to initially think that the fossil might be a very small avian dinosaur. Text 2 begins by noting the discovery of a second fossil similar to the one discussed in Text 1, then explains that based on detailed studies of both fossils, paleontologists think that the two creatures were probably unusual lizards, even though the skulls appeared avian at first. This suggests that the paleontologists in Text 2 recognize that the fossils do indeed look like they could be related to birds. For this reason, the paleontologists in Text 2 would most likely say that the initial thought of the researchers in Text 1—that the fossil was avian—is understandable, even if the fossil is probably not avian but rather is from a lizard.

Choice B is incorrect because Text 2 indicates that the fossils initially looked avian, so the paleontologists described in Text 2 wouldn't be confused by the researchers in Text 1 initially thinking that *O. khaungraae* might be related to birds. The paleontologists would find that initial thought understandable, not confusing. *Choice C* is incorrect because Text 1 never mentions lizards, so it wouldn't make sense for the paleontologists in Text 2 to say that the researchers in Text 1 mistakenly assumed that *O. khaungraae* must be a lizard. *Choice D* is incorrect. Although the paleontologists in Text 2 might agree that the initial thought of the researchers in Text 1 was reasonable, nothing in Text 2 suggests that the two skulls were shaped differently.

QUESTION 10

Choice C is the best answer because it presents a description of how the human mind is like a flower that is directly supported by the text. The text compares the needs of a "fragile and lovely flower" to those of the speaker's "tender mind": both need to be fed if they're going to survive. Without such feeding, they'll "beginneth straightway to languish," or weaken. Thus, the text suggests that the human mind is like a flower in that they both need proper nourishment in order to thrive.

Choice A is incorrect because the text doesn't address the passage of time or describe either the human mind or a flower as becoming increasingly vigorous. *Choice B* is incorrect because the text doesn't suggest that human minds or flowers draw strength from changes in weather. The references to rain in the text pertain to a flower's need for water rather than the general effects of changing weather. *Choice D* is incorrect because the text doesn't suggest that the human mind or a flower will persist regardless of challenging circumstances. In fact, the text indicates that they'll both languish right away if not given what they need.

QUESTION 11

Choice C is the best answer because it most effectively uses data from the table to complete the statement about the forestry student's project. The table shows five types of maple trees, each tree's maximum height, and whether each tree is native to North America. The text indicates that the student needs to recommend a maple tree that's native to North America and won't reach a height greater than 60 feet. The red maple is the only tree listed in the table that meets these criteria: its maximum height is 60 feet—meaning that it won't grow higher than 60 feet—and it's native to North America.

Choice A is incorrect because the text states that the student needs to recommend a tree that's native to North America and won't grow higher than 60 feet, but the table shows that the maximum height of the silver maple is 70 feet. *Choice B* is incorrect because the text states that the student needs to recommend a tree that's native to North America and won't grow higher than 60 feet, but the table shows that the maximum height of the sugar maple is 75 feet. *Choice D* is incorrect because the text states that the student needs to recommend a tree that's native to North America and won't grow higher than 60 feet, but the table shows that the Norway maple isn't native to North America.

QUESTION 12

Choice C is the best answer because it would most directly support the student's claim about the motivation for including explanatory notes with the stand-alone volume of the poem. The text explains that the poem had previously been published without the notes in a quarterly journal. It stands to reason that readers who had purchased the journal issue containing the poem would be unlikely to purchase an unchanged version of the poem in a stand-alone volume. However, the inclusion of notes in that volume would encourage the purchase of a stand-alone volume, since the later text would differ from the original by including the author's own explanation of the poem. Therefore, if it were true that the publishers of the stand-alone volume had requested the notes to make the book attractive to readers who already had a copy of the journal issue, this fact would support the student's claim that the notes were included primarily as a marketing device.

Choice A is incorrect because the student's claim is about the motivation for including the explanatory notes in the stand-alone volume, not about changes that might have been made to the poem itself for publication in that volume; moreover, the text never suggests that such changes were made. *Choice B* is incorrect because the student's claim is about why the explanatory notes were included in the stand-alone volume, not about how the notes affected readers' and critics' subsequent experience of the poem. *Choice D* is incorrect because the fact that the poet drafted multiple versions of the explanatory notes doesn't directly address the issue of whether the notes were intended as a marketing device, as the student claims; the correspondence would support this claim only if it showed that the poet had revised the notes specifically to make them useful to the marketing of the stand-alone volume.

QUESTION 13

Choice B is the best answer because it most effectively illustrates the claim that Amal imagines the people he sees are carefree even when engaged in work. In the quotation, Amal observes that the flower seller's daughter is "flower gathering," or working, as the text indicates. Moreover, Amal notes that the daughter's feet "seem so glad" and her "anklets jingle so merrily," suggesting that Amal believes that the flower seller's daughter is cheerful.

Choice A is incorrect because the quotation makes no observation about the cheerful mood of the flower seller's daughter. *Choice C* is incorrect because the quotation discusses how Amal envisions his future, not the feelings of the flower seller's daughter. *Choice D* is incorrect because the quotation discusses Amal's wishes, not the feelings of the flower seller's daughter.

QUESTION 14

Choice D is the best answer because it accurately describes data from the table that support Rodriguez and colleagues' assertion about the classifications of the five new gas exoplanets. The text describes two categories of gas planets: hot Jupiters, which have a mass of at least 0.25 Jupiters and an orbital period of less than 10 days, and warm Jupiters, which have the same mass characteristic but have orbital periods of more than 10 days. According to the table, four of the gas exoplanets discovered by Rodriguez and colleagues have a mass of at least 0.25 Jupiters and an orbital period of less than 10 days, while one of the planets has a mass of at least 0.25 Jupiters and an orbital period of more than 10 days. These data therefore support Rodriguez and colleagues' assertion that four of the new exoplanets are hot Jupiters and one is a warm Jupiter.

Choice A is incorrect because it doesn't accurately describe the data from the table. Although the table shows that TOI-628 b has a mass equivalent to 6.33 Jupiters, the table also shows that one of the planets—TOI-1478 b—does indeed have an orbital period of more than 10 days. *Choice B* is incorrect because it doesn't accurately describe the data from the table. Although the table does show that the masses of the five planets range from 0.85 to 6.33 Jupiters, the table also shows that TOI-1478 b has an orbital period of 10.180 days, not 153 days. *Choice C* is incorrect. According to the table, TOI-1333 b has an orbital period of only 4.720 days, not more than 10 days. Additionally, although the table does show that all the planets have a radius between 1.060 and 1.771 Jupiters, the text indicates that a planet may be classified as a hot Jupiter or a warm Jupiter based on its mass and orbital period, not on its radius, making the information about the range of the five planets' radius values irrelevant.

QUESTION 15

Choice A is the best answer because it uses data from the graph to effectively support Charles and Stephens's claim about how level of information affects voters. The graph shows the probability of voting for both high- and low-information voters in seven categories of political orientation. Charles and Stephens claim that "the more informed voters are about politics...the more likely they are to vote." This statement correctly asserts that the graph shows a higher probability of voting for high-information voters than for low-information voters at each of the seven political orientations. Thus, this statement accurately cites data from the graph that support Charles and Stephens's claim about how level of information affects voters.

Choice B is incorrect. Although this statement is correct that the only probability in the graph below 50% is for low-information voters categorized as independent (orientation 4), the claim in question is about the relative likelihood that low- and high-information voters will vote, and without some reference to high-information voters, this statement cannot help support such a comparison. *Choice C* is incorrect. Although this statement is correct that the highest probabilities of voting for low-information voters are at the ends of the orientation scale (1 and 7), the claim in question is about the relative likelihood that low- and high-information voters will vote, and without some reference to high-information voters, this statement cannot help support such a comparison. *Choice D* is incorrect because the graph does not give any information about how many people are represented in any of the categories, so this statement is not based on data from the graph. Furthermore, even if we did have this information, the claim is about how level of information affects voters' probability of voting, not whether they're likely to strongly identify with a particular political party.

QUESTION 16

Choice D is the best answer because it presents a finding that, if true, would support the researchers' prediction about the language nest model of education. The text states that Morcom and Roy studied the effects of the language nest model of education on students at an Anishinaabe school, and they found that the model—which is used with students during pre-K or elementary school—increased students' fluency in the Anishinaabe language and pride in Anishinaabe culture. The researchers predicted that the students' positive early experiences with the Anishinaabe language would lead them to be more likely to later share the language with younger generations. If former students maintain full fluency and cultural pride after finishing secondary and higher education, it follows that they would be both able and motivated to share what they know with others; this would likely result in a higher probability of transmitting the language to younger generations, as the researchers predict.

Choice A is incorrect because finding that Anishinaabe adults who didn't attend the school feel approximately the same degree of cultural pride as those adults who did attend wouldn't support the researchers' prediction that former students will be more likely to share their knowledge with younger generations. This finding would identify a similarity between the groups rather than a factor that might make former students more likely than other adults to transmit the language to younger people. *Choice B* is incorrect because finding that new students experience increased performance in language fluency and academics would suggest that the school has a positive effect on students when they attended but wouldn't reveal anything about those students' later actions as adults (such as their likelihood of sharing their knowledge with younger generations). *Choice C* is incorrect because finding that Anishinaabe adults who attended the school are equally likely to stay in the community as adults who didn't attend the school wouldn't support the researchers' prediction that former students will be more likely to share their knowledge with younger generations. This finding would identify a similarity between the groups rather than a factor that might make former students more likely than other adults to transmit the language to younger people.

QUESTION 17

Choice A is the best answer because it most accurately describes Gibson's approach to art. As the text explains, Gibson, who is Cherokee and Choctaw, transforms punching bags into art pieces by applying (or attaching) to them beadwork and elements of Native dressmaking, including leather fringe and the jingles of the jingle dress. The text goes on to say that in most Native communities, the art forms of beadwork and dressmaking are traditionally practiced by women. Therefore, Gibson's approach to art consists of creating original works by drawing from traditional Native art forms.

Choice B is incorrect because the text doesn't indicate that Gibson designs dresses influenced by boxing but instead that he turns punching bags, which are used in boxing, into works of art by applying elements of Native dressmaking to them. *Choice C* is incorrect. Although Gibson does incorporate beadwork into his art, the text never mentions the colors or patterns that he uses or suggests that his art defies the expectations that people might have about color and pattern in beadwork. *Choice D* is incorrect. Because Gibson incorporates Native art forms into his own original artwork, it can be inferred that he has been influenced by other Native artists, but the text never suggests that non-Native artists have influenced him.

QUESTION 18

Choice B is the best answer. The convention being tested is finite and nonfinite verb forms within a sentence. A main clause requires a finite verb to perform the action of the subject (in this case, "people in the Americas"), and this choice supplies the finite past perfect tense verb "have used" to indicate what people in the Americas used the gourd for.

Choice A is incorrect because the nonfinite to-infinitive "to use" doesn't supply the main clause with a finite verb. *Choice C* is incorrect because the nonfinite participle "having used" doesn't supply the main clause with a finite verb. *Choice D* is incorrect because the nonfinite participle "using" doesn't supply the main clause with a finite verb.

QUESTION 19

Choice B is the best answer. The convention being tested is the coordination of main clauses within a sentence. This choice correctly uses a comma and the coordinating conjunction "but" to join the first main clause ("the Alvarez...out") and the second main clause ("it left...extinctions").

Choice A is incorrect because when coordinating two longer main clauses such as these, it's conventional to use a comma before the coordinating conjunction. *Choice C* is incorrect because it results in a run-on sentence. The two main clauses are fused without punctuation and/or a conjunction. *Choice D* is incorrect because it results in a comma splice. Without a conjunction following it, a comma can't be used in this way to join two main clauses.

QUESTION 20

Choice A is the best answer. The convention being tested is finite and nonfinite verb forms within a sentence. A main clause requires a finite verb to perform the action of the subject (in this case, "embryos"), and this choice supplies the clause with the finite present tense verb "enter" to indicate how the embryos achieve diapause.

Choice B is incorrect because the nonfinite to-infinitive "to enter" doesn't supply the main clause with a finite verb. *Choice C* is incorrect because the nonfinite participle "having entered" doesn't supply the main clause with a finite verb. *Choice D* is incorrect because the nonfinite participle "entering" doesn't supply the main clause with a finite verb.

QUESTION 21

Choice D is the best answer. The convention being tested is the use of verbs to express tense. In this choice, the present tense verb "is," used in conjunction with the word "today," correctly indicates that Paik is currently considered the first video artist.

Choice A is incorrect because the future-indicating verb "will be" doesn't indicate that Paik is currently considered the first video artist. *Choice B* is incorrect because the past perfect tense verb "had been" doesn't indicate that Paik is currently considered the first video artist. *Choice C* is incorrect because the past tense verb "was" doesn't indicate that Paik is currently considered the first video artist.

QUESTION 22

Choice D is the best answer. The convention being tested is punctuation between a verb and a preposition. When, as in this case, a verb ("is added") is immediately followed by a preposition ("whenever"), no punctuation is needed.

Choice A is incorrect because no punctuation is needed between the verb and the preposition. *Choice B* is incorrect because no punctuation is needed between the verb and the preposition. *Choice C* is incorrect because no punctuation is needed between the verb and the preposition.

QUESTION 23

Choice D is the best answer. The convention being tested is the use of verbs to express tense. In this choice, the present tense verb "survives" correctly indicates that the wood frog regularly survives subfreezing temperatures by producing large amounts of glucose.

Choice A is incorrect because the past perfect verb "had survived" doesn't indicate that the wood frog regularly survives subfreezing temperatures by producing large amounts of glucose. *Choice B* is incorrect because the past tense verb "survived" doesn't indicate that the wood frog regularly survives subfreezing temperatures by producing large amounts of glucose. *Choice C* is incorrect because the conditional verb "would survive" doesn't indicate that the wood frog regularly survives subfreezing temperatures by producing large amounts of glucose.

QUESTION 24

Choice A is the best answer. "Meanwhile" logically signals that the action described in this sentence (Obinze's move to London to pursue a career) is simultaneous with the action described in the previous sentence (Ifemelu's move to the United States). The first sentence establishes that the actions take place around the same time, referring to the characters' "divergent experiences" following high school.

Choice B is incorrect because "nevertheless" illogically signals that the information in this sentence about Obinze's move to London is true despite the previous information about Ifemelu's move to the United States. Instead, as the first sentence establishes, Obinze's move and Ifemelu's move are related, parallel experiences that occur around the same time. *Choice C* is incorrect because "secondly" illogically signals that the information in this sentence is a second point or reason separate from the previous information about Ifemelu's move to the United States. Instead, as the first sentence establishes, Obinze's move and Ifemelu's move are related, parallel experiences that occur around the same time. *Choice D* is incorrect because "in fact" illogically signals that the information in this sentence emphasizes, modifies, or contradicts the previous information about Ifemelu's move to the United States. Instead, as the first sentence establishes, Obinze's move and Ifemelu's move are related, parallel experiences that occur around the same time.

QUESTION 25

Choice C is the best answer. "Similarly" logically signals that the activity described in this sentence (Nancy Tuttle Craig distributing Votes for Women Tea in her Los Angeles grocery stores) is like the activity described in the previous sentence (the Woman's Suffrage Party selling Equality Tea at fairs in San Francisco). Together, the two examples support the preceding claim that "activists across the state sold tea to promote the cause of suffrage."

Choice A is incorrect because "for example" illogically signals that the activity described in this sentence exemplifies the activity described in the previous sentence. Instead, the two activities are similar, and both support the preceding claim about selling tea to promote women's right to vote. *Choice B* is incorrect because "to conclude" illogically signals that the activity described in this sentence concludes or summarizes the information in the previous sentences. Instead, the activity is similar to the one described in the previous sentence, and both support the preceding claim about selling tea to promote women's right to vote. *Choice D* is incorrect because "in other words" illogically signals that the activity described in this sentence paraphrases the activity described in the previous sentence. Instead, the two activities are similar, and both support the preceding claim about selling tea to promote women's right to vote.

QUESTION 26

Choice B is the best answer. The sentence effectively explains an advantage of infilling: it's less invasive than using a power grinder.

Choice A is incorrect. The sentence identifies a disadvantage of power grinding; it doesn't explain an advantage of infilling. *Choice C* is incorrect. The sentence identifies the two techniques park rangers use; it doesn't explain an advantage of infilling. *Choice D* is incorrect. The sentence indicates that power grinding and infilling are different in one aspect; it fails to explain an advantage of infilling.

QUESTION 27

Choice D is the best answer. The sentence effectively describes *Unwoven Light* to an audience unfamiliar with Park, noting that Soo Sunny Park is a Korean American artist and that the 2013 work consists of colorful prisms formed by light passing through iridescent tiles.

Choice A is incorrect. The sentence describes aspects of *Unwoven Light* but doesn't mention who Park is; it thus doesn't effectively describe the work to an audience unfamiliar with Park. *Choice B* is incorrect. Although the sentence indicates when the work was created and who Park is, it lacks descriptive details and thus doesn't effectively describe *Unwoven Light*. *Choice C* is incorrect. The sentence mentions Park and describes an aspect of *Unwoven Light*—the chain-link fence—but doesn't effectively describe the overall work to an audience unfamiliar with the artist.

Math

Module 1
(22 questions)

QUESTION 1

Choice C is correct. It's given that t represents the number of seconds after the bus passes the marker. Substituting 2 for t in the given equation $d = 30t$ yields $d = 30(2)$, or $d = 60$. Therefore, the bus will be 60 feet from the marker 2 seconds after passing it.

Choice A is incorrect. This is the distance, in feet, the bus will be from the marker 1 second, not 2 seconds, after passing it. *Choice B* is incorrect and may result from conceptual or calculation errors. *Choice D* is incorrect. This is the distance, in feet, the bus will be from the marker 3 seconds, not 2 seconds, after passing it.

QUESTION 2

Choice D is correct. The equation of a line in the xy-plane can be written as $y = mx + b$, where m represents the slope of the line and $(0, b)$ represents the y-intercept of the line. It's given that the slope of the line is $\frac{1}{9}$. It follows that $m = \frac{1}{9}$. It's also given that the line passes through the point $(0, 14)$. It follows that $b = 14$. Substituting $\frac{1}{9}$ for m and 14 for b in $y = mx + b$ yields $y = \frac{1}{9}x + 14$. Thus, the equation $y = \frac{1}{9}x + 14$ represents this line.

Choice A is incorrect. This equation represents a line with a slope of $-\frac{1}{9}$ and a y-intercept of $(0, -14)$. *Choice B* is incorrect. This equation represents a line with a slope of $-\frac{1}{9}$ and a y-intercept of $(0, 14)$. *Choice C* is incorrect. This equation represents a line with a slope of $\frac{1}{9}$ and a y-intercept of $(0, -14)$.

QUESTION 3

The correct answer is $\frac{1}{5}$. Since the number 5 can also be written as $\frac{5}{1}$, the given equation can also be written as $\frac{x}{8} = \frac{5}{1}$. This equation is equivalent to $\frac{8}{x} = \frac{1}{5}$. Therefore, the value of $\frac{8}{x}$ is $\frac{1}{5}$. Note that 1/5 and .2 are examples of ways to enter a correct answer.

Alternate approach: Multiplying both sides of the equation $\frac{x}{8} = 5$ by 8 yields $x = 40$. Substituting 40 for x into the expression $\frac{8}{x}$ yields $\frac{8}{40}$, or $\frac{1}{5}$.

QUESTION 4

Choice B is correct. It's given that triangle *ABC* is congruent to triangle *DEF*. Corresponding angles of congruent triangles are congruent and, therefore, have equal measure. It's given that angle *A* corresponds to angle *D*, and that the measure of angle *A* is 18°. It's also given that the measures of angles *B* and *E* are 90°. Since these angles have equal measure, they are corresponding angles. It follows that angle *C* corresponds to angle *F*. Let $x°$ represent the measure of angle *C*. Since the sum of the measures of the interior angles of a triangle is 180°, it follows that $18° + 90° + x° = 180°$, or $108° + x° = 180°$. Subtracting 108° from both sides of this equation yields $x° = 72°$. Therefore, the measure of angle *C* is 72°. Since angle *C* corresponds to angle *F*, it follows that the measure of angle *F* is also 72°.

Choice A is incorrect. This is the measure of angle *D*, not the measure of angle *F*. *Choice C* is incorrect. This is the measure of angle *E*, not the measure of angle *F*. *Choice D* is incorrect. This is the sum of the measures of angles *E* and *F*, not the measure of angle *F*.

QUESTION 5

Choice B is correct. Applying the commutative property of multiplication, the expression $(m^4 q^4 z^{-1})(mq^5 z^3)$ can be rewritten as $(m^4 m)(q^4 q^5)(z^{-1} z^3)$. For positive values of x, $(x^a)(x^b) = x^{a+b}$. Therefore, the expression $(m^4 m)(q^4 q^5)(z^{-1} z^3)$ can be rewritten as $(m^{4+1})(q^{4+5})(z^{-1+3})$, or $m^5 q^9 z^2$.

Choice A is incorrect and may result from multiplying, not adding, the exponents. *Choice C* is incorrect and may result from conceptual or calculation errors. *Choice D* is incorrect and may result from conceptual or calculation errors.

QUESTION 6

Choice C is correct. The median of a data set represented in a box plot is represented by the vertical line within the box. It follows that the median mass of the gazelles in group 1 is 25 kilograms, and the median mass of the gazelles in group 2 is 24 kilograms. Since 25 kilograms is greater than 24 kilograms, the median mass of group 1 is greater than the median mass of group 2.

Choice A is incorrect. The mean mass of each of the two groups cannot be determined from the box plots. *Choice B* is incorrect. The mean mass of each of the two groups cannot be determined from the box plots. *Choice D* is incorrect and may result from conceptual or calculation errors.

QUESTION 7

Choice B is correct. Since the point (x, y) is an intersection point of the graphs of the given equations in the *xy*-plane, the pair (x, y) should satisfy both equations, and thus is a solution of the given system. According to the first equation, $y = 76$. Substituting 76 in place of y in the second equation yields $x^2 - 5 = 76$. Adding 5 to both sides of this equation yields $x^2 = 81$. Taking the square root of both sides of this equation yields two solutions: $x = 9$ and $x = -9$. Of these two solutions, only −9 is given as a choice.

Choice A is incorrect and may result from conceptual or calculation errors. Choice C is incorrect and may result from conceptual or calculation errors. Choice D is incorrect. This is the value of coordinate y, rather than x, of the intersection point (x, y).

QUESTION 8

Choice A is correct. It's given that the estimate for the proportion of the population that has the characteristic is 0.49 with an associated margin of error of 0.04. Subtracting the margin of error from the estimate and adding the margin of error to the estimate gives an interval of plausible values for the true proportion of the population that has the characteristic. Therefore, it's plausible that the proportion of the population that has this characteristic is between 0.45 and 0.53.

Choice B is incorrect. A value less than 0.45 is outside the interval of plausible values for the proportion of the population that has the characteristic. Choice C is incorrect. The value 0.49 is an estimate for the proportion based on this sample. However, since the margin of error for this estimate is known, the most appropriate conclusion is not that the proportion is exactly one value but instead lies in an interval of plausible values. Choice D is incorrect. A value greater than 0.53 is outside the interval of plausible values for the proportion of the population that has the characteristic.

QUESTION 9

Choice A is correct. A system of two linear equations in two variables, x and y, has zero points of intersection if the lines represented by the equations in the xy-plane are distinct and parallel. The graphs of two lines in the xy-plane represented by equations in slope-intercept form, y = mx + b, are distinct if the y-coordinates of their y-intercepts, b, are different and are parallel if their slopes, m, are the same. For the two equations in the given system, y = 2x + 10 and y = 2x − 1, the values of b are 10 and −1, respectively, and the values of m are both 2. Since the values of b are different, the graphs of these lines have different y-coordinates of the y-intercept and are distinct. Since the values of m are the same, the graphs of these lines have the same slope and are parallel. Therefore, the graphs of the given equations are lines that intersect at zero points in the xy-plane.

Choice B is incorrect. The graphs of a system of two linear equations have exactly one point of intersection if the lines represented by the equations have different slopes. Since the given equations represent lines with the same slope, there is not exactly one intersection point. Choice C is incorrect. The graphs of a system of two linear equations can never have exactly two intersection points. Choice D is incorrect. The graphs of a system of two linear equations have infinitely many intersection points when the lines represented by the equations have the same slope and the same y-coordinate of the y-intercept. Since the given equations represent lines with different y-coordinates of their y-intercepts, there are not infinitely many intersection points.

QUESTION 10

Choice C is correct. In the xy-plane, the graph of a linear function can be written in the form f(x) = mx + b, where m represents the slope and (0, b) represents the y-intercept of the graph of y = f(x). It's given that the graph of the linear function f, where y = f(x), in the xy-plane contains the point (0, 2). Thus, b = 2. The slope of the graph of a line containing any two points (x_1, y_1) and (x_2, y_2) can be found using the slope formula, $m = \dfrac{y_2 - y_1}{x_2 - x_1}$. Since it's given that the graph of the linear function f contains the points $(0, 2)$ and $(8, 34)$, it follows that the slope of the graph of the line containing these points is $m = \dfrac{34 - 2}{8 - 0}$, or $m = 4$. Substituting 4 for m and 2 for b in $f(x) = mx + b$ yields $f(x) = 4x + 2$.

Choice A is incorrect. This function represents a graph with a slope of 2 and a y-intercept of $(0, 42)$. *Choice B* is incorrect. This function represents a graph with a slope of 32 and a y-intercept of $(0, 36)$. *Choice D* is incorrect. This function represents a graph with a slope of 8 and a y-intercept of $(0, 2)$.

QUESTION 11

The correct answer is 24. The equation $\dfrac{24x}{ny} = 4$ can be rewritten as $\left(\dfrac{24}{n}\right)\left(\dfrac{x}{y}\right) = 4$. It's given that $\dfrac{x}{y} = 4$. Substituting 4 for $\dfrac{x}{y}$ in the equation $\left(\dfrac{24}{n}\right)\left(\dfrac{x}{y}\right) = 4$ yields $\left(\dfrac{24}{n}\right)(4) = 4$. Multiplying both sides of this equation by n yields $(24)(4) = 4n$. Dividing both sides of this equation by 4 yields $24 = n$. Therefore, the value of n is 24.

QUESTION 12

Choice D is correct. It's given that the function w models the volume of liquid, in milliliters, in a container t seconds after it begins draining from a hole at the bottom. The given function $w(t) = 300 - 4t$ can be rewritten as $w(t) = -4t + 300$. Thus, for each increase of t by 1, the value of $w(t)$ decreases by $4(1)$, or 4. Therefore, the predicted volume, in milliliters, draining from the container each second is 4 milliliters.

Choice A is incorrect. This is the amount of liquid, in milliliters, in the container before the liquid begins draining. *Choice B* is incorrect and may result from conceptual errors. *Choice C* is incorrect and may result from conceptual errors.

QUESTION 13

Choice C is correct. Because the value of the investment increases each year, the function that best models how the value of the investment changes over time is an increasing function. It's given that each year, the value of the investment increases by 0.49% of its value the previous year. Since the value of the investment changes by a fixed percentage each year, the function that best models how the value of the investment changes over time is an exponential function. Therefore, the function that best models how the value of the investment changes over time is an increasing exponential function.

Choice A is incorrect and may result from conceptual errors. *Choice B* is incorrect and may result from conceptual errors. *Choice D* is incorrect and may result from conceptual errors.

QUESTION 14

The correct answer is 80. Subtracting the second equation in the given system from the first equation yields $(24x + y) - (6x + y) = 48 - 72$, which is equivalent to $24x - 6x + y - y = -24$, or $18x = -24$. Dividing each side of this equation by 3 yields $6x = -8$. Substituting -8 for $6x$ in the second equation yields $-8 + y = 72$. Adding 8 to both sides of this equation yields $y = 80$.

Alternate approach: Multiplying each side of the second equation in the given system by 4 yields $24x + 4y = 288$. Subtracting the first equation in the given system from this equation yields $(24x + 4y) - (24x + y) = 288 - 48$, which is equivalent to $24x - 24x + 4y - y = 240$, or $3y = 240$. Dividing each side of this equation by 3 yields $y = 80$.

QUESTION 15

The correct answer is 7. When an equation is of the form $y = ax^2 + bx + c$, where a, b, and c are constants, the value of y reaches its minimum when $x = -\dfrac{b}{2a}$. Since the given equation is of the form $y = ax^2 + bx + c$, it follows that $a = 1$, $b = -14$, and $c = 22$. Therefore, the value of y reaches its minimum when $x = -\dfrac{(-14)}{2(1)}$, or $x = 7$.

QUESTION 16

Choice A is correct. The x-intercept of a graph in the xy-plane is the point on the graph where $y = 0$. It's given that function h is defined by $h(x) = 4x + 28$. Therefore, the equation representing the graph of $y = h(x)$ is $y = 4x + 28$. Substituting 0 for y in the equation $y = 4x + 28$ yields $0 = 4x + 28$. Subtracting 28 from both sides of this equation yields $-28 = 4x$. Dividing both sides of this equation by 4 yields $-7 = x$. Therefore, the x-intercept of the graph of $y = h(x)$ in the xy-plane is $(-7, 0)$. It's given that the x-intercept of the graph of $y = h(x)$ is $(a, 0)$. Therefore, $a = -7$. The y-intercept of a graph in the xy-plane is the point on the graph where $x = 0$. Substituting 0 for x in the equation $y = 4x + 28$ yields $y = 4(0) + 28$, or $y = 28$. Therefore, the y-intercept of the graph of $y = h(x)$ in the xy-plane is $(0, 28)$. It's given that the y-intercept of the graph of $y = h(x)$ is $(0, b)$. Therefore, $b = 28$. If $a = -7$ and $b = 28$, then the value of $a + b$ is $-7 + 28$, or 21.

Choice B is incorrect. This is the value of b, not $a + b$. *Choice C* is incorrect and may result from conceptual or calculation errors. *Choice D* is incorrect. This is the value of $-a + b$, not $a + b$.

QUESTION 17

The correct answer is 27,556. The area of a square is s^2, where s is the side length of the square. Let x represent the length of each side of square B. Substituting x for s in s^2 yields x^2. It follows that the area of square B is x^2. It's given that square A has side lengths that are 166 times the side lengths of square B. Since x represents the length of each side of square B, the length of each side of square A can be represented by the expression $166x$. It follows that the area of square A is $(166x)^2$, or $27,556x^2$. It's given that the area of square A is k times the area of square B. Since the area of square A is equal to $27,556x^2$, and the area of square B is equal to x^2, an equation representing the given statement is $27,556x^2 = kx^2$. Since x represents the length of each side of square B, the value of x must be positive. Therefore, the value of x^2 is also positive, so it does not equal 0. Dividing by x^2 on both sides of the equation $27,556x^2 = kx^2$ yields $27,556 = k$. Therefore, the value of k is 27,556.

QUESTION 18

Choice C is correct. On the line of best fit, an x-value of 25.5 corresponds to a y-value between 8 and 8.5. Therefore, at $x = 25.5$, 8.2 is closest to the y-value predicted by the line of best fit.

Choice A is incorrect and may result from conceptual errors. *Choice B* is incorrect and may result from conceptual errors. *Choice D* is incorrect and may result from conceptual errors.

QUESTION 19

Choice C is correct. It's given that the measure of angle *R* is $\frac{2\pi}{3}$ radians, and the measure of angle *T* is $\frac{5\pi}{12}$ radians greater than the measure of angle *R*. Therefore, the measure of angle *T* is equal to $\frac{2\pi}{3} + \frac{5\pi}{12}$ radians. Multiplying $\frac{2\pi}{3}$ by $\frac{4}{4}$ to get a common denominator with $\frac{5\pi}{12}$ yields $\frac{8\pi}{12}$. Therefore, $\frac{2\pi}{3} + \frac{5\pi}{12}$ is equivalent to $\frac{8\pi}{12} + \frac{5\pi}{12}$, or $\frac{13\pi}{12}$. Therefore, the measure of angle *T* is $\frac{13\pi}{12}$ radians. The measure of angle *T*, in degrees, can be found by multiplying its measure, in radians, by $\frac{180}{\pi}$. This yields $\frac{13\pi}{12} \times \frac{180}{\pi}$, which is equivalent to 195 degrees. Therefore, the measure of angle *T* is 195 degrees.

Choice A is incorrect. This is the number of degrees that the measure of angle *T* is greater than the measure of angle *R*. *Choice B* is incorrect. This is the measure of angle *R*, in degrees. *Choice D* is incorrect and may result from conceptual or calculation errors.

QUESTION 20

Choice B is correct. It's given that the formula $P = C(2)^{rt}$ gives the number of bacteria in a growth medium, where *r* and *C* are constants and *P* is the number of bacteria *t* hours after the initial measurement. It's also given that a scientist initially measures 12,000 bacteria in the growth medium. Since the initial measurement is 0 hours after the initial measurement, it follows that when *t* = 0, *P* = 12,000. Substituting 0 for *t* and 12,000 for *P* in the given equation yields $12{,}000 = C(2)^{r(0)}$, or $12{,}000 = C(2)^0$, which is equivalent to 12,000 = *C*. It's given that 4 hours later, the scientist measures 24,000 bacteria, or when *t* = 4, *P* = 24,000. Substituting 4 for *t*, 24,000 for *P*, and 12,000 for *C* in the given equation yields $24{,}000 = 12{,}000(2)^{4r}$. Dividing each side of this equation by 12,000 yields $2 = 2^{4r}$, or $2^1 = 2^{4r}$, which is equivalent to 1 = 4*r*. Dividing both sides of this equation by 4 yields $\frac{1}{4} = r$. Therefore, the value of *r* is $\frac{1}{4}$.

Choice A is incorrect. This is the value of the reciprocal of *C*. *Choice C* is incorrect. This is the value of the reciprocal of *r*. *Choice D* is incorrect. This is the value of *C*.

QUESTION 21

The correct answer is −3. Squaring both sides of the given equation yields $(x - 2)^2 = 3x + 34$, which can be rewritten as $x^2 - 4x + 4 = 3x + 34$. Subtracting 3*x* and 34 from both sides of this equation yields $x^2 - 7x - 30 = 0$. This quadratic equation can be rewritten as $(x - 10)(x + 3) = 0$. According to the zero product property, $(x - 10)(x + 3)$ equals zero when either *x* − 10 = 0 or *x* + 3 = 0. Solving each of these equations for *x* yields *x* = 10 or *x* = −3. Therefore, the given equation has two solutions, 10 and −3. Of these two solutions, −3 is the smallest solution to the given equation.

QUESTION 22

Choice C is correct. Subtracting the expression $(x - 29)$ from both sides of the given equation yields $0 = (x - a)(x - 29) - (x - 29)$, which can be rewritten as $0 = (x - a)(x - 29) + (-1)(x - 29)$. Since the two terms on the right-hand side of this equation have a common factor of $(x - 29)$, it can be rewritten as $0 = (x - 29)(x - a + (-1))$, or $0 = (x - 29)(x - a - 1)$. Since $x - a - 1$ is equivalent to $x - (a + 1)$, the equation $0 = (x - 29)(x - a - 1)$ can be rewritten as $0 = (x - 29)(x - (a + 1))$. By the zero product property, it follows that $x - 29 = 0$ or $x - (a + 1) = 0$. Adding 29 to both sides of the equation $x - 29 = 0$ yields $x = 29$. Adding $a + 1$ to both sides of the equation $x - (a + 1) = 0$ yields $x = a + 1$. Therefore, the two solutions to the given equation are 29 and $a + 1$. Thus, only $a + 1$ and 29, not a, are solutions to the given equation.

Choice A is incorrect and may result from conceptual or calculation errors.
Choice B is incorrect and may result from conceptual or calculation errors.
Choice D is incorrect and may result from conceptual or calculation errors.

Math

Module 2
(22 questions)

QUESTION 1

Choice B is correct. 10% of a quantity means $\frac{10}{100}$ times the quantity. Therefore, 10% of 470 can be represented as $\frac{10}{100}$(470), which is equivalent to 0.10(470), or 47. Therefore, 10% of 470 is 47.

Choice A is incorrect. This is 10% of 370, not 10% of 470. *Choice C* is incorrect. This is 90% of 470, not 10% of 470. *Choice D* is incorrect. This is 470 – 10, not 10% of 470.

QUESTION 2

Choice B is correct. The height of each bar in the bar graph given represents the number of students that voted for the activity specified at the bottom of the bar. The bar for activity 3 has a height that is between 35 and 40. In other words, the number of students that chose activity 3 is between 35 students and 40 students. Of the given choices, 39 is the only value between 35 and 40. Therefore, 39 students chose activity 3.

Choice A is incorrect and may result from conceptual errors. *Choice C* is incorrect. This is the number of students that chose activity 5, not activity 3. *Choice D* is incorrect and may result from conceptual errors.

QUESTION 3

The correct answer is 40. Subtracting 5 from both sides of the given equation yields $4x = 160$. Dividing both sides of this equation by 4 yields $x = 40$. Therefore, the solution to the given equation is 40.

QUESTION 4

The correct answer is 9. It's given that the customer spent $27 to purchase oranges at $3 per pound. Therefore, the number of pounds of oranges the customer purchased is 27\left(\frac{1 \text{ pound}}{\$3}\right)$, or 9 pounds.

QUESTION 5

The correct answer is 2. Substituting 8 for $f(x)$ in the given equation yields $8 = 4x$. Dividing the left- and right-hand sides of this equation by 4 yields $x = 2$. Therefore, the value of x is 2 when $f(x) = 8$.

QUESTION 6

Choice A is correct. It's given that $g(x) = x^2 + 9$. Substituting 25 for $g(x)$ in this equation yields $25 = x^2 + 9$. Subtracting 9 from both sides of this equation yields $16 = x^2$. Taking the square root of each side of this equation yields $x = \pm 4$. It follows that $g(x) = 25$ when the value of x is 4 or −4. Only 4 is listed among the choices.

Choice B is incorrect and may result from conceptual or calculation errors.
Choice C is incorrect and may result from conceptual or calculation errors.
Choice D is incorrect and may result from conceptual or calculation errors.

QUESTION 7

Choice D is correct. The y-intercept of a graph in the xy-plane is the point at which the graph crosses the y-axis. The graph shown crosses the y-axis at the point $(0, 8)$. Therefore, the y-intercept of the graph shown is $(0, 8)$.

Choice A is incorrect and may result from conceptual or calculation errors.
Choice B is incorrect and may result from conceptual or calculation errors.
Choice C is incorrect and may result from conceptual or calculation errors.

QUESTION 8

Choice C is correct. It's given that the cost of renting a tent is $11 per day for d days. Multiplying the rental cost by the number of days yields $11d$, which represents the cost of renting the tent for d days before the insurance is added. Adding the onetime insurance fee of $10 to the rental cost of $11d$ gives the total cost c, in dollars, which can be represented by the equation $c = 11d + 10$.

Choice A is incorrect. This equation represents the total cost to rent the tent if the insurance fee was charged every day. *Choice B* is incorrect. This equation represents the total cost to rent the tent if the daily fee was $(d + 11)$ for 10 days. *Choice D* is incorrect. This equation represents the total cost to rent the tent if the daily fee was $10 and the onetime fee was $11.

QUESTION 9

Choice D is correct. The expression $\dfrac{4}{4x - 5} - \dfrac{1}{x + 1}$ can be rewritten as $\dfrac{4}{4x - 5} + \dfrac{(-1)}{x + 1}$. To add the two terms of this expression, the terms can be rewritten with a common denominator. Since $\dfrac{x + 1}{x + 1} = 1$, the expression $\dfrac{4}{4x - 5}$ can be rewritten as $\dfrac{(x + 1)(4)}{(x + 1)(4x - 5)}$. Since $\dfrac{4x - 5}{4x - 5} = 1$, the expression $\dfrac{-1}{x + 1}$ can be rewritten as $\dfrac{(4x - 5)(-1)}{(4x - 5)(x + 1)}$. Therefore, the expression $\dfrac{4}{4x - 5} + \dfrac{(-1)}{x + 1}$ can be written as $\dfrac{(x + 1)(4)}{(x + 1)(4x - 5)} + \dfrac{(4x - 5)(-1)}{(4x - 5)(x + 1)}$, which is equivalent to $\dfrac{(x + 1)(4) + (4x - 5)(-1)}{(x + 1)(4x - 5)}$. Applying the distributive property to each term of the numerator yields $\dfrac{(4x + 4) + (-4x + 5)}{(x + 1)(4x - 5)}$, or $\dfrac{(4x + (-4x)) + (4 + 5)}{(x + 1)(4x - 5)}$. Adding like terms in the numerator yields $\dfrac{9}{(x + 1)(4x - 5)}$.

Choice A is incorrect and may result from conceptual or calculation errors.
Choice B is incorrect and may result from conceptual or calculation errors.
Choice C is incorrect and may result from conceptual or calculation errors.

QUESTION 10

Choice D is correct. It's given that the graph shows the linear relationship between x and y. The given graph passes through the points $(0, -5)$, $(1, -3)$, and $(2, -1)$. It follows that when $x = 0$, the corresponding value of y is -5, when $x = 1$, the corresponding value of y is -3, and when $x = 2$, the corresponding value of y is -1. Of the given choices, only the table in choice D gives these three values of x and their corresponding values of y for the relationship shown in the graph.

Choice A is incorrect. This table represents a relationship between x and y such that the graph passes through the points $(0, 0)$, $(1, -7)$, and $(2, -9)$. *Choice B* is incorrect. This table represents a relationship between x and y such that the graph passes through the points $(0, 0)$, $(1, -3)$, and $(2, -1)$. *Choice C* is incorrect. This table represents a linear relationship between x and y such that the graph passes through the points $(0, -5)$, $(1, -7)$, and $(2, -9)$.

QUESTION 11

The correct answer is 70. Based on the figure, the angle with measure $110°$ and the angle vertical to the angle with measure $x°$ are same side interior angles. Since vertical angles are congruent, the angle vertical to the angle with measure $x°$ also has measure $x°$. It's given that lines s and t are parallel. Therefore, same side interior angles between lines s and t are supplementary. It follows that $x + 110 = 180$. Subtracting 110 from both sides of this equation yields $x = 70$.

QUESTION 12

Choice D is correct. The perimeter of a figure is equal to the sum of the measurements of the sides of the figure. It's given that the rectangle has a length of 4 inches and a width of 9 inches. Since a rectangle has 4 sides, of which opposite sides are parallel and equal, it follows that the rectangle has two sides with a length of 4 inches and two sides with a width of 9 inches. Therefore, the perimeter of this rectangle is $4 + 4 + 9 + 9$, or 26 inches.

Choice A is incorrect. This is the sum, in inches, of the length and the width of the rectangle. *Choice B* is incorrect. This is the sum, in inches, of the two lengths and the width of the rectangle. *Choice C* is incorrect. This is the sum, in inches, of the length and the two widths of the rectangle.

QUESTION 13

Choice D is correct. To express j in terms of k and m, the given equation must be solved for j. Dividing each side of the given equation by 8 yields $j = \dfrac{k + 15m}{8}$.

Choice A is incorrect. This is equivalent to $8j = k + 120m$. *Choice B* is incorrect. This is equivalent to $8j = 8k + 15m$. *Choice C* is incorrect. This is equivalent to $\dfrac{j}{8} = k + 15m$.

QUESTION 14

Choice A is correct. The given point, $(8, 2)$, is located in the first quadrant in the xy-plane. The system of inequalities in choice A represents all the points in the first quadrant in the xy-plane. Therefore, $(8, 2)$ is a solution to the system of inequalities in choice A.

Alternate approach: Substituting 8 for *x* in the first inequality in choice A, *x* > 0, yields 8 > 0, which is true. Substituting 2 for *y* in the second inequality in choice A, *y* > 0, yields 2 > 0, which is true. Since the coordinates of the point (8, 2) make the inequalities *x* > 0 and *y* > 0 true, the point (8, 2) is a solution to the system of inequalities consisting of *x* > 0 and *y* > 0.

Choice B is incorrect. This system of inequalities represents all the points in the fourth quadrant, not the first quadrant, in the *xy*-plane. *Choice C* is incorrect. This system of inequalities represents all the points in the second quadrant, not the first quadrant, in the *xy*-plane. *Choice D* is incorrect. This system of inequalities represents all the points in the third quadrant, not the first quadrant, in the *xy*-plane.

QUESTION 15

Choice B is correct. The equation representing a linear model can be written in the form $y = a + bx$, or $y = bx + a$, where *b* is the slope of the graph of the model and (0, *a*) is the *y*-intercept of the graph of the model. The scatterplot shows that as the *x*-values of the data points increase, the *y*-values of the data points decrease, which means the graph of an appropriate linear model has a negative slope. Therefore, $b < 0$. The scatterplot also shows that the data points are close to the *y*-axis at a positive value of *y*. Therefore, the *y*-intercept of the graph of an appropriate linear model has a positive *y*-coordinate, which means $a > 0$. Of the given choices, only choice B, $y = -1.9x + 10.1$, has a negative value for *b*, the slope, and a positive value for *a*, the *y*-coordinate of the *y*-intercept.

Choice A is incorrect. The graph of this model has a *y*-intercept with a negative *y*-coordinate, not a positive *y*-coordinate. *Choice C* is incorrect. The graph of this model has a positive slope, not a negative slope, and a *y*-intercept with a negative *y*-coordinate, not a positive *y*-coordinate. *Choice D* is incorrect. The graph of this model has a positive slope, not a negative slope.

QUESTION 16

Choice A is correct. Since it's given that the account balance, $A(t)$, in dollars, after *t* years can be modeled by an exponential function, it follows that function *A* can be written in the form $A(t) = Nr^t$, where *N* is the initial value of the function and *r* is a constant related to the growth of the function. It's given that the initial balance of the account is $36,100.00, so it follows that the initial value of the function, or *N*, must be 36,100.00. Substituting 36,100.00 for *N* in the equation $A(t) = Nr^t$ yields $A(t) = 36,100.00r^t$. It's given that the account balance after 13 years, or when $t = 13$, is $68,071.93. It follows that $A(13) = 68,071.93$, or $36,100.00r^{13} = 68,071.93$. Dividing each side of the

equation $36,100.00r^{13} = 68,071.93$ by 36,100.00 yields $r^{13} = \frac{68,071.93}{36,100.00}$. Taking

the 13th root of both sides of this equation yields $r = \sqrt[13]{\frac{68,071.93}{36,100.00}}$, or

r is approximately equal to 1.05. Substituting 1.05 for *r* in the equation $A(t) = 36,100.00r^t$ yields $A(t) = 36,100.00(1.05)^t$, so the equation $A(t) = 36,100.00(1.05)^t$ could define *A*.

Choice B is incorrect. Substituting 0 for *t* in this function indicates an initial balance of $31,971.93, rather than $36,100.00. *Choice C* is incorrect. Substituting 0 for *t* in this function indicates an initial balance of $31,971.93, rather than $36,100.00. Additionally, this function indicates the account balance is decreasing, rather than increasing, over time. *Choice D* is incorrect. This function indicates the account balance is decreasing, rather than increasing, over time.

QUESTION 17

The correct answer is 9. The given equation can be rewritten as $5|4 - x| = 25$. Dividing each side of this equation by 5 yields $|4 - x| = 5$. By the definition of absolute value, if $|4 - x| = 5$, then $4 - x = 5$ or $4 - x = -5$. Subtracting 4 from each side of the equation $4 - x = 5$ yields $-x = 1$. Dividing each side of this equation by -1 yields $x = -1$. Similarly, subtracting 4 from each side of the equation $4 - x = -5$ yields $-x = -9$. Dividing each side of this equation by -1 yields $x = 9$. Therefore, since the two solutions to the given equation are -1 and 9, the positive solution to the given equation is 9.

QUESTION 18

The correct answer is 6. Applying the distributive property to the expression $ry^4(15y - 9)$ yields $15ry^5 - 9ry^4$. Since $90y^5 - 54y^4$ is equivalent to $ry^4(15y - 9)$, it follows that $90y^5 - 54y^4$ is also equivalent to $15ry^5 - 9ry^4$. Since these expressions are equivalent, it follows that corresponding coefficients are equivalent. Therefore, $90 = 15r$ and $-54 = -9r$. Solving either of these equations for r will yield the value of r. Dividing both sides of $90 = 15r$ by 15 yields $6 = r$. Therefore, the value of r is 6.

QUESTION 19

Choice D is correct. It's given that the expression $w(w + 9)$ represents the area, in square centimeters, of a rectangular cutting board, where w is the width, in centimeters, of the cutting board. The area of a rectangle can be calculated by multiplying its length by its width. It follows that the length, in centimeters, of the cutting board is represented by the expression $(w + 9)$.

Choice A is incorrect. This expression represents the area, in square centimeters, of the cutting board, not its length, in centimeters. *Choice B* is incorrect. This expression represents the width, in centimeters, of the cutting board, not its length. *Choice C* is incorrect. This is the difference between the length, in centimeters, and the width, in centimeters, of the cutting board, not its length, in centimeters.

QUESTION 20

Choice D is correct. All the tables in the choices have the same three values of x, so each of the three values of x can be substituted in the given inequality to compare the corresponding values of y in each of the tables. Substituting 3 for x in the given inequality yields $y > 13(3) - 18$, or $y > 21$. Therefore, when $x = 3$, the corresponding value of y is greater than 21. Substituting 5 for x in the given inequality yields $y > 13(5) - 18$, or $y > 47$. Therefore, when $x = 5$, the corresponding value of y is greater than 47. Substituting 8 for x in the given inequality yields $y > 13(8) - 18$, or $y > 86$. Therefore, when $x = 8$, the corresponding value of y is greater than 86. For the table in choice D, when $x = 3$, the corresponding value of y is 26, which is greater than 21; when $x = 5$, the corresponding value of y is 52, which is greater than 47; when $x = 8$, the corresponding value of y is 91, which is greater than 86. Therefore, the table in choice D gives values of x and their corresponding values of y that are all solutions to the given inequality.

Choice A is incorrect. In the table for choice A, when $x = 3$, the corresponding value of y is 21, which is not greater than 21; when $x = 5$, the corresponding value of y is 47, which is not greater than 47; when $x = 8$, the corresponding value of y is 86, which is not greater than 86. *Choice B* is incorrect. In the table for choice B, when $x = 5$, the corresponding value of y is 42, which is not greater than 47; when $x = 8$, the corresponding value of y is 86, which is not greater than 86.

Choice C is incorrect. In the table for choice C, when $x = 3$, the corresponding value of y is 16, which is not greater than 21; when $x = 5$, the corresponding value of y is 42, which is not greater than 47; when $x = 8$, the corresponding value of y is 81, which is not greater than 86.

QUESTION 21

Choice B is correct. It's given that $g(x) = f(x - 1)$. Since $f(x) = (x + 6)(x + 5)(x + 1)$, it follows that $f(x - 1) = (x - 1 + 6)(x - 1 + 5)(x - 1 + 1)$. Combining like terms yields $f(x - 1) = (x + 5)(x + 4)(x)$. Therefore, $g(x) = x(x + 5)(x + 4)$. The x-intercepts of a graph in the xy-plane are the points where $y = 0$. The x-coordinates of the x-intercepts of the graph of $y = g(x)$ in the xy-plane can be found by solving the equation $0 = x(x + 5)(x + 4)$. Applying the zero product property to this equation yields three equations: $x = 0$, $x + 5 = 0$, and $x + 4 = 0$. Solving each of these equations for x yields $x = 0$, $x = -5$, and $x = -4$, respectively. Therefore, the x-intercepts of the graph of $y = g(x)$ are $(0, 0)$, $(-5, 0)$, and $(-4, 0)$. It follows that the values of a, b, and c are 0, -5, and -4. Thus, the value of $a + b + c$ is $0 + (-5) + (-4)$, which is equal to -9.

Choice A is incorrect. This is the value of $a + b + c$ if $g(x) = f(x + 1)$.
Choice C is incorrect. This is the value of $a + b + c - 1$ if $g(x) = (x - 6)(x - 5)(x - 1)$.
Choice D is incorrect. This is the value of $a + b + c$ if $f(x) = (x - 6)(x - 5)(x - 1)$.

QUESTION 22

Choice A is correct. When a square is inscribed in a circle, a diagonal of the square is a diameter of the circle. It's given that a square is inscribed in a circle and the length of a radius of the circle is $\frac{20\sqrt{2}}{2}$ inches. Therefore, the length of a diameter of the circle is $2\left(\frac{20\sqrt{2}}{2}\right)$ inches, or $20\sqrt{2}$ inches. It follows that the length of a diagonal of the square is $20\sqrt{2}$ inches. A diagonal of a square separates the square into two right triangles in which the legs are the sides of the square and the hypotenuse is a diagonal. Since a square has 4 congruent sides, each of these two right triangles has congruent legs and a hypotenuse of length $20\sqrt{2}$ inches. Since each of these two right triangles has congruent legs, they are both 45-45-90 triangles. In a 45-45-90 triangle, the length of the hypotenuse is $\sqrt{2}$ times the length of a leg. Let s represent the length of a leg of one of these 45-45-90 triangles. It follows that $20\sqrt{2} = \sqrt{2}(s)$. Dividing both sides of this equation by $\sqrt{2}$ yields $20 = s$. Therefore, the length of a leg of one of these 45-45-90 triangles is 20 inches. Since the legs of these two 45-45-90 triangles are the sides of the square, it follows that the side length of the square is 20 inches.

Choice B is incorrect. This is the length of a radius, in inches, of the circle.
Choice C is incorrect. This is the length of a diameter, in inches, of the circle.
Choice D is incorrect and may result from conceptual or calculation errors.

Scoring Your Paper SAT Practice Test #3

Congratulations on completing an SAT® practice test.
To score your test, follow the instructions in this guide.

IMPORTANT: *This scoring guide is for students who completed the paper version of this digital SAT practice test.*

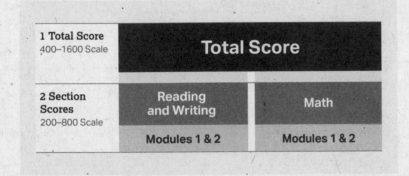

1 Total Score 400–1600 Scale	Total Score	
2 Section Scores 200–800 Scale	Reading and Writing	Math
	Modules 1 & 2	Modules 1 & 2

Scores Overview

Each assessment in the digital SAT Suite (SAT, PSAT/NMSQT®, PSAT™ 10, and PSAT™ 8/9) reports test scores on a common scale.

For more details about scores, visit **sat.org/scores**.

How to Calculate Your Practice Test Scores

The worksheets on pages 544 and 545 help you calculate your test scores.

GET SET UP

1 In addition to your practice test, you'll need the conversion tables and answer key at the end of this guide.

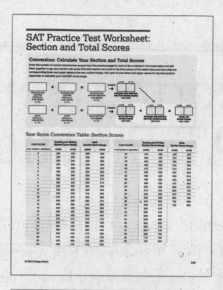

SCORE YOUR PRACTICE TEST

2 Compare your answers to the answer key on page 544, and count up the total number of correct answers for each section. Write the number of correct answers for each section in the answer key at the bottom of that section.

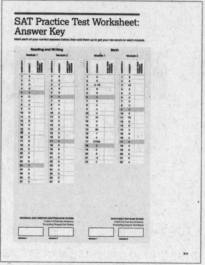

CALCULATE YOUR SCORES

3 Using your marked-up answer key and the conversion tables, follow the directions on page 545 to get your section and test scores.

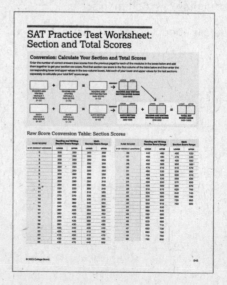

Get Section and Total Scores

Section and total scores for the paper version of this digital SAT practice test are expressed as ranges. That's because the scoring method described in this guide is a simplified (and therefore slightly less precise) version of the one used in Bluebook™, the digital test application.

To obtain your Reading and Writing and Math section scores, use the provided answer key to determine the number of questions you answered correctly in each section. These numbers constitute your *raw scores* for the two sections. Use the provided table to convert your raw score for each section into a *scaled score* range consisting of a "lower" and "upper" value. Add the two lower values together and the two upper values together to obtain your total score range.

GET YOUR READING AND WRITING SECTION SCORE

Calculate your SAT Reading and Writing section score (it's on a scale of 200–800).

1. Use the answer key on page 544 to find the number of questions in module 1 and module 2 that you answered correctly.

2. To determine your Reading and Writing raw score, add the number of correct answers you got on module 1 and module 2. **Exclude the questions in grayed-out rows from your calculation.**

3. Use the Raw Score Conversion Table: Section Scores on page 545 to turn your raw score into your Reading and Writing section score.

4. The "lower" and "upper" values associated with your raw score establish the range of scores you might expect to receive had this been an actual test.

GET YOUR MATH SECTION SCORE

Calculate your SAT Math section score (it's on a scale of 200–800).

1. Use the answer key on page 544 to find the number of questions in module 1 and module 2 that you answered correctly.

2. To determine your Math raw score, add the number of correct answers you got on module 1 and module 2. **Exclude the questions in grayed-out rows from your calculation.**

3. Use the Raw Score Conversion Table: Section Scores on page 545 to turn your raw score into your Math section score.

4. The "lower" and "upper" values associated with your raw score establish the range of scores you might expect to receive had this been an actual test.

GET YOUR TOTAL SCORE

Add together the "lower" values for the Reading and Writing and Math sections, and then add together the "upper" values for the two sections. The result is your total score, expressed as a range, for this SAT practice test. The total score is on a scale of 400–1600.

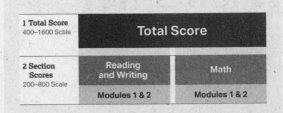

1 Total Score 400–1600 Scale	Total Score	
2 Section Scores 200–800 Scale	Reading and Writing	Math
	Modules 1 & 2	Modules 1 & 2

Your total score on this SAT practice test is the sum of your Reading and Writing section score and your Math section score. On this paper version of the digital SAT practice test, you'll receive a lower and upper score for each test section and the total score. This is the range of scores that you might expect to receive.

Use the worksheets on pages 544 and 545 to calculate your section and total scores.

SAT Practice Test Worksheet: Answer Key

Mark each of your correct answers below, then add them up to get your raw score on each module.

Reading and Writing

Module 1

QUESTION #	CORRECT	MARK YOUR CORRECT ANSWERS
1	B	
2	D	
3	C	
4	B	
5	A	
6	D	
7	A	
8	A	
9	A	
10	D	
11	A	
12	B	
13	A	
14	C	
15	A	
16	D	
17	D	
18	D	
19	C	
20	C	
21	B	
22	D	
23	C	
24	A	
25	D	
26	D	
27	C	

Module 2

QUESTION #	CORRECT	MARK YOUR CORRECT ANSWERS
1	B	
2	B	
3	C	
4	B	
5	D	
6	A	
7	D	
8	A	
9	A	
10	C	
11	C	
12	C	
13	B	
14	D	
15	A	
16	D	
17	A	
18	B	
19	B	
20	A	
21	D	
22	D	
23	D	
24	A	
25	C	
26	B	
27	D	

Math

Module 1

QUESTION #	CORRECT	MARK YOUR CORRECT ANSWERS
1	C	
2	D	
3	.2, 1/5	
4	B	
5	B	
6	C	
7	B	
8	A	
9	A	
10	C	
11	24	
12	D	
13	C	
14	80	
15	7	
16	A	
17	27556	
18	C	
19	C	
20	B	
21	−3	
22	C	

Module 2

QUESTION #	CORRECT	MARK YOUR CORRECT ANSWERS
1	B	
2	B	
3	40	
4	9	
5	2	
6	A	
7	D	
8	C	
9	D	
10	D	
11	70	
12	D	
13	D	
14	A	
15	B	
16	A	
17	9	
18	6	
19	D	
20	D	
21	B	
22	A	

READING AND WRITING SECTION RAW SCORE
(Total # of Correct Answers, Excluding Grayed-Out Rows)

Module 1

Module 2

MATH SECTION RAW SCORE
(Total # of Correct Answers, Excluding Grayed-Out Rows)

Module 1

Module 2

SAT Practice Test Worksheet: Section and Total Scores

Conversion: Calculate Your Section and Total Scores

Enter the number of correct answers (raw scores from the previous page) for each of the modules in the boxes below and add them together to get your section raw score. Find that section raw score in the first column of the table below and then enter the corresponding lower and upper values in the two-column boxes. Add each of your lower and upper values for the test sections separately to calculate your total SAT score range.

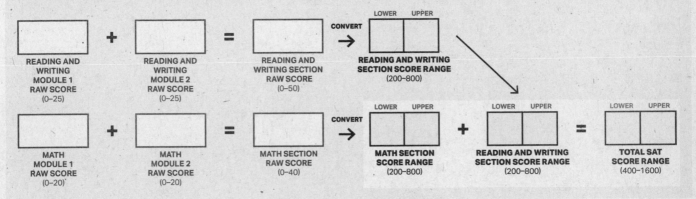

Raw Score Conversion Table: Section Scores

RAW SCORE (# OF CORRECT ANSWERS)	Reading and Writing Section Score Range		Math Section Score Range		RAW SCORE (# OF CORRECT ANSWERS)	Reading and Writing Section Score Range		Math Section Score Range	
	LOWER	UPPER	LOWER	UPPER		LOWER	UPPER	LOWER	UPPER
0	200	250	200	250	26	440	480	460	520
1	200	250	200	250	27	450	490	470	530
2	200	250	200	250	28	450	490	490	550
3	200	250	200	250	29	460	500	500	560
4	200	250	200	250	30	470	510	510	570
5	200	250	200	250	31	480	520	530	590
6	200	260	200	250	32	480	520	530	610
7	200	270	200	270	33	490	530	550	630
8	200	290	250	310	34	490	550	570	650
9	200	300	280	320	35	500	560	590	670
10	220	320	300	340	36	510	570	620	700
11	230	330	310	350	37	520	580	640	740
12	270	370	320	360	38	530	590	680	780
13	300	380	330	370	39	540	600	730	800
14	330	390	340	380	40	550	610	750	800
15	340	400	350	390	41	560	620		
16	360	400	350	390	42	580	640		
17	360	400	360	400	43	590	650		
18	370	410	370	410	44	600	660		
19	380	420	380	420	45	620	680		
20	390	430	390	430	46	630	710		
21	400	440	400	440	47	650	730		
22	400	440	410	450	48	680	760		
23	410	450	410	470	49	710	790		
24	420	460	430	490	50	750	800		
25	430	470	440	500					

The SAT®

Practice Test #4

Make time to take the practice test.
It is one of the best ways to get ready
for the SAT.

After you have taken the practice test, score it right away
using materials provided in *The Official Digital SAT Study Guide*.

This version of the SAT Practice Test is for students using
this guide. As a reminder, most students taking the
digital SAT will do so using Bluebook™, the digital testing
application. To best prepare for test day, download Bluebook
at **bluebook.app.collegeboard.org** to take the practice test in
the digital format.

Test begins on the next page.

Reading and Writing

27 QUESTIONS

1

Although critics believed that customers would never agree to pay to pick their own produce on farms, such concerns didn't _____ Booker T. Whatley's efforts to promote the practice. Thanks in part to Whatley's determined advocacy, farms that allow visitors to pick their own apples, pumpkins, and other produce can be found throughout the United States.

Which choice completes the text with the most logical and precise word or phrase?

A) enhance

B) hinder

C) misrepresent

D) aggravate

2

The artisans of the Igun Eronmwon guild in Benin City, Nigeria, typically _____ the bronze- and brasscasting techniques that have been passed down through their families since the thirteenth century, but they don't strictly observe every tradition; for example, guild members now use air-conditioning motors instead of handheld bellows to help heat their forges.

Which choice completes the text with the most logical and precise word or phrase?

A) experiment with

B) adhere to

C) improve on

D) grapple with

3

Set in a world where science fiction tropes exist as everyday realities, Charles Yu's 2010 novel *How to Live Safely in a Science Fictional Universe* traces a time traveler's quest to find his father. Because the journey at the novel's center is so _____, with the protagonist ricocheting chaotically across time, the reader often wonders whether the pair will ever be reunited.

Which choice completes the text with the most logical and precise word or phrase?

A) haphazard

B) premeditated

C) inspirational

D) fruitless

4

In a 2019 study, Jeremy Gunawardena and colleagues found that the single-celled protozoan *Stentor roeseli* not only uses strategies to escape irritating stimuli but also switches strategies when one fails. This evidence of protozoans sophisticatedly "changing their minds" demonstrates that single-celled organisms may not be limited to _____ behaviors.

Which choice completes the text with the most logical and precise word or phrase?

A) aggressive

B) rudimentary

C) evolving

D) advantageous

CONTINUE ▶

5

Some economic historians _____ that late nineteenth- and early twentieth-century households in the United States experienced an economy of scale when it came to food purchases—they assumed that large households spent less on food per person than did small households. Economist Trevon Logan showed, however, that a close look at the available data disproves this supposition.

Which choice completes the text with the most logical and precise word or phrase?

A) surmised

B) contrived

C) questioned

D) regretted

6

The following text is adapted from Karel Čapek's 1920 play *R.U.R. (Rossum's Universal Robots)*, translated by Paul Selver and Nigel Playfair in 1923. Fabry and Busman are telling Miss Glory why their company manufactures robots.

FABRY: One Robot can replace two and a half *workmen*. The human machine, Miss Glory, was terribly *imperfect*. It had to be removed sooner or later.

BUSMAN: It was too expensive.

FABRY: It was not *effective*. It no longer <u>answers</u> the requirements of *modern engineering*. Nature has no idea of keeping pace with *modern labor*.

As used in the text, what does the word "answers" most nearly mean?

A) Explains

B) Rebuts

C) Defends

D) Fulfills

7

In 2014, Amelia Quon and her team at NASA set out to build a helicopter capable of flying on Mars. Because Mars's atmosphere is only one percent as dense as Earth's, the air of Mars would not provide enough resistance to the rotating blades of a standard helicopter for the aircraft to stay aloft. For five years, Quon's team tested designs in a lab that mimicked Mars's atmospheric conditions. The craft the team ultimately designed can fly on Mars because its blades are longer and rotate faster than those of a helicopter of the same size built for Earth.

According to the text, why would a helicopter built for Earth be unable to fly on Mars?

A) Because Mars and Earth have different atmospheric conditions

B) Because the blades of helicopters built for Earth are too large to work on Mars

C) Because the gravity of Mars is much weaker than the gravity of Earth

D) Because helicopters built for Earth are too small to handle the conditions on Mars

8

In West Africa, jalis have traditionally been keepers of information about family histories and records of important events. They have often served as teachers and advisers, too. New technologies may have changed some aspects of the role today, but jalis continue to be valued for knowing and protecting their peoples' stories.

Which choice best states the main idea of the text?

A) Even though there have been some changes in their role, jalis continue to preserve their communities' histories.

B) Although jalis have many roles, many of them like teaching best.

C) Jalis have been entertaining the people within their communities for centuries.

D) Technology can now do some of the things jalis used to be responsible for.

Unauthorized copying or reuse of any part of this page is illegal.

CONTINUE

551

9

The following text is adapted from Jack London's 1903 novel *The Call of the Wild*. Buck is a sled dog living with John Thornton in Yukon, Canada.

Thornton alone held [Buck]. The rest of mankind was as nothing. Chance travellers might praise or pet him; but he was cold under it all, and from a too demonstrative man he would get up and walk away. When Thornton's partners, Hans and Pete, arrived on the long-expected raft, Buck refused to notice them till he learned they were close to Thornton; after that he tolerated them in a passive sort of way, accepting favors from them as though he favored them by accepting.

Which choice best states the main idea of the text?

A) Buck has become less social since he began living with Thornton.

B) Buck mistrusts humans and does his best to avoid them.

C) Buck has been especially well liked by most of Thornton's friends.

D) Buck holds Thornton in higher regard than any other person.

10

The Souls of Black Folk is a 1903 book by W.E.B. Du Bois. In the book, Du Bois suggests that upon hearing Black folk songs, he felt an intuitive and sometimes unexpected sense of cultural recognition: _____

Which quotation from *The Souls of Black Folk* most effectively illustrates the claim?

A) "[Black folk music] still remains as the singular spiritual heritage of the nation and the greatest gift of the Negro people."

B) "Ever since I was a child these songs have stirred me strangely. They came out of the South unknown to me, one by one, and yet at once I knew them as of me and of mine."

C) "Caricature has sought again to spoil the quaint beauty of the music, and has filled the air with many debased melodies which vulgar ears scarce know from the real. But the true Negro folk-song still lives in the hearts of those who have heard them truly sung and in the hearts of the Negro people."

D) "The songs are indeed the siftings of centuries; the music is far more ancient than the words, and in it we can trace here and there signs of development."

CONTINUE ➤

11

Percentage of Ondo State Small-Scale Farmers Who Are Female, by Main Crop Grown

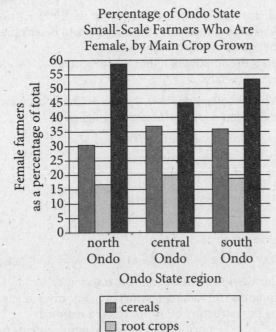

Geographer Adebayo Oluwole Eludoyin and his colleagues surveyed small-scale farmers in three locations in Ondo State, Nigeria—which has mountainous terrain in the north, an urbanized center, and coastal terrain in the south—to learn more about their practices, like the types of crops they mainly cultivated. In some regions, female farmers were found to be especially prominent in the cultivation of specific types of crops and even constituted the majority of farmers who cultivated those crops; for instance, _____

Which choice most effectively uses data from the graph to complete the example?

A) most of the farmers who mainly cultivated cereals and most of the farmers who mainly cultivated non–root vegetables in south Ondo were women.

B) more women in central Ondo mainly cultivated root crops than mainly cultivated cereals.

C) most of the farmers who mainly cultivated non–root vegetables in north and south Ondo were women.

D) a relatively equal proportion of women across the three regions of Ondo mainly cultivated cereals.

12

Scholars have noted that F. Scott Fitzgerald's writings were likely influenced in part by his marriage to Zelda Fitzgerald, but many don't recognize Zelda as a writer in her own right. Indeed, Zelda authored several works herself, such as the novel *Save Me the Waltz* and numerous short stories. Thus, those who primarily view Zelda as an inspiration for F. Scott's writings _____

Which choice most logically completes the text?

A) overlook the many other factors that motivated F. Scott to write.

B) risk misrepresenting the full range of Zelda's contributions to literature.

C) may draw inaccurate conclusions about how F. Scott and Zelda viewed each other's works.

D) tend to read the works of F. Scott and Zelda in an overly autobiographical light.

13

Herbivorous sauropod dinosaurs could grow more than 100 feet long and weigh up to 80 tons, and some researchers have attributed the evolution of sauropods to such massive sizes to increased plant production resulting from high levels of atmospheric carbon dioxide during the Mesozoic era. However, there is no evidence of significant spikes in carbon dioxide levels coinciding with relevant periods in sauropod evolution, such as when the first large sauropods appeared, when several sauropod lineages underwent further evolution toward gigantism, or when sauropods reached their maximum known sizes, suggesting that _____

Which choice most logically completes the text?

A) fluctuations in atmospheric carbon dioxide affected different sauropod lineages differently.

B) the evolution of larger body sizes in sauropods did not depend on increased atmospheric carbon dioxide.

C) atmospheric carbon dioxide was higher when the largest known sauropods lived than it was when the first sauropods appeared.

D) sauropods probably would not have evolved to such immense sizes if atmospheric carbon dioxide had been even slightly higher.

CONTINUE ▶

14

Known for her massive photorealistic paintings of African American figures floating or swimming in pools, Calida Garcia _____ was the logical choice to design the book cover for Ta-Nehisi Coates's *The Water Dancer*, a novel about an African American man who can travel great distances through water.

Which choice completes the text so that it conforms to the conventions of Standard English?

A) Rawles—

B) Rawles:

C) Rawles,

D) Rawles

15

In 2010, archaeologist Noel Hidalgo Tan was visiting the twelfth-century temple of Angkor Wat in Cambodia when he noticed markings of red paint on the temple _____ the help of digital imaging techniques, he discovered the markings to be part of an elaborate mural containing over 200 paintings.

Which choice completes the text so that it conforms to the conventions of Standard English?

A) walls, with

B) walls with

C) walls so with

D) walls. With

16

Cheng Dang and her colleagues at the University of Washington recently ran simulations to determine the extent to which individual snow _____ affect the amount of light reflecting off a snowy surface.

Which choice completes the text so that it conforms to the conventions of Standard English?

A) grain's physical properties'

B) grains' physical properties

C) grains' physical property's

D) grains physical properties

17

The Mission 66 initiative, which was approved by Congress in 1956, represented a major investment in the infrastructure of overburdened national _____ it prioritized physical improvements to the parks' roads, utilities, employee housing, and visitor facilities while also establishing educational programming for the public.

Which choice completes the text so that it conforms to the conventions of Standard English?

A) parks and

B) parks

C) parks;

D) parks,

Unauthorized copying or reuse of any part of this page is illegal.

CONTINUE

554

18

The Progressive Era in the United States witnessed the rise of numerous Black women's clubs, local organizations that advocated for racial and gender equality. Among the clubs' leaders _____ Josephine St. Pierre Ruffin, founder of the Women's Era Club of Boston.

Which choice completes the text so that it conforms to the conventions of Standard English?

A) was

B) were

C) are

D) have been

19

Eli Eisenberg, a genetics expert at Tel Aviv University in Israel, recently discovered that _____ have a special genetic ability called RNA editing that confers evolutionary advantages.

Which choice completes the text so that it conforms to the conventions of Standard English?

A) cephalopods, ocean dwellers that include the squid, the octopus, and the cuttlefish

B) cephalopods—ocean dwellers—that include the squid, the octopus, and the cuttlefish,

C) cephalopods, ocean dwellers that include: the squid, the octopus, and the cuttlefish,

D) cephalopods—ocean dwellers that include the squid, the octopus, and the cuttlefish—

20

A model created by biologist Luis Valente predicts that the rate of speciation—the rate at which new species form—on an isolated island located approximately 5,000 kilometers from the nearest mainland _____ triple the rate of speciation on an island only 500 kilometers from the mainland.

Which choice completes the text so that it conforms to the conventions of Standard English?

A) being

B) to be

C) to have been

D) will be

21

Award-winning travel writer Linda Watanabe McFerrin considers the background research she conducts on destinations featured in her travel books to be its own reward. _____ McFerrin admits to finding the research phase of her work just as fascinating and engaging as exploring a location in person.

Which choice completes the text with the most logical transition?

A) By contrast,

B) Likewise,

C) Besides,

D) In fact,

CONTINUE

22

While researching a topic, a student has taken the following notes:

- Bharati Mukherjee was an Indian-born author of novels and short stories.
- She published the novel *The Holder of the World* in 1993.
- A central character in the novel is a woman living in twentieth-century United States.
- Another central character is a woman living in seventeenth-century India.

The student wants to introduce the novel *The Holder of the World* to an audience already familiar with Bharati Mukherjee. Which choice most effectively uses relevant information from the notes to accomplish this goal?

A) Bharati Mukherjee's settings include both twentieth-century United States and seventeenth-century India.

B) In addition to her novel *The Holder of the World*, which was published in 1993, Indian-born author Bharati Mukherjee wrote other novels and short stories.

C) Bharati Mukherjee's novel *The Holder of the World* centers around two women, one living in twentieth-century United States and the other in seventeenth-century India.

D) *The Holder of the World* was not the only novel written by Indian-born author Bharati Mukherjee.

23

While researching a topic, a student has taken the following notes:

- Pterosaurs were flying reptiles that existed millions of years ago.
- In a 2021 study, Anusuya Chinsamy-Turan analyzed fragments of pterosaur jawbones located in the Sahara Desert.
- She was initially unsure if the bones belonged to juvenile or adult pterosaurs.
- She used advanced microscope techniques to determine that the bones had few growth lines relative to the bones of fully grown pterosaurs.
- She concluded that the bones belonged to juveniles.

The student wants to present the study and its findings. Which choice most effectively uses relevant information from the notes to accomplish this goal?

A) In 2021, Chinsamy-Turan studied pterosaur jawbones and was initially unsure if the bones belonged to juveniles or adults.

B) Pterosaur jawbones located in the Sahara Desert were the focus of a 2021 study.

C) In a 2021 study, Chinsamy-Turan used advanced microscope techniques to analyze the jawbones of pterosaurs, flying reptiles that existed millions of years ago.

D) In a 2021 study, Chinsamy-Turan determined that pterosaur jawbones located in the Sahara Desert had few growth lines relative to the bones of fully grown pterosaurs and thus belonged to juveniles.

CONTINUE

While researching a topic, a student has taken the following notes:

- Samuel Selvon was a Trinidadian author.
- *The Lonely Londoners* is one of his most celebrated novels.
- Selvon published the novel in 1956.
- It is about a group of men who emigrate from the Caribbean to Great Britain after World War II.
- Some of *The Lonely Londoners'* characters also appear in Selvon's later novel *Moses Ascending*.

The student wants to introduce Samuel Selvon and his novel *The Lonely Londoners* to a new audience. Which choice most effectively uses relevant information from the notes to accomplish this goal?

A) In 1956, Trinidadian author Samuel Selvon published one of his most celebrated novels, *The Lonely Londoners*, which is about a group of men who emigrate from the Caribbean to Great Britain after World War II.

B) Samuel Selvon wrote the novel *Moses Ascending* after he wrote *The Lonely Londoners*.

C) *The Lonely Londoners*, a celebrated novel that was published in 1956, depicts post–World War II Caribbean migration from the perspective of a Trinidadian author.

D) Some of the characters who appear in Samuel Selvon's *Moses Ascending* also appear in *The Lonely Londoners*.

While researching a topic, a student has taken the following notes:

- Seven species of sea turtle exist today.
- Five sea turtle species can be found in the Atlantic Ocean.
- One of those species is the Kemp's ridley sea turtle.
- Its scientific name is *Lepidochelys kempii*.
- Another of those species is the olive ridley sea turtle.
- Its scientific name is *Lepidochelys olivacea*.

The student wants to emphasize a similarity between the two sea turtle species. Which choice most effectively uses relevant information from the notes to accomplish this goal?

A) Among the seven species of sea turtle is the olive ridley sea turtle, which can be found in the Atlantic Ocean.

B) The Kemp's ridley sea turtle is referred to as *Lepidochelys kempii*, while the olive ridley sea turtle is referred to as *Lepidochelys olivacea*.

C) Both the Kemp's ridley sea turtle and the olive ridley sea turtle can be found in the Atlantic Ocean.

D) The Kemp's ridley sea turtle (*Lepidochelys kempii*) and the olive ridley sea turtle (*Lepidochelys olivacea*) are different species.

CONTINUE

26

While researching a topic, a student has taken the following notes:

- In 2019, Emily Shepard and colleagues in the UK and Germany studied the effect of wind on auks' success in landing at cliffside nesting sites.
- They found as wind conditions intensified, the birds needed more attempts in order to make a successful landing.
- When the wind was still, almost 100% of landing attempts were successful.
- In a strong breeze, approximately 40% of attempts were successful.
- In near-gale conditions, only around 20% of attempts were successful.

The student wants to summarize the study. Which choice most effectively uses relevant information from the notes to accomplish this goal?

A) For a 2019 study, researchers from the UK and Germany collected data on auks' attempts to land at cliffside nesting sites in different wind conditions.

B) Emily Shepard and her colleagues wanted to know the extent to which wind affected auks' success in landing at cliffside nesting sites, so they conducted a study.

C) Knowing that auks often need multiple attempts to land at their cliffside nesting sites, Emily Shepard studied the birds' success rate, which was only around 20% in some conditions.

D) Emily Shepard's 2019 study of auks' success in landing at cliffside nesting sites showed that as wind conditions intensified, the birds' success rate decreased.

27

While researching a topic, a student has taken the following notes:

- Abdulrazak Gurnah was awarded the 2021 Nobel Prize in Literature.
- Gurnah was born in Zanzibar in East Africa and currently lives in the United Kingdom.
- Many readers have singled out Gurnah's 1994 book *Paradise* for praise.
- *Paradise* is a historical novel about events that occurred in colonial East Africa.

The student wants to introduce *Paradise* to an audience unfamiliar with the novel and its author. Which choice most effectively uses relevant information from the notes to accomplish this goal?

A) Abdulrazak Gurnah, who wrote *Paradise* and later was awarded the Nobel Prize in Literature, was born in Zanzibar in East Africa and currently lives in the United Kingdom.

B) Many readers have singled out Abdulrazak Gurnah's 1994 book *Paradise*, a historical novel about colonial East Africa, for praise.

C) A much-praised historical novel about colonial East Africa, *Paradise* (1994) was written by Abdulrazak Gurnah, winner of the 2021 Nobel Prize in Literature.

D) *Paradise* is a historical novel about events that occurred in colonial East Africa, Abdulrazak Gurnah's homeland.

STOP

If you finish before time is called, you may check your work on this module only. Do not turn to any other module in the test.

Test begins on the next page.

Reading and Writing

27 QUESTIONS

DIRECTIONS

The questions in this section address a number of important reading and writing skills. Each question includes one or more passages, which may include a table or graph. Read each passage and question carefully, and then choose the best answer to the question based on the passage(s).

All questions in this section are multiple-choice with four answer choices. Each question has a single best answer.

1

In studying the use of external stimuli to reduce the itching sensation caused by an allergic histamine response, Louise Ward and colleagues found that while harmless applications of vibration or warming can provide a temporary distraction, such _____ stimuli actually offer less relief than a stimulus that seems less benign, like a mild electric shock.

Which choice completes the text with the most logical and precise word or phrase?

A) deceptive

B) innocuous

C) novel

D) impractical

2

New and interesting research conducted by Suleiman A. Al-Sweedan and Moath Alhaj is inspired by their observation that though there have been many studies of the effect of high altitude on blood chemistry, there is a _____ studies of the effect on blood chemistry of living in locations below sea level, such as the California towns of Salton City and Seeley.

Which choice completes the text with the most logical and precise word or phrase?

A) quarrel about

B) paucity of

C) profusion of

D) verisimilitude in

3

Whether the reign of a French monarch such as Hugh Capet or Henry I was historically consequential or relatively uneventful, its trajectory was shaped by questions of legitimacy and therefore cannot be understood without a corollary understanding of the factors that allowed the monarch to _____ his right to hold the throne.

Which choice completes the text with the most logical and precise word or phrase?

A) reciprocate

B) annotate

C) buttress

D) disengage

4

Researcher Haesung Jung led a 2020 study showing that individual acts of kindness can _____ prosocial behavior across a larger group. Jung and her team found that bystanders who witness a helpful act become more likely to offer help to someone else, and in doing so, can inspire still others to act.

Which choice completes the text with the most logical and precise word or phrase?

A) require

B) remember

C) foster

D) discourage

CONTINUE

5

The following text is adapted from *Indian Boyhood*, a 1902 memoir by Ohiyesa (Charles A. Eastman), a Santee Dakota writer. In the text, Ohiyesa recalls how the women in his tribe harvested maple syrup during his childhood.

Now the women began to test the trees—moving leisurely among them, axe in hand, and striking a single quick blow, to see if the sap would appear. <u>The trees, like people, have their individual characters; some were ready to yield up their life-blood, while others were more reluctant.</u> Now one of the birchen basins was set under each tree, and a hardwood chip driven deep into the cut which the axe had made. From the corners of this chip—at first drop by drop, then more freely—the sap trickled into the little dishes.

Which choice best describes the function of the underlined sentence in the text as a whole?

A) It portrays the range of personality traits displayed by the women as they work.

B) It foregrounds the beneficial relationship between humans and maple trees.

C) It demonstrates how human behavior can be influenced by the natural environment.

D) It elaborates on an aspect of the maple trees that the women evaluate.

6

The following text is from Charlotte Brontë's 1847 novel *Jane Eyre*. Jane, the narrator, works as a governess at Thornfield Hall.

I went on with my day's business tranquilly; but ever and anon vague suggestions kept wandering across my brain of reasons why I should quit Thornfield; and I kept involuntarily framing advertisements and pondering conjectures about new situations: these thoughts I did not think to check; they might germinate and bear fruit if they could.

Which choice best states the main purpose of the text?

A) To convey a contrast between Jane's outward calmness and internal restlessness

B) To emphasize Jane's loyalty to the people she works for at Thornfield Hall

C) To demonstrate that Jane finds her situation both challenging and deeply fulfilling

D) To describe Jane's determination to secure employment outside of Thornfield Hall

7

Musician Joni Mitchell, who is also a painter, uses images she creates for her album covers to emphasize ideas expressed in her music. For the cover of her album *Turbulent Indigo* (1994), Mitchell painted a striking self-portrait that closely resembles Vincent van Gogh's *Self-Portrait with Bandaged Ear* (1889). The image calls attention to the album's title song, in which Mitchell sings about the legacy of the postimpressionist painter. In that song, Mitchell also hints that she feels a strong artistic connection to Van Gogh—an idea that is reinforced by her imagery on the cover.

Which choice best describes the overall structure of the text?

A) It presents a claim about Mitchell, then gives an example supporting that claim.

B) It discusses Van Gogh's influence on Mitchell, then considers Mitchell's influence on other artists.

C) It describes a similarity between two artists, then notes a difference between them.

D) It describes the songs on *Turbulent Indigo*, then explains how they relate to the album's cover.

8

A study by a team including finance professor Madhu Veeraraghavan suggests that exposure to sunshine during the workday can lead to overly optimistic behavior. <u>Using data spanning from 1994 to 2010 for a set of US companies, the team compared over 29,000 annual earnings forecasts to the actual earnings later reported by those companies.</u> The team found that the greater the exposure to sunshine at work in the two weeks before a manager submitted an earnings forecast, the more the manager's forecast exceeded what the company actually earned that year.

Which choice best states the function of the underlined sentence in the overall structure of the text?

A) To summarize the results of the team's analysis

B) To present a specific example that illustrates the study's findings

C) To explain part of the methodology used in the team's study

D) To call out a challenge the team faced in conducting its analysis

9

Text 1
Most animals can regenerate some parts of their bodies, such as skin. But when a three-banded panther worm is cut into three pieces, each piece grows into a new worm. Researchers are investigating this feat partly to learn more about humans' comparatively limited abilities to regenerate, and they're making exciting progress. An especially promising discovery is that both humans and panther worms have a gene for early growth response (EGR) linked to regeneration.

Text 2
When Mansi Srivastava and her team reported that panther worms, like humans, possess a gene for EGR, it caused excitement. However, as the team pointed out, the gene likely functions very differently in humans than it does in panther worms. Srivastava has likened EGR to a switch that activates other genes involved in regeneration in panther worms, but how this switch operates in humans remains unclear.

Based on the texts, what would the author of Text 2 most likely say about Text 1's characterization of the discovery involving EGR?

A) It is reasonable given that Srivastava and her team have identified how EGR functions in both humans and panther worms.

B) It is overly optimistic given additional observations from Srivastava and her team.

C) It is unexpected given that Srivastava and her team's findings were generally met with enthusiasm.

D) It is unfairly dismissive given the progress that Srivastava and her team have reported.

CONTINUE

Credited Film Output of James Young Deer,
Dark Cloud, Edwin Carewe, and Lillian St. Cyr

Individual	Years active	Number of films known and commonly credited
James Young Deer	1909–1924	33 (actor), 35 (director), 10 (writer)
Dark Cloud	1910–1920	35 (actor), 1 (writer)
Edwin Carewe	1912–1934	47 (actor), 58 (director), 20 (producer), 4 (writer)
Lillian St. Cyr (Red Wing)	1908–1921	66 (actor)

Some researchers studying Indigenous actors and filmmakers in the United
States have turned their attention to the early days of cinema, particularly the
1910s and 1920s, when people like James Young Deer, Dark Cloud, Edwin
Carewe, and Lillian St. Cyr (known professionally as Red Wing) were involved in
one way or another with numerous films. In fact, so many films and associated
records for this era have been lost that counts of those four figures' output should
be taken as bare minimums rather than totals; it's entirely possible, for example,
that _____

Which choice most effectively uses data from the table to complete the example?

A) Dark Cloud acted in significantly fewer films than did Lillian St. Cyr, who is
credited with 66 performances.

B) Edwin Carewe's 47 credited acting roles includes only films made after 1934.

C) Lillian St. Cyr acted in far more than 66 films and Edwin Carewe directed
more than 58.

D) James Young Deer actually directed 33 films and acted in only 10.

Mosasaurs were large marine reptiles that lived in the Late Cretaceous period, approximately 100 million to 66 million years ago. Celina Suarez, Alberto Pérez-Huerta, and T. Lynn Harrell Jr. examined oxygen-18 isotopes in mosasaur tooth enamel in order to calculate likely mosasaur body temperatures and determined that mosasaurs were endothermic—that is, they used internal metabolic processes to maintain a stable body temperature in a variety of ambient temperatures. Suarez, Pérez-Huerta, and Harrell claim that endothermy would have enabled mosasaurs to include relatively cold polar waters in their range.

Which finding, if true, would most directly support Suarez, Pérez-Huerta, and Harrell's claim?

A) Mosasaurs' likely body temperatures are easier to determine from tooth enamel oxygen-18 isotope data than the body temperatures of nonendothermic Late Cretaceous marine reptiles are.

B) Fossils of both mosasaurs and nonendothermic marine reptiles have been found in roughly equal numbers in regions known to be near the poles during the Late Cretaceous, though in lower concentrations than elsewhere.

C) Several mosasaur fossils have been found in regions known to be near the poles during the Late Cretaceous, while relatively few fossils of nonendothermic marine reptiles have been found in those locations.

D) During the Late Cretaceous, seawater temperatures were likely higher throughout mosasaurs' range, including near the poles, than seawater temperatures at those same latitudes are today.

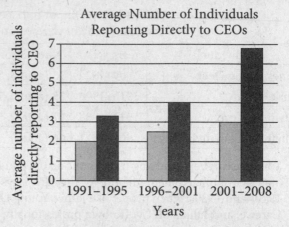

Average Number of Individuals Reporting Directly to CEOs

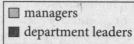

Considering a large sample of companies, economics experts Maria Guadalupe, Julie Wulf, and Raghuram Rajan assessed the number of managers and leaders from different departments who reported directly to a chief executive officer (CEO). According to the researchers, the findings suggest that across the years analyzed, there was a growing interest among CEOs in connecting with more departments in their companies.

Which choice best describes data from the graph that support the researchers' conclusion?

A) The average numbers of managers and department leaders reporting directly to their CEO didn't fluctuate from the 1991–1995 period to the 2001–2008 period.

B) The average number of managers reporting directly to their CEO was highest in the 1996–2001 period.

C) The average number of department leaders reporting directly to their CEO was greater than the average number of managers reporting directly to their CEO in each of the three periods studied.

D) The average number of department leaders reporting directly to their CEO rose over the three periods studied.

CONTINUE

13

Given that stars and planets initially form from the same gas and dust in space, some astronomers have posited that host stars (such as the Sun) and their planets (such as those in our solar system) are composed of the same materials, with the planets containing equal or smaller quantities of the materials that make up the host star. This idea is also supported by evidence that rocky planets in our solar system are composed of some of the same materials as the Sun.

Which finding, if true, would most directly weaken the astronomers' claim?

A) Most stars are made of hydrogen and helium, but when cooled they are revealed to contain small amounts of iron and silicate.

B) A nearby host star is observed to contain the same proportion of hydrogen and helium as that of the Sun.

C) Evidence emerges that the amount of iron in some rocky planets is considerably higher than the amount in their host star.

D) The method for determining the composition of rocky planets is discovered to be less effective when used to analyze other kinds of planets.

14

While attending school in New York City in the 1980s, Okwui Enwezor encountered few works by African artists in exhibitions, despite New York's reputation as one of the best places to view contemporary art from around the world. According to an arts journalist, later in his career as a renowned curator and art historian, Enwezor sought to remedy this deficiency, not by focusing solely on modern African artists, but by showing how their work fits into the larger context of global modern art and art history.

Which finding, if true, would most directly support the journalist's claim?

A) As curator of the Haus der Kunst in Munich, Germany, Enwezor organized a retrospective of Ghanaian sculptor El Anatsui's work entitled *El Anatsui: Triumphant Scale*, one of the largest art exhibitions devoted to a Black artist in Europe's history.

B) In the exhibition *Postwar: Art Between the Pacific and the Atlantic, 1945–1965,* Enwezor and cocurator Katy Siegel brought works by African artists such as Malangatana Ngwenya together with pieces by major figures from other countries, like US artist Andy Warhol and Mexico's David Siqueiros.

C) Enwezor's work as curator of the 2001 exhibition *The Short Century: Independence and Liberation Movements in Africa, 1945–1994* showed how African movements for independence from European colonial powers following the Second World War profoundly influenced work by African artists of the period, such as Kamala Ibrahim Ishaq and Thomas Mukarobgwa.

D) Enwezor organized the exhibition *In/sight: African Photographers, 1940 to the Present* not to emphasize a particular aesthetic trend but to demonstrate the broad range of ways in which African artists have approached the medium of photography.

CONTINUE

15

One challenge when researching whether holding elected office changes a person's behavior is the problem of ensuring that the experiment has an appropriate control group. To reveal the effect of holding office, researchers must compare people who hold elected office with people who do not hold office but who are otherwise similar to the office-holders. Since researchers are unable to control which politicians win elections, they therefore _____

Which choice most logically completes the text?

A) struggle to find valid data about the behavior of politicians who do not currently hold office.

B) can only conduct valid studies with people who have previously held office rather than people who presently hold office.

C) should select a control group of people who differ from office holders in several significant ways.

D) will find it difficult to identify a group of people who can function as an appropriate control group for their studies.

16

Compiled in the late 1500s largely through the efforts of Indigenous scribes, *Cantares Mexicanos* is the most important collection of poetry in Classical Nahuatl, the principal language of the Aztec Empire. The poems portray Aztec society before the occupation of the empire by the army of Spain, and marginal notes in *Cantares Mexicanos* indicate that much of the collection's content predates the initial invasion. Nonetheless, some of the poems contain inarguable references to beliefs and customs common in Spain during this era. Thus, some scholars have concluded that _____

Which choice most logically completes the text?

A) while its content largely predates the invasion, *Cantares Mexicanos* also contains additions made after the invasion.

B) although those who compiled *Cantares Mexicanos* were fluent in Nahuatl, they had limited knowledge of the Spanish language.

C) before the invasion by Spain, the poets of the Aztec Empire borrowed from the literary traditions of other societies.

D) the references to beliefs and customs in Spain should be attributed to a coincidental resemblance between the societies of Spain and the Aztec Empire.

CONTINUE

17

To humans, it does not appear that the golden orb-weaver spider uses camouflage to capture its _____ the brightly colored arachnid seems to wait conspicuously in the center of its large circular web for insects to approach. Researcher Po Peng of the University of Melbourne has explained that the spider's distinctive coloration may in fact be part of its appeal.

Which choice completes the text so that it conforms to the conventions of Standard English?

A) prey, rather,

B) prey rather,

C) prey, rather;

D) prey; rather,

18

Bonnie Buratti of NASA's Jet Propulsion Laboratory _____ data about Saturn's rings collected by the *Cassini* spacecraft when she made an interesting discovery: the tiny moons embedded between and within Saturn's rings are shaped by the buildup of ring material on the moons' surfaces.

Which choice completes the text so that it conforms to the conventions of Standard English?

A) studies

B) has been studying

C) will study

D) was studying

19

On July 23, 1854, a clipper ship called the *Flying Cloud* entered San Francisco _____ left New York Harbor under the guidance of Captain Josiah Perkins Creesy and his wife, navigator Eleanor Creesy, a mere 89 days and 8 hours earlier, the celebrated ship set a record that would stand for 135 years.

Which choice completes the text so that it conforms to the conventions of Standard English?

A) Bay and having

B) Bay. Having

C) Bay, having

D) Bay having

20

Bengali author Toru Dutt's *A Sheaf Gleaned in French Fields* (1876), a volume of English translations of French poems, _____ scholars' understanding of the transnational and multilingual contexts in which Dutt lived and worked.

Which choice completes the text so that it conforms to the conventions of Standard English?

A) has enhanced

B) are enhancing

C) have enhanced

D) enhance

CONTINUE

21

Hegra is an archaeological site in present-day Saudi Arabia and was the second largest city of the Nabataean Kingdom (fourth century BCE to first century CE). Archaeologist Laila Nehmé recently traveled to Hegra to study its ancient _____ into the rocky outcrops of a vast desert, these burial chambers seem to blend seamlessly with nature.

Which choice completes the text so that it conforms to the conventions of Standard English?

A) tombs. Built

B) tombs, built

C) tombs and built

D) tombs built

22

In 1937, Chinese American screen actor Anna May Wong, who had portrayed numerous villains and secondary characters but never a heroine, finally got a starring role in Paramount Pictures' *Daughter of Shanghai*, a film that _____ "expanded the range of possibilities for Asian images on screen."

Which choice completes the text so that it conforms to the conventions of Standard English?

A) critic, Stina Chyn, claims

B) critic, Stina Chyn, claims,

C) critic Stina Chyn claims

D) critic Stina Chyn, claims,

23

The Arctic-Alpine Botanic Garden in Norway and the Jardim Botânico of Rio de Janeiro in Brazil are two of many botanical gardens around the world dedicated to growing diverse plant _____ fostering scientific research; and educating the public about plant conservation.

Which choice completes the text so that it conforms to the conventions of Standard English?

A) species, both native and nonnative,

B) species, both native and nonnative;

C) species; both native and nonnative,

D) species both native and nonnative,

24

The Babylonian king Hammurabi achieved much during his forty-year reign. He conquered all of Mesopotamia and built Babylon into one of the most powerful cities of the ancient world. Today, _____ he is mainly remembered for a code of laws inscribed on a seven-foot-tall block of stone: the Code of Hammurabi.

Which choice completes the text with the most logical transition?

A) therefore,

B) likewise,

C) however,

D) for instance,

Unauthorized copying or reuse of any part of this page is illegal.

CONTINUE

568

25

In her poetry collection *Thomas and Beulah*, Rita Dove interweaves the titular characters' personal stories with broader historical narratives. She places Thomas's journey from the American South to the Midwest in the early 1900s within the larger context of the Great Migration. _____ Dove sets events from Beulah's personal life against the backdrop of the US Civil Rights Movement.

Which choice completes the text with the most logical transition?

A) Specifically,

B) Thus,

C) Regardless,

D) Similarly,

26

When designing costumes for film, American artist Suttirat Larlarb typically custom fits the garments to each actor. _____ for the film *Sunshine*, in which astronauts must reignite a dying Sun, she designed a golden spacesuit and had a factory reproduce it in a few standard sizes; lacking a tailor-made quality, the final creations reflected the ungainliness of actual spacesuits.

Which choice completes the text with the most logical transition?

A) Nevertheless,

B) Thus,

C) Likewise,

D) Moreover,

27

While researching a topic, a student has taken the following notes:

- Astronomers estimate that the number of comets orbiting the Sun is in the billions.
- 81P/Wild is one of many comets whose orbit has changed over time.
- 81P/Wild's orbit once lay between the orbits of Uranus and Jupiter.
- The comet's orbit is now positioned between the orbits of Jupiter and Mars.

The student wants to make and support a generalization about the orbits of comets. Which choice most effectively uses relevant information from the notes to accomplish these goals?

A) Astronomers estimate that the number of comets orbiting the Sun is in the billions; the comets' orbits may change over time.

B) Like Uranus, Jupiter, and Mars, billions of comets orbit the Sun.

C) One example of a comet is 81P/Wild, whose orbit around the Sun once lay between Uranus's and Jupiter's orbits but is now positioned between those of Jupiter and Mars.

D) A comet's orbit around the Sun may change over time: the orbit of comet 81P/Wild once lay between the orbits of Uranus and Jupiter but is now positioned between those of Jupiter and Mars.

STOP

**If you finish before time is called, you may check your work on this module only.
Do not turn to any other module in the test.**

Math

22 QUESTIONS

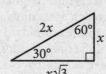

$A = \pi r^2$ $A = \ell w$ $A = \frac{1}{2}bh$ $c^2 = a^2 + b^2$ Special Right Triangles
$C = 2\pi r$

$V = \ell wh$ $V = \pi r^2 h$ $V = \frac{4}{3}\pi r^3$ $V = \frac{1}{3}\pi r^2 h$ $V = \frac{1}{3}\ell wh$

The number of degrees of arc in a circle is 360.

The number of radians of arc in a circle is 2π.

The sum of the measures in degrees of the angles of a triangle is 180.

CONTINUE →

For multiple-choice questions, solve each problem, choose the correct answer from the choices provided, and then circle your answer in this book. Circle only one answer for each question. If you change your mind, completely erase the circle. You will not get credit for questions with more than one answer circled, or for questions with no answers circled.

For student-produced response questions, solve each problem and write your answer next to or under the question in the test book as described below.

- Once you've written your answer, circle it clearly. You will not receive credit for anything written outside the circle, or for any questions with more than one circled answer.

- If you find **more than one correct answer**, write and circle only one answer.

- Your answer can be up to 5 characters for a **positive** answer and up to 6 characters (including the negative sign) for a **negative** answer, but no more.

- If your answer is a **fraction** that is too long (over 5 characters for positive, 6 characters for negative), write the decimal equivalent.

- If your answer is a **decimal** that is too long (over 5 characters for positive, 6 characters for negative), truncate it or round at the fourth digit.

- If your answer is a **mixed number** (such as $3\frac{1}{2}$), write it as an improper fraction (7/2) or its decimal equivalent (3.5).

- Don't include **symbols** such as a percent sign, comma, or dollar sign in your circled answer.

CONTINUE

1

If $x = 7$, what is the value of $x + 20$?

A) 13

B) 20

C) 27

D) 34

2

Data set X: 5, 9, 9, 13
Data set Y: 5, 9, 9, 13, 27

The lists give the values in data sets X and Y. Which statement correctly compares the mean of data set X and the mean of data set Y?

A) The mean of data set X is greater than the mean of data set Y.

B) The mean of data set X is less than the mean of data set Y.

C) The means of data set X and data set Y are equal.

D) There is not enough information to compare the means.

3

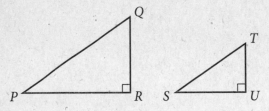

Note: Figures not drawn to scale.

Right triangles PQR and STU are similar, where P corresponds to S. If the measure of angle Q is 18°, what is the measure of angle S?

A) 18°

B) 72°

C) 82°

D) 162°

4

A rocket contained 467,000 kilograms (kg) of propellant before launch. Exactly 21 seconds after launch, 362,105 kg of this propellant remained. On average, approximately how much propellant, in kg, did the rocket burn each second after launch?

A) 4,995

B) 17,243

C) 39,481

D) 104,895

5

$$4x = 20$$
$$-3x + y = -7$$

The solution to the given system of equations is (x, y). What is the value of $x + y$?

A) −27

B) −13

C) 13

D) 27

6

A certain apprentice has enrolled in 85 hours of training courses. The equation $10x + 15y = 85$ represents this situation, where x is the number of on-site training courses and y is the number of online training courses this apprentice has enrolled in. How many more hours does each online training course take than each on-site training course?

Unauthorized copying or reuse of any part of this page is illegal.

572

CONTINUE ▶

7

Square X has a side length of 12 centimeters. The perimeter of square Y is 2 times the perimeter of square X. What is the length, in centimeters, of one side of square Y?

A) 6

B) 10

C) 14

D) 24

8

$$g(m) = -0.05m + 12.1$$

The given function g models the number of gallons of gasoline that remains from a full gas tank in a car after driving m miles. According to the model, about how many gallons of gasoline are used to drive each mile?

A) 0.05

B) 12.1

C) 20

D) 242.0

9

If $|4x - 4| = 112$, what is the positive value of $x - 1$?

10

$$\frac{1}{7b} = \frac{11x}{y}$$

The given equation relates the positive numbers b, x, and y. Which equation correctly expresses x in terms of b and y?

A) $x = \dfrac{7by}{11}$

B) $x = y - 77b$

C) $x = \dfrac{y}{77b}$

D) $x = 77by$

11

x	10	15	20	25
$f(x)$	82	137	192	247

The table shows four values of x and their corresponding values of $f(x)$. There is a linear relationship between x and $f(x)$ that is defined by the equation $f(x) = mx - 28$, where m is a constant. What is the value of m?

12

$$(5x^3 - 3) - (-4x^3 + 8)$$

The given expression is equivalent to $bx^3 - 11$, where b is a constant. What is the value of b?

13

$$y > 14$$
$$4x + y < 18$$

The point $(x, 53)$ is a solution to the system of inequalities in the xy-plane. Which of the following could be the value of x?

A) −9

B) −5

C) 5

D) 9

14

Bacteria are growing in a liquid growth medium. There were 300,000 cells per milliliter during an initial observation. The number of cells per milliliter doubles every 3 hours. How many cells per milliliter will there be 15 hours after the initial observation?

A) 1,500,000

B) 2,400,000

C) 4,500,000

D) 9,600,000

CONTINUE

15

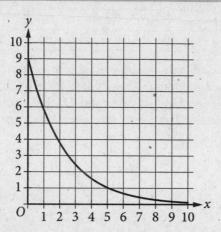

The graph gives the estimated number of catalogs y, in thousands, a company sent to its customers at the end of each year, where x represents the number of years since the end of 1992, where $0 \le x \le 10$. Which statement is the best interpretation of the y-intercept in this context?

A) The estimated total number of catalogs the company sent to its customers during the first 10 years was 9,000.

B) The estimated total number of catalogs the company sent to its customers from the end of 1992 to the end of 2002 was 90.

C) The estimated number of catalogs the company sent to its customers at the end of 1992 was 9.

D) The estimated number of catalogs the company sent to its customers at the end of 1992 was 9,000.

16

Which expression is equivalent to $\sqrt[7]{x^9 y^9}$, where x and y are positive?

A) $(xy)^{\frac{7}{9}}$

B) $(xy)^{\frac{9}{7}}$

C) $(xy)^{16}$

D) $(xy)^{63}$

17

The population of City A increased by 7% from 2015 to 2016. If the 2016 population is k times the 2015 population, what is the value of k?

A) 0.07

B) 0.7

C) 1.07

D) 1.7

18

Which of the following systems of linear equations has no solution?

A) $x = 3$
   $y = 5$

B) $y = 6x + 6$
   $y = 5x + 6$

C) $y = 16x + 3$
   $y = 16x + 19$

D) $y = 5$
   $y = 5x + 5$

CONTINUE

19

The first term of a sequence is 9. Each term after the first is 4 times the preceding term. If w represents the nth term of the sequence, which equation gives w in terms of n?

A) $w = 4(9^n)$

B) $w = 4(9^{n-1})$

C) $w = 9(4^n)$

D) $w = 9(4^{n-1})$

20

The minimum value of x is 12 less than 6 times another number n. Which inequality shows the possible values of x?

A) $x \leq 6n - 12$

B) $x \geq 6n - 12$

C) $x \leq 12 - 6n$

D) $x \geq 12 - 6n$

21

$RS = 20$
$ST = 48$
$TR = 52$

The side lengths of right triangle RST are given. Triangle RST is similar to triangle UVW, where S corresponds to V and T corresponds to W. What is the value of $\tan W$?

A) $\dfrac{5}{13}$

B) $\dfrac{5}{12}$

C) $\dfrac{12}{13}$

D) $\dfrac{12}{5}$

22

The graph of $9x - 10y = 19$ is translated down 4 units in the xy-plane. What is the x-coordinate of the x-intercept of the resulting graph?

STOP

**If you finish before time is called, you may check your work on this module only.
Do not turn to any other module in the test.**

Math

22 QUESTIONS

The questions in this section address a number of important math skills.
Use of a calculator is permitted for all questions.

Unless otherwise indicated:

- All variables and expressions represent real numbers.
- Figures provided are drawn to scale.
- All figures lie in a plane.
- The domain of a given function f is the set of all real numbers x for which $f(x)$ is a real number.

$A = \pi r^2$
$C = 2\pi r$

$A = \ell w$

$A = \frac{1}{2} bh$

$c^2 = a^2 + b^2$

Special Right Triangles

$V = \ell wh$

$V = \pi r^2 h$

$V = \frac{4}{3}\pi r^3$

$V = \frac{1}{3}\pi r^2 h$

$V = \frac{1}{3}\ell wh$

The number of degrees of arc in a circle is 360.

The number of radians of arc in a circle is 2π.

The sum of the measures in degrees of the angles of a triangle is 180.

CONTINUE

For multiple-choice questions, solve each problem, choose the correct answer from the choices provided, and then circle your answer in this book. Circle only one answer for each question. If you change your mind, completely erase the circle. You will not get credit for questions with more than one answer circled, or for questions with no answers circled.

For student-produced response questions, solve each problem and write your answer next to or under the question in the test book as described below.

- Once you've written your answer, circle it clearly. You will not receive credit for anything written outside the circle, or for any questions with more than one circled answer.

- If you find **more than one correct answer**, write and circle only one answer.

- Your answer can be up to 5 characters for a **positive** answer and up to 6 characters (including the negative sign) for a **negative** answer, but no more.

- If your answer is a **fraction** that is too long (over 5 characters for positive, 6 characters for negative), write the decimal equivalent.

- If your answer is a **decimal** that is too long (over 5 characters for positive, 6 characters for negative), truncate it or round at the fourth digit.

- If your answer is a **mixed number** (such as $3\frac{1}{2}$), write it as an improper fraction (7/2) or its decimal equivalent (3.5).

- Don't include **symbols** such as a percent sign, comma, or dollar sign in your circled answer.

CONTINUE

1

There are 55 students in Spanish club. A sample of the Spanish club students was selected at random and asked whether they intend to enroll in a new study program. Of those surveyed, 20% responded that they intend to enroll in the study program. Based on this survey, which of the following is the best estimate of the total number of Spanish club students who intend to enroll in the study program?

A) 11

B) 20

C) 44

D) 55

2

A machine makes large boxes or small boxes, one at a time, for a total of 700 minutes each day. It takes the machine 10 minutes to make a large box or 5 minutes to make a small box. Which equation represents the possible number of large boxes, x, and small boxes, y, the machine can make each day?

A) $5x + 10y = 700$

B) $10x + 5y = 700$

C) $(x + y)(10 + 5) = 700$

D) $(10 + x)(5 + y) = 700$

3

The scatterplot shows the relationship between two variables, x and y. A line of best fit is also shown.

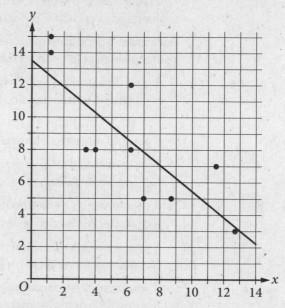

Which of the following equations best represents the line of best fit shown?

A) $y = 13.5 + 0.8x$

B) $y = 13.5 - 0.8x$

C) $y = -13.5 + 0.8x$

D) $y = -13.5 - 0.8x$

CONTINUE

4

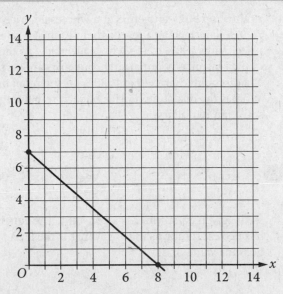

The point with coordinates $(d, 4)$ lies on the line shown. What is the value of d?

A) $\dfrac{7}{2}$

B) $\dfrac{26}{7}$

C) $\dfrac{24}{7}$

D) $\dfrac{27}{8}$

5

x	$f(x)$
-1	10
0	14
1	20

For the quadratic function f, the table shows three values of x and their corresponding values of $f(x)$. Which equation defines f?

A) $f(x) = 3x^2 + 3x + 14$

B) $f(x) = 5x^2 + x + 14$

C) $f(x) = 9x^2 - x + 14$

D) $f(x) = x^2 + 5x + 14$

6

The function f is defined by $f(x) = \dfrac{x + 15}{5}$, and $f(a) = 10$, where a is a constant. What is the value of a?

A) 5

B) 10

C) 35

D) 65

7

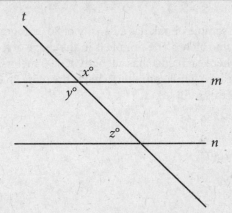

Note: Figure not drawn to scale.

In the figure, lines m and n are parallel. If $x = 6k + 13$ and $y = 8k - 29$, what is the value of z?

A) 3

B) 21

C) 41

D) 139

CONTINUE

8

Line p is defined by $2y + 18x = 9$. Line r is perpendicular to line p in the xy-plane. What is the slope of line r?

A) -9

B) $-\dfrac{1}{9}$

C) $\dfrac{1}{9}$

D) 9

9

A sample of oak has a density of 807 kilograms per cubic meter. The sample is in the shape of a cube, where each edge has a length of 0.90 meters. To the nearest whole number, what is the mass, in kilograms, of this sample?

A) 588

B) 726

C) 897

D) 1,107

10

$$P(t) = 290(1.04)^{\left(\frac{4}{6}\right)t}$$

The function P models the population, in thousands, of a certain city t years after 2005. According to the model, the population is predicted to increase by $n\%$ every 18 months. What is the value of n?

A) 0.38

B) 1.04

C) 4

D) 6

11

$$2(kx - n) = -\frac{28}{15}x - \frac{36}{19}$$

In the given equation, k and n are constants and $n > 1$. The equation has no solution. What is the value of k?

12

A gift shop buys souvenirs at a wholesale price of 7.00 dollars each and resells them each at a retail price that is 290% of the wholesale price. At the end of the season, any remaining souvenirs are marked at a discounted price that is 80% off the retail price. What is the discounted price of each remaining souvenir, in dollars?

13

$$x^2 - 34x + c = 0$$

In the given equation, c is a constant. The equation has no real solutions if $c > n$. What is the least possible value of n?

14

Data set A consists of the heights of 75 buildings and has a mean of 32 meters. Data set B consists of the heights of 50 buildings and has a mean of 62 meters. Data set C consists of the heights of the 125 buildings from data sets A and B. What is the mean, in meters, of data set C?

15

The expression $4x^2 + bx - 45$, where b is a constant, can be rewritten as $(hx + k)(x + j)$, where h, k, and j are integer constants. Which of the following must be an integer?

A) $\dfrac{b}{h}$

B) $\dfrac{b}{k}$

C) $\dfrac{45}{h}$

D) $\dfrac{45}{k}$

CONTINUE

16

$$y = -1.5$$
$$y = x^2 + 8x + a$$

In the given system of equations, a is a positive constant. The system has exactly one distinct real solution. What is the value of a?

17

Data Set A

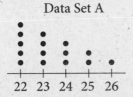

22 23 24 25 26

The dot plot represents the 15 values in data set A. Data set B is created by adding 56 to each of the values in data set A. Which of the following correctly compares the medians and the ranges of data sets A and B?

A) The median of data set B is equal to the median of data set A, and the range of data set B is equal to the range of data set A.

B) The median of data set B is equal to the median of data set A, and the range of data set B is greater than the range of data set A.

C) The median of data set B is greater than the median of data set A, and the range of data set B is equal to the range of data set A.

D) The median of data set B is greater than the median of data set A, and the range of data set B is greater than the range of data set A.

18

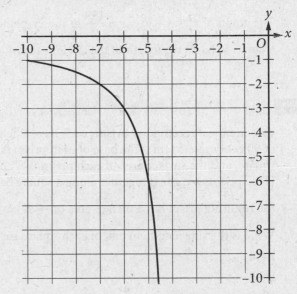

The rational function f is defined by an equation in the form $f(x) = \dfrac{a}{x + b}$ where a and b are constants. The partial graph of $y = f(x)$ is shown. If $g(x) = f(x + 4)$, which equation could define function g?

A) $g(x) = \dfrac{6}{x}$

B) $g(x) = \dfrac{6}{x + 4}$

C) $g(x) = \dfrac{6}{x + 8}$

D) $g(x) = \dfrac{6(x + 4)}{x + 4}$

19

$$57x^2 + (57b + a)x + ab = 0$$

In the given equation, a and b are positive constants. The product of the solutions to the given equation is kab, where k is a constant. What is the value of k?

A) $\dfrac{1}{57}$

B) $\dfrac{1}{19}$

C) 1

D) 57

CONTINUE

20

The graph of $x^2 + x + y^2 + y = \dfrac{199}{2}$ in the xy-plane is a circle. What is the length of the circle's radius?

21

Two identical rectangular prisms each have a height of 90 centimeters (cm). The base of each prism is a square, and the surface area of each prism is K cm^2. If the prisms are glued together along a square base, the resulting prism has a surface area of $\dfrac{92}{47} K$ cm^2.

What is the side length, in cm, of each square base?

A) 4

B) 8

C) 9

D) 16

22

In the xy-plane, a parabola has vertex $(9, -14)$ and intersects the x-axis at two points. If the equation of the parabola is written in the form $y = ax^2 + bx + c$, where a, b, and c are constants, which of the following could be the value of $a + b + c$?

A) -23

B) -19

C) -14

D) -12

STOP

**If you finish before time is called, you may check your work on this module only.
Do not turn to any other module in the test.**

The SAT®

Practice Test #4

ANSWER EXPLANATIONS

These answer explanations are for students using
The Official Digital SAT Study Guide.

Reading and Writing

Module 1
(27 questions)

QUESTION 1

Choice B is the best answer because it most logically completes the text's discussion of Booker T. Whatley. In this context, "hinder" means hold back or obstruct. The text explains that Whatley encouraged farms to allow customers on site to pick their own produce for a fee. He did so despite critics' concerns that the customers would never pay to do so. This context establishes that the critics' concerns didn't hinder Whatley's efforts to promote the practice.

Choice A is incorrect. The text indicates that critics' skepticism of the idea that customers would pay to pick their own produce didn't have some effect on Whatley's promotion of the practice. The text illustrates this assertion by describing Whatley's "determined advocacy" for the practice. This context suggests that critics' concerns didn't obstruct Whatley's efforts, not that critics' concerns didn't "enhance," or increase or improve, Whatley's efforts. *Choice C* is incorrect because in this context, "misrepresent" would mean portray inaccurately, and the text includes no information relevant to the issue of how Whatley's efforts were portrayed by critics of the practice of charging customers to pick their own produce. *Choice D* is incorrect. The text indicates that critics' skepticism of the idea that customers would pay to pick their own produce didn't have some effect on Whatley's promotion of the practice. The text illustrates this assertion by describing Whatley's "determined advocacy" for the practice. This context suggests that critics' concerns didn't obstruct Whatley's efforts, not that critics' concerns didn't "aggravate," or irritate or make more severe, Whatley's efforts.

QUESTION 2

Choice B is the best answer because it most logically completes the text's discussion of bronze- and brasscasting techniques used by the Igun Eronmwon guild. In this context "adhere to" would mean to act in accordance with. The text states that although members of the Igun Eronmwon guild typically do something with techniques that have been passed down since the thirteenth century, they "don't strictly observe every tradition." By establishing a contrast with not always following traditions, the context suggests that guild members do typically adhere to traditional techniques.

Choice A is incorrect because in this context "experiment with" would mean to do something new with. Although using motors rather than manual bellows is presented as a new approach, the text establishes a contrast between what the guild members typically do with techniques that have been passed down over centuries and the idea that the members "don't strictly observe every tradition." The phrase "experiment with" wouldn't support the contrast because regularly trying new things with the techniques would be an example of not strictly following all traditions. *Choice C* is incorrect because in this context "improve on" would mean to make better. Although using motors rather than manual bellows might be an improved approach, the text establishes a contrast between what the guild members typically do with techniques that have been passed down over centuries and the idea that the members "don't strictly observe every tradition." The phrase "improve on" wouldn't support the contrast because regularly making changes to the techniques would be an example of not strictly following all traditions. *Choice D* is incorrect because in this context "grapple with" would mean to try hard to solve a difficult problem. Although bronze- and brasscasting are likely challenging tasks, nothing in the text suggests that the guild members have any particular difficulties with the techniques passed down since the thirteenth century.

QUESTION 3

Choice A is the best answer because it most logically completes the text's discussion of Yu's novel. In this context, "haphazard" means marked by a lack of plan or order. The text indicates that the quest featured in the novel, which involves the protagonist bouncing across time, is chaotic and causes the reader to often wonder what will happen. This context suggests that the protagonist's journey seems to be marked by a lack of order.

Choice B is incorrect because the text indicates that the journey featured in Yu's novel involves a character "ricocheting chaotically," or bouncing in a disordered way, across time and causes the reader to often wonder what will happen. It wouldn't make sense to say that a chaotic journey seems "premeditated," or characterized by forethought and planning. *Choice C* is incorrect because the text doesn't give any indication that readers regard the journey in Yu's novel as "inspirational," or as causing extraordinarily creative or brilliant thoughts or actions; instead, the text focuses on the idea that the protagonist's journey is chaotic, or disordered, and doesn't give readers a clear sense of what will happen. *Choice D* is incorrect. Rather than suggesting that the journey featured in Yu's novel is "fruitless," or has an unsuccessful outcome, the text focuses on the idea that while reading about the protagonist's chaotic movements across time, readers are often unsure of what will happen—that is, they don't know whether the protagonist will be successful in finding his father.

QUESTION 4

Choice B is the best answer because it most logically completes the text's discussion of single-celled organism behavior. As used in this context, "rudimentary" means basic or unsophisticated. According to the text, a study of the single-celled protozoan *Stentor roeseli* showed that the organisms can switch strategies for escaping certain stimuli, "sophisticatedly 'changing their minds'" and using new strategies should other strategies fail. This context suggests that single-celled organisms may not be limited to behaviors that are basic or rudimentary, since the study showed that single-celled protozoans can respond complexly to irritating stimuli.

Choice A is incorrect because the text doesn't suggest that single-celled organisms may not be limited to behavior that is "aggressive," or threatening. Rather, the text suggests that single-celled organisms may not be limited to behaviors that are basic, since the study of *Stentor roeseli* showed that single-celled protozoans can respond complexly to irritating stimuli.

Choice C is incorrect because the text doesn't suggest that single-celled organisms may not be limited to behavior that is "evolving," or advancing. Rather, the text suggests that single-celled organisms may not be limited to behaviors that are basic, since the study of *Stentor roeseli* showed that single-celled protozoans can respond complexly to irritating stimuli. *Choice D* is incorrect because the text doesn't suggest that single-celled organisms may not be limited to behavior that is "advantageous," or helpful. Rather, the text suggests that single-celled organisms may not be limited to behaviors that are basic, since the study of *Stentor roeseli* showed that single-celled protozoans can respond complexly to irritating stimuli.

QUESTION 5

Choice A is the best answer because it most logically completes the text's discussion of late nineteenth- and early twentieth-century household food purchases. In this context, "surmised" means formed an idea or assumption with little evidence. The text explains that certain economic historians "assumed" that large and small households spent different amounts on food per person, but that another economist found this supposition to be false based on evidence from available data. This context suggests that the economic historians made an incorrect assumption without enough consideration of evidence.

Choice B is incorrect. In this context, "contrived" would mean brought about or created through trickery. Nothing in the text suggests that the economic historians were deliberately trying to trick people with a claim about food purchasing behaviors in late nineteenth- and early twentieth-century households; the text simply suggests that they made an assumption about those behaviors that another historian believes isn't supported by the available data. *Choice C* is incorrect because the text indicates that it's Logan and not the economic historians who "questioned," or doubted, the assumption that large and small households in the late nineteenth and early twentieth centuries spent different amounts on food per person; the economic historians are the ones who made that assumption to begin with. *Choice D* is incorrect because nothing in the text suggests that some economic historians "regretted," or felt sad or remorseful about, the food purchasing behaviors of late nineteenth- and early twentieth-century households. The text focuses on the idea that the economic historians made an assumption about those behaviors that may not be supported by available data, not on the historians' emotional response to what households did in the past.

QUESTION 6

Choice D is the best answer because as used in the text, "answers" most nearly means fulfills. In the text, Fabry and Busman claim that the robots manufactured by their company are more efficient than human workers, which they refer to as "the human machine." Fabry observes that the human machine "no longer answers the requirements of *modern engineering*." That is, human workers are incapable of meeting the rigorous needs of modern, industrialized workplaces.

Choice A is incorrect. Although in some contexts "answers" can mean explains, it doesn't have that meaning in this context because the topic under discussion is human beings' inability to perform labor efficiently, not their inability to engage in discussion or explanation. *Choice B* is incorrect. Although in some contexts "answers" can mean rebuts, or proves a claim or argument to be false, it wouldn't make sense to speak of proving requirements to be false; requirements might or might not be reasonable, but they can't be verified as truthful or untruthful, as claims or accusations can. *Choice C* is incorrect.

Although in some contexts, "answers" can mean defends against criticism, or justifies, it doesn't have that meaning in this context because the opinion that Fabry expresses is that human workers can no longer fulfill the requirements of modern workplaces, not that they have ceased to justify those requirements or to defend them against criticism; indeed, there is no suggestion in the text that workers ever defended those requirements.

QUESTION 7

Choice A is the best answer because it presents an explanation about a helicopter that is directly supported by the text. The text states that Mars's atmosphere is much less dense than Earth's, and as a result, the air on Mars doesn't provide the resistance required to support the blades of a helicopter built for Earth and to keep the helicopter aloft. In other words, a helicopter built for Earth can't fly on Mars because of the differences in the two planets' atmospheres.

Choice B is incorrect because instead of stating that the blades of helicopters built for Earth are too large to work on Mars, the text indicates that the helicopter built to fly on Mars actually has even longer blades than a helicopter built for Earth. *Choice C* is incorrect because the text never addresses the role of gravity on Mars or on Earth; instead, it focuses on atmospheric conditions. *Choice D* is incorrect because the text doesn't indicate that helicopters built for Earth are too small to operate in the conditions on Mars. In fact, the text states that the size of the helicopter built to fly on Mars is the same size as a helicopter built for Earth, even though it has longer blades that rotate faster.

QUESTION 8

Choice A is the best answer because it best states the main idea of the text. According to the text, jalis' traditional role has been to maintain information about families' histories and significant events. The text goes on to say that although technological changes have altered jalis' role somewhat, jalis are still valued for preserving the histories of their communities.

Choice B is incorrect because the text says nothing about jalis' views of the various tasks they perform. There is no information to support the idea that many jalis prefer teaching to other tasks. *Choice C* is incorrect because the text doesn't describe jalis as being sources of entertainment. Rather, jalis are presented as valued sources of knowledge. Additionally, the text gives no indication of how long jalis have been serving their communities. *Choice D* is incorrect because the main focus of the text is on jalis' role and their continued value despite the effects of technology, not on what technology can now do. Although the text indicates that jalis' role has changed as a result of technological changes, the text doesn't present any specific information about technology performing tasks that jalis once performed.

QUESTION 9

Choice D is the best answer because it most accurately states the main idea of the text. After establishing that Buck views most people "as nothing," the text explains that Buck won't acknowledge people other than Thornton unless they appear friendly toward Thornton, and even then he's only reluctantly accepting. Thus, the text focuses on the idea that Thornton has a special status in Buck's mind, with Buck holding him in higher regard than other people.

Choice A is incorrect because the text conveys that Buck isn't social with people other than Thornton but doesn't address Buck's life or temperament before he lived with Thornton. *Choice B* is incorrect because the text conveys that Buck doesn't really care about people other than Thornton and is aloof toward them. However, there's no indication that Buck mistrusts and avoids people generally; indeed, he accepts Thornton, who is a human. *Choice C* is incorrect because the text refers to random travelers praising and petting Buck and Thornton's partners giving Buck favors, but there's no indication that any of these people are Thornton's friends or that they have a particular fondness for Buck.

QUESTION 10

Choice B is the best answer because the quotation from *The Souls of Black Folk* illustrates the claim that Du Bois felt a sense of cultural recognition when he heard Black folk songs. In the quotation, Du Bois explains that for his entire life, Black folk songs "stirred [him] strangely." Even though they originated in the South, a region he wasn't familiar with, he knew the songs "as of me and of mine." That is, he identified strongly with them and associated them with his community. Therefore, Du Bois felt an intuitive sense of cultural recognition when he heard Black folk songs.

Choice A is incorrect. Although the quotation considers the cultural and spiritual value of Black folk music, it doesn't establish that this music inspired in Du Bois a sense of cultural recognition. *Choice C* is incorrect because this quotation addresses the cultural survival of Black folk songs despite attempts to caricature, or parody, them, not Du Bois's sense of cultural connection to them. *Choice D* is incorrect because the quotation indicates that the Black folk songs and music are old, "the siftings of centuries," instead of addressing how Du Bois felt when he heard the songs.

QUESTION 11

Choice C is the best answer because it uses data from the graph to effectively complete the example of Eludoyin and his colleagues' findings concerning female farmers in some regions of Ondo State, Nigeria. The graph presents values for the percentage of Ondo State small-scale farmers who are female, by type of crop and region. The graph shows that of the farmers mainly cultivating non-root vegetables, approximately 57% in north Ondo and approximately 54% in south Ondo are female; in other words, most of those farmers are female, which exemplifies the idea that female farmers make up the majority (more than half) of the farmers cultivating specific types of crops in some regions.

Choice A is incorrect because it inaccurately cites data from the graph: the graph shows that in south Ondo, most of the farmers mainly cultivating non-root vegetables are women (approximately 54%), but that only about 35% (less than half) of the farmers mainly cultivating cereals are women. *Choice B* is incorrect because it inaccurately cites data from the graph: the graph shows that more women in central Ondo mainly cultivate cereals than mainly cultivate root crops (approximately 36% and 20%, respectively). Additionally, it doesn't effectively complete the example because the graph shows that female farmers don't make up the majority (more than half) of the farmers for any type of crop in central Ondo. *Choice D* is incorrect because it doesn't effectively complete the example; it simply states that a relatively equal proportion of women across the three regions mainly cultivate cereals, which doesn't address the value for that proportion and thus doesn't show that a majority (more than half) of the farmers cultivating certain crops are female.

QUESTION 12

Choice B is the best answer because it most logically completes the text's discussion of Zelda Fitzgerald's contributions to literature. The text begins by saying that many scholars view Zelda mainly in terms of her marriage to F. Scott Fitzgerald and "don't recognize Zelda as a writer in her own right." The text then mentions a novel and "numerous short stories" that she wrote and that such scholars tend to ignore. Therefore, those scholars who focus on Zelda only as an inspiration for F. Scott's writings risk misrepresenting the full range of Zelda's contributions to literature.

Choice A is incorrect. Although the text does mention that Zelda Fitzgerald "likely influenced" her husband's literary work, its focus is on Zelda's own writing, not on her husband's writing or factors that might have influenced it. *Choice C* is incorrect because the text does not discuss F. Scott and Zelda Fitzgerald's opinions of each other's works. *Choice D* is incorrect. Although the text does suggest that F. Scott Fitzgerald's works were "likely influenced in part" by his marriage to Zelda, it does not discuss autobiographical interpretations of the works of either F. Scott or Zelda.

QUESTION 13

Choice B is the best answer because it presents the conclusion that most logically follows from the text's discussion of the relationship between atmospheric carbon dioxide and sauropod body size. The text establishes that sauropods evolved to reach enormous sizes, and it notes that some scientists have asserted that the cause of this phenomenon was increased plant production that resulted from increased atmospheric carbon dioxide. The text goes on to state, however, that atmospheric carbon dioxide levels didn't increase around the time of important periods in sauropods' evolution of larger body sizes. If significant periods of sauropod evolution toward larger sizes occurred without increased atmospheric carbon dioxide levels, that suggests that the evolution of larger sizes didn't depend on increased carbon dioxide in the atmosphere.

Choice A is incorrect because the text doesn't describe any fluctuations in atmospheric carbon dioxide, so there's no evidence in the text to support the conclusion that such fluctuations had different effects on different sauropod lineages. All that the text says about atmospheric carbon dioxide levels is that there weren't increases at particular points that correspond with key moments in sauropod evolution. *Choice C* is incorrect because the text indicates that there weren't significant increases in atmospheric carbon dioxide around the time of important periods in sauropods' evolution toward larger body sizes, not that atmospheric carbon dioxide was higher when the largest sauropods lived than when sauropods first appeared. *Choice D* is incorrect because the text indicates that atmospheric carbon dioxide levels didn't increase at important periods in sauropod evolution, not that higher levels would have affected that evolution. The text provides no information about how higher levels of atmospheric carbon dioxide might have affected sauropods.

QUESTION 14

Choice D is the best answer. The convention being tested is punctuation between a subject and a verb. When, as in this case, a subject ("Calida Garcia Rawles") is immediately followed by a verb ("was"), no punctuation is needed.

Choice A is incorrect because no punctuation is needed between the subject and the verb. *Choice B* is incorrect because no punctuation is needed between the subject and the verb. *Choice C* is incorrect because no punctuation is needed between the subject and the verb.

QUESTION 15

Choice D is the best answer. The convention being tested is punctuation use between sentences. In this choice, the period after "walls" is used correctly to mark the boundary between the first sentence ("In...walls") and the second sentence ("With...techniques"), which starts with a supplementary phrase.

Choice A is incorrect because it results in a comma splice. A comma can't be used in this way to mark the boundary between sentences. *Choice B* is incorrect because it results in a run-on sentence. The sentences ("In...walls" and "with...paintings") are fused without punctuation and/or a conjunction. *Choice C* is incorrect. Without a comma preceding it, the conjunction "so" can't be used in this way to join sentences.

QUESTION 16

Choice B is the best answer. The convention being tested is the use of plural and possessive nouns. The plural possessive noun "grains'" and the plural noun "properties" correctly indicate that the simulations involved multiple snow grains and that those snow grains had several properties.

Choice A is incorrect because the context requires the plural possessive noun "grains'" and the plural noun "properties," not the singular possessive noun "grain's" and the plural possessive noun "properties'." *Choice C* is incorrect because the context requires the plural noun "properties," not the singular possessive noun "property's." *Choice D* is incorrect because the context requires the plural possessive noun "grains'," not the plural noun "grains."

QUESTION 17

Choice C is the best answer. The convention being tested is the coordination of main clauses within a sentence. This choice uses a semicolon to correctly join the first main clause ("The Mission...parks") and the second main clause that begins with "it."

Choice A is incorrect. When coordinating two longer main clauses such as these, it's conventional to use a comma before the coordinating conjunction. *Choice B* is incorrect because it results in a run-on sentence. The two main clauses are fused without punctuation and/or a conjunction. *Choice D* is incorrect because it results in a comma splice. Without a conjunction following it, a comma can't be used in this way to join two main clauses.

QUESTION 18

Choice A is the best answer. The convention being tested here is subject-verb agreement. The singular verb "was" agrees in number with the singular subject "Josephine St. Pierre Ruffin."

Choice B is incorrect because the plural verb "were" doesn't agree in number with the singular subject "Josephine St. Pierre Ruffin." *Choice C* is incorrect because the plural verb "are" doesn't agree in number with the singular subject "Josephine St. Pierre Ruffin." *Choice D* is incorrect because the plural verb "have been" doesn't agree in number with the singular subject "Josephine St. Pierre Ruffin."

QUESTION 19

Choice D is the best answer. The convention being tested is the punctuation of a supplementary element within a sentence. In this choice, the dash after "cephalopods" pairs with the dash after "cuttlefish" to clearly separate the supplementary element "ocean dwellers that include the squid, the octopus, and the cuttlefish" from the rest of the sentence. This supplementary element functions to explain what cephalopds are, and the pair of dashes indicates that this element could be removed without affecting the grammatical coherence of the sentence.

Choice A is incorrect because it fails to use appropriate punctuation to separate the supplementary element that explains what cephalopods are from the rest of the sentence. *Choice B* is incorrect because it fails to use appropriate punctuation to separate the supplementary element that explains what cephalopods are from the rest of the sentence. *Choice C* is incorrect because it fails to use appropriate punctuation to separate the supplementary element that explains what cephalopods are from the rest of the sentence.

QUESTION 20

Choice D is the best answer. The convention being tested is finite and nonfinite verb forms within a sentence. Relative clauses, such as the one beginning with "that," require a finite verb, a verb that can function as the main verb of a clause. This choice correctly supplies the clause with the finite future tense verb "will be."

Choice A is incorrect because the nonfinite participle "being" doesn't supply the clause with a finite verb. *Choice B* is incorrect because the nonfinite to-infinitive "to be" doesn't supply the clause with a finite verb. *Choice C* is incorrect because the nonfinite to-infinitive "to have been" doesn't supply the clause with a finite verb.

QUESTION 21

Choice D is the best answer. "In fact" logically signals that the information in this sentence—that McFerrin finds the research phase of her work to be just as fascinating as travel—emphasizes and elaborates on the previous sentence's point that McFerrin regards background research as a rewarding activity.

Choice A is incorrect because "by contrast" illogically signals that the information in this sentence contrasts with the previous sentence's point about McFerrin's attitude toward background research. Instead, it emphasizes and elaborates on that point. *Choice B* is incorrect because "likewise" illogically signals that this sentence merely adds a second, similar point to the previous sentence's point about McFerrin's attitude toward background research. Instead, it emphasizes and elaborates on that point. *Choice C* is incorrect because "besides" illogically signals that this sentence provides a separate point in addition to, or apart from, the previous sentence's point about McFerrin's attitude toward background research. Instead, it emphasizes and elaborates on that point.

QUESTION 22

Choice C is the best answer. The sentence effectively introduces *The Holder of the World* to an audience already familiar with Mukherjee, explaining that the novel centers around two women and mentioning the author without providing any other identifying information.

Choice A is incorrect. The sentence provides a detail about Mukherjee's settings; it doesn't introduce, or even mention, the novel. *Choice B* is incorrect. The sentence provides introductory information about Mukherjee; it doesn't effectively introduce her novel to an audience already familiar with the author. *Choice D* is incorrect. The sentence provides introductory information about Mukherjee; it doesn't effectively introduce her novel to an audience already familiar with the author.

QUESTION 23

Choice D is the best answer. The sentence presents both the study and its findings, noting the study's date and the researcher's name as well as describing what the researcher determined about the jawbones and how she determined it.

Choice A is incorrect. While the sentence describes the study and the researcher's initial assessment, it doesn't present the study's findings. *Choice B* is incorrect. While the sentence describes the study and its focus, it doesn't present the study's findings or the name of the researcher who conducted it. *Choice C* is incorrect. While the sentence mentions the study's methodology and provides information about pterosaurs, it doesn't present the study's findings.

QUESTION 24

Choice A is the best answer. By noting that Selvon is a Trinidadian author and indicating that *The Lonely Londoners*, published in 1956, is about a group of men who emigrate from the Caribbean to Great Britain after World War II, the sentence effectively introduces Samuel Selvon and his novel to a new audience.

Choice B is incorrect. The sentence indicates the order in which two of Selvon's novels were written; it doesn't introduce Samuel Selvon and *The Lonely Londoners* to a new audience. *Choice C* is incorrect. While the sentence describes the novel *The Lonely Londoners*, it doesn't mention its author, Samuel Selvon, by name and thus doesn't effectively introduce him to a new audience. *Choice D* is incorrect. The sentence indicates that two of Selvon's novels include the same characters; it doesn't introduce Samuel Selvon and *The Lonely Londoners* to a new audience.

QUESTION 25

Choice C is the best answer. The sentence emphasizes a similarity between the two sea turtle species: both can be found in the Atlantic Ocean.

Choice A is incorrect. The sentence indicates that the olive ridley sea turtle is one of seven species of sea turtle; it fails to mention the Kemp's ridley sea turtle. *Choice B* is incorrect. The sentence emphasizes a difference between the two sea turtle species rather than a similarity. *Choice D* is incorrect. The sentence emphasizes a difference between the two sea turtle species rather than a similarity.

QUESTION 26

Choice D is the best answer. The sentence effectively summarizes the study, noting who conducted it, when it was conducted, and what its results showed: that auks' landing success rate decreased as wind conditions intensified.

Choice A is incorrect. While the sentence presents the methodology of the study—that is, the approach taken by the researchers—it fails to summarize the study as a whole. *Choice B* is incorrect. While the sentence presents the aim, or goal, of the study, it fails to summarize the study as a whole. *Choice C* is incorrect. While the sentence indicates what Shepard studied, it fails to mention a key factor: the effect of wind. It thus fails to summarize the study as a whole.

QUESTION 27

Choice C is the best answer. The sentence effectively introduces *Paradise* to an audience unfamiliar with the novel and its author, describing *Paradise* as a historical novel about colonial East Africa and its author as the winner of the 2021 Nobel Prize in Literature.

Choice A is incorrect. While the sentence introduces Abdulrazak Gurnah to an audience unfamiliar with the author, it doesn't effectively introduce *Paradise*. *Choice B* is incorrect. While the sentence provides background information about *Paradise*, it doesn't effectively introduce the novel to an audience unfamiliar with its author. *Choice D* is incorrect. While the sentence provides background information about *Paradise*, it doesn't effectively introduce the novel to an audience unfamiliar with its author.

Reading and Writing

Module 2
(27 questions)

QUESTION 1

Choice B is the best answer because it most logically completes the text's discussion of Ward and colleagues' findings. As used in this context, "innocuous" means mild or unharmful. The text describes the vibration and warming that Ward and colleagues used to alleviate itching as "harmless applications" and goes on to contrast these applications with another stimulus that actually offers more relief even though it seems to be stronger and "less benign." This context conveys the idea that vibration and warming were innocuous stimuli.

Choice A is incorrect because the text focuses on a distinction between harmless stimuli and those that seem to be less benign. Nothing in the text suggests that any of the treatments are "deceptive," or misleading; indeed, even the less effective ones are described as offering some relief. *Choice C* is incorrect because the text focuses on the amount of relief from itching offered by harmless stimuli and those that seem to be less benign. The text doesn't suggest that any of these stimuli are "novel," or original and new; heat, vibration, and electricity aren't new inventions. *Choice D* is incorrect because it wouldn't make sense to describe an application of vibration or warming as "impractical," or not suitable for use. The text indicates that these harmless applications are useful in that they offer at least some temporary relief.

QUESTION 2

Choice B is the best answer because it most logically and precisely completes the text's discussion of studies of altitude's effect on blood chemistry. In this context, "paucity of" means lack of. In describing the inspiration behind Al-Sweedan and Alhaj's research, the text uses the word "though" to suggest a contrasting relationship between two types of studies: those examining the effect on blood chemistry of living at a high altitude and those examining the effect on blood chemistry of living in locations below sea level. This contrasting relationship and the text's use of the word "many" provide context suggesting that there are few, if any, examples of the second type of study, whereas there are numerous examples of the first type.

Choice A is incorrect because it wouldn't make sense in context for there to be a "quarrel about," or open disagreement about, studies of the effect on blood chemistry of living in locations below sea level. The text's use of the words "though" and "many" suggests a contrasting relationship in terms of amount between two types of studies: those examining the effect on blood chemistry of living at a high altitude and those examining the effect on blood chemistry of living in locations below sea level. There's nothing in the text to suggest that the contrast between the two types of studies involves the extent to which researchers broadly agree or disagree about the contents of either type. *Choice C* is incorrect because it wouldn't make sense in context for there to be a "profusion of," or great abundance of, studies of the effect on blood chemistry of living in locations below sea level. The text's use of the words "though" and "many" suggests a contrasting relationship in terms of amount between two types of studies: those examining the effect on blood chemistry of living at a high altitude and those examining the effect on blood chemistry of living in locations below sea level. Rather than logically completing this contrast, "profusion of" would indicate that the two types of studies are similar in terms of amount, with many examples existing of both types. *Choice D* is incorrect because it wouldn't make sense in context for there to be a "verisimilitude in," or appearance of truth in, studies of the effect on blood chemistry of living in locations below sea level. The text's use of the words "though" and "many" suggests a contrasting relationship in terms of amount between two types of studies: those examining the effect on blood chemistry of living at a high altitude and those examining the effect on blood chemistry of living in locations below sea level. There's nothing in the text to suggest that the contrast between the two types of studies involves the extent to which either type of study presents an appearance of truth.

QUESTION 3

Choice C is the best answer because it most logically completes the text's discussion of the legitimacy of the reigns of French monarchs such as Hugh Capet and Henry I. As used in this context, "buttress" means to strengthen or defend. The text indicates that regardless of whether a French monarch's reign was significant or uneventful, each monarch faced questions about his right to the throne. The text goes on to say that in order to understand the path of a French monarch's reign, it's important to understand what contributed to the monarch's ability to "hold the throne." This context suggests that French monarchs such as Hugh Capet and Henry I had to buttress, or defend, their right to be monarch.

Choice A is incorrect. Saying that a monarch who is faced with questions about the legitimacy of his reign was able to "reciprocate" his right to the French throne would mean that he either returned his right to the throne or that he responded in kind to the challenge. Neither of these meanings would make sense in context because the text focuses on people who did reign as French monarchs and defended their right to do so. *Choice B* is incorrect because it wouldn't make sense in context to discuss factors that enabled a monarch to "annotate," or add notes to or explain, his right to the French throne. Nothing in the text suggests that the monarchs were writing notes about their right to the throne; instead, faced with questions about the legitimacy of their reign, the monarchs defended their right. *Choice D* is incorrect because it wouldn't make sense in context to discuss factors that enabled a monarch to "disengage," or withdraw his right to the French throne. The text focuses on an examination of people who reigned as French monarchs, not on people who didn't choose to rule.

QUESTION 4

Choice C is the best answer because it most logically completes the text's discussion of Jung and her team's study of acts of kindness. In this context, "foster" means encourage or promote the development of. The text indicates that Jung and her team found that seeing a helpful (or prosocial) act makes a bystander more likely to help someone else, which can in turn inspire additional people to help others. That is, the team showed that single acts of kindness can foster additional prosocial acts across a group.

Choice A is incorrect because nothing in the text suggests that Jung and her team found that single acts of kindness "require," or depend on or make obligatory, broader prosocial (or helpful) behavior across a group. There's no suggestion in the text that individual acts of kindness can only occur if other prosocial acts have already occurred, and the text indicates only that an act of kindness *can* inspire additional helpful acts, not that it necessarily will do so. *Choice B* is incorrect because the text focuses on a possible direct effect of individual acts of kindness, or single helpful actions, and it wouldn't make sense to suggest that actions can "remember," or hold a memory of, something. *Choice D* is incorrect because the text doesn't indicate that Jung and her team found that single acts of kindness can "discourage," or hinder, prosocial (or helpful) behavior across a group. On the contrary, the text states that Jung and her team found that seeing a helpful act makes a bystander *more* likely to help someone else, which can in turn inspire even more people to help others.

QUESTION 5

Choice D is the best answer because it best describes the function of the underlined sentence in the text's overall portrayal of how the women in Ohiyesa's tribe harvested maple syrup. The text states that the women used an axe to strike the maple trees in order to find out which ones would produce sap. The underlined sentence compares the trees to people, with the sap described as the trees' "life-blood." Some of the trees are ready to give out their sap, while others are unwilling to do so. Using personification, the sentence provides greater detail about the aspect of the maple trees—their potential to give sap—that the women are evaluating.

Choice A is incorrect because the personalities of the women are not discussed in the text. Although the underlined sentence does mention "individual characters," this reference is not to the women in the text but rather to the maple trees, which the sentence compares to people with individual character traits. *Choice B* is incorrect because the underlined sentence focuses on the trees' willingness or refusal to yield sap, not on the beneficial relationship between the women and the trees. Additionally, although the text does suggest that the women and their tribe benefit from the maple trees since the trees allow the women to harvest syrup, there is nothing in the text to suggest that the trees benefit from this relationship in turn. *Choice C* is incorrect because the underlined sentence is comparing maple trees to humans, not addressing the influence of the natural environment on how the actual humans in the text, the women, behave.

QUESTION 6

Choice A is the best answer because it most accurately describes the main purpose of the text, which is to show that while Jane calmly goes about her daily tasks, she is experiencing internal agitation about possibly seeking a new job. At the start of the text, Jane says, "I went on with my day's business tranquilly," indicating that she is outwardly calm. This outward calmness is then contrasted with her intense internal restlessness, as Jane says that thoughts of leaving her job keep running through her mind, that she is "involuntarily framing advertisements" (meaning that she can't stop herself from thinking up potential listings for jobs), and that she often wonders what new "situations" (or jobs) would be like.

Choice B is incorrect because the text gives no indication of Jane's feelings, either positive or negative, about the people she works for at Thornfield Hall. And rather than emphasizing that Jane feels particularly loyal to her employers, the text focuses on her constant consideration of leaving her job. *Choice C* is incorrect because the text gives no indication that Jane finds her current situation fulfilling, or satisfying. Given that much of the text is focused on Jane's thoughts about possibly leaving her job for a new one, it might be the case that she finds her situation challenging, but there is no evidence in the text that Jane also finds that situation satisfying—she says nothing positive about her current job at all, in fact. *Choice D* is incorrect because the text describes Jane as wondering about getting a new job, not as determined to definitely do so. Jane keeps thinking about reasons why she "should" quit her current job (indicating that she hasn't yet decided to) and imagining possible new situations she could find, but she says at the end of the text that these thoughts "might germinate and bear fruit if they could," meaning that the thoughts haven't yet led to a decision—that Jane isn't yet determined to get a new job somewhere else.

QUESTION 7

Choice A is the best answer because it accurately describes the organization of the elements within the text. The text begins with the claim that Joni Mitchell's album covers use images she creates in order to emphasize ideas embedded in her albums. It then goes on to provide an example of how Mitchell's self-portrait on the cover of *Turbulent Indigo* resembles a painting by Van Gogh, which the text indicates helps emphasize the strong connection Mitchell feels toward Van Gogh, a connection that is also expressed in the album's title song.

Choice B is incorrect because there are no references in the text to artists other than Joni Mitchell and Van Gogh. *Choice C* is incorrect because there is nothing in the text that calls attention to any similarities or differences between Joni Mitchell and Van Gogh. Instead, it mentions that Mitchell feels a strong "artistic connection" to Van Gogh. *Choice D* is incorrect because the text discusses the cover before referring to any songs, and it only references one song from the album not all the songs.

QUESTION 8

Choice C is the best answer because it best describes how the underlined sentence functions in the text as a whole. The first sentence presents the implications of Veeraraghavan's team's study: sunshine exposure during work hours can cause overly optimistic behavior. The underlined sentence then describes the data the team consulted and how they were used (comparing predictions about earnings to what the companies actually earned), and the final sentence presents what the team found in their examination of the data. Thus, the underlined sentence mainly functions to explain part of the methodology used in the team's study.

Choice A is incorrect because the underlined sentence explains in part how the team conducted their analysis of the effect of sunshine but doesn't address what the team found; a broad summary is instead given in the other two sentences. *Choice B* is incorrect because the underlined sentence doesn't present any specific examples from the team's comparisons of 29,000 earnings predictions to actual earnings; it simply explains in part how the team conducted their analysis. *Choice D* is incorrect because the underlined sentence simply explains in part how the team conducted their analysis; the text never mentions any challenges that the team encountered in their study.

QUESTION 9

Choice B is the best answer because it reflects how the author of Text 2 would most likely respond to Text 1 based on the information provided. Text 1 discusses the discovery of a regeneration-linked gene, EGR, in both three-banded panther worms (which are capable of full regeneration) and humans (who have relatively limited regeneration abilities). Text 1 characterizes this discovery as "especially promising" and a sign of "exciting progress" in understanding human regeneration. The author of Text 2, on the other hand, focuses on the fact that the team that reported the EGR finding pointed out that while EGR's function in humans isn't yet known, it's likely very different from its function in panther worms. Therefore, the author of Text 2 would most likely say that Text 1's enthusiasm about the EGR discovery is overly optimistic given Srivastava's team's observations about EGR in humans.

Choice A is incorrect because the author of Text 2 explains that Srivastava and her team explicitly reported that they haven't yet identified how EGR functions in humans; therefore, the author of Text 2 wouldn't say that Text 1's excitement is reasonable for the stated reason. Instead, the author of Text 2 would likely characterize Text 1's excitement as premature and overly optimistic. *Choice C* is incorrect because Text 1 does treat Srivastava's team's findings with enthusiasm; it describes the discovery of EGR in both three-banded panther worms and humans as promising and exciting. It would be illogical for the author of Text 2 to say that because most others treat the discovery with enthusiasm, Text 1's enthusiastic characterization of the discovery is unexpected. *Choice D* is incorrect because Text 1 isn't at all dismissive of Srivastava's team's findings; instead, Text 1 is optimistic about the EGR discovery, characterizing it as promising and exciting. There's nothing in Text 2 to suggest that the author of Text 2 would say that Text 1's praise for the discovery is dismissive, or disdainful.

QUESTION 10

Choice C is the best answer because it uses data from the table to effectively exemplify the idea that the film outputs of the four individuals included in the table should be considered bare minimums—that is, that we should assume that the individuals actually had higher outputs than those recorded. The table presents the years during which the individuals were active and the number of known films the individuals are credited in. The table indicates that Lillian St. Cyr has 66 film credits as an actor and that Edwin Carewe has 58 film credits as a director; it follows that if some films and records for the era were lost, it's possible that Lillian St. Cyr acted in far more than 66 films and that Edwin Carewe directed more than 58 films.

Choice A is incorrect because it doesn't effectively exemplify the idea that the film outputs of the four individuals included in the table should be considered bare minimums. Rather than addressing the idea that the individuals likely had higher outputs than those presented in the table, this choice simply compares data from the table to make the point that Dark Cloud has fewer credited acting roles than Lillian St. Cyr (35 and 66, respectively). *Choice B* is incorrect because it misrepresents data from the table, even though it may exemplify the idea that the film outputs of the four individuals included in the table should be considered bare minimums by implying that Edwin Carewe acted in more than 47 films. The table indicates that Edwin Carewe was active from 1912 to 1934, meaning that his 47 credited acting roles were in films made before or during 1934, not after that time. *Choice D* is incorrect because it doesn't effectively exemplify the idea that the film outputs of the four individuals included in the table should be considered bare minimums. Instead of addressing the idea that the individuals likely had higher outputs than those recorded, this choice suggests that James Young Deer actually acted in and directed fewer films than presented in the table (only 33 known films as a director instead of 35, and only 10 known films as an actor instead of 33).

QUESTION 11

Choice C is the best answer because it presents the finding that, if true, would best support Suarez, Pérez-Huerta, and Harrell's claim about mosasaurs. The text states that Suarez, Pérez-Huerta, and Harrell's research on mosasaur tooth enamel led them to conclude that mosasaurs were endothermic, which means that they could live in waters at many different temperatures and still maintain a stable body temperature. The researchers claim that endothermy enabled mosasaurs to live in relatively cold waters near the poles. If several mosasaur fossils have been found in areas that were near the poles during the period when mosasaurs were alive and fossils of nonendothermic marine reptiles are rare in such locations, that would support the researchers' claim: it would show that mosasaurs inhabited polar waters but nonendothermic marine mammals tended not to, suggesting that endothermy may have been the characteristic that enabled mosasaurs to include polar waters in their range.

Choice A is incorrect because finding that it's easier to determine mosasaur body temperatures from tooth enamel data than it is to determine nonendothermic reptile body temperatures wouldn't support the researchers' claim. Whether one research process is more difficult than another indicates nothing about the results of those processes and therefore is irrelevant to the issue of where mosasaurs lived and what enabled them to live in those locations. *Choice B* is incorrect because finding roughly equal numbers of mosasaur and nonendothermic marine reptile fossils in areas that were near the poles in the Late Cretaceous would suggest that endothermy didn't give mosasaurs any particular advantage when it came to expanding their range to include relatively cold polar waters, thereby weakening the researchers' claim rather than supporting it. *Choice D* is incorrect because finding that the temperature of seawater in the Late Cretaceous was warmer than seawater today wouldn't weaken the researchers' claim. Seawater in the Late Cretaceous could have been warmer than seawater today but still cold enough for endothermy to be advantageous to mosasaurs, so this finding wouldn't provide enough information to either support or weaken the researchers' claim.

QUESTION 12

Choice D is the best answer because it describes data from the graph that support the researchers' conclusion that there is a growing interest among CEOs in connecting with more departments in their companies. The graph shows the average number of individuals reporting directly to CEOs during three different time periods: the individuals are divided into managers and department leaders. The average number of department leaders directly reporting to their CEO during the 1991–1995 period was slightly more than three, during the 1996–2001 period it was four, and during the 2001–2008 period it was almost seven. Thus, the average number of department leaders reporting directly to their CEO rose over the three periods studied, which suggests that CEOs were connecting with more departments.

Choice A is incorrect because the average number of managers and department leaders reporting directly to their CEO rose for both categories between the 1991–1995 and 2001–2008 periods; thus, it isn't true that the average numbers didn't fluctuate. *Choice B* is incorrect because the average number of managers reporting directly to their CEO was highest in the 2001–2008 period, not in the 1996–2001 period. *Choice C* is incorrect.

Although it correctly describes a feature of the graph, the observation that more department leaders than managers are reporting to CEOs does not by itself address the question of whether CEOs are connecting with more departments over time—to address that question, one needs to know whether the number of department leaders reporting to CEOs is increasing over time.

QUESTION 13

Choice C is the best answer because it presents a finding that, if true, would weaken the astronomers' claim about the makeup of host stars and their planets. The text explains that because stars and planets begin forming from the same gas and dust, astronomers believe planets should be composed of the same materials as their host stars, but in equal or smaller quantities. The finding that the amount of iron in some rocky planets is much higher than the amount in their host star would weaken the astronomers' claim because it would show that some planets contain the same material as their host star, but in higher quantities.

Choice A is incorrect because a finding only about the makeup of stars, whether they've cooled or not, would provide no information about the makeup of planets. Thus, it wouldn't have any bearing on the claim that planets and their host stars are composed of the same materials in differing quantities. *Choice B* is incorrect because a finding about two host stars having similar proportions of certain materials wouldn't provide any information about the makeup of planets. Thus, it wouldn't be relevant to the claim that planets and their host stars are composed of the same materials in differing quantities. *Choice D* is incorrect because the text indicates that the astronomers' claim is based on a fact—that stars and planets begin forming from the same gas and dust in space—which would remain true regardless of the effectiveness of a method for analysis of compositions. The text does cite analysis of rocky planets in our solar system and the Sun, but only as a single piece of evidence that is consistent with the claim and not as the source of the claim; the finding that the method used for that analysis is less effective in other scenarios wouldn't weaken a claim that's based on knowledge of how stars and planets initially form.

QUESTION 14

Choice B is the best answer because it presents a finding that, if true, would most directly support the arts journalist's claim about Enwezor's work as a curator and art historian. In the text, the arts journalist asserts that Enwezor wished not just to focus on modern African artists but also to show "how their work fits into the larger context of global modern art and art history," or how their work relates to artistic developments and work by other artists elsewhere in the world. The description of *Postwar: Art Between the Pacific and the Atlantic, 1945–1965* indicates that Enwezor and Siegel's exhibition brought works by African artists together with works by artists from other countries, thus supporting the arts journalist's claim that Enwezor sought to show works by African artists in a context of global modern art and art history.

Choice A is incorrect because it describes a retrospective that wouldn't support the arts journalist's claim that Enwezor wanted to show how works by modern African artists fit into the larger context of global modern art and art history. The description of *El Anatsui: Triumphant Scale* indicates that the retrospective focused only on the work of a single African artist, El Anatsui. The description doesn't suggest that the exhibition showed how El Anatsui's works fit into a global artistic context. *Choice C* is incorrect because it describes an exhibition that wouldn't support the arts journalist's claim that Enwezor wanted to show how works by modern African artists relate to the larger context of global modern art and art history. The description of *The Short Century: Independence and Liberation Movements in Africa, 1945–1994* indicates that the exhibition showed how African artists were influenced by movements for independence from European colonial powers following the Second World War. Although this suggests that Enwezor intended the exhibition to place works by African artists in a political context, it doesn't indicate that the works were placed in a global artistic context. *Choice D* is incorrect because it describes an exhibition that wouldn't support the arts journalist's claim that Enwezor wanted to show how works by modern African artists relate to the larger context of global modern art and art history. The description of *In/sight: African Photographers, 1940 to the Present* indicates that the exhibition was intended to reveal the broad range of approaches taken by African photographers, not that the exhibition showed how photography by African artists fits into a global artistic context.

QUESTION 15

Choice D is the best answer because it presents the conclusion that most logically follows from the text's discussion of the challenge researchers face when studying the effects of holding elected office on a person's behavior. The text explains that it's hard for researchers to test for the effects that elected office has on people because finding people to serve as a control group is difficult. The text indicates that a control group needs to be made up of people who share characteristics of the group being tested but don't have the variable being tested (in this case, holding elected office). Because researchers aren't able to influence who wins elections, they're also unable to determine who would serve as an appropriately similar member of a control group. Thus, it logically follows that researchers will find it difficult to identify a group of people who can function as an appropriate control group for their studies.

Choice A is incorrect because the text focuses on the struggle to put together a control group for experiments; it doesn't suggest that finding information about politicians' behavior is difficult. *Choice B* is incorrect because the experiments mentioned in the text are testing the effects of holding elected office on a person's behavior. Studying people who have already held elected office wouldn't provide an opportunity to note any behavioral changes that the position might cause. *Choice C* is incorrect because the text defines people in a control group as those "who are otherwise similar to the office-holders"; selecting people who differ from the office-holders wouldn't fit the criteria for an appropriate control group.

QUESTION 16

Choice A is the best answer because it most logically completes the text. The text explains that the *Cantares Mexicanos* contains poems about the Aztec Empire from before the Spanish invasion. Furthermore, it indicates that notes in the collection attest that some of these poems predate the Spanish invasion, while some customs depicted are likely Spanish in origin. The implication is that some poems were composed before the invasion but the references to Spanish customs could have come about only after the invasion, and thus that the collection includes content that predates the invasion and also content from after the invasion.

Choice B is incorrect because the text clearly indicates that the collection is in Nahuatl, not Spanish, so the compilers' unfamiliarity with Spanish is irrelevant to whether the collection contains material composed after the Spanish invasion. *Choice C* is incorrect because the text mentions only the Aztec Empire and

Spain: there is no information about the relationship of Aztec literature to any traditions other than its own or Spain's. *Choice D* is incorrect because the text states that some of the poems make "inarguable references" to common Spanish customs, which conflicts with the idea that these references can reasonably be attributed to mere coincidence.

QUESTION 17

Choice D is the best answer. The convention being tested is the coordination of main clauses within a sentence. The semicolon is correctly used to join the first main clause ("To humans…prey") and the second main clause ("rather…approach"). Further, the comma after the adverb "rather" is correctly used to separate the adverb from the main clause ("the brightly…approach") it modifies, logically indicating that the information in this clause (how the spider's behavior appears to humans) is contrary to the information in the previous clause (how the spider's behavior does not appear to humans).

Choice A is incorrect because it results in a comma splice. Without a conjunction following it, a comma can't be used in this way to join two main clauses. *Choice B* is incorrect because it results in a run-on sentence. The two main clauses are fused without appropriate punctuation and/or a conjunction. *Choice C* is incorrect. Placing the comma between the first main clause "To humans…prey" and the adverb "rather" illogically indicates that the information in the first main clause is contrary to what came before, which doesn't make sense in this context.

QUESTION 18

Choice D is the best answer. The convention being tested is the use of verbs to express tense in a sentence. In this choice, the past progressive tense verb "was studying" is consistent with the other past tense verbs (e.g., "made" and "collected") used to describe Buratti's discovery. Further, the past progressive tense correctly indicates that an ongoing action in the past was occurring (she was studying) at the same time that another event occurred in the past (she made an interesting discovery).

Choice A is incorrect because the present tense verb "studies" isn't consistent with the past tense verbs used to describe Buratti's discovery. *Choice B* is incorrect because the present perfect progressive tense verb "has been studying" isn't consistent with the past tense verbs used to describe Buratti's discovery. *Choice C* is incorrect because the future tense verb "will study" isn't consistent with the past tense verbs used to describe Buratti's discovery.

QUESTION 19

Choice B is the best answer. The convention being tested is punctuation use between sentences. In this choice, the period after "Bay" is used correctly to mark the boundary between one sentence ("On…Bay") and another sentence that begins with a supplementary phrase ("Having…years"). Here, the supplementary phrase beginning with "having" modifies the subject of the second sentence, "the celebrated ship."

Choice A is incorrect. Without a comma preceding it, the conjunction "and" can't be used in this way to join sentences. *Choice C* is incorrect because it results in a comma splice. A comma can't be used in this way to join two sentences. *Choice D* is incorrect because it results in a run-on sentence. The sentences ("On…Bay" and "having…years") are fused without punctuation and/or a conjunction.

QUESTION 20

Choice A is the best answer. The convention being tested is subject-verb agreement. The singular verb "has enhanced" agrees in number with the singular subject "*A Sheaf Gleaned in French Fields,*" which is the title of a book of poems.

Choice B is incorrect because the plural verb "are enhancing" doesn't agree in number with the singular subject "*A Sheaf Gleaned in French Fields.*" *Choice C* is incorrect because the plural verb "have enhanced" doesn't agree in number with the singular subject "*A Sheaf Gleaned in French Fields.*" *Choice D* is incorrect because the plural verb "enhance" doesn't agree in number with the singular subject "*A Sheaf Gleaned in French Fields.*"

QUESTION 21

Choice A is the best answer. The convention being tested is punctuation use between sentences. In this choice, the period after "tombs" is used correctly to mark the boundary between one sentence ("Archaeologist...tombs") and another ("Built...nature").

Choice B is incorrect because it results in a comma splice. A comma can't be used in this way to mark the boundary between sentences. *Choice C* is incorrect. Without a comma preceding it, the conjunction "and" can't be used in this way to join the two sentences. *Choice D* is incorrect because it results in a run-on sentence. The sentences ("Archaeologist...tombs" and "Built...nature") are fused without punctuation and/or a conjunction.

QUESTION 22

Choice C is the best answer. The conventions being tested are punctuation use between titles and proper nouns and between verbs and integrated quotations. No punctuation is needed to set off the proper noun "Stina Chyn" from the title that describes Chyn, "critic." Because "Stina Chyn" is essential information identifying the "critic," no punctuation is necessary. Further, no punctuation is needed between the verb "claims" and the following quotation because the quotation is integrated into the structure of the sentence.

Choice A is incorrect because no punctuation is needed before or after the proper noun "Stina Chyn." Setting the critic's name off with commas suggests that it could be removed without affecting the coherence of the sentence, which isn't the case. *Choice B* is incorrect because no punctuation is needed before or after the proper noun "Stina Chyn." Setting the critic's name off with commas suggests that it could be removed without affecting the coherence of the sentence, which isn't the case. Additionally, no punctuation is needed between "claims" and the integrated quotation. *Choice D* is incorrect because no punctuation is needed between the verb "claims" and its subject, "critic Stina Chyn." Additionally, no punctuation is needed between the verb "claims" and the integrated quotation.

QUESTION 23

Choice B is the best answer. The convention being tested is the punctuation of items in a complex series (a series including internal punctuation). The semicolon after "nonnative" is correctly used to separate the first item ("growing diverse plant species, both native and nonnative") and the second item ("fostering scientific research") in the series of things that botanical gardens are dedicated to. Further, the comma after "species" is correctly used to separate the noun phrase "diverse plant species" and the supplementary phrase "both native and nonnative" that modifies it.

Choice A is incorrect because a comma (specifically, the comma after "nonnative") can't be used in this way to separate items in a complex series. *Choice C* is incorrect because a semicolon can't be used in this way to separate the noun phrase "diverse plant species" and the supplementary phrase "both native and nonnative" that modifies it. Further, a comma can't be used in this way to separate items in a complex series. *Choice D* is incorrect because it fails to use appropriate punctuation to separate the noun phrase "diverse plant species" and the supplementary phrase "both native and nonnative" that modifies it. Further, a comma can't be used in this way to separate items in a complex series.

QUESTION 24

Choice C is the best answer. "However" logically signals that the information in this sentence—that Hammurabi is mainly remembered for just a single achievement, the Code of Hammurabi—is contrary to what might be assumed from the previous information about Hammurabi's many achievements.

Choice A is incorrect because "therefore" illogically signals that the information in this sentence is a result of the previous information about Hammurabi's many achievements. Instead, this sentence makes a point that is contrary to what might be assumed from the previous information. *Choice B* is incorrect because "likewise" illogically signals that the information in this sentence is similar to the previous information about Hammurabi's many achievements. Instead, this sentence makes a point that is contrary to what might be assumed from the previous information. *Choice D* is incorrect because "for instance" illogically signals that this sentence exemplifies the previous information about Hammurabi's many achievements. Instead, this sentence makes a point that is contrary to what might be assumed from the previous information.

QUESTION 25

Choice D is the best answer. "Similarly" logically signals that the information in the sentence—that Dove situates Beulah's life in the context of the US Civil Rights Movement—is similar to the previous information about Thomas and the Great Migration. Both sentences support the first sentence's claim that Dove portrays her characters in the context of broader historical narratives.

Choice A is incorrect because "specifically" illogically signals that the information about Beulah in this sentence provides specific details elaborating on the previous information about Thomas. Instead, it's similar to the previous information about Thomas. *Choice B* is incorrect because "thus" illogically signals that the information about Beulah in this sentence is a result or consequence of the previous information about Thomas. Instead, it's similar to the previous information about Thomas. *Choice C* is incorrect because "regardless" illogically signals that the information about Beulah in this sentence is true despite the previous information about Thomas. Instead, it's similar to the previous information about Thomas.

QUESTION 26

Choice A is the best answer. "Nevertheless" logically signals that the information in this sentence—that the spacesuits Suttirat Larlarb designed for the film *Sunshine* were made in standard sizes in a factory—presents a notable exception to Larlarb's typical approach of custom-fitting garments to actors, which is described in the previous sentence.

Choice B is incorrect because "thus" illogically signals that the information in this sentence is a result or consequence of the previous information about Larlarb's typical approach of custom-fitting garments to actors. Instead, it presents a notable exception to Larlarb's typical approach. *Choice C* is incorrect because "likewise" illogically signals that the information in this sentence is similar to the previous information about Larlarb's typical approach of custom-fitting garments to actors. Instead, it presents a notable exception to Larlarb's typical approach. *Choice D* is incorrect because "moreover" illogically signals that the information in this sentence merely adds to the previous information about Larlarb's typical approach of custom-fitting garments to actors. Instead, it presents a notable exception to Larlarb's typical approach.

QUESTION 27

Choice D is the best answer. The sentence makes a generalization—that a comet's orbit around the Sun may change over time—and supports the generalization with the example of the orbit of comet 81P/Wild, which once lay between the orbits of Uranus and Jupiter but is now positioned between the orbits of Jupiter and Mars.

Choice A is incorrect. The sentence emphasizes the number of comets orbiting the Sun and makes a generalization about their orbits, but it doesn't support the generalization with an example. *Choice B* is incorrect. The sentence makes a generalization about comets and compares them to the planets Uranus, Jupiter, and Mars; it doesn't make and support a generalization about comets' orbits. *Choice C* is incorrect. While the sentence provides an example of a comet whose orbit has changed, it doesn't make a generalization about the orbits of comets.

Math

Module 1
(22 questions)

QUESTION 1

Choice C is correct. It's given that $x = 7$. Substituting 7 for x into the given expression $x + 20$ yields $7 + 20$, which is equivalent to 27.

Choice A is incorrect. This is the value of $x + 6$. *Choice B* is incorrect. This is the value of $x + 13$. *Choice D* is incorrect. This is the value of $x + 27$.

QUESTION 2

Choice B is correct. The mean of a data set is the sum of the values in the data set divided by the number of values in the data set. It follows that the mean of data set X is $\dfrac{5 + 9 + 9 + 13}{4}$, or 9, and the mean of data set Y is $\dfrac{5 + 9 + 9 + 13 + 27}{5}$, or 12.6. Since 9 is less than 12.6, the mean of data set X is less than the mean of data set Y.

Alternate approach: Data set Y consists of the 4 values in data set X and one additional value, 27. Since the additional value, 27, is larger than any value in data set X, the mean of data set X is less than the mean of data set Y.

Choice A is incorrect and may result from conceptual or calculation errors. *Choice C* is incorrect and may result from conceptual or calculation errors. *Choice D* is incorrect and may result from conceptual or calculation errors.

QUESTION 3

Choice B is correct. In similar triangles, corresponding angles are congruent. It's given that right triangles PQR and STU are similar, where angle P corresponds to angle S. It follows that angle P is congruent to angle S. In the triangles shown, angle R and angle U are both marked as right angles, so angle R and angle U are corresponding angles. It follows that angle Q and angle T are corresponding angles, and thus, angle Q is congruent to angle T. It's given that the measure of angle Q is 18°, so the measure of angle T is also 18°. Angle U is a right angle, so the measure of angle U is 90°. The sum of the measures of the interior angles of a triangle is 180°. Thus, the sum of the measures of the interior angles of triangle STU is 180 degrees. Let s represent the measure, in degrees, of angle S. It follows that $s + 18 + 90 = 180$, or $s + 108 = 180$. Subtracting 108 from both sides of this equation yields $s = 72$. Therefore, if the measure of angle Q is 18 degrees, then the measure of angle S is 72 degrees.

Choice A is incorrect. This is the measure of angle T.
Choice C is incorrect and may result from conceptual or calculation errors.
Choice D is incorrect. This is the sum of the measures of angle S and angle U.

QUESTION 4

Choice A is correct. It's given that the rocket contained 467,000 kilograms (kg) of propellant before launch and had 362,105 kg remaining exactly 21 seconds after launch. Finding the difference between the amount, in kg, of propellant before launch and the remaining amount, in kg, of propellant after launch gives the amount, in kg, of propellant burned during the 21 seconds: $467,000 - 362,105 = 104,895$. Dividing the amount of propellant burned by the number of seconds yields $\frac{104,895}{21} = 4,995$. Thus, an average of 4,995 kg of propellant burned each second after launch.

Choice B is incorrect and may result from conceptual or calculation errors.
Choice C is incorrect and may result from conceptual or calculation errors.
Choice D is incorrect and may result from finding the amount of propellant burned, rather than the amount of propellant burned each second.

QUESTION 5

Choice C is correct. It's given that $4x = 20$ and $-3x + y = -7$ is a system of equations with a solution (x, y). Adding the second equation in the given system to the first equation yields $4x + (-3x + y) = 20 + (-7)$, which is equivalent to $x + y = 13$. Thus, the value of $x + y$ is 13.

Choice A is incorrect. This represents the value of $-2(x + y) - 1$. *Choice B* is incorrect. This represents the value of $-(x + y)$. *Choice D* is incorrect. This represents the value of $2(x + y) + 1$.

QUESTION 6

The correct answer is 5. It's given that the equation $10x + 15y = 85$ represents the situation, where x is the number of on-site training courses, y is the number of online training courses, and 85 is the total number of hours of training courses the apprentice has enrolled in. Therefore, $10x$ represents the number of hours the apprentice has enrolled in on-site training courses, and $15y$ represents the number of hours the apprentice has enrolled in online training courses. Since x is the number of on-site training courses and y is the number of online training courses the apprentice has enrolled in, 10 is the number of hours each on-site course takes and 15 is the number of hours each online course takes. Subtracting these numbers gives $15 - 10$, or 5 more hours each online training course takes than each on-site training course.

QUESTION 7

Choice D is correct. The perimeter, P, of a square can be found using the formula $P = 4s$, where s is the length of each side of the square. It's given that square X has a side length of 12 centimeters. Substituting 12 for s in the formula for the perimeter of a square yields $P = 4(12)$, or $P = 48$. Therefore, the perimeter of square X is 48 centimeters. It's also given that the perimeter of square Y is 2 times the perimeter of square X. Therefore, the perimeter of square Y is 2(48), or 96, centimeters. Substituting 96 for P in the formula $P = 4s$ gives 96 = 4s. Dividing both sides of this equation by 4 gives 24 = s. Therefore, the length of one side of square Y is 24 centimeters.

Choice A is incorrect and may result from conceptual or calculation errors.
Choice B is incorrect and may result from conceptual or calculation errors.
Choice C is incorrect and may result from conceptual or calculation errors.

QUESTION 8

Choice A is correct. It's given that the function g models the number of gallons that remain from a full gas tank in a car after driving m miles. In the given function $g(m) = -0.05m + 12.1$, the coefficient of m is -0.05. This means that for every increase in the value of m by 1, the value of $g(m)$ decreases by 0.05. It follows that for each mile driven, there is a decrease of 0.05 gallons of gasoline. Therefore, 0.05 gallons of gasoline are used to drive each mile.

Choice B is incorrect and represents the number of gallons of gasoline in a full gas tank. *Choice C* is incorrect and may result from conceptual errors. *Choice D* is incorrect and may result from conceptual errors.

QUESTION 9

The correct answer is 28. The given absolute value equation can be rewritten as two linear equations: $4x - 4 = 112$ and $-(4x - 4) = 112$, or $4x - 4 = -112$. Adding 4 to both sides of the equation $4x - 4 = 112$ results in $4x = 116$. Dividing both sides of this equation by 4 results in $x = 29$. Adding 4 to both sides of the equation $4x - 4 = -112$ results in $4x = -108$. Dividing both sides of this equation by 4 results in $x = -27$. Therefore, the two values of $x - 1$ are $29 - 1$, or 28, and $-27 - 1$, or -28. Thus, the positive value of $x - 1$ is 28.

Alternate approach: The given equation can be rewritten as $|4(x - 1)| = 112$, which is equivalent to $4|x - 1| = 112$. Dividing both sides of this equation by 4 yields $|x - 1| = 28$. This equation can be rewritten as two linear equations: $x - 1 = 28$ and $-(x - 1) = 28$, or $x - 1 = -28$. Therefore, the positive value of $x - 1$ is 28.

QUESTION 10

Choice C is correct. Multiplying each side of the given equation by y yields the equivalent equation $\frac{y}{7b} = 11x$. Dividing each side of this equation by 11 yields $\frac{y}{77b} = x$, or $x = \frac{y}{77b}$.

Choice A is incorrect. This equation is not equivalent to the given equation.
Choice B is incorrect. This equation is not equivalent to the given equation.
Choice D is incorrect. This equation is not equivalent to the given equation.

QUESTION 11

The correct answer is 11. It's given that $f(x)$ is defined by the equation $f(x) = mx - 28$, where m is a constant. It's also given in the table that when $x = 10$, $f(x) = 82$. Substituting 10 for x and 82 for $f(x)$ in the equation $f(x) = mx - 28$ yields $82 = m(10) - 28$. Adding 28 to both sides of this equation yields $110 = 10m$. Dividing both sides of this equation by 10 yields $11 = m$. Therefore, the value of m is 11.

QUESTION 12

The correct answer is 9. The given expression can be rewritten as $(5x^3 - 3) + (-1)(-4x^3 + 8)$. By applying the distributive property, this expression can be rewritten as $5x^3 - 3 + 4x^3 + (-8)$, which is equivalent to $(5x^3 + 4x^3) + (-3 + (-8))$. Adding like terms in this expression yields $9x^3 - 11$. Since it's given that $(5x^3 - 3) - (-4x^3 + 8)$ is equivalent to $bx^3 - 11$, it follows that $9x^3 - 11$ is equivalent to $bx^3 - 11$. Therefore, the coefficients of x^3 in these two expressions must be equivalent, and the value of b must be 9.

QUESTION 13

Choice A is correct. It's given that the point $(x, 53)$ is a solution to the given system of inequalities in the xy-plane. This means that the coordinates of the point, when substituted for the variables x and y, make both of the inequalities in the system true. Substituting 53 for y in the inequality $y > 14$ yields $53 > 14$, which is true. Substituting 53 for y in the inequality $4x + y < 18$ yields $4x + 53 < 18$. Subtracting 53 from both sides of this inequality yields $4x < -35$. Dividing both sides of this inequality by 4 yields $x < -8.75$. Therefore, x must be a value less than -8.75. Of the given choices, only -9 is less than -8.75.

Choice B is incorrect. Substituting -5 for x and 53 for y in the inequality $4x + y < 18$ yields $4(-5) + 53 < 18$, or $33 < 18$, which is not true.
Choice C is incorrect. Substituting 5 for x and 53 for y in the inequality $4x + y < 18$ yields $4(5) + 53 < 18$, or $73 < 18$, which is not true.
Choice D is incorrect. Substituting 9 for x and 53 for y in the inequality $4x + y < 18$ yields $4(9) + 53 < 18$, or $89 < 18$, which is not true.

QUESTION 14

Choice D is correct. Let y represent the number of cells per milliliter x hours after the initial observation. Since the number of cells per milliliter doubles every 3 hours, the relationship between x and y can be represented by an exponential equation of the form $y = a(b)^{\frac{x}{k}}$, where a is the number of cells per milliliter during the initial observation and the number of cells per milliliter increases by a factor of b every k hours. It's given that there were 300,000 cells per milliliter during the initial observation. Therefore, $a = 300,000$. It's also given that the number of cells per milliliter doubles, or increases by a factor of 2, every 3 hours. Therefore, $b = 2$ and $k = 3$. Substituting 300,000 for a, 2 for b, and 3 for k in the equation $y = a(b)^{\frac{x}{k}}$ yields $y = 300,000(2)^{\frac{x}{3}}$. The number of cells per milliliter there will be 15 hours after the initial observation is the value of y in this equation when $x = 15$. Substituting 15 for x in the equation $y = 300,000(2)^{\frac{x}{3}}$ yields $y = 300,000(2)^{\frac{15}{3}}$, or $y = 300,000(2)^5$. This is equivalent to $y = 300,000(32)$, or $y = 9,600,000$. Therefore, 15 hours after the initial observation, there will be 9,600,000 cells per milliliter.

Choice A is incorrect and may result from conceptual or calculation errors.
Choice B is incorrect and may result from conceptual or calculation errors.
Choice C is incorrect and may result from conceptual or calculation errors.

QUESTION 15

Choice D is correct. The y-intercept of the graph is the point at which the graph crosses the y-axis, or the point for which the value of x is 0. Therefore, the y-intercept of the given graph is the point $(0, 9)$. It's given that x represents the number of years since the end of 1992. Therefore, $x = 0$ represents 0 years since the end of 1992, which is the same as the end of 1992. It's also given that y represents the estimated number of catalogs, in thousands, that the company sent to its customers at the end of the year. Therefore, $y = 9$ represents 9,000 catalogs. It follows that the y-intercept $(0, 9)$ means that the estimated number of catalogs the company sent to its customers at the end of 1992 was 9,000.

Choice A is incorrect and may result from conceptual or calculation errors. *Choice B* is incorrect and may result from conceptual or calculation errors. *Choice C* is incorrect and may result from conceptual or calculation errors.

QUESTION 16

Choice B is correct. For positive values of a and b, $a^m b^m = (ab)^m$, $\sqrt[n]{a} = (a)^{\frac{1}{n}}$, and $(a^j)^k = a^{jk}$. Therefore, the given expression, $\sqrt[7]{x^9 y^9}$, can be rewritten as $\sqrt[7]{(xy)^9}$. This expression is equivalent to $\left((xy)^9\right)^{\frac{1}{7}}$, which can be rewritten as $(xy)^{9 \cdot \frac{1}{7}}$, or $(xy)^{\frac{9}{7}}$.

Choice A is incorrect and may result from conceptual or calculation errors. *Choice C* is incorrect and may result from conceptual or calculation errors. *Choice D* is incorrect and may result from conceptual or calculation errors.

QUESTION 17

Choice C is correct. It's given that the population of City A increased by 7% from 2015 to 2016. Therefore, the population of City A in 2016 includes 100% of the population of City A in 2015 plus an additional 7% of the population of City A in 2015. This means that the population of City A in 2016 is 107% of the population in 2015. Thus, the population of City A in 2016 is $\frac{107}{100}$, or 1.07, times the 2015 population. Therefore, the value of k is 1.07.

Choice A is incorrect. This would be the value of k if the population in 2016 was 7% of the population in 2015. *Choice B* is incorrect. This would be the value of k if the population in 2016 was 70% of the population in 2015. *Choice D* is incorrect. This would be the value of k if the population increased by 70%, not 7%, from 2015 to 2016.

QUESTION 18

Choice C is correct. A system of two linear equations in two variables, x and y, has no solution if the graphs of the lines represented by the equations in the xy-plane are distinct and parallel. The graphs of two lines in the xy-plane represented by equations in slope-intercept form, $y = mx + b$, where m and b are constants, are parallel if their slopes, m, are the same and are distinct if their y-coordinates of the y-intercepts, b, are different. In the equations $y = 16x + 3$ and $y = 16x + 19$, the values of m are each 16, and the values of b are 3 and 19, respectively. Since the slopes of these lines are the same, and the y-coordinates of the y-intercepts are different, it follows that the system of linear equations in choice C has no solution.

Choice A is incorrect. The lines represented by the equations in this system are a vertical line and a horizontal line. Therefore, this system has a solution, $(3, 5)$, rather than no solution. *Choice B* is incorrect. The two lines represented by these equations have different slopes and the same y-coordinate of the y-intercept. Therefore, this system has a solution, $(0, 6)$, rather than no solution. *Choice D* is incorrect. The two lines represented by these equations are a horizontal line and a line with a slope of 5 that have the same y-coordinate of the y-intercept. Therefore, this system has a solution, $(0, 5)$, rather than no solution.

QUESTION 19

Choice D is correct. Since *w* represents the *n*th term of the sequence and 9 is the first term of the sequence, the value of *w* is 9 when the value of *n* is 1. Since each term after the first is 4 times the preceding term, the value of *w* is 9(4) when the value of *n* is 2. Therefore, the value of *w* is 9(4)(4), or $9(4)^2$, when the value of *n* is 3. More generally, the value of *w* is $9(4^{n-1})$ for a given value of *n*. Therefore, the equation $w = 9(4^{n-1})$ gives *w* in terms of *n*.

Choice A is incorrect. This equation describes a sequence for which the first term is 36, rather than 9, and each term after the first is 9, rather than 4, times the preceding term. *Choice B* is incorrect. This equation describes a sequence for which the first term is 4, rather than 9, and each term after the first is 9, rather than 4, times the preceding term. *Choice C* is incorrect. This equation describes a sequence for which the first term is 36, rather than 9.

QUESTION 20

Choice B is correct. It's given that the minimum value of *x* is 12 less than 6 times another number *n*. Therefore, the possible values of *x* are all greater than or equal to the value of 12 less than 6 times *n*. The value of 6 times *n* is given by the expression 6*n*. The value of 12 less than 6*n* is given by the expression 6*n* − 12. Therefore, the possible values of *x* are all greater than or equal to 6*n* − 12. This can be shown by the inequality $x \geq 6n - 12$.

Choice A is incorrect. This inequality shows the possible values of *x* if the maximum, not the minimum, value of *x* is 12 less than 6 times *n*. *Choice C* is incorrect. This inequality shows the possible values of *x* if the maximum, not the minimum, value of *x* is 6 times *n* less than 12, not 12 less than 6 times *n*. *Choice D* is incorrect. This inequality shows the possible values of *x* if the minimum value of *x* is 6 times *n* less than 12, not 12 less than 6 times *n*.

QUESTION 21

Choice B is correct. It's given that right triangle *RST* is similar to triangle *UVW*, where *S* corresponds to *V* and *T* corresponds to *W*. It's given that the side lengths of the right triangle *RST* are *RS* = 20, *ST* = 48, and *TR* = 52. Corresponding angles in similar triangles are equal. It follows that the measure of angle *T* is equal to the measure of angle *W*. The hypotenuse of a right triangle is the longest side. It follows that the hypotenuse of triangle *RST* is side *TR*. The hypotenuse of a right triangle is the side opposite the right angle. Therefore, angle *S* is a right angle. The adjacent side of an acute angle in a right triangle is the side closest to the angle that is not the hypotenuse. It follows that the adjacent side of angle *T* is side *ST*. The opposite side of an acute angle in a right triangle is the side across from the acute angle. It follows that the opposite side of angle *T* is side *RS*. The tangent of an acute angle in a right triangle is the ratio of the length of the opposite side to the length of the adjacent side. Therefore, $\tan T = \frac{RS}{ST}$. Substituting 20 for *RS* and 48 for *ST* in this equation yields $\tan T = \frac{20}{48}$, or $\tan T = \frac{5}{12}$. The tangents of two acute angles with equal measures are equal. Since the measure of angle *T* is equal to the measure of angle *W*, it follows that $\tan T = \tan W$. Substituting $\frac{5}{12}$ for $\tan T$ in this equation yields $\frac{5}{12} = \tan W$. Therefore, the value of $\tan W$ is $\frac{5}{12}$.

Choice A is incorrect. This is the value of sin *W*. *Choice C* is incorrect. This is the value of cos *W*. *Choice D* is incorrect. This is the value of $\frac{1}{\tan W}$.

QUESTION 22

The correct answer is $\dfrac{59}{9}$. When the graph of an equation in the form

$Ax + By = C$, where A, B, and C are constants, is translated down k units in the xy-plane, the resulting graph can be represented by the equation $Ax + B(y + k) = C$. It's given that the graph of $9x - 10y = 19$ is translated down 4 units in the xy-plane. Therefore, the resulting graph can be represented by the equation $9x - 10(y + 4) = 19$, or $9x - 10y - 40 = 19$. Adding 40 to both sides of this equation yields $9x - 10y = 59$. The x-coordinate of the x-intercept of the graph of an equation in the xy-plane is the value of x in the equation when $y = 0$. Substituting 0 for y in the equation $9x - 10y = 59$ yields $9x - 10(0) = 59$,

or $9x = 59$. Dividing both sides of this equation by 9 yields $x = \dfrac{59}{9}$. Therefore,

the x-coordinate of the x-intercept of the resulting graph is $\dfrac{59}{9}$. Note that 59/9,

6.555, and 6.556 are examples of ways to enter a correct answer.

Math

Module 2
(22 questions)

QUESTION 1

Choice A is correct. It's given that 20% of the students surveyed responded that they intend to enroll in the study program. Therefore, the proportion of students in Spanish club who intend to enroll in the study program, based on the survey, is 0.20. Since there are 55 total students in Spanish club, the best estimate for the total number of these students who intend to enroll in the study program is 55(0.20), or 11.

Choice B is incorrect. This is the best estimate for the percentage, rather than the total number, of students in Spanish club who intend to enroll in the study program. *Choice C* is incorrect. This is the best estimate for the total number of Spanish club students who do not intend to enroll in the study program. *Choice D* is incorrect. This is the total number of students in Spanish club.

QUESTION 2

Choice B is correct. It's given that it takes the machine 10 minutes to make a large box. It's also given that x represents the possible number of large boxes the machine can make each day. Multiplying 10 by x gives $10x$, which represents the amount of time spent making large boxes. It's given that it takes the machine 5 minutes to make a small box. It's also given that y represents the possible number of small boxes the machine can make each day. Multiplying 5 by y gives $5y$, which represents the amount of time spent making small boxes. Combining the amount of time spent making x large boxes and y small boxes yields $10x + 5y$. It's given that the machine makes boxes for a total of 700 minutes each day. Therefore $10x + 5y = 700$ represents the possible number of large boxes, x, and small boxes, y, the machine can make each day.

Choice A is incorrect and may result from associating the time of 10 minutes with small, rather than large, boxes and the time of 5 minutes with large, rather than small, boxes. *Choice C* is incorrect and may result from conceptual errors. *Choice D* is incorrect and may result from conceptual errors.

QUESTION 3

Choice B is correct. The line of best fit shown intersects the y-axis at a positive y-value and has a negative slope. The graph of an equation of the form $y = a + bx$, where a and b are constants, intersects the y-axis at a y-value of a and has a slope of b. Of the given choices, only choice B represents a line that intersects the y-axis at a positive y-value, 13.5, and has a negative slope, −0.8.

Choice A is incorrect. This equation represents a line that has a positive slope, not a negative slope. *Choice C* is incorrect. This equation represents a line that intersects the *y*-axis at a negative *y*-value, not a positive *y*-value, and has a positive slope, not a negative slope. *Choice D* is incorrect. This equation represents a line that intersects the *y*-axis at a negative *y*-value, not a positive *y*-value.

QUESTION 4

Choice C is correct. It's given from the graph that the points $(0, 7)$ and $(8, 0)$ lie on the line. For two points on a line, (x_1, y_1) and (x_2, y_2), the slope of the line can be calculated using the slope formula $m = \frac{y_2 - y_1}{x_2 - x_1}$. Substituting $(0, 7)$ for (x_1, y_1) and $(8, 0)$ for (x_2, y_2) in this formula, the slope of the line can be calculated as $m = \frac{0 - 7}{8 - 0}$, or $m = -\frac{7}{8}$. It's also given that the point $(d, 4)$ lies on the line. Substituting $(d, 4)$ for (x_1, y_1), $(8, 0)$ for (x_2, y_2), and $-\frac{7}{8}$ for m in the slope formula yields $-\frac{7}{8} = \frac{0 - 4}{8 - d}$, or $-\frac{7}{8} = \frac{-4}{8 - d}$. Multiplying both sides of this equation by $8 - d$ yields $-\frac{7}{8}(8 - d) = -4$. Expanding the left-hand side of this equation yields $-7 + \frac{7}{8}d = -4$. Adding 7 to both sides of this equation yields $\frac{7}{8}d = 3$. Multiplying both sides of this equation by $\frac{8}{7}$ yields $d = \frac{24}{7}$. Thus, the value of *d* is $\frac{24}{7}$.

Choice A is incorrect. This is the value of *y* when $x = 4$. *Choice B* is incorrect and may result from conceptual or calculation errors. *Choice D* is incorrect and may result from conceptual or calculation errors.

QUESTION 5

Choice D is correct. The equation of a quadratic function can be written in the form $f(x) = a(x - h)^2 + k$, where *a*, *h*, and *k* are constants. It's given in the table that when $x = -1$, the corresponding value of $f(x)$ is 10. Substituting -1 for *x* and 10 for $f(x)$ in the equation $f(x) = a(x - h)^2 + k$ gives $10 = a(-1 - h)^2 + k$, which is equivalent to $10 = a(1 + 2h + h^2) + k$, or $10 = a + 2ah + ah^2 + k$. It's given in the table that when $x = 0$, the corresponding value of $f(x)$ is 14. Substituting 0 for *x* and 14 for $f(x)$ in the equation $f(x) = a(x - h)^2 + k$ gives $14 = a(0 - h)^2 + k$, or $14 = ah^2 + k$. It's given in the table that when $x = 1$, the corresponding value of $f(x)$ is 20. Substituting 1 for *x* and 20 for $f(x)$ in the equation $f(x) = a(x - h)^2 + k$ gives $20 = a(1 - h)^2 + k$, which is equivalent to $20 = a(1 - 2h + h^2) + k$, or $20 = a - 2ah + ah^2 + k$. Adding $20 = a - 2ah + ah^2 + k$ to the equation $10 = a + 2ah + ah^2 + k$ gives $30 = 2a + 2ah^2 + 2k$. Dividing both sides of this equation by 2 gives $15 = a + ah^2 + k$. Since $14 = ah^2 + k$, substituting 14 for $ah^2 + k$ into the equation $15 = a + ah^2 + k$ gives $15 = a + 14$. Subtracting 14 from both sides of this equation gives $a = 1$. Substituting 1 for *a* in the equations $14 = ah^2 + k$ and $20 = ah^2 - 2ah + a + k$ gives $14 = h^2 + k$ and $20 = 1 - 2h + h^2 + k$, respectively. Since $14 = h^2 + k$, substituting 14 for $h^2 + k$ in the equation $20 = 1 - 2h + h^2 + k$ gives $20 = 1 - 2h + 14$, or $20 = 15 - 2h$. Subtracting 15 from both sides of this equation gives $5 = -2h$. Dividing both sides of this equation by -2 gives $-\frac{5}{2} = h$. Substituting $-\frac{5}{2}$ for *h* into the equation $14 = h^2 + k$ gives $14 = \left(-\frac{5}{2}\right)^2 + k$, or $14 = \frac{25}{4} + k$. Subtracting $\frac{25}{4}$ from both sides of this equation gives $\frac{31}{4} = k$. Substituting 1 for *a*, $-\frac{5}{2}$ for *h*, and $\frac{31}{4}$ for *k* in the equation $f(x) = a(x - h)^2 + k$ gives $f(x) = \left(x + \frac{5}{2}\right)^2 + \frac{31}{4}$, which is equivalent to $f(x) = x^2 + 5x + \frac{25}{4} + \frac{31}{4}$, or $f(x) = x^2 + 5x + 14$. Therefore, $f(x) = x^2 + 5x + 14$ defines f.

Choice A is incorrect. If $f(x) = 3x^2 + 3x + 14$, then when $x = -1$, the corresponding value of $f(x)$ is 14, not 10. *Choice B is incorrect.* If $f(x) = 5x^2 + x + 14$, then when $x = -1$, the corresponding value of $f(x)$ is 18, not 10. *Choice C is incorrect.* If $f(x) = 9x^2 - x + 14$, then when $x = -1$, the corresponding value of $f(x)$ is 24, not 10, and when $x = 1$, the corresponding value of $f(x)$ is 22, not 20.

QUESTION 6

Choice C is correct. It's given that $f(x) = \frac{x + 15}{5}$ and $f(a) = 10$, where a is a constant. Therefore, for the given function f, when $x = a$, $f(x) = 10$. Substituting a for x and 10 for $f(x)$ in the given function f yields $10 = \frac{a + 15}{5}$. Multiplying both sides of this equation by 5 yields $50 = a + 15$. Subtracting 15 from both sides of this equation yields $35 = a$. Therefore, the value of a is 35.

Choice A is incorrect. This is the value of a if $f(a) = 4$. *Choice B is incorrect.* This is the value of a if $f(a) = 5$. *Choice D is incorrect.* This is the value of a if $f(a) = 16$.

QUESTION 7

Choice C is correct. Vertical angles, which are angles that are opposite each other when two lines intersect, are congruent. The figure shows that lines t and m intersect. It follows that the angle with measure $x°$ and the angle with measure $y°$ are vertical angles, so $x = y$. It's given that $x = 6k + 13$ and $y = 8k - 29$. Substituting $6k + 13$ for x and $8k - 29$ for y in the equation $x = y$ yields $6k + 13 = 8k - 29$. Subtracting $6k$ from both sides of this equation yields $13 = 2k - 29$. Adding 29 to both sides of this equation yields $42 = 2k$, or $2k = 42$. Dividing both sides of this equation by 2 yields $k = 21$. It's given that lines m and n are parallel, and the figure shows that lines m and n are intersected by a transversal, line t. If two parallel lines are intersected by a transversal, then the same-side interior angles are supplementary. It follows that the same-side interior angles with measures $y°$ and $z°$ are supplementary, so $y + z = 180$. Substituting $8k - 29$ for y in this equation yields $8k - 29 + z = 180$. Substituting 21 for k in this equation yields $8(21) - 29 + z = 180$, or $139 + z = 180$. Subtracting 139 from both sides of this equation yields $z = 41$. Therefore, the value of z is 41.

Choice A is incorrect and may result from conceptual or calculation errors. Choice B is incorrect. This is the value of k, not z. *Choice D is incorrect.* This is the value of x or y, not z.

QUESTION 8

Choice C is correct. It's given that line r is perpendicular to line p in the xy-plane. This means that the slope of line r is the negative reciprocal of the slope of line p. If the equation for line p is rewritten in slope-intercept form $y = mx + b$, where m and b are constants, then m is the slope of the line and $(0, b)$ is its y-intercept. Subtracting $18x$ from both sides of the equation $2y + 18x = 9$ yields $2y = -18x + 9$. Dividing both sides of this equation by

2 yields $y = -9x + \dfrac{9}{2}$. It follows that the slope of line p is -9. The negative reciprocal of a number is -1 divided by the number. Therefore, the negative reciprocal of -9 is $\dfrac{-1}{-9}$, or $\dfrac{1}{9}$. Thus, the slope of line r is $\dfrac{1}{9}$.

Choice A is incorrect. This is the slope of line p, not line r. *Choice B* is incorrect. This is the reciprocal, not the negative reciprocal, of the slope of line p. *Choice D* is incorrect. This is the negative, not the negative reciprocal, of the slope of line p.

QUESTION 9

Choice A is correct. It's given that the sample is in the shape of a cube with edge lengths of 0.9 meters. Therefore, the volume of the sample is 0.90^3, or 0.729, cubic meters. It's also given that the sample has a density of 807 kilograms per 1 cubic meter. Therefore, the mass of this sample is 0.729 cubic meters $\left(\dfrac{807 \text{ kilograms}}{1 \text{ cubic meter}}\right)$, or 588.303 kilograms. Rounding this mass to the nearest whole number gives 588 kilograms. Therefore, to the nearest whole number, the mass, in kilograms, of this sample is 588.

Choice B is incorrect and may result from conceptual or calculation errors. *Choice C* is incorrect and may result from conceptual or calculation errors. *Choice D* is incorrect and may result from conceptual or calculation errors.

QUESTION 10

Choice C is correct. It's given that the function P models the population of the city t years after 2005. Since there are 12 months in a year, 18 months is equivalent to $\dfrac{18}{12}$ years. Therefore, the expression $\dfrac{18}{12}x$ can represent the number of years in x 18-month periods. Substituting $\dfrac{18}{12}x$ for t in the given equation yields $P\left(\dfrac{18}{12}x\right) = 290(1.04)^{\left(\frac{4}{6}\right)\left(\frac{18}{12}x\right)}$, which is equivalent to $P\left(\dfrac{18}{12}x\right) = 290(1.04)^x$. Therefore, for each 18-month period, the predicted population of the city is 1.04 times, or 104% of, the previous population. This means that the population is predicted to increase by 4% every 18 months.

Choice A is incorrect and may result from conceptual or calculation errors. *Choice B* is incorrect. Each year, the predicted population of the city is 1.04 times the previous year's predicted population, which is not the same as an increase of 1.04%. *Choice D* is incorrect and may result from conceptual or calculation errors.

QUESTION 11

The correct answer is $-\dfrac{14}{15}$. A linear equation in the form $ax + b = cx + d$ has no solution only when the coefficients of x on each side of the equation are equal and the constant terms are not equal. Dividing both sides of the given equation by 2 yields $kx - n = -\dfrac{28}{30}x - \dfrac{36}{38}$, or $kx - n = -\dfrac{14}{15}x - \dfrac{18}{19}$. Since it's given that the equation has no solution, the coefficient of x on both sides of this equation must be equal, and the constant terms on both sides of this equation must not be equal. Since $\frac{18}{19} < 1$, and it's given that $n > 1$, the second condition is true. Thus, k must be equal to $-\frac{14}{15}$. Note that $-14/15$, $-.9333$, and -0.933 are examples of ways to enter a correct answer.

QUESTION 12

The correct answer is 4.06. It's given that the retail price is 290% of the wholesale price of $7.00. Thus, the retail price is $7.00\left(\frac{290}{100}\right)$, which is equivalent to $7.00(2.9), or $20.30. It's also given that the discounted price is 80% off the retail price. Thus, the discounted price is $20.30\left(1 - \frac{80}{100}\right)$, which is equivalent to $20.30(0.20), or $4.06.

QUESTION 13

The correct answer is 289. A quadratic equation of the form $ax^2 + bx + c = 0$, where a, b, and c are constants, has no real solutions when the value of the discriminant, $b^2 - 4ac$, is less than 0. In the given equation, $x^2 - 34x + c = 0$, $a = 1$ and $b = -34$. Therefore, the discriminant of the given equation can be expressed as $(-34)^2 - 4(1)(c)$, or $1{,}156 - 4c$. It follows that the given equation has no real solutions when $1{,}156 - 4c < 0$. Adding $4c$ to both sides of this inequality yields $1{,}156 < 4c$. Dividing both sides of this inequality by 4 yields $289 < c$, or $c > 289$. It's given that the equation $x^2 - 34x + c = 0$ has no real solutions when $c > n$. Therefore, the least possible value of n is 289.

QUESTION 14

The correct answer is 44. The mean of a data set is computed by dividing the sum of the values In the data set by the number of values in the data set. It's given that data set A consists of the heights of 75 buildings and has a mean of 32 meters. This can be represented by the equation $\frac{x}{75} = 32$, where x represents the sum of the heights of the buildings, in meters, in data set A. Multiplying both sides of this equation by 75 yields $x = 75(32)$, or $x = 2{,}400$ meters. Therefore, the sum of the heights of the buildings in data set A is 2,400 meters. It's also given that data set B consists of the heights of 50 buildings and has a mean of 62 meters. This can be represented by the equation $\frac{y}{50} = 62$, where y represents the sum of the heights of the buildings, in meters, in data set B. Multiplying both sides of this equation by 50 yields $y = 50(62)$, or $y = 3{,}100$ meters. Therefore, the sum of the heights of the buildings in data set B is 3,100 meters. Since it's given that data set C consists of the heights of the 125 buildings from data sets A and B, it follows that the mean of data set C is the sum of the heights of the buildings, in meters, in data sets A and B divided by the number of buildings represented in data sets A and B, or $\frac{2{,}400 + 3{,}100}{125}$, which is equivalent to 44 meters. Therefore, the mean, in meters, of data set C is 44.

QUESTION 15

Choice D is correct. It's given that $4x^2 + bx - 45$ can be rewritten as $(hx + k)(x + j)$. The expression $(hx + k)(x + j)$ can be rewritten as $hx^2 + jhx + kx + kj$, or $hx^2 + (jh + k)x + kj$. Therefore, $hx^2 + (jh + k)x + kj$ is equivalent to $4x^2 + bx - 45$.

It follows that $kj = -45$. Dividing each side of this equation by k yields $j = \dfrac{-45}{k}$. Since j is an integer, $-\dfrac{45}{k}$ must be an integer. Therefore, $\dfrac{45}{k}$ must also be an integer.

Choice A is incorrect and may result from conceptual or calculation errors.
Choice B is incorrect and may result from conceptual or calculation errors.
Choice C is incorrect and may result from conceptual or calculation errors.

QUESTION 16

The correct answer is $\dfrac{29}{2}$. According to the first equation in the given system, the value of y is -1.5. Substituting -1.5 for y in the second equation in the given system yields $-1.5 = x^2 + 8x + a$. Adding 1.5 to both sides of this equation yields $0 = x^2 + 8x + a + 1.5$. If the given system has exactly one distinct real solution, it follows that $0 = x^2 + 8x + a + 1.5$ has exactly one distinct real solution. A quadratic equation in the form $0 = px^2 + qx + r$, where p, q, and r are constants, has exactly one distinct real solution if and only if the discriminant, $q^2 - 4pr$, is equal to 0. The equation $0 = x^2 + 8x + a + 1.5$ is in this form, where $p = 1$, $q = 8$, and $r = a + 1.5$. Therefore, the discriminant of the equation $0 = x^2 + 8x + a + 1.5$ is $(8)^2 - 4(1)(a + 1.5)$, or $58 - 4a$. Setting the discriminant equal to 0 to solve for a yields $58 - 4a = 0$. Adding $4a$ to both sides of this equation yields $58 = 4a$.

Dividing both sides of this equation by 4 yields $\dfrac{58}{4} = a$, or $\dfrac{29}{2} = a$. Therefore, if the given system of equations has exactly one distinct real solution, the value of a is $\dfrac{29}{2}$. Note that 29/2 and 14.5 are examples of ways to enter a correct answer.

QUESTION 17

Choice C is correct. The median of a data set with an odd number of values, in ascending or descending order, is the middle value of the data set, and the range of a data set is the positive difference between the maximum and minimum values in the data set. Since the dot plot shown gives the values in data set A in ascending order and there are 15 values in the data set, the eighth value in data set A, 23, is the median. The maximum value in data set A is 26 and the minimum value is 22, so the range of data set A is $26 - 22$, or 4. It's given that data set B is created by adding 56 to each of the values in data set A. Increasing each of the 15 values in data set A by 56 will also increase its median value by 56 making the median of data set B 79. Increasing each value of data set A by 56 does not change the range, since the maximum value of data set B is $26 + 56$, or 82, and the minimum value is $22 + 56$, or 78, making the range of data set B $82 - 78$, or 4. Therefore, the median of data set B is greater than the median of data set A, and the range of data set B is equal to the range of data set A.

Choice A is incorrect and may result from conceptual or calculation errors.
Choice B is incorrect and may result from conceptual or calculation errors.
Choice D is incorrect and may result from conceptual or calculation errors.

QUESTION 18

Choice C is correct. It's given that $f(x) = \dfrac{a}{x + b}$ and that the graph shown is a partial graph of $y = f(x)$. Substituting y for $f(x)$ in the equation $f(x) = \dfrac{a}{x + b}$ yields $y = \dfrac{a}{x + b}$. The graph passes through the point $(-7, -2)$. Substituting -7 for x and -2 for y in the equation $y = \dfrac{a}{x + b}$ yields $-2 = \dfrac{a}{-7 + b}$. Multiplying each side of this equation by $-7 + b$ yields $-2(-7 + b) = a$, or $14 - 2b = a$. The graph also passes through the point $(-5, -6)$. Substituting -5 for x and -6 for y in the equation $y = \dfrac{a}{x + b}$ yields $-6 = \dfrac{a}{-5 + b}$. Multiplying each side of this equation by $-5 + b$ yields $-6(-5 + b) = a$, or $30 - 6b = a$. Substituting $14 - 2b$ for a in this equation yields $30 - 6b = 14 - 2b$. Adding $6b$ to each side of this equation yields $30 = 14 + 4b$. Subtracting 14 from each side of this equation yields $16 = 4b$. Dividing each side of this equation by 4 yields $4 = b$. Substituting 4 for b in the equation $14 - 2b = a$ yields $14 - 2(4) = a$, or $6 = a$. Substituting 6 for a and 4 for b in the equation $f(x) = \dfrac{a}{x + b}$ yields $f(x) = \dfrac{6}{x + 4}$. It's given that $g(x) = f(x + 4)$. Substituting $x + 4$ for x in the equation $f(x) = \dfrac{6}{x + 4}$ yields $f(x + 4) = \dfrac{6}{x + 4 + 4}$, which is equivalent to $f(x + 4) = \dfrac{6}{x + 8}$. It follows that $g(x) = \dfrac{6}{x + 8}$.

Choice A is incorrect. This could define function g if $g(x) = f(x - 4)$. Choice B is incorrect. This could define function g if $g(x) = f(x)$. Choice D is incorrect. This could define function g if $g(x) = f(x) \cdot (x + 4)$.

QUESTION 19

Choice A is correct. The left-hand side of the given equation is the expression $57x^2 + (57b + a)x + ab$. Applying the distributive property to this expression yields $57x^2 + 57bx + ax + ab$. Since the first two terms of this expression have a common factor of $57x$ and the last two terms of this expression have a common factor of a, this expression can be rewritten as $57x(x + b) + a(x + b)$. Since the two terms of this expression have a common factor of $(x + b)$, it can be rewritten as $(x + b)(57x + a)$. Therefore, the given equation can be rewritten as $(x + b)(57x + a) = 0$. By the zero product property, it follows that $x + b = 0$ or $57x + a = 0$. Subtracting b from both sides of the equation $x + b = 0$ yields $x = -b$. Subtracting a from both sides of the equation $57x + a = 0$ yields $57x = -a$. Dividing both sides of this equation by 57 yields $x = \dfrac{-a}{57}$. Therefore, the solutions to the given equation are $-b$ and $\dfrac{-a}{57}$. It follows that the product of the solutions of the given equation is $(-b)\left(\dfrac{-a}{57}\right)$, or $\dfrac{ab}{57}$. It's given that the product of the solutions of the given equation is kab. It follows that $\dfrac{ab}{57} = kab$, which can also be written as $ab\left(\dfrac{1}{57}\right) = ab(k)$. It's given that a and b are positive constants. Therefore, dividing both sides of the equation $ab\left(\dfrac{1}{57}\right) = ab(k)$ by ab yields $\dfrac{1}{57} = k$. Thus, the value of k is $\dfrac{1}{57}$.

Choice B is incorrect and may result from conceptual or calculation errors. Choice C is incorrect and may result from conceptual or calculation errors. Choice D is incorrect and may result from conceptual or calculation errors.

QUESTION 20

The correct answer is 10. It's given that the graph of $x^2 + x + y^2 + y = \frac{199}{2}$ in the

xy-plane is a circle. The equation of a circle in the xy-plane can be written in the form $(x - h)^2 + (y - k)^2 = r^2$, where the coordinates of the center of the circle are (h, k) and the length of the radius of the circle is r. The term $(x - h)^2$ in this equation can be obtained by adding the square of half the coefficient of x to both sides of the given equation to complete the square. The coefficient of x is 1.

Half the coefficient of x is $\frac{1}{2}$. The square of half the coefficient of x is $\frac{1}{4}$. Adding $\frac{1}{4}$

to each side of $(x^2 + x) + (y^2 + y) = \frac{199}{2}$ yields $\left(x^2 + x + \frac{1}{4}\right) + (y^2 + y) = \frac{199}{2} + \frac{1}{4}$, or

$\left(x + \frac{1}{2}\right)^2 + (y^2 + y) = \frac{199}{2} + \frac{1}{4}$. Similarly, the term $(y - k)^2$ can be obtained by adding

the square of half the coefficient of y to both sides of this equation, which yields

$\left(x + \frac{1}{2}\right)^2 + \left(y^2 + y + \frac{1}{4}\right) = \frac{199}{2} + \frac{1}{4} + \frac{1}{4}$, or $\left(x + \frac{1}{2}\right)^2 + \left(y + \frac{1}{2}\right)^2 = \frac{199}{2} + \frac{1}{4} + \frac{1}{4}$. This

equation is equivalent to $\left(x + \frac{1}{2}\right)^2 + \left(y + \frac{1}{2}\right)^2 = 100$, or $\left(x + \frac{1}{2}\right)^2 + \left(y + \frac{1}{2}\right)^2 = 10^2$.

Therefore, the length of the circle's radius is 10.

QUESTION 21

Choice B is correct. Let x represent the side length, in cm, of each square base. If the two prisms are glued together along a square base, the resulting prism has a surface area equal to twice the surface area of one of the prisms, minus the area of the two square bases that are being glued together, which yields

$2K - 2x^2$ cm^2. It's given that this resulting surface area is equal to $\frac{92}{47}K$ cm^2,

so $2K - 2x^2 = \frac{92}{47}K$. Subtracting $\frac{92}{47}K$ from both sides of this equation yields

$2K - \frac{92}{47}K - 2x^2 = 0$. This equation can be rewritten by multiplying $2K$ on the

left-hand side by $\frac{47}{47}$, which yields $\frac{94}{47}K - \frac{92}{47}K - 2x^2 = 0$, or $\frac{2}{47}K - 2x^2 = 0$.

Adding $2x^2$ to both sides of this equation yields $\frac{2}{47}K = 2x^2$. Multiplying both

sides of this equation by $\frac{47}{2}$ yields $K = 47x^2$. The surface area K, in cm^2,

of each rectangular prism is equivalent to the sum of the areas of the two square bases and the areas of the four lateral faces. Since the height of each rectangular prism is 90 cm and the side length of each square base is x cm, it follows that the area of each square base is x^2 cm^2 and the area of each lateral face is $90x$ cm^2. Therefore, the surface area of each rectangular prism can be represented by the expression $2x^2 + 4(90x)$, or $2x^2 + 360x$. Substituting this expression for K in the equation $K = 47x^2$ yields $2x^2 + 360x = 47x^2$. Subtracting $2x^2$ and $360x$ from both sides of this equation yields $0 = 45x^2 - 360x$. Factoring x from the right-hand side of this equation yields $0 = x(45x - 360)$. Applying the zero product property, it follows that $x = 0$ and $45x - 360 = 0$. Adding 360 to both sides of the equation $45x - 360 = 0$ yields $45x = 360$. Dividing both sides of this equation by 45 yields $x = 8$. Since a side length of a rectangular prism can't be 0, the length of each square base is 8 cm.

Choice A is incorrect and may result from conceptual or calculation errors.
Choice C is incorrect and may result from conceptual or calculation errors.
Choice D is incorrect and may result from conceptual or calculation errors.

QUESTION 22

Choice D is correct. The equation of a parabola in the *xy*-plane can be written in the form $y = a(x - h)^2 + k$, where *a* is a constant and (*h*, *k*) is the vertex of the parabola. If *a* is positive, the parabola will open upward, and if *a* is negative, the parabola will open downward. It's given that the parabola has vertex (9, −14). Substituting 9 for *h* and −14 for *k* in the equation $y = a(x - h)^2 + k$ gives $y = a(x - 9)^2 - 14$, which can be rewritten as $y = a(x - 9)(x - 9) - 14$, or $y = a(x^2 - 18x + 81) - 14$. Distributing the factor of *a* on the right-hand side of this equation yields $y = ax^2 - 18ax + 81a - 14$. Therefore, the equation of the parabola, $y = ax^2 - 18ax + 81a - 14$, can be written in the form $y = ax^2 + bx + c$, where $a = a$, $b = -18a$, and $c = 81a - 14$. Substituting −18*a* for *b* and 81*a* − 14 for *c* in the expression $a + b + c$ yields $(a) + (-18a) + (81a - 14)$, or $64a - 14$. Since the vertex of the parabola, (9, −14), is below the *x*-axis, and it's given that the parabola intersects the *x*-axis at two points, the parabola must open upward. Therefore, the constant *a* must have a positive value. Setting the expression $64a - 14$ equal to the value in choice D yields $64a - 14 = -12$. Adding 14 to both sides of this equation yields $64a = 2$. Dividing both sides of this equation by 64 yields $a = \dfrac{2}{64}$, which is a positive value. Therefore, if the equation of the parabola is written in the form $y = ax^2 + bx + c$, where *a*, *b*, and *c* are constants, the value of $a + b + c$ could be −12.

Choice A is incorrect. If the equation of a parabola with a vertex at (9, −14) is written in the form $y = ax^2 + bx + c$, where *a*, *b*, and *c* are constants and $a + b + c = -23$, then the value of *a* will be negative, which means the parabola will open downward, not upward, and will intersect the *x*-axis at zero points, not two points. *Choice B* is incorrect. If the equation of a parabola with a vertex at (9, −14) is written in the form $y = ax^2 + bx + c$, where *a*, *b*, and *c* are constants and $a + b + c = -19$, then the value of *a* will be negative, which means the parabola will open downward, not upward, and will intersect the *x*-axis at zero points, not two points. *Choice C* is incorrect. If the equation of a parabola with a vertex at (9, −14) is written in the form $y = ax^2 + bx + c$, where *a*, *b*, and *c* are constants and $a + b + c = -14$, then the value of *a* will be 0, which is inconsistent with the equation of a parabola.

Scoring Your Paper SAT Practice Test #4

Congratulations on completing an SAT® practice test.
To score your test, follow the instructions in this guide.

IMPORTANT: *This scoring guide is for students who completed the paper version of this digital SAT practice test.*

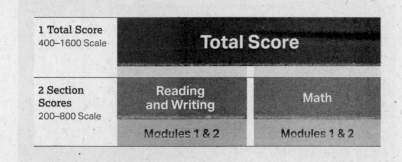

1 Total Score 400–1600 Scale	Total Score	
2 Section Scores 200–800 Scale	Reading and Writing	Math
	Modules 1 & 2	Modules 1 & 2

Scores Overview

Each assessment in the digital SAT Suite (SAT, PSAT/NMSQT®, PSAT™ 10, and PSAT™ 8/9) reports test scores on a common scale.

For more details about scores, visit **sat.org/scores**.

How to Calculate Your Practice Test Scores

The worksheets on pages 626 and 627 help you calculate your test scores.

GET SET UP

1 In addition to your practice test, you'll need the conversion tables and answer key at the end of this guide.

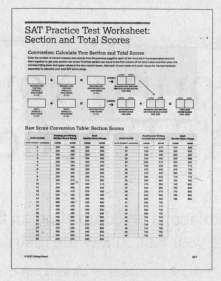

SCORE YOUR PRACTICE TEST

2 Compare your answers to the answer key on page 626, and count up the total number of correct answers for each section. Write the number of correct answers for each section in the answer key at the bottom of that section.

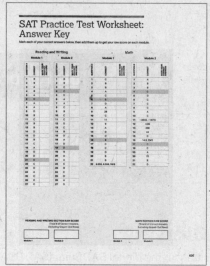

CALCULATE YOUR SCORES

3 Using your marked-up answer key and the conversion tables, follow the directions on page 627 to get your section and test scores.

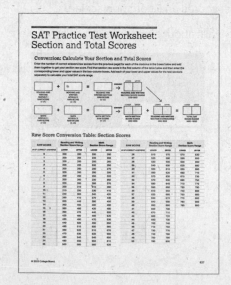

Get Section and Total Scores

Section and total scores for the paper version of this digital SAT practice test are expressed as ranges. That's because the scoring method described in this guide is a simplified (and therefore slightly less precise) version of the one used in Bluebook™, the digital test application.

To obtain your Reading and Writing and Math section scores, use the provided answer key to determine the number of questions you answered correctly in each section. These numbers constitute your *raw scores* for the two sections. Use the provided table to convert your raw score for each section into a *scaled score* range consisting of a "lower" and "upper" value. Add the two lower values together and the two upper values together to obtain your total score range.

GET YOUR READING AND WRITING SECTION SCORE

Calculate your SAT Reading and Writing section score (it's on a scale of 200–800).

1. Use the answer key on page 626 to find the number of questions in module 1 and module 2 that you answered correctly.

2. To determine your Reading and Writing raw score, add the number of correct answers you got on module 1 and module 2. **Exclude the questions in grayed-out rows from your calculation.**

3. Use the Raw Score Conversion Table: Section Scores on page 627 to turn your raw score into your Reading and Writing section score.

4. The "lower" and "upper" values associated with your raw score establish the range of scores you might expect to receive had this been an actual test.

GET YOUR MATH SECTION SCORE

Calculate your SAT Math section score (it's on a scale of 200–800).

1. Use the answer key on page 626 to find the number of questions in module 1 and module 2 that you answered correctly.

2. To determine your Math raw score, add the number of correct answers you got on module 1 and module 2. **Exclude the questions in grayed-out rows from your calculation.**

3. Use the Raw Score Conversion Table: Section Scores on page 627 to turn your raw score into your Math section score.

4. The "lower" and "upper" values associated with your raw score establish the range of scores you might expect to receive had this been an actual test.

GET YOUR TOTAL SCORE

Add together the "lower" values for the Reading and Writing and Math sections, and then add together the "upper" values for the two sections. The result is your total score, expressed as a range, for this SAT practice test. The total score is on a scale of 400–1600.

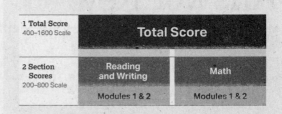

1 Total Score 400–1600 Scale	Total Score	
2 Section Scores 200–800 Scale	Reading and Writing	Math
	Modules 1 & 2	Modules 1 & 2

Your total score on this SAT practice test is the sum of your Reading and Writing section score and your Math section score. On this paper version of the digital SAT practice test, you'll receive a lower and upper score for each test section and the total score. This is the range of scores that you might expect to receive.

Use the worksheets on pages 626 and 627 to calculate your section and total scores.

SAT Practice Test Worksheet: Answer Key

Mark each of your correct answers below, then add them up to get your raw score on each module.

Reading and Writing

Module 1

QUESTION #	CORRECT	MARK YOUR CORRECT ANSWERS
1	B	
2	B	
3	A	
4	B	
5	A	
6	D	
7	A	
8	A	
9	D	
10	B	
11	C	
12	B	
13	B	
14	D	
15	D	
16	B	
17	C	
18	A	
19	D	
20	D	
21	D	
22	C	
23	D	
24	A	
25	C	
26	D	
27	C	

Module 2

QUESTION #	CORRECT	MARK YOUR CORRECT ANSWERS
1	B	
2	B	
3	C	
4	C	
5	D	
6	A	
7	A	
8	C	
9	B	
10	C	
11	C	
12	D	
13	C	
14	B	
15	D	
16	A	
17	D	
18	D	
19	B	
20	A	
21	A	
22	C	
23	B	
24	C	
25	D	
26	A	
27	D	

Math

Module 1

QUESTION #	CORRECT	MARK YOUR CORRECT ANSWERS
1	C	
2	B	
3	B	
4	A	
5	C	
6	5	
7	D	
8	A	
9	28	
10	C	
11	11	
12	9	
13	A	
14	D	
15	D	
16	B	
17	C	
18	C	
19	D	
20	B	
21	B	
22	6.555, 6.556, 59/9	

Module 2

QUESTION #	CORRECT	MARK YOUR CORRECT ANSWERS
1	A	
2	B	
3	B	
4	C	
5	D	
6	C	
7	C	
8	C	
9	A	
10	C	
11	-.9333, -14/15	
12	4.06	
13	289	
14	44	
15	D	
16	14.5, 29/2	
17	C	
18	C	
19	A	
20	10	
21	B	
22	D	

READING AND WRITING SECTION RAW SCORE
(Total # of Correct Answers, Excluding Grayed-Out Rows)

Module 1

Module 2

MATH SECTION RAW SCORE
(Total # of Correct Answers, Excluding Grayed-Out Rows)

Module 1

Module 2

SAT Practice Test Worksheet: Section and Total Scores

Conversion: Calculate Your Section and Total Scores

Enter the number of correct answers (raw scores from the previous page) for each of the modules in the boxes below and add them together to get your section raw score. Find that section raw score in the first column of the table below and then enter the corresponding lower and upper values in the two-column boxes. Add each of your lower and upper values for the test sections separately to calculate your total SAT score range.

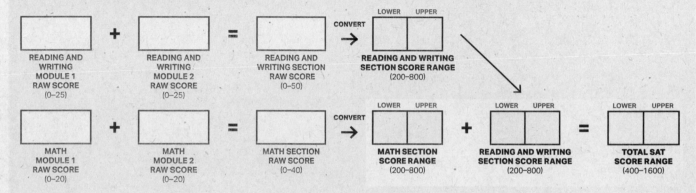

Raw Score Conversion Table: Section Scores

RAW SCORE (# OF CORRECT ANSWERS)	Reading and Writing Section Score Range LOWER	UPPER	Math Section Score Range LOWER	UPPER	RAW SCORE (# OF CORRECT ANSWERS)	Reading and Writing Section Score Range LOWER	UPPER	Math Section Score Range LOWER	UPPER
0	200	260	200	260	26	510	570	570	630
1	200	260	200	260	27	520	580	590	650
2	200	260	200	260	28	530	590	600	660
3	200	260	200	260	29	540	600	620	680
4	200	260	200	270	30	550	610	630	690
5	200	260	200	300	31	560	620	650	710
6	200	260	200	320	32	570	630	670	730
7	200	260	230	350	33	570	630	690	750
8	200	260	290	370	34	580	640	710	770
9	200	310	310	390	35	590	650	730	790
10	210	330	330	410	36	610	650	740	800
11	240	360	340	420	37	620	660	750	800
12	290	410	370	430	38	630	670	770	800
13	320	440	390	450	39	640	680	780	800
14	350	450	400	460	40	650	690	780	800
15	380	460	420	480	41	660	700		
16	390	470	440	500	42	670	710		
17	420	480	460	520	43	680	720		
18	430	490	470	530	44	690	730		
19	440	500	490	550	45	700	740		
20	450	510	500	560	46	710	750		
21	460	520	510	570	47	730	770		
22	470	530	530	590	48	740	780		
23	480	540	540	600	49	750	790		
24	490	550	550	610	50	780	800		
25	500	560	560	620					